Q & A

In the series *Asian American History and Culture*, edited by
Cathy Schlund-Vials, Shelley Sang-Hee Lee, and Rick Bonus. Founding editor,
Sucheng Chan; editors emeriti, David Palumbo-Liu, Michael Omi,
K. Scott Wong, and Linda Trinh Võ.

Also in this series:

A list of additional titles in this series appears at the back of this book

Q & A

Voices from Queer Asian North America

Edited by

MARTIN F. MANALANSAN IV,
ALICE Y. HOM, and
KALE BANTIGUE FAJARDO

Preface by DAVID L. ENG

TEMPLE UNIVERSITY PRESS
Philadelphia • *Rome* • *Tokyo*

TEMPLE UNIVERSITY PRESS
Philadelphia, Pennsylvania 19122
tupress.temple.edu

Library of Congress Cataloging-in-Publication Data

Names: Manalansan, Martin F., 1960– editor. | Hom, Alice Y., 1967– editor.
  | Fajardo, Kale Bantigue, editor. | Eng, David L., writer of preface.
Title: Q & A : voices from queer Asian North America / edited by Martin F.
  Manalansan IV, Alice Y. Hom, and Kale Bantigue Fajardo.
Other titles: Q & A (Temple University Press : 1998) | Asian American
  history and culture.
Description: Philadelphia : Temple University Press, 2021. | Series: Asian
  American history and culture | This book is a follow-up to Q & A: Queer
  in Asian America edited by David L. Eng and Alice Y. Hom, published in
  1998. | Includes bibliographical references and index. | Summary: "This
  book offers a vibrant array of contemporary Asian North American LGBT
  scholarship and cultural productions from essays, poetry, visual art,
  and memoirs of activists and scholars"— Provided by publisher.
Identifiers: LCCN 2020045499 (print) | LCCN 2020045500 (ebook) | ISBN
  9781439921081 (cloth) | ISBN 9781439921098 (paperback) | ISBN
  9781439921104 (pdf)
Subjects: LCSH: Asian American gays—Social conditions. | Asian American
  lesbians—Social conditions. | Asian American bisexuals—Social
  conditions. | Gays—North America—Identity. | Lesbians—North
  America—Identity. | Transgender people—North America—Identity. |
  Bisexuals—North America—Identity. | Queer theory.
Classification: LCC HQ73.3.N7 .Q113 2021 (print) | LCC HQ73.3.N7 (ebook)
  | DDC 306.76089/95073—dc23
LC record available at https://lccn.loc.gov/2020045499
LC ebook record available at https://lccn.loc.gov/2020045500

Printed in the United States of America

9 8 7 6 5 4 3 2 1

Contents

Preface

Alice Y. Hom and I coedited *Q & A: Queer in Asian American* over twenty years ago. It represented our concerted attempt to bring Asian American studies together with queer studies. Our efforts were motivated by an unwavering belief that race and sexuality are intertwined and indissociable categories produced in a long history of liberal— which is to say, racial—capitalism. Looking back now over the table of contents of the original 445-page volume published in 1998 and consisting of twenty-six pathbreaking contributions by both scholars and activists, I realize that *Q & A* was one of the very first collections to map out what has coalesced in the ensuing decades as the interdisciplinary field of "queer of color critique." This realization fills me with gratitude for our contributors and a certain amount of pride in our collective achievement. It also gives me the occasion to acknowledge, once again, the incisive vision of Professor Sucheng Chan and Temple University Press editor-in-chief Janet Francendese for their steadfast support of a project whose success was profoundly uncertain at the time. Looking now at the contents of *Q & A: Voices from Queer Asian North America,* a.k.a. *Q & A 2.0,* curated by Alice, Kale Bantigue Fajardo, and Martin F. Manalansan IV, I am suffused with similar feelings for what the three coeditors have achieved in this wide-ranging follow-up collection. This is an instance of queer pride that I can endorse with enthusiasm.

When Alice and I started gathering the authors and materials for *Q & A* in 1995, we were still graduate students in history and in comparative literature, respectively—two fields organized in a highly disciplinary fashion. Much has changed in the subsequent twenty-odd years. (I, for one, have less hair and fantasize about retirement on an all-too-frequent basis.) However, much has also remained the same, as political possibilities and catastrophes ebb and flow. As we have moved from Generation X to Y and now to Z, we have witnessed significant capital accumulation in East, Southeast, and South Asia, reconfiguring Asian American identity into a decidedly neoliberal global context. With the proliferation of multiple "Asias," Asian American studies has evolved to encompass critical and comparative race studies. At the same time, gender and sexuality studies have expanded to encompass queer and trans studies. I do not mean to suggest that these significant social, political, and intellectual shifts have taken place in a linear or progressive manner. On the contrary, these developments remain uneven and recursive. For instance, to cite one modest example, I experience a distinct and uncanny sense of déjà vu when I realize that *Q & A* already contained in 1998 a prescient transgender roundtable underscoring the "groundlessness" of trans sex—how body, gender identity, sexual orientation, and sexual object choice are aligned in indeterminate ways.

It is worth highlighting that across these various historical and intellectual shifts, the insights of queer of color critique (as well as the abiding influence of women of color feminisms) have remained constant. The understanding that gender, sex, and race are intertwined assemblages and that they index complex histories of settler colonialism and contingent futures of global capital serves as both a critical unconscious and an important political and theoretical asset for queer Asian American scholars. Since 1998, we have experienced the fallout of 9/11 and an unending Islamaphobic "war on terror" under the shadows of empire. The United States elected its first black president in what was naively proclaimed a colorblind age, followed by an openly white supremacist president and administration, as right-wing nationalist, authoritarian, and populist movements grow all over the world. In the Global North, for those with access to health care, AIDS has gone from a death sentence to a manageable chronic disease, even as it persists unabated in the Global South. Numerous financial crises and austerity regimes have resulted in the mass disenfranchisement of the racialized poor while the wealthiest of the global elite have further elevated their fortunes. Humanitarian, epidemiological, and climatological emergencies of unprecedented scale continue to engulf the planet as borders are closed, migrants are caged, loved ones are separated, and protestors are shot and imprisoned. All the while, environmental habitats and a growing number of nonhuman species become extinct.

As all this unfolds, normative LGBTQ subjects in the West, as elsewhere, have been further incorporated into (neo)liberal structures of rights and recognition, markets and property, and marriage and kinship. In 1998, the idea of legalized same-sex marriage in the United States was unthinkable. Today, more and more homonormative and homonationalist subjects are being interpellated into the logics of queer liberalism and pinkwashing as the "homosexual question" comes to frame human rights agendas with increasing frequency. The morphing capacities of both queerness and race demonstrate that LGBTQ alignments with nationalist and racist ideologies cannot be seen as aberrations but rather as constitutive of the queer liberal rights program itself. In such a polarized climate, it is unsurprising that critical race and queer studies continue to be contested both inside and outside of the academy for their social, political, and cultural interventions. At the same time, we also witness how the uneven institutionalization of these fields lays bare the fact that both ethnic and queer studies sometimes constitute themselves as their own exceptionalist brands of U.S. area studies, signing on to liberal projects of representation and assimilation with equal measures of alacrity and cynicism. The academy is in many ways a reflection of the world at large, a world that can hardly be described as a story of liberal progress, justice, and freedom.

Voices from Queer Asian North America comes, then, at a very opportune moment. Queer Asian American scholars have always paid heightened attention to the transnational histories of U.S. national identity and belonging. As they have interrogated the politics of (im)migration, citizenship, diaspora, colonization, dispossession, and displacement, they have provided trenchant analyses of changing structures of family and kinship. They have reshaped the fields of American studies, area studies, and diaspora studies, not to mention gender and sexuality studies, in indelible ways, insistently asking what populations are deemed valuable and worthy of protection and what processes of relationality and sociality are left out of our current social imaginaries and arrangements. This welcome (re)collection—a deliberate mix of contributions from academics, activists, community organizers, creative writers, and visual artists—underscores the vital expansion of our queer archive to incorporate histories and experiences outside the Global North, written and thought in languages other than English. It plumbs new geographies, identities, desires, bodies, and communities not yet acknowledged as well as queer cultural productions and performances that harness new theoretical frameworks and political possibilities for exploration. It pushes us in the direction of the not-yet-here, pointing to more capacious horizons. For that, we must all be thankful.

David L. Eng
Richard L. Fisher Professor of English
University of Pennsylvania

Q & A

Journeys, Itineraries, Horizons

An Introduction

Martin F. Manalansan IV, Alice Y. Hom,
and Kale Bantigue Fajardo

I. Q & A in the Twenty-First Century

Over twenty years ago, David L. Eng and Alice Y. Hom edited *Q & A: Queer in Asian America*, which was to become a canonical work in Asian American studies and queer studies.[1] Lauded by scholars, activists, artists, and community members, this award-winning work was one of the first anthologies to offer a critical yet sensitive collection of a variety of Asian American queer voices. What does it mean to publish *Q & A* in the twenty-first century? What does a book about the queerness of Asians in the Americas do in shedding light on recent events that seem at first to be radical departures from the late twentieth century when the first iteration of *Q & A* was launched? At that time, the AIDS pandemic was a major public concern, LGBT studies was slowly gaining institutional ground, struggles for gay marriage and for gays in the military were the prime issues in many LGBT activist agendas, and queerness was becoming a resonant umbrella signifier and as an analytic. But where are we now?

We, the editors, gesture to both the material presence and affective aspirations of a collectivity and to a fragile yet crucial coalition of multiple communities. Have queers come a long way since "the maiden voyage," as Dana Takagi termed it in her formative essay that chronicled the advent of gay and lesbian studies focusing on Asian Americans?[2] Or have we lost our way in the midst of the increasing xenophobic, brutal, and increasingly blatant violent inequalities wrought by a world filled with populists, white supremacists, capitalists, unabashed homophobes, and transphobes? AIDS is still a raging problem in the Global South and in Black and Latinx communities in the United States; poverty and violence pervade communities of color in North America; refugees are being turned away or incarcerated at various borders; reproductive health and transgender rights are being threatened. Despite the initial celebration of the gay marriage ruling and marveling at the triumphs of the transgender revolution, there is more work to be done and even more daunting obstacles to surmount. We need to think of these events more as way stations to something better and more capacious, to other horizons, and to the not-yet-here. Currently, we all live in an era where political regimes are dismantling the progressive political and cultural advances LGBTQ communities have gained, and these regimes are cruelly devastating the fruitful coalitions that have formed through the years. This collection is built around these realities, and its relevance is buoyed by the vital aspirations and struggles for our endurance and survival.

Q & A is not a mere sequel to the original volume. It is not an additional appendage to an original site. First, it is a series of continuing meditations and conversations on enduring questions, issues, and struggles that have persisted and vexed Asian North American LGBTQ individuals, communities, and agendas. These conversations are by no means linear. In fact, as the array of scholarly and creative works proves, this anthology's trajectories are multiple and often multidirectional. By imagining alternative ways to confront these issues, this volume reframes seemingly vexing chronic issues by thinking beyond preset ideas, frameworks, political stances, and emotional composures.

Second, this volume is a space for opening new vistas, geographies, experiences, bodies, identities, and communities that have not, until this moment, been acknowledged if not made visible. It is clear that many other voices and communities were not part of the first iteration of Q & A. Political groups, queer studies, and cultural productions in the twenty-first century have indeed given rise to movements that have questioned the canonization of LGBT/queer studies in both popular culture and in the academy. In this regard, writings about transgender phenomena, disability, and settler colonialism are placed at the forefront of this volume. The editors envision these works not as mere additives but rather as complex vectors that reshape if not upend the typical idea of queerness as always renegade sexuality and sociality bounded by Euro-American historical and cultural exigencies.

Which Asia? Whose Asia? What Is "Queer Asian America"? What Does "Queer Asian America" Do?

The "queer Asian America" that the subtitle alludes to is no longer tethered to its long-standing mainstream political and cultural strictures. Asian

America is not anchored to the politically demarcated geography and situated history but rather is constituted by multistranded postnational temporal and spatial convergences and entanglements. This anthology aims to conceptually and politically reconfigure these strictures within and across scales of body, city, nation, region, and global. We are not discarding the value of the original idea for the title, and this volume is sensitive to the decades of vibrant intellectual work in Asian American studies as well as political organizing and coalition building in various Asian American LGBTQ activist groups. That said, we recognize that this volume comes out of this current period of ongoing growth not only in critical ethnic studies and American studies but also in the emergence of area studies–based queer studies.

What, then, is the "Asia" in queer Asian America? Or more appropriately, what does the idea of a queer Asian America do in relation to the idea of "Asia"? First, we recognize the ongoing effects of the vestiges of imperial domination, neocolonial infringements, and other political maneuvers of an increasingly vexed "empire" of the United States of America. These enduring vestiges have spurred migrations and return migrations between Asia and North America. Asian Americans have had the long history of historical exclusion in the realm of immigration history and citizenship; the Chinese Exclusion Laws of the nineteenth century and Filipinos as "national wards" (not citizens) in the early twentieth century are just a few prime examples of the fraught relationship of Asians in the North American continent with the nodes of race, nationhood, and citizenship, embroiled as they were in the classed, sexualized, and gendered dimensions of difference. We continue to recognize and appreciate the particularity of the experiences of Asian American and Asian Canadian queers in terms of these legacies and conditions.

That said, this anthology also confronts the promise and limitation of a "queer Asian America" despite its postnationalist, transregional, and transnational repositionings and aspirations. We have involved people in Canada and other places not just to have more expansive geographic inclusivity but also to question the very perimeters of our conceptual, theoretical, cultural, and political understandings. Queer Asian America is part of a set of transnational entanglements and nodes that considers its emplacement not as a central hub but rather as a point of convergences, encounters, and possible collisions or clashes. We acknowledge and are sensitive to the fact that much of the early scholarship in queer Asian American studies has been seen as imposing a Euro-American–centric view of "Asian" queerness, especially in light of the glaring institutional and economic disparities. However, we hope to harvest the playful yet critical openness of "queer" in light of the various contingencies that face scholarship and activism in Asian America and Asia. We also recognize the new politico-economic power matrix involving China. We appreciate and are constantly learning from emerging contemporary cross-national, intra-Asian political and cultural queer institutions and practices.

This collection further "queers" the meanings of "Asian" and "America" by not simply forging a cumulative diverse gathering of queer-identified voices, bodies, and experiences but by expanding the contours' spatial and temporal boundaries that enfold issues of decoloniality; sovereignty; and cross-border, cross-racial, and imperial entanglements from the United States–Mexico nexus to those of Israel and Palestine. Therefore, this volume dismantles Asian America by including issues and debates beyond the confines of the United States of America; by questioning conceptual, geographic, and historical boundaries; and through breaking down epistemologies of queer as emanating only from specific conditions that cannot be easily universalized. We also recognize the need to accelerate the growth of transnational and inter- or intraregional networks of scholars, activists, and cultural producers to further complicate the understandings of queer and "Asia."

To echo and relocate Howard Chiang's and Alvin K. Wong's felicitous concept of "Queer Asia as Critique," this volume envisions a queer Asian America as part of a dialogical assemblage of queer *Asias* (emphasis ours) by approaching meanings and materialities surrounding queerness through an open-ended approach.[3] We aim to defuse and "reorient" queer Asian American studies' Global North–centric optics by enhancing continuing efforts to listen and learn from queer Asian Studies and other paradigms. This volume attempts to take on the gnarled, enmeshed relationships between desires, bodies, social hierarchies, and cultural meanings across temporal and spatial scales. We take inspiration from ongoing developments in queer Sinophone studies, critical regional studies, and frameworks such as the "transpacific."[4] We seek to frame our locations and cultural productions in the political and academic institutions of North America and the privileges we enjoy within these unequal geopolitical realities. That said, we look forward to strengthening ongoing institutional and informal cooperative efforts between scholars in area and ethnic studies, and between those based in North America and in Asia.

What does "queer" in "queer Asian America" do? This collection's understanding of queer comes from the emergence and dissemination of queer of color critique and the continuing legacy of women of color feminism. "Queer" is not just about nonheterosexual desire and coupling or non-normative gender behavior. In fact, it reinforces what has been offered in the first iteration of Q & A, that sex can never be divorced from its complex entanglements with gender, class, race, and ethnicity.[5] Diasporic migration itself is a queer process as it uncovers and dismantles the normative masculinist carapace of nationhood[6] and emplaces the "migrant" or diasporic subject within unstable, nonheteronormative, and often precarious states of being. In other words, Asians, who compose some of the biggest numbers of migrants and mobile subjects crossing borders both in North America and in other parts of the world, wittingly or unwittingly participate in this queering or a political and cultural process of exfoliating layers of normative, often violent precepts of social order and deviance. This anthology is one of many ongoing efforts to translate, transfer, discard, or refuse circulating ideas of queer scholarship and activism that highlight the perils of universalism and the rich potentials of multiple "particulars." We seek to participate in the ongoing broad discussions between queer studies scholars, artists, and activists in the North and South because many of our contributors straddle this troubled divide.

The Work of Cultural Production and Activism

A significant distinction of this volume is that it has a noticeable decrease in academic essays—significantly less than the first *Q & A*. It includes more contributions from activists, community organizers, creative writers, and visual artists. The editors have their own varying histories and experiences with nonacademic locations that will be evident in the acknowledgments piece that consists of the editors' individual odysseys. Queer cultural producers have always been the pivotal fulcrum for energizing theoretical frameworks and political agendas. Cultural productions and community work have always been a major part of a queer vision of the world and have always been intertwined. The editors strongly believe that instead of paying mere lip service to this important mesh of relationships, visions, and institutions, this volume is committed to centering the work and voices of these groups of social agents who have been influential both within and outside the ivory tower of academia. One example is the Trinidadian Canadian filmmaker Richard Fung, whose canonical cinematic oeuvre and his classic essay "Looking for My Penis" have been major sources of inspiration for generations of Asian North American queers.[7] The contributions of Fung and other Asian North American poets, filmmakers, and visual, musical, and performance artists have been the persistent sparks—the creative triggers—that animate and fuel ongoing questions and creative responses to the possibilities of queer Asian America.

This collection's emphasis on cultural production sheds light on affects, postures, ideas, and feelings that undergird queer activism, education, and scholarship that often circumvent the imposition of universalist, neoliberal metrics. Indeed, personal testimonies, poetry, and visual arts are more often seen as unwieldy, unruly, and unscholarly—exemplifying a queerness that often evades neoliberal governance "standards," measures, and modernist empiricism. The cultural genres represented in this collection offer this mode of queerness that not only informs but often also inspires, unsettles, and amuses, among other things. In other words, these cultural genres animate and propel movement into new goals, visions, agendas, and horizons.

Like many anthologies, this work is never a complete one. We admit that what we present in the following pages is a mere glimpse or a snapshot of what is happening now—after twenty years. We do not aspire to be the final word. Instead, we humbly offer this anthology not as a kind of denouement or triumphant conclusion but rather as fodder and fuel to animate and energize future dialogues and fiery debates. In the spirit of queer in queer theory and studies, this volume aspires (à la José Esteban Muñoz) to that horizon of things that are yet to be, working through and investing in struggles from the past and in the present for that distant future.[8] With tempered optimism and a fervent aspirational outlook, the essays in this collection move us further toward that ever-shifting vanishing point as we look around ourselves in the midst of multiple swirling collective energies and desire, and with burning hope, we reach out to the world.

II. Itineraries: An Unruly Map of Chapters

There is already something amiss when we try to put order in an otherwise recalcitrant collection. Recalcitrance is not just idiosyncratic willfulness but rather is based on the creative paths and trajectories of many of these works. Some people might call it "scholarship lite" since there are not a lot of scholarly citational practices in poetry and other creative genres. However, we assert that the inclusion of various creative works implies that there is no singular way in which critical thought can be formulated and channeled. We want to expand the goal of this collection from this limited notion of critical thought to a more expansive idea of the fostering of sensibilities—skills that enable people to empathize and make meaningful connections that escape the neoliberal metrics of higher education and knowledge production in general.

We confess that writing this part of the introduction was quite uncomfortable. Is it mere bad curatorial or editorial skills, or is it in a discomfort at trying to rein in the multiple genres? Recalcitrance is not mere direct refusal or resistance. Rather, the various contributions point to the ways in which things never comfortably fit in unitary or coherent parts. They connect and converse to various conversations within and outside this collection. For the sake of the reader and under pressure from publication conventions, we tried to commit to paper the various fragile and contentious connections between works. This part is a normative mandate from above, so we invite the readers to peruse, skim, and read with abandon. This is a messy map, so please revel in the mingling of voices, images, and ideas. Feel free to design your own routes of reading.

Part I, Enduring Spaces and Bodies

This set of visual art, poetry, scholarly essays, autobiographical meditations, and analyses of histories and popular culture gestures to enduring everyday racial, gender, and sexual experiences of misrecognition, microaggressions, loss, and trauma when racialized Asian bodies—for example, Chinese, Pinay, Tamil, Jewish, Korean, femme, feminine presenting, gender noncon-forming, transgender, transmasculine, queer, mixed race, mother, immi-grant, and "foreign"—are on the line, called into question, pathologized, marginalized, or violated. Danni Lin creates "portraits of inadequacy" through large scroll paintings that combine "Western masterpiece materials and Chinese symbolism." The paintings also include self-portraits that sug-gest the artist's complex relationship with Chinese-ness and queerness. Kim-berly Alidio's poem, "All the Pinays are straight, all the queers are Pinoy, but some of us," evokes shame, grief, pain, an *LOL in your face* queer femme Pinay fierceness. Jih-Fei Cheng deconstructs and problematizes the "Chinese Jew" figure in the context of science, race, and labor. Cheng argues that the "reprisal of the Chinese Jew" in current scholarship, popular literature, and genetics research complicates, and even undoes, the racial/ethnic categories of "Chinese," "Jewish," "Asian," and by extension "Chinese American," "Jew-ish American," and "Asian American." Performance poet and spoken word and hip-hop artist D'Lo reflects on personal experiences to discuss their queerness and how their mother/amma inspired and became a part of their creative processes and performances. Mixing personal, creative, and schol-arly voices, Patti Duncan also interrogates her mixed-race family histories across generations and from the subjectivity of a mother writing to her son. In addressing various historical fragments related to the personal and po-litical, race, gender, sexuality, and U.S. empire, Duncan also reveals healing and wholeness. Douglas S. Ishii compares and contrasts two television shows about Chinese diasporic family lives, *Fresh off the Boat* (United States) and *Family Law* (Australia), to discuss the concept of "lateral diasporas" and "queer adaptations," which "reorient vertical relationships" and reveal alter-native intimacies and socialities. As a group, contributors use art, poetry, hybrid writing, and critical scholarship to reveal how a queer lens that fierce-ly takes into account other axes of difference and structures of power (e.g., race/racial formation, imperialism, militarization) also facilitates important personal and political critiques that put the spotlight on racial, gender, and sexual injustices, and just as crucial, how we can create racial, gender, and sexual justice through visual art, poetic forms, memory work, and reflexive and critical diasporic scholarship.

Part II, Queer Unsettlings: Geographies, Sovereignties

This part, comprised primarily of academic essays plus a set of poems, offers different ways of considering queer Asian subjects and subjectivities in local and global economies of desire situated largely outside of the continental United States in locales such as mainland Southeast Asia, the Philippines, Hawaiʻi, Palestine, the United Kingdom, South Africa, and the U.S./Mexico border. The essays and poems describe what happens or may happen when queer Asian American subjects travel, crossing different national borders as a result of immigration or displacement resulting from war; tourism; returns to homelands, occupied places, or sites of apartheid. Through unflinching poetry, Việt Lê provides us an itinerary of queer and refugee desire, displacement, and pleasures. Kim Compoc analyzes racial and sexual border zones in Ang Lee's 2005 film *Brokeback Mountain* and R. Zamora Linmark's 2011 novel *Leche* to unpack complicated race and class politics that intersect on queer brown bodies in motion. Sony Coráñez Bolton writes of Filipinx houseboys and housemaids in Bryon Escalon Roley's 2001 novel *American Son*. Coráñez Bolton argues that the novel reveals how Asian American experience is inevitably refracted through and changed by the U.S.–Mexican corridor in early 1990s post-riots Los Angeles. Vanita Reddy addresses queer South Asian desires, Blackness, and the apartheid state in South Africa in Shamim Sarif's 2008 novel *The World Unseen*. Reddy's essay "foregrounds the role that intimacy, affect, and aesthetics play in comparative racialization, particularly between Black and Asian diasporic populations." Jennifer Lynn Kelly addresses "pink washing, tourism, and the (in)visibility of Israeli state violence" through critical analyses of gay tourism materials and reflections on fieldwork at pride events such as those in Palestine and Israel. Kelly ultimately argues, "Israeli state violence is thus not rendered invisible by Israeli gay tourist initiatives, but rather it is selectively celebrated as both necessary and justified." Finally, Reid Uratani develops the concepts of "Asian Settler abstraction" and "administrative aloha" through his critical analysis of gay tourism materials in Hawaiʻi. Ultimately, Uratani suggests that "Hawaiʻi becomes legible as a confluence of contingent historical processes whose efficacies are dispersed and resistant to tidy narrations."

This part is highly significant in that it includes some of the latest queer Asian American studies scholarship on tourism. While the field of queer studies (broadly defined) has focused on the phenomenon of "gay tourism," and in the field of feminist studies there has been attention on (gendered, racialized, classed, and placed) sex work and sex tourism, scholarship in the field of Asian American studies in the last couple of decades seemed to stall. Essays in this part reignite and reanimate important conversations regarding tourism and differently situated mobilities. They also describe and analyze other types of border crossings, not just through geography or spaces but when particular bodies cross established (or policed) racial and class lines in different temporal moments—for example, in the context of settler colonialism as argued by Uratani; neocolonialism from the contributions of Lê, Compoc, and Coráñez; and racial apartheid as discussed by Reddy. The scholars in this part also model how to closely read and interpret literary and cinematic works. They demonstrate how the seemingly fleeting moments in the queer economy of desire when traveling, moving, staying still, getting settled, crossing borders, hanging out in cafés, walking on streets, dancing in clubs, organizing for social justice, feeling alive and present, and fucking your lover(s) are laced with power and pleasure always; complicity and privilege oftentimes; resistance, decoloniality, radicalism, feminism, longing, beauty, shame, loss, and resilience sometimes.

Part III, Building Justice: Queer Movements in Asian North America

The authors in this part—Eric Estuar Reyes, Eric C. Wat, Amy Sueyoshi, Sasha Wijeyeratne, Glenn D. Magpantay, and Kim Tran—are scholars, teachers, and activists who also participate in the movements they document and analyze. From their particular perches, they invite the reader to ponder the multiple spaces, identities, and contexts of the activism of queer Asians from local, national, and international perspectives. Amy Sueyoshi's article provides a broad overview of queer Asian and Pacific Islander (API) history from the nineteenth century to the present while the other authors— Sasha Wijeyeratne, Glenn D. Magpantay, Eric Reyes and Eric Wat, and Kim Tran—offer specific lived experiences and examples of how our horizons have shifted given what others have done before us. How can we imagine different possibilities for our future? How can we connect the everyday experiences to larger political narratives? Where do we succeed in moving beyond identity politics and engaging in the hard work of solidarity practices? The essays by Eric Reyes and Eric Wat and by Kim Tran include the voices and the singing of those on the frontlines in the past and in the current day. The authors recognize they are not in a position to make grand speculations, but they allow for the multiplicity and provide a mapping of where we've been and how we've made our change for API LGBTQ communities. Sasha Wijeyeratne's essay provides an on-the-ground account of their activism in grassroots organizations around solidarity and allyship. Glenn D. Magpantay's essay provides a macro-level account of political organizing, community building, and advocacy by API LGBTQ organizations across the United States.

The articles by Reyes and Wat, Sueyoshi, Wijeyeratne, Tran, and Magpantay knit together the many ways API LGBTQ communities have worked toward justice in small and big ways, how we have invited our families and broader communities in our lives, and how organizing continues to be a critical way to make change. From an oral history roundtable discussion to a personal narrative, historical overviews, and connecting cultural production, we are witnessing the continuation of legacies, one that tells the stories of solidarity, the challenges within our own families and communities, and how we shift our own understandings between and among generations of LGBTQ Asian Americans.

Part IV, Messing up the Archives and Circuits of Desire

The works in this part examine politics of histories—as in LGBT dominant "mainstream" history (read: white, male, gay, and U.S. American), as well as dominant Asian American histories (read: straight and/or heteronormative and gender conforming). Who gets to set the terms of Asian American queer history? How does Asian American queer history "mess up" the archive not as a mere "repository" of facts but as a space for dwelling and struggle?

Ching-In Chen's poetry subtly suggests the forms and locations of intimate histories through the flow of desire and history in various locations such as Sumatra and Manila and their containment through and in letters, oral histories, and baskets. Joyce Gabiola confronts the vicissitudes of actual "official" archives and challenges their institutional strictures and their racialization. Chris A. Eng revisits the historicity of the Japanese internment camps by productively reframing them in terms of kitsch and camp. C. Winter Han and Paul Michael Leonardo Atienza engage with virtual archives of gay sociality. Han takes Craigslist as a historical and cultural arena where tensions of interracial desires and intimacies are troubled and unsettled. Through a life history of a Filipino American gay man, Atienza examines Grindr as a location where pleasures and perils of online dating apps are the grounds by which shifting racialized standards of gay male desirability complicate the technology's promise of efficient and fulfilling sociosexual encounters. Anthony Yooshin Kim and Margaret Rhee's essay offers a reflective response to Jee Yeun Lee's provocation from the 1998 volume that maps out contemporary routes and challenges of queer Korean American studies.

The artists and scholars in this part collectively illustrate how and why queer histories and queer Asian and American critical engagement with archives, special collections, objects, historiography, and narratives produces critical insights. They show how queerness may playfully and powerfully disrupt dominant, well-known, but now tired histories and established conventional gender binaries, imperial racial hierarchies, and (hetero)normative notions of the past. In so doing, as a group, they show us how to queerly interpret histories with an intersectional attention to race, class, gender, sexuality, and location, and they point out the possibilities and pleasures messing with archives and reimagining different queer and Asian futurities.

Part V, Burning Down the House—Institutional Queerings

Social institutions have queer potentials despite their roles in maintaining and propping up power and inequality. The essays in this part lay out the varied sites and places where a queer intersectional analysis offers alternative sets of queer collective action and ways of being that interrogate the limits and possibilities of social institutions. From universities to mental health fields to religious settings, the essays offer a productive and radical set of institutional restructuring and reconfiguration that departs from neoliberal metrics of success and failure. In Long T. Bui's essay, the military complex might seem to be an odd site for exploring queerness, but he argues that the experiences and tactics of Asian American soldiers such as Dan Choi have effectively been a major source of critical insights about the facile connections between military service and "good legitimate citizenship." John Paul Catungal portrays the university as another place of queer navigation and disruption, particularly as higher education (in this case Canadian) has become entrenched in the unjust and rabidly inhumane precepts of neoliberal capitalism. However, with the presence of faculty of color and the deployment of queer of color critique, the university is made habitable and even a more vibrant site of learning despite ongoing precarity in the academic field. Queering the curriculum through intersectional approaches is one strategy in which the "house" of learning is transformed from a factory of professional skilled workers for the labor economy to agents for imagining and building the foundations for alternative educational futures. The mental health field is often considered a race-blind public service field, but the terrain is filled with inequalities, and more important, it is rife with the destructive processes of the privatization and monetization of "mental health well-being." To counter this trend, Mimi Khúc argues for a "queer" rethinking of clinical mainstream definitions of mental health issues according to the contingencies of racialized, classed, and gendered immigrant experiences and the works of Asian American critical theorists. Three essays involve the queer dimensions of religious institutions, practices, and experiences. May Farrales's essay focuses on the Catholic Church in Canada and its influence on Filipinx Canadian lives, not as easy extensions of each other but rather as complicated by the challenges of race, class, and everyday life. Spirituality and sexuality are not antipodal extremes but rather are intersecting lines of ideas and practices that complicate Filipinx Canadian lives. In other words, migration to Canada is not a "secularizing" process but involves other queer possibilities, even with the presence of religion. Sung Won Park offers his "personal theological reflection" as a Korean American transman who envisions the possibilities for Korean American immigrant churches to be transformed from institutions of transphobia into welcoming spaces through minjung theology. Pahole Sookkasikon unpacks the queer Orientalist underpinnings of the tensions surrounding two Thai temples in Berkeley, California, and Los Angeles and lays out the literal and figurative nourishing religious processes and rituals involved in Thai American community activist formation against heteronormative Orientalized neighborhood zoning politics.

Part VI, Mediating Queer

Scholars and writers in this part collectively explore the vicissitudes of Asian-ness and queerness in various media and sensorial regimes. Kay Ulanday Barrett's poetry evokes meaning-making worlds in various intimate encounters, including those of YouTube imagery, that enable various affective intensities and emotional stances around such intimacies and disabilities. The essays by Thea Quiray Tagle, Thomas Xavier Sarmiento, and Casey Mecija focus on queer Filipinx performativities' postcolonial "excesses." Using the cinematic production on the Andrew Cunanan murders, Sarmiento argues that these excesses elude racial and sexual legibilities in the United States; "excess" here is used in the geographic and spatial sense, whereby Filipinx subjects do not neatly align with the nation (Philippines) or with the diaspora (United States), or with either dominant East and West Coast perspectives or established LGBTQ cultures, and are instead routed through the Midwest region. Quiray Tagle and Mecija point to corporeal excesses (as in gyrating bodies or monsters and vampires) by thinking through queerness via (racialized) Filipinx kids and notions of queer childhood and futurity. Emily Raymundo offers an important critical analysis on a revised contemporary version and production of *M Butterfly* in the context of Trump-era "post-multiculturalism." The part is rounded out by Xine Yao's critical essay on a graphic novel where tarot cards and the occult play a central role in a queer mixed Japanese Canadian teen character's "disiden-tificatory tactics," which anticipate later popular QTPOC (Queer and Trans People of Color) tarot cards. The scholars and writers collectively show how queerness and Asian-ness are navigated and mediated through a range of popular culture, media, literature, and poetry. Contributors model for us to closely read diverse kinds of texts to reveal how race and queerness operate in surprising, unexpected, and complex ways.

Part VII, Finding One's Way: Routes of Lives and Bodies

Contributors in this part collectively use autobiographical writing and po-etry to remember and reinscribe powerful personal and family-related ex-periences concerning bodies, health, disability, gender transitions, bodily trauma, death, healing, resilience, and social action. The contributors in this part remind us that the personal is still political in the twenty-first century and that taking the time to remember and write important life moments as queer Asians has the power to touch others. This is not a concluding part. It is one that refuses termination or redemption but rather prefers a collection of moments of dwelling and lingering amid dreams, deaths, and illness. These works are not mere displays of emotions but are powerful illustrations of how queers of color confront, endure, and survive various vicissitudes and contingencies. What is perhaps stunning in all of these contributions is that they form a generous and brave commensal set of narratives about struggles that are always kept under wraps, submerged in the unconscious, or cast into the realm of forgetting. They are not emotional stalemates, final endpoints, or dramatic endings but rather pivotal nodes of healing or "mov-ing on" toward more complete itineraries of intimacies and histories.

Leslie Mah and Maiana Minahal read and rewrite their (queer, racial-ized, gendered, and classed) bodies and address how difficult it can be to navigate health-care systems and medical diagnoses; how healing journeys take many twists and turns; and how biology is not destiny. Kinship and the familial are ties that bind yet also set queer free. They are not always the spaces of incarceration that mainstream LGBTQ narratives often portray them to be. As a parent, Marsha Aizumi also recalls how (Asian) queer politics, sensibilities, orientations, connections, and personal and commu-nity knowledge have the power to transform lives and heal different kinds of bodies and identities. Karen Tongson embraces the memory of her grand-mother, Mamang, as pivotal in her own self-formation. Syd Yang offers a meditation about healing that weaves the biological, the historical, and the diasporic. traci kato-kiriyama's poem is a reverie about intimacies of places and people that blur both the past and the future.

The works in this part collectively echo and complicate past LGBTQ anthologies from the 1980s and 1990s that always included a significant number of autobiographical narratives. The anthologies from back in the day were a way to write from queer and Asian perspectives or as queer people of color (to give a few examples of featured positionalities and subjectivities), and readers in various communities often eagerly awaited them to find representations of themselves and their experiences. Thus, this part can be seen as significantly building on and dialoguing with the aforementioned literary legacies. Finally, readers of this part have the opportunity to bear witness to writers' personal truths and memories. Thus, as they read these queer Asian personal narratives, there is a strong possibility and hope that they will be deeply moved and hopefully forge some connection and the beginning of an emotional and political attunement that can animate and energize their own healing journeys.

III. Inspirations and Hope: Foundations and Futures

Part I, Enduring Spaces and Bodies

This collection of works gestures to enduring ideas of political and conceptual genealogies, openings, and inaugural thoughts about being in a queer racialized world.

Danni Lin
Kimberly Alidio
Jih-Fei Cheng
D'Lo
Patti Duncan
Douglas S. Ishii

Part II, Queer Unsettlings: Geographies, Sovereignties

This part is a series of conceptual and theoretical reconfigurations as it highlights issues of queerness in relation to settler colonialism and other political forms of spatial inhabitation and divisions.

Việt Lê
Kim Compoc
Sony Coráñez Bolton
Vanita Reddy
Jennifer Lynn Kelly
Reid Uratani

Part III, Building Justice: Queer Movements in Asian North America

This set of essays and works revolves around varied interrogations about the provocative intimacy between social justice and queerness.

Eric Estuar Reyes and Eric C. Wat
Amy Sueyoshi
Sasha Wijeyeratne
Kim Tran
Glenn D. Magpantay

Part IV, Messing up the Archives and Circuits of Desire

This set of writing engages with multiple political and cultural implications of various fields or dwelling spaces of knowledge and desire from academic fields to various cultural forms.

Ching-In Chen
Joyce Gabiola
Chris A. Eng
C. Winter Han
Paul Michael Leonardo Atienza
Anthony Yooshin Kim and Margaret Rhee

Part V, Burning Down the House—Institutional Queerings

This part lays out the varied sites and places where a queer intersectional analysis offers alternative sets of collective action and ways of being. From universities to the mental health field to various religious settings, the essays offer a productive and often radical set of queer reconfigurations of institutions and social structures.

Long T. Bui
John Paul Catungal
Mimi Khúc
May Farrales
Sung Won Park
Pahole Sookkasikon

Part VI, Mediating Queer

This set of essays explores the vicissitudes of Asianess and queerness in various media and sensorial regimes.

Kay Ulanday Barrett
Thomas Xavier Sarmiento
Casey Mecija
Thea Quiray Tagle
Emily Raymundo
Xine Yao

Part VII, Finding One's Way: Routes of Lives and Bodies

This set of essays, poems, and artwork offer multiple meditations and affective inquiries into diasporic contingencies, precarity, mourning, and the future as framed within a queer of color vantage.

Marsha Aizumi
Syd Yang
Leslie Mah
Maiana Minahal
Karen Tongson
traci kato-kiriyama

Acknowledgments and Itineraries: To Whom? For Whom? From Where? To Where?

This book, like many intellectual and political projects, is a journey, or more appropriately a conglomeration of ongoing and future travels. While a book is a site and a location for collective world making, we suggest that we take location not as a bounded site but, as James Clifford has wisely described it, as an itinerary, a process, and an unfolding.[9] In the spirit of this unfolding and in trying to present the coming together of three editors, we turn to our own individual voyages to complicate our seemingly unitary voice and singular destination in this volume.

Q & A is a product of various legacies, travails, and travel. One of the pillars of this anthology's was formed on the basis of the three editors' visions and experiences. How did the three of us come together? "Together" here is not a fusion but rather a set of crossings of political, intellectual, and social networks and visions. While this might seem unusual if not seemingly narcissistic, we want to highlight the importance of the personal with the social, as this collection is a tribute to the necessary connections between individual and collective endeavors and aspirations. In other words, coediting is a form of queer connection not merely between queer identified persons per se but rather about the uncomfortable yet productive juxtaposition of lives and projects. This connection or togetherness is future oriented not in terms of reproducibility but as an enduring coalitional commitment to reaching the horizon of a queer Asian America. In this part, we combine the biographical as a way to acknowledge, give thanks, and recognize the generosity of people who have buoyed our lives and fueled the energies behind this endeavor. We have crafted brief narratives of our individual personal odysseys and professional itineraries that have led us to this project that in turn become the platforms for recognizing debts and offering gratitude.

Alice Y. Hom

When *Q & A: Queer in Asian America* reached the milestone of its twentieth anniversary publication in 2018, I couldn't help but feel a bit of pride and disbelief that this anthology continues to be taught in a variety of courses ranging from queer studies, ethnic studies, and gender studies and is still relevant to a broad audience. When I meet queer Asian Americans of a certain age, I typically get an excited reaction, and they share how *Q & A* made a difference in their lives or inspired them to get involved with the queer Asian American community. As a community historian with a fascination with dates, I acknowledged the anniversary by writing a personal essay about what it meant for this anthology to be published. I did a quick phone interview with David L. Eng, the coeditor, and we reminisced about project and what it meant for us in our lives.

The significance of *Q & A* was its "narrative plentitude," a term coined by Viet Thanh Nguyen, at a time when that wasn't a reality for Asian American queers in academia or in our communities. This anthology brought together academics, activists, and cultural workers who submitted articles, roundtable interviews, personal essays, and artwork that represented a vibrant queer Asian America. David still gets emails from gay Asian Americans who struggle with the whiteness of the queer community and the dominant racial images of masculinity that don't reflect Asian American men. They share the difficulties of being an academic in a racist institution or department and the difficulties of coming out. I'm often approached at community events with people telling me *Q & A* made them feel like they belonged and even helped them in their coming out.

When David and I set out to collect articles for *Q & A*, we were both graduate students immersed in our academic pursuits while simultaneously involved in community activism with the Asian American queer community. I was in my first year as a Ph.D. student in a history program and knew I wanted to conduct research on lesbians of color and trace the activism of these women in various social movements. I loved being a graduate student because I could focus on the research and write about communities who were erased and marginalized within the published books and articles I read in the academy. I wanted to ensure community voices were heard, documented, and shared with the academic and wider public audience. Since I was trained in Asian American Studies Masters Program at UCLA, I felt indebted to the teachings of the early Asian American movement activists from the 1960s and 1970s, a time when the phrase "serve the people" was the rallying cry.

While I completed my Ph.D. program, I also knew that a tenure-track teaching position was not my end goal. I never wanted to become a professor, and I took jobs that allowed me to blend my academic endeavors with community organizing. I worked at Occidental College as the director of the Intercultural Community Center, where I worked on issues of diversity, equity, and inclusion, and social justice, which provided me the opportunity to work with students and faculty on intersectionality issues and allowed me to teach outside of the classroom. Cocurricular workshops, trainings, and programs became the way for me to make a difference.

The last fifteen years of my professional career has been in the philanthropy sector, where I focused on advocacy for increased funding to people of color and LGBTQ communities, specifically LGBTQ Asian American communities. Lack of funding continues to be a critical issue for Asian American issues and communities, and I worked at Asian Americans/Pacific Islanders in Philanthropy as the director of the Queer Justice Fund to address this need. AAPIP's Queer Justice Fund provided funding to support the fragile infrastructure and build the capacity of LGBTQ AAPI organizations with paid staff. In terms of my activism and community work, I came to a full-circle moment where I used to document and write about the LGBTQ Asian American organizing and community, and in the late 2000s I began funding them. Now in my career, I'm the director of equity and social justice at Northern California Grantmakers and can work at a larger scale of moving foundations to practice racial equity with an intersectional lens in their grant making and within the internal policies and operations of organizations.

When presented with the opportunity to revisit *Q & A* and work on a new anthology for the times we are in now, I was intrigued because the academic work is not as a close to me since I left working in higher education. I spoke with David, and he declined because his current work wasn't in queer studies. While I'm not in academia anymore, I wanted to make sure that this anthology had community voices and experiences and included activists, artists, and creatives. When I learned that Martin F. Manalansan IV and Kale Fajardo would be the other coeditors, I was excited to work with the both of them, having known them over the years.

In some ways, because *Q & A* was one of the earliest anthologies to gather personal, political, and academic essays on queer Asian Americans, it had the pressure of being a lot of things to different people. Some friends of mine have critiqued the anthology as being too academic, and others shared that it was great blend of different types of articles. I see this anthology as a product of the times, and it couldn't resonate for all people. It makes me think about the groups who formed early on and who dealt with the tensions of some people left out, or how the group focused on political activities while others wanted more social activities. The one group had to bear the burden of creating a space of belonging, and it couldn't be everything for everyone. The tensions and the critiques provided a generative space where people formed other groups and focused on the issues important to them. This new anthology is a product of this current time period, and we have more communities and a larger body of work to draw from.

There are many people to thank who have helped in my journey to where I am professionally and personally. I'd like to offer my appreciation and gratitude for their support, encouragement, and love over the years. A deep bow of thanks David L. Eng because this anthology wouldn't exist if we hadn't crossed paths at the Association of Asian American Studies conferences and he asked me if I wanted to coedit the first *Q & A*. Everyone needs a best friend like Diep Tran, someone who is there to say no when you're about to do something silly and to cheer you on when the fear seems overwhelming. A close circle of friends always helps when you need a meal, a shoulder to lean on, a writing buddy, an accountability partner, or someone to be with. A grateful bow to my chosen family: Maylei Blackwell, Gisele Fong, Noelle Ito, Ingin Kim, Sami Iwata, Laila Mehta, Marie Morohoshi, Tei Okamoto, Eric C. Wat, Kayva Yang, and Karen Yin. I want to thank my birth family, especially my mom; sisters Anita, Anna, and Angela; and my brother Wellington. They have all provided care and comfort.

To my professors and teachers from the academic world, I'd like to thank Janet Farrell Brodie, King-kok Cheung, Robert Dawidoff, Deena Gonzalez, Don Nakanishi, Eve Oishi, and Vicki L. Ruiz. They saw potential in me; encouraged me to focus on race, gender, and sexuality; and generously offered their expertise and time when I needed it the most. There are some people who come into your life for a reason, and these two amazing leaders, Jacki Rodriguez and Peggy Saika, showed me how one can be empathetic, progressive, and generous in the workplace. I'd also like to acknowledge and thank the healers, activists, and community builders in the LGBTQ Asian American communities. Lastly, much love and appreciation to Martin F. Manalansan IV and Kale Bantigue Fajardo, whose brilliance and dedication helped bring this anthology to life, and a thousand handclaps to Paul Michael (Mike) Leonardo Atienza, who managed and oversaw this project with humor, diligence, and expertise. The final nod of acknowledgment goes to the all the contributors of this anthology—thank you for sharing your gifts.

Kale Bantigue Fajardo

I am deeply honored to be a coeditor for this new queer and Asian American anthology. I offer a deep bow to my coeditors, Alice Y. Hom and Martin F. Manalansan IV, for inviting me into this project and for the important conversations we had as we coedited this book. I offer a deep bow to Paul Michael Leonardo Atienza, who strongly supported this project through important administrative assistance. He did a wonderful job keeping things organized and trying to keep us on schedule. He is an important part of this book, and we are grateful for his contributions. I also offer a deep bow to all of the contributors who took the time to write, reflect, edit, and submit their work. There are so many amazing writers, scholars, activists, and artists in this anthology, and so many powerful stories, insights, analyses, and critiques. I absolutely appreciate the contributors' commitments to queer Asian American lives, communities, the field of queer Asian American studies (and other allied fields), as well as everyone's commitment and modeling of engaged writing and living.

I am tasked with writing a little bit about my role in coediting or cocurating this anthology. I thought I would begin by talking about Alice and Martin since they are the ones who invited me to this project. Both of them represent two parts of my life that were previously somewhat separate but have become more integrated in the last two decades, and for that I am grateful. The 1990s were an exciting time, when many LGBTQ Asian Americans moved to and converged in the Bay Area to find "community" (if they weren't homegrown), and at the time the Bay Area was generally (more) affordable, unlike today. During most of the 1990s, I lived in Santa Cruz, primarily living and working as a graduate student at the University of California, Santa Cruz, studying cultural anthropology, feminist studies, and Philippine studies. I would drive up Highway 1 for an hour and a half to hang out in San Francisco and to be with other queer people of color, including queer Asian Americans, because although Santa Cruz had a queer POC scene, it was tiny and pretty marginalized. I met Alice at one of those queer Chinese Lunar New Year banquets that have been going on for years and decades! If I recall correctly, Alice was also a graduate student in Southern California. In the San Francisco queer Asian American community during this decade, many of us often went to pride parades, attended house parties together, danced together at queer/POC/Asian American clubs, attended the queer Asian American film shorts at the annual San Francisco LGBTQ film festivals, and attended other community-based cultural and political events. We developed friendships, and yes, we hooked up and were involved in "sticky (Asian American) relationships." Although Alice was an academic and a historian during this time period, our friendship did not revolve around academic matters or an academic community. It was more about cultural and political community building in the Bay and in California as young queer Asian Americans.

As a graduate student and junior ethnographer and anthropologist, I didn't centrally study queer Asian or Filipinx phenomena in the early to mid-1990s. I had other interests such as the sea, seafaring and shipping, migrant masculinities, the Filipinx diaspora, and globalization. Since this time, as a scholar I have queered all of these things and phenomena in my scholarship, and I am now generally considered a queer and trans Asian/ Filipinx American studies scholar and researcher. When I first met Alice, though, my academic life and my (queer/trans) personal and community life were more separate.

Fast-forward to 2005, when I first officially met Martin F. Manalansan IV. He had already published *Global Divas*, and I was still (re)writing *Filipino Crosscurrents*, my first ethnographic book. I really wanted his help on this project because I was strengthening the queer analytical thread of my research and book, and I knew Martin was a foundational queer Asian/ Filipinx American/diaspora studies scholar and anthropologist. *Global Divas* is an important book that queered Filipinx migration, and I was studying Filipino seamen in the global shipping industry, so his book offered an important model of scholarship and writing. At first I was hesitant to contact Martin because we were both up for the same job at the University of Minnesota, Twin Cities, the previous year, and I wasn't sure how he would react to me. (Minnesota hired me as a more junior scholar compared to Martin. Sometimes departments choose junior folks over senior folks due to financial issues or whatever specific needs the faculty may have. I am glad that we are now in the same department.) In spite of my hesitancy, I emailed Martin and asked him if he would read my dissertation and share feedback, critique, and questions with me. He immediately said yes, and he generously wrote me back with three to four pages of single-spaced comments, which was incredibly helpful as I revised my dissertation into a book. Martin has mentored me in other important ways. For example, he co-organized a Filipinx studies conference at the University of Illinois in 2008 (where he was teaching at the time), and he invited me and many other junior scholars to share our research and learn from more senior colleagues. Through this conference, we were able to further develop a Filipinx studies network and community. Thus, meeting Martin was a major moment in my life where my queer Asian/Filipino life became more integrated with my academic professional life.

It is through my collegial and community relationships with Alice and Martin and the connected roots and routes of queer Asian/Filipinx/American communities in California, Minnesota, and the Midwest that I have introduced here that inform my contribution to this anthology. Alice, Martin, and I have a lot of overlapping communities and networks, and perhaps this is what makes this book work, but it may also be a shortcoming. My networks and communities are generally California/West Coast based, and are now also more connected to Minnesota and the Midwest. I suggested many of the folks who are rooted and routed in these places.

To close, I want to say a few words about what I find most exciting about this anthology. To me, after many decades of separation or geographic exclusivity, I find it exciting to see and read how queer Asian American studies comfortably and fluidly moves both inside and outside of the borders of the United States and Asian America. Queer Asian American studies is a global field, and the various inter- and intra-regional interconnections that are made in this anthology are highly important. They signal complex and important solidarities with diverse places and people. I am also deeply excited and moved by the fierce writing by transgender, gender-nonconforming, and femme folks in this book. They reveal our multiple, complex, and powerful consciousness and our abilities to survive, change, heal, and thrive in cis-supremacist, white supremacist, patriarchal, and heteronormative dominant social conditions. The scholarly essays in this book are also excellent. They offer wonderful models for how to do close readings of various texts and fields and how to engage theories of culture and power, and I am confident these essays will be of importance in our classrooms. Last but not least, I am deeply moved by the poetry and autobiographical writing in this book. Many of the writers cut to the chase and teach us in succinct, clear, and compelling ways what it means to be queer and Asian in the twenty-first century, and they remind us that individual lives and the personal matter, but perhaps more important, when placed in a larger social field and context (like this book), the autobiographical and the personal become even more powerful.

Martin F. Manalansan IV

David Eng and Alice Y. Hom first approached me for a possible contribution to the first *Q & A* volume. At that time, I was in the second half of my decade-long involvement in AIDS and HIV prevention activism and research in New York City. David generously took me out to lunch and asked me about the possibility of submitting my essay. Due to the unforgiving nature of nonprofit work and the tumult of living in late twentieth-century New York City under the throes of a Giuliani-led massive gentrification, I was both physically and emotionally exhausted. I decided against doing so, and it is a decision I have always regretted. Not that I would have made a great contribution, but I felt that the publication of *Q & A* was a milestone in the emergence of queer studies as a vibrant critical approach in Asian and

Asian American studies. This was further solidified when I was hired into a tenure-track position in anthropology and Asian American studies at the University of Illinois, Urbana-Champaign, with a dissertation on Filipino gay men in New York City—a piece of research many people, including my adviser, were skeptical of finding any kind of institutional support in academia. The presence of queer studies in Asian American studies and in the other ethnic studies fields have led one former colleague in Latino studies to declare with more than a tinge of exasperation, "The queers have taken over ethnic studies." That kind of backhanded compliment reminded me of the crucial role that queer studies and queer critique have played and continue to play even in the most progressive and marginalized academic fields and interdisciplines.

The AIDS pandemic was the major historical linchpin that transformed and reoriented my own work. I know that it was a crucial turning point for many people's lives. By 1988, initial efforts to transform myself into an area studies scholar of Southeast Asia, particularly Indonesia, were dramatically altered after I read reports of a more than 200 percent increase in Asian and Pacific Islanders AIDS cases in San Francisco. At the same time, I was a bewildered witness to the illness experiences and deaths of many Asian American friends across the country, particularly New York City. It was then that I abandoned my dreams of becoming a traditional ethnographer immersed in the bucolic dailiness of a small Sumatran village and started a project that became my dissertation and then book, *Global Divas*.

In many ways, my academic experiences and the foray into AIDS prevention education, research, and activism mirrored a generation of Asian American queers who came of age in the 1980s and 1990s. The pandemic was at first seen as a white gay male disease and then, particularly in the U.S. northeast, the epidemic of mostly Black and Latino communities. Asians, due to many stereotypical Orientalist conceptions, were not seen as a "problem" and in fact were isolated from the ravages of the pandemic. Nothing could be further from the truth, as my years at the Gay Men's Health Crisis and the Asian Pacific Islander Coalition on HIV/AIDS would attest. Asian North Americans were caught in the swirl and turbulence of these late twentieth-century health and social crises. It is ironic that while many would think that the AIDS pandemic is over with the invention and use of such drugs as PREP and the possibility of an eventual cure, African American and Latino communities are still being ravaged, and new strains of the virus have been found. It is still a disease on a rampage around the world, including several Asian countries such as the Philippines.

When my colleagues and I were working in the late 1990s and early 2000s, we were conscious and encouraging of each other's work, but we were not directly working on building a "school of thought." Rather, we were very aware of the political and intellectual malaise caused by the post-Reagan neoliberal policies that have filtered through and infused, if not infected, the life worlds of many institutions and quotidian spaces. Through our mutual encouragement and friendships that cut across academic and ethnoracial boundaries, we were able to offer through individual and collective efforts, critical optics, and strategic embodied immersion and engagement with the experiences of immigrants, racial minorities, working-class subjects, communities of color refugee experiences, disability issues, settler colonialism, and struggles around indigeneity.

Today, I find myself in a somewhat uncomfortable institutional position as an "elder" or senior scholar. While I acknowledge the privileges of having a senior tenured position in a research university and my rather egocentric ambivalence about the physical imprints of aging, I refuse to abandon my continuing adherence to learning from my colleagues and allies in the struggle. My location here has been a product of mentorship and friendship with people in Filipino studies, queer studies, and critical ethnic studies such as Marlon Bailey, Christine Balance, Nerissa Balce, Joi Barrios LeBlanc, Rick Bonus, Lucy Mae San Pablo Burns, Rosa Castillo, Joshua Chambers-Letson, Richard Chu, Cathy Cohen, Christa Craven, Denise Cruz, Arnaldo Cruz Malave, Deidre de la Cruz, Robert Diaz, Lisa Duggan, David Eng, Yen Le Espiritu, Roderick Ferguson, Anna Gonzalez, Gayatri Gopinath, Jack Halberstam, Grace Hong, Allan Punzalan Isaac, E. Patrick Johnson, Bill Johnson Gonzalez, Ellen Lewin, Eng-Beng Lim, Lisa Lowe, Larry Lafountaine, Jeffrey McCune, Victor Mendoza, Ellen Moodie, Ghassan Moussawi, Jose Muñoz, Chantal Nadeau, Ramón Rivera-Servera, Richard T. Rodriguez, Robyn Rodriguez, Joseph Ruanto-Ramirez, Siobhan Somerville, Eric Wat, and Margot Weiss. I also extend my deep appreciation to the faculty and staff of Asian American studies at the University of Illinois at Urbana-Champaign: Pallassana Balgopal, Jose B. Capino, Clark Cunningham, Augusto Espiritu, Kat Fuenty, Maryam Kashani, Susan Koshy, Soo Ah Kwon, Christine Lyke, Mimi Thi Nguyen, A. Naomi Paik, Yoon Pak, Junaid Rana, and Lila Sharif. When I started this project, my dear friend, colleague, and mentor Nancy Abelmann passed away. Nancy was one of the main driving forces and creative energies behind Asian American studies at Illinois. She remains an inspiration to me and many others. This work hopefully will do justice to her valuable legacy.

After almost twenty years at Illinois, I moved to another vibrant community at the University of Minnesota, Twin Cities. Here, I found and am grateful for the camaraderie of such colleagues as Aren Aizura, Bianet Castellanos, Brenda Child, Jigna Desai, Erin Durban, Miranda Joseph, David Karjanen, Karen Ho, Juliana Hu Pegues, Erika Lee, Lorena Muñoz, Kevin Murphy, Elaine Tyler May, Jennifer Pierce, Elliot Powell, Sima Shakhsari, David Valentine, and Terrion Williamson.

I also want to recognize the continuing warmth of friends and colleagues in the Philippines: Fras Abaya, Oscar Campomanes, Gary Devilles, Patrick Flores, John Labella, Laura Samson, and Roland Tolentino. Of course, my dear high school friends who are still (like Rick Bonus and me) naturally young-looking and fabulous: Bobby Abastillas, Alonzo Gatuslao, Ariel Reyes, Manolo Tanquilut, and Ria Vera Cruz.

I am indebted to and in awe of the courageous, bold ideas and paradigms of a new generation of scholars, some of whom are listed in the bibliography at the end of the introduction, entitled "Inspirations and Hopes: Foundations and Futures." Admittedly, it is an incomplete list of works that have inspired and continue to inspire me to persist on learning and listening. I continue to discover new ideas and worlds from former and current graduate students and junior scholars in anthropology, Asian American studies, and queer studies such as Constancio Arnaldo, Dilara Çalişkan, John Paul Catungal, John Cho, Genevieve Clutario, Joseph Coyle, May Farrales, Dohye Kim, Kareem Khubchandani, Dai Kojima, Ferdie Lopez, John Musser, Khoi Nguyen, Monica F. W. Santos, Demiliza Saramosing, Chris Tan, Stan Thangaraj, and James Welker.

From my coeditors and myself, our heartfelt thanks to the brilliance, diligence, and tenacity of Paul Michael (Mike) Leonardo Atienza, who has been a major pillar of this project. Without Mike, this project will never have seen fruition.

Finally, I will always be indebted to my family dispersed across several countries and continents. I continue to thrive and survive through remembered intimate events and anticipated homecomings.

NOTES

1. David L. Eng and Alice Y. Hom, eds., *Q & A Queer in Asian America* (Philadelphia: Temple University Press, 1998).

2. Dana Takagi, "Maiden Voyage: Excursion into Sexuality and Identity Politics in Asian America," in *Asian American Sexualities: Dimensions of the Gay and Lesbian Experience*, ed. Russell Leong (New York: Routledge, 1996), 21–36.

3. Howard Chiang and Alvin K. Wong, "Asia Is Burning: Queer Asia as Critique," *Culture, Theory and Critique* 58, no. 2 (2017): 121–126.

4. See Anjali Arondekar and Geeta Patel, "Area Impossible: Notes toward an Introduction," *GLQ: A Journal of Lesbian and Gay Studies* 22, no. 2 (2016): 151–171; Shu-mei Shih, Chien-hsin Tsai, and Brian Bernards, eds, *Sinophone Studies: A Critical Reader* (New York: Columbia University Press, 2013); and Megan Sinnott, "Borders, Diaspora, and Regional Connections: Trends in Asian 'Queer' Studies," *The Journal of Asian Studies* 69, no. 1 (2010): 17–31.

5. See Cathy Cohen, "Punks, Bulldaggers, and Welfare Queens: The Radical Potential of Queer Politics?" *GLQ* 3 (1997): 437–465; Rodrick A. Ferguson, *Aberrations in Black: Toward a Queer of Color Critique* (Minneapolis: University of Minnesota Press, 2004).

6. Gayatri Gopinath, *Impossible Desires: Queer Diasporas and South Asian Public Cultures* (Durham, NC: Duke University Press, 2005).

7. Richard Fung, "Looking for My Penis: The Eroticized Asian in Gay Video Porn," in *How Do I Look? Queer Film and Video*, ed. Bad Object-Choices (Seattle: Bay Press, 1991), 145–168.

8. José Esteban Muñoz, *Cruising Utopia: The Then and There of Queer Futurity* (New York: New York University Press, 2009).

9. James Clifford, *Routes: Travel and Translation in the Late Twentieth Century* (Cambridge: Harvard University Press, 1997).

SELECTED BIBLIOGRAPHY

This is not a typical bibliography. This list includes works cited in this introduction as well as an incomplete yet exciting abbreviated glimpse of queer studies work and of queer diasporic works that have inspired and influenced the expansive *Q & A* project. We encourage readers to use this list as a core of an ever-expanding constellation of scholars, activists, and cultural producers that are continuing the struggle on multiple fronts.

Adur, Shweta M., and Bandana Purkayastha. "(Re)Telling Traditions: The Language of Social Identity among Queer South Asians in the United States." *South Asian Diaspora* 9, no. 1 (2017): 1–16.

Albrecht, Charlotte Karem. "Why Arab American History Needs Queer of Color Critique." *Journal of American Ethnic History* 37, no. 3 (2018): 84–92.

Alimahomed, Sabrina. "Thinking Outside the Rainbow: Women of Color Redefining Queer Politics and Identity." *Social Identities* 16, no. 2 (March 2010): 151–168.

Alumit, Noel, Anjali Arondekar, Dan Bacalzo, Eugenie Chan, Sylvia Chong, Richard Fung, Cathy Irwin, et al. *Embodying Asian/American Sexualities.* Lanham, MD: Lexington Books, 2009.

Antwi, Phanuel, Richard Fung, Christine Kim, and Helen Hok-Sze Leung. "Richard Fung's Re: Orientations in Vancouver." *Asian Diasporic Visual Cultures and the Americas* 4, no. 1–2 (2018): 165–178.

Arondekar, Anjali. "Thinking Sex with Geopolitics." *WSQ: Women's Studies Quarterly* 44, no. 3 (2016): 332–335.

———. "Time's Corpus." In *Comparatively Queer*, edited by W. Spurlin, J. Hayes, and Margaret R. Higonnet, 113–128. New York: Palgrave Macmillan, 2010.

Balance, Christine Bacareza. "Notorious Kin." *Journal of Asian American Studies* 11, no. 1 (February 2008): 87.

Bow, Leslie. "Transracial/Transgender: Analogies of Difference in Mai's America." *Signs: Journal of Women in Culture and Society* 35, no. 1 (September 2009): 75.

Bui, Long T. "Breaking into the Closet: Negotiating the Queer Boundaries of Asian American Masculinity and Domesticity." *Culture, Society and Masculinities* 6, no. 2 (Fall 2014): 129–149.

Caluya, Gilbert. "'The Rice Steamer': Race, Desire and Affect in Sydney's Gay Scene." *Australian Geographer* 39, no. 3 (2008): 283–292.

Catungal, John Paul. "Ethno-Specific Safe Houses in the Liberal Contact Zone: Race Politics, Place-Making and the Genealogies of the AIDS Sector in Global-Multicultural Toronto." *ACME: An International E-Journal for Critical Geographies* 12, no. 2 (2013): 250–278.

———. "The Lessons of Travel: Teaching Queer Asian Canada through Joella Cabalu's *It Runs in the Family* and Alejandro Yoshizawa's *All our Father's Relations.*" *TOPIA* 38 (2017): 93–101.

Chan, Connie S. "Don't Ask, Don't Tell, Don't Know: Sexual Identity and Expression among East Asian-American Lesbians." In *The New Lesbian Studies: Into the Twenty-First Century*, edited by Bonnie Zimmerman, Toni A. H. McNaron, and Margaret Cruikshank, 91–97. New York: Feminist, 1996.

Chan, Kenneth. "Rice Sticking Together: Cultural Nationalist Logic and the Cinematic Representations of Gay Asian-Caucasian Relationships and Desire." *Discourse: Journal for Theoretical Studies in Media and Culture* 28, no. 2–3 (Spring 2008): 178–196.

Chang, Stewart. "Is Gay the New Asian? Marriage Equality and the Dawn of a New Model Minority." *Asian American Law Journal* 23, no. 1 (June 2016): 5.

Chatterjee, Sandra. "Impossible Hosting: D'Lo Sets an Undomesticated Stage for South Asian Youth Artists." *Women and Performance* 16, no. 3 (2006): 443–462.

Chen, Aimin. "Another Powerful Voice on the New Millennium American Stage: A Study of Asian American Playwright Chay Yew and His Two Plays." *Foreign Literature Studies* 35, no. 2 (April 2013): 92–99.

Chen, Jian Neo. "Trans Riot: Transmasculine of Colour Expressions and Embodiments in the Films of Christopher Lee." *Asian Diasporic Visual Cultures and the Americas* 4, no. 3 (2018): 297–312.

Chen, Kuan-Hsing. "Asia as Method: Overcoming the Present Conditions of Knowledge Production." In *Asia as Method: Toward Deimperialization*, edited by Kuan-Hsing Chen, 211–285. Durham, NC: Duke University Press, 2010.

Chen, Mel Y. *Animacies: Biopolitics, Racial Mattering, and Queer Affect.* Durham, NC: Duke University Press, 2012.

———. "Everywhere Archives: Transgendering, Trans Asians, and the Internet." *Australian Feminist Studies* 25, no. 64 (2010): 199–208.

Cheng, Patrick S. "From a 'Far East Coast Cousin': Queer Asian Reflections on Roger A. Sneed's *Representations of Homosexuality.*" *Black Theology* 10, no. 3 (2012): 292–300.

———. "Gay Asian Masculinities and Christian Theologies." *Cross Currents* 61, no. 4 (December 2011): 540–48.

———. "'I Am Yellow and Beautiful': Reflections on Queer Asian Spirituality and Gay Male Cyberculture." *Journal of Technology, Theology, and Religion* 2, no. 3 (2011): 1–21.

———. "The Rainbow Connection: Bridging Asian American and Queer Theologies." *Theology and Sexuality* 17, no. 3 (2011): 235–264.

———. "A Three-Part Sinfonia: Queer Asian Reflections on the Trinity." *Journal of Race, Ethnicity, and Religion* 2 (2012): 1–23.

Chiang, Howard, and Alvin K. Wong. "Asia Is Burning: Queer Asia as Critique." *Culture, Theory and Critique* 58, no. 2 (2017): 121–126.

———. "Queering the Transnational Turn: Regionalism and Queer Asias." *Gender, Place and Culture* 23, no. 11 (2016): 1643–1656.

Chou, Rosalind S. *Asian American Sexual Politics: The Construction of Race, Gender, and Sexuality.* Lanham, MD: Rowman and Littlefield, 2012.

Choudhury, Prajna Paramita. "The Violence That Dares Not Speak Its Name: Invisibility in the Lives of Lesbian and Bisexual South Asian American Women." In *Body Evidence: Intimate Violence Against South Asian Women in America*, edited by Shamita Das Dasgupta, 126–138. New Brunswick, NJ: Rutgers University Press, 2007.

Chung, Y. Barry, and Anneliese A. Singh. "Lesbian, Gay, Bisexual, and Transgender Asian Americans." *Asian American Psychology: Current Perspectives* (2009): 233–246.

Clifford, James. *Routes: Travel and Translation in the Late Twentieth Century*. Cambridge, MA: Harvard University Press, 1997.

Cohen, Cathy J. "Punks, Bulldaggers, and Welfare Queens: The Radical Potential of Queer Politics?" *GLQ: A Journal of Lesbian and Gay Studies* 64, no. 2 (May 1997): 437–465.

Coloma, Roland Sintos. "'Too Asian?' On Racism, Paradox and Ethno-nationalism." *Discourse: Studies in the Cultural Politics of Education* 34, no. 4 (2013): 579–598.

———. "White Gazes, Brown Breasts: Imperial Feminism and Disciplining Desires and Bodies in Colonial Encounters." *Paedagogica Historica* 48, no. 2 (2012): 243–261.

Coráñez Bolton, Sony. "Deconstructing Filipino Studies: Queer Reading beyond U.S. Exceptionalism." *GLQ: A Journal of Lesbian and Gay Studies* 19, no. 4 (2013): 575–577.

Cynn, Christine. "'[T]he Ludicrous Transition of Gender and Sentiment.'" *Journal of Asian American Studies* 19, no. 2 (June 2016): 237–62.

David, Emmanuel. "Purple-Collar Labor: Transgender Workers and Queer Value at Global Call Centers in the Philippines." *Gender and Society* 29, no. 2 (2015): 169–194.

———. "Transgender Archipelagos." *Transgender Studies Quarterly* 5, no. 3 (2018): 332–354.

David, Emmanuel, and Christian J. P. Cruz. "Deaf Turns, Beki Turns, Transformations: Toward New Forms of Deaf Queer Sociality." *Feminist Formations* 30 no. 1 (2018): 91–116.

Davies, Sharyn Graham. *Gender Diversity in Indonesia: Sexuality, Islam and Queer Selves*. London: Routledge, 2010.

de Guzman, Ben, and Alice Y. Hom. "Crossing Intersections: Challenges Facing Asian American, Native Hawaiian, Pacific Islander and Lesbian, Gay, Bisexual, Transgender Youth: Exploring Issues and Recommendations." *AAPI Nexus* 9, no. 1–2 (Fall 2011): 4–10.

Diaz, Robert G. "Queer Unsettlements." *Journal of Asian American Studies* 19, no. 3 (October 2016): 327–50.

Diaz, Robert G., Marissa Largo, and Fritz Pino, eds. *Diasporic Intimacies: Queer Filipinos and Canadian Imaginaries*. Evanston, IL: Northwestern University Press, 2017.

Dyer, Hannah, and Casey Mecija. "Leaving to Love: Filipina Caregivers and the Queer Kinship of Transnational Childcare." *World Futures* 74, no. 7–8 (2018): 542–558.

Eguchi, Shinsuke. "Cross-National Identity Transformation: Becoming a Gay 'Asian-American' Man." *Sexuality and& Culture* 15, no. 1 (March 2011): 19–40.

———. "Queer Intercultural Relationality: An Autoethnography of Asian–Black (Dis) Connections in White Gay America." *Journal of International & Intercultural Communication* 8, no. 1 (February 2015): 27.

Ellawala, Themal I. "Mismatched Lovers: Exploring the Compatibility between LGBTQ+ Identity Theories and Gender and Sexual Plurality in Sri Lanka." *Sexuality and Culture* 22, no. 4 (December 2018): 1321–1339.

Émon, Ayeshah, and Christine Garlough. "Refiguring the South Asian American Tradition Bearer: Performing the 'Third Gender' in *Yoni Ki Baat*." *Journal of American Folklore* 128, no. 510 (Fall 2015): 412–437.

Eng, Chris A. "'Give It up, Kwang': Disavowing Asian Labor and Queer/Trans of Color Critique in *Hedwig and the Angry Inch*." *Theatre Journal* 70, no. 2 (2018): 173–193.

———. "Queer Genealogies of (Be) Longing: On the Thens and Theres of Asian America in Karen Tei Yamashita's I Hotel." *Journal of Asian American Studies* 20, no. 3 (2017): 345–372.

Eng, David L. *The Feeling of Kinship: Queer Liberalism and the Racialization of Intimacy*. Durham, NC: Duke University Press, 2010.

Engebretsen, Elisabeth L., Hongwei Bao, and William F. Schroeder, eds. *Queer/Tongzhi China: New Perspectives on Research, Activism and Media Cultures*. Copenhagen, Denmark: Nordic Institute of Asian Studies Press, 2015.

Fajardo, Kale Bantigue. *Filipino Crosscurrents: Oceanographies of Seafaring, Masculinities, and Globalization*. U of Minnesota Press, 2011.

——. "Transportation: Translating Filipino and Filipino American Tomboy Masculinities through Global Migration and Seafaring." *GLQ: A Journal of Lesbian and Gay Studies* 14, no. 2–3 (2008): 403–424.

Ferguson, Roderick. *Aberrations in Black: Toward a Queer of Color Critique*. Minneapolis: University of Minnesota Press, 2003.

Ferrão, R. Benedito. "Gay Globalization via Goa in My Brother . . . Nikhil." *Journal of Creative Communications* 6, no. 1–2 (2011): 141–147.

Fung, Richard. "How Do I Look? Queer Film & Video," In *Bad Object-Choices*, edited by Bad Object-Choices, 145–168. Seattle: Bay, 1991.

Furth, Charlotte. "Becoming Alternative? Modern Transformations of Chinese Medicine in China and the United States." *Canadian Bulletin of Medical History* 28, no. 1 (2011): 5–41.

Gopinath, Gayatri. *Impossible Desires: Queer Diasporas and South Asian Public Cultures*. Durham, NC: Duke University Press. 2005.

——. *Unruly Visions: The Aesthetic Practices of Queer Diaspora*. Durham, NC: Duke University Press, 2018.

Haas, Astrid. "Discourses of Belonging: Language and Identities in Gay Asian American Drama." In *Moving Migration: Narrative Transformations in Asian American Literature*, edited by Johanna C. Kardux and Doris Einsiedel, 139–160. Contributions to Asian American Literary Studies 5. Münster: Lit, 2010.

Hahm, Hyeouk Chris, and Chris Adkins. "A Model of Asian and Pacific Islander Sexual Minority Acculturation." *Journal of LGBT Youth* 6, no. 2–3 (April 2009): 155–173.

Han, C. Winter. *Geisha of a Different Kind: Race and Sexuality in Gaysian America*. New York: New York University Press, 2015.

Haritaworn, Jin. "Shifting Positionalities: Empirical Reflections on a Queer/Trans of Colour Methodology." *Sociological Research Online* 13, no. 1 (2008): 1–12.

Hegarty, Benjamin. "The Value of Transgender: Waria Affective Labor for Transnational Media Markets in Indonesia." *Transgender Studies Quarterly* 4, no. 1 (2017): 78–95.

Hochberg, Gil Z. "Introduction: Israelis, Palestinians, Queers: Points of Departure." *GLQ: A Journal of Lesbian and Gay Studies* 16, no. 4 (2010): 493–516.

Homma, Yuko, and Elizabeth M. Saewyc. "The Emotional Well-Being of Asian-American Sexual Minority Youth in School." *Journal of LGBT Health Research* 3, no. 1 (2007): 67–87.

Huang, Jill, Eric C. Chen, and Joseph G. Ponterotto. "Heterosexual Chinese Americans' Experiences of Their Lesbian and Gay Sibling's Coming Out." *Asian American Journal of Homosexuality* 7, no. 3 (2016): 147–158.

Hwahng, Sel J. "The Western 'Lesbian Agenda' and the Appropriation of Non-Western Transmasculine People." In *Gender and the Science of Difference: Cultural Politics of Contemporary Science and Medicine*, edited by Jill A. Fisher, 164–186. New Brunswick, NJ: Rutgers University Press, 2011.

Hwahng, Sel J., and Alison J. Lin. "The Health of Lesbian, Gay, Bisexual, Transgender, Queer, and Questioning People." In *Asian American Communities and Health: Context, Research, Policy, and Action*, edited by Jill A. Fisher, 226–282. New Brunswick, NJ: Rutgers University Press, 2009.

Kang, Dredge Byung'chu. "Eastern Orientations: Thai Middle-Class Gay Desire for 'White Asians.'" *Culture, Theory and Critique* 58, no. 2 (2017): 182–208.

Kanuha, Valli Kalei. "'Relationships So Loving and So Hurtful': The Constructed Duality of Sexual and Racial/Ethnic Intimacy in the Context of Violence in Asian and Pacific Islander Lesbian and Queer Women's Relationships." *Violence against Women* 19, no. 9 (September 2013): 1175–1196.

Kapadia, Ronak K. "Sonic Contagions: Bird Flu, Bandung, and the Queer Cartographies of MIA." *Journal of Popular Music Studies* 26, no. 2–3 (2014): 226–250.

Khan, Faris A. "Powerful Cultural Productions: Identity Politics in Diasporic Same-Sex South Asian Weddings." *Sexualities* 14, no. 4 (August 2011): 377.

Khubchandani, Kareem. *Ishtyle: Accenting Gay Indian Nightlife*. Ann Arbor: University of Michigan Press, 2020.

———. "Lessons in Drag: An Interview with LaWhore Vagistan." *Theatre Topics* 25, no. 3 (2015): 285–294.

———. "Terrifying Performances: Black-Brown-Queer Borrowings in *Loins of Punjab Presents*." *Journal of Asian American Studies* 19, no. 3 (October 2016): 275–297.

Kina, Laura, and Jan Christian Bernabe, eds. *Queering Contemporary Asian American Art*. Seattle: University of Washington Press, 2017.

Kleisath, C. M. "The Costume of Shangri-La: Thoughts on White Privilege, Cultural Appropriation, and Anti-Asian Racism." *Journal of Lesbian Studies* 18, no. 2: 142–157.

Kojima, Dai. "Bootstraps, Sugar Daddies, Silence and Civility: A Queer Reflection on Japanese Endurance." *TOPIA* 38 (2017): 115–122.

———. "Migrant Intimacies: Mobilities-in-Difference and Basue Tactics in Queer Asian Diasporas." *Anthropologica* (2014): 33–44.

———. "Trans-Pacific Imaginaries and Queer Intimacies in the Ruins of Middlesex." *The Goose* 17, no. 1 (2018): 57.

Kojima, Dai, John Paul Catungal, and Robert Diaz. "Introduction: Feeling Queer, Feeling Asian, Feeling Canadian." *TOPIA* 38 (2017): 69–80.

Kumashiro, Kevin, ed. *Restoried Selves: Autobiographies of Queer Asian/Pacific American Activists*. New York: Routledge, 2004.

Lavin, Maud, Ling Yang, and Jing Jamie Zhao, eds. *Boys' Love, Cosplay, and Androgynous Idols: Queer Fan Cultures in Mainland China, Hong Kong, and Taiwan*. Hong Kong: Hong Kong University Press, 2017.

Leong, Russell. *Asian American Sexualities: Dimensions of the Gay and Lesbian Experience*. New York: Routledge, 2014.

Lim, Eng-Beng. *Brown Boys and Rice Queens: Spellbinding Performance in the Asias*. New York: New York University Press, 2014.

Luu, Thang D., and Monit Cheung. "GLBT Vietnamese-Americans: Building a Conceptual Framework to Examine Minority Help-Seeking Behavior." *Journal of GLBT Family Studies* 6, no. 4 (2010): 365–380.

Ly, Lynn. "Beyond Refusal: Queer Transpacific Feminism During the Vietnam War." *TOPIA* 38 (2017): 145–154.

———. "(Im)Possible Futures: Liberal Capitalism, Vietnamese Sniper Women, and Queer Asian Possibility." *Feminist Formations* 29, no. 1 (2017): 136–160.

Magpantay, Glenn D. "The Future of the LGBTQ Asian American and Pacific Islander Community in 2040." *AAPI Nexus* 14, no. 2 (Fall 2016): 33–47.

Manalansan IV, Martin F. "Queer Worldings: The Messy Art of Being Global in Manila and New York." *Antipode* 47, no. 3 (June 2015): 566–579.

———. "The 'Stuff' of Archives: Mess, Migration, and Queer Lives." *Radical History Review* 2014, no. 120 (2014): 94–107.

Martin, Fran, Peter Jackson, Mark McLelland, and Audrey Yue, eds. *AsiaPacifiQueer: Rethinking Genders and Sexualities*. Champaign: University of Illinois Press, 2010.

Masequesmay, Gina. "How Religious Communities Can Help LGBTIQQ Asian Americans to Come Home." *Theology and Sexuality* 17, no. 3 (2011): 319–335.

Masequesmay, Gina, and Sean Metzger, eds. *Embodying Asian/American Sexualities*. Lanham, MD: Rowman and Littlefield. 2010.

Mayo Jr., James B. "Hmong History and LGBTQ Lives: Immigrant Youth Perspectives on Being Queer and Hmong." *Journal of International Social Studies* 3, no. 1 (2013): 79–91.

McIntosh, Dawn Marie D., Dreama G. Moon, and Thomas K. Nakayama. "Queerness as Strategic Whiteness: A Queer Asian American Critique of Peter Le." In *Interrogating the Communicative Power of Whiteness*, edited by Dreama G. Moon, Dawn Marie D. McIntosh, Thomas K. Nakayama, 43–59. Abingdon, Oxon: Routledge, 2018.

Munoz, Jose. *Cruising Utopia: The Then and There of Queer Futurity*. New York: New York University Press, 2009.

Nadal, Kevin L., and Ben Cabangun. *Working with Asian American/Pacific Islander Gay Men Living with HIV/AIDS: Promoting Effective and Culturally Appropriate Approaches*, edited by Leo Wilton, 225–246. New York: Springer, 2017.

Nadal, Kevin L., and Melissa J. H. Corpus. "'Tomboys' and 'Baklas': Experiences of Lesbian and Gay Filipino Americans." *Asian American Journal of Psychology* 4, no. 3 (September 2013): 166–175.

Narui, Mitsu. "Understanding Asian/American Gay, Lesbian, and Bisexual Experiences from a Poststructural Perspective." *Journal of Homosexuality* 58, no. 9 (2011): 1211–1234.

Ngo, Bic. "The Importance of Family for a Gay Hmong American Man: Complicating Discourses of 'Coming Out.'" *Hmong Studies Journal* 13 (2012): 1–27.

Ngo, Bic, and Melissa Kwon. "A Glimpse of Family Acceptance for Queer Hmong Youth." *Journal of LGBT Youth* 12, no. 2 (2015): 212–231.

Nguyen, Hoang Tan. *A View from the Bottom: Asian American Masculinity and Sexual Representation*. Durham, NC: Duke University Press, 2014.

Ocampo, Anthony C., and Daniel Soodjinda. "Invisible Asian Americans: The Intersection of Sexuality, Race, and Education among Gay Asian Americans." *Race, Ethnicity and Education* 19, no. 3 (May 2016): 480–499.

Ong, Aihwa. "Introduction: An Analytics of Biotechnology and Ethics at Multiple Sites." In *Asian Biotech: Ethics and Communities of Fate*, edited by Aihwa Ong and Nancy N. Chen, 1–51. Durham, NC: Duke University Press, 2010. Electronic book.

Operario, Don, Chong-Suk Han, and Kyung-Hee Choi. "Dual Identity among Gay Asian Pacific Islander Men." *Culture, Health and Sexuality* 10, no. 5 (June 2008): 447–461.

Patel, Alpesh Kantilal. *Productive Failure: Writing Queer Transnational South Asian Art Histories*. Oxford: Oxford University Press, 2017.

Pha, Kong Pheng, Louisa Schein, and Pao Lee Vue. "Hmong Sexual Diversity: Beginning the Conversation." *Hmong Studies Journal* 16 (2015): 1.

Phua, Voon Chin. "Contesting and Maintaining Hegemonic Masculinities: Gay Asian American Men in Mate Selection." *Sex Roles* 57 no. 11–12 (December 2007): 909–918.

Ponce, Martin Joseph. *Beyond the Nation: Diasporic Filipino Literature and Queer Reading*. New York: New York University Press, 2012.

———. "José Garcia Villa's Modernism and the Politics of Queer Diasporic Reading." *GLQ: A Journal of Lesbian and Gay Studies* 17, no. 4 (2011): 575–602.

———. "Pinoy Posteriority." *Filipino Studies: Palimpsests of Nation and Diaspora*, edited by Martin F. Manalansan IV and Augusto Espiritu, 251–273. New York: New York University Press, 2016.

Puar, Jasbir K. *The Right to Maim: Debility, Capacity, Disability*. Durham, NC: Duke University Press, 2017.

———. *Terrorist Assemblages: Homonationalism in Queer Times*. Durham, NC: Duke University Press, 2007.

———. "'The Turban Is Not a Hat': Queer Diaspora and Practices of Profiling." *Sikh Formations* 4, no. 1 (2008): 47–91.

Quero, Hugo Córdova, and Michael Sepidoza Campos. *Queering Migrations towards, from, and beyond Asia*. New York: Palgrave Macmillan, 2014.

Reddy, Chandan. *Freedom with Violence: Race, Sexuality, and the US State*. Durham, NC: Duke University Press, 2011.

Sam, Kosal, and Susan Finley. "A Teacher's Journey: A First-Person Account of How a Gay, Cambodian Refugee Navigated Myriad Barriers to Become Educated in the United States." *International Journal of Qualitative Studies in Education (QSE)* 28, no. 6 (July 2015): 714–729.

Sarmiento, Thomas X. "Diasporic Filipinx Queerness, Female Affective Labor, and Queer Heterosocial Relationalities in *Letters to Montgomery Clift*." *Women, Gender, and Families of Color* 5, no. 2 (2017): 105–128.

Serquiña Jr., Oscar Tantoco. "Out and About: Migrant Bakla, Perverse Intimacies, and the Musical of Migration in Liza Magtoto's *Care Divas*." *Kritika Kultura* 27 (2016): 199–248.

Shakhsari, Sima. "From Homoerotics of Exile to Homopolitics of Diaspora: Cyberspace, the War on Terror, and the Hypervisible Iranian Queer." *Journal of Middle East Women's Studies* 8, no. 3 (Fall 2012): 14–40, 157.

Shih, Shu-mei. "Against Diaspora: The Sinophone as Places of Cultural Production," in *Global Chinese Literature: Critical Essays*, edited by Jing Tsu and David Wang, 29–48. Leiden, the Netherlands: Brill, 2010.

Shimizu, Celine Parreñas. "Screening Shirtless AZN Men: The Full Frontal Power of Intimate Internet Industries." *Positions* 24, no. 1 (February 2016): 231–252.

———. *Straitjacket Sexualities: Unbinding Asian American Manhoods in the Movies*. Palo Alto, CA: Stanford University Press, 2012.

Sieber, Patricia. "The Crucible of Space, Time, and Words: Female Same-Sex Subjectivities in Contemporary Chinese-language Contexts." In *The Cambridge History of Gay and Lesbian Literature*, edited by Ellen Lee McCallum and Mikko Tuhkanen, 512–528. Cambridge: Cambridge University Press, 2014.

Sinott, Megan. "Borders, Diaspora and Regional Connections: Trends in Asian Queer Studies." *Journal of Asian Studies* 69, no. 1 (2010): 17–31.

Sohn, Stephen Hong. "Burning Hides What It Burns." *Journal of Asian American Studies* 17, no. 3 (October 2014): 243.

———. *Inscrutable Belongings: Queer Asian North American Fiction*. Palo Alto, CA: Stanford University Press, 2018.

Strayhorn, Terrell L. "Beyond the Model Minority Myth: Interrogating the Lived Experiences of Korean American Gay Men in College." *Journal of College Student Development* 55, no. 6 (September 2014): 586–594.

Strings, Sabrina, and Long T. Bui. "'She Is Not Acting, She Is': The Conflict between Gender and Racial Realness on RuPaul's Drag Race." *Feminist Media Studies* 14, no. 5 (2014): 822–836.

Sueyoshi, Amy. *Discriminating Sex: White Leisure and the Making of the American "Oriental."* Champaign: University of Illinois Press, 2018.

———. "Miss Morning Glory: Orientalism and Misogyny in the Queer Writings of Yone Noguchi." *Amerasia Journal* 37, no. 2 (2011): 2–27.

———. "Queer Asian American Historiography." In *The Oxford Handbook of Asian American History*, edited by Eiichiro Azuma and David Yoo, 267–278. New York: Oxford University Press, 2016.

———. *Queer Compulsions: Race, Nation, and Sexuality in the Affairs of Yone Noguchi.* Honolulu: University of Hawai'i Press, 2012.

Sung, M. R., D. M. Szymanski, and C. Henrichs-Beck. "Challenges, Coping, and Benefits of Being an Asian American Lesbian or Bisexual Woman." *Psychology of Sexual Orientation and Gender Diversity* 2, no. 1 (2019): 52–64.

Takagi, Dana. "Maiden Voyage: Excursion into Sexuality and Identity Politics in Asian America." In *Asian American Sexualities: Dimensions of the Gay and Lesbian Experience*, edited by Russell Leong, 21–36. New York: Routledge, 1996.

Takemoto, Tina. "Looking for Jiro Onuma: A Queer Meditation on the Incarceration of Japanese Americans during World War II." *GLQ: A Journal of Lesbian and Gay Studies* 20, no. 3 (July 2014): 241–275.

Tan, Jia. "Beijing Meets Hawai'i: Reflections on Ku'er, Indigeneity, and Queer Theory." *GLQ: A Journal of Lesbian and Gay Studies* 23, no. 1 (2017): 137–150.

Tan, Jonathan. "From Classical Tradition Maintenance to Remix Traditioning: Revisioning Asian American Theologies for the 21st Century." *Journal of Race, Ethnicity, and Religion* 3, no. 2–3 (2012): 1.

Tongson, Karen. *Relocations: Queer Suburban Imaginaries.* New York: New York University Press, 2011.

Trang, M. L., and N. Yu. "Ideological and Philosophical Underpinnings of Attitudes toward Sexual Minorities in Vietnamese Society." *Sexuality and Culture* (2018): 1–14.

Velasco, Gina. "Performing the Filipina 'Mail-Order Bride': Queer Neoliberalism, Affective Labor, and Homonationalism." *Women and Performance: A Journal of Feminist Theory* 23, no. 3 (2013): 350–372.

Winter, Sam. "Cultural Considerations for the World Professional Association for Transgender Health's Standards of Care: The Asian Perspective." *International Journal of Transgenderism* 11, no. 1 (January 2009): 19–41.

Wong, Nicholas. "Saving Face: Unveiling or Covering Up Asian American Experiences?" *Asian Cinema* 21, no. 2 (Fall–Winter 2010): 254–267.

Wong, Sau-ling C. "Circuits/Cycles of Desire." *Amerasia Journal* 37, no. 1 (April 2011): 87–114.

Wu, Cynthia. *Sticky Rice: A Politics of Intraracial Desire.* Temple University Press, 2018.

Yapp, Hentyle. "To Punk, Yield, and Flail: Julie Tolentino's Etiolations and the Strong Performative Impulse." *GLQ: A Journal of Lesbian and Gay Studies* 24, no. 1 (2018): 113–138.

Yue, Audrey. "Critical Regionalities in Inter-Asia and the Queer Diaspora." *Feminist Media Studies* 11, no. 1 (2011): 131–138.

Zhang, C. Y. "When Feminist Falls in Love with Queer: Dan Mei Culture as a Transnational Apparatus of Love." *Feminist Formations* 29, no. 2 (2017): 121–146.

Zhang, Eric. "Memoirs of a GAY! Sha: Race and Gender Performance on RuPaul's *Drag Race*." *Studies in Costume and Performance* 1, no. 1 (2016): 59–75.

PART I

Enduring Spaces and Bodies

"Shanghai, Hong Kong, Egg Fu Yung, Fortune Cookie Always Wrong"

DANNI LIN

"Shanghai, Hong Kong, Egg Fu Yung, Fortune Cookie Always Wrong," 2019. Oil paint on canvas and mixed media, 84 × 216 in. (By Danni Lin)

All the Pinays are straight, all the queers are Pinoy, but some of us

Kimberly Alidio

hold our femme gaze straight into the cosmos

behold a supernova of fat negation

know Mark Aguhar as the real babaylan

have mothers young enough to be transfemmes never to reach 26

                        Blessed be

our ugly grief

our helpless beauty

this very moment of utterance incarnate in an absent brown body

joining us

alive painfully so

strand us alone together

                      I will never not

want to be violent with you (dare you to say

this isn't love, queen)

pray for

her resurrection every easter

"I'm just so bored and so pretty and not white"

LOL YOUR PINAY SELF

LOL YOUR SUBCONSCIOUS DECOLONIAL INDIGENEITY

LOL RECOVERY AS AN ESCAPE HATCH FROM REAL NEGOTIATIONS

LOL CARING THAT WHITE PEOPLE THINK OUR BODIES ARE CHEAP

LOL THINKING ONLY WHITE PEOPLE THINK OUR BODIES ARE CHEAP

LOL THINKING WHITE POETS MATTER AT ALL

LOL FRETTING OVER OUR FAILED TOKENIZATION

LOL AGENCY AND THE COURAGE TO SPEAK

LOL CENTERING OURSELVES IN THE NARRATIVE

LOL PRETTY TRAUMA POETRY AT OUR NATION'S CAPITAL

LOL RESPECTABILITY POLITICS

LOL SLUT SHAMING

LOL LANGUAGE SHAMING

LOL MOTHER TONGUE

LOL THE MOTHERLAND

LOL PRECOLONIAL PARADISE FOLKTALES

LOL UTOPIA UNTOUCHED BY QUEER PINAY RUIN ACROSS TIME &
    SPACE

LOL YOUR LOLA

LOL YOUR HIYA

LOL YOUR WALANG HIYA

LOL OUR TENDER EMOTIONALITY

AUTHOR'S NOTE

"All the Pinays are straight, all the queers are Pinoy, but some of us" was originally published in the book of poetry, *After projects the resound* (Black Radish Books, 2016). It quotes Mark Aguhar's Call Out Queen, and takes its title from Akasha (Gloria T.) Hull, Patricia Bell Scott, and Barbara Smith's *All the Women Are White, All the Blacks Are Men, But Some of Us Are Brave: Black Women's Studie*s (Feminist Press at CUNY, 1982).

The Hybridity of Race

Genetics, Geopolitics, and the Queer Genealogy
of the "Chinese Jew"

JIH-FEI CHENG

In August 2012, the *Jewish Journal of Greater Los Angeles*, or simply the *Jewish Journal*, featured a cover photograph with the caption "The Jews of China: Their past and our future." The inside description read, "Kids eating Matzah in Kaifeng, China." Together, two stories made the case that the People's Republic of China (PRC) plays a crucial role in determining the futures of Jewish studies and the nation-state of Israel. In "The Jews of Kaifeng," David N. Myers speculates that Judeo-Persians migrated during the medieval period to the ancient capital city of Kaifeng, Henan. The article touts the religious and cultural revitalization of today's Kaifeng Jews as an effort led by Shavei Israel,[1] an Israel-based organization that "reaches out and assists Lost Tribes and 'Hidden Jews' seeking return to the Jewish people."[2] In his second article, "Jewish Studies Flourish in China," Myers names the modern-day PRC as "one of the most promising in terms of growth" for Jewish studies.[3] He cites the "riches of American Jewish literature" and the influential role American Jews have played in institutionalizing Jewish studies in the PRC, such as the endowment funded by "Los Angeles Jewish philanthropists Diane and Guilford Glazer."[4] Myers marvels at the rapid economic development of the PRC and comments on how the fervor for Jewish studies among the PRC's graduate students rivals that of graduate students in the United States.[5] "Encountering these students made clear how remarkable and worthy an enterprise Jewish studies in China is," Myers proclaims. "It's important for China, it's important for the field—and, it almost goes without saying, it's important for Jews that the Chinese develop an informed understanding of their past and present in the 21st century."[6]

The *Jewish Journal*'s double-article feature underscores the critical importance of the figure of the "Chinese Jew" in auguring, even building, diplomatic relations between the PRC and Israel. Furthermore, it highlights the fundamental role that knowledge produced about "Chinese Jews" plays in reconfiguring contemporary geopolitics and global power. To understand the stakes, this chapter examines the shifting terrain of racial and ethnic identifications as we move from the twentieth century, known as the "American

Century," further into the twenty-first century, dubbed by scholars like economist and Pulitzer Prize–winner Joseph E. Stiglitz the "Chinese Century."[7] Specifically, it argues that the recent return to focus and debate the existence of Chinese Jews illuminates how the battle between the United States and the PRC for global authority occurs at the molecular level. To understand the implications at hand for science, politics, and the global economy, this chapter outlines an interdisciplinary historical approach to studying the fields of knowledge that construct race and ethnicity.

The transfer in global hegemony is prompted by the growing military and economic might of the PRC, wherein the PRC's defense spending ranks second only to the United States.[8] Meanwhile, the yuan begins to replace the dollar as a standard for international currency.[9] Nation-states formerly dependent upon U.S. military, financial, and political aid, such as Israel, proceed toward carefully and gradually negotiating ways to simultaneously gain or shift diplomatic allegiance to the PRC. What at first blush may seem an imminent turn toward yet another new world order actually entails a transformation in ideology through various social, cultural, and even biological spheres—a process that early twentieth-century anti-fascist political theorist Antonio Gramsci described as the changes that occur in the field of "common sense."[10] The case of the Chinese Jew underscores how the shift in common sense hinges upon race, particularly contestations over racial mixing, as a primary tool for organizing the scholarly and popular knowledges that inform the practices of social relations, biological determinism, securing national borders, and forging geopolitical alliances.

Racial mixing, I contend, is a concept that holds power not simply through the exercise of one field of study's dominance over the other. Rather, as I will show, ideas about racial mixing gain traction through the movements of the concept across fields, including the studies of science, labor, and race and ethnicity, as well as through the adaptations of the concepts of race and racial mixing across national identities and geographical borders. Following the scholarly articles and debates contemplating the authenticity of Chinese Jews, this essay tracks how the various knowledge regimes that produce uneven and contradictory meanings about race and ethnicity nonetheless work together to actively reshape historical memories about social, biological, and transnational ties. To define the "Chinese Jew," scholars, as well as popular publications like the *Jewish Journal*, have examined the histories of exclusion, migration, agricultural labor, cultural memory, religion, and genetics, to name a few far-ranging fields, that gave rise to the seemingly distinct experiences of Chinese and Jews. As such, race itself is a hybrid concept—one that becomes a powerful tool for organizing, institutionalizing, and popularizing knowledge about the terms for social and national belonging across disciplines and international lines.

My analysis and use of the case of the Chinese Jew to demonstrate the hybridity of race[11] brings together the emergent scholarship in transpacific studies and Sinophone studies with the extant literature on Asian American studies, Indigenous studies, settler colonial studies, and queer studies. It seeks to historicize contemporary geopolitics by attending to how race and ethnicity and the hemispheric Americas and Asia Pacific regions have been shaped by the United States and the PRC as settler societies, respectively and concomitantly. I draw upon previous research that I have conducted on the role of racialized labor in agricultural industrialization that led to the founding of virology and genetics, as well as insights gleaned from my own family history. To be clear, I am not interested in proving that I am queer *and* Chinese *and* Jewish *and* American, or that Chinese Jews exist. Instead, I address the figure of the Chinese Jew as a strange, or queer, case to underline how the ongoing formations of race and ethnicity involve collusions between the United States, the imperial Qing (1644–1911), and the modern republic of China, since at least the late nineteenth century. The disputes over the definitions and categorizations for race, ethnicity, and national identity become especially sharp when we consider the United States and the PRC as two colonial powers whose strategies for global dominance reflect one another. Queer analyses, then, are utilized to bring to the fore the embedded contradictions regarding race and ethnicity, as well as the contentious assertions of heteropatriarchal nationalisms, that appear when researchers and state institutions are faced with questions about racial mixing.

Molecularizing the Chinese Jew

During early October 2013, subscribers to a humanities and social sciences email listserv on Asian studies, *H-Asia*, raised discussion of the Kaifeng Jews. The focus was on Jewish genetics, especially the published writings of U.S.-born Israeli translator, literary critic, and novelist Hillel Halkin. Ian Welch of the Australian National University, Canberra, submitted a post to *H-Asia* citing Halkin's assertion that "The Cohen name is associated with 'kohanim' descendants of Moses" and that "the DNA of the kohanim has been traced in a number of instances, including an African tribe, the Lemba, who have long nurtured a belief in descent from ancient Jews."[12] Welch then asked whether anyone knew of "reports on the DNA of the ancient Jewish community of Kaifeng, China."[13]

Halkin's article "Jews and their DNA," published in the U.S. magazine *Commentary*, maintains "3 to 5 percent of all male Jews have certain . . . Y-chromosome haplotypes or DNA markers"[14] that are traceable to a "common ancestor . . . that is, close to the period in which Aaron and his brother Moses are situated by biblical chronology."[15] Several *H-Asia* responders weighed in, speculating that "the Kaifeng Jewish community . . . share the same Y chromosome found in Iraqi Jews."[16] Thread participant Micha'el Tanchum, of Asia and Middle East Units Truman Research Institute for the Advancement of Peace at the Hebrew University of Jerusalem, referenced two of Halkin's articles also published in *Commentary*, "Wandering Jews— And Their Genes" and "Jews and Their DNA," as well as Halkin's book *Across the Sabbath River: In Search of a Lost Tribe of Israel*. Tanchum elaborated upon those living on the "Indian-Burmese border [who] have been reclaiming their Israelite heritage. . . . They . . . [have] been recognized by the Israeli government" and, based upon "genetic testing [have] shown a relation." Tanchum continues, "With Jews from Kaifeng, it is important to determine if some of these people came with the ancient migrations of the 'lost tribes' or later migrations [after] the Jews were exiled by the Roman Empire."[17]

Another respondent to the thread, Professor Sue Fawn Chung of the University of Nevada, Las Vegas, seemed to provide caution against perceiving race, ethnicity, or group affiliation and identity as genetic traits. In terse form, she wrote, "In the late 1970s I had lunch with a Boston U professor because of his interest in the Kaifeng Jews. He told me that when he was in Israel after WWII, he encountered a community of Chinese Jews who had tried to settle there but found the discrimination uncomfortable. Years later he [visited] the area again but the colony had left and he asked me if I knew where they went. I did not."[18]

Why would genetics be used to determine one's identification as Chinese and/or Jewish? Originally penned in 1950 in response to the Nazi holocaust, the revised 1978 "Declaration on Race and Racial Prejudice" by the United Nations Educational, Scientific and Cultural Organization (UNESCO) laid commitment to prevent racism, eugenics, and genocide.[19] As a number of scholars have shown, the growing trend toward accepting genetic markers as correspondent to race and/or ethnicity rely on faulty assumptions regarding the discreteness of social identities and the stability of histories and geographies while also enforcing the belief that all societies are patrilineal.[20] Thus, the return to biological determinisms for race, in this case through genomic science, should sound alarms against eugenic science. However, while we might remain wary of the eugenic ends for genomic science, we should not be so quick to engage in the wholesale dismissal of the field. Furthermore, if we disregard genomic science as racist unto itself, then we recommit to a presentist conception of genetics.

Rather, we should draw comparisons between the studies of genetics, race and ethnicity, cultural memory, and family history. In doing so, we find certain paradoxes that emerge in spite of race and ethnicity becoming fixed as identities and categories. By extension, we also foreground the modes by which genetics is mobilized in the service of racial and ethnic supremacy, heteropatriarchal family formations, nationalism, and geopolitics. By crossing the fields of science, ethnic studies, and cultural studies, we enable the historicization of genetics as contiguous or fundamental and not simply new additions to the histories and scholarship on race, gender, and sexuality.

A Queer Genealogy of the Chinese Jew

Intellectual and political interests vested in the cultural memory regarding Chinese Jews have long existed. My own paternal grandfather was born in Henan Province, of which Kaifeng is the capital, shortly after the end of the Manchu ethnic rule of the Qing Dynasty and the founding of the republic in 1912. He informed me as a child that our family might derive from Jewish ancestry. Nonetheless, my family ethnically identifies as Han and as Mandarin speakers, although my maternal and paternal grandmothers speak Ningbo and Fukienese, respectively. Both grandmothers came of age in Shanghai during the early twentieth century and learned Shanghainese. My parents understand these languages or topolects, as well as Taiwanese Hokkien, whereas I was taught only Mandarin as a child.

I was born in Houston, Texas, and was initially raised in Austin until the age of ten. I was often asked, "Where are you from? Do you speak Chinese? Why haven't you been to China?" These imposed categories of nationalistic and linguistic identification with the PRC became further fraught because I grew up in predominantly white neighborhoods, including Orange County, California, where I faced bullying in school as one of the few racial and ethnic minority students who was also a small and feminine boy who wanted to grow into an adult woman.

In the context of my parents' immigration to the United States in the late 1960s, after the Immigration Reform Act of 1965 struck down anti-Asian quotas in response to Black-led social movements, their Han identification was somewhat abandoned because of the limited recognition of difference and available forms of categorical identification in the new country, the United States. My parents became "Chinese" from the "Taiwan Republic of China." Although they continue to claim U.S. and Taiwanese dual citizenship, they do not identify ethnically as Taiwanese or Taiwanese Americans, but as *waishengren,* or "foreigners" (literally, "provincial outsiders"), to the land and people of Taiwan. They are patriotic children of the Kuomintang (KMT), or Nationalist military and government who, in 1949, were defeated by the Chinese Communist Party in the post–World War II struggle for power over modern China. The KMT then enforced "administrative control" over the island of Taiwan, which had previously operated with a level of autonomy from the Qing empire. Therein commenced the period of "White Terror" whereby the KMT violently suppressed Taiwanese leftist, independence, and pro-Japanese movements.[21] In spite of promising a democratic constitution, the KMT maintained martial law until 1987, a duration of thirty-nine years—the longest period of martial law in modern history next to Syria and Israel. Presently, the PRC wishes to reclaim Taiwan as a province under a "One China" policy. Meanwhile, the Democratic Progressive Party, led by the nation's first Taiwanese and Paiwan Indigenous mixed and woman president, Tsai Ing-Wen, continues to assert Taiwanese independence.

These contestations over nation, identity, land, belonging, and historical, cultural, and family memories are important to the discussion at hand because they complicate, and even undo, U.S. and Western racial and ethnic classifications such as Chinese and Chinese American. They also confound notions of Asian and Asian American since Chinese and Chinese American often occupy the center and focus of these categorical definitions. As troubled Anglophone identifications, they reveal the enduring settler colonial constructions of power—forged through the combined investments in white supremacy, Han ethnosupremacy, the dispossession of Natives, and anti-Blackness—that form the terms for difference and the categories for race, ethnicity, gender, sexuality, and racial and ethnic mixing. These socially, politically, and legally constructed categories are naturalized when they are left unquestioned and instituted through the study of genetics (and virology).

Coining the usage of the term "Sinophone" to name an emergent academic field, Shu-mei Shih inaugurated the careful study of the hegemony and conflations of the national identity termed "Chinese." "Chinese" refers most often to Han peoples and the Sinitic script that corresponds to the Mandarin language spoken in Beijing. Sinophone studies attends to the global operations of Han ethnosupremacy and settler colonialism by analyzing how racial and ethnic minorities who reside in the regions occupied by the PRC engage and transform the dominant Sinitic language and culture. Alongside this, Sinophone studies also investigates how Sinitic peoples who are located outside of the PRC engage and transform the major languages of the regions in which they live. This includes writings by Sinitic peoples in other language contexts, including Anglophone, Hispanophone, and Francophone literatures.[22]

For instance, Hsinya Huang argues that the Indigenous writers of Taiwan who engage the Sinitic script of Han settlers "convert" the trauma of dispossession and "cultural nothingness into insight" to narrativize their otherwise traditionally oral ways for cultural preservation and tribal survival.[23] Thus, the Indigenous writers of Taiwan, some of whom may identify as mixed Han, are able to embed in the archives of Sinitic writing various interventions into the settler colonial hegemony of Han peoples who may attempt to erase Indigeneity or co-opt Indigenous resistance into narratives of Han-led Taiwanese nationalism. Furthermore, there are contradictions over national, racial, and ethnic identities that are nestled in the texts of the dominant language. By exploiting these paradoxes, Sinophone writers articulate local, family, and personal memories that contest national borders, identities, and the occupations of Native lands.

Readers of these minor literatures are instead led to the "orphaned," "contaminated," and "degenerate" records that are repressed, rendered inauthentic, or estranged from what Robb Hernández describes as the "compulsory heterosexuality . . . of archival thinking."[24] Hernández instead offers "queer genealogy" as a way to trace the "detritus" from the archives of nationalism, gender binarism, and compulsory heterosexuality. Here, I apply queer, Sinophone, Indigenous, and settler colonial analyses to trace the figure of the racially mixed subject that endures by crossing categories and scales of molecular, biological, social, and national categories and distinctions.

The Intimacies of the "Mulato": From the Racial to the Molecular

To understand the queer genealogy of the Chinese Jew—heretofore Sinitic Jew—we must return to the historical figure of the mixed-race subject— mulatto in English, *mulato* in Spanish. Lisa Lowe begins her book *The Intimacies of Four Continents* by quoting Cuban anthropologist Fernando Ortiz, who described "'peoples from all four quarters of the globe' who labored in the 'new world' to produce tobacco and sugar for European consumption." Observing that sugar linked the histories of colonial settlers, Native peoples, and slave labor, followed by Sinitic and other migrants, Ortiz comments that sugar was "'mulatto' from the start."[25] This "mulatto" figure, as I will show, is historically critical to our understanding of the microbiological world, particularly virology and genetics. Lowe's quote from Ortiz underscores how the mulatto as a colonial term and figure for racial and ethnic mixing—but also, in Ortiz's usage, a descriptor for the Black and Indigenous transcultural processes of sugar and tobacco production and consumption—draws into the present the enduring histories of slave labor, Indigenous dispossession, and Asian "coolie" labor across the Americas and the Pacific.

With respect to histories of racial mixing, Lowe states,

> The British colonial conflation of the Chinese with indigenous and racially mixed people expresses this moment in the history of

coloniality, in which a racial taxonomy gradually emerged both to manage and modernize labor, reproduction, and society among the colonized, as well as to rationalize the conditions of creolized mixing and to discipline the range of potential "intimacies" among them.[26]

To foreground these potential intimacies, Lowe, like Hernández, advocates for a reading of "absences" and "forgotten subjects" in archives to attend to the "aporia . . . often belied by discrepant tone or insistent repetitions, and rhetorical anomalies that obscure omissions, tensions, or outright illogic."[27]

Through my historical research on virology and genetics, I found that the *mulato* figure stages the intimacies between race, gender, sexuality, and cross-species intermingling in the archives of late nineteenth-century industrial agricultural science and post-chattel slavery agribusiness. From these knowledge archives emerge the studies of viruses and genetics. Following the queer genealogy for the *mulato* signifier throughout the archives of science reveals how colonial categories for race, gender, and sexuality function as antecedents to modern virology and genetics. I focus here first on the emergence of the field of genetics while drawing from my earlier research on viruses.

There are at least two distinct yet overlapping histories for the field of genetics. Around 1865, the "father of modern genetics," Austrian friar Gregor Mendel, proposed a theory for genetic heredity using his cultivation of pea plants to demonstrate the process of what he called "Versuche über Pflanzenhybriden," or "Experiments in Plant Hybridization." He generated an argument for the theory of genetic inheritance by differentiating and tracking the patterns in the quality, color, brightness, and other visual and textural cues of the pea plants he would breed. In turn, he demonstrated that offspring inherited traits from their parents via what we now call genes. It is crucial to point out that the category of "hybrid" must presume the hereditary purity of the two pea plants prior the event of genetic "mixing." However, Mendel's study does little to prove the pure heredity of his plants' origins. We must simply trust Mendel's accounting of events as empirical fact. Let us compare the historical crossings of Sinitic and Jewish migrants to demonstrate this case in point.

Mendel's publication of "Experiments in Plant Hybridization" in German would remain untranslated and widely unread for some time,[28] until the late nineteenth and early twentieth centuries waves of immigration to the United States by Jewish immigrants seeking refuge from persecution in Europe. At the same time, Asian "coolie" agricultural workers arrived to supplant the newly freed Black laborers. Asian laborers, who often toiled in slave-like conditions, undermined the Black demand for equal wages to white workers in the postslavery economy.[29] Late nineteenth-century and early twentieth-century Jewish and Chinese immigrants to the United States, and across the West, endured xenophobic and racist views that Jews and Sinitic peoples were both genetically inferior and prone to disease, which curbed their entry and settlement. This promulgated social isolation and geographic ghettoization for those who did migrate.[30]

The perception of Jews and Muslims as pathological groups extends to sixteenth-century Iberia, wherein Catholicism was enforced through blood purity statues (*limpieza de sangre*) that presumed that Jewish and Muslim lineage could be passed down, mother to child, through blood and breast milk in spite of religious conversion to Christianity. María-Elena Martínez argues that this gave rise to the modern concept of race, tying concerns over blood purity to sexual (and later biological) reproduction and heredity.[31] Likewise, the Euro-American colonial belief that smallpox, syphilis, and the Black Death originated from Imperial and, later, modern China also served to historically mark Sinitic peoples as "contagious" and racially distinct. Nineteenth- and twentieth-century Sinitic, Mexican, and Japanese immigrant laborers were targeted for discrimination using public health and sanitary codes that eventually helped shape the United States' public health bureaucracy and industrialize its agriculture.[32] The racialization of Asians maintained scientific belief in their inherently physical and genetically manifested "foreignness," "backwardness," and "idiocy."[33]

Meanwhile, the scientific credence that lent to the perception that European-descent Jews are physically different from that of their Anglo-Saxon counterparts served contradictory ends. Medical geneticist Harry Orstrer published his book *Legacy: A Genetic History of the Jewish People* in 2012, the same year as David N. Myers's double-feature article on Sinitic Jews in the *Jewish Journal*. Orstrer further attests to the recently increased attention to the supposed racial and ethnic genetics of Jews. He argues that the nineteenth-century and early twentieth-century involvement of European immigrant Jewish scholars, medical doctors, and anthropologists in the United States to determine what diseases "seem to cluster among the Jewish peoples" resulted in the establishment of the field of population genetics.[34] To pushback against eugenicist science, and to dispel the myth that Jews had higher rates of tuberculosis (TB), which was an accusation that was used to bar Jews from entry to the United States, New Yorker and Russian Jewish immigrant, physician, and self-taught anthropologist Maurice Fishberg compared cranial measurements and catalogued skin pigmentation among Jews living across continents to identify whether Jews were indeed a race. While Fishberg disproved that TB and diabetes were higher among Jewish populations, he found that a progressive neurodegenerative condition, Tay-Sachs disease, was more common among Jews.[35] Simultaneously, he found that physiognomic appearances between

Jewish men and women differed enough to throw doubt on whether Jews were pure in their genetic makeup. Jewish women's cranium sizes varied more greatly than that of men, and Jewish women tended to be darker in skin color. Although Fishberg declared in 1906 that Jews are not a race, he nonetheless asserted that Jews have a discernable "look."[36] He proclaimed, "One can pick out a Jew from among a thousand non-Jews without difficulty."[37]

Proponents that Jews "constituted a single race" included Joseph Jacobs, "the leading Jewish physical anthropologist" at the turn of the twentieth century in England who immigrated to the United States in 1901 to become the editor of the *Jewish Encyclopedia*. Jacobs declared, "Wherever such a type had been socially or racially selected, the law of inheritance discovered by G. Mendel would imply that hybrids tend to revert to it, and a certain amount of evidence has been given for the potency of the Jewish side in mixed marriages."[38] Mendelian genetics was revived through the field of population genetics. Hence, although population genetics was meant to combat anti-Semitic, and specifically anti-Jewish, discrimination, it emphasized visually and physically identifiable traits as the source for establishing racial and ethnic differences even (or especially) in the case of racial and ethnic mixing.

To concede to the conclusions drawn by Mendelian genetics, however, we must draw upon the record of Mendel's visual gaze and textural sensibilities to calibrate our evaluations of physical difference. His concept of hybridization rests upon notions of "origin" and "purity" about the pea plants that he used, which the canon of modern genetics leaves largely unchallenged. Yet if we trace the etymology of the term "hybrid," we find that it derives from the Latin term *hybrida*, which is a variant of *ibrida*, or "mongrel." *Ibrida* operates under the influence of an ancient Greek term that translates into the contemporary English terms "hubris" and "outrage." Furthermore, *ibrida* is a cognate to the Latin terms *iber* and *imbrum*. *Iber* is the root word for the term "Iberian," which is a term that historians such as Martínez have used to refer to the early transatlantic, southern European region of Spanish and Portuguese empires. Meanwhile, *imbrum* refers to the contemporary English word "mule." Finally, the second meaning of the term "hybrid," after "mongrel," is a "person born of a Roman father and foreign mother, or of a freeman and a slave."[39]

The term "mule," or *mula* in Spanish and Portuguese, serves as the root for the word *mulato*. In my published research on the founding of the first virus in the tobacco plant, I also draw upon the work of Fernando Ortiz, and the figure of the *mulato*, to analyze the first recorded observation of what we now describe as viral infection. Tracing the scientific and historical records for the discovery of the inaugural virus, I came upon the earliest documented accounting for viral infection in the tobacco plant to a racialized Spanish phrase, *el tabaco se ha mulato*, loosely translated into English as "the tobacco has become mulatto." The phrase appears in the late nineteenth-century travel writing of French colonial scientist Jules Crevaux as he journeyed through post–Spanish independence Colombia. I theorized the literary translations and visualizations of the phrase across scientific and historical texts to track the refraction of racial, gender, and sexual discourses in virology. I argue that the phrase refers to the dispossessed Indigenous and Black subjects of the nascent Colombian republic and their resistance to subjection when forced to work the tobacco fields.[40]

In the transit between the late ancient to modern periods—from ancient Rome to modern nation-states—the term *mulato* paves a queer genealogy for racialization; slavery; the rape of African enslaved and Indigenous peoples, particularly women; and the emergence of what we now categorically call racially mixed subjects. We continue to apply this meaning of *mulato* to our understandings of virology and genetics in order to reinscribe race and the fantasy of "purity," "origins," and "mutation," as well as infection, degeneracy, and terror. The hybridity of race across the scales of species and subcellular existence was exemplified by the 2014 *CNN News* headline "Ebola: The Isis of Biological Agents?" which ratcheted up racialized and geopolitical anxieties over the outbreak of the Ebola virus in parts of western Africa. The histories of race, virology, and genetics are mutually entwined. For instance, viruses have played a crucial role in our understanding of the purpose and structure of DNA. Viruses helped to clarify that DNA and not proteins carry the material for genetic inheritance.[41] With the growth of consumer genetics companies that propose to unlock the "truth" of one's ancestry and identity, we hold fast to the belief that race is embedded in a sequence of nucleotides which are referred to as the blueprint for life.

Still, genetics research has also served to uncover historical inequities based upon racial and biological traumas. According to Alondra Nelson, genetic conceptions of race are increasingly important to establish the terms for the reparations and reconciliation of racial trauma. For instance, she discusses the use of genetics among African Americans who wish to trace their ancestry to particular African peoples and nations to establish belonging and citizenship, which follows a particular genealogy of family history otherwise broken by slavery.[42] Genotyping has also helped scientists to identify how viruses like HIV replicate and to record patterns of viral spread. For example, scientists were able to utilize virus genotyping to identify how, in 1969, sixteen-year-old African American and reportedly homeless Robert Rayford of St. Louis, Missouri, died with HIV.[43] Rayford's case is considered one of the earliest known instances of HIV infection in the United States, which challenges the well-touted "patient zero" narrative of HIV and AIDS that focused on the outbreak among North American white gay men around 1981.

Meanwhile, genetic research has also operated as an arm of the U.S. empire. Examining the development of genetic research labs in Singapore, Aihwa Ong shows how U.S.-based genetic research and consumer initiatives have been exported and adapted globally, translating and transforming racial and ethnic categories and national sensibilities in their new locales.[44] As Kim TallBear demonstrates, genetic testing has remained contentious for Native Americans who are often forced by the U.S. government to rely upon it for tribal recognition. At times it has radically altered notions of tribal belonging to suit heteropatriarchal, blood-based kinships. Nonetheless, it serves the vital purposes for determining tribal enrollment and the potential to leverage Indigenous self-determination before the settler state.[45]

Consumer genetics companies like AncestryDNA offer any paying customer a panel of their racial genetic markers using a DNA sample derived from a self-administered cheek swab. Customers are not prompted to ask whether the categories for race and ethnicity, gender, and geography are accurate, or to even question how these categories can change and how they are undergoing constant challenge. Furthermore, as Nadia Abu El-Hajj argues, genetic consumerism reinscribes race and summons consumers to be self-responsible and engage in preventative care for diseases that are associated with specific racial and ethnic populations.[46] As of this writing, no U.S. federal or local laws prevent privately owned databases for genetic consumerism from selling the information to health insurance companies, security and defense corporations, or any government—U.S. or otherwise.

To trace queer genealogies and problematize the configuration of race as genetics, we must recall Hillel Halkin, who argued in favor for the genetic testing of Jews using "Y-chromosome haplotypes or DNA markers."[47] Alondra Nelson reminds us that while the Y-chromosome DNA "is passed mostly unchanged from fathers to sons—women do not have a Y chromosome."[48] Thus, the racialization of genetics cannot account for matrilineal societies or genetic chimerism. It refuses to recognize intersex subjects or any form of nonbinary gender. In addition, it cannot concede to the possibilities of nonheterosexual, nonprocreative, and nonblood kinship—which would then rattle the notions of race and ethnicity, genetic and property inheritance, and nationalism. Racialization through genetics research and consumerism induces a sense of racial and ethnic homogeneity, heteropatriarchal family, and community that can shed light on and generate a sense of care for historical racial and biological traumas. Yet it can also contradict the aims of reconciliation and reparations by coercing history, community, and identity into the terms of race, gender, and sexuality within the settler colonial imaginary. Finally, by coercing community and care, the molecularization of race in genetics and virology can enforce the surveillance of intimacies and invoke the militarized defense of the ideological, social,

geopolitical, and physical borders for white supremacist and Han ethnosupremacist, heteropatriarchal nationalisms in the United States, Israel, and the
PRC—even if, or especially when, these nationalisms are placed in tension.

Here is where the intimacies of the *mulato* figure within colonial scientific archives can trace queer genealogies at the level of racialized molecules
to anticipate the simultaneous shifts in geopolitics and biomedical research.
According to Mel Y. Chen, the "animacy hierarchy" is the indelible tie between life and its "ostensible opposite . . . deadness . . . the abject, the object"
such that racialized subjects and inanimate objects variously share the characteristics of lower sentience and value.[49] Chen's notion of "queer animacies" lends itself to a queer genealogy that pays heed to the instances in
which human and nonhuman animals, and nonsentient objects, forge intimacies through the porousness, or "transness," of animating features that
articulate the intentional mixings of species, substances, and objects even
as the differences among each are partitioned and infused with colonial
power.[50]

The PRC's expanding global influence includes settler colonial investments in mining in Namibia, engaging in oil and defense contracts in Saudi
Arabia, and sponsoring Han ethnosupremacist settlements on Uyghur
Muslim minority lands while engaging in Islamophobic campaigns to ban
various beards, headwear, and clothing associated with Islam. The PRC's
state-sponsored massive interment of Muslim ethnic and religious minorities in concentration camps have been described as genocidal. In this sense,
the PRC's Han ethnosupremacy mirrors back the United States' own white
supremacist settler colonialism. This includes the United States' dispossess-
sion of Indigenous peoples, its enslavement and mass incarceration of African descended peoples, and its internment of Japanese Americans during
World War II. It also includes investments in the Israeli occupation of Palestinian lands and peoples, the racialization of "Muslims" in the enduring
Global War on Terror, the U.S. occupation of the Pacific, and the intensified
militarization of the U.S.-Mexico border leading to the growing detention
of refugees from Latin America and elsewhere.

While the historical and cultural memory of Sinitic Jews is not new, the
emphasis on this identitarian designation, and the potential for genetically
verifiable racial and ethnic mixing, serve a cautionary tale for affirming
heteropatriarchal intimacies that function in the interest of geopolitical re-
alignment. In the meantime, Sinitic Jews living in the PRC must face xenophobia, anti-Semitism, and laws imposed against religious assembly; those
living in Israel must face xenophobia and racism; and Sinitic Jews living in
the United States occupy the social space of endless deferral for the authenticity and belonging of either/or identity, or both identities.

ACKNOWLEDGMENTS

My gratitude to volume editors Kale Fajardo, Alice Hom, and Martin Manalansan, as well as managing editor Paul Michael Leonardo Atienza. This essay benefited from conversations and support from R. Benedito Ferrão, Anjali Nath, Esmat Elhalaby, Gayatri Gopinath, Christopher Chien, Stephen Sheehi, Arnika Fuhrmann, Dina Al Kassim, Jonathan M. Hall, and more. Any oversights and errors are mine.

NOTES

1. David N. Myers, "The Jews of Kaifeng," 15.

2. Shavei Israel website, http://www.shavei.org/.

3. David N. Myers, "Jewish Studies Flourish in China," 14.

4. Ibid., 15.

5. Ibid., 14.

6. Ibid., 15.

7. Joseph E. Stiglitz, "The Chinese Century."

8. Nian tian et al., "Trends in World Military Expenditure, 2016."

9. Nelson Eshe, "Europe's Central Banks Are Starting to Replace Dollar Reserves with Yuan."

10. Antonio Gramsci, *Selections from the Prison Notebooks*, 430–33, 625.

11. Tavia Nyong'o argues that racial hybridity functions paradoxically as the enduring trauma of modernity and slavery, as well as a future-oriented ideal. Tavia Nyong'o, *The Amalgamation Waltz: Race, Performance, and the Ruses of Memory* (Minneapolis: University of Minnesota Press, 2009).

12. Ian Welch, "H-ASIA: DNA Studies and Chinese Jews—2 Responses," October 2, 2013, *H-Asia* email listserv.

13. Welch, "H-ASIA: DNA Studies and Chinese Jews."

14. Hillel Halkin, "Wandering Jews—And Their Genes."

15. Hillel Halkin, "Jews and Their DNA."

16. Micha'el Tanchum, "H-ASIA: DNA Studies and Chinese Jews—2 Responses," October 2, 2013, *H-Asia* email listserv.

17. Ibid.

18. Ibid.

19. United Nations Educational, Scientific and Cultural Organization, "Declaration on Race and Racial Prejudice."

20. Nadia Abu El-Haj, *The Genealogical Science*; Jonathan Kahn, *Race in a Bottle*; Alondra Nelson, *The Social Life of DNA*; Kim TallBear, *Native American DNA*.

21. Formosan Association for Public Affairs, "Taiwan's History: An Overview."

22. Shu-mei Shih, "What Is Sinophone Studies?" 1–16.

23. Hsinya Huang, "Sinophone Indigenous Literature of Taiwan: History and Tradition," 251.

24. Robb Hernández, "Drawn from the Scraps: The Finding AIDS of Mundo Meza," 74.

25. Lowe, *The Intimacies of Four Continents*, 2.

26. Ibid., 32.

27. Ibid., 5–6.

28. Amanda Andrei, "'Experiments in Plant Hybridization' (1866), by Johann Gregor Mendel."

29. Moon-Ho Jung, *Coolies and Cane: Race, Labor, and Sugar in the Age of Emancipation.*

30. Nayan Shah, *Contagious Divides Epidemics and Race in San Francisco's Chinatown*; Natalia Molina, *Fit to Be Citizens? Public Health and Race in Los Angeles, 1879–1940.*

31. María-Elena Martínez, *Genealogical Fictions: Limpieza de Sangre, Religion, and Gender in Colonial Mexico.*

32. Nayan Shah, *Contagious Divides Epidemics and Race in San Francisco's Chinatown*; Natalia Molina, *Fit to Be Citizens?.*

33. Mel Y. Chen, "'The Stuff of Slow Constitution': Reading Down Syndrome for Race, Disability, and the Timing That Makes Them So," 235–248.

34. Harry Orster, *Legacy: A Genetic History of the Jewish People* (London: Oxford University Press, 2012), 1–2.

35. Ibid., 6–8.

36. Ibid., 13–4.

37. Ibid., 14.

38. Ibid., 15.

39. "Hybrid," Online Etymology Dictionary, accessed March 10, 2017, http://www.etymonline.com/index.php?term=hybrid.

40. Jih-Fei Cheng, "'El tabaco se ha mulato': Globalizing Race, Scientific Observation, and Viruses in the Late Nineteenth Century."

41. Ibid.

42. Nelson, *The Social Life of DNA.*

43. Theodore Kerr, "AIDS 1969: HIV, History, and Race."

44. Aihwa Ong, *Fungible Life: Experiment in the Asian City of Life* (Durham, NC: Duke University Press, 2016).

45. TallBear, *Native American DNA.*

46. Abu El-Hajj, *The Genealogical Science.*

47. Halkin, "Wandering Jews—And Their Genes."

48. Nelson, *The Social Life of DNA*, 18–19.

49. Mel Y. Chen, *Animacies: Biopolitics, Racial Mattering, and Queer Affect*, 30.

50. Ibid., 126.

BIBLIOGRAPHY

Abu El-Haj, Nadia. *The Genealogical Science: The Search for Jewish Origins and the Politics of Epistemology.* Chicago: Chicago University Press, 2012.

Andrei, Amanda. "'Experiments in Plant Hybridization' (1866), by Johann Gregor Mendel." *The Embryo Project Encyclopedia*, September 4, 2013. Accessed April 12, 2017. https://embryo.asu.edu/pages/experiments-plant-hybridization-1866-johann-gregor-mendel.

Chen, Mel Y. *Animacies: Biopolitics, Racial Mattering, and Queer Affect.* Durham, NC: Duke University Press, 2013.

———. "'The Stuff of Slow Constitution': Reading Down Syndrome for Race, Disability, and the Timing That Makes Them So." *Somatechnics* 6, no. 2 (2016): 235–248.

Cheng, Jih-Fei. "El tabaco se ha mulato: Globalizing Race, Scientific Observation, and Viruses in the Late Nineteenth Century." *Catalyst: Feminism, Theory, Technoscience* 1, no. 1 (2015). Accessed March 1, 2018. http://catalystjournal.org/ojs/index.php/catalyst/article/view/cheng/112.

Eshe, Nelson. "Europe's Central Banks Are Starting to Replace Dollar Reserves with Yuan." *Quartz*, January 16, 2018. Accessed February 7, 2018. https://qz.com/1180434

/europes-central-banks-are-starting-to-replace-us-dollar-reserves-with-the-chinese
-yuan/.

Formosan Association for Public Affairs. "Taiwan's History: An Overview." Accessed March 21, 2017. http://www.fapa.org/generalinfo/Taiwan%27s_history.htm.

Gramsci, Antonio. *Selections from the Prison Notebooks*. London: ElecBook, 1999. Transcribed from the edition published by Lawrence and Wishart, London, 1971, 430–433, 625. Accessed March 1, 2018. http://abahlali.org/files/gramsci.pdf.

Halkin, Hillel. "Jews and Their DNA." *Commentary*, September 1, 2008. Accessed April 25, 2015. https://www.commentarymagazine.com/article/jews-and-their-dna/.

———. "Wandering Jews—And Their Genes." *Commentary*, September 1, 2000. Accessed April 25, 2015. https://www.commentarymagazine.com/article/wandering-jews%E2%80%94and-their-genes/.

Hernández, Robb. "Drawn from the Scraps: The Finding AIDS of Mundo Meza." *Radical History Review* 2015, no. 122 (2015): 70–88.

H-Net. "H-ASIA: DNA Studies and Chinese Jews—2 Responses." Email listserv: *H-Asia*. October 2, 2013.

Huang, Hsinya. "Sinophone Indigenous Literature of Taiwan: History and Tradition." In *Sinophone Studies: A Critical Reader*, 242–254. New York: Columbia University Press, 2013.

Jung, Moon-Ho. *Coolies and Cane: Race, Labor, and Sugar in the Age of Emancipation*. Baltimore: Johns Hopkins University Press, 2006.

Kahn, Jonathan. *Race in a Bottle: The Story of BiDil and Racialized Medicine in a Post-Genomic Era*. New York: Columbia University Press, 2013.

Kerr, Theodore. "AIDS 1969: HIV, History, and Race," in "AIDS and Memory." Special Issue, *Drain* 13, no. 2 (2016). Accessed March 10, 2017. http://drainmag.com/aids-1969-hiv-history-and-race/#ftn9.

Lowe, Lisa. *The Intimacies of Four Continents*. Durham, NC: Duke University Press, 2015.

Martínez, María-Elena. *Genealogical Fictions: Limpieza de Sangre, Religion, and Gender in Colonial Mexico*. Stanford, CA: Stanford University Press, 2008.

Molina, Natalia. *Fit to Be Citizens? Public Health and Race in Los Angeles, 1879–1940*. Berkeley: University of California Press, 2006.

Myers, David N. "Jewish Studies Flourish in China." *Jewish Journal*, August 15, 2012. Accessed April 25, 2015. http://www.jewishjournal.com/cover_story/article/jewish_studies_flourish_in_china_20120815/.

———. "The Jews of Kaifeng." *Jewish Journal*, August 15, 2012. Accessed April 25, 2015. http://www.jewishjournal.com/cover_story/article/jewish_studies_flourish_in_china_20120815/.

Nelson, Alondra. *The Social Life of DNA: Race, Reparations, and Reconciliation After the Genome*. Boston: Beacon, 2016.

Online Etymology Dictionary. Entry: hybrid (n.) *Online Etymology Dictionary*. http://www.etymonline.com/index.php?term=hybrid. Accessed: March 10, 2017.

Orster, Harry. *Legacy: A Genetic History of the Jewish People*. London: Oxford University Press, 2012.

Shah, Nayan. *Contagious Divides Epidemics and Race in San Francisco's Chinatown*. Berkeley: University of California Press, 2001.

Shavei Israel website. Accessed April 25, 2015. http://www.shavei.org/.

Shih, Shu-mei. "What Is Sinophone Studies?" Introduction to *Sinophone Studies: A Critical Reader*, 1–16. New York: Columbia University Press, 2013.

Stiglitz, Joseph E. "The Chinese Century." *Vanity Fair,* January 2015. Accessed July 31, 2016. http://www.vanityfair.com/news/2015/01/china-worlds-largest-economy.

TallBear, Kim. *Native American DNA: Tribal Belonging and the False Promise of Genetic Science.* Minneapolis: University of Minnesota Press, 2013.

Tian, Nan tian, et al. "Trends in World Military Expenditure, 2016." Stockholm International Peace Institute. *SIPRI Fact Sheet.* April 2016. Accessed March 1, 2017. https://www.sipri.org/sites/default/files/Trends-world-military-expenditure-2016.pdf.

United Nations Educational, Scientific and Cultural Organization. "Declaration on Race and Racial Prejudice." November 27, 1978. Accessed August 10, 2016. http://portal.unesco.org/en/ev.php-URL_ID=13161&URL_DO=DO_TOPIC&URL_SECTION=201.html.

Sewing Patches through Performance

D'Lo

I had a pair of jeans when I was younger, say twelve. It was my last year as a boy, a time where I would soon transition into being a girl. It was also a year before my older and only sister died. I loved those jeans, and I wore them every day, wearing them out at the knees. When the first knee showed a tear, Amma asked if she could patch it. I said no—I wanted my jeans to be free in their self-expression. But inevitably, as the hole over my right knee was getting bigger and another hole was starting over the left knee, Amma asked me again if she could patch it. And again I said no.

Finally the day came. While I was putting my leg through the pantleg, my foot went straight into the hole instead, so I told Amma she could patch them. My Amma knows how to sew; it's something many Tamil Sri Lankan girls are taught to do when they are younger, especially when they were discouraged from pursuing further studies, and especially when they were encouraged to become good wives and mothers. Amma knows how to patch from behind and sew over, she knows how to make things that are of use, and she knows how to sew dresses and sari blouses and many other things I have worn or had repaired by her expert hands.

The next day, I came home, and she had patched a stiff square over each of the holes, but the left knee's square patch was rotated diamond-wise. I put on the jeans and looked like a dork. I told her that maybe I didn't need to wear the jeans anymore, and she laughed and said, "That's what I was hoping." Having holes in your clothes might be a Tamil atrocity, but I wondered why she went through all that trouble and insisting if she simply wanted me to trash the jeans in the first place.

I asked Amma for freedom to say I am queer. She says no. I say, Please let me make sense of this life by talking about it in the open. She says no.

It might not be fair to her, the way I have sewn together bits of my Amma's story regarding me. Sometimes fairness is irrelevant when it comes to struggling to make sense of the holes of your own story. What I have heard from her, and heard of her, mixed with these memories of mine and my own queerstory—it all makes up the lens from which I have experienced my life, love, and art as a queer and trans masculine person. Here I am, a queer Tamil Sri Lankan American in my truth, and my truth rages hard against the consistent defaulting to my Amma's Tamil Sri Lankan denial or selective amnesia.

What I can say I've patched together about her is that she is a spirit woman, an incredibly mystical and magical being, a woman who becomes more childlike as she gets older. She is also the Amma who raised me: strict, disciplinarian, safekeeper of rituals and superstitions, paranoid over what would become of her bicultural children in America. She is all-loving and ignorantly racist, desiring to be godly while being judgmental. She is someone whom many turn to for comfort, and somehow I still can't say she's completely in touch with her own pain of losing two daughters, though somewhere along the way she faced it all and emerged light.

I write this piece to honor my journey with my Amma. And in this honoring, may I honor my story, queer as it is, to convince myself that though I am not what she hoped for, I am possibly more. Today I honor my spirit for the first time in this story. My trans spirit, my boy self, my masculinity—gentle and fiercely feminist. D'Lo—girl child, turned sunchild.

The Threads

I can imagine what my Amma's eyes saw when looking at her first child in the days after she was born. I picture my sister with chocolate skin, with a head full of hair and sweet, beautiful features, and I imagine that my Amma is having a hard time connecting to the fact that she has become a mother. Amma calls it "baby blues" when she tells me about those days in Colombo. "Postpartum" sounds foreign and unrelatable, definitely too sterile for a mother who is supposed to bond immediately with her child in a land where one barely talked about depression.

I wonder about the details—the quiet moments of thought as she verbalizes her past. I imagine and wonder, because as I ask her questions, she tells me she has forgotten. I have come to understand forgetfulness and denial as friends, tools sharpened for survival, used to continue to live in the most primitive way, to find the strength to eat, sleep, and work. Indeed, denial's river runs deep in our brown bodies.

She claims she doesn't remember much, but from time to time, I am caught off guard with a precious story from her past, and I try to catch them as they emerge like dust from an ancient vault. Usually, however, she finds comfort in repeating stories of her mother and her brothers, speaking of them as if they were all honorable and without mistake. Of course, her memories have never held truthful to the way life changes people, but at least she has the memories—memories that create order, for the life of chaos hers could've been.

After my birth in Queens four years after my sister, memories are what I have too. Maybe they are constructed from audio recordings, pictures, videos, poems I've written, and letters I've sent to exes, but they are memories nonetheless, on the shelf with the stuff that needn't be reconstructed, because some events you can't shake no matter how hard you jostle your mind.

Perhaps I am not a hopeless romantic but a dramatic romantic when I say that I have always felt Amma's eyes on me. I remember the fondness she had over me when I was younger, or maybe this is another constructed feeling cocreated from an audio tape of her asking me questions when I was three. Amma asked me, "Vut do you hav in yoh head?" I answered, "Uh, mud!" She seemed to love the answer. She seemed to be very fond of me.

I felt her eyes on me when I played outside by myself after we moved to a hick town in Southern California. I felt her eyes on me like surveillance cameras at banks, right after I ran away from home—and I wasn't wrong, because she was the one who found me. I felt them less so after my sister died, and then it became my eyes on her. I felt hers needlessly or needfully back on me throughout high school with the threat of boys, and then again on me almost finished with college, both curiously and disappointedly, after I announced my queerness. I felt them not only when I left for New York but also while I walked or biked from borough to borough. I felt them every time I lit up a cigarette and took a swig. And when I visited LA, back into a Tamil community function, I even felt her eyes slip off my bald head with shame the minute I stepped into the room. Those days, my heart broke repeatedly under the weight of her eyes on me; her eyes that spoke the weight of her wonder, "I don't know how I could have a child like you"—that I was a source of disgust and that she craved some sort of normalcy. I cannot expect Amma to not have ever thought, "I wish Krishani were alive."

The Holes

I was thirteen when my seventeen-year-old sister, Krishani, died in a plane crash at LAX. One can imagine my parents' response to this devastation. I wish I knew how to mourn, or even that it was allowed, because all I remember feeling was immense fear. I really believed from an even younger age that my queerness would be buffered by the distraction of my sister's accomplishments and her allyship to me, even if the latter was just an assumption. Now that I was left to navigate the waters of coming out alone, I tried to keep busy until I could get the hell out of Lancaster.

So of course, it was only a matter of months at UCLA before my queerness came out full-fledged to the world. And four years later, to my parents, it all came out—or rather I did. And not without a pop, bang, or boom . . .

So off I went to New York, with no real understanding of how uprooting myself from my support system of queer chosen family would be a first of many blows—a rite of passage, if you will, into what felt like adulthood.

The Patchwork

In 2003, one of the very first monologues I wrote was from my Amma's voice.

The comedic monologue was the Amma character speaking to the audience about how she was absorbing the information that her daughter was "a gay," and that this gender nonconforming child of hers was, against her desires, indeed a boy, and how all this was foreign to her because there were "no gays in Sri Lanka." The character also shares that she first thought she was to blame for her child's queerness, but then she realized the truth: that it was really her husband's fault. She further shares that she wishes for her child's safety and that she probably wouldn't have such a hard time with this "gay business" if her first daughter hadn't died, because queerness was a death of sorts all over again.

The character is both loosely and tightly based on my Amma: my actual Amma doesn't wear a sari every day, but the character does—with a long plait—which my Amma also doesn't wear but once had. But fabric wrapped tightly and a tight long plait: in the theater, they say, "Show, don't tell."

Additionally, and more importantly, the character shares things that my mother never openly shared with me. I simply knew my Amma thought them—the remorse, the pain, the regrets over how her life had turned out. But the minor fictionalized bits were vehicles for the larger chunks of her truth to be carried by.

Side note: The monologue has changed from when I first wrote it in 2003 to how I do it today in 2015. It also dips more dramatically in theater settings than on the college and university circuit, but nonetheless it has been one of my more powerful, impactful, and emotion-stirring pieces by the mere fact that most people, but particularly queer people and more particularly queer people of color, on this planet have some strained relationship with a family member from whom they are seeking love and acceptance.

It was 2004, and I was invited as an artist to perform at the Prakriti Festival in Chennai. I was also there with my cousin Tanisha, helping her with her academic research, while another academic turned friend, Sandra, was doing research on my work.

Amma was with us because we had just finished a pilgrimage. I had also completed my last visit to a swami's ashram to appease Amma. She kept sending me to one swami or guru after another in hopes that they could change me. All these holy people couldn't be bothered with my queerness and tried to get Amma to also not be bothered by it. Amma couldn't stop being bothered. Furthermore, she was heartbroken every time one of holy ones essentially told her that "gay was okay." My poor Amma.

Right before my performance, I remember Amma telling me, "Don't talk about gay." I reminded her that being queer was precisely why I was asked to come to perform. She didn't understand and tried to convince me, "No, these people are Indian, and they won't like to hear about it." At this point, I remembered what had happened five years prior when I begged my parents to come to a show of mine in the hopes that if they saw that other people, other South Asians, really loved me and my work for the fact that I was queer, then just maybe my parents would be comforted enough to change their own understanding and tolerance around my queerness. They didn't come, and I had just learned to not expect them to be in support of my career or as an openly queer person.

But five years later, I figured Amma had no say in a performance I was invited to do, and it was up to her whether she felt like coming. She was too intrigued and curious to stay back, so she tagged along.

I came out on stage, and in the sea of over one thousand people, my eyes immediately found Amma, feeling her nervousness even from far away. I saw the reflections in her specs, her shoulders stiff, smooshed between Tanisha and Sandra, who were both smiling. I started with my intro, which was a mix of jokes and crowd work to get an understanding of the audience. Within seconds, the audience started laughing and responding, and I saw Amma looking around her in shock. It seemed that she would always be in shock that people enjoyed me. I then went into my first piece, a slowed down hip-hop piece, and then changed onstage, discreetly, into the character of "Amma."

Suddenly I was the one who was nervous. I was well aware that I was performing this version of my Amma in front of my actual Amma, yet it only really hit me on the first lines of the monologue. Because the stakes were high, I knew I had to believe in me—the integrity and vulnerability I try to walk with—so much so that the honor and reverence I put into that performance changed the way I performed that piece forever.

I was even given a standing ovation. I knew I had done the piece justice; I had done Amma justice. I would like to believe that through this fictionalized version of herself, she finally was able to air her grievances without sounding like a demon; she could be seen with all her contradictions without judgment. But most important, I believe it was the first time she felt seen by me, her child; the person whom she couldn't communicate with, the person she didn't know she needed understanding from.

I'm not saying that this moment changed things immediately, because my parents' shame over me only started leaving a couple of years ago, but I can say that these tiny but strong moments definitely helped heat the steel tracks to curve a new path for us both to travel on. I understand that this moment in 2004 was, for me, another rite of passage in checking my ego—that in order to make any changes, I really had to make the first move. We both wanted each other to change. Neither of us could. No one was to blame. (Though I still believe parents should do better.) My immigrant Amma knows denial as a coping mechanism more so than tools like self-reflection and processing feelings. I thank America for introducing me to therapy.

The Desired Pattern

In 2012, I was invited to go on a six-city tour of India with my stand-up storytelling show. My work had evolved in different ways, but the premise was still the same: using stories from my life to talk about navigating this world as a queer person without societal rite of passages and family support, while trying to stay alive and stay away from self-sabotage.

After finishing the tour, I went to Sri Lanka, and my parents again happened to be there as well. A month prior, I had told a friend in Colombo, Ruhanie, that I would be finding my way to Colombo. Ruhanie booked a venue, and before I knew it, I was scheduled to perform at the Punchi Theater in Sri Lanka.

My tech rehearsal was scheduled for the day after I arrived, and I told Amma she could come to the tech. (It's a long story, but I felt like it would be wise for her to not come see the actual show.) Ruhanie picked up Amma and me, and we made our way to the theater. In the car, Ruhanie told us that performances like mine were rare in Sri Lanka due to the queer factor, and she asked how I was feeling. She also asked Amma how she felt about the fact that I was going to perform in Sri Lanka.

Out of the blue, Amma tells us both a story that I was hearing for the very first time. Apparently, either while I was in her womb or shortly after I was born, Amma brought me to Sri Lanka. She went outside the house, and a chatrakaran (holy/wise/psychic guy?) came to congratulate my Amma on her newborn boy. Amma corrected him and said, "No, I had a girl." He responded, "No, a boy," and walked off.

As much as this was a shock to hear from Amma's mouth, it made sense that she felt free to tell me this—that Ruhanie's question triggered that vault to open yet once again. I could be trying to sew again here, but to me, her sharing this story was a marker that she was finally accepting that which she could not change.

After much hesitation, I told Amma that she could come if she wanted to, and so she did. Amma sat with my cousin and laughed alongside everyone. After the show, she was bombarded like a celebrity and joked with everyone that she was going to take a cut of my performer fees because my material was largely about my journey with her.

THE PATCH

I realize that my journey has been one of healing my broken heart, but more specifically it has been finding my way back to being fondly seen through my Amma's eyes. I wish it weren't true, but if I told you that my world was off-kilter, especially while the storm she and I brewed shook every point between Lancaster and Brooklyn, it would be an understatement. I needed her love and acceptance more than even I knew.

I can say that through the fights and the yelling and yearning to be seen by one another, I felt groundless. I would search for grounding thinking that I would find it in my career path, or on occasion with women that I had the chance to exchange love with. But for me, it is true what they say: there is nothing like an Amma's love, and I wanted to be the light of her eye again and tell her that my head was still filled with mud.

I needed her love to feel grounded and like I had a place in this world, so that it was okay that I chose to stay alive because I belonged. And the more I grew, the more she accepted me. But even more surprising is how my Amma grew the more she felt seen by me. We sewed patches over each other's holes.

ACKNOWLEDGMENT

This piece is dedicated to all the beautiful Tamil, Sri Lankan, South Asian, API, Southeast Asian, and Asian queers. May you share this story with your parents if you need a tool to crack open their hearts to you.

nine genealogies (of un/belonging)[1]

Patti Duncan

> From A Far / What nationality / or what kindred and relation / what
> blood relation / what blood ties of blood / what ancestry / what race
> generation / what house clan tribe stock strain / what lineage extrac-
> tion / what breed sect gender denomination caste / what stray ejection
> misplaced / Tertium Quid neither one thing nor the other / Tombe des
> nues de naturalized / what transplant to dispel upon
> —Theresa Hak Kyung Cha, *Dictée*[2]

i. "exile"[3]

"Where are you from?" they always ask. "No, where are you really from?"
And then, "But how did your parents meet?"

How did you come to be? How did you come to exist? How did you come to
exist *here*? Why are you here? Why are you here? Why are you here?

ii. "You move. You are being moved. You are movement."

Dear Chance,

Let me begin by telling you how much I love you. The day you were
born was probably the happiest day of my life. I am amazed by you
every day, and I'm so honored to be your mother.

There's so much I want to pass on to you—things I hope to teach
you and share with you. Already I notice that you seem to inherit
some traits from me. I'm thrilled that you love music and art and
books as much as I do. And I love and appreciate your deep compassion for others, and for the earth and all beings. Your commitment
to justice and equity mirrors my own, and I like to imagine that you
get that from me.

But even as I celebrate these connections, I am also aware of
some more difficult legacies. I know that you inherit a complex family history, the effects of intergenerational trauma, and the ghosts of
our collective past. As a mixed race Korean American daughter of a
Korean immigrant woman and white male former U.S. soldier, I
have grown up in the shadow of a war no one wants to remember.

And the geopolitical history of the Korean War continues to structure the unequal power relationship between the United States and Korea, as well as relations within our own family. I tell you this not to worry you, but because I want "to keep the pain from translating itself into memory" (Cha, 140). Even more so, as a family history, I want to "document the map of [our] journey" (Cha, 140). I want to displace time. I would move history for you if I could.

iii. "The memory is the entire. The longing in the face of the lost."

The ultrasound is grainy, hard to read. I spend hours looking at it, imagining the little face, the hands, the feet. I believe this little being is on their way to meet me, joining the past and the future to create a present in which we will exist together. I know my child carries the weight of our family history. But I also know somehow that they will weave it together in a way that makes them free.

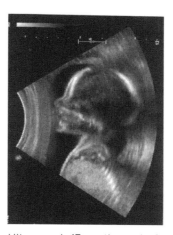

Ultrasound. (From the author)

iv. "neither one thing nor the other"

Growing up mixed race in America meant being interrogated on a regular basis about my racial and ethnic heritage: "Where are you from?" or "What are you?" When my childhood responses didn't satisfy, the questions became more aggressive: "Well, how did your parents meet?" "What's your nationality?" "Can I guess your background?" Growing up mixed race meant enduring the constant scrutiny of the nonmixed, who never tried to hide their feelings of superiority, illustrated by comments like, "It must be so hard to be mixed," or, "You must feel caught between two worlds," and other, more insidious remarks: "Mixed race people are so exotic," or, "Mixed race people are so beautiful." I learned to live with ambiguity as I was frequently subjected to such contradictory statements and assumptions. Growing up mixed race meant feeling invisible, always having to justify my existence and my identity. It meant apologizing to one community or another, for never being enough. Sometimes it meant passing, or being passed over by those who needed to categorize or quantify my racial identity for their own comfort. It meant feeling different, other, wrong. At other times, I was accused of selling out one race or the other. Frequently, it was implied that I was not "Asian enough" or "Korean enough." When I was very young, my (Asian) mother was occasionally mistaken for my nanny. When people found out my (white) father had served in the U.S. military and had been stationed in South Korea, they frequently asked if my mother had been a prostitute. Growing up mixed race meant assumptions about who I am, who my parents are, and what my experiences must be.

In "If I Could Write This in Fire, I Would Write This in Fire," Michelle Cliff interweaves her memories of growing up as a light-skinned, mixed race girl in Jamaica with a searing critique of the colonialism and racism that continue to shape the lives of the people living there.[4] She writes, "*Looking Back:* to try and see when the background changed places with the foreground. To try and locate the vanishing point: where the lines of perspective converge and disappear. Lines of color and class. Lines of history and social context. Lines of denial and rejection. When did *we* (the light-skinned middle-class Jamaicans) take over for *them* as oppressors? I need to see when and how this happened."[5] In her writing—a blend of poetry and prose, critical analysis and autobiographical writing—Cliff explores themes of privilege and power, as well as the complex workings of internalized oppression. With painful honesty, she plunges into questions of her own complicity with systems of colorism and classism. Such writing reminds us, as Mari Matsuda suggests, that "at the end of all this theorizing, there is a body."[6] It grounds feminist theories of power and privilege in the intimate space of personal experience, rooted in embodiment and material reality.

In some of my writing, I explore similar themes through my own family history, specifically by reflecting on my experience as a mixed race woman. I am interested in mixed race experience and especially the ways in which race and gender intersect to produce certain kinds of narratives about and experiences for mixed race people. I seek to intervene in a discourse that suggests our lives are always already tragic yet somehow exotic, and to understand the social locales in which these narratives and representations are produced, as well as the social, political, and economic conditions that enable such constructions. I believe it is critical to interrogate the gendered racialization of such discourses about mixed race people in order to explore the ways in which systems of oppression intersect and interact.

Within the Asian Pacific American communities of my childhood, mixed race individuals were associated with Asian women who had children with U.S. soldiers during and after war or armed conflict. The U.S. military presence in South Korea, Vietnam, Japan, and the Philippines, for example, produced the conditions that led to the birth of large numbers of mixed race children. For local populations, U.S. militarism has resulted in poverty, violence, and the creation of a sex economy characterized by unequal power relations, economic disparities, and language and cultural barriers between U.S. troops and local communities. Also, the gendered, racialized, and sexualized encounters that frequently occur in such contact zones have resulted in the stigmatization of mixed race children, assumed to be associated with both prostitution and U.S. occupation of the homeland.

Born the daughter of a Korean immigrant woman and a U.S. serviceman, I grew up very aware of how my mother and I were perceived. I witnessed the discrimination she faced within U.S. society, but the disparagement from other Koreans was even more painful and difficult to comprehend—the contemptuous looks, ridicule, avoidance, and rejection from various Korean people and organizations, and at community events. As her mixed race daughter, I experienced it too, in the form of constant reminders that neither she nor I could ever be Korean enough to fully belong in the Korean community of my hometown.

But still, I grew up dreaming of Korea. I imagined it as the answer to all my questions and problems, the mysteries of growing up in a mixed race military household, where my mother's alienation and displacement were constant themes of my childhood. As a child, I spoke only a smattering of Korean; I was encouraged to speak English only at school and in other public places. I ate *bulgogi* and *kimchi* in private with my mother, knowing that most of my U.S. friends would not appreciate her Korean cooking. I outgrew the *hanbok* my mother brought for me from Korea, and for a period of time, I think I tried to assimilate as much as I could into a typical (white) American adolescence. But I was constantly questioned about my race, a persistent reminder of my lack of belonging. I witnessed my mother's encounters with American racism and anti-Asian sentiments, and when I saw other Koreans ignore her or make fun of her, my own pain mirrored hers. I know she made friends with other women like herself who had married U.S. soldiers and had mixed race children in the United States. But when my mother talked about home, she always meant Korea, and I too began to imagine Korea as my home and my birthright.

v. "resistant to memory"

> You return and you are not one of them . . . They comment upon
> your inability or ability to speak. Whether you are telling the truth
> or not about your nationality. They say you look other than you say.
> As if you didn't know who you were. You say who you are but you
> begin to doubt. (Cha, 56–57)

To memory, and the other things I lost.
My first language.
My mother.
My sister.
The war claimed many things, not just then and not just now.

I inherit my mother's trauma, untranslatable but always present.

vi. "Refugees. Immigrants. Exiles."

> When did you leave the country why did you leave this country why
> are you returning to the country. (Cha, 57)

What does it mean to "look Korean," anyway? What if I don't pass as white,
but I'm somehow never seen as Korean enough, especially in Korea? But
race isn't skin color or facial features or hair texture. Race is socially constructed, shaped by histories and social, economic, and political systems.
Also, race shapes and is structured by gender, class, sexuality, nation, and
other social categories and systems. Processes of racialization are also systems of power. To be mixed race Korean American invokes a long history of
colonialism, war, military occupation, militarized violence, and other forms
of state violence. We embody this history, we carry it in our blood, and we
wear it on our faces.

What does it mean to look queer, or lesbian, or bisexual? How do we
account for all the ways we go unseen every day?

vii. "Mother, I dream you just to be able to see you."

> Dear Mother,
> I'm writing again, hoping you'll read this. You refuse the past. You
> always have. And while I am finally able to acknowledge and accept
> that, I continue to feel haunted by our collective, familial history.

Dear Mother,
"Nothing has changed, we are at a standstill. I speak in another tongue now, a second tongue a foreign tongue. All this time we have been away. But nothing has changed. A stand still" (Cha, 80).

Dear Ma,
There is so much I want to tell you, but "there are chasms between us."[7]

Dear Mother,
ahnyoung hasehyo. Are you at peace?[8]

Interpretive sketch of partitioned Korean peninsula by Paul Michael L. Atienza. (Courtesy of Paul Michael L. Atienza)

viii. "Mother tongue is your refuge."

Chance, this year you will turn seven. When I look at your little face, so sweet and open, I imagine the world in front of you full of possibilities and hope. Remember this: in Maria P. P. Root's "Bill of Rights for Racially Mixed People" (7), she states: "I have the right not to justify my existence in this world."[9] This is what I hope for you: that you will grow up with a sense of community and belonging, taking pride in all the parts of who you are, and that you will know that we are whole—just as we are—and that we never need to apologize for or justify our mixed race identities.

ix. "Why resurrect it all now. From the Past. History, the old wound."

> There is a chronology that is useful to keep in mind, but the story I want to tell is about the ways in which the figure of the *yanggongju* gets its very life from the effects of trauma, and the temporality of trauma is never faithful to linear timelines.
>
> —GRACE CHO, *Haunting*[10]

I know why you had to return to the place of such loss.
Burdened by the weight of memories.
Full of untold stories.
In my bones I feel it too. Always returning, always letting go, always losing.
The images haunt my dreams too, memories like nightmares,
buried deep in skin and heart.

AUTHOR'S NOTE

A version of this essay was previously published in *Mixed Korean: Our Stories*, edited by Cerrissa Kim, Katherine Kim, Sora Kim-Russell, and Mary-Kim Arnold (Bloomfield, Indiana: Truepeny Publishing Company, 2018). Reprinted with permission. Earlier versions of some of this writing have been previously published as "In Search of Other 'Others': Exploring Representations of Mixed Race Asian Pacific Americans," in *Women's Lives: Multicultural Perspectives*, 6th ed., edited by Gwyn Kirk and Margo Okazawa-Rey (Mountain View, CA: Mayfield, 2012), 145–151; and as "The Marginalization of Korean Military Wives," in *Borderlands 2: It's a Family Affair*, a zine edited by Nia King (Denver, CO, 2008), available at the Queer Zine Archive Project.[11]

NOTES

1. The title of this piece references the nine "chapters" (based on nine muses) of Theresa Hak Kyung Cha's *Dictée* and allows me to experiment with the concept of genealogy as family history, kinship narratives, and historical records.
2. Theresa Hak Kyung Cha, *Dictée* (Berkeley, CA: Third Woman, 1995).
3. All headings in quotation marks are from Cha's *Dictée*.
4. Michelle Cliff, "If I Could Write This in Fire, I Would Write This in Fire," in *The Land of Look Behind: Prose and Poetry* (Ithaca, NY: Firebrand, 1985), 57–76.
5. Cliff, "If I Could Write This in Fire, I Would Write This in Fire," 62.
6. Mari J. Matsuda, *Where Is Your Body? And Other Essays on Race, Gender, and the Law* (Boston: Beacon, 1996).
7. This is a quotation from Merle Woo's well-known work "Letter to Ma," published in *This Bridge Called My Back: Writings by Radical Women of Color*, edited by Cherríe Moraga and Gloria Anzaldúa (New York: Kitchen Table: Women of Color, 1983), 140–147.
8. Here, I invoke Nami Mun's review of the novel *Human Acts* by Han Kang, in which Mun writes, "In Korean, 'Hello' (*ahnyoung hasehyo*) literally translates to 'Are

you at peace?' This question-greeting is delivered as a statement, of course, but a certain poignancy can't be ignored—especially if one considers the violent history of the Korean peninsula." Nami Mun, "The Author of 'The Vegetarian' Takes on Korea's Violent Past," *The New York Times* Book Review, January 10, 2017, https://www.nytimes.com/2017/01/10/books/review/han-kang-human-acts.html?_r=0.

9. Maria P. P. Root, "A Bill of Rights for Racially Mixed People," in *The Multiracial Experience: Racial Borders as the New Frontier,* edited by Maria P. P. Root (Thousand Oaks, CA: Sage, 1996), 3–14.

10. Grace M. Cho, *Haunting the Korean Diaspora: Shame, Secrecy, and the Forgotten Korean War* (Minneapolis: University of Minnesota Press, 2008), 4.

11. *Borderlands 2: It's a Family Affair,* a zine edited by Nia King (Denver, CO, 2008), available at the Queer Zine Archive Project.

Lateral Diasporas and Queer Adaptations in *Fresh Off the Boat* and *The Family Law*

Douglas S. Ishii

The 1990s flashback series *Fresh Off the Boat* (2015–2020) centers the Taiwanese American Huang family upon their move to the suburbs of Orlando, Florida, from Washington, DC's Chinatown. *Fresh Off the Boat* renewed conversations about racial stereotypes from its place in the American Broadcasting Company's lineup of single-camera family sitcoms. The adaptation of food celebrity Eddie Huang's memoir into this brand, and his departure from the show's production, was much discussed around the series's 2015 premiere. Meanwhile, across the Pacific, *The Family Law* (2016–2019) follows the Queensland-based Chinese Australian family as the parents divorce. The program, loosely based on Benjamin Law's memoir and cowritten by him, aired as part of the Special Broadcasting Service's appeal to Australian ethnic minorities. Comparisons abound, as both series are coming-of-age sitcoms inspired by Asian diasporic memoirs to tap into multicultural market segments. Their stories gesture to the contradiction of the families' hardships with national mythologies of meritocracy and centralize adolescent protagonists who are particularly out of place because of the regions they inhabit. However, coverage of *The Family Law* has generally not mentioned *Fresh Off the Boat* and vice versa, with exceptions like one December 2015 post by Angry Asian Man, "'The Family Law' is Australia's Answer to 'Fresh Off the Boat.'"[1] This chapter argues that looking sideways across settler states of the Asian Pacific offers a necessarily queer diasporic critique.

The categorization of these media texts reflects the minoritizing racialization of Asians within white settler nation-states. *Fresh Off the Boat* is celebrated as Asian American, both as its aura of critical citizenship that recalls the Asian American Movement and the neoliberal appropriation of that language that makes marketization feel like social change. "Asian American" clusters race, identity, community, flattened difference, and bureaucratic diversity simultaneously.[2] Timothy Yu argues that "Asian Australian" does not possess the prevalence of its U.S. counterpart and has been used by publishers to locate Australian poets of Asian descent outside of the nation and its canon. As Yu argues, the reclamation of "Asian Australian" as an analogy of "Asian American" at best names the local conditions of racialization through the nation-frame in a diasporic travel of a U.S. concept.[3] The TV adaptation of *The Family Law* illustrates this uneven portability. Many of the show's advertisements are packaged through the Chinese Australian mother Jenny, as SBS makes clear its targeted marketing to the Chinese diaspora. Even as its mainstream Australian coverage insists upon the program's "universal appeal," *The Family Law* forces confrontation with the Orientalist baggage of previous representations.[4] This shift reflects that the country's sizeable and growing Chinese, Indian, Filipinx, and Vietnamese populations are not only immigrants but domestically born citizens.[5]

Timothy Yu calls the plural tensions between Asian and Australian the "poetic ambivalence" of simultaneously belonging and not belonging to the nation. I look queerly sideways to call this a lateral diaspora. It has been two decades since David Eng, Gayatri Gopinath, and Martin Manalansan, among others, mobilized diaspora and queerness to critique the imbrications of cultural nationalism and compulsory heterosexuality. Critical race scholarship and activism have used diaspora as a conceptual tool to facilitate politics that refuse the insularity of the nation and appeals to the state. Yet as an object of post–Cold War knowledge, diaspora has subordinated a "here" of minority experience to a "there" of a global elsewhere for cultural fascination, military mastery, and resource expropriation—a heteronormative, vertical relation that authenticates as it creates distance. If this use of diaspora organizes a "here" and "there," certain race radicalisms function "inward" and "outward." Activists turn inward to grapple with socioeconomic and political cleavages in Asian American communities to confront their frustration not only with the model minority myth but also with model minority subjectivities. Calls for solidarity with Black freedom and indigenous sovereignty turn outward to declare that we are over complicity—which can claim innocence regarding our own embeddedness. Lateral diasporas thus serve as a praxis for thinking, acting, and feeling across nation-states. It is not a restored kinship but a reckoning with assemblages of racialization and dispossession from the overlapping realities of Asian diasporas.

Spatial estrangement, as a point of comparison between *Fresh Off the Boat* and *The Family Law*, makes evident how region mediates race and nation. Gayatri Gopinath theorizes region in two ways. For one, region challenges the assimilation of the local into the global, the "here" and the "there," as impelled by processes such as transnational capital, the heteronormative imperatives of the nation, the imperialism of U.S.-centric gay politics, and homophobia within diasporic formations.[6] For another, it is a rubric for "the particularities of gender and sexual logics in spaces that exist in a tangential relation to the nation, but that are simultaneously and irreducibly marked by complex national and global processes."[7] Region is thus both eccentric and deconstructive. However, I depart from Gopinath's understanding of region as inherently resistive, and I trace the normative desires that the phantasm of region expresses through nationalist grammars. In *Fresh Off the Boat* and *The Family Law*, region's mediation magnifies Asian difference and incorporates it into the settler nation's multicultural exceptionalisms. Region, as a scale that aligns with, subtends, and exceeds national territory, appears and disappears in ways that, following Jodi Byrd, make the Asian immigrant "native" to settler colonization.[8]

Because racial difference administers their adolescent, second-generation protagonists' sexuality, *Fresh Off the Boat* and *The Family Law* invite an analysis of adaptation in its twinned senses, of transmedia rewritings and immigrant sociology. In terms of aesthetic form, I analyze the visibilities of the pop memoir and the family sitcom. I borrow from Lauren Berlant and Sianne Ngai to dwell in the detachments and proximities enacted through the cathexis and catharsis of comedy, or "investment in the joke and the relief of release from it."[9] Comedy produces "a scene of affective mediation and expectation" motivated by "what it means to be out of control"—an anxiety rooted in the layers of meaning that laughter blurs, collapses, and reconstitutes.[10] In terms of racial form, Lisa Lowe reminds that the trope of generational difference "contribute[s] to the aestheticizing commodification of Asian American *cultural* differences, while denying the immigrant histories of material exclusion."[11] This liberal abstraction synchronizes the settler time of nationhood with the normative maturation of the racialized citizen, as getting over their racialization completes settler multiculturalism.[12]

Lateral diasporas can reorient vertical relationships that reproduce discourses of "good" and "bad" offspring: cultural hierarchy, which presumes the literary text more authentic and valuable than its media rewriting, and generational thinking, which organizes liberal progress narratives through reproduction.[13] If, as Gopinath argues, region is the remainder, recuperating these remainders through lateral diaspora considers the adaptations of racial difference within a normativizing form like the situation comedy as representational correlations of Asian incorporation in settler multiculturalism.

Both narrative universes treat region as the disappointing exception to the inclusivity of the settler nation. *Fresh Off the Boat* is based in Orlando, Florida. Yet outside of the series pilot, in which the father Louis declares their new home to be "the Wild West," references to the U.S. South are scant. Orlando represents the homogeneous whiteness of suburbia in which the Huangs confront the racialization of their upward mobility. This collapse of place into abstract cultural geography facilitates the sitcom's commentary on tokenism, Orientalism, and media stereotype, as well as minoritized agency. Yet this avowal and disavowal of specificity registers how the sitcom's underwriting liberalism scapegoats region for the national predominance of white supremacy. As the series departs from its source text, it alternates between nineties hypernostalgia, metacommentary, and family romance. In the season 2 episode "Year of the Rat," matriarch Jessica tries to find ethnic community for the Lunar New Year in the Orlando Asian Culture Club and instead finds white Asiaphiles. The laughability of the Asia-philes elicits sympathy from the imagined viewer's "good" inclusive whiteness as this "bad" whiteness that heightens her alienation. The generalized spatiality of this scenario less reflects the family's secondary migration to the South than their leaving Chinatown, thus maintaining Jessica's adaptation as the goal.

This gesture of the American South as synecdoche via race and exception via U.S. liberal sexuality shapes the Huang family for television adaptation. The transit from memoir to sitcom adapts Louis from unexpressive father to corny sitcom dad, and Jessica no longer haunts as the abusive force of judgment from Huang's narrative. *Fresh Off the Boat* the memoir ends with Huang, over two decades later, now a former drug dealer and law school dropout, detailing his "Asian American" restaurant Baohaus. It ends not with Baohaus's February 2010 review in the *New York Times* but with Jessica celebrating the April 2010 review in *The World Journal*, which Huang footnotes as "the preeminent newspaper for overseas Chinese people" (272). This Jessica epitomizes the diasporic distance between the Asian America proffered throughout the text and the insular space she inhabits. Though Huang refuses to be the U.S. model minority, this Jessica discovers his success not through Baohaus's national buzz but its belated recognition in the diaspora—which Huang writes for humor based on its seeming removal from relevance.

In *Fresh Off the Boat* the sitcom, the narrative focus on Jessica finds humor in her overbearing expectations of her sons but also lands emotional beats in her own anxieties about parenting. She takes from Eddie the role of co-ensemble lead with Louis and is adapted not only from immigrant to American but also from domineering mother to flustered sitcom mom. In the season 2 episode "Boy II Man," Jessica coaches Honey—Jessica's white neighbor, best friend, stepmother to one of Eddie's love interests, and often the butt of the joke—to be less permissive with her stepdaughter. Honey then advises Jessica to speak to her adolescent Eddie as a friend. Against the trope of the immigrant mother fighting her American children, this advice leads Jessica to an unusual but intimate moment of personal sharing from mother to son. This scene is less a disassociation from racialized "Tiger parenting" discourse and more an affirmation of the bourgeois family. Such formal conventions of the family sitcom thus reinforce heteronormativity, which here appears at once universal yet specific, through liberal sentimentality as U.S. cultural citizenship.

One of the few emplaced mentions of Florida occurs not because of race but because of sexuality. When patriarch Louis discovers that his middle son Emery hides a cache of martial arts films featuring topless men, he assumes that Emery, portrayed as artistic and emotionally expressive, is gay. Louis fumbles a speech about puberty and tolerance and in the process stammers, "Although we're not in the best state . . . for . . ." before Emery explains that he was looking for a macho role model. The specter of the gay child brings the region's exceptionalism to bear because U.S. sitcom liberalism seems more politically amenable to addressing pervasive homophobia than systemic racism. The joke's cathexis locates that bias in a someone else who presumably is not consuming the diversity family brand. Its catharsis takes place as the tightly wound sitcom dad, here the audience surrogate, exhales his relief in a knot of difference, youth, and safety.[14] The actual sexual coming-of-age arc belongs to Eddie's neighbor, ex-girlfriend, and best friend Nicole, which culminates in the sixth episode of season 4, "A League of Her Own." Nicole comes out to her stepmother in front of Jessica as she frets over how to tell her significantly older father, Marvin. Jessica alternates between flustered and dismissive of Nicole's plight, and she accidentally spoils Nicole's coming out. Marvin nevertheless accepts his daughter with open arms. Contradicting Louis's previous hesitation about homosexuality in the language of region, sexual liberalism, attributed to the white family, enacts the emotional promise of cultural citizenship: the freedom to be happy.

Fresh Off the Boat thus elides region to elide difference through the twinned processes of adaptation. The same holds true for *The Family Law*, which takes place in Sunshine Coast, Queensland—a fact that underwrites author Benjamin Law's experiences of racial isolation and tokenization in the 1990s. The narrative unfolds in a region known for its whiteness because of its seasonal tourist industry, in a metropolis with a lower Asian population than most. As in *Fresh Off the Boat* the series, *The Family Law* adaptation disarticulates a "good," inclusive whiteness from a "bad," intolerant whiteness. This is evident in the series 1 finale when oldest sister Candy's white, buffoonish fiancé Wayne reveals that he has not told his parents about their engagement because "they wouldn't understand." He tearfully tells the Laws, "It's not like they're KKK." Ben adds, "Don't you mean One Nation?" This joke, premised on a kinder liberal whiteness, holds region as the nation's xenophobic remainder while acknowledging the trans-Pacific project of white supremacy. It further makes the Asian diasporan "native" to the nation's exceptionalism, as Ben reaffirms Australia's multicultural present, first made official in policy in 1978, by identifying One Nation as aberration. Yet, their Sunshine Coast exists out of time. The pilot episode opens on an image of a beach at sunset. The camera then pans out to unveil the image as a photograph within the kitsch of a Chinese restaurant. This juxtaposition of the still paradise and hectic diasporic space frames the bicultural world of the Laws and its racialized dynamic of progress and inertia, of nation and race—which invites deconstruction through the lens of lateral diasporas.

This arrested temporality that opens the series is also a sentimental melancholy, like the image frozen in time and the child's image of his parents. As in *Fresh Off the Boat* the TV series, the narrative attends to the mother's development. The series 1 arc of *The Family Law* begins when the mother, Jenny, hears the term "deadbeat" on TV. She asks her son Ben, the protogay protagonist, what it means, and he responds, "It's, like, someone who can't be relied on." She applies it to her husband, Danny, and kicks him out of the family house. TV Jenny thus becomes a modern subject via her gay son, as he indirectly impels her feminist self-possession. This arc adapts how Law the memoirist pokes fun at his immigrant mother's misuse of words—which does not include "deadbeat," as Jenny and Danny divorce by the end of the third essay without much consequence. The TV family thus stages Australian sexual modernity, represented by a divorce that leads to greater happiness, against the temporal inertia of their culturalized racialization. The television program about the gay son is not queer, in that his protosexuality aligns Jenny with the liberal promises of the settler nation.

Australian sexual modernity makes possible the TV Law's adaptation by eliding the global Chinese diaspora. In both versions of *The Family Law*, Jenny arrives to Australia via Malaysia. The essay that introduces this route, "You've Got a Friend," is sandwiched between two essays on Law coming of age as a gay man. The first, "Toward Manhood," is on Law's failing hegemonic masculinity and his inconsequential coming out to his mother. The second, "God Camp," is on being a child at the titular month-long retreat and how much he missed his parents. "You've Got a Friend" tells of a family visit to Jenny's friend Clara, who lives in Ipoh, Malaysia, with her husband, Wayne, as devout Christians. The essay engages a poetics of denial: as Clara and Wayne grow uncomfortable with the children asking about mosques and Malaysia's Muslim majority, a rift begins to grow between Jenny and Clara. Jenny wanders away, and Clara panics, revealing that she lives in Islamophobic fear. The essay ends with a final conversation in which Clara tells Jenny through a toothy grin, "As long as you are a Christian, I'll be your friend" (119). God camp is not where Law experiences religion as discipline, and, against Orientalist expectations of homophobia, the immigrant mother and domestic son dyad does not damage Ben. Instead, Clara's religious identity accumulates sexual antagonism and repression.

The fifth TV episode, "Everything's Coming Up Roses," traces this path of relocation without the differential racialization through religion suggested in the memoir. The episode begins with Jenny, listless over not only her martial separation but also her eldest son's move out of the family house. Ben thus calls on her best friend from Malaysia, Aunty Rose. Rose, like Clara, is a devout Christian. Unlike Clara, Rose hints at a deep homophobia: after Ben makes a dramatic entrance and exit to announce his acting camp, she asks Jenny, "Do you think he chooses to be like this?" Jenny responds that Ben "was born this way" but also calls him a "triple threat." Jenny misrecognizes Rose's coded language. Ben's inclination toward the arts acts either as obfuscation or metonym of his sexual orientation, which is only hinted at in his love of acting, his occasionally shrill voice, and his disgust when his long-suffering gal pal kisses him. During an act II conversation, as Rose tries to drive a wedge between Jenny and her children, the camera focuses on Rose stroking Jenny's arm. When Danny and the children stage a final act III confrontation to stop Jenny from accompanying Rose to Malaysia, Rose throws down an ultimatum: her or the children. Jenny triumphantly chooses the kids. Rose screams from the backseat of her departing cab, "You break my heart again!" Rose's possessiveness is her repressed lesbian desire, which is maligned for its visibility—unlike Ben's undiscovered sexuality. Her denied queerness projects onto a pathological elsewhere— one that is not only Chinese but also the remainder of Muslim Malaysia, and thus need not explain its repressiveness.

These poetics of denial read back into *Fresh Off the Boat* through the slippery relationship of the Huangs to colonized Asia. Actor Randall Park's suspicion of portraying accents appeared in press coverage alongside mentions of his background in Asian American studies, and Louis Huang loses his accent after the first few episodes.[15] Season 2 retroactively characterizes Louis's longer acculturation through his love of Jon Hughes films. A season 3 flashback scene in "The Flush," evocative of the show's self-reflexivity, places Louis alongside Asian American pop culture greats Jeremy Lin, Ali Wong, and Ming-Na Wen. Further, his point of origin has been retconned as Taiwan. These slippages express region as remainder, in the incomplete consolidation of China in *Fresh Off the Boat*, as well as Taiwan's palimpsestic history as the Republic of China—just as the incomplete erasure of Islamic Malaysia from *The Family Law* makes impossible a monolithic Chinese Australia. The originary "there" is revealed the inauthentic counterpart.

By recuperating these remainders as lateral diasporas, I have destabilized certain strands of diasporic discourse to locate the erasures that make Asian diasporans model consumers of the white settler nation. The sideways look across the queerness of region and adaptation does not seek a global completion of Asian community, but highlights parallel sites that do not recognize each other within the inward pull of settler nation-frame. Lateral diasporas thus can connect us through a queer relationality that inhabits the planet outside of the colonial partition of space installed through dispossession and genocide—the "here" of multicultural settlement and the "there" of reproductive origins.

NOTES

1. One exception mentions *Fresh Off the Boat* as an "international success" and an international model for Australia, but not a point of solidarity. Shaad D'Souza, "Diversity on Australian TV Is Still Pretty Terrible. Whose Job Is It to Fix That?" *Junkee*, 10 December 2015, http://junkee.com/diversity-on-australian-tv-is-still-pretty-terrible -whose-job-is-it-to-fix-that/70710

2. See Shalini Shankar, "Racial Naturalization, Advertising, and Model Consumers for a New Millennium," *Journal of Asian American Studies* 16, no. 2 (2013): 159–188; Soo Ah Kwon, "The Politics and Institutionalization of Panethnic Identity," *Journal of Asian American Studies* 16, no. 2 (2013): 137–157.

3. Timothy Yu, "On Asian Australian Poetry," *Southerly* 73, no. 1 (2013): 75–88.

4. See Michael Idato, "The Family Law: Authentic Comedy with Universal Appeal," *The Sydney Morning Herald*, January 12, 2016, https://www.smh.com.au/entertainment /tv-and-radio/the-family-law-authentic-comedy-with-universal-appeal-20160112-gm 44jn.html.

5. This is suggested by the increase between the 2011 and 2016 censuses as well as the growing gap in the 2016 census between birthplace and ancestry numbers for these groups. "Australia: Community Profile," *.id*, accessed April 7, 2018, https://profile .id.com.au/australia.

6. Gayatri Gopinath, "Queer Regions: Locating Lesbians in *Sancharram*," in *A Companion to Lesbian, Gay, Bisexual, Transgender, and Queer Studies*, edited by George E. Haggerty and Molly McGarry (Malden, MA: Blackwell Publishing, 2007), 342.

7. Ibid., 343.

8. Jodi A. Byrd, *The Transit of Empire: Indigenous Critiques of Colonialism* (Minneapolis: University of Minnesota Press, 2011). See also Iyko Day, *Alien Capital: Asian Racialization and the Logic of Settler Colonial Capitalism* (Durham, NC: Duke University Press, 2016).

9. Lauren Berlant and Sianne Ngai, "Comedy Has Issues," *Critical Inquiry* 43 (2017): 245.

10. Ibid., 239.

11. Lisa Lowe, *Immigrant Acts: On Asian American Cultural Politics* (Durham, NC: Duke University Press, 1997), 63, emphasis original.

12. See Anne Anlin Cheng, *The Melancholy of Race: Psychoanalysis, Assimilation, and Hidden Grief* (Oxford: Oxford University Press, 2001), and Hortense J. Spillers, "Mama's Baby, Papa's Maybe: An American Grammar Book," *Diacritics* 17 no. 2 (1987): 64–81.

13. For the latter, see Chris A. Eng, "Queer Genealogies of (Be)Longing: On the Thens and Theres of Asian America in Karen Tei Yamashita's *I Hotel*," *Journal of Asian American Studies* 20, no. 3 (2017): 345–372.

14. Youngest child Evan, who enacts the precocious child trope and circulates among the white housewives of the homeowner's association, serves as a rather queer surrogate for non-normativity.

15. Fresh Air, "Actor Randall Park Says 'Fresh Off the Boat' Is Comedy Without the Cliché," *National Public Radio*, October 14, 2015, https://www.npr.org/2015/10/14/448278570/actor-randall-park-says-fresh-off-the-boat-is-comedy-without-the-clich.

PART II

Queer Unsettlings

Geographies, Sovereignties

Khmer Alphabet

Not a language I loved at first like French: seductive
murmurs, coy tilt of the head, dusk
in a dusty *patisserie*; Khmer is harsh:

midday sun on Sihanouk Boulevard
palms swaying in impossible heat, slanting shadows

of colonial edifices, pristine relics of splendored desire.
Sanskrit looks like prayer, embers and incense, hot instant noodles,
mudras, corporate logos—alien and familiar, home and

faraway. I want you to say you love me in Khmer,
I want to speak it like my mother

tongue (father *logos*), I want to French kiss you head on,
palm to palm, heat to heat, I want

to forget it takes a lifetime to learn.

Galaxies Like Blood

The iron in our blood was formed in stars,
billions of years ago, trillions of miles away.
—PEROT MUSEUM OF NATURAL SCIENCE, Dallas

The stars, this raft. Guide us.
in moonlight and midnight ink, the ocean wide as galaxies
   No north star to guide us
        Refuge, refuse, refusal.

We are not refugees
   Seeking pity, redemption, your gift
of freedom (the ironies
of freedom).

The iron in my blood
The iron in my blood

I willed the astronomy of fear and hope
my compass—breathe, breathe, breathe:
survive.

   Surface: skin, air, blood, water.

   Surface: rise, rise
   buoyant tides,   so many drowned
                      bloated skin pale face moon-
                      light starlight starboard

Our children huddled

       a raft and stars

I come from lifetimes away.

Teeth and Chairs (Phnom Penh)

> Anonymous, mass produced objects contain a collective and equally
> extraordinary message: Whoever you are . . . at least in this small way,
> be well.
>
> —ELAINE SCARRY, *The Body in Pain: The Making and Unmaking of the World*

Q: What objects did you leave behind?
A: My life.

Pain, the unmaking of the world.

A city bled of inhabitants, 1970s, only ghosts
reside in these halls.

Whoever you are

mass of anonymous dead, mere
objects

anonymous
mass produced objects . . . a comb, empty chairs, a piano
in the middle of empty streets, open cupboards, stacks of paper

in this small way

The city barren, no marks
of life.

And what do I know
of pain who receive these flickering images,
stereotypical stories
decades after the fact, an afterimage, after—
fact: a prodigal son's despair (Rami, did you find your
father's ghost?);

young
students, architects, artists, engineers, 102 survivors, returned
gathering in the shadows,
Royal University in 1980,

counting their dead kin for the GDR cameramen, recounting
their world undone
counting their days, ways to
make the world
make their way

this brave new world—

What has become of them?

Whoever you are

The afterlife of trauma

Rami, here is your father, a snapshot in time
a small image, a small object
among thousands, Tuol Sleng, black and white

stacks of paper
confessions

only ghosts reside in these halls

Whoever you are

Former "Pearl of the Orient," wats and waterways; chronic,
centrifugal, the rivers churn.

Now this city, once barren
bears no marks
of its pain—

Night's neon casing, sulfur;
teenage boys—rooster strut hair, laughing
speeding ablaze (red taillights), the long bright
boulevard, glimmering high-rises, past the rotten
teeth of buildings, humid zoom into the future

the past sweats through our pores, almost invisible
cooled by dark's motorcycle throttle rush, sticky skin

of billboards, skeleton pile
of buildings, construction.

The making of the world? Repopulate it:
objects in lieu of loved ones lost,

chattering sidewalks overflowing, waiting
chairs and tables, fluorescent seeth
noodles, bread, balloons, exhaust and asphalt.

Anonymous mass objects
mass graves
graven images
billboards.

Whoever you are

Comb, shoe, piano in the street, black and white photographs staring empty
into the future which is now decades past . . .

Q. What object
lessons will you leave behind?
A. My life.
Q. What message do you bear?

Whoever you are
(the least) at least . . .

be well.

The rivers churn.

Pornography of Days

Give me your beauty, all of it
    undone, radiant, un-
        furled like a flag, fag

    When it's unbearable
        epithets, epigraphs, epigrams
Grin and bare it, epic
Give me skin and teeth and breath, heave, hurl
        burden and heft

        skin and screen
The stills suspended
Cock ass balls
    Yeah, like that
    I want it like that

male grief
    Let me hear you hot
        freeze-frame, gasp, silence, groan
    the same curious poses
        bared, grin-and-bear-it
        till exhaustion
        then again and again
throttle, thrust blind repetition,
    the coupling of days on end

this parade of fleshly days spread
    eagle all-American patriotic patriarchal
      until marred   numb
    lions and tigers and bears there's no place like
        homo, give me

    your splendored heat, cadaver
    cold this empty room. Old Glory,
        make me whole.

LDR (Amsterdam ←→ San Francisco) (for Wai)

You are photographs, pixels, voice—
           mornings slicing in your kitchen
                  you: wish, idea, desire, void

I never understood
        Vermeer's shifts
        of light, banal, broken—art history
                book Ben-Day dots
        technology impales tenderness

    —until the brick passageways
    the bone white broken
light streaming through your halls
        strolling on Binnendraaierij, holding
              your pale hand, tender

light, pallid flesh, paint—wish, want, an idea
    about love, the everyday
    I want

              to live with you. But living
a life—its wide canals,
      passageways so pristine in paintings and pixels

    —not mortar grit
      bricks broken,
      not mundane
arguments, anger. Understand I never
            want those things.

A relationship: the long sharp doorways
    in Dutch paintings—only glimpse, knife slice
      of broken light, life half
          hidden in hallways

In those paintings—so many times   a lone figure,
            lost in thought, yearning
                    beyond the frame

    these windowsills beating
            shards of light, pale, tender.

Samsara *(A prayer for Geshela Gyeltsen)*

Fly droning in the suburban temple
suddenly stops.
            Do you believe in reincarnation?
            Geshela asks. *You've been my mother,*
            brother, father, sister through thousands of lives.

Sitting on crimson
pillows on crimson carpet—
not my blood

relatives, these strangers
nodding, *yes.*
What forms does one take

after a lifetime, after exhaustion?
Who believes in countless cycles
of winged joys and hunger, circling
samsara not remembering—slow buzzing,
then shedding of husk, another life.

I willfully forget my
reincarnations this life: high
school dropout, angry son,
refugee insect, unfaithful lover,
sparrow-child; let me begin

again, let me forge myself anew, a
believer in small kindnesses

under the gaze of this dying

Tibetan monk. I forget and
forget. Light shifts across walls,
Sunday again.
Endless suburban lawns midday:

sprinklers hissing,
thousands of small sorrows
remembered,

spraying arcs that leave no trace
but green and void,

yes, tell me again and
again.

"Eighteen Levels of Hell" (Đai Nam Amusement Park, Sài Gòn)

I held your trembling hand, you
couldn't see: the afterlife, jagged
      dark corners, neon horror

              upon horror, turn by turn.
      Mother, I can
protect you from falling.

This life, we couldn't
         see, it turns

dark

     I couldn't

falling

Impossible Poem (Paññāsāstra University, Phnom Penh)

The bright young things, bright young things so eager and hungry, hungry to go to school in America, a chance, a change, distant horizon, your bright future famished. Worm-eaten photograph: mother and fresh-faced friends, black and white radiant. Đà Nẵng beach scene, smiling, decades past, distant water horizon, war horizon; sun-squinting, oh the bright

You're Here, You're Queer, but You're Still a Tourist

Kim Compoc

In Ang Lee's Oscar-winning 2005 film *Brokeback Mountain*, Jack Twist and Ennis Del Mar's relationship comes to a crisis when it is learned that Jack has made several illicit trips to Mexico.[1] While both men know about the other's wife and children, the idea of this particular infidelity so angers Ennis that he threatens Jack's life. The scene ends with them on the ground in tears and Ennis begging Jack to leave him. If Ennis's performance of rugged cowboy masculinity falters, viewers are reminded of the pressures of homophobic violence and unemployment that threaten his psychic and material well-being. Indeed, the film provokes considerable empathy for men like this, closeted in rural America where most people were and are trying to survive, with no working concept of being out and proud. In addition, the superb acting and direction capture an intimacy between men almost unmatched in Hollywood before or since. The success of the film has been useful not just for North American gay men but for queers around the world, many of whom had to fight censorship laws to view it.

Despite these achievements, the representation of Mexicans and Mexico in the film opens up important questions. From this scene and one other, Mexico is portrayed as nothing more than the place you go to get your needs met when the homophobia back home gets too intense. In essence, Mexico operates as a metonym for a brothel. Even more, Jack is indignant in being questioned about these trips across the border, which relieve him from the pressures of the closet: "Yeah I've been to Mexico, is there a fuckin' problem?" The man Jack has sex with in Mexico is unnamed and utters but one word, "Señor?" before they walk into the shadows together. In every way he conforms to what M. Jacqui Alexander calls the "'queer fetishized native' who is made to remain silent within his local economy in order to be appropriately consumed."[2] Viewers are not encouraged to direct sympathies to this man at all. He remains the flat, anonymous character who conveniently disappears from the scene once the tourist's desire is fulfilled. Jack's "taste for brown bodies," to use Hiram Perez's term, extends U.S. neocolonial agendas with a queer twist. When Jack insists, "You have no idea how bad it gets," I direct my curiosity to how bad it might get for that Mexicano who may or may not be gay but sure needs that American dollar to survive.

In R. Zamora Linmark's 2011 novel *Leche*, another gay American ventures across another border, in this case the Philippines. Linmark provides a sobering meditation on neocolonialism, diasporic longing, and multigenerational servitude, but the seriousness is repeatedly derailed by the protagonist's catty self-centeredness and voracious libido. In contrast with *Brokeback Mountain*, however, Vince de los Reyes cannot get laid. If Manila is a character, Linmark paints her as a decidedly uncooperative one, repeatedly refusing to provide services, sexual or otherwise, in the way this *balikbayan* (Tagalog for "returnee") expects. I argue *Leche* offers a pedagogy on the anxiety of the queer Filipino cosmopolitan whereby the self-possession of the "first-worlder" is contingent upon a "third-world" willingness to provide services on demand. Vince is an antihero that enables readers to interrogate queer travel practices that too often reinstall colonial routes of desire.

Leche begins with an excerpt from Vince's college textbook, *Decolonization for Beginners: A Filipino Glossary*, "**balikbayan**, *noun*. 1. coined by the Marcos regime in 1973 for U.S.-based Filipinos returning to visit the motherland and witness its vast improvements, attributed to martial law. 2. unwitting propagator of martial law propaganda. 3. potential savior of the Philippine economy. *See also* **Overseas Filipino Workers, brain drain.**"[3] Right away Linmark sets up the framework and the set of questions at hand: if one is truly interested in a decolonized Philippines, what is the role of the privileged class coming back from abroad? The year is 1991, so martial law is no longer in place, but great inequality still remains after the Marcos dictatorship. Vince considers himself a Filipino, and he is returning to the Philippines for the first time since childhood. However, the Manila airport staff explains it's the passport, not place of birth, that determines which line to stand in: "You *were* a Filipino. . . . You're *now* a balikbayan with a U.S. passport. You need to stand over there with the other *foreigners*."[4] Vince resists this designation of foreigner and guards his Filipino identity throughout the text. Having grown up in Hawaiʻi, he has no other identity to assign himself. Furthermore, his connection to his place of birth combined with his knowledge of colonization of the Philippines sets him apart from casual, uneducated tourists. However, it's clear that Vince has crossed a border into a now unfamiliar place, a city that offers him a privileged status as a balikbayan, but never the deep, horizontal camaraderie of the compatriot. But what provokes the most anxiety is that Manila never offers him a proper vacation.

For Vince, the heat, the traffic, and the inconveniences of third-world life contrast strikingly with the comforts of his Waikīkī condo. In Manila, he has a maid and a driver, and all his expenses are paid. But barely four days into his trip, he complains to his brother:

> The longer I am here the more I'm convinced that everything in this city conspires to vex me. Either that, or this is where Mercury goes retrograde. I can't buy a pack of AA batteries without popping a blood vessel. The cashier put the batteries on a tray behind the others and told me I had to wait, but I was the only one ready to make a purchase. I lost it. I started shouting. Two guards with guns had to escort me out.[5]

In this same postcard, he refers to Manila as "a dump." This is no nostalgic journey to the motherland; there are no scrumptious descriptions of the food, or the latest music, or the hippest slang. Manila provides many things to complain about, especially the scheduled blackouts, or "brown outs," a rationing of water and electricity that even the wealthy neighborhoods must endure. On page after page of ranting, Vince's true coconut colors come out: brown on the outside, tourist on the inside.

Perhaps Vince would be more patient with the rationing and quirks of the retail sector if he could only satisfy his voracious libido. After all, he's a confident, educated, gay man, unfettered by homophobic or racist self-hatred. Even more, he's a good-looking mestizo, who just won first runner-up at a "Mr. Pogi" (Tagalog for "cutie pie") contest back in Honolulu. But despite these credentials, Vince cannot get laid, not by the ever-patient taxi driver Dante or by the brainy museum worker Jonas. He almost hooks up with a guy who flirts with him in a mall parking lot, only to realize he's being solicited. "You like that? . . . It's yours for three hundred pesos."[6] Vince knows how difficult it is to support oneself in the Philippines, and in a previous section he reflects on poverty and injustice, reminding readers, "The average daily wage is equal to the price of a McDonald's Happy Meal."[7] Nonetheless he's shocked: "'You want me to pay you twelve dollars for sex?' Vince asks, stunned. 'You think I'm free?' The postcard thief zips up his pants. 'Pucha, Pare, this is not America. I'm giving you the best deal pero kung ayaw mo, e di huwag.' Translation: no money, no honey."[8] On the next page, Vince is writing home again, this time calling Manila "a shithole."[9]

Despite his Clare Danes–like tantrums, Vince becomes indignant when people repeatedly refer to him as an American, a foreigner, and refuse him his Filipino identity. When prospective hookup Jonas asks him what he thinks of Manila, Vince carefully tries not to offend him and answers, "Chaotic, depressing, surreal." "'There's nothing surreal about Manila,' Jonas replies, matter-of-factly. 'It's only surreal because Manila's no longer part of your world.'"[10] Smart and educated, Jonas knows history and film, and when the hip club Leche is open. Unlike any other character, Jonas can talk to Vince as an equal, despite their decidedly unequal positions in terms of privilege and mobility. Jonas is the Filipino and must endure the problems of his country as his material reality; Vince is the balikbayan who can comprehend the problems of the Philippines only as they affect his injured diasporic identity. Their lunch is cut short because Jonas must take the long bus home to care for his mother. Vince picks up the check, and they agree to meet at the club later on that night. After so many failed attempts to find connection—sexual or otherwise—in the motherland, Jonas offers a glimmer of hope; perhaps Manila's not so bad after all.

If one scene suggests that Vince's relationship with the Philippines might differ from Jack Twist's relationship with Mexico, it's when he finally enters Leche. It's at this notorious dance club that Vince must again confront the soul-crushing depth of oppression in the Philippines, causing a momentary crisis between his decolonized, conscious side and his first-world, entitled side so eager to get laid. The space itself captures this same dysphoria: museum in the daytime and sex club at night. Tita G explains, "We're in the third world, Vicente, so we have to multitask in order to make it to tomorrow."[11] The building is a kind of palimpsest of Filipino historical trauma, having been there for centuries: first as a milk distribution center under the Spanish, then as an orphanage during the Philippine-American War, and then as a headquarters and torture chamber during the Japanese occupation. In short, all three of the colonial masters have had their way with this space. Even more chilling, Vince learns that the famous director Boca Bino decided to document the story of comfort women, or "the Lolas" (grandmothers) as they are called, and chose Leche to do the filming. Upon learning this, Vince finally steps outside himself long enough to contemplate what it means that these elderly women had been retraumatized here in the place of their horrific and systemized violation: "Vince remains quiet, but has a mouthful of words in his head: but young and innocent girls were raped and tortured in these rooms, and Boca has achieved nothing except to exploit the Lolas's ordeal, cheapen their suffering, capitalize on their sorrows by turning their victimization into a two-hour melodrama."[12] As in multiple scenes in the novel, Vince learns again that history is always alive. History demands our attention in the present. History demands we respond with our best ethical selves. In this regard, Vince disappoints again. His moment of revulsion at Boca is only a temporary departure from the task at hand. Three drinks later, Vince is back to nursing his libido: Where is Jonas? He never shows up.

Though Vince was initially shocked at the idea of paying for sex, once at Leche, his resistance falters as he sees the opportunity to hook up with two guys. Having already paid a handsome year's membership to the club, he prepares to negotiate the price like his nanny Yaya Let taught him to do at "the open market": "Start from the bottom and stay there as long as possible."[13] Vince steadies himself for haggling. He reasons that the two men "are not the only pricks in Leche that're for rent."[14] After a much-needed first kiss, he realizes that these men are "strictly queer for pay," but again, he's not diverted.[15] They settle on the price, but they refuse to have sex there, insisting he come to Makati next Wednesday instead. Will they show? The reader doesn't get to find out. What's notable is how again and again, Manila takes Vince's money, refuses his touristic desire, and in doing so preserves a bit of its dignity. Linmark seems to make us ask the question: Who has time to complain about the colonizer when there are so many balikbayans here doing the work for them?

In "Your Grief Is Our Gossip: Overseas Filipinos and Other Spectral Presences," Vicente Rafael describes the hatred that Filipinos feel for these touristic Filipino Americans:

> Their easy association with Western consumer products and their access to a powerful North American state apparatus mark them as different: they represent the fulfillment of Filipino desires realizable only outside of the Philippines. However, what adds to their difference is this: that they are unable to respond to the envy of others with a show of empathy. While they seem to possess everything, they in fact lack a sense of humility . . . Indeed, they do nothing else but point out what the Philippines lacks, thereby appearing shameless and arrogant.[16]

Rafael contrasts the figure of the shameless and arrogant balikbayan with that ubiquitous figure of globalization's crisis: the Overseas Contract Workers, or OCWs. Working abroad in 178 countries, the remittances of the OCWs are the backbone of the fragile Philippine economy. While the former is a cosmopolitan tourist, the latter hasn't even seen her family, let alone had a vacation, in many years. The OCW is the alienated worker in every sense of the word. Vince might be Mr. Pogi "cutie pie" in Honolulu, but his conformity to this stereotype marks an ugliness that is obvious and familiar to the Filipinos in Manila. This resentment raises important questions from both postcolonial and queer perspectives. Vince is not a white Western heterosexual tourist going to exploit the abject Filipina sex worker. He is not an American soldier on R & R. He is not even a lonely gay man like Jack Twist. But he has in common some of the same expectations and sense of entitlement of these colonial figures. Importantly, the book is set in the early 1990s, a time when, as M. Jacqui Alexander points out, advertisers "came out" of their own closet, no longer ashamed to court the gay dollar for fear of losing straight customers. As a result, gay tourists were directed to imperial geographies, pink-washing colonialism under a banner of rainbow solidarity. In "Imperial Desire/Sexual Utopias: White Gay Capital and

Transnational Tourism," Alexander draws attention to the threat tourism poses for queer social justice advocates to work across national borders: "If we invoke a common experience of (sexual) queerness as the ground on which to establish *global* solidarity communities, where is this queer 'native' to fit? Who is this 'native' within the discourses of anthropology, fetishized as sexual other at the inauguration of imperialism, now recolonized by white gay capital through tourism?"[17] Put another way, what potential really is there for queers to work in solidarity with each other given these colonial divisions, these inequalities exacerbated through global capitalism? What strategies might we employ as literary critics to interrupt first-world entitlement, be it straight, queer, Filipino, or otherwise?

Some might argue that Vince deserves to be treated with more generosity given that he is a racialized subject and that his return to his place of his birth must be contextualized within a proper Filipino historical context. For example, Robert Diaz argues the queer balikbayan's unique relationship to homecoming and Vince's "failed return" can be read as a rejection of "redressive nationalism" and the heteronorms of diasporic citizenship. He writes:

> Redressive nationalisms valorize specific identities in the name of repairing past dictatorial, colonial, and imperial violence, even as these nationalisms occlude certain subjectivities and communities in the act of animating such reparative sentiments. Redressive nationalisms reproduce and espouse normative kinship structures and ultimately delineate which subject so worthy of inclusion in the wholesale attempt to "repair" the broken nation-state.[18]

Diaz's reminds us that in both the pre- and post-martial law era, the Philippines promoted the balikbayan program to keep flows of transnational capital flowing both through tourism and remittances. Vince's failures to consume Manila's tourist sites as a proper balikbayan are distinctly queer and, by extension, sympathetic.

However, I argue that Vince's behavior makes a different set of analytics is necessary. He demonstrates perfectly what Hiram Pérez has described as a "cosmopolitan mobility that originates with the white body but can be mortgaged from it."[19] Although Vince is a brown body himself, his passport, his class privilege, and the mobility these enable put him at arm's distance from working-class Philippine nationals. Further, his lack of humility in the face of his class privilege and the entitlement he feels to have his sexual and consumer desires be fulfilled confirm his role as a neocolonial figure not unlike Rafael's "ugly balikbayan," queerness notwithstanding. Further, Vince's ability to articulate a decolonial politics on the first pages of the book puts his behavior under scrutiny in a different way. He enters Leche with the desire to consume Filipino flesh, and no history lesson will divert him from this task, not even if the sex must take place in the very building where the comfort women were tortured. As Vince is denied his release, so is the reader. The Philippines has a hundred serious problems, and unfulfilled tourist desire is not one. To return to Perez, "If a racialized homoerotics converges with U.S. empire to consolidate gay modernity . . . then gay men committed to antiracist, leftist critiques are obligated to disentangle their own 'intimate investments' from the projects of U.S. imperialism."[20] Vince's journey reminds tourists, balikbayans, and readers alike that we must interrogate our desires, even or especially as our own bodies emerge in new territories with new power over others.

By way of conclusion, I offer these final observations toward a reading strategy that is both queer and decolonial. First, we must denaturalize touristic ways of looking at colonized land and bodies. Both *Brokeback Mountain* and *Leche* feature extremely compelling stories that contain liberatory agendas. But as Jasbir Puar, M. Jacqui Alexander, and Hiram Perez as have pointed out, LGBT movements for national acceptance align with heteropatriarchal white supremacy of the U.S. nation-state, the result being a homonationalism that is not just exclusionary but ultimately pro-imperialist. It's still important to denaturalize that touristic gaze, even with the queer ethnic minority returning to the homeland.

Second, it's important to denaturalize borders and the colonial assumptions that accompany them. What is the story of power of that particular border? Who crosses the border for work? Who crosses for pleasure? What are the consequences for disobeying the rules? As "free trade" organizations like Asia-Pacific Economic Cooperation and World Trade Organization continue to dissolve national borders and the protections they allegedly offer, the movement of human beings has become both necessary and criminalized. Border police and other measures to provide "security" for a country's elite must be put into contrast with those whose lives are defined by insecurity, a point unevenly explored by queer writers, but a defining characteristic of Philippine life across the diaspora.

Third, we must ask in what ways texts invite readers to comply with regressive politics. *Brokeback Mountain* is a working-class rural story, and the focus on class oppression might encourage readers to ignore its race politics. *Leche* is a gay diasporic Filipino story, and the focus on gay and colonial oppression might encourage readers to ignore its class politics. Vince seeks relief from the psychic wound that comes from being a diasporic subject. The novel ends without his being able to find it. It's antinostalgic in that sense; the Philippines is not what he had hoped for in terms of the desire for home, or the desire for flesh outside the home. The ending disappoints if we see Vince as a hero who deserves to get what he wants. But if we see Vince as not as decolonized as he purports himself to be, then his failure to get what he wants is a disciplining of that desire and his bourgeois sense of entitlement. It's a discipline long overdue.

ACKNOWLEDGMENTS

Thank you to Candace Fujikane, Noʻu Revilla, Amalia Bueno, and the late Paul Lyons for their assistance and feedback on this essay.

NOTES

1. *Brokeback Mountain*, directed by Ang Lee (Los Angeles: Universal Studios Home Entertainment, 2006).

2. M. Jacqui Alexander, "Imperial Desire/Sexual Utopias: White Gay Capital and Transnational Tourism," in *Pedagogies of Crossing: Meditations on Feminism, Sexual Politics, Memory, and the Sacred* (Durham, NC: Duke University Press, 2005), 70.

3. R. Zamora Linmark, *Leche* (Minneapolis: Coffee House, 2011), 1.

4. Ibid., 44.

5. Ibid., 187.

6. Ibid., 179.

7. Ibid., 103.

8. Ibid., 179.

9. Ibid., 180.

10. Ibid., 262.

11. Ibid., 286.

12. Ibid., 281–282.

13. Ibid., 294.

14. Ibid., 294.

15. Ibid., 295.

16. Vince L. Rafael, "Your Grief Is Our Gossip: Overseas Filipinos and Other Spectral Presences," *Public Culture* 9, no. 2 (1997): 271–272.

17. Alexander, "Imperial Desire/Sexual Utopias," 69.

18. Robert Diaz, "Failed Returns: The Queer Balikbayan in R. Zamora Linmark's *Leche* and Gil Portes's *Miguel/Michelle*," in *Global Asian American Popular Cultures*, edited by Shilpa Davé et al. (New York: New York University Press, 2016), 336.

19. Hiram Pérez, *A Taste for Brown Bodies: Gay Modernity and Cosmopolitan Desire* (New York: New York University Press, 2015), 2.

20. Linmark, *Leche*, 9.

Filipinx and Latinx Queer Critique

Houseboys and Housemaids in the
U.S.-Mexican Borderlands

Sony Coráñez Bolton

The novel *American Son* (2001) by Filipino American author Brian Ascalon Roley narrates the coming of age of the protagonist Gabriel, or Gabe. Gabe possesses a queerness that far exceeds the conventional variability of identity that is commonplace in minority *bildungsroman*.[1] The book is set in post-riots Los Angeles in the early 1990s, and Asian American identity, U.S. colonization of the Philippines, and queerness are refracted through and changed by the U.S.-Mexican borderlands. Gabe develops a racial and sexual identity that evades monolithic categorization. He is represented almost as if he is a blank canvas that accrues unstable racial meaning at the intersection of Mexican American and Filipino American identities. This is especially evident as he examines his own reflection several times throughout his narration when others often mistake him for white:

> Suddenly I notice my reflection in the mirrored glass and it appears so obviously Asian I almost stop in my tracks. My eyes look narrow, and my hair straight and coarse and black. He must be blind. I have slender Asian hips, and my cheekbones are too high. The way the sunlight hits my face you cannot even make out my eyes. My eyes jerk away. Everyone will be able to tell. I might even look Mexican, but not white.[2]

The "he" that Gabe accuses of being blind is the white top. Gabe's not uncommon narrative introspection binds racial identification with the queer desire of the white daddy for the brown Asian boy and his "slender . . . hips."[3] Stone, a white middle-aged tow-truck driver who picks up a fifteen-year-old Gabe after he runs away from home, brings him to a hotel to facilitate a surreptitious meeting with his worried mother. Gabe asks Stone, "So why'd you pay for my hotel room?" to which Stone responds, "Do I have to have a reason? . . . Come on, buddy, don't look at me like that. What the hell do you think this is about?"[4] The inference of colonial desire of the "white top" for the Asian "bottom"—a figure produced through the colonialist conflation of "Asian with anus"—shapes Gabe's moments of existential self-reflection, which demonstrate the ways that racialization is a concatenated process in the borderlands where racial error turns out to be less exceptional than one might initially surmise.[5] Indeed, Gabe eventually and more fully embraces the racial misrecognition of being Mexican, undoubtedly influenced by his older brother, Tomas. Tomas performs Mexican drag throughout the novel much to the chagrin of their mother, Ika. The boys' mestizo appearance helps to facilitate a racial ambiguity that activates various racial signifiers related to Mexican masculinity, Asian femininity, and whiteness. Gabe and Tomas's Filipino diasporic experience in the borderlands is foreclosed to their very dark-skinned mother, Ika, who cannot Americanize in the same ways—she is an "impossible subject" too perverse to assimilate.[6] Indeed, Ika is alienated from Americanness by her estranged and abusive white American husband, who early in the novel is satisfyingly cast out of the family's life by Tomas after a violent altercation in which Gabe is struck and Ika is threatened.

A facile but reasonable reading of *American Son* would be consumed with the ways that Asian American masculinity is amended in the U.S.-Mexican borderlands. In this case, Filipino racial ambiguity occasions a masculinist Mexican drag to rehabilitate the perverse femininities that normally attach to Asian American male bodies. Ethnic masculinity perhaps affords an agency to avoid the white top's gaze. Gabe's *bildung* presents an evolution of Asian "houseboy" to "Cholo gangster" wherein the problem of queerness and abject femininity is resolved through the criminal entanglements that condition ethnic masculinities along the border. Nevertheless, in this essay, I cannot exclusively focus on the "pathological" masculinities that the queer narrative eye of *American Son* inevitably elicits its reader to ponder. While it is a productive exercise to recuperate the houseboy or the "joy of the castrated boy" as it has been put by queer critics like Joon Oluchi Lee,[7] or even to imagine a politics that would question the criminalization of Latino and Black masculinities as part and parcel of a queer political agenda envisioned by the likes of Cathy Cohen,[8] I shift focus to the "racialized gendered" labor dynamics of the borderlands.[9] I argue that the queerness of racial ambiguity enables an inclusive critique of border economies that profit on the racialized and feminized distribution of economic vulnerability. That is, through the sexual economies invoked by the figure of the houseboy, I think through the political and discursive economies of the feminization of migrant and domestic labor. In doing so, I explore how the Asian houseboy and the Mexican migrant domestic worker help us to re-genealogize the U.S.-Mexican borderscape as a transpacific encounter.

I suggest that the relationship of the queer femininity of Asian American masculinity to the perverse femininity of *mexicana* migrant labor articulates a "transpacific borderlands" as an expansive critical apparatus. In this essay, I attempt to capture the ways that asymmetrical economic relations in global racial capitalism have shaped both Filipinx/Latinx affinities and inhibited ethnic studies from genealogizing these affinities' co-construction of the border. I channel Ascalon Roley's queer novel to stage a transpacific border reading between the Philippines and the U.S. Southwest. This border affinity between two sites colonized by the Spanish and the United States is consolidated through the queer discourses of Spanglish and the queer and thoroughly unexpected codeswitching of Filipino border Spanglish that the novel productively captures—what Roley calls "flip, peasant Spanish."[10] What might it mean for queer of color theories to see two queer Filipinxs speaking Spanglish in the U.S.-Mexican borderlands?

Queer Flip Spanglish: A Housemaid and Houseboy's Tale

Gabe's development is told through a clear recognition of the pathological criminalities that inform American understandings of Latino masculinity in the U.S. borderlands of Los Angeles. Tomas, Gabe's older brother,

> is the son who helps pay the mortgage by selling attack dogs to rich people and celebrities. He is the son who keeps our mother up late with worry. He is the son who causes her embarrassment by showing up at family parties with his muscles covered in gangster tattoos and his head shaved down to stubble and his eyes bloodshot from pot. He is really half white, half Filipino but dresses like a Mexican, and it troubles our mother that he does this. She cannot understand why if he wants to be something he is not he does not at least try to look white. He is also the son who says that if any girlfriend criticized our mother or treated her wrong he would knock the bitch across the house.[11]

Meanwhile, Gabe is "the son who is quiet and no trouble, and [helps their] mother with chores around the house."[12] Tomas relies on a racial misrecognition in the borderlands whereby his Filipino body can inhabit a Mexican masculinity. Through a performative stylization of his body, which he has "covered in gangster tattoos" as well as shaving his head, he "dresses like a Mexican." Thus, it is not simply an access to Mexicanness that the author wishes to highlight but rather a performative articulation of a criminal pathologized masculinity whose toxicity is emblematized by "knock[ing] [a] bitch across the house" who might disrespect his mother. The novel proposes that there is something about Filipinoness within the borderlands that allows for the inherence of racial error whereby mestizo features are interchangeable (even across the Pacific!) with a completely different group collapsing the categories of Latino and Asian American. The abjection of Asian

American femininity and an embrace of racialized misogyny conspire in an embrace of racial-sexual deviance.[13] On the other hand, Gabe, the "son who is quiet and no trouble" and who helps their mother with chores around the house, is presented as perhaps the more familiar characterization for Asian Americans in U.S. minority fiction—a docile stereotype that *American Son* traffics in. Nevertheless, this model minority is not necessarily completely understood as such. Gabe, our queer protagonist, is quite literally the boy who helps around the house; he is the houseboy.

One of our first introductions to Gabe is through a violent homophobic appraisal from his brother Tomas: "Sit down. If the client sees you standing there like that he's gonna think you're my houseboy."[14] This is one of the central racial and sexual tensions articulated in this novel: a pronounced desire to distance oneself from Asian American feminization.[15] The houseboy and the Asian American male femininities that are marked with this sexual figure racially configure Asian American men to a particular kind of feminized relationship to capital. The houseboy cites a colonial genealogy of racialized sexual labor limited to the domestic sphere, thus implying diminished capacity and agency given the political economy of the border.[16] Meanwhile, Tomas is able to participate in different kinds of economic exchanges through the performance of a Mexicanness that is available to him in the borderlands. He performs Mexican drag to sell German attack dogs to wealthy Hollywood clientele. His studied appearance, his white Pontiac, and his Virgen de Guadalupe tattoo all give needed racial credibility at once enabled and delimited by his Filipino version of Spanglish. Tomas arrives at a potential client's house who is interested in purchasing an attack dog from a legit "Cholo gangster." Gabe and Tomas arrive at a mansion, and Tomas

> stops and lowers his window before a white intercom perched on a metal stand. Tomas pushes a red button. We wait. He tries again and after a minute a lady's voice that sounds Mexican—probably the maid—asks what we want.
>
> We've come to sell some dogs, he says into the box.
>
> Again, the sound of static. Then the crackled voice comes on and says they don't take solicitors.
>
> No, listen, Tomas says. We have the dogs with us now.
>
> We no take solicitations, it says.
>
> Then the static clicks off.
>
> Tomas frowns and hits the side of the intercom and presses the button. I already talked to the señor of the casa, he says to the voice when it comes on again.
>
> You speak to him already?

Sí.

There is a pause, and then the voice says *okay* and the gate swings open. Its iron bottom scrapes along the driveway. You'd think they'd get a faster motor if they can afford a house like this, he says.

That was really great Spanish, Tomas, I say.

Fuck you, he says.[17]

When they are in the mansion, Tomas asks who he assumes to be the "Mexican maid" during his sale pitch: "Hey do you think you could get us a glass of water or something? . . . It's getting hot in here." Gabe (the younger brother) "stiffens" at this request as he recognizes that Lucinda is "not the maid." Annoyed, Lucinda, the "maid," asks them:

Ustedes son hermanos?

[Tomas] looks like he doesn't understand but doesn't want her to know this.

She wants to know if we're brothers, I tell him.

I know that.

He glares at me and I shut up, but she faces me now and expects an answer.

Sí.

Yo creo que no.

I nod. Mi madre tampoco lo cree.

She bites her lip and thinks a moment.

Se parecen por la forma de sus ojos, she says, and then turns to Tomas: You do not seem so. But I can tell it in the shape of your eyes.[18]

The Filipino's Chicano drag, reliant on the criminal pathologies that attach to the Chicano male body in a post LA Riots Los Angeles, is disrupted by the maid. This climaxes into physical violence against Gabe (who can speak Spanish for reasons not explained in the novel):

His knuckles hit me hard . . . salty blood floods my mouth . . . the concrete meet[s] my temple. . .

Don't you fucking talk disrespect to me.

I wasn't disrespecting you.

Don't you overstand me with your Flip, peasant Spanish![19]

Anzaldúa's *Borderlands/La Frontera* postulates that one of the constitutive features of "mestiza consciousness" is the affirmation of linguistic sovereignty. She writes, "Deslenguadas. Somos los del español deficiente" [The

108 / Sony Coráñez Bolton

(women who are) foul-mouthed. We are those of deficient Spanish].[20] The state of being "deslenguada" affirming the existence of "deficient Spanish" is consonant with Anzaldúa's famous crip-of-color reorientation of the border as an "herida abierta" or open wound.[21] This open wound shapes "theoretical subjects" that shuttle between different desires and identifications that evade expectations of stability and stasis.[22] Chicana feminist theorists like Anzaldúa, Norma Alarcón, Maria Cotera, and Chela Sandoval postulate a queer insistence on deficiency and variability that is not reliant on normative coherence or good grammar.[23] "Flip, peasant Spanish" may add to the inventories of defective Spanishes that are captured by Chicana feminist thought. Might this peasant, flip Spanish of Filipino-Chicano fiction be one of the very instantiations of "deficient Spanishes" that Chicana feminists theorize yet perhaps did not intend? What kind of Latinx subject is the Filipino American? Could Latinx studies account for the Filipinx subject?[24]

However, it is not necessarily only a knowledge of Spanish that enables an insight into Lucinda's life that is foreclosed to Tomas—a foreclosure against which he can only violently rage. What kind of feminism can or should the queer Filipino houseboy elicit? And how can Chicana feminist and border thought help queer Asian American studies paint a more complete picture of the maneuvers of global racial capital? Gabe, the "houseboy," recognizes that Lucinda, the Mexican woman in the scene, is not a maid. I suggest that this scene demonstrates an affinity between the "houseboy" and the "Mexican maid" because of their similar station in the sexual-gendered politics of global racial capital. Of course, neither Gabe nor Lucinda is actually a domestic servant. Nevertheless, their racialized bodies are mapped within the U.S.-Mexico borderlands through problematic representational tropes that circulate in the political and economic environment of Los Angeles. As such, Tomas assumes that Lucinda has a predetermined relationship to menial domestic labor. His hyperbolic ethnic masculinity unavoidably traffics in the logics of dispossession that structure racialized-gendered labor in the U.S.-Mexican borderlands. And the houseboy is the object of disdain who suffers the punishment.

Dos X: Filipinx and Latinx Cultural Critique

American Son demonstrates that the overlaps between Latinx and Filipinx cultural politics are not simply parallel formations. Far from an analogical comparative wherein one political formation simply borrows the "x" from another as a mode of recognition, solidarity, and affinity, I suggest that the "x" represents a queer dialectic that can aid in genealogizing the seemingly diffuse patchwork of political possibilities of Latinx and Filipinx formations that have formed as a response to the historical intersections of U.S. and

Spanish colonialisms. The "dos x" of "Filipinx" and "Latinx" furnish a queer reading that connects the Philippine archipelago, the U.S.-Mexican borderlands, Filipinx and Latinx Americas within a transpacific framing. Filipinx and Latinx queer critique demonstrates the inherent "intimacies" of a transpacific borderlands.[25] "X" marks how colonialism and imperialism have rendered opaque the obvious—Spanish and U.S. empires have historically dislocated the colonial and postcolonial cultural formations of Filipino America and Latino America, and "dos x" demonstrates a potential for mutual political recognition in which the disarticulatory technologies of overlapping imperialisms can be vitiated.

As scholars like Tom Sarmiento have indicated, the use of "x" in "Filipinx" is a citation of the queering of language invoked in Latinx communities.[26] The variability of the "x" as a placeholder calls attention to the disciplinary operations of gender binaries in ordering the lives of diasporic subjects. The "x" in Filipinx is productive in attending to the inaccuracies, inconsistencies, and imprecisions that may inhere in political gestures meant to capture the complexities of the lives of queer subjects, perhaps for those Filipinx that inhabit and shape the U.S. borderlands. Following in line with the queer and feminist genealogies of the U.S.-Mexican borderscape's shaping of the hybrid identifications of Chicanx (or Xicanx) cultures, languages, and politics, Filipinx is similarly invested in modes of queer and gender inclusive discourses. To wit, Joseph Martin Ponce has imagined queer diasporic reading practices, aligned with queer diasporas scholars like Gayatri Gopinath and Martin Manalansan, that articulate multiple "modes of address" that are not captured by the literary and cultural rubrics of heteronational literature.[27]

What should be the methods, theories, and objects of analysis of both Filipinx and Latinx studies? The borrowing of the "x" carries an opportunity to rethink the ways that queer political projects can demonstrate how we forgot that we forgot about Latinx and Filipinx historical, cultural, and political intimacies.[28] In this essay, I have attempted to account for the "x" as a queer of color gesture that takes femininity seriously as a space of transpacific encounter.[29] The queering that the "x" highlights should not have the effect of effacing the critical contributions of Filipina and Chicana feminisms. Nevertheless, an easy and complete embrace of "Filipina" as the central organizing rubric through which we materialize critique and politics may allow to go underremarked the transphobia that can obtain in seemingly "progressive" feminist analysis. It is the estimation of this author that Filipinx, as well as Latinx, should be a feminist project. More specifically, I argue that Filipinx and Latinx queer critique should scrutinize the feminized vulnerabilities that are distributed via racialized capital. Indeed, there is a shared struggle in terms of the ways that the state maligns gender deviant bodies. While critical distinctions between the subjectivities of different groups should be maintained, the political invocation of a Filipinx or Latinx critique should understand how the state promulgates regimes of racial, sexual, and gender discipline that profit off of our inability to imagine alternative queer coalitions across national and ethnic lines of difference. I see the affinities of Filipinx and Latinx cultures as a potential framework and mode of thought can aid us in imagining political alliance across racial formations, geographic location, and intersecting colonial histories that can do the work of making us less governable.

NOTES

1. David Palumbo Liu, *Asian/America: Historical Crossings of a Racial Frontiers* (Palo Alto, CA: Stanford University Press, 1999).

2. Brian Ascalon Roley, *American Son* (New York: W. W. Norton, 2001), 90.

3. Eng-Beng Lim, *Brown Boys and Rice Queens: Spellbinding Performance in the Asias* (New York: New York University Press, 2013).

4. Roley, *American Son*, 111.

5. Richard Fung, "Looking for My Penis: The Eroticized Asian in Gay Video Porn," in *Q&A: Queer in Asian America*, edited by David Eng and Alice Hom (Philadelphia: Temple University Press, 1998), 115–134; David Eng, *Racial Castration: Managing Masculinity in Asian America* (Durham, NC: Duke University Press, 2001); Hoang Tan Nguyen, *A View from the Bottom: Asian American Masculinity and Sexual Representation* (Durham, NC: Duke Univeristy Press, 2014).

6. Gayatri Gopinath, *Impossible Subjects: Queer Diasporas and South Asian Public Culture* (Durham, NC: Duke University Press, 2005).

7. Joon Oluchi Lee, "The Joy of the Castrated Boy," *Social Text* 23, no. 3–4 (Fall–Winter 2005): 35–36.

8. Cathy Cohen, "Punks, Bulldaggers, and Welfare Queens: The Radical Potential of Queer Politics?" *Gay and Lesbian Quarterly* 3, no. 4 (1997): 437–465.

9. Lisa Lowe, *Immigrant Acts: On Asian American Cultural Politics* (Durham, NC: Duke University Press, 1996).

10. "Flip" is an outdated and derogatory term for a Filipino person.

11. Roley, *American Son*, 15.

12. Ibid., 15.

13. See Victor Román Mendoza, *Metroimperial Intimacies: Fantasy, Racial-Sexual Governance, and the Philippines in US Imperialism, 1899–1913*, (Durham, NC: Duke University Press, 2015) for a compelling analysis of how racial and sexual power collude in the maneuvers of U.S. imperial statecraft.

14. Roley, *American Son*, 18.

15. Mendoza, *Metroimperial Intimacies*.

16. Lim, *Brown Boys and Rice Queens*.

17. Roley, *American Son*, 43.

18. Ibid., 46.

19. Ibid., 54.

20. Gloria Anzaldúa, *Borderlands/La Frontera: The New Mestiza* (San Francisco: Aunt Lute, 1987), 80.

21. Jina Kim, "Toward a Crip-of-Color Critique: Thinking with Minich's 'Enabling Whom?'" *Lateral: Journal of the Cultural Studies Association* 6, no. 1 (2017), https://doi.org/10.25158/L6.1.14; Rod Ferguson, *Aberrations in Black: Toward a Queer of Color Critique* (Minneapolis: University of Minnesota Press, 2003).

22. Norma Alarcón, "The Theoretical Subjects of *This Bridge Called My Back and Anglo-American Feminism*," in *Criticism in the Borderlands: Studies in Chicano Literature, Culture, and Ideology*, edited by Hector Calderón and José David Saldívar (Durham, NC: Duke University Press, 2001), 28–40.

23. Norma Alarcón, "The Theoretical Subjects of *This Bridge Called My Back and Anglo-American Feminism*"; María Eugenia Cotera, *Native Speakers: Ella Deloria, Zora Neale Hurston, Jovita González, and the Poetics of Culture* (Austin: University of Texas Press, 2008); Chela Sandoval, *Methodology of the Oppressed* (Minneapolis: University of Minnesota Press, 2000).

24. Nicole M. Guidotti-Hernández, "Affective Communities and Millenial Desires: Latinx, or Why My Computer Won't Recognize Latina/o," *Cultural Dynamics* 29, no. 3 (2017): 141–159; Macarena Gómez-Barris and Licia Fiol-Matta, "Introduction: *Las Américas Quarterly*," *American Quarterly* 66, no. 3 (2014): 493–504.

25. Lisa Lowe, *Intimacies of Four Continents* (Durham, NC: Duke University Press, 2015).

26. Tom X. Sarmiento, "Diasporic Filipinx Queerness, Female Affective Labor, and Queer Heterosocial Relationalities in *Letters to Montgomery Clift*," *Women, Gender, and Families of Color* 5, no. 2 (Fall 2017): 105–128.

27. Joseph Martin Ponce, *Beyond the Nation: Diasporic Filipino Literature and Queer Reading* (New York: New York University Press, 2012); Gayatri Gopinath, *Impossible Subjects*; Martin Manalansan, *Global Divas: Filipino Gay Men in the Diaspora* (Durham, NC: Duke University Press, 2003).

28. The doubled elision that I explore here is inspired by Sarita See's diagnosis of the ways that the Filipino American War is doubly disarticulated from mainstream U.S. history and culture. For more on what she calls a "the disarticulation of the empire," see Sarita Echavez See, *The Decolonized Eye: Filipino American Art and Performance* (Minneapolis: University of Minnesota Press, 2009), 16–23.

29. For more on the ways that femininity shapes Philippine cultural formation, see Denise Cruz, *Transpacific Femininities: The Making of the Modern Filipina* (Durham, NC: Duke University Press, 2012).

Queer South Asian Desire, Blackness, and the Apartheid State

Vanita Reddy

This article is part of a larger project that foregrounds the role that intimacy, affect, and aesthetics play in comparative racialization, particularly between Black and Asian diasporic populations. By intimacy, I mean forms of relationality that remain "inaccessible and unseen" within the historical registers of colonial and postcolonial state governance[1] and that surface more readily within the domains of the aesthetic and the representational. In mobilizing affect and intimacy as the basis of comparative racialization, I have in mind an Afro-Asian queer feminist framework that extends the insights of Grace K. Hong and Roderick Ferguson, in their groundbreaking coedited volume *Strange Affinities: The Gender and Sexual Politics of Comparative Racialization* (2011). Hong and Ferguson acknowledge the danger of flattening out incommensurate histories of racialization on the basis of commonality. At the same time, Hong observes in a related project that refusing coalitional models on the basis of racial exceptionalism "risks replicating the totalizing narratives of liberal political modernity that are in fact where such logics of exceptionalism originate."[2] Hong and Ferguson turn to women of color feminisms—an incomplete political project that is taken up through queer of color critique—to show how this critical framework has been "underexamined"[3] for its fracturing of discrete racial formations through their sexual and gender variegations.[4] Women of color feminisms, they argue, lay bare how "racialized communities are not homogenous but instead have always policed and preserved the difference between those who are able to conform to categories of normativity, respectability, and value and those who are forcibly excluded from such categories."[5] Hong and Ferguson thus highlight how differences within racial groups gain traction within and against processes of valuation and devaluation across racial groups.

Drawing upon Hong and Ferguson's useful framing of women of color feminisms as "a set of comparative analytics rather than as a description of an identity category,"[6] this chapter takes up the representation of South Asian lesbian desire in British Asian director Shamim Sarif's 2000 novel and 2007 independent film *The World Unseen*. It shows that lesbian desire discloses the gendered and sexual structures of "normativity, respectability, and value" through which Asian and Black populations maintain their racial discreteness in South Africa under apartheid. Queer desire, rather than cohering a legible lesbian identity, instead opens onto a broader critique of racial segregation and possibilities for cross-racial intimacies. These intimacies challenge the logics of racial separatism that underwrite both state and diasporic racisms.

Set in 1952 apartheid South Africa, Sarif's novel and film tell the story of friendship and burgeoning sexual attraction between two diasporic Indian women, Amina and Miriam. Amina is a recently arrived Indian immigrant who co-owns a local café in Pretoria. Miriam is the recently arrived housewife of a dry goods shop owner, Omar, who lives in Delhof, a small town outside of Pretoria. Miriam and Amina's friendship and romance are complexly intertwined with a set of interracial sexual intimacies: Amina's Colored business partner Jacob's romance with a Dutchwoman, Magdalene; Omar's sister Rehmat's marriage to a white Dutchman, James; Miriam's sister-in-law Jehan's secret romance with a Black man; and Amina's grandmother's rape by a Black worker. It is also intertwined with Amina's friendship and business partnership with Jacob.

While all of these narratives populate the novel in more or less equal measure, it is the lesbian romance between Amina and Miriam that characterizes much of the dramatic action in the film, and that has been the focus of much popular and critical reception of both the film and novel. Undoubtedly, Sarif's openly lesbian identity, her South African Indian heritage (her parents fled South Africa for Britain in the 1960s to escape apartheid), and her previous lesbian novel (2000) and film (2008) by the same name, *I Can't Think Straight*, have shaped the characterization of Sarif's work within the genre of lesbian romance and queer independent film.

Yet above and beyond any claims to identity, I understand the representation of lesbian desire in *The World Unseen* as operating within a decolonization framework. This is a framework advanced by LGBT groups who have leveraged queer politics to contest the characterization of post-apartheid South Africa as a multiracial "rainbow nation." The post-apartheid South African constitution outlawed discrimination based on sexual orientation. But under South Africa's ruling National Party from 1948–1994, homosexuality was a crime punishable by up to seven years in prison. Recently, nonwhite LGBT groups have made demands for legal reforms by arguing that it was colonial-era laws, such as anti-sodomy statutes, that "formalized legal and social prohibitions on same-sex sexual behavior and introduced homophobia into these societies."[7] Mobilizing the decolonial framing of homophobia leveraged by South African queer of color activism,

The World Unseen routes lesbian desire through the racial violence of apartheid; it frames homophobia as intertwined with colonial-era racisms. Within this framing, homophobia is an effect of the colonial state's laws mandating racial separatism.

In addition to its foregrounding of lesbian desire within the historical context of apartheid, Sarif's film is notable for its representation of *Indian* identities within prevailing South African national narratives. The queer South African scholar Jordache Ellapen observes that state histories of the post-apartheid period—particularly those narrated by the Truth and Reconciliation Commission, which focuses on apartheid atrocities from 1960 to 1994—erase earlier historical traumas of slavery, Indian indenture, and Indian migration. These histories also position the Black, heteromasculinist subject at the center of the apartheid and post-apartheid nation. Such state narratives, Ellapen argues, code the Indian as always already queer, "evoked through stereotypes of excess, such as the exploitative merchant, or through lack and impotency, through stereotypes of the emasculated or effeminate Indian man in African nation."[8] Such gendered nationalist narratives also work to position Black Africans and Indians in an antagonistic relationship to each other.

My queer comparative framework is certainly in conversation with Ellapen. Yet for Ellapen, the diasporic Indian subject is implicitly gendered male, since effeminacy and access to capital are so often ascribed to Asian male subjects. Ellapen is also concerned with how representations of the Indian diasporic subject unsettle heteronormative Blackness as representative of the post-apartheid nation. Somewhat differently from Ellapen, I shift focus to the way that representations of queer diasporic female subjectivity destabilize a range of gendered and sexual normativities upon which racial singularities (Black, white, Colored, Indian) depend.

In *The World Unseen*, Amina and Miriam come from families who belong to a merchant class of Indian migrants called passenger Indians. Passenger Indians were "distinct from the indentured Indians who were brought to Natal as British colonial subjects to work on sugarcane plantations and coal mines."[9] Unlike indentured Indians, they maintained close ties to their ancestral villages in India and practiced endogamous marriage.[10] These forms of diasporic ethnic insularity among passenger Indians converge with the apartheid state's mandates of racial separatism. Amina's and Miriam's romance develops against the backdrop of the 1946 South African Indian Congress Party's protests against the Ghetto Bill, which curtailed Indian ownership of land in white areas;[11] the passage of the 1949 Prohibition of Mixed Marriages Act, which prohibited "European" and "non-European" intermarriage;[12] and the 1950 Group Areas Act, which limited property ownership among nonwhites by eliminating mixed race neighborhoods. Though differentiated in their racial logic and producing different forms of racial inequality, these laws were intended to ensure the strict separation of different racial groups in South Africa: Black, white, Colored, and Indian. Through different standards for land tenure and ownership; occupation of land along racial lines; white expropriation of Black, Colored, and Indian land; and the prohibition of marriage across racial groups, the apartheid state actively discouraged interracial intimacies, sexual or otherwise.

Amina's queerness in Sarif's film and novel is coded through various acts of racial and gender impropriety that are in direct opposition to these apartheid state laws: her political activism (such as her protesting of the Ghetto Bill), which emerges against her family's selective opposition to apartheid laws; her racial ambiguity (the Indian community gossips about her visibly curly hair, which codes her as partially Black); and her economic independence as a co-owner of the Location Café. Her gender impropriety takes the form of having taken multiple (and, as rumor has it, Black) female lovers, her questioning of the inevitability of marriage within the diasporic family, and her gender non-normative presentation (she dresses in slacks, shirts, and hats). Amina might be understood as the referent for Sarif's titular unseen, insofar as her queerness represents the illegibility of the Indian and even the Indian lesbian as an impossible subject of the apartheid nation. Yet within the queer comparative framework I have outlined, the unseen refers more broadly to a constellation of intimacies that violate racialized norms of respectability.

Diasporic lesbian desire in *The World Unseen* consistently emerges within a range of gendered improprieties that reveal how social devaluation within Black and Asian populations is deeply relational, operating across these populations. Here, I focus on two aspects of Sarif's novel and film to demonstrate how lesbian desire is bound up in the unsettling of the colonial state's racial management of Indian, Black, and Colored populations. First, I show that the sharing of labor and capital between Coloreds and Indians allows Amina to negotiate the diasporic community's heteronormative injunctions, allowing for cross-racial intimacies that exceed the state's scrutinizing gaze. Second, I focus on the representation of the Black African man as an embodiment of proletarian labor and as a racial-sexual threat to diasporic femininity. I argue that this representation of Black masculinity emerges as the limit case for Afro-Asian intimacies. Yet, this limit is itself predicated upon the social devaluation of Indian women's bodies within the diasporic family. In other words, the devaluation of Black men under the apartheid state and the devaluation of Indian women within the diasporic family are distinct and uneven forms of social devaluation; but they (must) operate in tandem to shore up the apartheid state's logic of racial separatism.

Both the novel and film's opening scene make clear the way in which apartheid law relied upon the racialized stratifications of labor and capital. In the beginning of the novel, a white police officer bursts into the Location Café, which is located in an Indian and Colored area of Pretoria. Black workers are eating while on their lunch break alongside Colored (and one hidden white) patrons. The officer demands to see the workers' passes after reminding Amina that Blacks are not permitted to eat in the same place as "non-Blacks."[13] A pass is an identity document that Black South Africans were required to carry with them at all times when traveling to urban areas.[14] One of the workers shows the officer a travel permit—a document that allowed Blacks, Indians, and Coloreds to travel outside their racially designated districts—but tells him she doesn't have a pass because she is Colored and "not Black." The officer responds, "You look like a bloody *kaffir* [an Afrikaans racial slur for 'Black'] to me." The officer's response betrays the way in which legal definitions of race were policed by an arbitrary visual economy (distinguishing between Colored and Black).

As part of the racial stratifications of capital, this scene also alludes to laws that prohibit Indians and Coloreds from participating as equal actors in property and business ownership. Despite his "apparent role as manager"[15] of the café (and therefore Amina's employee), Jacob is actually Amina's business partner: "a helpful lawyer had assisted [Amina and Jacob] in drawing up a secret power of attorney for Jacob and the partnership was now widely acknowledged, yet closely guarded by those around them."[16] Amina's partnership with Jacob thus disrupts a dominant apartheid narrative that positions Indians economically above Blacks and Coloreds.

The café is a space in which Amina and Jacob determine the conditions of their labor outside not only the scrutinizing gaze of the apartheid state but also the diasporic community. Amina's camaraderie with Blacks and Coloreds contrasts sharply with the ethnic insularity of other Pretoria Indians, whose social interactions take place almost exclusively among other Indians within the Asiatic Bazaar and who remain wary of interactions with Blacks, even when they employ their labor.[17] For example, Omar warns Miriam not to "be friendly" with the Black workers in his shop lest they "take advantage" of Indians.[18] Even Amina's father, who chooses to live outside of the Asiatic Bazaar in Springs rather than among his Indian co-ethnics, betrays his economic self-interest in challenging apartheid laws. Like some diasporic subjects, Amina's father protests the apartheid state's differential treatment of Indians and their limited access to property under apartheid. Yet these protests are highly motivated by a set of class investments that remain unconcerned with the proletarianization of Black and Colored labor. Her father's primary motivation for listening to the "latest news of the National Party," which came to power on the basis of its apartheid policies, is to "find out whether the newest apartheid laws might affect his business. His interest in his country's politics had always been predicated on the practical rather than the ethical."[19] Amina's business partnership with Jacob thus might be understood as an ethical betrayal of ethnic singularities that are reproduced through economic self-interest.

In addition to disrupting the apartheid state's racial economies, the sharing of Indian and Colored labor and capital is significant for the way that it disrupts the diasporic community's gendered economies. Throughout the novel and film, Amina is represented as anomalous among Indian women in Pretoria for remaining unmarried and for working and earning a wage outside the home. (Even Miriam, who, as she says, helps Omar "mind the shop" in Delhof, is not paid for her labor.) Her friendship with Jacob thus allows Amina to live outside the diasporic community's codes of sexual respectability. She builds a "room of her own"[20] behind the café, ostensibly to be closer to her work, but also, it is rumored, to have sex with (Black) women. In the novel, police officers "had . . . searched [Amina's] room and the café a couple of times before, once looking for a Black woman that Amina was rumored to have been involved with, but they found nothing."[21] In the film, Amina's sexual interest in Black women is referenced more obliquely—on a break from managing the Café, she dances playfully with one of the Black female staff, as Indian patrons looks on in disapproval.

In addition to allowing Amina and Jacob to determine the conditions of their labor and allowing Amina to escape the demands of compulsory heterosexuality within the diasporic family, the café provides political sanctuary for other subjects who must escape the racisms of the apartheid state. When Miriam's sister-in-law, Rehmat, has to flee from the police because they have discovered her marriage to a white Dutchman, Amina hides her in the storage closet of her bedroom, which is attached to the back of the café. When the police visit Amina to ask if she is hiding Rehmat in her room, Amina replies, "You know as well as I do that I've had some women in here," for which she receives a slap across the face and is called "a stinking queer."[22] Rehmat's hiding place is in the proverbial closet, the space in which Amina previously has hidden women lovers and in which she hangs her wardrobe of men's clothing. The café, in its blurring of private and public intimacies—of Amina's work life and her erotic life, of Colored and Indian capital, and everyday camaraderie between Indians, Blacks, and Coloreds—reveals the tenuousness of the apartheid state's management of intimacies through the racial stratifications of capital.

Here I consider the Black African man as the limit case for such intimacies. With the exception of John and Robert, the hired Black men who work for Omar in his shop, and an unnamed Black man who is hit by a car, the only other representations of Black men in Sarif's texts are those depicting them as embodiments of violent masculinity, namely in the stories of Amina's grandmother Begum and Omar's sister Jehan. The figure of the Black man thus appears either as an embodiment of racialized labor or as a racial-sexual threat to Indian femininity.

As mentioned earlier, the Indian community speculates about Amina's mixed race identity as a result of her grandmother Begum's sexual relationship with a Black man. We later learn that Begum has been raped by a Black man and becomes pregnant with a daughter, Amina's mother. Omar's sister, Jehan, is likewise rumored to have had an affair with a Black man. Though the Jehan narrative is omitted in the film, in the novel Jehan lives in a secluded room in the upstairs of Omar's house because she has gone mad, allegedly from contracting syphilis. Within the colonial imagination, syphilis was constructed as a particularly African disease, rooted in the sexual pathology of Black men.[23] Omar's sister-in-law, Farah, tells Miriam that Jehan had a *kaffir* boyfriend and that the family "only *preferred* to think that Jehan had been raped" (my emphasis).[24] Farah explains to Miriam that Jehan's "inherent mental slowness"[25] led to her romantic feelings toward her Black lover. Jehan's madness is thus not only the effect of her sexual relationship with a Black man through medicalizing discourses of Black contagion. Curiously, it is also its cause, a symptom of her prior mental illness. Within the racial logic of the apartheid state and the diasporic family, then, sexual desire between Asian women and Black men is rendered impossible: any expression of romantic feeling between Jehan and Begum on the one hand, and Black men on the other, is constructed as inherently pathological. This conflation of intimate relations—of romance and sexual violence—between Black men and Indian women reveals a gendered racist logic in which violence, rather than love, desire, and eroticism, is figured as the only viable form of intimacy between Blacks and Asians.

These constructions of Black men certainly invoke an essentially violent and pathological Black masculinity. More tellingly, however, they point back to the *diasporic family* as the primary agent of gendered violence. Before narrating to Miriam the story of Begum's exile, Amina tells her that Begum's story "begins with the beatings."[26] The novel then flashes back to the year 1892 in Pretoria, as Begum's family chants, "Slut, slut, whore bitch."[27] As they chant, they beat Begum into a state of unconsciousness for giving birth to a mixed race daughter. Later, they kidnap her firstborn son before exiling her and her daughter to India. For Amina to claim that Begum's story "begins" with domestic violence and not with rape means that Amina implicitly contests the diasporic community's construction of the rape as the central gendered trauma of Begum's life. The flashback and Amina's narration of it destabilize what might otherwise appear as a naturalization of violent Black masculinity—the stereotype of the Black male rapist. Instead, Amina's retelling of Begum's first-person account of the rape, as opposed to her family's third-person account, reveals a representational crisis around sexual violence, in which the rape obscures the sexual violence of the diasporic family. In the novel, Amina recalls Begum telling her, "Even if [her family] believed she had been raped, she would be worthless to her husband now."[28] Begum's foregone conclusion about her diminished value within the family thus reinforces practices of misogyny within the diasporic family that are entrenched prior to the scene of rape. In keeping with this entrenchment, Begum's admonition to Amina is to be wary of "the dangers of losing yourself in a marriage, or being ruled by family."[29] This warning is in sharp contrast to that of Omar and Farah earlier in the novel for Amina to be wary of the sexual predation of Black men. Amina's memory of Begum's story thus centers the diasporic family and its racist patriarchal structure, rather than Black masculinity, as a prior and primary agent of sexual violence.

Later, in both the film and the novel, Miriam, for her part, challenges these ideas about Indian sexual propriety and Black contagion. She goes out of her way to help an unnamed Black man who is hit by a car driven by a white Dutchman and who is left bleeding by the side of the road. The film sequence emphasizes physical closeness and touch between Miriam and the Black man, a departure from the requisite distance that Miriam keeps with John and Robert under the watchful eye of her husband. She wraps her arms around him to hold up his weight, and in doing so, his blood stains her skin and her dress. On the one hand, this scene complicates both romantic and violent exchanges between Black men and Indian women by revealing the Black man's social devaluation under apartheid law—he is literally left to die by the side of the road. On the other hand, this scene may seem to invite a revision of the white woman as savior figure that dominates colonialist narratives by replacing her with the Indian woman as savior. However, I would suggest that this scene also complicates such a reading. Despite Miriam telling him that she is Indian, an admission that is intended to reassure him that she is not invested in the white supremacist logic of apartheid, the man reacts by pulling away from her touch and stumbling off into the night. Lest he be accused of fraternizing with Indian women, he flees the scene, and in doing so, reveals Miriam's powerlessness to "save" him.

This scene also positions the Black man's social powerlessness in relation to Miriam's. Miriam's attempts to save him—revealed by the blood stains on her skin and dress—earn her a devastating beating from Omar because he suspects that Miriam has gone in search of him. Omar's retributive violence against Miriam for touching the Black man operates in tandem with the Black man's fears of the state's retributive violence for receiving that touch. Furthermore, Miriam's beating redoubles the scene of familial violence toward Begum: both are the result of the diasporic family's perceptions about Black contagion. Here, as in both Jehan's and Begum's stories, the social devaluation of Black life within the apartheid state—the Black man left to die on the side of the road, and even the proletarianization of Black labor that is figured through John's and Robert's roles as hired help in Omar's shop—is reinforced by and reinforces the social devaluation of Indian women within the diasporic family. Amina, Jehan, Begum, and Miriam are connected across historical time through a range of gender and sexual improprieties—interracial sex, lesbian desire, and bodily proximities to Blackness—in which the social devaluation of Indian women within diasporic communities is sustained by its relation to the social devaluation of Blackness under the apartheid state.

I conclude by returning to the opening scenes of quotidian cross-racial intimacies in the Location Café. During the police raid of the café, an officer shoots a bullet into the air that ricochets off the ceiling and strikes a glass-framed, black-and-white photograph of Begum holding an infant (presumably Amina's mother) in her arms. When the officers leave, Amina picks up the pieces of the photo, her face distraught. Jacob comes up behind her, puts his arms around her waist, and holds her while she gazes at the photo. This scene registers Begum's connection to Amina and Amina's connection to Jacob, in an expression of what Grace Hong has called a "shared queerness."[30] Amina's identification with her grandmother occurs not through a generational narrative of heteronormative gender. Rather, it occurs through a queer generational narrative of sexual impropriety that remains unassimilable to the diasporic family form (and indeed, that is only knowable through Amina's preservation of her grandmother's memory and story). Jacob's identification with Amina occurs not on the basis of racial and sexual sameness but rather through the way that racial impropriety marks his mixed race body, which is also, differently, part of Amina's queer inheritance. Diasporic queerness, rather than cohering a lesbian identity that has remained "unseen" within post-apartheid histories of the apartheid nation, emerges as a comparative analytic for examining the deeply relational structures of Afro-Asian intimacies.

NOTES

1. Ann Laura Stoler, "Intimidations of Empire: Predicaments of the Tactile and Unseen," in *Haunted by Empire: Geographies of Intimacies in North American History*, edited by Ann Laura Stoler (Durham, NC: Duke University Press, 2006), 16.

2. Grace Kyungwon Hong, "Comparison and Coalition in the Age of Black Lives Matter," *Journal of Asian American Studies* 20, no. 2 (2017): 275.

3. Grace Kyungwon Hong and Roderick A. Ferguson, introduction to *Strange Affinities: The Gender and Sexual Politics of Comparative Racialization*, edited by Grace Kyungwon Hong and Roderick A. Ferguson (Durham, NC: Duke University Press, 2011), 2.

4. Hong and Ferguson refer in particular to two seminal texts: *This Bridge Called My Back: Writings by Radical Women of Color* and the "A Black Feminist Statement" by the Combahee River Collective.

5. Grace Kyungwon Hong and Roderick A. Ferguson, *Strange Affinities: The Gender and Sexual Politics of Comparative Racialization*, edited by Grace Kyungwon Hong and Roderick A. Ferguson (Durham, NC: Duke University Press, 2011), 2.

6. Ibid., 1.

7. Ashley Currier, "Decolonizing the Law: LGBT Organizing in Namibia and South Africa," *Studies in Law, Politics, and Society* 54 (2011): 18.

8. Jordache Ellapen, "From Black to Brown: Race, Diaspora, and Post-Apartheid South Africa" (dissertation, Indiana University, 2015), 215.

9. Ibid., 223.

10. Ibid., 223.

11. This bill divided up land into controlled areas, in which Indians could not purchase new land and were allowed only to lease it from whites, and uncontrolled areas, in which both whites and Indians could own land. "'Ghetto Act' or the Asiatic Land Tenure and Indian Representation Act No 28 of 1946 Is Passed," *South African History Online: Towards a People's History*, September 30, 2019, http://www.sahistory.org.za/dated-event/ghetto-act-or-asiatic-land-tenure-and-indian-representation-act-no-28-1946-passed.

12. This act was also used to prohibit intermarriage between non-European groups as well, such as between Indians and Blacks or Indian and Coloreds.

13. Shamim Sarif, *The World Unseen* (London: Enlightenment, 2011), 11.

14. Pass documents can be traced to slave history at the Cape; they continued to be used during the tenure of the Group Areas Act.

15. Shamim Sarif, *The World Unseen*, 11.

16. Ibid., 12.

17. Ibid., 24.

18. Ibid., 28.

19. Ibid., 226.

20. I am riffing on Virginia Woolf's oft-cited twentieth-century protofeminist novel title *A Room of One's Own*.

21. Sarif, *The World Unseen*, 170.

22. Ibid., 175.

23. See, for example, Meghan Vaughn's chapter "Syphilis and Sexuality: the Limits of Colonial Medical Power" in her book *Curing Their Ills: Colonial Power and African Illness* (Stanford, CA: Stanford University Press, 1991). Writing about syphilis in particular, Vaughn argues that contrary to dominant representations of sexual illness in nineteenth-century colonial Africa in which "female sexuality became the focus of shared attention from colonial medics, administrators, and African male elders," "male sexuality was a more immediate problem because men appeared to be more autonomous in the conduct of their sexual relations and because it was men, more than women, who peopled the colonial cities and constituted the labor force" (130).

24. Sarif, *The World Unseen*, 46.

25. Ibid., 36.

26. Ibid., 132.

27. Ibid., 134.

28. Ibid., 135.

29. Ibid., 141.

30. Grace Kyungwon Hong, "'A Shared Queerness': Colonialism, Transnationalism, and Sexuality in Shani Mootoo's 'Cereus Blooms at Night,'" *Meridians* 7, no. 1 (2006): 89.

Pinkwashing, Tourism, and Israeli State Violence

JENNIFER LYNN KELLY

ork at the intersection of Asian American studies, comparative
colonial studies, and queer studies necessarily takes as its subject
shared settler logics in transnational contexts, gendered colonial
constructs, and the violence of forced displacement as it coexists with neoliberal celebrations of multicultural tolerance.[1] For this reason, both pinkwashing and Palestine—as sites of inquiry and sites of colonial logics and
practices in Southwest Asia—need not exist at the margins of Asian American studies but have much to illuminate at its center. Pinkwashing, in the
context of Palestine/Israel, is often understood as the methods through
which Israel circulates an image of itself as a gay-friendly oasis in efforts
to position Israel as "the only democracy in the Middle East" and divert
attention away from its human rights violations.[2] In this essay, drawing
from discursive analysis of Israeli gay tourism materials and field-based
research in Palestine, I complicate the notion that pinkwashing functions
solely to occlude Israeli state violence in order to instead ask, How and in
what ways does pinkwashing in fact work to put state violence on display
and render it justifiable? And through what strategies might we refocus
our attention on the contours of colonial rule it simultaneously obscures
and celebrates?

I first analyze Israeli gay tourist initiatives, both city-sponsored pride
events and state-sponsored LGBTQ birthright initiatives, in order to explore what precisely is rendered "visible" and "invisible" in Israel's attempts
to showcase its gay-friendliness. I argue that gay tourism to Israel physically routes tourists away from witnessing the everyday violence of Israel's
racialized segregation, yet it simultaneously celebrates IDF soldiers and in-
oculates against critiques of militarized violence by positioning it as integral
to the maintenance of diversity, the promise of safety from violence, and the
guarantee of gay tourist mobility. These initiatives avoid analysis of the occupation while implicitly justifying it, eclipse certain images of militarism
while celebrating others, and legitimate Israeli state violence and settler-
colonialism by rewriting them as security and defense. Israeli state violence

is thus not rendered invisible by Israeli gay tourist initiatives; rather, it is selectively celebrated as both necessary and justified.[3]

Meanwhile, Palestinian solidarity tour itineraries route tourists through sites of state violence in order to disrupt the logic of Israel as a purveyor of "rights" and "freedom." Solidarity tours, though fraught and often unwieldy, seek to (re)center the conversation on displacement, racism, and colonialism. Palestinian solidarity tour initiatives thus function as an embodied response to Israeli pinkwashing campaigns, even when they don't directly engage questions of Israeli pinkwashing. As such, they allow us to reject the terms pinkwashing seeks to entrench and instead refocus our attention on practices that expose, negotiate, and resist the practices and processes of settler colonialism.

Brand Israel, the Promise of Nonviolence, and Occupation as a Precondition

In September 2010, on the heels of an $88 million gay marketing campaign launched by the Tel Aviv Municipality and the Ministry of Tourism, Tel Aviv was nominated as the "Sexiest Place in the World" and "Best Breakout Destination" by MTV's gay travel magazine *Trip Out*. The narratives advanced in the virtual guidebooks that accompanied the marketing of Tel Aviv as "the world's newest gay capital" pivoted on the promise of protection from homophobic violence, with Tel Aviv positioned as a place where gays could be "fun, free, and fabulous." For gay tourists, Israel needed to be both recognizable and extraordinary in its capacity to "out-gay" the United States in its promise of gay-friendliness and safety.[4] The now defunct "Frequently Asked Questions" section of *Gay Tel Aviv Guide*, for example, emphasized that Tel Aviv needs no designated gay areas because it's all gay-friendly and that any battles for gay rights not yet won are precisely that—not yet, a situation described as "constantly evolving in favor of the gay community," positioning gay marriage and military service as the twinned teleological end goals of gay rights.[5] The FAQ was later replaced by an advertisement for Atraf, "Tel Aviv's #1 gay dating app that lets you meet guys wherever you are and keeps you updated about current and future gay events in Tel Aviv."[6] *Gay Tel Aviv Guide* evidently no longer needs to make the case for the safety of gay Tel Aviv; it need only evidence the ubiquity of gay opportunity.

Central to *Gay Tel Aviv Guide*'s early platform was the celebration of LGBTQ equality within the IDF, lauding the abolishment of restrictions against gays serving in the military.[7] Meanwhile, in June 2012, the Israeli Army's official Facebook page posted a controversial image of two male IDF soldiers holding hands on a Tel Aviv street alongside the caption, "It's Pride

Month. Did you know that the IDF treats all of its soldiers equally? Let's see how many shares you can get for this photo."[8] Add to this a July 2016 *The Times of Israel* piece, which celebrated the IDF as more progressive than the state itself.[9] This circulation of images and examples from the IDF across multiple platforms of Israeli (and U.S.) image-crafting reveals the centrality—and not the omission—of the military in efforts to showcase Israel's gay-friendliness.

Further, this promise of protection against homophobic violence is sutured to the rhetoric of protection against terrorist violence. The safety promised to internationals by the Ministry of Tourism hinges also on the construction of Israel as a model counterterrorist state. In the wake of 9/11, as Naomi Klein has argued, Israel marketed itself specifically to the United States and Europe as an "Exhibit A" for fighting terrorism, positioning itself as having been "fighting terrorism since [its] birth."[10] This characterization worked to obscure the foundational violence of the State of Israel, paint Israelis as innocent victims and Palestinians as irrationally violent, and draw a parallel between the United States and Israel as suffering "victimization at the hands of terrorists."[11] Israel's proliferation of high-tech firms, privatized spy companies, and arsenal of counterterrorism technologies are, first, funded in large part by American aid and with American weapons.[12] Israel's ties to Western counterterrorist academic centers and institutions and its role in training U.S. soldiers in the war on terror also help shape this referential terrain that buttresses Israel's "other" branding of itself as both ally and sponsor in the United States' war on terror.[13] Further, the marketing of Israel's counterterrorism and surveillance technologies has aided in the militarization of policing elsewhere, with Israeli-developed technologies of surveillance first tested on Palestinians in Gaza and the West Bank and then exported for crowd control in and outside of the United States.[14] Indeed, while the United States manufactures the tear gas Israel uses against Palestinians, U.S. police forces routinely train in Israel under the auspices of "counterterrorism training," bringing strategies, tactics, and technologies back to the United States to use against, for example, Black Lives Matter protesters.[15] In this way, these two narratives are advanced by the state in conjunction: one of safety from homophobic violence in invitations to be "fun, free, and fabulous"[16] in Tel Aviv, and one of safety from broadly defined "terrorists" in invitations to invest in and be protected by Israel's counterterrorism and surveillance technologies.

Israel's strategic positioning as a model for the United States in terms of its marketable and marketed counterterrorist and surveillance techniques, military technologies, and gay inclusiveness is inextricably tied to its construction of a racialized enemy that is characterized both by illegitimate violence and regressive social mores. In keeping with the claims of scholars like Lila Abu-Lughod, Saba Mahmood, and Leti Volpp, who have delineated the coalescence of orientalism with colonial feminisms in the rhetoric and practice of the United States' "war on terror," many scholars and activists have detailed the extent to which Israeli state and nonstate actors represent Palestinians as irreparably homophobic in efforts to shore up Israel's self-representation as a gay paradise.[17] State-sanctioned Israeli gay tourism initiatives laud Israel as a progressive, tolerant, multicultural oasis in the Middle Eastern desert and marshal such rhetoric in support of its state practices of militarization and in efforts to recruit both tourists and investments from Europe and the United States. These gay tourist initiatives function through a historically racialized construction of safety and danger wherein the potential gay tourist is hailed to partake in the temporary purchase of safety where he (it is almost exclusively "he") can hold hands with his partner in public in a walled-in nation without the threat of either homophobic violence or terrorism, safe from the violence allegedly endemic to Palestinians.[18] This characterization of Palestinians as irreparably homophobic and irrationally violent does the ideological work of not just eclipsing the brutal violence of Israeli occupation but in fact rewriting it as a precondition for the safety of gay travel and the protection of gay life. This state-sanctioned and simultaneous branding of Israel as both a gay-friendly paradise and a counterterrorism expert thus compels us to critically interrogate the racialized ways in which freedom of mobility, the rhetoric of security, and the (in)visibility of state violence function within the context of Israel's settler colonial military occupation.

While militarism is an implicit undercurrent in many attempts to brand Israel as a gay-friendly oasis, other organized gay tours explicitly celebrate militarization and state violence as that which protects the freedoms they are commemorating. The state-sponsored Taglit-Birthright Israel, which provides (predominantly American) Jewish young adults aged eighteen to twenty-six with free ten-day trips to Israel, hosts annual LGBTQ tours. These tours simultaneously celebrate the IDF and work to market Israel as a land of acceptance, tolerance, and possibility for queer youth.[19] Unlike the ostensible erasures of violence and occupation one can read in invitations to party, cruise, and lounge beachside in Tel Aviv, the promotional materials for Taglit Birthright Tours (called Faglit by its tongue-in-cheek participants) legitimate an exclusively Jewish claim to the land, narrate Israeli state practice entirely from the standpoint of victimization and defense of the "modern miracle state," and overtly valorize the IDF. In addition to underscoring Israeli "diversity," online brochures for previous iterations of Taglit's "Original Rainbow Trip" promised stories of "Jerusalem's glory during the time of Herod to the Jewish people's longing for Jerusalem throughout the generations," discursively constructing all Jewish people as sharing the same historical goal in their longing for Jerusalem and, by extension, supporting Israel's contemporary and consistently expanding control over Jerusalem.[20] These materials promised that tourists would be taken to Jaffa, which has "always been the entry port to the ancient land of Israel," a clear omission of how Jaffa functioned as the "epicenter of the Palestinian economy before the 1948 Nakba" and was characterized as the Bride of the Sea of historic Palestine.[21] These narratives write a seamless Jewish claim to the land, erasing any history of either Palestine or Palestinians.

Earlier iterations of these LGBTQ Birthright tours took guests to the Western Wall on the same day that they were introduced to gay life in Israel, juxtaposing historical Jewish suffering with contemporary gay Jewish liberties.[22] On the 2013 sample itinerary of the tour, the "night out in Tel Aviv" was bracketed by a visit to the Tel Aviv Pride Center and a tour of Independence Hall and first Prime Minister David Ben-Gurion's house, both homages to the establishment of the state. In 2019, the trips end in Tel Aviv for the pride parade and nights out to check out the drag scene, inviting tourists to either "head home or stay on," and offering discounted extensions for "Birthright Plus," an array of food tours, art and culture tours, or "diversity tours" that introduce tourists to the "many faces of Israel."[23] Current tours additionally laud Israel as a "startup nation," aligning Israel with Silicon Valley, positioning the state as an economic wonder, and promising "Instagram likes" for camel rides.[24] Day two of the 2019 LGBTQ trip interpellates the tourist to see Israel as their new home, an implicit nod toward the potentiality of the tourist on Birthright to make *aliyah* and move to Israel; the heading on the itinerary for tourists' second day reads, "Welcome Home." In this context, while Israel denies Palestinians the Right of Return to their homes, it welcomes, via the Law of Return, queer Jewish American youth "home," twinning LGBTQ rights and freedom of mobility for Jewish American youth with the expansion of the Israeli state at the expense of Palestinians on their own land.

Organized gay Jewish youth tours to Israel are, not by default but by design, nationalist endorsements of Israeli state practice. Further, with soldiers as guides, as is common in Taglit-Birthright writ large, the tours are explicitly tied to celebrations of the IDF and Israel's military expertise. Taglit-Birthright Israel's central selling point in 2014, in answer to the question of why potential tourists should choose Taglit, is that their tours offer "more Israeli soldiers (they're with you for all ten days, instead of the usual five), more social action, and WIFI on all of our buses."[25] This positioning of increased military presence, "more social action," and technological convenience as the reasons to choose Taglit demonstrates the centrality of the IDF to their organized LGBT tour. In this way, the tour extends the rhetoric of protection of gays to that of national protection, which positions struggles against homophobia as synonymous with the occupation, rendering the occupation not invisible but in fact visible and deemed necessary.

The narratives advanced in the promotional material for these trips are ones that celebrate queer and multicultural diversity, write a seamless history of Jewish claim to the land, and refuse to recognize Palestinian claims or historical ties to the land. These invitations paint Israel at large as a queer-friendly, progressive haven and Tel Aviv in particular as a party for queer youth. They celebrate Israeli diversity and promise to leave tourists with an understanding of Israel's acceptance of "the other," but they provide itineraries that celebrate Israeli statehood, legitimate Jewish claim to the land, and preclude analyses of Israel's historical and contemporary military occupation while celebrating the prowess of the Israeli military. In doing so, they wed narratives of LGBTQ inclusion to state endorsements of militarization, which implicitly and inevitably position the latter as a precondition for the former.

In gay tourism to Israel, then, we see three state-sanctioned Israeli branding initiatives that are not at odds but are in fact functioning in concert: (1) Israel's "Brand Israel," which attempts to make Israel legible, particularly to American youth, by downplaying Israel's association with both religion and war and instead highlighting displays of culture and democracy; (2) Israel's endeavor to brand itself since 9/11 as an expert and resource for the United States' "war on terror"; and (3) Israel's celebration of the IDF as responsible for protecting a Jewish demographic majority in Israel, Israeli multiculturalism, and LBTQ freedoms.[26] Israel thus works to promulgate a gay-friendly multicultural image—notwithstanding, for example, the inequality experienced by Palestinian citizens of Israel, the documentation of abuse against Thai and Filipino workers within its borders, or the indefinite detention of Eritrean and Sudanese asylum seekers in Israel.[27] Alongside this image, Israel promulgates a defense of and justification for Israel's militarized colonization of Palestinian land. In this formulation, queer multicultural mobility via tourism—the capacity for an array of gay tourists to visit Israel, move freely, and kiss their partners in public with no need for "designated areas"—is positioned as possible only because of the violence enacted by the Israeli army, itself positioned as a partner in U.S. war-waging.

The Promise of Mobility and the Exposure of Immobility

The attempts to market Tel Aviv as a gay hotspot traffic in a sustained emphasis on borderlessness and queer multicultural mobility. They invite gay tourists to use the "cultural and social oasis"[28] of Tel Aviv as a "jumping off point" for all of Israel, inviting gay tourists to explore Jerusalem, the Dead Sea, Haifa, and Masada.[29] These invitations tell gay tourists staying in Tel

Aviv that their mobility is unparalleled. As the *Gay Tel Aviv Guide* put it, "Within 1–2 hours drive you can be in magical tourist sites during the day, and easily return to Tel Aviv to catch a party at night."[30] These invitations are predicated on the question of movement, proximity, and images of borderlessness. Borderlessness is similarly performed every time a tourist bus from Israel travels to Bethlehem or the Dead Sea. Unlike Palestinians or tourists traveling from the West Bank into Jerusalem via Checkpoint 300 in Bethlehem or the Qalandia Checkpoint in Ramallah, Israeli tour buses coming into the West Bank enter no checkpoint; tourists show no passports and see no armed guards. The Wall opens for them to let the bus through, allowing them to believe they have simply just been "to Israel." Within this discursive logic and conceptual grammar, Israel becomes the guarantor of freedom of movement for gays, and repressive state violence is simultaneously legitimated and disavowed.

In a strategy that attempts to fashion decolonial praxis out of tourist itineraries, Palestinians in the West Bank, and across Historic Palestine, have issued calls for international tourists to "come and see" the devastating effects of colonial rule on their lives. These calls underscore the restriction of Palestinian movement—and Palestinian movement building—in the context of ongoing Israeli settler colonialism.[31] If solidarity tourists entering Palestine/Israel announce, at Ben Gurion International Airport in Tel Aviv, that they are going to Palestine, they will be subject to a lengthy interrogation and possibly refused entry. Palestinian guides and organizers collaborated, in 2012, to call attention to this restriction of visitors by crafting the "Welcome to Palestine" campaign, or the Flytilla (referencing the Flotillas that have attempted to break the siege on Gaza), wherein international activists flew to Ben Gurion and declared that they were going to Palestine. These activists were not let in the country and many were not even allowed to board Israel-bound planes in their home countries. The imposition of restrictions on visitors to Palestine is an attempt by the Israeli state to circumscribe international solidarity efforts in the name of "security." Highlighting the militarized, policed state of surveillance, control, restriction of movement, and bars against being visited, Palestinian organizers have stressed, "Even prisoners are allowed visits."[32]

Solidarity tour organizers guide tourists through Palestinian land across the West Bank that is bisected and trisected by Israeli-only roads connecting Israeli settlements to one another. West Bank tour guides will explain, "I can see Jerusalem from where I'm standing, but I can get to Copenhagen easier than I can get to Jerusalem." Palestinian guides in the West Bank will negotiate the movement of tourists from Bethlehem to Jerusalem via a "trade-off" at Checkpoint 300, where an international volunteer will guide tourists through the checkpoint on foot since the groups' West Bank

Palestinian guides cannot go with them. Tourists will move easily through the checkpoints, waving their passports for bored Israeli soldiers to glance at, while Palestinians in line have to produce IDs and permits and potentially face harassment, additional screening, and denial of entry. On the other side of the checkpoint, the internationals have a new guide for the day, and they make their way to Jerusalem.

On guided political tours through the Old City of Jerusalem, tourists will see armed civilian settlers, settlers' armed bodyguards in plain clothes, groups of heavily armed young Israeli soldiers on every corner, homes settlers have taken over, and the grates above Palestinian markets to catch the trash settlers throw. They will file into a bus to hear a detailed and thorough explanation of Israeli apartheid in the Eastern part of Occupied Jerusalem and witness its effects, from the lack of infrastructure and unpaved roads in East Jerusalem to the Wall cutting through Abu Dis and severing the route that had long served as a throughway from Jerusalem to Jericho and segregating Palestinian communities from their former neighbors.

In Hebron, tourists will witness and reenact the segregation that characterizes the city. They will learn that Shuhada Street—now closed to Palestinians, emptied of stores, and home to only soldiers, settlers, and tourists—was once a Palestinian market so busy, one guide tells tourists, that he used to have to hold hands with his father in order to not get lost in the bustling marketplace. They will leave their guide to walk down Shuhada Street, witnessing how the street is closed to Palestinians, even those whose homes are still on the street and who have to enter their homes from the back, who have cages around their patios to protect them from the debris the settlers throw, who have signs in their windows that read. "You are witnessing apartheid." Tourists will take in Shuhada Street, the main road through the city closed off to the 177,000 Palestinians who live in Hebron with access only to tourists, the 500 settlers who live there, and the 1,500–2,000 soldiers who protect them. Here, tourists will witness the 2,400 stores that have been closed under military orders or due to closures and checkpoints, and the more than 1,000 emptied Palestinian homes.[33] At each entrance to Shuhada Street and elsewhere in Hebron, tourists witness Palestinians detained at checkpoints, searched at every stop. Tourists leave Hebron with a tangible understanding of their freedom of mobility and an awareness of the restriction of the mobility of Palestinians at every turn. They also understand the way in which their mobility is tied to the presumed and policed absence of Palestinians—if soldiers guarding checkpoints know they have a Palestinian guide, they might not be let in.[34]

This precarity and contingency of movement is set in sharp contrast to the image Israel puts forth in invitations to station oneself in Tel Aviv as a jumping off point for the entire country, a home base from which to explore what Israel has to offer. These fragmented itineraries beg the question: What can we gain from having a capacious understanding of responses to pinkwashing? What does it mean to resist the logic of pinkwashing while not expressly addressing questions of gay rights? If we understand Israeli PR campaigns to be using gay rights as a diversion tactic, then in what ways does changing the conversation from questions of LGBTQ advances to questions of freedom of movement actually allow us to refocus our attention on practices that expose and resist the processes of settler colonialism?

Rerouted Itineraries: Conceptual and Material Interventions

Pinkwashing is a strategy whose logics are not circumscribed to questions of gay rights. Candace Fujikane has argued that, through yellowwashing, Israel uses Asian American figures like Daniel Inouye, who is himself a Japanese settler in Hawai'i, to bolster Israel's claim to liberal multiculturalism and to disappear its settler solidarities with the United States.[35] An array of think pieces countering Israeli greenwashing initiatives pepper the pages of anti-Zionist journals like *The Electronic Intifada*, pointing to the many ways in which Israel touts its environmental advocacy to obscure its human rights violations.[36] Yet analyzing the multiple ways in which Israel brands itself—as "counterterrorism expert" with unmatched military prowess alongside its alleged role as multicultural, queer-friendly, environmentally conscious oasis—in tandem with an analysis of its severe restrictions on Palestinian mobility enables us to ask not only what pinkwashing disappears but also what it enables, produces, and celebrates.

In the wake of a 2012 queer delegation to Palestine, organized by Sarah Schulman, Jasbir Puar wrote,

> During the course of our 7 day LGBTIQ delegation, which was the first of its kind to the West Bank, we were part of countless discussions about various routes of travel and how many and what kinds of checkpoints would be encountered on a chosen route; how easy or difficult would they be to traverse; what kinds of delays could be anticipated. Our visiting delegation of U.S. citizens experienced the bodily and logistical discombobulation of always needing to be hyperaware of how one is transiting through the ever-shifting boundaries between Israel and the West Bank. Questions about the treatment of homosexuals in the West Bank or the Gaza Strip fail to take into account the constant and omnipresent restrictions on mobility, contact, and organizing necessary to build any kind of queer presence and politics.[37]

With this delegation as an exception, Palestinian-led solidarity tours do not explicitly address gay tourism or Israeli pinkwashing campaigns. However, all of them, regardless of the extent to which they bring up "gay rights," disrupt the logic of pinkwashing and its attendant logic of mobility by using the movement of internationals to highlight the immobility of Palestinians.

The itineraries of these tours, routed in ways that render visible the restrictions on Palestinian mobility, ask what it would mean to see solidarity tourism—queer and otherwise—as an embodied response to pinkwashing. What does it mean to strategize against the logic of an initiative without explicitly addressing or defining that initiative? What does it mean to centralize the question of freedom of movement in the collective struggle to define and resist settler colonialism in Palestine/Israel? To what extent does centralizing (im)mobility avoid the pitfall of having the conversation on the terms set by pinkwashing campaigns and their central focus on LGBTQ advances, gay rights, modernity, liberalism, and gay visibility as a barometer for progressive politics? Further, might reorienting analysis toward the problem of (im)mobility avoid the discursive logic and conceptual grammar that underpin pinkwashing campaigns' mystification of repressive state violence as tolerance and progress?

Reoriented along these lines, it is worth exploring the ways in which solidarity tourism—in spite of all the limitations of tourism as a vehicle for decolonization—potentially offers a material deconstruction of the central premises of pinkwashing that not only divert attention away from the question of settler-colonial military occupation and onto the question of gay rights but simultaneously celebrate the violent quotidian work of the Israeli military. Palestinian tour guides and organizers, by way of narration and itinerary, attempt to center the discussions of their tours on colonialism, apartheid, land expropriation, severed communities, checkpoints, detention, and restrictions on movement. Solidarity tourists, then, are expected to participate in a conversation that does not relegate the question of displacement and immobility to the sidelines in favor of talk about progress and gay visibility. In showcasing colonialism and revealing restrictions on mobility, solidarity tourism, a fraught and constantly reworked strategy, seeks to intervene in the coalescing (and not contradictory) narratives advanced by Israeli pinkwashing, among other forms of "washing," and refocus the discussion on "migration, displacement, colonialism, racism, and the lives of people in war zones and occupation"—sites of inquiry at the very center of Asian American studies.[38]

ACKNOWLEDGMENTS

I want to thank Kale Fajardo, Alice Y. Hom, and Martin Manalansan for the invitation to contribute to this volume. I first presented this work at the Homonationalism and

Pinkwashing Conference at CUNY Graduate Center and Center for Gay and Lesbian Studies in New York in April 2013, and I am grateful to the moderator, co-panelists, and audience members for engagement with my work. Portions of this essay appeared in *GLQ: A Journal of Lesbian and Gay Studies* (January 2020) and I am grateful to the editors of the Queer In/Security Dossier in which it appeared for engaging with my arguments pinkwashing and Israeli gay tourist initiatives.

NOTES

1. For work at the intersections of Asian American studies and transnational settler colonial studies, see Iyko Day, *Alien Capital: Asian Racialization and the Logic of Settler Colonial Capitalism* (Durham, NC: Duke University Press, 2016). For readings that place the archives of liberalism within the same analytic frame as colonial state archives, see, Lisa Lowe, *The Intimacies of Four Continents* (Durham, NC: Duke University Press, 2015). For work on the coalescence of forced displacement and celebrations of multicultural tolerance, see Mimi Nguyen, *The Gift of Freedom: War, Debt, and Other Refugee Passages* (Durham, NC: Duke University Press, 2012). And for work in queer studies and Asian American studies that challenges the teleological positioning of assimilation as gay modernity, alongside its evacuation of questions of immigration, diaspora, and racialized and gendered citizenship, see Martin Manalansan, *Global Divas: Filipino Gay Men in the Diaspora* (Durham, NC: Duke University Press, 2003). My analysis of pinkwashing in Palestine/Israel grows from this careful attention in Asian American studies to the space where liberalism, colonialism, and depoliticized and decontextualized celebrations of gay identity meet.

2. Important discussions and debates on pinkwashing include work by Ali Abunimah, Nada Elia, Haneen Maikey, Maya Mikdashi, Jasbir Puar, Jason Ritchie, Heike Schotten, Sarah Schulman, and Mikki Stelder, among others. A primary way in which Israel traffics in pinkwashing is through its well-funded campaign "Brand Israel," which markets the country as gay-friendly. For more on the relationship between pinkwashing and Brand Israel, see Sarah Schulman, "A Documentary Guide to Brand Israel and the Art of Pinkwashing," *Mondoweiss: The War of Ideas in the Middle East* (November 30, 2011) and Nada Elia, "Gay Rights with a Side of Apartheid," *Settler Colonial Studies* 2, no. 2 (2012): 49–68. For more on pinkwashing as a diversionary tactic, see Ali Abunimah, "Pinkwash, Greenwash, Hogwash: How Israel uses Sex and Marketing to Distract from Apartheid," *Electronic Intifada* (July 13, 2013), accessed June 25, 2014, http://electronic intifada.net/blogs/ali-abunimah/pinkwash-greenwash-hogwash-ali-abunimah-israels -use-sex-and-marketing-distract. For critiques on the limits of homonationalism as an explanatory analytic framework vis-à-vis pinkwashing, see Jason Ritchie, "Pinkwashing, Homonationalism, and Israel–Palestine: The Conceits of Queer Theory and the Politics of the Ordinary," *Antipode: A Radical Journal of Geography* (June 3, 2014): 1–19. For debates on the relationship(s) between pinkwashing, pinkwatching, and complicity in imperial projects, see Jasbir Puar and Maya Mikdashi, "Pinkwatching and Pinkwashing: Interpenetration and Its Discontents," *Jadaliyya* (August 9, 2012), accessed June 25, 2014, http://www.jadaliyya.com/pages/index/6774/pinkwatching-andpinkwashing_interpen etration-and-, and Haneen Maikey and Heike Schotten's response, "Queers Resisting Zionism: On Authority and Accountability Beyond Homonationalism" (October 10, 2012), accessed June 25, 2014, http://www.jadaliyya.com/pages/index/7738/queers-resisting -Zionism_on-authority-and-accounta. For a contextualization of the implications of this debate and its aftermath, see Mikki Stelder, "Other Scenes of Speaking: Listening to

Palestinian Queer Anti-Colonial Critique." *Journal of Palestine* 47, no. 3 (2018): 45–61. Some of the debates around pinkwashing were crystallized in the 2013 Homonationalism and Pinkwashing conference at the City University of New York, which prompted keynote speaker Haneen Maikey to ask the audience, in an effort to remind them of the limits of an identity-based solidarity in the face of unchecked settler colonialism, "Are you in solidarity with Palestine or with the queers in Palestine?" Haneen Maikey, keynote lecture, Homonationalism and Pinkwashing Conference, CUNY Graduate Center and Center for Gay and Lesbian Studies, New York (April 11, 2013).

3. For an extended version of my argument here, see "Israeli Gay Tourist Initiatives and the (In)Visibility of State Violence," Queer In/Security Dossier, edited by Tallie Ben Daniel and Hilary Berwick, *GLQ: A Journal of Lesbian and Gay Studies*, 26, no. 1 (January 2020): 160–173.

4. Jacqui Alexander argues that gay guidebooks like these become "travel curriculum on which gay tourists can rely" precisely because "the threat of homophobic violence can express itself swiftly and with grave consequences." She also theorizes that the friendliness of the people at the tourist sites flagged in gay tour guides "needs to be more intimate and personable than the friendliness of even the most gay friendly corporations in the United States." Jacqui Alexander, *Pedagogies of Crossing: Meditations on Feminism, Sexual Politics, Memory, and the Sacred* (Durham, NC: Duke University Press, 2005), 81.

5. "Frequently Asked Questions," *Gay Tel Aviv Guide*, last accessed April 30, 2013, http://www.gaytlvguide.com/start-here/frequently-asked-questions?

6. Ibid.

7. "Gay Rights in Israel," *Gay Tel Aviv Guide*, last accessed June 27, 2014, http://www.gaytlvguide.com/start-here/gay-rights-in-israel. The website, in its entirety, is now inaccessible.

8. "Gay Pride Month: Israel Defense Forces Facebook Photo Stirs Controversy," *Huffington Post*, June 11, 2012, accessed March 7, 2018, http://www.huffingtonpost.com/2012/06/11/gay-pride-israel-defense-forces-photo_n_1587666.html.

9. Judah Ari Gross, "For Gay Soldiers, the IDF Seen as More Progressive Than the State," *The Times of Israel*, July 5, 2016, accessed March 26, 2018, https://www.timesofisrael.com/for-gay-soldiers-idf-seen-as-more-progressive-than-the-state/.

10. Naomi Klein, *The Shock Doctrine: The Rise of Disaster Capitalism* (New York: Metropolitan, 2007), 428–435.

11. See Derek Gregory's *The Colonial Present: Afghanistan, Palestine, Iraq* (New York: Wiley-Blackwell, 2004) for a discussion of the political implications of the parallels drawn between Israel and the United States in post-9/11 American and Israeli public spheres.

12. For more on the "war on terror's" homeland security boom and Israel's economy, see Naomi Klein, *The Shock Doctrine*, 435–436.

13. For more on counterterrorism technologies funded by American aid and with American weapons, see Gregory, *The Colonial Present*, 117. For more on Israel's ties to western counter-terrorist academic centers, see Jasbir Puar, *Terrorist Assemblages: Homonationalism in Queer Times* (Durham: Duke University Press, 2007), 55.

14. See Jewish Voice for Peace, "Deadly Exchange Report Reveals the Extent of Massive Training Programs between US Law Enforcement and Israeli Police, Military and the Shin Bet," September 12, 2018, https://jewishvoiceforpeace.org/deadlyexchangereport/.

15. In addition to the Deadly Exchange Report (Jewish Voice for Peace 2018), for more on U.S. police departments, receiving training from Israeli military forces and

using "skunk water," a tactic tested on Palestinians, on protestors in Ferguson, see Domenica Ghanem, "Why We Should Be Alarmed That Israeli Forces and U.S. Police Forces Are Training Together," *Foreign Policy in Focus*, June 7, 2018, accessed February 15, 2020, https://fpif.org/why-we-should-be-alarmed-that-israeli-forces-and-u-s-police-are-training-together/.

16. "Tel Aviv Pride 2018 with OUTStanding Travel," last accessed March 26, 2018, http://israel.siguez.com/tel-aviv/tel-aviv-israel/tel-aviv-pride-2018-with-outstanding-travel?ctchbv4jk4.

17. On colonial feminism that accompanied the United States's invasion of Afghanistan, see Lila Abu-Lughod, "Do Muslim Women Really Need Saving? Anthropological Reflections on Cultural Relativism and Its Others," *American Anthropologist* 104, no. 3 (September 2002): 783–790; Saba Mahmood and Charles Hirschkind, "Feminism, the Taliban, and the Politics of Counter-Insurgency," *Anthropological Quarterly* 75, no. 2 (Spring 2002): 339–354; Leti Volpp, "The Citizen and the Terrorist," *University of California Los Angeles Law Review* 49 (June 2002): 5. On pinkwashing and its colonial implications, see Elia, "Gay Rights with a Side of Apartheid"; Haneen Maikey and Jason Ritchie, "Israel, Palestine, and Queers," *Monthly Review*, April 28, 2009, accessed May 1, 2013, http://mrzine.monthlyreview.org/2009/mr280409.html; Jasbir Puar, *Terrorist Assemblages*; Jasbir Puar, "Israel's Gay Propaganda War," *The Guardian*, July 1, 2010; and Jason Ritchie, "How Do You Say 'Come Out of the Closet?' in Arabic? Queer Activism and the Politics of Visibility in Israel-Palestine," *GLQ: A Journal of Gay and Lesbian Studies* 16, no. 4 (2010): 557–575. See also Nadine Naber, Sa'ed Atshan, Nadia Awad, Maya Mikdashi, Sofian Merabet, Dorgham Abusalim, and Nada Elia, "On Palestinian Studies and Queer Theory," *Journal of Palestine Studies* 47, no. 3 (2018): 62–71.

18. See, especially, Jasbir Puar's discussion of how this violence is constructed as religious rather than political and the ways in which Palestinian queers are read through the lens of Islamic fundamentalism instead of the struggle for self-determination and statehood (Puar, *Terrorist Assemblages*, 17).

19. Taglit's Birthright trip is paid for by private philanthropists, the Israeli government, and umbrella organizations like North American Jewish Federations, Keren Hayesod, and the Jewish Agency for Israel. See also Spencer Kornhaber, "A Queer Tour of Israel: Out and About in a Nation with Identity Issues," *The Atlantic*, July 2014, accessed March 20, 2018, https://www.theatlantic.com/magazine/archive/2014/07/out-and-about-in-israel/372272/.

20. The Israel Experience, "LGBTQ: The Original Rainbow Trip," sample itinerary, accessed April 30, 2013, http://www.freejourney toisrael.org/trips-2/specialty-trips/lgbtq-the-rainbow-trip/lgbtq-sample-itinerary/.

21. Sami Abu Shehadeh and Fadi Shbaytah, "Jaffa: From Eminence to Ethnic Cleansing," *Electronic Intifada*, February 26, 2009, accessed May 7, 2013, http://electronicintifada.net/content/jaffa-eminence-ethnic-cleansing/8088.

22. Tour itineraries foreground the importance of archaeology in Israel and offered tours of the Western Wall tunnels, describing each tour as an "unforgettable journey through time," eliding the ways in which archeological tunnels, shaking the foundations of Palestinian homes, make Palestinians' lives in today's East Jerusalem precarious. The tour also paired exploration of the landscape with lessons on "security and borders" from Malkia, a kibbutz bordering Lebanon and established on Palestinian village lands, eclipsing the history of the Haganah's violent takeover of the village. Walid Khalidi, *All That Remains: The Palestinian Villages Occupied and Depopulated by Israel in 1948* (Washington, DC: Institute for Palestine Studies, 1992), 470–471.

23. "Birthright Israel Plus: Extend Your Adventure," *Birthright Israel*, last accessed July 16, 2019, https://www.birthrightisrael.com/extend.

24. Ibid.

25. See Taglit-Birthright Israel, "FAQ," accessed June 24, 2014, http://www.freejour neytoisrael.org/faqs/.

26. See Nathaniel Popper, "Israel Aims to Improve Its Public Image," *The Forward*, October 14, 2005, accessed May 7, 2013, http://forward.com/articles/2070/israel-aims -to-improve-its-public-image/. For more on Brand Israel, see Sarah Schulman, "A Documentary Guide to Brand Israel and the Art of Pinkwashing."

27. On the experiences of Palestinian citizens in Israel, see Sharri Plonski, *Palestinian Citizens of Israel: Power, Resistance and the Struggle for Space* (New York: I. B. Tauris, 2017). On Human Rights Watch documentation of abuse against Thai workers in Israel, see Human Rights Watch, "Israel: Serious Abuse of Thai Migrant Workers," accessed April 11, 2018, https://www.hrw.org/news/2015/01/21/israel-serious-abuse-thai-migrant -workers. On Filipino workers in Israel, see Ruth Marglalit, "Israel's Invisible Filipino Work Force," *New York Times*, May 3, 2017, accessed April 11, 2018, https://www.nytimes.com /2017/05/03/magazine/israels-invisible-filipino-work-force.html, and *Transit*, directed by Hannah Espia, Cinemalaya (July 2013). On the detention of African migrant workers, see Human Rights Watch, "Israel: Don't Lock Up Asylum Seekers," accessed April 11, 2018, https://www.hrw.org/news/2018/01/22/israel-dont-lock-asylum-seekers.

28. "Discover Tel Aviv: The Tel Aviv Gay Vibe," Tel Aviv Gay Vibe, accessed April 30, 2013, http://telavivgayvibe.atraf.com/template/default.aspx?PageId=8.

29. "Israel: Do, See, Go," Gay Tel Aviv Guide, accessed March 11, 2013, http://www .gaytlvguide.com/do-see-go/travel-israel.

30. Ibid.

31. The West Bank is completely severed from Gaza, where the entire population of 1.8 million Palestinians is enclosed under Israeli blockade. Further, Palestinians in the diaspora are often denied entry to their homeland at Ben Gurion Airport or at Allenby Bridge constructing the border between the West Bank and Jordan. Additionally, contact between Palestinian citizens of Israel and Palestinians in the West Bank, Gaza, and the diaspora is foreclosed through Israeli restrictions on Palestinian movement across Palestine/Israel.

32. Robert Naiman, citing campaign organizer Mazin Qumsiyeh in "Welcome to Palestine: 'Even Prisoners Are Allowed Visits,'" *Al Jazeera*, April 14, 2012, accessed May 14, 2013, http://www.aljazeera.com/indepth/opinion/2012/04/201241484657679358 .html. While this statement has the rhetorical effect of underscoring how Israel isolates Palestinians from the rest of the world, Israel, like other carceral states, often does not allow prisoners visits. In defiance of international law, Israel itself banned visits entirely for prisoners from Gaza in the years between 2007 and 2012, and has continued to severely restrict them even after the ban was lifted (B'Tselem. 2019. "Court-Sanctioned Vengeance: HCJ Upholds Ban on Family Visits for Hamas Prisoners from Gaza." B'Tselem: The Israeli Information Center for Human Rights in the Occupied Territories. July 14, 2019. https://www.btselem.org/gaza_strip /20190714_court_sanc tioned_vengeance.).

33. B'Tselem, "Hebron City Center," accessed April 1, 2013, http://www.btselem.org /hebron.

34. For a longer discussion of the itineraries I briefly describe here, see Jennifer Lynn Kelly, "Asymmetrical Itineraries: Militarism, Tourism, and Solidarity in Occupied

Palestine," special issue, Tours of Duty/Tours of Leisure, edited by Vernadette Vicuña Gonzalez, Jana K. Lipman, and Teresia Teaiwa, *American Quarterly* 68, no. 3 (September 2016): 723–745.

35. Candace Fujikane, "Against the Yellowwashing of Israel: The BDS Movement and Liberatory Solidarities across Settler States," in *Flashpoints for Asian American Studies*, ed. Cathy Schlund-Vials (New York: Fordham University Press, 2018): 150–172.

36. Accessed April 10, 2018, https://electronicintifada.net/tags/greenwashing.

37. Jasbir Puar, "The Golden Handcuffs of Gay Rights: How Pinkwashing Distorts Both LGBTIQ and Anti-Occupation Activism," *The Feminist Wire*, January 30, 2012, accessed April 11, 2018, http://www.thefeministwire.com/2012/01/the-golden-handcuffs-of-gay-rights-how-pinkwashing-distorts-both-lgbtiq-and-anti-occupation-activism/.

38. As one of the central reasons for supporting the boycott of Israeli academic institutions, in response to the 2005 Palestinian call for boycott, divestment, and sanctions, the Asian American Studies Association 2013 Resolution reads, "Whereas the Association for Asian American Studies seeks to foster scholarship that engages conditions of migration, displacement, colonialism, and racism, and the lives of people in zones of war and occupation." (Association of Asian American Studies, "Resolution to Support the Boycott of Israeli Academic Institutions," https://aaastudies.org/wp-content/uploads/2020/01/aaas-4_20_13-conference-resolution-to-support-the-boycott-of-israeli-academic-institutions-revised.pdf, last accessed December 20, 2020.)

Asian Settler Abstraction and Administrative Aloha

Reid Uratani

n late 2017, I stepped into the downtown Seattle Barnes and Noble hoping
to source images for a presentation on tourism advertising. Among the
racks of travel magazines I was startled to see a volume titled *Lei*—a term
I recognize as ʻŌlelo Hawaiʻi (Native Hawaiian language)—and drawn in
further by the model on its cover. The model's particularity is the implicit
focus of the image, a shot pulled from one of the issue's features on "casual,
active wear for adventuring around Honolulu."[1] "Born in Spain and raised
in Oahu," the model self-identifies as "a Korean, Native American, German,
and Spanish trans-masculine person (they/them)."[2] *Lei*—a magazine "for
the LGBT traveler"—and its cover model are fruitful visualizations of the
logics animating queerness, race, and ethnicity in Hawaiʻi and a useful
entry point for my argument that one of their key structuring rationales
centers on the term "aloha."[3]

A host of scholarship accounting for the complex history of Hawaiʻi's
relation to U.S. imperialism, multiculturalism, film, and television commonly notes both the exoticism with which the islands are narrated and the
tacit economies of racial power they presuppose and affirm. My discussion
centralizes "aloha" as a fundamental discourse in this rendering of Hawaiʻi.
"Aloha" in my analysis operates not only as a heuristic for the more explicit
evocations of paradise found in tourism advertising but also as a logical
principle organizing the subtler labor of hegemony. In this essay, I underscore the mobilization of aloha as a type of affective ideology by state and
corporate interests in specifying it as "administrative aloha."

My encounter with *Lei* in a Seattle bookstore indexes my relation to
Hawaiʻi. I was born and raised in Honolulu, among the fourth generation of Japanese settlers in the United States (*yonsei*), but only found the
vocabulary to articulate my unease with the sentimentality of "aloha"
from afar. In its most widely circulated sense, "aloha" as administrative
is a colonial logic. It is an ideology attuned to simultaneously elicit touristic consumption, pacify Hawaiʻi residents and Kanaka Maoli (indigenous Hawaiians), and acquiesce to the terms of reality recognized by the

metropole (both the state of Hawai'i and Washington, DC).[4] This reality is marked by the red herring of a multicultural polity (itself a gloss of diversity obscuring interethnic hierarchies of structural advantage). This reality invests indigenous bodies through administrative "aloha," but only within a circumscribed horizon of possibility, and only to particular ends (performers, cultural practitioners, military personnel) where the potential of recognizing—let alone changing—the terms of reality are obviated.[5] This reality assuages the strangeness of "aloha's" transliterations and even deploys this same term as recourse to foreclose challenges to its organization of the status quo.[6]

Before returning to discuss *Lei* and similar expressions of administrative "aloha," I begin by canvassing the history of race and ethnicity vis-à-vis indigeneity in Hawai'i. Next, I examine the political and economic efficacies of administrative aloha and its recent expansions. I then concretize my discussion in the history of same-sex rights claims in Hawai'i in order to better contextualize the solicitations of administrative aloha marshaled in queer tourism.

Race, Ethnicity, and Indigeneity in Hawai'i

Hawai'i as a geopolitical site is patterned by multiple logics of varying scales—island, interisland, state, interstate, national, international. These coexist but do not neatly coincide with other logics, most notably the temporalities of historical memory and geological activity. However, these analytics cloud the individual and social frames that have patterned the modern history of Hawai'i as an object of collective nostalgia. My discussion of the discourse of aloha aims to specify this experiential register. Here, I articulate contemporary Hawai'i as an effect of what Michel Foucault describes as the "exteriority of accidents."[7] Viewed as "accident," Hawai'i becomes legible as a confluence of contingent historical processes whose efficacies are dispersed and resistant to tidy narrations.

As a state, Hawai'i possesses the largest nonwhite population in the union.[8] With a visible indigenous presence, substantial influences from Chinese, Japanese, Filipino communities, along with recent migrations from Southeast Asia and Micronesia, the persistence of social and cultural demarcations in the islands eludes racial classification, especially when evaluated along a white/black binary. In my discussion, the delineation of race (structural determinations characterizing bodily appearance), ethnicity (heritage traced along kinship lines), and indigeneity (heritage grounded in relation to territory) in Hawai'i is blurred by the production of a discourse of "local," often mobilized by ethnic groups against indigenous claims to land.[9] I return to this point later.

Accounts of the incorporation of the Hawaiian Islands into the United States' territorial imaginary must awkwardly minimize either the complex political reality of Kanaka Maoli or the violence by which they were displaced in portraying Hawai'i as a "racial melting pot."[10] From isolation at the time of the arrival of James Cook in 1779, the islands' estimated populace of three hundred thousand to one million Native Hawaiians endured the rapid succession of both ideological (capitalism, Christian evangelism, land tenure reform) and visceral (death, disease, and immigration) changes relentlessly destabilizing and overcoding Kanaka Maoli culture. By 1900, the Kingdom of Hawai'i had been overthrown, the islands were annexed by the United States, and an early territorial census counted less than forty thousand Native Hawaiians.[11]

The one hundred years spanning these historical landmarks narrates multiple processes of inundating reform and retrofit. Cook himself failed to find a northwest passage for the British empire, but the voyage firmly established the Hawaiian Islands on naval cartographies. Increased international commerce gradually led to the sustained residence of European and American foreigners in Hawai'i as businessmen, missionaries, and political advisors to the monarchy, but also to the spread of diseases like influenza to which the indigenous people had no resistance.[12] Rapid depopulation required the burgeoning sugar industry import large labor forces from several countries, the first wave of contract laborers arriving from China in 1852.[13] New economic sanctions in the late nineteenth century motivated white sugar planters to overthrow the monarchy in 1893, aiming to circumvent tariffs through annexation by the United States.

Local, Imperial

The territorial government of Hawai'i, formed through the islands' annexation to the United States, reinforced the sugar oligarchy's racialized control of plantation labor. Continuous immigration of contract workers from China, Japan, and the Philippines facilitated white plantation managers' domination of numerically larger labor groups. Linguistic division, threat of violent suppression, and manipulation of interethnic conflict were constant checks to labor organizing.[14] An unintended consequence of this plantation history was the gradual production of "local," a synthesis of laborers' experiences grounded in opposition to the racialized hierarchy of the planter class.

"Local," as a cultural common ground among plantation laborers, takes on greater significance with statehood. When the United States entered World War II following the 1941 Japanese bombing of Pearl Harbor, U.S. citizens of Japanese ancestry in Hawai'i were not subjected to the internment process facing those on the continent. As the largest ethnic group in

Hawai'i at the time, internment was logistically impossible. Further, Hawai'i's Japanese-American labor force was necessary to maintain the war effort in the islands. Heightened surveillance and regulation throughout the period of martial law, in addition to the battlefield accomplishments of the *Nisei* (second generation Japanese-American) in the 100th and 442nd divisions, further soured Japanese in Hawai'i to the racial stratifications of the territorial leadership.[15] After the war, Japanese contributions to labor organizing among plantation workers and support of union-backed politicians culminated in the 1954 Democratic Revolution, where Democrat candidates won the majority of seats in both houses of the Hawai'i Territorial Legislature for the first time.[16]

The postwar politicization of Japanese in Hawai'i patterns the emergence of "local" in a manner parallel to the Democratic Revolution. Unlike the generic sense of local—as sustained residence or birthplace—"local" in Hawai'i signifies a vague history of interethnic collaboration against white domination. Posed as an amalgam of plantation Asian and Native Hawaiian cultures, "local" as an identity tacitly defines its racial parameters (non-white) as it blurs interethnic differences. "Local" in this way abstracts from its historical conditions by stifling questions about its own qualifications— one is not local if one asks how to be local.

Displayed as evidence of the state's apparent multicultural harmony, local actively confuses application of sociological heuristics like race and ethnicity while obviating others, especially with regard to claims to land. This maneuver is apparent in claims that localness supersedes and outmodes racial difference, compelling a color-blind view of all Hawai'i residents while effectively denying indigeneity. In this case, local becomes anti–Native Hawaiian.[17]

As the ideology of localness, "aloha" elaborates a Kanaka Maoli concept of familial attachment into a byword for depoliticization. A ubiquitous greeting or a valence of love, "aloha" possesses a substantial record of institutionalization in Hawai'i. According to Keiko Ohnuma, its emergence as a public concern coincides with both the 1959 admission of the Territory of Hawai'i into the union as well as the expansion of commercial jet engine service.[18] "Administrative aloha" was effectively born in the wake of these developments, and the new Democratic leadership mobilized it to redirect the Hawai'i economy from agriculture to the nascent visitor industry.[19]

The state government of Hawai'i began branding the Hawaiian Islands from its inception, adopting "The Aloha State" as its nickname. In 1982, the Hawai'i State Legislature intensified commitment to the brand identity by passing the Aloha Spirit Law, which defines "aloha" as "mutual regard and affection [extending] warmth in caring with no obligation in return" at the same time as it codifies this sense of the term as an ethos in government practices. It is this central patterning of "aloha" as "welcome" that is flexibly manipulated by the (neoliberal) state to incorporate select social groups insofar as they prove to be lucrative niche markets.[20]

Queerness in Hawai'i

Administrative "aloha" indexes the state of Hawai'i's changing relation to queerness not through civic demonstrations and legislative appeals but via market research. For Matthew Link, the author of the 1999 *Rainbow Handbook Hawai'i: The Islands' Ultimate Gay Guide*, a formal extension of "aloha" to queer travelers was unthinkable in 2002; he recounts meetings with the Hawai'i Visitors and Convention Bureau (HVCB) proposing a marketing plan in coordination with Hawai'i gay business owners:

> After the course of two meetings with the Bureau, we were given the cold shoulder and basically told that they did not have the budget for such an undertaking. . . . They had no means in place for specialized campaigns, and that they 'target no one group in particular.'[21]

The modern history of same-sex rights claims in Hawai'i can be characterized in terms of court decisions but also in economic briefs in a vein similar to Link's. In this section, I canvas the legal history of same-sex recognitions in Hawai'i, its mutating relation to the economic pressures of an increasingly visible queer tourism market, and the ways in which "aloha" has been proffered by proponents of same-sex rights.

The case history of LGBT rights claims in Hawai'i most visibly begins from 1991, when three same-sex couples were denied marriage licenses by the state department of health.[22] In *Baehr v. Lewin*, the couples sought redress through Hawai'i courts but unintentionally prompted legislative pushback against same-sex rights claims from both the state and federal governments. In Washington, DC, implications of the Hawai'i suit garnered the attention of Congress, and the Defense of Marriage Act was passed and signed into law by President Clinton in 1996. In Hawai'i, a 1998 referendum to empower the legislature to define marriage as "between one man and one woman" was approved by 69 percent of Hawai'i voters, effectively mooting the standing of the pro-marriage plaintiffs in the lawsuit and silencing the viability of same-sex marriage in Hawai'i for over a decade.[23]

The economic argument for same-sex rights is less defined, as the evaluation of liberties in terms of cost-benefit analyses is an unpalatable metric in political transcripts. Nevertheless, the presence of economic appeals and even academic studies touting the value of fortifying Hawai'i's branding of diversity through legal recognition is noteworthy. A 2010 report by the UCLA Williams Institute on Sexual Orientation and Gender Identity Law and Public Policy underlines the potential job creation civil unions might entail, estimating an annual contribution of roughly $5,000,000 to the Hawai'i economy.[24] A study authored by University of Hawai'i economics professor Sumner La Croix offered a more compelling statement for the 2013 legislative session, projecting an impact of over $200,000,000 over a three-year period, or almost $200,000 per day.[25]

Interest in revisiting the matter of same-sex unions only gained traction in 2010, when a bill to legalize same-sex civil unions passed the state house and senate but was vetoed by then governor Linda Lingle. Two years later, as Senate Bill 232, civil unions legislation passed through both chambers of the Hawai'i State Legislature and was signed by then newly elected Governor Neil Abercrombie in February 2012.[26] Concurrent with landmark decisions from the U.S. Supreme Court striking down the Defense of Marriage Act (*United States v. Windsor*) and upholding same-sex marriage in California (*Hollingsworth v. Perry*), Abercrombie called for a special legislative session in October 2013, and the Hawai'i Marriage Equality Act was passed and signed into law by December 2013.[27]

The state of Hawai'i wasted little time integrating queerness into the commercial ambit of "administrative aloha." *Lei*, the magazine with which I began this account, is a product of this commitment. The issue I stumbled across—an accident—is the fourth of *Lei*'s annual publications, the first appearing in late 2013. While the feature article from which the image is pulled does not relay any claim to localness, the coordinates through which the model self-identifies—"Korean, Native American, German, and Spanish trans-masculine person (they/them)"—invoke the array of geographical sites that Hawai'i, patterned through administrative aloha as a "racial melting pot," proclaims as evidence of its multicultural makeup. Importantly, the model does not resemble older iterations of queer travel marketing to Hawai'i. Almost exclusively catered to gay male leisure travelers, these either openly presented Kanaka Maoli figures as sexual commodities or modeled the rarefied forms of Gauguin's primitivism. In fact, both are appropriate descriptions of the artwork featured on Link's *Rainbow Handbook. Lei* contrasts this with the slick aesthetics of state-funded, research-driven cosmopolitanism.[28] In its production of queer tourist marketing, *Lei*'s minimalism supplants overblown ostentation while phenotype (or its manipulation by image processing) abstracts from echoes of "the noble savage."

Lei, as a glossy invitation to queer tourists, is awkwardly introduced through "Letters of Aloha" from the Hawai'i state governor and the CEO of the state tourism agency. In the words of Governor David Ige,

> We encourage you to come discover a collection of beautiful islands that is remarkable in every respect and meet our people, who embrace the 'aloha spirit,' a mindset and way of life unmatched anywhere. . . .

As you enjoy the warmth of our hospitality, you will discover what I believe is the root of Hawai'i's appeal, the diversity of our people, the loveliness of this place, and the core values of our host culture in welcoming all visitors with acceptance and friendship.[29]

Ige and Hawai'i Tourism Authority (HTA) head George Szigeti employ the word "aloha" nine times in their generic greetings, arguing for its unique value alongside the fact of the state's "diverse" population as hospitality in itself. The global expansion of administrative "aloha" to queer markets is already underway, as the HTA announced results from its first LGBT market studies in 2016, with foci in three national markets—the United States (particularly Western markets like Seattle), Canada, and China.[30] In late 2017, the HTA published reports from preliminary studies of LGBT markets in Japan and Taiwan.[31]

Conclusion

As Keiko Ohnuma describes the experience of "aloha," "What makes (Hawai'i) appear so civilized (placid, slow-paced) to outsiders is this willingness to accept patiently and silently the many daily irritations that come with rapid, uneven development, crumbling infrastructure, a third-world economy, and an entrenched political regime hell-bent on luring more tourists, industry, hotels, and military installations—all in the interest of exemplifying that gracious social lubricant that has been called Hawai'i's 'gift to the world.'"[32] In this depiction, administrative "aloha" operates as a place-based fantasy—a narrativization of a culture's common sense or status quo, akin to other region-specific sensibilities like "Minnesota nice," "Seattle freeze," or even "Portland weird." They are the logics underpinning the continuity of a culture's social reality. Only recognizable as such in periods of crisis, the breakdown of these fantasies—the metaphysical confusion engendered in their failure to sufficiently rationalize the status quo—invites questioning of previously unquestioned values. Contemporary symptoms include disagreements over construction of rapid transit on O'ahu and solutions to homelessness.

Administrative "aloha," like mythic multiculturalism, homonormativity, and other schemes of incorporation, domesticates through recognition—it defangs opposition and perniciously disappears the conditions of protest in exchange for an abstract promise of inclusion and the dream of a carefree everydayness, a normal life.[33] Importantly, administrative "aloha" is disproportionate in its efficacy. My determinations, my sociocultural position as Asian or Japanese, make my relation to aloha relatively contingent—an accident. Someone whose identity is even partially determined by residence in Hawai'i or by Kanaka Maoli ancestry is less mobile—the conditions under which that person might elect to move and reject aloha are not as generous. Place has variable investment, a point that advocates of administrative aloha desperately obscure.[34]

Administrative aloha tacitly patterns opportunity over generations, obliging social reproduction to recognize that aloha qua tourism is unquestionable. To Haunani-Kay Trask's depiction of Kanaka Maoli resigned to participate in Hawai'i's visitor industry as performers in Waikiki hula shows and luau, "aloha" codes these scenes as inescapable. "Aloha" coerces its individual and collective avatars to a future of servitude in a tourist economy subject to Hawai'i's diminishing environment. To elaborate "aloha" as ideological is not to suggest that adopting coldness as a state ethos amounts to progress. Rather, it aims to produce a minimal difference, a critical difference, in accounting for the present. "Aloha" as it continues to be administrated is a misnomer for the opportunity cost of a sustainable economy, sentimentally obfuscated and fatalistically resigned to environmental destruction and intensified militarization.[35]

ACKNOWLEDGMENTS

Thank you to Suzanne Uratani for assistance in vetting source material.

NOTES

1. "Work It Out," *Lei*, 2017, 52.

2. Carter Schneider, "About," accessed March 26, 2018, http://www.carterschneider.com/about.

3. In this text, I distinguish the terms "LGBT" and "queer" by using the former when describing identity-based rights claims and the latter to note modes of desire and embodiment that exceed state recognition. "Queer" in my rendering echoes Eric O. Clarke's use of the term "indeterminate erotic expression." See Eric O Clarke, *Virtuous Vice: Homoeroticism and the Public Sphere* (Durham, NC: Duke University Press, 2000), 26.

4. "Spa Resorts in Hawaii | Mauna Lani Bay Hotel & Bungalows—Spa & Fitness," accessed March 17, 2018, https://www.maunalani.com/hawaii-spa-resorts.

5. Haunani-Kay Trask, *From a Native Daughter: Colonialism and Sovereignty in Hawai'i*, rev. ed. (Honolulu: University of Hawai'i Press, 1999), 140.

6. Stephanie Nohelani Teves, "Aloha State Apparatuses," *American Quarterly* 67, no. 3 (2015): 717.

7. Michel Foucault, "Nietzsche, Genealogy, History," in *The Foucault Reader*, edited by Paul Rabinow (New York: Pantheon, 1984), 81.

8. Judy Rohrer, *Staking Claim: Settler Colonialism and Racialization in Hawai'i* (Tucson: University of Arizona Press, 2017), 80.

9. Hokulani K. Aikau et al., "Indigenous Feminisms Roundtable," *Frontiers: A Journal of Women Studies* 36, no. 3 (2015): 86.

10. Jonathan Y. Okamura, *Ethnicity and Inequality in Hawai'i* (Philadelphia: Temple University Press, 2008), 8.

11. Robert C. Schmitt, *Demographic Statistics of Hawaii: 1778–1965* (Honolulu: University of Hawai'i Press, 1968), 25.

12. Noenoe K. Silva, *Aloha Betrayed: Native Hawaiian Resistance to American Colonialism* (Durham, NC: Duke University Press, 2004), 24.

13. Rohrer, *Staking Claim*, 61.

14. Jonathan Y. Okamura, *From Race to Ethnicity: Interpreting Japanese American Experiences in Hawai'i* (Honolulu: University of Hawai'i Press, 2014), 24.

15. Okamura, *Ethnicity and Inequality in Hawai'i*, 196.

16. Candace Fujikane, "Introduction: Asian Settler Colonialism in the U.S. Colony of Hawai'i," in *Asian Settler Colonialism: From Local Governance to the Habits of Everyday Life in Hawai'i*, edited by Candace Fujikane and Jonathan Okamura (Honolulu: University of Hawai'i Press, 2008), 5.

17. The Hawai'i group "Aloha 4 All" exemplifies this move, aiming to curtail institutions designated for Kanaka Maoli through the framework of American jurisprudence. Arguing that these resources are by nature racially discriminatory, the group leaders deny the specificity of indigenous Hawaiians' relation to Hawai'i. See Rohrer, *Staking Claim*, 146.

18. Keiko Ohnuma, "'Aloha Spirit' and the Cultural Politics of Sentiment as National Belonging," *The Contemporary Pacific* 20, no. 2 (2008): 370.

19. Okamura, *From Race to Ethnicity*, 104.

20. Clarke, *Virtuous Vice*, 13.

21. Matthew Link, "A Case-Study in Contradictions: Hawaii and Gay Tourism," in *Gay Tourism: Culture, Identity and Sex*, edited by Stephen Clift, Michael Luongo, and Carry Callister (New York: Continuum, 2002), 85.

22. *Baehr v. Lewin*, 74 Haw. 530 (1993).

23. Jonathan Goldberg-Hiller, *The Limits to Union: Same-Sex Marriage and the Politics of Civil Rights* (Ann Arbor: University of Michigan Press, 2002), 1.

24. Naomi G. Goldberg, Brad Sears, and M. V. Lee Badgett, "Potential Impact of HB444 on the State of Hawai'i," June 1, 2010, 1, https://williamsinstitute.law.ucla.edu /experts/lee-badgett/hb444-impact-hawaii/.

25. Sumner La Croix and Lauren Gabriel, "The Impact of Marriage Equality on Hawai'i's Economy and Government: An Update After the U.S. Supreme Court's Same-Sex Marriage Decisions," accessed February 8, 2018, http://www.uhero.hawaii.edu/news /view/244.

26. Chad Blair, "Hawaii Civil Unions Signed into Law," *Honolulu Civil Beat*, February 24, 2011, http://www.civilbeat.org/posts/2011/02/24/9233-hawaii-civil-unions-signed -into-law.

27. Mileka Lincoln, "Hawaii Becomes 15th State to Legalize Same-Sex Marriage," accessed March 26, 2018, http://www.hawaiinewsnow.com/story/23960302/breaking -gov-abercrombie-signs.

28. Derek Rushbrook, "Cities, Queer Space, and the Cosmopolitan Tourist," *GLQ: A Journal of Lesbian and Gay Studies* 8, no. 1–2 (2002): 188.

29. David Y. Ige, George D. Szigeti, and State of Hawai'i: Hawai'i Tourism Authority, "Letters of Aloha," *Lei*, 2017, 14.

30. "Target Lifestyle Segments—Hawaii Tourism Authority," accessed March 21, 2018, http://www.hawaiitourismauthority.org/research/reports/target-lifestyle-seg ments/.

31. Hawai'i Tourism Authority, "Hawaii Tourism Authority Issues LGBT Travel Studies for Japan, Taiwan Markets," accessed March 26, 2018, https://governor.hawaii .gov/newsroom/latest-news/hawaii-tourism-authority-issues-lgbt-travel-studies-for-japan -taiwan-markets/.

32. Ohnuma, "'Aloha Spirit' and the Cultural Politics of Sentiment as National Belonging," 365.

33. Lisa Duggan, *The Twilight of Equality?: Neoliberalism, Cultural Politics, and the Attack on Democracy* (Boston: Beacon, 2003), 50.

34. Teves, "Aloha State Apparatuses," 721.

35. Okamura, *From Race to Ethnicity*, 217.

BIBLIOGRAPHY

Aikau, Hokulani K., Maile Arvin, Mishuana Goeman, and Scott Morgensen. "Indigenous Feminisms Roundtable." *Frontiers: A Journal of Women Studies* 36, no. 3 (2015): 84–106.

Blair, Chad. "Hawaii Civil Unions Signed into Law." *Honolulu Civil Beat*, February 24, 2011. http://www.civilbeat.org/posts/2011/02/24/9233-hawaii-civil-unions-signed -into-law.

Clarke, Eric O. *Virtuous Vice: Homoeroticism and the Public Sphere.* Durham, NC: Duke University Press, 2000.

Duggan, Lisa. *The Twilight of Equality?: Neoliberalism, Cultural Politics, and the Attack on Democracy.* Boston: Beacon, 2003.

Foucault, Michel. "Nietzsche, Genealogy, History." In *The Foucault Reader*, edited by Paul Rabinow, 76–100. New York: Pantheon, 1984.

Fujikane, Candace. "Introduction: Asian Settler Colonialism in the U.S. Colony of Hawai'i." In *Asian Settler Colonialism: From Local Governance to the Habits of Everyday Life in Hawai'i*, edited by Candace Fujikane and Jonathan Okamura, 1–42. Honolulu: University of Hawai'i Press, 2008.

Goldberg, Naomi G., Brad Sears, and M. V. Lee Badgett. "Potential Impact of HB444 on the State of Hawai'i." Los Angeles: Williams Institute, June 1, 2010. https://williams institute.law.ucla.edu/experts/lee-badgett/hb444-impact-hawaii/.

Goldberg-Hiller, Jonathan. *The Limits to Union: Same-Sex Marriage and the Politics of Civil Rights.* Ann Arbor: University of Michigan Press, 2002.

Hawai'i Tourism Authority. "Hawaii Tourism Authority Issues LGBT Travel Studies for Japan, Taiwan Markets." Accessed March 26, 2018. https://governor.hawaii.gov /newsroom/latest-news/hawaii-tourism-authority-issues-lgbt-travel-studies-for-japan -taiwan-markets/.

Ige, David Y., George D. Szigeti, and State of Hawai'i: Hawai'i Tourism Authority. "Letters of Aloha." *Lei*, 2017.

La Croix, Sumner, and Lauren Gabriel. "The Impact of Marriage Equality on Hawai'i's Economy and Government: An Update After the U.S. Supreme Court's Same-Sex Marriage Decisions | UHERO." Honolulu: UHERO, The Economic Research Organization at the University of Hawai'i, February 2013. http://www.uhero.hawaii.edu /news/view/244.

Lincoln, Mileka. "Hawaii Becomes 15th State to Legalize Same-Sex Marriage." Accessed March 26, 2018. http://www.hawaiinewsnow.com/story/23960302/breaking-gov-ab ercrombie-signs.

Link, Matthew. "A Case-Study in Contradictions: Hawaii and Gay Tourism." In *Gay Tourism: Culture, Identity and Sex*, edited by Stephen Clift, Michael Luongo, and Carry Callister, 63–87. New York: Continuum, 2002.

Ohnuma, Keiko. "'Aloha Spirit' and the Cultural Politics of Sentiment as National Belonging." *The Contemporary Pacific* 20, no. 2 (2008): 365–394.

Okamura, Jonathan Y. *Ethnicity and Inequality in Hawai'i*. Philadelphia: Temple University Press, 2008.

———. *From Race to Ethnicity: Interpreting Japanese American Experiences in Hawai'i*. Honolulu: University of Hawai'i Press, 2014.

Rohrer, Judy. *Staking Claim: Settler Colonialism and Racialization in Hawai'i*. Tucson: University of Arizona Press, 2017.

Rushbrook, Derek. "Cities, Queer Space, and the Cosmopolitan Tourist." *GLQ: A Journal of Lesbian and Gay Studies* 8, no. 1–2 (2002): 183–206.

Schmitt, Robert C. *Demographic Statistics of Hawaii: 1778–1965*. Honolulu: University of Hawai'i Press, 1968.

Schneider, Carter. "About." Carter Schneider's Portfolio. Accessed March 26, 2018. http://www.carterschneider.com/about.

Silva, Noenoe K. *Aloha Betrayed: Native Hawaiian Resistance to American Colonialism*. Durham, NC: Duke University Press, 2004.

"Spa Resorts in Hawaii | Mauna Lani Bay Hotel & Bungalows—Spa & Fitness." Accessed March 17, 2018. https://www.maunalani.com/hawaii-spa-resorts.

"Target Lifestyle Segments—Hawaii Tourism Authority." Accessed March 21, 2018. http://www.hawaiitourismauthority.org/research/reports/target-lifestyle-segments/.

Teves, Stephanie Nohelani. "Aloha State Apparatuses." *American Quarterly* 67, no. 3 (2015): 705–26.

Trask, Haunani-Kay. *From a Native Daughter: Colonialism and Sovereignty in Hawai'i*. Rev. ed. Honolulu: University of Hawai'i Press, 1999.

"Work It Out." *Lei*, 2017.

PART III

Building Justice

Queer Movements in Asian North America

In All Our Splendid Selves

A Roundtable Discussion on Queer API Activism
in Three Political Moments

Eric Estuar Reyes and Eric C. Wat

Queer Asian and Pacific Islander (API) activism has always been a part of a broader struggle for social justice. For queer APIs in particular who are engaged on multiple fronts, whether within ourselves, our families, or across our various communities of belonging, the fight has always been about a sense of togetherness, a sense of place, a sense of home. As Karin Aguilar-San Juan succinctly wrote in the first *Q&A*, "Precisely because of the high price at which queer Asian America purchases a sense of home, our motivation toward building community and enacting justice must be stronger" (Aguilar-San Juan 1998, 38). In this essay, we share the voices of four queer API activists in Southern California who have helped us build and enact justice stronger for ourselves and others.

The four activists, Ric Parish, Gina Masequesmay, Jury Candelario, and riKu Matsuda, agreed to meet with us to share their stories in early 2018.[1] While these four, and our own two voices, surely cannot represent the full range of social justice work in LGTBQ communities, we offer this essay as a window into the challenges and successes of queer API activism in Southern California from the early 1990s to the late 2010s.[2] The essay is clearly Western-centric, and specifically Southern California–centric. Regardless, the essay provides us with insights into three moments in the past twenty or so years that represent focal points for queer API activism: HIV and AIDS, marriage equality, and trans rights. We use "moments" instead of "movement" to emphasize the temporal aspect of social change activism—each has a time, a place, and a set of actors in which specific strategies work (or don't work). In a political moment, an issue may achieve enough momentum in a community or meaningfulness in someone's life to spur them to action, broadening the base for a movement. Political moments also offer movement activists an opportunity to link current struggle to address broader inequities, build allyship, and pivot their work after a setback or victory. This essay describes how the panelists' stories of activism illustrate these political moments at work and raise important questions as our community prepares for the next moment in political organizing.

The four panelists were invited because of their history with the three political moments of HIV and AIDS, marriage equality, and trans rights. We also tried to bring diverse experiences to the table in terms of ethnicity, gender identity, nativity, and age, with the caveat that four people cannot represent the spectrum of identities in the queer API community.

Ric Parish, a Filipino African American gay man living with HIV, is one of the cofounders of Asian Pacific AIDS Intervention Team (APAIT) in 1992. In 1991, Ric met Joël B. Tan, another APAIT cofounder, while protesting against California Governor Pete Wilson's veto of AB 101, which would have prohibited discrimination in housing and employment on the basis of sexual orientation. Joël subsequently invited Ric to a meeting of Colors United Action Coalition (CUAC), and from there Ric began his lifelong involvement in social justice struggles. Focusing on antiracist, anticlassist, and antiheteropatriarchal politics, CUAC reached out to other LGBTQ radical groups of the time, such as AIDS Coalition to Unleash Power (ACT-UP) and Queer Nation. Through these attempts to collaborate, Ric learned the different ways that HIV phobia, racism against APIs, and ignorance about gendered and sexual diversities pervaded these so-called radical groups, who don't all share the same priorities, values, and practices. As a result, he was committed to carving out a viable space for queer people of color community organizing. During the early years of APAIT, he pioneered treatment advocacy for people living with HIV and helped develop its first groundbreaking social marketing campaign, "Love Your Asian Body" (1992), which addressed deep stigmas around same-sex desire between API men. APAIT was also one of the earliest AIDS service organizations to develop women's and transgender programming.

Gina Masequesmay, a Vietnamese American immigrant lesbian, has engaged with social justice issues in Vietnamese American, API, and LGBTQ communities for nearly the past twenty-five years. In the 1990s, she worked as a community organizer with East-West Community Partnership before returning to graduate school at UCLA. While at UCLA, she conducted ethnographic research at Asian Pacific AIDS Intervention Team and co-organized Mahu, a queer API student organization. In the community, she was instrumental in the development of Ô-Môi, a support group for Vietnamese lesbians, bisexual women, and FTM transgenders. In this essay, she discussed transgender inclusion in Ô-Môi in the late 1990s and her experience organizing a queer Vietnamese contingent at the Tet parades in Little Saigon, especially during those years when marriage equality drew a lot of controversies in that community. She is currently professor of Asian American Studies at California State University at Northridge, where she has taught since 2004. As an academic, she has published numerous essays on LGBTQ issues, including her ethnographic research on both APAIT and

Ô-Môi. More recently, as she delves more deeply into her spiritual identity, Gina has turned to addressing queer concerns in the Buddhist community by organizing a LGBTQ Buddhist retreat in the Plum Village tradition and starting a dialogue with monks and nuns about inclusive language in order to help them connect with LGBTQ communities.

Jury Candelario, a Filipino American gay man and an immigrant, has worked at the Asian Pacific AIDS Intervention Team since 1995 and has been its director since 2003. He began his AIDS activism as a buddy for people living with HIV. Over the years, he welcomed new opportunities and expanded his leadership roles in HIV and AIDS, both locally and nationally. As part of the "second generation" of APAIT activists and with the mentorship of APAIT's founding director, Dean Goishi, Jury soon found himself challenging the status quo within institutions at the local, state, and national levels. He has worked with a range of groups including National Association of People with AIDS, White House Initiative on Asian Americans and Pacific Islanders, Office of National AIDS Policy, State of California Legislature Health Committee, National Minority AIDS Council, American Public Health Association, Asian Pacific Policy and Planning Council, and the California State Asian Pacific Islanders Community Action Network. He was also a cofounder of the local Act Now against Meth Coalition. Under his leadership, APAIT has successfully adapted to the changing AIDS funding structure and thrived as the agency, through cultivating relationships with other communities of color as well as embracing the trans community and nurturing its leaders. Jury was also a founding member of API Equality-LA, which spearheaded the marriage equality campaign locally in the API community.

riKu Matsuda has been a social justice activist since high school and has worked at the Los Angeles County Commission on Human Relations for the past seventeen years, where he leads the commission's work to end violence against trans and nonbinary communities. A transman of both Japanese and White heritage, riKu began youth organizing in 1995 at his high school in Antelope Valley. Identifying as a lesbian at the time, riKu sought out a lesbian of color community at California State University, Long Beach, where he received his undergraduate degree. After college, he was recruited by Californians for Justice to organize young people around several ballot initiatives at the time, including Prop 22, which defined marriage only as something between a man and a woman. He then worked as a youth organizer at Khmer Girls in Action in Long Beach (2001–2003) on reproductive health issues. His activism mirrored his gender transition, initially working on youth and lesbian of color issues and over the years focusing on trans rights and queer human rights. In addition to his work at the commission, he cofounded qteam, a radical collection of queer and trans youth of color, and cochaired Okaeri 2014: A Nikkei LGBTQ Gathering. Since 2003, riKu has been the host and programmer for the weekly radio program "Flip the Script" on KPFK, a progressive public radio station in LA.

Discussion: The Three Political Moments

We facilitated the discussion to help the four panelists map out their history of activism within each of the three political moments: HIV and AIDS, marriage equality, and trans rights. The following is a synthesis of our conversation.

HIV and AIDS

> We were pushing on all fronts. We were pushing against a system, a healthcare system, that didn't recognize us as sexual beings, therefore we were not "at risk". We were pushing against a community that was in fear, and total silence, to get them to come forward and just talk about HIV and AIDS. And we were pushing against this overall perception of what it meant to be queer API.
>
> —RIC PARISH

HIV and AIDS did not mark the genesis of queer API organizing. Prior to the AIDS epidemic, organizations by and for API lesbians and gay men had formed around the United States since the seventies and early eighties.[3] Many of them were inspired by the first National March on Washington for Lesbian and Gay Rights in 1979 or by the innate desire to create safe space, after experiencing alienation in the broader Asian American or Gay Liberation Movements. Many of these organizations were support groups for API lesbians and gay men, where they could safely socialize with each other and provide support against racism, sexism, and homophobia from the outside world. However, attempts to be more politically active often created tension among a membership who preferred to remain anonymous.[4]

The AIDS epidemic offered a unique space for API lesbians and gay men to build a more outward-facing movement. At a protest against then Governor Pete Wilson's veto of AB 101 in 1991, Ric Parish remembers meeting a group of Filipinos, especially a gay man holding up a sign that said, "Drop Wilson into Mount Pinatubo." Ric said to himself, "I need to meet him." That man turned out to be Joël B. Tan, who later invited Parish to an organization he was forming called Colors United Action Coalition. Ric recalls, "They were a group of progressive, mostly college-age students, who wanted to see change." Recognizing how discrimination in housing and employment against LGBT people (which AB 101 would have outlawed) was connected to healthcare access and HIV and AIDS discrimination, the API caucus within CUAC began working with a working committee within Asian/Pacific Lesbians and Gays (A/PLG) called the AIDS Intervention Team, which was providing education and support for mostly A/PLG members. Despite its name, by the early 1990s, A/PLG did not have any lesbian members.[5] Ric observes, "We brought the lesbians in. That was shocking to them.[6] Suddenly the tail is wagging the dog."

Dean Goishi, an A/PLG cofounder who was heading up the AIDS Intervention Team at the time, shares that the general membership was not invested in working on HIV and AIDS because they did not think they were at risk. And the CUAC contingent of younger activists were not interested in the social mission of A/PLG, let alone paying its membership dues.[7] In 1992, the AIDS Intervention Team formally separated from A/PLG, and Dean, Ric, and Joël went on to cofound Asian Pacific AIDS Intervention Team (APAIT), which is still in existence today. The history of the local AIDS movement is yet another example of the tension that arose when a lesbian and gay organization negotiated between its original mission of providing a safe space for its members and its potential role to be a more public advocate for the community. In some way, the AIDS movement benefited from the established network and infrastructure at the time while at the same time challenged its insular strategies, marking a significant moment in the evolution of our community.

Doing AIDS work in the API community was challenging early on. Ric says, "What was really frustrating is that there was this idea that API gay men did not get AIDS because the numbers [incidence rate] were so low. We had always submitted that the numbers are low because nobody's getting tested." This misconception of low risk in the API community gave API gay men a false sense of confidence, exemplified by the indifference among A/PLG's general membership. The "low numbers" also had funding and policy implications: it became a justification for the county not to allocate resources to address the epidemic in API community. Ric continues, "So the first thing we had to do is, we had to go into the bars, do outreach, and get people to get tested. That was a huge challenge in and of itself. . . . The owner of Mugi's [a gay Asian bar in Hollywood, which is now Thai Town] told us, 'You're going to scare away all our customers with this AIDS stuff.' He put us way in the corner by the exit door. But we pushed, and we pushed. We were pushing on all fronts. We were pushing against a healthcare system that didn't recognize us as sexual beings, therefore we were not 'at risk.' We were pushing against a community that was in fear and total silence . . . We were pushing against this overall perception of what it meant to be queer API."

The major push came in 1992, when APAIT developed its first social marketing campaign to encourage HIV testing called "Love Your Asian

Body." The idea was sparked at a coffeehouse in West Hollywood, where Ric and Joël overheard a Filipino gay man at the next table complaining how his nose was "so flat." Ric recalls that Joël stood up and said, "Honey, love yo' Asian body." Ric instantly thought it sounded like "a good tagline." The campaign included a series of four postcards to be distributed during outreach. All four featured images of queer, sex-positive, Asian-Asian intimacy. The models, all APAIT staff or volunteers, were naked or seminaked, straddling or touching each other. The postcards were provocative and sexy. Three of them were gay male-identified, and one lesbian-identified. These postcards were also placed as advertisements in the gay newspapers. As a campaign, the images created a new image of Asian queer sexuality that was specifically for and by the API LGBTQ community.

These provocatively sexy and joyously fun images contradicted the preponderance of public health messages about AIDS at the time, which were prohibitive, alienating, and downright depressing. Even more significant was how the campaign also challenged the prevailing sexual ideology in the gay community that prized white men over men of color and denied gay Asian men their sexual agency.[8] Translated in five Asian languages, the "Love Your Asian Body" campaign pervaded Los Angeles County. Ric adds, "We did radio spots. We did posters. We just papered LA with this testing campaign. It had mixed results, but it got people talking . . . In order to create a community, we got to get people to come forward and be part of the community." APAIT became a space for many progressive LGBTQ API individuals to test out their new identities, find communities, and hone their activism.

Gina Masequesmay was such an individual. When Gina came to APAIT, she was a UCLA graduate student looking for a community organization for her ethnography assignment. Gina was no stranger to political activism. She was a community organizer prior to her graduate studies, but she had not explicitly worked on LGBTQ issues. She was interested in APAIT because, she says, "I had some inkling that maybe I'm gay but not quite sure." Her ambivalence must have been palpable. When her contact at APAIT introduced her to Unhei Kang, APAIT volunteer coordinator, he said, "This is Gina. She's in the process of coming out." Unhei asked Gina if she was a lesbian, to which she replied, "I'm about to find out."

More than a space for young LGBTQ APIs to develop their sexual identity and political analysis, APAIT worked with and supported other LGBTQ API organizations that were proliferating in Southern California in the 1990s.[9] For example, APAIT staff person Unhei Kang and APAIT advisory board member Connie Wong cochaired Los Angeles Asian Pacific Islander Sisters, an organization for API lesbians and bisexual women, and collaborated on many events such as safer sex workshops and dances.[10] Another APAIT staff Diep Tran expanded her outreach activities to include events she helped plan with Ô-Môi, which she also belonged to, with the blessings of Dean Goishi, then the APAIT director.[11] Similarly, Gina also recalls that Ô-Môi received some resources in the beginning from another community organization in Orange County, which, after some advocacy by Gay Vietnamese Alliance (GVA) leaders, was starting to allocate its HIV funding beyond gay men.

Early AIDS activism has always been about more than just the disease. Ric and other API members within CUAC saw the connection between AIDS and broader discrimination against LGBTQ people and used the AIDS movement as a vehicle to address multiple issues. Their organizing created a social space for a new generation to build critical self-consciousness, self-esteem, and political empowerment, which ultimately shaped a new collective identity. By advocating for people with HIV, one of the most marginalized groups in our communities, early AIDS activists found the need to combat homophobia and racism everywhere—on different levels (individual, family, community), in different institutions (businesses, schools, government), and in cultural representations (or lack thereof). Their success uplifted all LGBTQ API, regardless of their HIV status.

APAIT continues this work on multiple fronts, under the current leadership of Jury Candelario. He recalls a recent incident in 2016, when Christopher Street West (CSW), which organizes the annual pride parade and festival in West Hollywood, featured mainstream pop acts like Carly Rae Jepsen and Charli XCX and planned to raise ticket prices to the event while "cutting historical components like the Dyke March and Trans Social." APAIT spearheaded a #NotMyPride campaign with diverse community partners, blasting CSW for "a blatant commercialization of Pride and a disregard of Los Angeles' LGBT community history and legacy."[12] In response to this community pressure, CSW eventually restored programming for women's and trans communities and made the event more accessible.[13] This example shows how APAIT continues to challenge and adapt to emerging (and sometime repeated) instances where ostensible social justice groups hypocritically recreate systems of oppression. A year later, with the dawn of the Trump administration, APAIT joined forces with CSW and other groups. Peter Cruz, then associate director at APAIT and a leader of the #NotMyPride campaign the year before, represented the agency on the planning committee to turn the annual pride parade into a #Resist march to voice a collective opposition to the Trump administration.

Jury believes that such coalition efforts are both the continuing legacy of API AIDS activism in Los Angeles as well as the key to APAIT's growth in the future. He points to how his outlook grew from his experience working his first job at APAIT as the substance use coordinator, as part of a Gay Men of Color Consortium project in the mid-1990s. Jury recalls, "I had this excitement of getting to work with other communities of color, and to this very day, that's still a very impactful process for me. Leading into the fourth decade of the epidemic, recognizing that we're in a diverse city like Los Angeles, we've approached our delivery of services to address the issues of communities of color, not just Asians. I think that's how we continue to survive today. Outside of Hawai'i, we're the only API-led [AIDS service] organization that's funded by the Centers for Disease Control on HIV within the 48 contiguous states." He cites an example of "next-level" coalition building across communities and sectors: APAIT partners with the Children's Hospital Los Angeles, the LGBT Center, and TransLatin@ Coalition to run a Trans Wellness Center that is colocated at APAIT's office in Koreatown.

Marriage Equality

> We weren't just angry, but we wanted to make change in a positive way, and we used same-sex marriage. Even though I didn't care for that that much, because marriage [is a] patriarchal institution.
> —GINA MASEQUESMAY

While HIV and AIDS created an immediate sense of urgency and crisis, its direct impact on API LGBTQ communities as a rallying cry for mobilizing political and social action is very different than marriage equality. Three panelists, Jury, Gina, and riKu, who were active at different points in the fifteen-year struggle for marriage equality in California,[14] might not have chosen marriage equality as the top priority for their activism. But like HIV and AIDS, the political moment made this issue a viable vehicle for these activists to confront homophobia and fundamental human rights in API LGBTQ communities.

In 2000, riKu was an undergraduate student at California State University, Long Beach. Having been a high school student activist and identifying as a lesbian at the time, he was looking for youth organizing opportunities, especially those related to lesbians of color. riKu was recruited by Erin O'Brien, an organizer at Californians for Justice, a statewide organization that was organizing students locally against both Prop 21[15] and Prop 22. riKu believes that Erin approached him because of their "hapa and queer connection"; like riKu at the time, Erin is a biracial queer woman. riKu accepted the job offer because of the opportunity to work with youth to talk about queer issues in the community. "I wasn't quite thinking marriage is something we need now," riKu explains. He recalls being harassed by a man on campus who thought that marriage should be between a man and a woman. "We fought and we fought, and I tried to get him kicked off campus. It was a lot." The episode angered him so much that despite his reservations about the marriage institution, he began to see its "radical" potential to rattle the status quo. He wasn't alone.

In 2005, hundreds of Chinese Americans led by the conservative Christian clergies came together in San Gabriel Valley to protest against same-sex marriage and LGBTQ equality. The organizing from LGBTQ activists to counter this protest spurred the beginning of API Equality-Los Angeles (APIELA). At its tenth-year anniversary, cofounder Marshall Wong reflected on this incident: "It was a jarring sight: hundreds of Chinese people, young and old, led by religious extremists, carrying signs with hateful messages denigrating the LGBT community. Even more distressing was that these protests went virtually unchallenged, and coverage by the Chinese-language media made it appear that homophobia was a Chinese cultural norm."[16] Jury, also a cofounder, states that the deliberate attack from the Christian right in "our own community" demanded a response and catapulted same-sex marriage as a priority civil rights issue for community leaders like him, Marshall, and other APIELA cofounders. Jury adds, "We were social workers, lawyers, all activists in our own right. But we said, 'Let's come together and address this.'" When the religious conservatives turned out in the San Gabriel Valley again ten years later to oppose the 2015 Supreme Court decision to legalize same-sex marriage, APIELA members were ready with their counterprotests that dwarfed their opponents.[17]

Of all the activities APIELA did to promote marriage equality, the one that attracted the most participation from members and allies was marching in the annual Lunar New Year parade in Los Angeles Chinatown. At its peak in 2009, a few months after Prop 8 was passed, the marriage equality contingent organized by APIELA brought out over two hundred people. The queer API contingent continued to be the largest in the parade in subsequent years. Their presence was widely reported in ethnic Chinese media. The sheer size, length, and noise level of the contingent, as well as the cheering from supporters among the spectators in this very public yet ethnic-specific space, challenged the prevailing ideology that same-sex marriage was inconsistent with cultural norms in the Chinese community. Although "it got better and better over the years" in terms of participation and community reception, Jury thinks that the first year they marched is a unique form of activism because it caused the most disruption. "Just being out and proud in a relatively conservative community that doesn't necessarily accept LGBTQ, let alone this issue of marriage equality, address the whole core mission of API Equality LA, which is to change hearts and minds, one individual, one family, at a time."

Queer Vietnamese, at least in Northern California, have an even longer tradition of marching in their community's Tet Parade, though their contingent was not always organized around the marriage equality struggle but for more general visibility and representation. Gina remembers going to San Jose and marching with her peers as early as 2004. "Chị [older sister] Vương [Nguyễn] was the key person," Gina says. "She started a one-hour radio program [in San Jose] on Sunday to talk about gay issues. And so we marched with the radio station, and [were] shunned by other programs that didn't want to be associated with us." In later years, the contingent grew so big that the organizers could register as a group separate from the radio station. It was not until 2010 when Ô-Môi (where Gina played a leadership role) and Gay Vietnamese Alliance (GVA) organized their own queer contingent in the Tet Parade in Orange County. Spurred by the news coverage of LGBTQ teen suicides, the organizers decided that they should have a more visible presence in the Viet communities. She recalls, "The people who live in Orange County didn't want to be out, because they didn't want to be harassed afterwards. So it was mostly folks from outside of Orange County who came down to march. That first one was pretty successful. There was hate and resistance by the community, but we pushed forward. I think we debunked some of the stereotypes that they had."

The queer contingent in Orange County highlighted marriage equality in their message at the parade to match the festivity of the new year. They wanted to project a positive message that "LGBTIQ folks are part of the Vietnamese family and we need to protect and love each other." By then, Ô-Môi and GVA already had some ideas on how to incorporate that message in a more culturally appropriate way from their experience marching in San Jose's Tet Parade. In that parade, Gina recalls two straight women had marched in tuxes as part of the contingent as a same-sex couple. "They were not even lesbians," Gina says. "They were allies who wanted to help out. [The tuxes] just doesn't feel right with the Vietnamese cultural aspect of it. So if we're going to do same-sex marriage, we're going to do it more in a Vietnamese way. We were dressed up in more traditional *áo dài*. I think that worked better. That was the thing that caught people's attention. 'Oh, they're not scary men-women who are trying to convert our children. They actually look really nice. They look cute.' There were these surprise commentaries, like how good we looked. I think that helped the change in the perception of our community members."

The choice of clothing was more than just a matter of what was worn (i.e., the more culturally appropriate *áo dài* vs. the Western formal wear), but it was also about who was wearing it (i.e., women wearing men's clothes, in the case of the parade in San Jose). The adjustment also had to do with local conditions: In Orange County, the Interfaith Council of Vietnamese America had taken a public stance that homosexuality was anti-Vietnamese. As a result, the organizers wanted to change negative stereotypes about LGBTQ people and opted not to shock the community with cross-dressing. But their decision did not come without controversy. Gina recalls, "That became a struggle within the community. There were folks who were like 'We're here. We're queer. Get used to it.' They were ready to come in all aspects of our splendid selves. But others said, 'No, one step at a time. Let's make it palatable first. Once they're okay, then we will up it a notch every year.'"

Some parade organizers and Vietnamese American community leaders, like the conservative Interfaith Council, tried to exclude the queer contingent in subsequent years. Even the ethnic Vietnamese media tried to provoke a fight. Gina explains, "Every year they [the Vietnamese newspapers] ask queer couple to kiss and they would take pictures and then make a big deal. 'Oh, my God, they're kissing.' As if it's something really horrible. But then there were women dancing on poles in these convertibles, and that's not very family-friendly." Ironically, their vitriol provoked a strong reaction from the local community that had been relatively dormant. Gina says, "For a while, we had had several series of news articles in the Vietnamese American community about LGBT issues, but people didn't seem to pay attention as much until the Tet Parade in Little Saigon. [Same-sex marriage] became somehow a lot bigger because that is so symbolic for the Vietnamese. I think these protests and attempts to reject us were helpful for the community to become more open about it."

As a result of this public debate, Gina continues, "A younger group of folks from Orange County stood up and said *No!* and fought back." This resistance gave rise to Viet Rainbow of Orange County (VROC).[18] So in the span of those years, Gina highlights noticeable cultural shifts in the local Vietnamese American community, not only in terms of the emergence of a younger and more grassroots leadership but also in terms of allies, like parents and friends. Gina observes that these allies are "speaking out and lending support." More significantly, "their Vietnamese are a lot better, so that helps, too, because we [queers] are kind of considered whitewashed, Westernized." Against the religious backlash, Gina also sees the beginning of some change in the religious sector; individual faith leaders had called the organizers to offer private support and encouragement. She laments, though, that these faith leaders are not ready to "be in public and stand up for [us] because [they] don't want to create conflict. So we always had non-Vietnamese religious folks walking with us."

Trans Rights

> All of us know that we didn't turn trans at eighteen. I want our communities to think about newborn people as people who have so much potential, and not map onto our little baby bodies these identities.
> —RIKU MATSUDA

Unlike HIV and AIDS and marriage equality, there hasn't been a consolidated movement for trans rights in the local API communities in Southern California. With the passing of the marriage equality moment, some movement activists are considering how to pivot from that victory to prioritize issues important to the trans population. Much of the discussion among the four panelists about trans rights focused on the possibility of the moment, and they raised important questions for the future of our community organizing.

Although there has not been a cohesive movement (yet), trans rights arguably have shown up in the history of local queer API activism in specific moments, with varying results. In HIV and AIDS activism, the first social marketing campaign at APAIT targeting API transwomen, called "Bionic Woman," was started by the first transgender staff in the mid-1990s. Since then, the trans presence at APAIT, as staff or clients, has flourished under Jury's leadership. He notes how HIV funding is one of the few federal funding streams that name the trans community as a specific target population even as API-specific funding has declined. By creating a supportive institution and culture at APAIT, Jury has helped trans staff to broaden their work beyond HIV and AIDS to engage with broader trans rights through community building and political activism.

In local queer Vietnamese women's organizing, transgender issues were not so easily supported at the beginning. In her participant observation study in 2002, Gina documents the challenges faced by Ô-Môi as it tried to involve transgender members from its initial roots as a queer Vietnamese women's space in the late 1990s and early 2000s.[19] For example, when a member came out as male-identified early on, he challenged Ô-Môi's mission and membership policy. Gina recalls, "We didn't really work it out. Some of us who wanted to learn did learn, and try to be more respectful in the language that we use. But others were horrible. They talked about trans people as 'women who hate their bodies.'" The challenges to inclusion reflected a lack of understanding about transgender identity and experience that not all members were ready to rectify at the time.

Another critical challenge is to move away from the assumption that how we talk and fight for social justice can be expressed universally across languages. The incorrect assumption that linguistic language is the same as cultural language has a significant implication in promoting trans rights in immigrant communities. For instance, Gina quips that journalists and community leaders in the Vietnamese community were often confused about the names that queer Vietnamese activists had used to identify themselves. She says, "People didn't know who we were. We were using formal [Sino-]Vietnamese. We didn't use the negative Vietnamese terms, so they didn't understand. We had these names and they were just like, 'It's too long,' or they were confused what the words meant." Ô-Môi had a newsletter and listserv, and organizers were used to translating between Vietnamese and English. In doing so, they had created a vocabulary. However, she continues, "Recently I had to do something, so I looked back at my list of vocabulary words translated into Vietnamese, and I thought, 'Oh my God, this stuff is so outdated.' And then all these new terms, like 'cisgenderism.' Shoot, how am I going to translate that?" Gina expresses the challenge of translating emerging ways of understanding gender fluidity into Vietnamese language both linguistically and culturally.

Drawing parallels from Gina's experiences with Tet parades, riKu highlights the trans community's struggle for visibility. He has witnessed trans activists stopping pride parades in Los Angeles, Long Beach, and San Diego "to do a direct action, like a die-in, to talk about the murders of trans people, or violence against trans people. That's been amazing to see." One key difference he sees is that these actions were more transgressive and confrontational than the "respectability politics" espoused by the marriage equality activists in ethnic-specific spaces.

As the panelists delved deeper into the discussion around trans rights, the idea of allies or allyship emerged as an important concept. In political movements, allies are individuals who take on another's struggle as their own even though they may not directly benefit from it. In fact, most allies have some form of privilege that the population affected by an issue could not claim, and allies often use this privilege in support of the struggle, while making room for others to direct the movement.[20] Allyship is not important only to trans movement. The AIDS movement count many women as its allies. In marriage quality, as discussed above, much of the cultural change in our communities was the result of activists working with straight allies.

The Okaeri conferences, which sought "to welcome and provide a safe and productive space" for LGBTQ members of the Nikkei community and their families and allies, demonstrate a unique API-specific model of culture change through allyship. For instance, riKu, who cochaired the first conference in 2014, remembers hearing grandmothers talk openly about their lesbian granddaughters. That year, riKu's cochair on the planning committee was Marsha Aizumi, mother of a trans man and an author and advocate.[21] Both trans presence and the idea of allyship were even more evident in the conference in 2016. In addition to a significant number of trans plenary speakers, workshop facilitators, and conference participants, some of the workshops included "Genderful Self," "Allyship Teach-In," and "Intergenerational Trauma and Healing." The workshop on "Acceptance and Love" was geared toward parents "to keep families connected" and sought to shift the burden of gaining acceptance from queer folks to their straight allies.

Okaeri 2016's opening keynote featured former congressman Mike Honda, his daughter Michelle Honda-Phillips, and her nine-year-old trans daughter Malisa Phillips. On the other end of the age spectrum, the morning plenary on "Transgender Voices" (moderated by riKu) included Hoshina Seki, the president of the American Buddhist Study Center and an octogenarian transgender woman who had just begun her transition in her sixties. During Q&A, Seki shared that she wanted to be known as a woman, intimating that passing was the ultimate goal. This caused quite a stir among younger trans conferencegoers during later breakout sessions, who took umbrage at Seki's belief in passing as the end goal for trans rights. riKu thinks that the younger trans participants were "pushing back against the [male-female] binary and prescriptive ways of being trans." This intergenerational disagreement underscores how Seki developed her trans identity in a different era under a different gender and sexual ideology and norm, and how a much more public and collective trans identity has evolved since the late twentieth century. Similar to how HIV and AIDS provided a platform for many API LGBTQ to develop a more outward-facing and justice-oriented identity, the current trans rights moment can create new possibilities for this generation of activists.

The panelists also agreed that the current political moment around trans rights heightens their expectations of allyship. riKu explains, "I think we should be talking about sex positivity with the straight cisgenders. People who are raising kids, even though they're cool with us, because they're related to us, or they grew up with us, they're not cool if we are *their* kids. They're not there yet. We're one more generation away from, 'You're queer. Yes! I thought so. I hope so.' All of us know that we didn't turn trans at eighteen. I want our communities to think about newborn people as people who have so much potential, and not map onto our little baby bodies these identities." Similarly, Gina cites Marsha Aizumi as a model of allyship. She says, "Even with accepting parents, they feel bad because they think your life will be harder. That's just parents being parents, I guess. But some parents like Marsha are like, 'Well, I'm going to make our society a better world.' And she goes out and does that, which is really amazing." Both riKu and Gina are issuing a clarion call for allies to go beyond individual acceptance and private support to collective activism and public advocacy.

Reflections and Conclusion

The four panelists discussed how queer API activism in the three political moments of HIV and AIDS, marriage equality, and trans rights contributed to cultural shifts in the local API community. Ric recounted how in the fight against AIDS, activists had to combat racism in the LGBTQ community and homophobia in the API community. In so doing, they created a space for a younger generation to cultivate an intersectional identity based on social justice. Jury reminded us the importance of building coalitions with other communities and embracing the more marginalized populations in our communities. Gina cautioned us about the challenges of changing community norms and confronting our own biases so that we could be more inclusive. riKu shared her aspirations about the kind of allyship that can make trans issues front and center of our queer API organizing. Together, the panelists provide clear illustrations of how the experience of social justice activism in API LGBTQ communities almost inevitably begins with and continues to be about shifting cultural norms, behaviors, practices, and expectations.

In our reflections, we were particularly captivated by the panelists' discussion on allyship. Gina and riKu talk about how straight allies have been instrumental in their respective work in the Viet and Nikkei communities, respectively. The panelists' call for allyship—the public, activist kind[22]—will be key to our current political moment. In the fight for trans rights, we wonder whether we should conceive allies beyond straight people and call out cisgender gay, lesbian, and bisexual people as well for their role in the movement. Some local organizations are still trying to pivot from the marriage equality victories and hold on to volunteers and activists—straight and queer—who may find it's "just not as fun to be involved in [the movement]."[23] As we have learned from Ric and Jury about the AIDS movement, a collective struggle on behalf of one of the most marginalized populations (i.e., people living with HIV) can lift up and empower the entire LGBTQ community. Similarly, a community unified in advancing trans rights can ultimately improve the quality of life of cisgender queer people. How do we harness the energy from political moments that had some success, like HIV and AIDS and marriage equality, and channel it in the service of more challenging struggles to come?

We know that a cursory history of local queer API activism will not yield a blueprint for everyone in our community. Instead of ending with a broad call for action, we'd like to share one of riKu's stories about a key moment in his evolution as a queer API activist. In 2000, riKu attended a Nikkei conference, where he met a lot of young people who were mixed race and queer.

> I felt like all my stuff got seen at the same time. There were other people who didn't look anything like me, but we felt each other so much. The conference was about changing Nikkei culture to think about "What's next?" And they didn't have very much about mixed people. They didn't have very much about queer people. So we felt

like, Radical folks, have our own space. I took that with me, in all my work, and feeling like "Okay, I have a home. I can always find a home."

No matter how much history is behind us, much of our work is still creating our own space and finding home. And as you think about "what's next?" we wish your continuous activism, like riKu's, be a wondrous journey of imagination and discovery, inclusion and camaraderie.

NOTES

1. The roundtable consisted of the four panelists and both authors and was held on February 25, 2018, in Los Angeles. The two-hour discussion was recorded and transcribed. We submitted the final version to the panelists for review and clarifications. This essay clearly does not include the entirety of the panelists' discussion. Rather than providing simply transcribed text, we sought to provide unfamiliar readers with a context to understand the importance and meaningfulness of each of the panelist's stories. This methodology is similar to the one coauthor Wat has used with Steven Shum for the roundtable discussion essay that was published in the first *Q&A: Queer in Asian America*, 166–184.

2. For other ethnographic narratives, see Alice Y. Hom's groundbreaking "Stories from the Homefront"; K. K. Kumashiro, *Restoried Selves: Autobiographies of Queer Asian-Pacific-American Activists*; M. Manalansan, *Global Divas: Filipino Gay Men in the Diasporas*.

3. In Los Angeles, Asian/Pacific Lesbians and Gays was founded in 1980. In her essay "Asian Lesbians in San Francisco: Struggles to Create a Safe Space, 1970s–1980s," Trinity Ordoña wrote that Asian American Feminists, cofounded by Canyon Sam and Doreena Wong, began in 1977 in San Francisco. Since then, Wong continued to be instrumental in developing other LGBT API organizations, including cofounding API Equality-LA with Jury Candelario and other community leaders.

4. For example, see Ordoña's discussion of Asian Women's Group in her essay. Also see Eric C. Wat's account of Asian and Pacific Lesbians and Gays in his book *The Making of a Gay Asian Community: An Oral History of Pre-AIDS Los Angeles*.

5. Not too long afterward, A/PLG will change its name to Asian/Pacific Gays and Friends, to reflect the large number of non-Asians in its membership and somewhat in its leadership. API lesbians also began to organize among themselves into Asian/Pacific Lesbians and Friends, and later Los Angeles Asian Pacific Islander Sisters (LAAPIS). The early experiment in cogender organization among API lesbians and gay men was short-lived.

6. Many of these women were UCLA students, so they were not different from A/PLG members just in terms of gender identity but also in age.

7. Interview with coauthor Eric C. Wat, Lake Alfred, FL, July 19, 2017.

8. For more on this racial hierarchy in the gay community, see Eric C. Wat, *The Making of a Gay Asian Community: An Oral History of Pre-AIDS Los Angeles*; C. Winter Han, *Geisha of a Different Kind: Race and Sexuality in Gayasian America*; and essays by Richard Fung and Sandip Roy in *Q&A: Queer in Asian America*, edited by David L. Eng and Alice Y. Hom.

9. For instance, APAIT provided small grants to smaller and volunteer-run LGBTQ API organizations to host community events and set up hotlines. These organizations were ethnic and language specific (Chinese, Filipino, Japanese, Korean, South Asian, and Vietnamese), gender specific (Los Angeles Asian Pacific Islander Sisters), or both (Ô-Môi).

10. Interviews with coauthor Eric C. Wat, Oakland, CA, November 10, 2017 (Kang) and Los Angeles, December 10, 2017 (Wong).

11. Interview with coauthor Eric C. Wat, Los Angeles, CA, October 30, 2017 (Tran).

12. Tre'vell Anderson and Hailey Branson-Potts, "LA Pride Has Sold Out and Become 'Gay Coachella,' Critics Say," *Los Angeles Times,* May 20, 2016.

13. Christopher Street West, "A Letter from the Board of Directors," http://myemail .constantcontact.com/A-Letter-From-the-Board-of-Directors.html?soid=110154475524 5&aid=eiGokllf8N0.

14. In California, Prop 22 in 2000 recognized marriage only between a man and a woman. It was approved with 61.4 percent of the votes but was struck down in 2008 by the California Supreme Court. Prop 8 in 2008 amended the state's constitution in California to ban same-sex marriage. It was approved with 52.2 percent of the votes but was ruled unconstitutional by the California Supreme Court in 2010. In 2015, the U.S. Supreme Court, in its *Obergefell v. Hodges* decision, finally declared the constitutionality of same-sex marriage for the entire country.

15. Passed by voters in California in 2000, Prop 21 increased the penalty for juvenile offenders as young as fourteen and required them to be tried as adults for certain crimes.

16. Marshall Wong, "Supporters of LGBT Equality Rally against Homophobia in the San Gabriel Valley."

17. Ibid.

18. In 2013, VROC's application to march in the Tet Parade in Orange County was denied by organizers. VROC leaders organized a contingent of 250 Viet LGBT and allies who "came roaring with pride. Although sidelined, we demonstrated our existence as members of the community and demanded that our voices be heard. Our vibrant presence represented human diversity and the continued transformation of the Vietnamese diaspora." See VROC website, http://www.vietroc.org/about-us/history/. Also see "Interview with Hieu Nguyen, Viet Rainbow of Orange County," in *Many Bridges, One River: Organizing for Justice in Vietnamese American Communities,* edited by thuan nguyen and Vy Nguyen, 143–149.

19. Gina Masequesmay, "Negotiating Multiple Identities in a Queer Vietnamese Support Group."

20. For more description of "allies" or "allyship," see https://theantioppression network.com/allyship/ and http://www.guidetoallyship.com/. Also see G. M. Russell and J. S. Bohan, "Institutional Allyship for LGBT Equality: Underlying Processes and Potentials for Change."

21. See M. Aizumi and A. Aizumi, *Two Spirits, One Heart.*

22. We also want to define "activism" broadly. In a note to the coauthors after the roundtable discussion, Gina writes, "I want to emphasize that [in] the destigmatizing work and the advocacy for resources that were done was a collective achievement, we often forget all the conditions that made such work possible. I just happened to be accessible to be interviewed but that there were numerous individuals who made the work possible. So, the emphasis should be on the collective and not a few leaders. From individuals who volunteered their time and money to decorate the first LGBT float in the

2004 San Jose Parade, to the individuals who volunteered to be our security team on that first parade in Little Saigon when we weren't sure how safe it would be to march, to the visionary and daring leaders of these marches, to the allies who gathered their friends to show up at the marches as marchers and audience/witnesses, to the bilingual translators who make our message accessible, and to allies who featured us in the Vietnamese press. Everyone contributed what they could to advance our cause. That is, everyone can be part of social change and let us not lionize charismatic leaders to the point that we feel inadequate to participate in the change we want to see in society." Her comment also reminds one of the coauthors about the idea of "anonymous activism" from George Lipsitz in his work about Ivory Perry, who contributed decades of movement work, though not necessarily recognized as a leader. Lipsitz contends that mass movements depend on people like Perry. He writes, "The anonymity of his activism suggests layers of social protest activity missing from most scholarly accounts, while the persistence of his involvement undermines prevailing academic judgments about mass protests as outbursts of immediate anger and spasmodic manifestation of hysteria." George Lipsitz, *A Life in the Struggle: Ivory Perry and the Culture of Opposition*.

23. J. Bryan Lowder, "The Real Dangers of Same-Sex Marriage." Also see an interview with Lowder, "After Marriage Equality, What's Next for the LGBT Movement," *NPR All Things Considered*, June 28, 2015, https://www.npr.org/2015/06/28/418327652/after-marriage-equality-whats-next-for-the-lgbt-movement.

REFERENCES

Aizumi, M., and A. Aizumi. 2012. *Two Spirits, One Heart*. Bronx, NY: Magnus.

Anderson, T., and H. Branson-Potts. 2016. "LA Pride Has Sold Out and Become 'Gay Coachella,' Critics Say." *Los Angeles Times*. Retrieved on March 8, 2018. http://www.latimes.com/local/california/la-me-10102020-gay-pride-boycott-notourpride-snap-story.html.

Eng, D. L., and A. Y. Hom. 1998. *Q & A: Queer in Asian America*. Philadelphia: Temple University Press.

Han, C. W. 2015. *Geisha of a Different Kind: Race and Sexuality in Gaysian America*. New York: New York University Press.

Hom, A. Y. 1994. "Stories from the Homefront: Perspectives of Asian American Parents with Lesbian Daughters and Gay Sons." *Amerasia Journal* 20, no. 1: 19–32. doi:10.17953/amer.20.1.fw4816q23j815423.

Kumashiro, K. K. 2004. *Restoried Selves: Autobiographies of Queer Asian-Pacific-American Activists*. New York: Harrington Park.

Leong, R. 1996. *Asian American Sexualities: Dimensions of the Gay and Lesbian Experience*. New York: Routledge.

Lipsitz, G. 2011. *A Life in The Struggle: Ivory Perry and the Culture of Opposition*. 2nd ed. Philadelphia: Temple University Press.

Lowder, J. B. 2015. "The Real Dangers of Same-Sex Marriage." *Slate*. Retrieved on March 8, 2018. http://www.slate.com/blogs/outward/2015/06/25/some_unintended_consequences_of_marriage_equality_worth_taking_seriously.html.

Magantay, G. 2016. The Future of the LGBTQ Asian American and Pacific Islander Community in 2040. *AAPI Nexus: Policy, Practice and Community* 14, no. 2: 33–47.

Manalansan, M. 2003. *Global Divas: Filipino Gay Men in the Diasporas*. Durham, NC: Duke University Press.

Masequesmay, G. 2003. Negotiating Multiple Identities in a Queer Vietnamese Support Group. *Journal of Homosexuality* 45, no. 2–4: 193–215.

nguyen, t., and V. Nguyen. 2017. "Interview with Hieu Nguyen, Viet Rainbow of Orange County." In *Many Bridges, One River: Organizing for Justice in Vietnamese American Communities,* edited by thuan nguyen and Vy Nguyen. Los Angeles: UCLA Asian American Studies Center Press.

Ordoña, T. 2003. Asian Lesbians in San Francisco: Struggles to Create a Safe Space, 1970s–1980s. In. *Asian/Pacific Islander Women: A Historical Anthology,* edited by Shirley Hune and Gail M. Nomura. New York: New York University Press.

Russell, G. M., and J. S. Bohan. 2016. "Institutional Allyship for LGBT Equality: Underlying Processes and Potentials for Change." *Journal of Social Issues* 72, no. 2: 335–354. doi:10.1111/josi.12169.

Wat, E. C. 2002. *The Making of a Gay Asian Community: An Oral History of Pre-AIDS Los Angeles.* Lanham: Rowman and Littlefield.

Wong, M. 2015. "Supporters of LGBT Equality Rally against Homophobia in the San Gabriel Valley." *Pacific Citizen.* Retrieved on March 8, 2018. https://www.pacific citizen.org/supporters-of-lgbt-equality-rally-against-homophobia-in-the-san-gabriel -valley/.

Manservants to Millennials

A Brief Queer APA History

AMY SUEYOSHI

On July 1, 2015, the Respect after Death Act (California Assembly Bill 1577) took effect in California, enabling transgender people to record their chosen gender on their death certificates. Few people, however, know of the Asian American activism central in the passage of this bill. When trans man Christopher Lee, of mixed Chinese and Polish ancestry, killed himself in 2012, the coroner listed him as female on his death certificate. Troubled by their friend's misgendering, Chinese Mexican Chino Scott-Chung brought the death certificate to the attention of the Transgender Law Center, which initiated and lobbied for the passage of AB 1577. Three years later, Japanese American Kris Hayashi stood at the helm of the Transgender Law Center as its executive director when the organization celebrated the passage of the bill.[1] Yet when CBS reported on the victory, they featured only Masen Davis, the organization's former executive director, and in doing so erased the existence of all three Asian activists with a single broadcast.[2] Indeed, queer Asian Pacific Americans are more often overlooked rather than highlighted despite their incredible engagement in sociopolitical change.

Same-sex affairs certainly existed in early Asian Pacific American history even if those engaged in such intimacies did not identify as gay or lesbian. Nineteenth-century imperial zealots wrote of uninhibited sexuality in the Pacific as they sought refuge from the stigma of their own same-sex proclivities at home. Western writer Charles Warren Stoddard described the Pacific Islands as a sexual utopia that not even "California where men are tolerably bold" could provide.[3] In Hawai'i, a young man named Kána-aná took in Stoddard, fed him, "petted [him] in every possible way," and hugged him like "a young bear" each night as they fell asleep.[4] Literary critic Lee Wallace asserts that Pacific Islander same-sex sexualities so powerfully informed nineteenth-century Western imaginings of masculinity that "male homosexuality as we have come to understood it . . . was constituted in no small part through the collision with Polynesian culture."[5]

For the unlucky ones, the criminal court system etched their illicit activities into historical record. Authorities in 1890s San Francisco arrested a number of Chinese men impersonating women to attract fellow country-men for sex work.[6] So prevalent did incidents of South Asian men anally penetrating young white men appear that criminal courts in the 1910s and 1920s began to blame "Oriental depravity" for promoting degeneracy among America's transient youth, a population particularly susceptible to sodomy.[7] Alaskan canneries at which Japanese and Chinese immigrants labored also became productive sites of business for male sex workers, most often Chinese, African American, or Portuguese, in the 1920s and 1930s.[8]

Even at the turn of the century, some individuals explicitly identified as queer. Kosen Takahashi, an illustrator for *Shin Sekai*, one of San Francisco's earliest Japanese American newspapers, declared himself an "utmost queer Nipponese." Takahashi, who had earlier shared kisses with Yone Noguchi, missed him sorely when Noguchi went tramping from San Francisco to Los Angeles. Noguchi, a poet in his own right, played a formative role in the literary modernist movement through his affair with Charles Warren Stoddard, the aforementioned writer and lover of Kána-aná.[9]

In 1889, ten years before Kosen Takahashi pined away over Yone Nogu-chi's absence as he tramped to Los Angeles, Ah Yane gave birth to Margaret Chung in Santa Barbara, California. By the 1920s, Chung would become a successful physician, the first American surgeon of Chinese descent. Chung, known for wearing mannish attire, drove a sleek blue sports car around San Francisco and led many of her contemporaries, including lesbian poet Elsa Gidlow, to speculate that she might be a lesbian. Gidlow actively courted Chung, drinking bootleg liquor at a local speakeasy of Chung's choosing in San Francisco's North Beach. Later in the 1940s, Chung raised funds and supported the formation of the Women's Army Corps (WAC) and Women Accepted for Volunteer Emergency Services (WAVES) in hopes of joining the U.S. Navy. However, government officials would never accept Chung's application to join WAVES due to rumors about her lesbianism.[10]

The postwar period marked a shift for queer Asian Pacific American life as it did for the larger LGBT community as more explicitly queer activism took root. In the mid-1950s, when Daughters of Bilitis (DOB), the first les-bian civil and political rights group in the United States formed, Filipina Rose Bamberger played a crucial role in gathering a handful of women, in-cluding Del Martin and Phyllis Lyon, who would later become known as the founders. Bamberger invited a group of six women to join her and her part-ner Rosemary Sliepen for drinks and dinner at their home in San Francisco on Friday, September 21, 1955. Yet the purpose of DOB, a secret group of women gathered for private events versus a public organization pushing for political reform, came to divide the group. Bamberger left DOB in early 1956, refusing to be a part of an organization that hoped to welcome men and heterosexual women working publicly toward legislative changes. No doubt, an outward-facing DOB would increase the possibility that her own lesbianism become more public.[11]

Bamberger had reason to protect herself from instability that public knowledge of her sexuality might bring. During the 1950s, she had a different job nearly every year as a machine operator, brush maker, or factory worker, and she changed residences at least five times. Without job security and little residential stability, the consequences of coming out for Bamberger would have likely been unfathomable to bear.[12]

Ten years after Bamberger left the group, Chinese American Crystal Jang attended a few San Francisco DOB meetings in search of other lesbians and still found the group, as well as the lesbian bars she frequented, to be "all white." When she turned to leftist groups working for Third World liberation, the broader Asian American movement seemed "very male."[13] Jang would not be alone in her sense of alienation. Activist Gil Mangaoang described himself as being in state of "schizophrenia" during the 1970s, trapped between his involvement in a homophobic Asian American political community and his intimate life in a racist LGBTQ community.[14] He matriculated into the City College of San Francisco in 1970 after being discharged from the U.S. Airforce. On campus, Mangaoang joined the Filipino Club, became an officer on the student council, and worked with other student groups of color to establish an ethnic studies program. He and other student activists negotiated with the administration to ensure that courses in Filipino history and Tagalog be included in the curricula.[15] Mangaoang, impatient for change within the college, soon after began doing volunteer work at the International Hotel (I-Hotel), a low-income residence hotel at the corner of Jackson and Kearny Streets in San Francisco that housed many *manong*, or elderly Filipino men. It stood as the last bastion of the San Francisco's Manilatown and became an early site of panethnic Asian American activism as the city tore sought to tear down the building in the late 1960s as part of urban renewal.[16] Countless other Asian gay and lesbian activists and writers such as Daniel Tseng, Kitty Tsui, and Helen Zia have reported on how people of color and queer progressive spaces remained unable to accommodate queer people of color in the 1970s.[17]

Still, APA queers remained committed to social justice and forged their own paths for community engagement. In the 1960s, Crystal Jang and her women friends began a petition at the City College of San Francisco calling for women students on campus to be allowed to wear pants and successfully changed the dress code.[18] In 1978 Jang, who had recently become a middle school PE teacher, publicly spoke against the Briggs Initiative, which would have legalized the firing of all LGBT teachers and those who supported them.[19] When she appeared in the local newspapers as a result, she became one the faces of the anti–Briggs Initiative movement, participating in a rally with the United Educators of San Francisco despite the risk of losing her job.[20]

Gil Mangaoang also forged a space where he could be both queer and Asian in his activism for social change. Through his work at the I-Hotel, Mangaoang became a member of the Kalayaan Collective and would become one of the early members of Katipunan ng mga Demokratikong Pilipino (KDP), memorialized as the first revolutionary Filipino nationalist group in the United States. Headquartered in Oakland, California, KDP appeared to be the only organization within the Asian American movement that accepted queer members. At least ten lesbians and two gay men comprised the membership and leadership of the organization.[21]

On the East Coast, bar patrons at New York City's Stonewall Inn in 1969 fought back against police harassment, marking what many historians cite as the beginning of the gay rights movement. Yet three years earlier in 1966, in San Francisco's Tenderloin District, sex worker and activist Tamara Ching, of Native Hawaiian, Chinese, and German descent, fought back against police harassment with other street queens at Compton's Cafeteria. The revolt in which Ching and other queens participated initiated new transgender advocacy programs within the San Francisco Police Department and the city's Department of Public Health.[22] Queers in New York and soon after across the nation organized to form the Gay Liberation Front (GLF) to demand sexual liberation for all people. As GLF branches popped up across the country, Japanese American Kiyoshi Kuromiya cofounded the Gay Liberation Front–Philadelphia in 1970.[23]

Within a decade, queer Asians from across the nation gathered in Washington, DC, at the first National Third World Lesbian and Gay Conference in 1979. The conference, organized by the National Coalition of Black Gays, took place at Howard University.[24] According to poet Michiyo Cornell, the meeting was "the first time in the history of the American hemisphere that Asian American gay men and lesbians joined to form a network of support."[25] Cornell, who would later change her last name to Fukaya, would go on to organize Vermont's first queer pride celebration, called "Lesbian and Gay Pride," in 1983.[26] Four years later, Asian lesbian and bisexual women organized the first West Coast Asian Pacific Lesbian Retreat in Sonoma, California, in 1987, drawing eighty people, mostly from the San Francisco Bay Area. For Asian lesbians, the 1980s marked a time of momentous community building. A burgeoning network of individuals created newsletters, held potlucks, formed softball teams, and published books, coalescing into what sociologist Karin Aguilar-San Juan characterized as a "movement."[27]

Poet Kitty Tsui, whom Aguilar-San Juan remembers as "proud, defiant, no bullshit woman, the dyke we all wanted to be," took up bodybuilding and won bronze in 1986 and gold in 1990 at Gay Games I and II, held respectively in San Francisco and Vancouver.[28] Her muscled body also prominently appeared in the renegade lesbian erotica magazine *On Our Backs* in 1988 and 1990, as well as in New York City's *Village Voice*. Tsui may have been the first Asian lesbian to appear on the cover of both publications. In 1995, she published *Breathless*, a book of SM erotica in which sex mingled with fermented bean curd, beef tendons, and bitter melon. Tsui created intense scenes of pleasure, pain, and Chinese food and won the Firecracker Alternative Book (FAB) Award for *Breathless* in 1996.[29]

During the 1980s, many queer Asians defiantly sought to find each other. In New York City, two mixed heritage Asians, Katherine Hall and Chea Villanueva, formed Asian Lesbians of the East Coast in 1983.[30] In Los Angeles, queer Asian American activists formed Asian Pacific Lesbians and Gays (A/PLG) in 1980, the first organization of its kind in Southern California. The group would later become over run with "rice queens"—a term used to describe white men interested in relationships with Asians based largely on their ethnicity. Four years later in 1984, Steve Lew and Prescott Chow formed the Gay Asian Rap Group (GARP) in Long Beach, California, to nurture gay Asian leadership. As more gay API men within A/PLG defected to GARP, the two organizations became distinctly different. GARP would later become the Gay Asian Pacific Support Network (GAPSN) in 1989 to create a space specifically for API men.[31]

Queer South Asians contributed significantly to the explosion of queer API community groups in the 1980s. In 1985 and 1986, queer South Asians first in Brooklyn, New York, and then second in the San Francisco Bay Area formed two different groups, Anamika and Trikone, respectively, to address the specific needs of LGBTQ people of South Asian descent from countries such as Afghanistan, Bangladesh, India, Sri Lanka, Pakistan, Bhutan, Nepal, Myanmar (Burma), and Tibet. The two organizations would be part of a half dozen groups that emerged in the following years across North America, the United Kingdom, and India.[32]

The 1980s simultaneously marked mass devastation for the gay male community due to the U.S. government's nonresponse to the AIDS epidemic. Populations of color found themselves in a particular public health crisis due to disparate funding for services and education as well as presumptions within their own communities that HIV and AIDS was only a "white disease."[33] Queer activists of color across the nation quickly organized to provide support. On the West Coast, Asian American Recovery Services (AARS) in San Francisco established the Asian AIDS Project (AAP) in 1987, the first organization to target APIs for HIV and AIDS prevention. In the same year, AARRS would call Asian American city leaders to initiate the Asian AIDS Taskforce (AAT), a group committed to mobilizing community-wide resources in the fight against AIDS. The Japanese

American Cultural and Community Center of Northern California hosted these early meetings in Japan Town.[34] The following year, the Gay Asian Pacific Alliance (GAPA) implemented an informal support group for HIV-positive gay Asians later called GCHP. Chinese American Steve Lew served a critical role in these early efforts as a key organizer, educator, and role model for other HIV-positive men.[35] In 1990, when Vince Crisostomo left New York and traveled across the country with his Jewish boyfriend to live in San Francisco, he found community and family with GAPA, the Asian AIDS Project, and particularly Steve Lew. Crisostomo's boyfriend, who had AIDS, could also access the organization's services, and AAP offered Crisostomo a job in their theater program after he had applied for seven other jobs without success.[36]

Asian Pacific Americans took formative roles in AIDS activism in other parts of the United States as well as the world. In 1989, just two years after the formation of the Asian AIDS Project in San Francisco, Kiyoshi Kuromiya, who earlier formed the Philadelphia branch of Gay Liberation Front, founded Critical Path, one of the earliest and most comprehensive resources available to the public for treating HIV.[37] Crisostomo, who was Chamorro, would also become the first publicly out HIV-positive Pacific Islander at World AIDS Day in 1991 and become directly involved in bringing increased HIV and AIDS awareness and education to Guam. In 2000, Crisostomo would return to Guam to become the executive director for the first funded community-based organization to do AIDS work in the Pacific.[38]

AIDS organizing in the 1980s and 1990s both gathered and nurtured countless community-minded APA activists committed to promoting Asian Pacific American health and well-being in the queer and transgender communities and to eradicating broad-based fear based on gender, sexuality, or HIV status. Tamara Ching from the Compton's Cafeteria revolt worked as an AIDS education outreach worker for the AAP and oversaw a support group for the API transgender community for GCHP as the "God Mother of Polk [Street]."[39] Transwoman Nikki Calma, better known as "Tita Aida,"[40] who also worked at the Asian AIDS Project in 1990s, became a community icon through her advocacy work, a host to countless fundraisers, and one of three women to be featured in the first API transgender public service announcement in 2008.[41]

On the stage, queers who might otherwise enjoy musical theater spoke out against the 1991 production of *Miss Saigon*. On April 6 in New York City, queers of color, leftist Asian Americans regardless of sexual orientation and gender diversity, antiracist white gays, bisexuals, lesbians, and the Actors' Equity Association joined hands with Asian Lesbians of the East Coast (ALOEC) and Gay Asian and Pacific Islander Men of New York (GAPIMNY) to protest two prominent LGBTQ institutions' use of Cameron

Mackintosh's musical *Miss Saigon* as their annual fundraiser extravaganza. ALOEC and GAPIMNY had long been in conversation with the two hosts, Lambda Legal Defense and Education Fund and New York City's Lesbian and Gay Community Services Center, to cancel their fundraiser at this musical that promoted damaging images of submissive "Orientals" and used yellow face to make one of its white actors appear Asian.[42] While the fundraiser took place as scheduled, the protest marked the formation of an incredible coalition of various communities publicly denouncing racism, misogyny, and Orientalism. Organizer Yoko Yoshikawa remembers, "James Lee taped a neon pink triangle to his leather jacket, emblazoned with the words: 'San Francisco-born Gay Man of Korean Descent.' On any other night, he could have been bashed for that. But that night, his back was covered. Gray-haired Japanese American wives and mothers and brash young white men from Queer Nation marched side by side. Dykes in dreads, campy queens, leftists of all persuasions: we owned Broadway."[43]

Queer API publications continued to flourish through the 1990s. Asian Pacific Islander lesbians and bisexual women produced *The Very Inside,* an anthology of over one hundred pieces edited by Sharon Lim-Hing in 1994.[44] Other activists published landmark texts on not exclusively queer APAs. In 1991, mixed heritage Lani Ka'ahumanu co-edited *Bi Any Other Name* with Loraine Hutchins, and the anthology has become recognized as the "Bi-ble" of the bisexual movement.[45]

The most widely read queer API writing of the 1990s was Olympic medalist Greg Louganis's autobiography *Breaking the Surface,* in which he publicly came out as HIV positive after nearly a decade of rumors in professional sports that he was gay. Louganis, an adoptee of mixed Samoan and white ancestry, endured a childhood of persecution being called "nigger" as well as "sissy." He went on to win four gold medals in diving—the three-meter springboard and the ten-meter platform in 1984 and 1988. *Breaking the Surface* became a New York Times #1 Best Seller in 1995, initiating his public persona as a gay rights activist. As the first prominent athlete to come out as gay, Louganis faced tremendous challenges in professional sports that impacted him emotionally and lost him millions of dollars in endorsements.[46]

Queer Asian America continues to grow tremendously in the new millennium, particularly with the expansion of the Web. Countless blogs from queer Asians fill the Internet expounding upon the importance of community engagement and queer empowerment. Online forums for queer South Asians such as KhushList, SAGrrls, DesiDykes, GayBombay, and Khushnet.com have multiplied.[47] A queer Vietnamese American support group in Southern California called Ô-Môi took advantage of the Internet to grow ninefold from its initial six members in 1995 to fifty-four members by 2000.[48] Most notably, a younger generation of queer APIs are taking interest in the histories of their LGBTQ predecessors and deploying their research online. Queer advocacy organizations API Equality in both Northern and Southern California have initiated oral history projects (the "Pioneers Project" in Los Angeles and "Dragon Fruit Project" in San Francisco) and have sponsored educational workshops on API queer history as well as Wikipedia Hackathons.[49] Artists have more actively illuminated APA history in their creative works. In 2012, artist Tanya Wischerath recognized Tamara Ching, who revolted against police at Compton's Cafeteria in 1966 in a mural along Clarion Alley in San Francisco.[50] Two years later, filmmakers spotlighted Kumu Hinaleimoana Wong-Kalu's transformative work in the classroom teaching love, honor, and respect for indigeneity and gender diversity.[51] For APA activists, sexual freedom, economic justice, and gender and racial equity are inextricably intertwined in their fight for a more compassionate and inclusive world.

NOTES

This essay is an excerpt from an earlier version published with the National Parks Foundation titled "Breathing Fire." https://www.nps.gov/articles/lgbtqtheme-asianpacific.htm.

1. "Remembering Christopher Lee as Respect after Death Act Takes Effect," *Transgender Law Center*, July 7, 2015, accessed July 30, 2015, http://transgenderlawcenter.org/archives/11746. Lee cofounded the San Francisco Transgender Film Festival in 1997.

2. Jan Mabry, "'Respect after Death' Act Takes Effect Giving Transgenders Right to Have Chosen Gender on Death Certificates," *CBS San Francisco*, July 1, 2015, accessed July 30, 2015, http://sanfrancisco.cbslocal.com/2015/07/01/respect-after-death-act-takes-effect-giving-transgenders-right-to-have-chosen-gender-on-death-certificates.

3. Amy Sueyoshi, *Queer Compulsions: Race, Nation, and Sexuality in the Affairs of Yone Noguchi* (Honolulu: University of Hawai'i Press, 2012), 16.

4. Charles Warren Stoddard, *South Sea Idyls* (New York: Charles Scribner's Sons, 1926), 24.

5. Lee Wallace, *Sexual Encounters: Pacific Texts, Modern Sexualities* (Ithaca, NY: Cornell University Press, 2003).

6. Peter Boag, *Re-dressing the America's Frontier Past* (Berkeley: University of California Press, 2011), 149.

7. Nayan Shah, "Between 'Oriental Depravity' and 'Natural Degenerates': Spatial Borderlands and the Making of Ordinary Americans," *American Quarterly* 57, no. 3 (September 2005): 703–725.

8. Chris Friday, *Organizing Asian American Labor: The Pacific Coast Canned-Salmon Industry, 1870–1942* (Philadelphia: Temple University Press, 1994), 45–55, 114.

9. Sueyoshi, *Queer Compulsions*, 54, 83. Noguchi is better known today as the father of acclaimed artist Isamu Noguchi.

10. Judy Tzu-Chun Wu, *Doctor Mom Chung of the Fair-Haired Bastards: The Life of a Wartime Celebrity* (Berkeley: University of California Press, 2005).

11. See Marcia M. Gallo, *Different Daughters: A History of the Daughters of Bilitis and the Rise of the Lesbian Rights Movement* (Emeryville, CA: Seal, 2007), 4, 5, 8.

12. *Polk's San Francisco City Directories, 1950–1959* (San Francisco: R. L. Polk).

13. Interview with Crystal Jang, conducted by author, January 31, 2012, San Francisco, California.

14. Eric C. Wat, *The Making of a Gay Asian Community: An Oral History of Pre-AIDS Los Angeles* (New York: Rowman and Littlefield, 2002), 102.

15. Gil Mangaoang, "From the 1970s to the 1990s: Perspective of a Gay Filipino American Activist," in *Asian American Sexualities: Dimensions of the Gay and Lesbian Experience*, edited by Russell Leong (New York: Routledge, 1996), 102–103.

16. Estella Habal, *San Francisco's International Hotel: Mobilizing the Filipino American Community in the Anti-Eviction Movement* (Philadelphia: Temple University Press, 2007).

17. Daniel Tseng, "Slicing Silence: Asian Progressives Come Out," in *Asian Americans: The Movement and the Moment*, edited by Steve Louie and Glenn K. Omatsu (Los Angeles: UCLA Asian American Studies Center Press, 2001); Kitty Tsui, *The Words of a Woman who Breathes Fire* (Argyle, NY: Spinsters Ink, 1983); Helen Zia, *Asian American Dreams: The Emergence of an American People* (New York: Farrar, Straus, and Giroux, 2000).

18. Interview with Crystal Jang, conducted by author, January 31, 2012, San Francisco, California.

19. Karen Graves, "Political Pawns in and Educational Endgame: Reflections on Bryant, Briggs, and Some Twentieth Century School Questions," *History of Education Quarterly* 53, no. 1 (February 2013): 1–20.

20. Interview with Crystal Jang, conducted by author, January 31, 2012, San Francisco, California; Crystal Jang, email message to author, October 17, 2015.

21. Mangaoang, "From the 1970s to the 1990s," 103–109; Trinity Ann Ordona, "Coming Out Together: An Ethnohistory of the Asian and Pacific Islander Queer Women's and Transgendered People's Movement of San Francisco" (PhD diss., University of California, Santa Cruz, 2000).

22. Susan Stryker, *Transgender History* (Berkeley, CA: Seal, 2008), 63–66, 74, 75.

23. Interview with Kiyoshi Kuromiya, conducted by Marc Stein. See Marc Stein, "Kiyoshi Kuromiya, June 17, 1997," *Outhistory.org*, 2009, accessed July 14, 2014, http://out history.org/exhibits/show/philadelphia-lgbt-interviews/interviews/kiyoshi-kuromiya. Marc Stein, *City of Sisterly and Brotherly Loves: Lesbian and Gay Philadelphia, 1945–1972* (Philadelphia: Temple University Press, 2004).

24. Tseng, "Slicing Silence," 231.

25. Michiyo Cornell, "Living in Asian America," in Leong, *Asian American Sexualities*, 83.

26. Shervington, *A Fire Is Burning, It Is in Me*, 145; Chuck Stewart, ed., *Proud Heritage: People, Issues, and Documents of the LGBT Experience* (Santa Barbara, CA: ABC-CLIO, 2015), 1208.

27. Karin Aguilar-San Juan, "Landmarks in Literature by Asian American Lesbians," *Signs* 18, no. 4 (Summer 1993): 37.

28. Aguilar-San Juan, "Landmarks in Literature by Asian American Lesbians," 936.

29. *On Our Backs* 5, no. 1 (Summer 1988); *On Our Backs* 7, no. 2 (November–December 1990); Interview with Kitty Tsui, conducted by author, December 22, 2014, Long Beach, California. Kitty Tsui, *Breathless* (Ithaca, NY: Firebrand Books, 1996).

30. Ordona, "Coming Out Together," 219; Emi Minemura, "Asian Pacific Islander Lesbian and Bisexual Women in North America: Activism and Politics" (master's thesis, Michigan State University, 1996), 10.

31. Wat, *The Making of a Gay Asian Community*, 110, 115, 166–167.

32. Nayan Shah, "Sexuality, Identity, and the Uses of History," in *Q&A: Queer in Asian America*, edited by David L. Eng and Alice Y. Hom (Philadelphia: Temple University Press, 1998), 141.

33. Deborah Gould, *Moving Politics: Emotion and ACT UP's Fight against AIDS* (Chicago: University of Chicago Press, 2009); Nancy E. Stoller, *Lessons from the Damned: Queers, Whores, and Junkies Respond to AIDS* (New York: Routledge, 1998), 63–79.

34. Letter from Davis Y. Ja, July 14, 1987, Folder Meeting Minutes: General, 1987, Carton 1, Asian/Pacific AIDS Coalition 96–14, GLBT Historical Society, San Francisco, California.

35. Stoller, *Lessons from the Damned*, 64.

36. Interview with Vince Crisostomo conducted by Toby Wu, November 13, 2013, San Francisco, California.

37. Interview with Kiyoshi Kuromiya, conducted by Marc Stein, http://outhistory .org/exhibits/show/philadelphia-lgbt-interviews/interviews/kiyoshi-kuromiya.

38. Interview with Vince Crisostomo, conducted by Toby Wu, November 13, 2013, San Francisco, California.

39. Tamara Ching, "Piece of Mind: Stranger in Paradise," *A. Magazine* 3, no. 1 (March 31, 1994): 85.

40. "Tita Aida," translated as "Auntie AIDS" in Tagalog, is a fantastical trans-mogrification of AIDS from a deadly disease into a familiar feminine figure. Martin Manalansan, *Global Divas: Filipino Gay Men in the Diaspora* (Durham, NC: Duke University Press, 2003).

41. Anonymous, "PSA Targeting API Transgender Communities for World AIDS Day," *AsianWeek,* December 5, 2008, 17; Celeste Chan, "Tita Aida—A Community Icon," *Hyphen Magazine,* July 26, 2014, accessed June 5, 2016, http://hyphenmagazine.com /blog/2014/7/26/tita-aida-community-icon.

42. Yoko Yoshikawa, "The Heat Is on Miss Saigon Coalition: Organizing across Race and Sexuality," in *Q&A: Queer in Asian America*, 41–56; Alex Witchel, "Actor's Equity Attacks Casting of 'Miss Saigon,'" *New York Times,* July 26, 1990, accessed June 5, 2016, http://www.nytimes.com/1990/07/26/theater/actors-equity-attacks-casting-of-miss -saigon.html.

43. Yoshikawa, "The Heat Is on Miss Saigon Coalition," 55.

44. Sharon Lim-Hing, *The Very Inside: An Anthology of Writing by Asian and Pacific Islander Lesbian and Bisexual Women* (Toronto: Sister Vision Press, 1994).

45. Ordona, "Coming Out Together," 292.

46. Greg Louganis, *Breaking the Surface* (New York: Random House, 1994); Larry Reibstein and Gregory Beals, "Public Glory, Secret Agony," *Newsweek* 125, no. 10 (March 6, 1995): 48.

47. Mala Nagarajan, "Queer South Asian Organizing in the United States," *Trikone Magazine* 28, no. 1 (Summer 2014): 4–7.

48. Gina Masequesmay, "Becoming Queer and Vietnamese American: Negotiating Multiple Identities in an Ethnic Support Group of Lesbians, Bisexual Women, and Female-to-Male Transgenders" (PhD diss., University of California, Los Angeles, 2001).

49. API Equality-LA website, accessed August 1, 2015, http://apiequalityla.org; API Equality-Northern California website, accessed August 1, 2015, http://www.apiequality nc.org.

50. Caitlin Donohue, "Trans Activists Honored in Clarion Alley Mural," *San Francisco Bay Guardian Online,* October 24, 2012, accessed November 2, 2015, http://www.sfbg

.com/pixel_vision/2012/10/24/trans-activists-honored-clarion-alley-mural. Web page no longer online; see archived link at https://web.archive.org/web/20150911001552 /http://www.sfbg.com/pixel_vision/2012/10/24/trans-activists-honored-clarion-alley -mural.

51. *Kumu Hina: The True Meaning of Aloha*, directed by Dean Hamer and Joe Wilson (Qwaves, 2014).

From Potlucks to Protests

Reflections from Organizing Queer and Trans API Communities

SASHA WIJEYERATNE

When I first came on staff at the National Queer Asian Pacific Islander Alliance (NQAPIA), I had been organizing in Queer and Trans Asian Pacific Islander (QTAPI) communities for five years. I had been part of organizations built around developing shared community and support, organizing around LGBTQ immigrants' rights and reform, creating our own mental health services, and more. I was drawn to the potential to organize our communities around the issues that impact our lives, to stake our place in the movement through our bodies and our work, and to not just create alternatives but also change the systems that hurt us.

I joined NQAPIA soon after Mike Brown's murder catapulted the Black Lives Matter movement into international prominence. All around the country, Asian Pacific Islander (API) or Asians for Black Lives collectives were forming, doing the critical work of organizing Asian and API people to put our bodies on the line for Black liberation. Asian and API people offered to follow and support Black leadership in a multitude of ways, from fundraising to forming hard and soft blockades with their bodies.

I was involved in these spaces in multiple cities across the country. I found political home in these spaces, and yet as a queer, gender nonconforming, South Asian person, there was often something that felt missing from the dominant analyses and praxis. These spaces often replicated a "white allyship" model of organizing, where white people are urged to use their privilege without actually engaging their own lives, self-interest, or needs. Calls for allyship from white communities often ask people to become "race traitors," to prioritize broad values of social justice and liberation over their day-to-day material privilege.

As queer and trans Asian and API organizers, our communities experience more racial privilege than Black, Indigenous, and Latinx communities, yet we still experience oppression and material costs from racism and queerphobia. How would our strategies shift and our power grow if we engaged people through both the material conditions of their lives and a desire for solidarity?[1] When we say, "When Black people get free, everybody gets free,"[2] what did that mean for API people? This analysis isn't new—grassroots Asian organizations like Freedom Inc.,[3] PrYSM,[4] DRUM,[5] CAAAV,[6] and more have been putting forth this analysis for years.

We grounded our queer and trans API organizing in this analysis. How could we organize the margins of our communities—trans people and femmes, gender nonconforming people, Muslim queers, darker-skinned APIs, working-class queers, and more—around our own material needs as a way to organize more deeply in solidarity with the Movement for Black Lives?[7] How would this transform our existing QTAPI community organizing, which is often centered around potlucks and community building? Within the context of the movement moment we were in and using tools that we suspected would resonate with our base, we embarked on a series of experiments to build QTAPI political power.

We began by making visible the costs of racism and queerphobia within our own communities. We created a media piece called "#QAPIsforBlackLives"[8] with organizers who were South Asian, Southeast Asian, trans and trans femme, working-class, and organizing in solidarity with the Movement for Black Lives. They shared stories about their experiences with police violence—watching family members violated by police in their own homes, experiencing harassment for being gender nonconforming, being blamed for a friend's murder by the police, feeling guttural fear in the blare of sirens. These organizers described how their experiences of police violence and power crafted their understandings and practices of organizing. Instead of understanding themselves as "Asian race traitors," they organized from a place of shared investment and a deep personal and community commitment to undoing the systems that hurt Black people the most and that have ripple effects across our queer and trans API communities.

We wanted to create even more space in NQAPIA for those at the margins of our communities to share their stories. Our next experiment was a deeper dive into political education with our base. We held a week of action called "Redefine Security," based on questioning ideas of "safety" that leave our communities feeling profiled and unsafe. Seven QTAPI people shared their own stories of being shamed and harassed by the Transportation Security Authority (TSA), targeted through police informants, pulled over while driving, and targeted while doing sex work.[9] These stories, along with the #QAPIsforBlackLives video, opened up unexpected space for people across our communities to share their stories. Suddenly, stories were emerging from people I had known for years, breaking the silence that tells us that these experiences are normal, that this profiling is for our own safety. Through tears, rage, and fear, QTAPI people shared stories of getting targeted and assaulted by TSA, harassed by police in the street and in their homes, and carrying the constant anxiety that "safety" would actually mean violence.

As we listened to these stories, a few themes emerged. From our Muslim and trans base, we heard endless stories about profiling at the airport. For trans folks, the new full body scanners led to physical violation by TSA agents unable to read our bodies in the binary of their machines and protocols. For Muslim folks, and those perceived to be Muslim, being pulled aside for "random questioning" and invasive searches hadn't felt random for years. And of course, for those living at the intersections of these identities, the harassment and violations intensified. This mirrored the surveillance of Black travelers, and especially the marking of Black women's hair, as inherently dangerous.[10] When TSA agents couldn't "read" our bodies with their eyes and machines, they resorted to touch, making invasive body checks, hair checks, and more our new normal.[11] Though there are privileges—especially around class, documentation, and ability—in accessing airports, we decided to organize against TSA as a starting point. This issue was deeply and widely felt across the margins of our communities and brought us into the fight against profiling, policing, and surveillance.

These stories, unearthed through political education, made it clear that community building and potlucks weren't enough. We needed power and strategy. Up to this point, most of the organizations in NQAPIA primarily organized through shared social and community space. This work is deeply political—in a world where our communities throw us out, abuse us, and even kill us, surviving and creating our own beloved spaces is a political act. And yet it's not enough. As we build community through potlucks, social gatherings, and community space, we also need to build political power to challenge the forces we're up against.

Our next experiment was to build enough political power to shift the practices of policing and surveillance that target our communities. A few of our queer and trans Muslim and South Asian members suggested using 9/11 as a launching and mobilizing event in 2016. Islamophobia didn't start on 9/11, but the aftermath of the Twin Towers falling marked an increase in Islamophobia, similar to what we are living through under Trump's Muslim bans. On 9/11 the collective remembering of the United States vilifies a "Muslim enemy," and racist, violent patriotism runs rampant. For many of our community members, this is a day when people choose not to leave their homes if they can, where we make phone calls to our loved ones to make sure that everyone made it home in the evening.

Responding to our base's experiences of Islamophobia, transphobia, and racism, we developed a campaign targeted at one of the root causes of this profiling, policing, and surveillance: the Department of Homeland Security (DHS). DHS houses the TSA and was formed as a national security response after 9/11. Specifically, our target was DHS Secretary Jeh Johnson. We were excited for the possibility to change a system that seemed invincible yet was only thirteen years old, and to build campaign alliances with other Black, people of color, and queer trans people of color movements and organizations from a place of solidarity and shared struggle.

After building through storytelling and political education and deciding to embark on an experiment to build political power, we took it to the streets. We organized a guerilla street theater action called #15YearsLater, on the fifteenth anniversary of 9/11. We went to gentrifying areas of Washington, DC, and erected pop-up "checkpoints," replicating the violation, fear, and indignity of "random" profiling in our communities for white people in these historically Black and Latinx neighborhoods. As people stepped through our checkpoint, we asked them the questions that we were used to being asked: "Where are you from? Oh, I've heard that DC has become a hotbed of terrorist activity lately." "Whom are you going to meet? Where? Why?" "That name sounds Christian. Are you Christian? Well, then, we'll need to hold you for investigation." White participants had varying reactions, from disbelief to understanding, from rage to curiosity.

There were multiple goals for this action. We created controversy around our DHS target, getting Johnson's name into DC and national media.[12] We collected postcards aimed at Johnson and DHS, with the goal of pressuring them into abolitionist reforms.[13] Perhaps most important, we continued building the capacities of our base to have these conversations. We spent four hours the day before training people across our communities—trans and queer Muslims, QTAPI people, cis straight Asian folks, non-API people of color—to break down complicated policies into everyday language, centering the impact that these policies have on our people. We built political power by leaning into the strengths of our queer and trans community's ways of organizing and creating a sense of family and safety on a day when most of us would rather hide.

The pressure worked. We got noticed by DHS through pressuring them from the outside and used that leverage to build avenues on the inside. We were invited to submit a model policy that could shift their practices of profiling by taking away some of DHS's power. We had a long road ahead to really make those shifts, but we opened a door that we never imagined possible, and we were ready to keep building power.

The 2016 election marked the end of our campaign. We made a strategic decision not to fight even for abolitionist reforms under Trump and the shifting terrain of DHS leadership. Any victories we sought were too likely to be turned against us and used to recriminalize our communities. Despite the abrupt ending, we claimed this work and campaign as a victory for NQAPIA and QTAPI organizing.

There were certainly limitations and failures in our work—that's why these were experiments! To name a few: tackling the entire Department of

Homeland Security led to powerful base building on our end but was a national target too large for our current capacity, base, and power. As we worked to organize from the margins of our communities, we were still working on building base, particularly within working-class communities. Though there are certainly working-class members of our base, the majority of the people we organized were middle to upper-middle class. We continued to struggle with how to fight for the issues impacting our people and show up through a solidarity lens, without falling back on "white allyship" models.

And even with those limitations, there are a few lessons that I am proud to draw from our work and that I hope can be useful for other QTAPI organizers. Again, to name a few: we deepened our solidarity work in a queer and trans API context to work from a place of shared material needs and targets, not just a place of using our privilege. We brought the margins of our communities to the center of our work through base building, leadership development, and shared power, which had ripple effects across NQAPIA and QTAPI communities. We harnessed the strengths of our community's ways of building, through potlucks and storytelling, and used these tools to build toward political power.

I am proud of the ways that NQAPIA and QTAPI people and organizations across the country have organized and built people power from potlucks to protests. I am excited for our people to harness the brilliance from our lessons, celebrate and learn from our failures, and continue to transform our organizational and political homes, our movements, and our worlds.

AUTHOR'S NOTE

From *Queer and Trans Migrations: Dynamics of Illegalization, Detention, and Deportation*. Copyright 2020 by the Board of Trustees of the University of Illinois. Used with permission of the University of Illinois Press.

NOTES

1. I have written about this previously through a lens of "selfish solidarity." Sasha Wijeyeratne, "Towards a 'Selfish Solidarity': Building Deep Investment in the Movement for Black Lives," *To Speak a Song*, February 29, 2016, https://tospeakasong .com/2016/02/29/towards-a-selfish-solidarity-building-deep-investment-in-the-move ment-for-black-lives/.

2. Alicia Garza, "A Herstory of the #BlackLivesMatter Movement," *The Feminist Wire*, October 7, 2014, http://www.thefeministwire.com/2014/10/blacklivesmatter-2/.

3. Freedom Inc, http://freedom-inc.org/.

4. Providence Youth Student Movement, http://www.prysm.us/.

5. Desis Rising Up and Moving, http://www.drumnyc.org/.

6. CAAAV: Organizing Asian Communities, http://caaav.org/.

7. "Platform," The Movement for Black Lives, https://policy.m4bl.org/platform/.

8. National Queer Asian Pacific Islander Alliance, "#QAPIsforBlackLives," YouTube video, April 8, 2016, https://www.youtube.com/watch?v=Gorrtv1bw70.

9. #RedefineSecurity Story Bank, last modified September 23, 2017, http://www.nqa pia.org/wpp/category/redefinesecurity/redefinesecurity-stories/.

10. See Brenda Medina and Thomas Frank, "TSA Agents Say They're Not Discriminating against Black Women, but Their Body Scanners Might Be," *ProPublica*, April 17, 2019, https://www.propublica.org/article/tsa-not-discriminating-against-black-women -but-their-body-scanners-might-be.

11. #RedefineSecurity Story Bank, https://www.nqapia.org/wpp/redefinesecurity -sahar-shafqat/.

12. There is more information in our Race Files article, "Jeh Johnson, Can You Hear Us Now?": https://www.racefiles.com/2016/09/16/jeh-johnson-can-you-hear-us-now -15yearslater-queer-trans-muslims-and-south-asians-demand-an-end-to-racial-and -religious-profiling/.

13. Based on Mariame Kaba's work: http://www.truth-out.org/news/item/22604 -prison-reforms-in-vogue-and-other-strange-things.

Sing Freedom, Sing

Kim Tran

January 19, 2015, was a sunny day in Oakland, California. It was made warmer still by at least two thousand marchers gathered at Fruitvale Station, a stop on the Bay Area Rapid Transit system. Six years prior, early on New Year's Day, Johannes Mehserle killed unarmed Hayward man Oscar Grant at this working-class hub. To conclude a ninety-six-hour campaign to reclaim Martin Luther King Jr.'s "radical" legacy and to inaugurate the newly formed Third World Resistance contingent, it was apropos that a crowd the *San Francisco Chronicle* labeled "strikingly diverse"[1] convened at this location to acknowledge, mourn, and protest the lives and deaths of Black people at the hands of police. On this Monday, signs proclaimed solidarity with the nascent Black Lives Matter movement. They read, "Palestinian for Black Resistance," "White silence = violence," and the largest banner, "Third World for Black Power." A small cohort of twelve stood behind a banner that read, "Viet Unity 4 Black Power."

Viet Unity (VU) formed in 2004 in the Bay Area. It was created "as a response to the needs for a progressive/radical voice and presence in the Vietnamese American community."[2] In 2017, the newest branch of Viet Unity in the city of San Jose, California, established the Bà Triệu School of Consciousness, a social justice incubator program seeking to instill culturally specific organizing analysis and skills in high school students in the region. Bà Triệu is the youth-oriented companion to its almost identical sister program, Hai Bà Trưng School for Organizing (HBT). Viet Unity members are activists who participate in direct actions and protests as well as nonreformist reform at the municipal level. Many participants have either matriculated from or helped to plan one of its two racial justice schools. Viet Unity has facilitated Hai Bà Trưng for seven years in various states and cities throughout the country including throughout Vietnamese diasporic hubs of California's Bay Area and Orange County. On this day, the marchers (apart from myself) were graduates, teachers, or both of HBT.

At the head of the day's contingent was one of Viet Unity's earliest founders, Thuyet Pham.[3] Thuyet is a refugee, one of Vietnam's self-proclaimed "boat people" whose family settled in Oakland nearly thirty years ago. She was a major planner in the lead up to the day's events in the streets of east Oakland. Following the initial procession out of the train station and onto International Boulevard, Pham led the group in a rendition of "Bốn Phương Trời."

I pause on the singing of "Bốn Phương Trời" by marchers as a moment indicative of queer movement-making in which sonic affect transcends racial antagonism and the strictures of diaspora. Moreover, I claim "Bốn Phương Trời" as a relational Vietnamese protest song that draws upon a specific ethnic positionality to carve out solidarity with Black Lives Matter. Ultimately, I argue "Bốn Phương Trời" is a multitudinous affective instance that evinces Vietnamese American solidarity as a queer diasporic praxis.

"Bốn Phương Trời" is meant to be sung by four different quadrants in the fashion of call and response. Because the group was small, Pham designated roles and parts for groups of three, herself excluded. The song consists of only one verse repeated. Roughly translated, it states:

> We come home from the different cardinal directions to share
>   happiness
> There's no difference between us when it comes to communicating
> Holding hands and sharing words or affection.

As Viet Unity ambled down International Avenue, they linked arms behind the Viet Unity 4 Black Power and sang "Bốn Phương Trời." Together, the small group reimagined the relationship between Black and Vietnamese Americans through urban space.

Despite changing demographics,[4] Oakland has always boasted racial diversity. In the 2010 Census, the city had 34.5 percent white, 25.4 percent Latino, 16.7 percent Asian, and 28 percent Black inhabitants.[5] Oakland's Black American population can be traced back to World War II, when the small port town experienced an influx of Black residents seeking work in the military industrial complex. Ruth Wilson Gilmore calls this specific California migration "post-Keynesian militarism," a system in which the state's "relative stability depended on interlacing the military complex with consumer and producer goods manufacturing, agriculture, resource-extraction industries, and high levels of consumption."[6] Hot war led to military spending and jobs that also expanded education. However, with the end of World War II, labor—particularly in Black families—remained segregated in quickly diminishing lower skilled occupations. Over a handful of decades, economic crisis resulting from a decrease in military assembly-line work and a heightened number of immigrants who threatened white supremacy coincided to produce hyper incarceration and racial apartheid.

While Gilmore's work focuses on anti-Black hostility and the ascension of the prison industrial complex in California, a cross-racial coalition was also forged in the smithy of unemployment and economic recession. In the radicalized hands of Bobby Seale and Huey Newton, 1966 marked the formation of the Black Panther Party for Self Defense (BPP). Alongside national efforts to protect Black people through street patrols and community initiatives, the BPP offered refuge to the North Vietnamese and sent a small contingent to the Southeast Asian peninsula in 1970. It was also during this period that Martin Luther King Jr. nominated Thich Nhat Hanh for the Nobel Peace Prize in 1967, calling him "an apostle of peace and non-violence" with the potential to "build a monument to ecumenism, to world brotherhood, to humanity." The symbiotic history of cross-racial coalition between Black and Vietnamese American communities undergirds the contrasting inimitable specter of Black and Asian conflict in the California metropolitan imaginary.

A few hundred miles away and a handful of decades later, the Los Angeles Uprisings of 1992 birthed a landscape of controlling images foundational to understanding the relationship between Black and Asian Americans. The long-lasting stain of the "riots" prompted police reform, a quinquennial study[7] measuring racial tension in the city, and even an official rechristening[8] of the area from South Central to "South Los Angeles" in an attempt to erase the perception of racial unrest associated with its previous moniker. Entrapped between the bookends of acrimony past and present, Thuyet Pham had one narrow option: heed the triangulating force of Black and Asian conflict. Instead, Pham chose an alternative trajectory. In leading Viet Unity through Bốn Phương Trời, Viet Unity performed what Tamara Roberts calls a sono-racialization, or "racial possibilities that confound dominant offerings even as they draw on its constitutive elements."[9] Sono-racializations reimagine the relationship of Afro-Asia through interracial music. They trouble the divisive racial categorizations and structures of stereotypes and racial antagonism between Black and Asian communities through embodied articulations of cross-racial music and sound.

"Bốn Phương Trời" sutures the four cardinal directions of north, east, south, and west. In the context of a revived Third World Resistance and a march for Black lives, the song takes on new meaning and circuitry. It becomes a sonic and affective bridging of the well-tread "directions" of racial tropes and contestation with the prospect of a forthcoming and always already historical Afro Asian coalition. Emphasizing both a sense of unity and the distance between the "four corners," "Bốn Phương Trời" evokes transgression of racial division as well as geospatial distance. Through a simple repetitive proclamation, Viet Unity contests the legacy that pits the relative valorization of Asian Americans against the criminality of their Black counterparts.

The protesters repeated the song four times, increasing in volume and fervor. In so doing, they exemplified the transformation of this children's song into an anthem. As an invaluable part of the "movement repertoire," anthems are a methodology, a means "for announcement, camaraderie, and dissent."[10] Though many scholars have charted the ways protest music offers and illustrates a not yet actualized a pathway toward social change, these analyses can be limited to intra-racial and intra-ethnic application.[11] But "Bốn Phương Trời" depicts an anthem couched in the "shared desire to cross racial lines rather than the commonality of race, culture, musical style or geography."[12] It is an anthem sung in the explicit spirit and offering of coalition that is at once a refusal of unidimensional politics and an ethnically specific declaration of solidarity.

The cross-racial impetus behind "Bốn Phương Trời" is further indicative of its queer and affective underpinnings. For Roberts, sono-racial collaborations are the result of intentional "gestures" toward "interracial rapport." Thematically, "Bốn Phương Trời" employs two mechanisms with which to overcome racial division in the context of the protest: happiness and affection. Specifically,

> *We come home from the different cardinal directions to share*
>   *happiness*
> *Holding hands and sharing words or* affection. *(emphasis added)*

In this refrain, the emotions of happiness and affection—both physical and spoken—are tools with which to mend embodied and cultural division between Vietnamese and Black communities. If affect is "the emotions [that] operate to 'make' and 'shape' bodies as forms of action which also involve orientations towards others,"[13] this anthem reflects a particular affective circuitry. "Bốn Phương Trời" simultaneously implies a closing of space and a broadening of Vietnamese diasporic social habitus to include and indeed—encourage—affection for Black community and the injustice of their mortality. Happiness and affection become an invitation to care, and then to build, solidarity, whatever that may mean. Finally, the vague yet assertive quality of "Bốn Phương Trời" points to an explicitly queer methodology of movement making.

By both eschewing and highlighting the material importance of touch (holding hands), "Bốn Phương Trời" carves space for Vietnamese and Black solidarity as a queer praxis that hinges upon an alternative form of kinship. In "Friendship as a Way of Life," Michel Foucault contributes a seminal reconceptualization of affective ties through homosexuality, arguing compellingly for homosexuality's expansive qualities. Specifically Foucault claims,

"Homosexuality is an historic occasion to re-open affective and relational virtualities, not so much through the intrinsic qualities of the homosexual, but due to the biases against the position he occupies; in a certain sense diagonal lines that he can trace in the social fabric permit him to make these virtualities visible."[14] According to Foucault, gay men render new forms of affective ties conspicuous and accessible due to their oppositional positionality. By illuminating friendship as an alternative to sexually oriented relationality, Foucault contributes a novel trajectory for Vietnamese diasporic solidarity with the Black Lives Matter movement.

Applied to "Bốn Phương Trời," Foucault's formulation encourages a reading of the song that highlights a queer refusal of the rigid rubrics of anti-Black racism and honorary whiteness that has restricted Asian American solidarity both past and present. Sung in the space of east Oakland, in a moment of Black loss, "Bốn Phương Trời" directly contravenes the narratives of irrefutable difference and inimitable racial antagonism. Instead, it uses a culturally specific sonic affect to suture Vietnamese and Black communities together in both protest and fate.

NOTES

1. Steve Rubenstein, Kale Williams, and Vivian Ho, "Martin Luther King Jr. Day Rallies Strike Chord across Bay Area," *SFGate*, January 19, 2015, https://www.sfgate.com/bayarea/article/Final-Freedom-Train-rides-toward-San-Francisco-6025326.php.

2. The conservatism of the Vietnamese diaspora has been well documented by Caroline Kieu Linh in her book *Transnationalizing Viet Nam: Community, Culture, and Politics in the Diaspora* (Philadelphia: Temple University Press, 2012).

3. Name anonymized.

4. The Urban Displacement Project finds a mass exodus of Black residents due to region wide gentrification since the early 2000s.

5. 2010 Census.

6. Ruth Wilson Gilmore, *Golden Gulag: Prisons, Surplus, Crisis, and Opposition in Globalizing California* (Berkeley, CA: University of California Press, 2007).

7. Fernando Guerra, Brianne Gilbert, and Berto Solis, "LA Riots 25 Years Later," https://lmu.app.box.com/s/it0e448kjmhz2jg1s39eht0g8ye63yhr.

8. Calvin Sims, "In Los Angeles, It's South-Central No More," *New York Times*, April 10, 2003, http://www.nytimes.com/2003/04/10/us/in-los-angeles-it-s-south-central-no-more.html.

9. Roberts, Tamara, *Resounding Afro Asia: Interracial Music and the Politics of Collaboration* (New York: Oxford University Press, 2016), 37.

10. Shana L. Redmond. *Anthem: Social Movements and the Sound of Solidarity in the African Diaspora* (New York: New York University Press, 2013), 178.

11. See "The Making of African American Identity: Vol. III, 1917–1968/Protest/Singing/3. Bernice Johnson Reagon, 'In Our Hands: Thoughts on Black Music,'" accessed January 11, 2021, http://nationalhumanitiescenter.org/pds/maai3/protest/text3/text3read.htm; Redmond, *Anthem*.

12. Redmond, *Anthem*, 5.

13. Ahmed, Sara. *The Cultural Politics of Emotion*. Edinburgh: Edinburgh University Press, 2004.

14. "Friendship as a Lifestyle: An Interview with Michel Foucault," *Gay Information* 7 (Spring 1981): 4–6; "Friendship as a Way of Life," ed. S. Lotringer, trans. John Johnston, *Foucault Live (interviews, 1961–1984)* (New York: Semiotext(e), 1996), pp. 308–312.

Building a Queer Asian Movement

Building Communities and Organizing for Change

GLENN D. MAGPANTAY

Since the first *Q&A: Queer in Asian America* anthology, the lesbian, gay, bisexual, transgender, and queer (LGBTQ) Asian American, South Asian, Southeast Asian, and Pacific Islander (API) community has considerably matured. Yet challenges and frustrations still abound. According to the U.S. Census, APIs are the nation's fastest growing racial minority group. Immigrants from Asia are the largest segment of immigrants (both legal and undocumented) coming to the United States. More and more are coming out as LGBTQ. The Williams Institute at UCLA School of Law estimated 325,000, or 2.8 percent of all API adults in the United States, identify as LGBT.[1]

However, the community is often overlooked, and their needs are marginalized. LGBTQ APIs still suffer from invisibility, isolation, and stereotyping. LGBTQ APIs experience a truism that "All the gays are white; all the Asians are straight. Where do I belong?" Even in areas where there are large people of color populations, APIs feel submerged to larger African American or Latinx populations.

This essay will offer a historical overview of LGBTQ API communities and their organizing and community-building work since the last publication of *Q & A: Queer in Asian America* in 1998 to today's era in the 2020s. It will review local and national infrastructures that have been the basis for building communities.[2] Then it will review LGBTQ API organizing around a political agenda. This essay will offer future leaders and activists a sustainable model to build API LGBTQ communities and advance social change.

Development of Infrastructure to Build Community

In the 1980s, progressive movements connected and sparked organizing efforts amongst LGBTQ APIs. Lesbians and bisexual women were at the forefront in forming regional and national API groups such as the Asian Pacific Lesbian Bisexual Transgender Network (APLBTN), Asian Lesbians of the East Coast, and Trikone in San Francisco. The 1990s brought about increased public visibility for LGBTQ APIs, which inspired the formation of local LGBTQ API groups. In the early 2000s, several local LGBTQ API organizations formed. There were only thirty-five local LGBTQ API community organizations across the nation in 2005; today, there are nearly fifty. So much of the history of LGBTQ API organizing and community-building work has been shepherded through these organizations.

In an effort to learn from each other, leaders of LGBTQ API organizations convened at the National Gay and Lesbian Task Force's 2005 Creating Change conference in Oakland, California. There, organizational leaders shared stories of successes, challenges, and issues. They discovered that they all faced internal organizational challenges (e.g., organizational transitions, burnout, lack of involvement) and external frustrations about general invisibility, racism, and anti-immigrant bias in the gay community, as well as homophobia in the Asian community. Many felt that they were not connected with one another, and they were constantly reinventing the wheel. Basic organizational survival was immediate for some of them. They lamented over the lack of a national organization specifically for LGBTQ APIs. They envied LLeGO the Latin@ Lesbian and Gay Organization and the Black Lesbian and Gay Leadership Forum.

These leaders knew that they needed to regularly network to share ideas and that they could not each do it by themselves. Therefore, they formed a working group for a national organization that eventually became the National Queer Asian Pacific Islander Alliance.[3] NQAPIA was founded as a federation of LGBTQ API organizations to build the organizational capacity of local groups, develop leadership, invigorate grassroots organizing, and challenge homophobia and racism.

Almost all groups are all-volunteer run. Most groups are not formally incorporated as tax-exempt 501(c)(3) nonprofits. Some have only been around for less than five years, while others have endured for over twenty-five years. Being an all-volunteer-run organization presents obvious limitations in capacity and, at times, tenuous survival. On the other hand, it also allows for freedom from nonprofit limitations and the flexibility to more directly and quickly address emerging community needs.

Sustainable and enduring LGBTQ API organizations tend to engage in five distinct classes of activities: social, peer support, educational, outreach, and political.[4] They provide essential networking spaces where they can connect with people of common heritage and experiences. These spaces provide peer support for those coming out of the closet or simply looking to connect with their cultural identity. Educational activities include workshops, guest speakers, or discussion groups on a variety of topics.

This education work overlaps with efforts to promote visibility. LGBTQ APIs are often frustrated at how most of gay culture is an image of white gay hegemony and that women, transgender persons, South Asians, and Pacific Islanders are exceptionally absent. To address these frustrations, groups embark on a variety of outreach activities.

Almost all LGBTQ API organizations participate in annual LGBTQ Pride events. LBT women's groups and women members of multigender groups regularly participate in annual Dyke Marches. However, only half of organizations participate in API cultural-specific events, such as Lunar New Year or Tết, Diwali, or nation-specific Independence Day festivals. Before 2005, it seemed that LGBTQ APIs were more out as Asians in the LGBTQ community and more closeted in Asian communities. This has significantly shifted over the past fifteen years, where we could now also be LGBTQ in our Asian communities.

So much of the API community does not speak or read English. Almost half (43 percent) of the nation's Asian Americans over the age of eighteen are limited English proficient, and four out of five (81 percent) speak a language other than English in their homes. Yet resources and information about LGBTQ are almost all exclusively in English. The LGBTQ community does not engage non-English-speaking Americans.

This invisibility has promoted bias. For example, the Chinese-language newspaper *World Journal* published a national editorial in support of a federal constitutional amendment limiting marriage to only men and women. In 2004, Chinese Christian churches organized a multilingual rally against same-sex marriage in San Francisco. In response, LGBTQ API groups developed multilingual education campaigns about being LGBTQ.

Their approach to message development had to be culturally competent. They found that the traditional in-your-face approach of many gay activists, and Americans in general, turned off many foreign-born Asians. The messages needed to be more subtle, yet still affirming, in order to promote LGBTQ API acceptance.

Organizing and Advocacy

All LGBTQ API groups engage in some form of political advocacy or activism, but the frequency and manner vary tremendously. They all advocate for LGBTQ rights and frequently speak out against defamatory images and articles in the media. For example, groups in Los Angeles and New York protested the *Details* magazine's 2004 "Gay or Asian?" feature that mocked gay Asian men. SALGA in New York organized protests against the detention, deportation, and special registration of South Asians after 9/11. Sometimes groups express international solidarity by protesting human rights violations against LGBTQs abroad, such as Intro 377, the recriminalization of homosexual sodomy in India.

In 2000, the White House Initiative on Asian American and Pacific Islanders sought testimony on the needs of LGBTQ APIs.[5] Two hearings specifically involved representatives from the LGBTQ API community. This was arguably the first formal articulation of an LGBTQ API political agenda. In both hearings, witnesses spoke of a federally funded national needs assessment and the necessity that social services address the particular needs of LGBTQ APIs.

The campaign for marriage equality galvanized LGBTQ API groups, especially in California. API Equality Northern California and API Equality Los Angeles were founded in response to the 2008 anti-same-sex marriage Proposition 8. Both organizations hired staff, translated educational materials, and organized volunteers. They generated multiple stories about API same-sex couples in the ethnic media. They developed significant organizational infrastructure and, since Prop 8, have continued to advance the interests of LGBTQ APIs through advocacy, organizing, and storytelling.

Pushback and Strategic Utility

There was some pushback, however, to the organizational activism. In 2009, many LGBTQ API group leaders reported tensions in their organizations regarding balancing social and political activities. They had to negotiate between competing factions. A sizeable portion of their memberships were more focused on social activities and had a distaste for political activism. Another portion believed that their groups had a duty to be politically engaged and to speak up for LGBTQ APIs. Invariably, when the political was perceived as predominating (even if it was not with regard to actual hours), there were complaints that the groups became "too political," and members left.

Looking deeper, more of the socially oriented leaders and members tended to be immigrants or foreign-born. Those who were more political were U.S.-born. Indeed, some APIs came from countries with a history of government repression where speaking out had direct consequences. Some APIs are taught to be silent, but history has shown that silences lead to our demise. We must speak out.

One group leader noted that they use social events to build a political base; social events build their core group of volunteers and act as an entry point for new members. Once a part of the group, new members gain an awareness of community concerns and problems.

Another organizational leader said, "Simply existing as a gay Asian safe space was a political act in itself." Simply hosting API-only meetings was a recognition of racism and homophobia—and for women's groups, of sexism in society. He observed that people often came to "political consciousness" by going to organizational events, where discussions about racism and LGBTQ concerns would occasionally and organically emerge. These processes were highly effective in bringing more people to awareness.

The blending of political and social activities is essential. One longtime leader, Daniel Bao, noted that the history of the LGBTQ API community consisted of strong local social groupings and political regional organizing. To some extent, most of the social groups were predominantly men's groups—namely GAPIMNY, GAPA, and GAPSN—and regional political groups were predominantly East Asian women's groups, such as APLBTN and Asian Lesbians of the East Coast. Both networks were especially strong in the 1990s. Today, the LGBTQ API groups that have endured are those that balance general activities catering to larger numbers of people with more niche activities catering to people who seeking social, peer support, and educational opportunities.

Since then, men's groups have grown to be more political. Some, such as GAPIMNY and AQUA, have affirmatively worked to examine their role in the struggle against sexism. Many lesbian women activists joined broader women's issues or intersectional work to combat domestic violence and human trafficking. More recently founded LBTQ women's organizations since 2010 have become more social. Today, most LGBTQ API groups are multigender and mix both social and social justice activities.

Building a Queer Asian Agenda

Most of this activism has been reactionary. LGBTQ APIs have struggled to discern an affirmative political agenda that is both intersectional and inclusive. It must speak to the realities of LGBTQ APIs' lived experiences. Such an agenda must be multi-issue, encompassing racial justice, LGBTQ rights, women's rights, trans justice, and more. And it could be intersectional, where there is a unique area that bring together these lived realities. The lives of LGBTQ APIs involve complex intersections of being racial and ethnic, linguistic, sexual, gender, immigrant, and economic minorities.

Two breakthrough surveys helped to uncover this agenda. In 2004, the National Gay and Lesbian Task Force Policy Institute commissioned an LGBTQ API study, "Living at the Margins."[6] At the time, it was the most expansive and comprehensive study of LGBTQ APIs across the United States. LGBTQ APIs said that the most important issues they faced were immigration (40 percent), hate violence and harassment (39 percent), and lack of media representation (39 percent). In 2009, NQAPIA's descriptive directory of LGBTQ API groups, "Queer Asian Compass," found that LGBTQ API groups had or were working on multilingual anti-homophobia educational campaigns, media defamation, immigrants' rights and issues, and marriage equality.

LGBTQ Immigrants' Rights

Immigrants' rights became a unifying issue for LGBTQ APIs, first and foremost because many LGBTQ APIs are immigrants. According to the Census, Asian Americans are the fastest growing racial group in the nation, largely due to immigration. Two-thirds of all Asian Americans are foreign-born, and one-third (34 percent) are not citizens. Approximately one million Asian Americans are undocumented.

Asian immigration is outpacing Latino immigration. Today, 37 percent of all immigrants in the United States are from Asian countries. The Williams Institute at UCLA School of Law found that the immigrant population is disproportionately Asian. APIs comprised a larger share of LGBTQ immigrant populations, with 15 percent of undocumented LGBTQ adults and 35 percent of documented LGBTQ adults identifying as API.[7]

Moreover, immigrants have come under attack. After September 11, 2001, immigrants, particularly South Asian immigrants, became targets of racial profiling, detention, and deportation. Many LGBTQ APIs in the country were immigrants, most often as H1B professional workers or F-1 student visa holders.

For immigrants who are LGBTQ, residing in the United States can provide them with the freedom to be who they are. When their visas expire or when they are deported, they are sent back to countries and families that are less receptive, or even hostile, to homosexuality and gender nonconformity; they return to the closet and a life of denial.

Over the years, the specific agenda for immigrants' rights has grown out from responding to Newt Gingrich's 2006 congressional proposal, which made being an undocumented immigrant criminal, as well as a legal liability for those who know and harbor undocumented immigrants. The Catholic Church and social services agencies took to the streets in massive demonstrations. After Barack Obama's election, a new hope arose for the possibility of comprehensive immigration reform. Those failed attempts led to the Movement of Dreamers, where young people brought to the United States as children. When Congress failed to pass the Dream Act, Obama created the Deferred Action for Childhood Arrivals (DACA) program. Many LGBTQ API Dreamers are DACA recipients.

Before same-sex marriage was legalized, the agenda for LGBTQ immigrants' rights has been largely single-issue and narrowly focused on same-sex binational couples. While all couples deserve recognition, same-sex binational couples were actually a very small proportion among LGBTQ immigrants. Moreover, an agenda of immigrants' rights is usually not based on the benefit of Americans. The LGBTQ API community needed an all-encompassing immigrants' rights agenda.

The national campaign for LGBTQ API immigrants' rights was a multifaceted effort that brought together grassroots mobilization, storytelling and communications, training, and education.

NQAPIA's campaign on immigrants' rights spoke to the real-life experiences of diverse LGBTQ APIs. A statement of LGBTQ API unifying of principles included

- legalization of undocumented immigrants;
- expanded visa programs for students and workers (both low-wage and professional);
- legal protections to guard against racial profiling, detentions, and deportations;
- fewer restrictions in applying for political asylum; and
- protection of family immigration, including extending family sponsorship for binational same-sex couples.

In 2010, LGBTQ API organizations hosted community forums across the country where immigrant speakers put a tangible face on the campaign and told stories of being undocumented, denied asylum, or separated from their partners or families. Articles and opinion editorials raised the concerns of LGBTQ API immigrants in the *Huffington Post* and LGBT, Asian ethnic, and online news media outlets, including *India West*, *Philippine News*, DC's *MetroWeekly*, and Boston's *Rainbow Times*.[8]

This work had three long-term impacts. One impact was alliance building. NQAPIA brought together mainstream LGBTQ rights organizations to support communities of color, as well as mainstream API groups to support LGBTQ inclusive immigrations reform. NQAPIA pushed both API and LGBTQ national advocacy groups to appreciate an intersectional analysis that connected immigrants' rights and LGBTQ justice.

Second, the efforts united diverse constituencies. The campaign had broad resonance and brought together groups that were occasionally in competition to work collaboratively towards a shared goal. Examples include seeking green cards for both low-wage and professional workers, as well as bringing together East Asian and South Asian communities.

Third, efforts led to organized actions, community forums, and press conferences. Local leaders learned basic community-organizing skills such as working with the media, volunteer coordination, and spokesperson development. These core skills prove useful for many other efforts and can help develop diverse local networks of LGBTQ API activists across the country to lead further social change initiatives.

Family Acceptance

Another area of work focused on family acceptance. LGBTQ people can get married, but I ask, "Who will come to the wedding?" Marriage is not only an important legal right but also a familial recognition of our partners. Parental acceptance of their LGBTQ children and their children's partners is still needed.

Indeed, while most Americans support the right for same-sex couples to legally marry,[9] many APIs are less accepting, if not opposed. In 2012, the Asian American Legal Defense and Education Fund (AALDEF) polled 9,096 Asian American voters in fourteen states and in twelve Asian languages on Election Day. It was the largest multilingual exit poll of its kind, and it was the first time that API support for LGBTQ issues had been polled on such a national and representative scale.[10] AALDEF found that only about one-third (37 percent) of Asian American voters supported the right of same-sex couples to legally marry, whereas almost half (48 percent) were opposed.

The greatest opposition came from Asian Americans who were foreign-born, limited English proficient, and older. This cut makes up the largest portion of the Asian American electorate today. Only one-fifth (21 percent) of Asian American voters polled were born in the United States, and 79 percent were foreign-born citizens who naturalized. The majority support did not break by gender, college education, or Democratic Party affiliation.

Usually, the parents who are visible and publicly proclaim that they love their gay kids are almost all white or only verbalize this in English. Few API parents have stepped forward to say the same.[11] Traditional cultural attitudes sometimes dissuade such outness. API parents are often stuck in a "time warp" when it comes to awareness about LGBTQ people. Parents tell their children that "there are no gays back home" or share their perception of LG-BTQs as all being "transsexual prostitutes." That is what they remember from when they immigrated to the United States in the 1960s, 1970s, and 1980s. Today, the LGBTQ community has flourished abroad. There are sizable LGBTQ pride celebrations and public parades in Manila, Mumbai, Beijing, Taipei, Hanoi, and Seoul.[12] Unfortunately, Asian parents in the United States today never saw those parades, so they understand being gay only as something that would never happen back at home. Among APIs, homosexuality is still often viewed as a Western influence. LGBTQs in the community are hidden or sequestered. There is a belief that LGBTQ APIs should not be out so as not to bring shame or embarrassment to the family. API LGBTs themselves sometimes buy into this fallacy. To address this conundrum, NQAPIA partnered with Asian Pride Project (APP) on a family acceptance campaign.[13]

NQAPIA placed APP's PSAs of API parents who love their LGBTQ kids on international channels, namely Sinovision, Television Korea, and ZeeTV, which reached twenty-six million households. Along with the PSAs, NQAPIA distributed translated leaflets in twenty-five Asian and Pacific languages about being LGBTQ. Supportive API parents also held twenty-four family acceptance workshops in collaboration with NQAPIA.

The long-term term impact is to enhance LGBTQ API visibility in Asian ethnic communities, promote understanding, and support parents so that more LGBTQ young people can come out, be accepted, and be celebrated in their families.

Conclusion

LGBTQ API organizations across the United States work hard to provide a safe and supportive space for LGBTQ APIs. They provide an array of social, supportive, political, and educational activities. They reach out to educate their members and the broader community. They also speak out in support of the community. They challenge racism in the LGBTQ community and homophobia in Asian American communities.

Some groups have been around for twenty years, are incorporated, and have hired professional staff. Others are just starting out. Organizations have launched visibility campaigns, multilingual efforts, and safe spaces for the more vulnerable, forgotten, and marginalized identities of the community. Some are heavily involved in efforts for the right to marriage, whereas others seek rights for immigrants. Taken together, these efforts build LGBTQ API communities and advocacy in profound ways.

NOTES

1. Angeliki Kastanis and Gary J. Gates, "LGBT Asian and Pacific Islander Individuals and Same-sex Couples." The Williams Institute, UCLA School of Law. September 2013: 1. https://williamsinstitute.law.ucla.edu/wp-content/uploads/LGBT-API-People-Couples-Sep-2013.pdf.

2. For a more detailed review, see Glenn D. Magpantay, "TIGER: A Sustainable Model for Building LGBTQ AAPI Community," *Harvard JFK Asian Amer. Policy Review* 30 (2020): 5–15.

3. There were other prior efforts to form a national organization. APLBTN was a successful network in the 1990s but struggled at bringing in new women to take on leadership. Asian and Pacific Islanders for Human Rights (APIHR) hosted a convening at Creating Change in Portland in 2002 and announced its intention to being a national organization with no support or buy-in from others outside of Los Angeles, where it was based. LGBTQ API conferences such as DesiQ hosted by Trikone in San Francisco and Lotus Roots in Seattle never developed beyond simply being conferences.

4. National Queer Asian Pacific Islander Alliance (NQAPIA), *Queer Asian Compass: A Descriptive Directory of Lesbian, Gay, Bisexual, and Transgender (LGBTQ) Asian American, South Asian, and Pacific Islander (AAPI) organizations* (New York, July 2009).

5. President's Advisory Commissions on Asian Americans and Pacific Islanders, "A People Looking Forward, Action for Access and Partnerships in the 21st Century (Interim Report to the President and the Nation)," January 2001.

6. Alain Dang and Mandy Hu, "National Gay and Lesbian Task Force Policy Institute, Asian Pacific American Lesbian, Gay Bisexual and Transgender People: A Community Portrait," 2004.

7. Gary Gates, "LGBTQ Adult Immigrants in the United States," The Williams Institute UCLA School of Law, March 2013.

8. Deepa Iyer, Op-Ed, "LGBT South Asians and Immigration Reform," *India West*, July 19, 2013; Ben de Guzman, Opinion-Editorial, "National Coming Out Day and 'Coming Out' for Immigration Reform," *Philippine News*, October 11, 2014; Maxwell Ng, Debasri Roy, "Immigration Reform Needs Comprehensive Approach from the LGBT Community: Boston Asian Americans Weigh In," *Rainbow Times*, June 4, 2013, http://www.therainbowtimesmass.com/immigration-reform-needs-comprehensive-approach-from-the-lgbt-community-boston-asian-americans-weigh-in/; Ben de Guzman, "All LGBT Immigrants Need to Be Considered in Immigration Reform," *Huffington Post*, January 31, 2013, https://www.huffpost.com/entry/lgbt-immigrants_b_2582643.

9. Scott Clement and Robert Barnes, "Poll: Gay-Marriage Support at Record High," *Washington Post*, April 23, 2015.

10. Chi-Ser Tran, Glenn D. Magpantay, and Margaret Fung, "The Asian American Vote 2012," The Asian American Legal Defense and Education Fund, 2013, http://aaldef.org/Asian%20American%20Vote%202012.pdf.

11. Marsha Aizumi, "Op-ed: Embracing the Role of Asian Mother to a Trans Son," *The Advocate*, May 27, 2015, http://www.advocate.com/commentary/2015/05/27/op-ed-embracing-role-asian-mother-trans-son.

12. Thom Senzee, "PHOTOS: Taiwan Pride 2014 Is All About Marriage Equality." *The Advocate*, October 27, 2014, http://www.advocate.com/pride/2014/10/27/photos-taiwan-pride-2014-all-about-marriage-equality; Yogesh Pawar, "Seventh Edition of Mumbai Gay Pride Gets Bigger and Bolder, Attracts People from across the World," *DNA India*, February 2, 2014; "Thousands March in Seoul for S Korea's Gay Pride Parade," Channel NewsAsia, June 28, 2015.

13. NQAPIA, "PSA Campaign," May 22, 2015, http://www.nqapia.org/wpp/category/psa-campaign/; "South Asian Parents Who Love Their LGBTQ Kids," http://www.nqapia.org/wpp/south-asian-parents-who-love-their-lgbt-kids-psa/; "Japanese Parents Who Love Their LGBTQ Kids," http://www.nqapia.org/wpp/japanese-parents-who-love-their-lgbt-kids-psas/.

PART IV

Messing up the Archives and
Circuits of Desire

inspector of journals makes introductions

Fan & Basket plot escape from Peabody
Essex Museum/a birthright[1]

CHING-IN CHEN

winter sibling mold and fire   **a birthright**
                                born with an army
line a desk   *in my father's tongue. She was one who*
build paper
drown records   *lined coats and gushed*
kept men with failing bodies

                                            pork
                                fat, one who fasted
                        tomatoes, sizzled without mushrooms.

    Mocha, Red Sea, Lisbon, Madeira, Manila, Sumatra, India, China, Aus-
tralia, Sandwich and Marquesas Island

                    We marveled often at his dissolving
                                mouth, hard
                                    sweat on pan,

        this matchmaker of tiny details
                                crafted no inheritance
                                but what teeth procured, familiar
        young man   *dark between lips*
        of bitten seas

---

1. From *recombinant* (Berkeley, CA: Kelsey Street Press, 2017).

On (En)countering the Archival Sidekick

Joyce Gabiola

August is the most suffocating time of the year to be in the southern region of Texas, but for the most part, I was happy to be there—most certainly to hang out with family and longtime friends and devour as much Tex-Mex and Vietnamese food as my digestive system could handle. I was also looking forward to the explicit purpose of the overdue visit to my home state: inquiry. I had returned to conduct a research study that asked if symbolic annihilation—the underrepresentation, trivialization, or erasure of marginalized groups[1]—applies to LGBTQ+[2] Asian Americans and Pacific Islanders in Texas archives. While I was excited to conduct my first solo re-search project in four Texas cities, I was also highly anxious about being back in my home state against the backdrop of our current political climate, less than a year following a devastating presidential election in which a busi-nessperson with reality TV experience but no foreign relations experience somehow became the leader of the United States. While I feel very safe being in and traveling to/from Houston and Austin, I cannot say the same is true for College Station and Denton, two small Texas cities that are home to two institutions with significant LGBTQ+ archival collections. As I traveled alone on the road to and from these small cities, I experienced a high level of anxiety. As a queer, masculine-presenting, female-assigned person of color, I did not want to draw attention to myself, although I am certain I stood out. I was conscious of this, so in case I had to interact with someone who hates people who look like me and what I may represent based on their worldview, I was certain to smile and speak within my higher register in an attempt to mark myself "female," the gender identifier I was assigned at birth. All of this was to appear nonthreatening in white heteropatriarchal environments. All of this emotional labor in pursuit of research.

August 7, 2017.[3] I was already overcome with anxiety over the fact that I had to drive alone to College Station and stay overnight. The anxiety intensi-fied that morning because it was raining hard as I was leaving Houston. I was en route to continue my research study at Texas A&M University (TAMU), a historically conservative institution in a small, historically conservative

Texas city.[4] Overall, this was not an ordinary research trip; it was intense and made me ponder the precarity of my position on campus, in that city and state, and in my own profession . . . and even in the reading room of the archives.[5]

This study was not required; no one made me do it. In fact, I created the research opportunity for myself and even applied for and was awarded an institutional research grant that fully funded the project. I knew exactly what I was requiring of myself from the beginning, and I felt apprehensive, but the purpose of the entire study was important to me not only as a doctoral student in archival studies armed with a research question about the representation of LGBTQ+ Asian Americans and Pacific Islanders in Texas archives but also as a queer Filipinx Texan, hoping to see representations of people with whom I identify in archives—their preserved existence as part of the historical record. Even though I felt my safety was precarious as a queer, masculine-presenting, female-assigned person of color, I moved forward with this particular leg of the research trip because the entire study and experience was personally meaningful. Ironically, although I was studying the presence or absence of LGBTQ+ Asian Americans and Pacific Islanders in Texas archives, I was concerned with making myself invisible.

As I looked through materials in the Don Kelly Research Collection of Gay Literature and Culture in Texas A&M University's Cushing Memorial Library and Archives, I came across a minute representation of and information about LGBTQ+ Asians. In addition to a handful of books, such as *Queer Asian Cinema: Shadows in the Shade*, that include black-and-white photographs of what could be perceived as queer depictions, most of the materials did not originate from or are not specific to Texas.

- Southern California
  - Newsletters of Asian/Pacific Lesbians and Gays, Inc. (Los Angeles)
  - *Pacific Coast Times* (San Diego)
- New York
  - One issue of *PersuAsian*, the "Newsmagazine for the Gay Asian & Pacific Islander Men of New York"
  - Two issues of *Out & About*, a defunct travel magazine that was tailored for gay and lesbian travelers, featuring articles about "gay Asia"
  - One issue of *POZ* Magazine with Kiyoshi Kuromiya on the cover
  - Issue 99 (May 22, 1990) of *OutWeek* with a group of Asians on the cover linked to the featured article by Nina Reyes titled "Asians and Pacific Islanders Look for Unity in a Queer World"

- Detroit
- One issue of *Gay Liberator* (July 1973) with an article titled "Gays in China"
- Boston
  - *Gay Community News* (vol. 14, no. 38, April 12–18, 1987), with a cover article titled "Chinese Author Pai Hsien Yung Speaks on Attitudes toward Gay Men and Lesbians in Taiwan"
- Pittsburgh
  - *Out* (no. 164, November 1990) with an article titled, "On Relationships and 'Rice Queens'" about playwright David Henry Hwang and *M. Butterfly*[6]

Materials in the collection directly connected to Texas are *Paz y Liberación*, an international newsletter about gay liberation (with a Houston mailing address), and one newsletter, "The BUZZ of Dragonflies," from the Dragonflies of Dallas (January–February 1995).[7] The collection also contains a noticeable amount of materials about Yukio Mishima, a Japanese writer, poet, actor, and film director, that may lead one to conclude that the creator and donor of the collection had a particular interest in Mishima. Based solely on these archival materials, we know that there was and is, at the very least, a LGBTQ+ Asian American and Pacific Islander presence in California and New York in the 1980s and one queer Asian group, the Dragonflies of Dallas, in the mid-1990s. Considering the collection creator and donor is a white gay man,[8] it seems that he had a particular interest in queer Asian culture and the stories and images of gay Asian males. While I was pleased to see a semblance of Asian representation, I could not help but think that this group of people remains marginalized in this archival collection. They are not at the forefront of their depictions; although a significant part of the collection, they are "just an element to someone else's story."[9] They are archival sidekicks to a white, Western male narrative.

The most notable item for me in the collection is issue 6 (Summer 1980) of the *Gay Insurgent: A Gay Left Journal*, which features a black-and-white photograph on the cover that documents "gay Asians" at the 1979 March on Washington for Lesbian and Gay Rights.[10] They are holding up a banner that reads, "We're Asians / Gay & Proud." I was so taken aback when I came across this journal issue that I had to pause and sit back in my seat, shocked, taking in deep breaths. While the photograph is not specific to Texas, it is obviously significant. As I interrogate power structures in and of archives, I wondered whether this cover photograph would be more significant to me if I found the journal in an archival collection that was created and donated by an Asian person from Texas, whether or not they identify along the LGBTQ+ spectrum. For me, the answer is yes. In fact, if the journal was preserved by a community-based archives, that is even more significant. Institutional archives are beholden to funders, bureaucratic processes, and the research needs of an academic majority while being restricted by institutional policies and standardized archival practices that lead to the symbolic annihilation of marginalized groups in the historical record. Through a legacy of colonialism and white supremacy, many institutional archives in the United States are filled with archival materials that reflect white dominance, and although institutions are increasingly more motivated to diversify their collections, we might ask a series of questions. Are institutional archivists ethically prepared to steward materials that document the rich histories of historically erased groups? And if a LGBTQ+ collection is housed at a historically conservative institution in a historically conservative city that upholds laws that discriminate against LGBTQ+ people, what is required for a queer, masculine-presenting, female-assigned person of color to negotiate in order to access materials that may document representations of their own community? If the physical environment of a city or institution is inaccessible or precarious for someone who identifies across the intersectional, ever-evolving LGBTQ+ spectrum, for whom is the LGBTQ+ collection intended?

According to a 2018 report by the Women Archivists Section of the Society of American Archivists, 88 percent of American archivists in the profession identify as white, 63 percent as heterosexual, and 98 percent as within the gender binary, and 9 percent are directly or indirectly (self, or via parents and family) connected to an immigrant experience.[11] This means that collections housed in most of the country's archival repositories are informed and controlled by a worldview that is not aligned with the varying, intersectional realities of LGBTQ+ Asians and their respective communities. Archivists more or less adhere to standardized archival practices steeped in the traditions of an imperialistic, white supremacist cisheteropatriarchal society in order to preserve materials that document the lived realities of marginalized communities. This, along with their well-meaning initiatives to diversify their collections and extend the breadth of their holdings intended to serve the scholarly pursuits of a self-proclaimed "diverse" academic community, leads to the further marginalization or trivialization of underrepresented groups in archives. As mentioned previously, archival representations of LGBTQ+ Asians become archival sidekicks that are preserved within the confines of the narratives that belong to white, cis collection donors.

We can counter the archival sidekick found in institutional archives by proactively preserving our own "stuff" that materially connects us to history. We can control our own representation and maintain authority over the extent to which we are visible in archives and the ways in which we exist in the historical record, but perhaps you should first ask yourselves a question.

Is the history of you important? Upon asking this question during the semistructured focus groups and interviews of my research study,[12] I was met with silence, or rather the sound of intentional thinking. Participants hesitated to affirm that their history is important, even though to themselves they had already determined it to be so. Their readiness to convey that their own history is indeed important and to permit that determination to stand on its own without qualifying it seemed to be difficult, but certainly that is not surprising. The significance of this discomfort is connected to the preservation of materials that document the lived experiences of LGBTQ+ Asian Americans, which impacts representation in the historical record but also provides insight into the power structure that controls archives and further marginalizes vulnerable people and groups.

When asked if their history is important, none of the participants were alone in their discomfort while distancing the self from the importance of preserving one's history. Some voiced that the importance of their history is interconnected with and dependent on the histories and perspectives of others. Ching-In Chen, a Chinese American writer and teacher who identifies as queer, genderqueer, and gender fluid, responded,

> Yes, because I'm a writer, but I think . . . maybe because of my social-
> ization, it makes me uncomfortable to say that. I feel more comfort-
> able talking about other people's stories and histories being pre-
> served. I know that I'm part of that. . . . I feel like everyone's history
> is important and contributes to the social fabric of that community
> or that society. I want to know about different people's histories. But
> I also feel this resisting impulse when you're asking me about wheth-
> er my history is important.[13]

Addie Tsai, a biracial writer, poet, and teacher, identifies as queer and nonbinary. On whether her history is important, she explained,

> I do write about my queerness, my Asianness, my biraciality. The
> places where I feel liminal in terms of gender or ways that I feel
> people have wanted me to be a certain gender expression, and all the
> kinds of relationships I have. So, I guess, in that case, I feel like, that
> my work would be important to others. I mean, I was thinking about
> like, I probably would've come out earlier if I knew Asian queer
> people existed. Just if I saw what that looks like. But the only thing I
> even came close to seeing was most often white or black, and not
> dealing with the issues of family that I knew that I would have to
> contend with. And having no real figures to talk to about those
> things. So, I imagine that that would be a really sort of benefit of our

stories being out there. It's just that the more stories there are, the more people can connect themselves to them. So I guess it's hard for me to say yes 'cause I'm like, I'm not that important.[14]

Melanie Pang, a queer, cisgender Chinese Filipina American who has lived in Texas her entire life, responded to the question by first asking a couple of clarifying questions:

Of me as a person? . . . Important for the world to know? I am told that I have a story that is worth listening to, so I guess yes? I don't know, I feel weird saying that, but . . .[15]

Melanie proceeded to describe her experience giving a talk about social work and LGBTQ issues to an eighth grade class that was comprised of mostly Asian students at a private school. She opened her talk with,

"Has anyone in here had their parents tell them how their life should be when they're older? Like what profession you should be, what your life will look life. . . . [Everyone raised their hands] Cool, so you understand what it's like to have your parents decide for you that basically you're going to become a doctor. You're going to get married, and it's going to be to the opposite gender." They really clicked with that. They really understood, like, oh, having those expectations, it doesn't feel great to have those expectations placed upon you just like it's not great to have this heteronormativity placed upon you. . . . One of the girls wrote a letter and gave it to the counselor to mail to me. It basically said, "I never heard a speaker like you before. I think it's great what you're doing for the LGBTQ community. You're giving a voice. . . . It's even better because you're a person of color." This is an eighth grade girl. . . . Yeah, it's just having her taking the time . . . to sit down and write a letter to me and tell me that I'm unlike anyone else who's come to talk to them was really eye-opening for me. Kinda made me realize that, yeah, there are other people out there, even if this kid doesn't identify as queer or whatever. It's just that someone could relate to them on a certain level— that that was valued. That's what brings me to say yes.[16]

In good company with his fellow community members, T. Le, a gay Vietnamese university administrator, said,

I wanna say yes and no. But I wanna say yes. Because I wanna be that one example that I was looking for when I was a kid. . . . Now that [I am] older, I am like, "Yeah, my life mattered." And I want people to know that I did this. . . . I wanna leave a legacy or something behind.[17]

Reflecting on their own experiences, Addie, Melanie, and T. Le imagine that others might consider their histories important as a way to relate or be comforted in the fact that they are not alone. Certainly, across time and place throughout the American South, there are folks who are searching for such stories to connect. While access to materials that document these histories is significant, it also intensifies their vulnerability. Will others use this information in a way for which it was not intended? And to what extent do institutional archivists (in Texas) possess the knowledge and sensitivity to represent the nuances of Ching-In, Addie, Melanie, and T. Le's histories? If our personal papers are deposited in institutional archives, to what extent will our narratives be misrepresented, trivialized, devalued, or marginalized as a mere element of commodified diversification in the pursuit of knowledge?

Koomah, an interdisciplinary artist who is Japanese (Ainu, an Indigenous ethnic minority), Brazilian, intersex, gender fluid, pansexual, and queer, added to the discussion.

We can start giving our stories, but it's like, it kinda goes back to: where are our queer Asian elders and their stories? 'Cause we don't have that. And we don't know where to find that. We can make it for the future, but it feels almost like a loss. Like we're missing something, and it's something that we could've definitely benefited from, but at least our generation will not have that. Which, is sad. . . . I almost feel like I've let people down. I don't know if that's even, we were talking about this immediate need to feel humble. But like, there's also this immediate need to take the blame for the inaction on that. Even though I know it's not my fault. But at the same time, I feel like it's my not doing anything about it. Whether that is cultural or just my own shit, I don't know.[18]

Koomah continued, "I'm not that important, my story is not that important, there are much more important people than me' is the kind of mindset that we have to break through and get past. That's tough."[19] The directive that Koomah urges—that we need to get past the idea that one's story is "not that important" to preserve—is the simple point of this essay. The unsettled feeling that Ching-In, Addie, Melanie, T. Le, and Koomah experience prompted by the thought of their own history being important involves a tension in which they acknowledge the importance of their histories and stories but do not believe they are important enough to preserve on their own. How, then, will these materials be preserved, and who will lead or participate in the charge? Community-based archival initiatives have existed for years, but none explicitly focus on LGBTQ+ Asian Americans and/or Pacific Islanders in the American South.

On February 23, 2013, the White House Initiative on Asian Americans and Pacific Islanders (WHIAA/PI) Texas Regional Conference was held at the University of Houston, Central Campus. Hesitant but determined, a cisgender male of Filipino descent and a cisgender female of Thai descent, both in their thirties, scrambled along the row of seats to reach the mic stand. They stood together as they shared their names and occupations and, in the face of the unnamed landscape of Asian heterosexuality, asserted themselves as being part of the LGBTQ community. They affirmed, "We are your friends and family, your sons, your daughters, your cousins, your aunts, your uncles, your teachers, your doctors. . . . We are here. Do not forget about us." I was not present to witness this moment, but my lesbian friend of this anecdote told me they were met with applause. It was as though that mic stand was seemingly meant just for them to create that particular moment for posterity. As a queer Filipinx American who grew up in Houston not knowing of any other queer Filipinxs or Asians until college, this moment is especially significant because today it confirms the historical existence, however recent, of people with whom I racially and ethnically identify and their willingness to be visible, thriving in a shared geographic place governed by laws designed to discriminate against us. There is power and resistance in my friends' willingness to be visible and to demand that they not be forgotten by the larger Asian American community in Houston. Alas, while I can believe this meaningful moment transpired and also share the story with others as fact, there is no documentation—on paper or as digital content—that this particular moment took place. It is possible that my friends' joint statement was recorded or that they were photographed, but by whom and for what purpose?

As we've heard before, if we do not tell our own stories, they will be told by someone else. As Koomah mentioned, the histories and stories of queer Asian elders in and of Texas are already lost. One thing is certain: our histories (comprised of unique individual narratives that intersect with and enrich others) and materials that directly connect us to these histories can be found if we embrace the notion that we have not only the power to be the stewards of our own histories but also the responsibility to imagined others to connect with them through the historical record. The following question warrants another go, and I encourage you to invite others into the conversation: Is the history of you important?

NOTES

1. Gaye Tuchman, "Introduction: The Symbolic Annihilation of Women by the Mass Media," in *Hearth and Home: Images of Women in the Mass Media*, edited by Gaye Tuchman, Arlene Kaplan Daniels, and James Benet (New York: Oxford University Press,

1978), 3–38; Michelle Caswell, "Seeing Yourself in History: Community Archives in the Fight Against Symbolic Annihilation," *The Public Historian* 36, no. 4 (2014): 26–37.

2. LGBTQ+ (lesbian, gay, bisexual, trans, queer+) denotes the open, ever-evolving spectrum of intersecting identities regarding gender, gender expression, and sexuality.

3. Having lived through two major floods while living in Houston, hard rainfall is a trigger. This was ten days before Tropical Storm Harvey formed, which eventually grew into a Category 4 hurricane that devastated areas in Texas and Louisiana. "Hurricane Harvey Aftermath," CNN, 2017. https://www.cnn.com/specials/us/hurricane-harvey.

4. Human Rights Campaign, 2019 Municipal Equality Index Scorecard, https://assets2.hrc.org/files/images/resources/MEI-2019-College_Station-Texas.pdf?_ga=2.108371970.1200395307.1582139894-876556945.1582139894; Hannah Brennan, "Is 'Closet Station' Closing Up? A Look at a College's Newly Found Tolerance," LGBTQ NATION, January 19, 2020, https://www.lgbtqnation.com/2020/01/closet-station-closing-look-texas-ams-newly-found-tolerance/. Related to this: When my older sister was an undergraduate student at TAMU, the KKK held a rally in the field next to her apartment building. Additionally, around the time of my research trip, the leader of the "alt-right" was invited to speak on campus, and the riots in Charlottesville had just occurred. Moreover, the general listserv of the Society of American Archivists (SAA), affectionately known as #thatdarnlist on Twitter, was occupied with a tense, provocative discussion about a panel that was held during its annual meeting only a couple of weeks prior, which focused on the notion of "dismantling white supremacy in archives."

5. A bright light of my experience in TAMU's archives was my short but pleasant interaction with the esteemable Rebecca Hankins (associate professor and archivist of Africana studies, women and gender studies, race and ethnic studies, and Arabic language). With her presence, I was comforted knowing that I had access to not only her expert knowledge in regard to the LGBT collection but also her familiarity with navigating, as a person of color (although we are not monoliths), research in the reading room of a predominantly white, conservative institution.

6. Don Kelly Research Collection of Gay Literature and Culture, Cushing Memorial Library and Archives, Texas A&M University, College Station, TX.

7. Ibid.

8. Megan Smith, "Aggies Embrace LGBT Culture," *OutSmart*, March 1, 2015, https://www.outsmartmagazine.com/2015/03/aggies-embrace-lgbt-culture/.

9. Melanie Pang, individual phone interview, August 21, 2017. In the interview, Pang refers to the representation of Asian Americans in forms of media as elements to someone else's story.

10. Steve Nowling, National March on Washington for Lesbian and Gay Rights, October 14, 1979, *Gay Insurgent: A Gay Left Journal* no. 6 (1980), cover, Don Kelly Research Collection.

11. Society of American Archivists, Women Archivists Section, "The 2017 WArS /SAA Salary Survey: Initial Results and Analysis," accessed March 6, 2018, https://www2.archivists.org/sites/all/files/WArS-SAA-Salary-Survey-Report.pdf.

12. The call for research participants invited people of Asian and/or Pacific Islander descent, but none of the participants were of Pacific Islander descent.

13. Ching-In Chen, individual interview, Houston, TX, August 4, 2017. I obtained consent to cite them by name and attribute quotations to them in publications.

14. Addie Tsai, focus group, Houston, TX, August 18, 2017. I obtained consent to cite her by name and attribute quotations to her in publications.

15. Pang, 2017. I obtained consent to cite her by name and attribute quotations to her in publications.

16. Ibid.

17. T. Le, focus group, Houston, TX, August 18, 2017. I obtained consent to cite him by name and attribute quotations to him in publications.

18. Koomah, focus group, Houston, TX, August 18, 2017. I obtained consent to cite them by name and attribute quotations to them in publications.

19. Ibid.

Camp Objects

Orientalist Kitsch and Trashy Re-Collections
of the Japanese American Incarceration

Chris A. Eng

Trash, kitsch, or camp? Orientalist objects clutter the cultural landscape. Mustard yellow faces, buck-toothed grins, and slanted eyes constitute a recognizable repertoire of racial tropes that embellish their surfaces, projecting fantasies of a Far East and Orientalizing Asian-raced bodies into alien others. Given the prominent "culturalization of Asia in the United States through objects," as Leslie Bow submits, "Oriental *things* come to assume heightened symbolism."[1] That is, the persistent repertory of Orientalist visualizations materializes not only on the screen and the stage but also through physical objects: baubles, trinkets, tchotchkes, and other collectibles. Grappling with the legacies of such racial iconography, political projects grounded in cultural nationalism most commonly assert that racial minorities must reject objecthood to emerge as full subjects. The Oriental is the fake, a mere imitative copy of "real" Asian American bodies and histories distorted for the viewing pleasures of mainstream audiences. In order for the Asian American to flourish, the Oriental must die.

Rather than outright rejecting such Orientalia, what might it mean to more fully reckon with their effects and affects? Approaching Kandice Chuh's conceptualization of "subjectlessness" slantwise, I postulate "objectfulness" to apprehend the object (relation)s that cluster and orbit around the imaginaries of "Asian America(n)."[2] Accordingly, I follow the lead of Asian Americanists for reappraising objecthood in spite of the risks. Cultural and academic accounts customarily construe racialization in terms of objectification: "stereotyping reduces Asians and Asian Americans to objects of curiosity and desire or hatred, fear, and abuse."[3] Meanwhile, renewed scholarly attention to objects in studies of new materialisms too often elide considerations of social difference while also reproducing an "ahistorical compulsion."[4] In contrast to these tendencies, Joseph Jeon argues that apprehending objects as "racial things" can activate a "defamiliarizing function" and "access alternative histories."[5] Likewise, Tina Chen reassesses the "Asiancy" that objecthood affords to deflate preoccupations with resistance that underscore agency and subjecthood as the key objectives.[6] These efforts join Anne Anlin Cheng's appeal "to take seriously what it means to live as an object, an aesthetic supplement."[7] Heeding these calls, I ask, What are the potential uses and implications of reorientating our critical endeavors toward those despised objects of (Asian) American past-times?

This chapter turns to the prints of Roger Shimomura, which decidedly do not kill the Oriental but rather flagrantly place it front and center. His hybrid artwork takes up an ostensibly improper aesthetic approach in portraying the incarceration of Japanese Americans during World War II. A sansei Japanese American artist, Shimomura was interned as a child at the Minidoka camp in Hunt, Idaho. Reveling in the playful, irreverent, and humorous, Shimomura's prolific oeuvre explores three main themes: "appropriation and manipulation of traditional Japanese prints," depictions of the incarceration, and the reworking of popular American cultural icons.[8] His engagement with these three themes through creative juxtapositions provides unique insight into how "the heterosexual stability of the patriotic white American male icon emerges only in contrast to the resolute linking of queerness with Japaneseness."[9] By foregrounding the Oriental, Shimomura induces a reassessment of how queerness correlates with the incarceration through what might be called "debased aesthetics." The aesthetics animating such racist iconography is debased insofar as it fails to reach the cultural ideals of high art. Moreover, this categorization indexes the means of aestheticization that ascribe negative social values to specific bodies based on racial difference.[10] Therefore, the debased aesthetics of racial kitsch inspires affective responses of "disgust [which] apprehends the object as a kind of body that we are not. . . . It draws a boundary, not only against the object's complicit audiences, but also against the object itself."[11] Yet the aesthetic effects are by no means immaterial and inconsequential.

Refusing to turn away from these fake images, Shimomura playfully explores the capabilities of Asiancy by proliferating debased objects. As John Tchen notes, "Shimomura's handmade drawings of mass-produced reproductions effectively thumb his nose at aesthetic, hierarchic judgments on copying as derivative. He gleefully copies the racist copyists, understands they're systemic to the politics and culture, and bombards our visual field with japs, rats, and chinks so we can't avert our attention."[12] In so doing, Shimomura's artwork illuminates a category of Orientalist kitsch to theorize the ways in which processes of aestheticization embedded in such iconography correspond with the formal mechanisms of enemy racialization that rationalized the structures of confinement. Put otherwise, these objects come to queer Japanese Americans through a racializing logic that imposes "phantasms of orientalness" to characterize them as inauthentic and derivative.[13] In revisiting the debased repertoire of Orientalist kitsch, Shimomura's 2013 exhibition *Prints of Pop (& War)* recollects the camps of

Japanese American incarceration through the cultural practice of queer camp by reframing and recycling pop images of the Oriental, "enemy Jap." In this way, my formulation of "camp objects" follows Shimomura to examine the multiple aesthetic forms surrounding the iconography of Orientalist kitsch that circulated before, during, and after the incarceration as prominent artifacts of the camps. Through his art, Shimomura reanimates the modes of dissent emanating from Orientalist kitsch, elucidating the ways that queer camp can object to the racial structures that underwrite the pasts and aftermath of the incarceration.

Asian as Kitsch?

Shimomura's artwork starkly contrasts more prevalent treatments of the Japanese American incarceration. Manifesting in tones of black and white, documentary photography, most famously those by Ansel Adams and Dorothea Lange, have been a favored antidote to the erasure of these camps from national history. Yet as Elena Tajima Creef pointedly contends, "That we continue to be drawn to either Adams's heroic or Lange's tragic modes of visual narrative tells us much about the appeal of such binary poles of representation and its impact on the selective nature of our national historical memory."[14] The predominance of these dichotomous representational modes between the heroic and the tragic is perhaps unsurprising since they most readily conjure forms of major affect such as pride, sorrow, or anger, which are often perceived as inherently political insofar as they incite catharsis as "grander passions" that move us toward collective action.[15] These photographs evoke such affects to affirm claims to national belonging over and against the pervasive fearmongering that accused Japanese Americans of being inherently suspect, duplicitous, and indelibly alien on the sole basis of race.

Far from adhering to hues of black and white, Shimomura highlights the colorful imagery of the Oriental that saturated the popular national imaginary. By refusing "any wished-for escape from the shame of America's racial past,"[16] his artwork leads the way for a provocation made by Elaine Kim: to "disobediently claim and articulate the 'trashy heart of history.'"[17] Although this might resemble Maxine Hong Kingston's famous assertion to "claim America," Kim departs from a celebratory nationalist stance; instead, she identifies and urges a grappling with the detritus at the heart of history. Moreover, whereas Kim uses "trashy heart" to signify racist representations and their dehumanizing effects, the short story from which she draws this phrase intimates a more facetious interpretation.[18] In contrast to the former, which conveys a sense of seriousness and gravity, the latter registers the lowbrow, the trite, and the trivial. In camp fashion, we might read these two

meanings as deeply interconnected. Shimomura's passion for collecting fe-
licitously pairs these two valences of the trashy together: "racist memorabil-
ia-assembling took over his life . . . Little ghastly yellow men (and gee-shees)
in the guise of salt and pepper shakers, vases, lamps, fun masks, *ad nause-
um* populate his kitchen, his bathroom, and his bed. These things are literally everywhere as they are in the US political culture."[19] Elaborating upon
the means by which these figurations connect and rationalize on the macro
level exclusionary laws and policies while also circulating on the micro level
through affective economies of pleasures and desires, Shimomura's collections prompt a different understanding of this trash: kitsch.

Revisiting "kitsch" can offer a productive scrutiny of the operations of
U.S. Asiatic racialization that contemplates alternative aesthetic strategies
for reckoning with their discomfiting iconography. Clement Greenberg famously defined kitsch as anti-art, the epitome of a commercialized, debased
culture that exists exclusively for consumption by the masses.[20] Most sinis-
ter, Greenberg warns, is that its proliferation under industrialization threatens the chances for developing a more matured, sophisticated culture because kitsch masquerades as art. Put differently, kitsch is defined by its
aspirations toward and inevitable failure at achieving the ideals of art.
Kitsch is art's degraded Other, doomed to a status of pure derivativeness.
Racial kitsch, however, does not strive to attain any artistic standard. Furthermore, its consumers are not duped into a false aesthetic appreciation of
these kitsch objects as high art. In stark contrast, racial kitsch objects and
the enjoyment they arouse in gleeful consumers stem precisely from their
imitative qualities, artificiality, and lack of authenticity.

Ironically, the failed seriousness of kitsch that compels its indictment
fuels the pleasures that Orientalist kitsch affords. From the menacing to the
comical, Orientalist kitsch privileges performative effect over representational accuracy. Even the most offensive depiction of the enemy Jap might
align with what Josephine Lee discerns of the infamous comic opera *The
Mikado*, that it "disavows any serious intention to represent Japan faith-
fully."[21] Given that "authenticity becomes a moot point," the act of denouncing these objects as inaccurate proves futile.[22] Instead, it becomes necessary
to interrogate how the modes of aestheticization embedded in these objects
of Orientalist kitsch synchronize with the processes of racialization for the
Asian body. These images and material artifacts of kitsch not only visualize
how Asian-raced bodies are *"made* Oriental," but also provide object lessons
for reading these bodies as Oriental.[23] The derivative nature of kitsch affirms
notions of alienness associated with the Oriental, varyingly translating into
characteristics of Asian inscrutability, inauthenticity, theatricality, and em-
ulation.[24] In the case of Japanese Americans, the racial figure of the enemy
Jap imbued the derivative attribute of the Oriental with the menacing force

of duplicity, which corroborates their "divided allegiance." Consequently, their purportedly innate loyalty toward Japan was used to discredit any claims of patriotism toward the United States as always suspect. In short, the aestheticization of Japanese American bodies as derivative affirmed political anxieties that their allegiance is purely imitative, thereby rationalizing the need for confinement.

Shimomura's campy treatments of the Oriental posit Asian bodies as kitsch. Kitsch, in its failed aspirations to the lofty standards of real art, productively illustrates the racialization of Asian Americans as failed imitators whose foreignness render them unassimilable to the sacred bonds of American citizenship. This dynamic is dramatized through the extensive collection of Orientalist memorabilia that Shimomura often exhibits alongside his prints. As kitsch commodities purchased, collected, and displayed within the domestic space of American homes, these objects illuminate the vexed attachments that the Oriental inspires.[25] Although racial kitsch invites viewers to revel in its irreverence, its allure reinforces the difference and distance of Asian bodies from the U.S. national body politic. Hence, rather than condemning these objects and images wholesale, Shimomura works through camp to interrogate how the failed authenticity of these objects facilitates the ascription of duplicity characteristic of the enemy Jap.

Re-collecting Camp

The iconography and commodities of Orientalist kitsch substantiate economies of racial enjoyment that not only upheld structures of incarceration but also gesture toward their lingering afterlives. By engaging with Orientalist kitsch as the trashy heart of history, Shimomura's debased aesthetics demonstrates how "camp is a rediscovery of history's waste."[26] Specifically, Shimomura's distinctive practice of camp draws upon its conventional playfulness with troubling cultural hierarchies of taste while questioning how such aesthetic judgments have been implicated in the biopolitics of race. Shimomura explores the relationship between the Oriental and the "popular" by drawing on renowned cultural icons as well as conventions of pop art.[27] Whereas pop art became most successful in reclaiming the popular as high culture, Shimomura demands that his audience apprehend racial kitsch as embodying that which cannot be recuperated into the folds of high art, an emblem of the popular that we would rather ignore and relegate to the past. By insisting that we confront this "unsalvageable material," Shimomura beckons a consideration of how debased aesthetics modulates common sense about what constitutes Americanness and that which is considered alien to its parameters.[28]

Yellow No Same, No. 11, 1992. Color lithograph, 5 1/2 × 10 in. (Courtesy of Roger Shimomura)

The Spring 2013 exhibition *Prints of Pop (& War)* highlights these contemplations by curating his prints alongside an extensive collection of objects and racist memorabilia referencing the enemy Jap or Oriental other. His allusion to traditional Japanese prints drags in elements of supposed foreign difference that were used to racialize Japanese Americans as enemies. Analyzing Shimomura's artwork as enacting queer camp nuances how his incongruous juxtapositions of pop art and *ukiyo-e* spectacularly visualize the Oriental to problematize the modes of enemy racialization that justified the incarceration. Two prints in the exhibition, one from the series *Yellow No Same* (1992) and one from *Mix & Match* (2001), exemplify this campy aesthetic strategy. Through twelve color lithographs, the first series challenges the presumed equivalence between Japanese and Japanese Americans, calling into question the visual maneuvers that facilitated this conflation. Each image follows a similar pattern. Barbed wire cuts across the face of one or two individuals in the background as small objects or clothing accessories adorn the Asian-raced face(s) to signal a form of Americanism. In the foreground, a traditional Japanese figure, donning face paint and elaborate hairstyles or headwear, looms large.

In *Yellow No Same, No. 11*, the stoic expression of the soldier in the background mirrors the enigmatic look of the Kabuki actor in the foreground, who eclipses the face of a second soldier to the left. The direction of their eyes suggests that each is obliquely staring at the other. The Kabuki actor is especially fitting since Japan has historically been trapped within a *"theatricalizing discourse"* in which the United States framed the Japanese as theatrical, duplicitous, lacking interiority, and overly invested in artifice.[29] This figure, like the bright yellow backdrop, conjures discourses of Yellow

Mix & Match: No. 1, 2001. Color Lithograph, 22 × 30 in. (Courtesy of Roger Shimomura)

Peril that posed the Japanese as a menacing, sexualized threat. Meanwhile, the image also hints at a commonality between these two personages, who become linked not by assumptions of racial or ethnic sameness, but rather through the allegorical function of the barbed wire. This spatial mode of partition both separates and connects the two in their experiences of U.S. enemy racialization. Thus, the series refuses to operate by the logics of encampment to argue for a true enemy deserving of incarceration.

The figuration of the actor is part of Shimomura's strategy of drawing upon tropes from the Japanese pop art tradition of *ukiyo-e*, which appeared since the early seventeenth century of the Edo period. By placing it in this context, Shimomura emphasizes both the use of this form as pop art in Japan and the Orientalist construction of Asians that have permeated the popular U.S. imaginary. Although such practices may be construed as replicating Orientalist fantasies of Japan, Shimomura complicates this reductive imagery by nuancing how these visual techniques circulated as a popular art form intended for the Japanese masses. Whereas this lithograph, and the series more generally, visualizes the Orientalizing processes that conflated the Japanese and Japanese Americans to make incarceration possible, other prints draw out how this logic came to define Asian Americans against the (white) American citizen by juxtaposing Japanese and U.S. pop art forms. In *Mix & Match: No. 1*, two panels of the diptych play on Roy Lichtenstein's iconic *Kiss* series, which features in varying positions a kiss between a white man and woman.

Shimomura's series dramatizes heteronormative romance privileged in the popular media of comics and movies sealed with a kiss. The negative space between the two images replicates the format of the panels in comic strips. The relationship between these two images, their commonalities and differences, and the role of racial and sexual difference in facilitating the conditions of (im)possibility for romantic intimacy are embedded within whiteness. When it comes to heterosexual coupling, this print elucidates the cultural norms that dictate how the races can or cannot "mix and match." It gestures toward the distinct ways in which Asian American men and women are sexualized. In the left panel, the golden hair accessories Orientalize the depicted woman. With the majority of her facial features obscured, a hint of her red lips and exposed shoulder peek out from under the body of the white man, which is superimposed onto her. The romantic intimacy of the white man and the Asian woman is made acceptable only by shrouding her with qualities of foreignness. Conversely, on the right, the foreignness of the Asian man is not conveyed through any adornments but rather is inscribed onto his body through his facial features. While his buck teeth and slanted eyes are common to Orientalist illustrations of Asian men, this image also alludes to the character of Joe Jitsu, speaker of "broken" English and subordinate sidekick who briefly appeared in the cartoon series of *Dick Tracy* in 1961. The physical proximity of Joe Jitsu and the blonde woman, a nod to Lichtenstein, paired with their ambiguous facial expressions indicate potential danger. This coupling reflects tropes of Yellow Peril that circulate fears of miscegenation by depicting predatory Asian men preying on innocent white women. Donning a trench coat and hat, this replica of Joe Jitsu further invokes discourses that framed Japanese Americans as potential spies whose loyalty to America is suspect. Like the Kabuki actor, the spy symbolizes the impossibility of allegiance.

Shimomura draws attention to how specific racial caricatures substantiate broader cultural stereotypes and political anxieties. He shows that the construction of this seemingly benign sidekick relies upon the same tropes that were legible in the many anti-Japanese images that circulated in newspapers during World War II. In so doing, this print and his larger oeuvre compel us to account for the multiple manifestations and political effects of the "popular." Questioning how Orientalist kitsch buttressed the racial logics of incarceration, Shimomura's artwork deploys queer camp aesthetics toward other objectives, redirecting the humor, theatricality, and incongruity that is often indicative of stereotypical racial farce toward crafting grounds for materialist anti-racist critiques. He illustrates opportunities for queer camp to interrogate the visual fields that naturalize Asian Americans as alien others.

Shimomura's insistence on foregrounding the racial caricatures of Orientalist kitsch enacts a "temporal drag," wherein putatively obsolete histories and their pastness drag into the present.[30] These aesthetic practices thus amplify the multivalent temporalities of camp that Ann Pellegrini detects: "Camp . . . is both 'anticipatory,' in its ability to imagine different social worlds, *and* a form of historical memory, in its willful retention of despised or devalued love objects."[31] By collecting and exhibiting racist memorabilia, Shimomura extends the campy strategy of reclaiming cultural waste. His debased aesthetics indexes the historicity of the Japanese American incarceration and, in querying the role of culture in consolidating national consensus around it, proves that these representations exceed any demarcated confines of the past. Rather, by tarrying with these objects, Shimomura elucidates the ways in which they intimately shape our present and provide powerful points of departure for objecting to the now while demanding more utopian futures.

ACKNOWLEDGMENTS

Thank you to the editors, reviewers, and especially Paul Michael (Mike) Leonardo Atienza for his tireless labor. Emily Hue inspired this writing, and Douglas S. Ishii provided valuable feedback on an earlier draft; thank you for being my friends.

NOTES

1. Leslie Bow, "Fetish," in *The Routledge Companion to Asian American and Pacific Islander Literature*, edited by Rachel C. Lee (New York: Routledge, 2014), 124; emphasis original.

2. Kandice Chuh, *Imagine Otherwise: On Asian Americanist Critique* (Durham, NC: Duke University Press, 2003), 9.

3. Josephine Lee, Yuko Matsukawa, and Imogene L. Lim, *Re/Collecting Early Asian America: Essays in Cultural History* (Philadelphia: Temple University Press, 2002), 9.

4. Joseph Jonghyun Jeon, *Racial Things, Racial Forms: Objecthood in Avant-Garde Asian American Poetry* (Iowa City: University of Iowa Press, 2012), xxiii.

5. Jeon, *Racial Things*, xxiii, xxiv. For more, see Chad Shomura, "Object Theory and Asian American Literature," in *The Oxford Research Encyclopedia of Asian American Literature and Culture*, edited by Josephine Lee (New York: Oxford University Press, 2020), 659–674.

6. Tina Chen, "Agency/Asiancy," in *The Routledge Companion to Asian American and Pacific Islander Literature*, 65. On engagements between new materialisms and race through literary form, see Michelle N. Huang, "Rematerializations of Race," *Lateral* 6, no. 1 (2017).

7. Anne Anlin Cheng, *Ornamentalism* (New York: Oxford University Press, 2019), 19.

8. Emily Stamey, Roger Shimomura, and Helen Foresman Spencer Museum of Art, *The Prints of Roger Shimomura: A Catalogue Raisonné, 1968–2005* (Seattle: Spencer Museum of Art, the University of Kansas; in association with the University of Washington Press, 2007), 16.

9. David L. Eng, *Racial Castration: Managing Masculinity in Asian America* (Durham, NC: Duke University Press, 2001), 136.

10. This insight thinks alongside what Crystal Parikh observes as the "'negative' or 'critical' humanism" theorized through Shimomura's artwork. Crystal Parikh, "Introduction to Roger Shimomura and *Prints of Pop (& War)*," *Prints of Pop (& War): Spring 2013 Gallery Exhibition* (New York: Asian/Pacific/American Institute Publication, 2013), 13.

11. Tavia Nyong'o, "Racial Kitsch and Black Performance," *The Yale Journal of Criticism* 15, no. 2 (2002): 371.

12. John Kuo Wei Tchen, "Who Is Roger Shimomura?" in *Prints of Pop (& War)*, 7.

13. Karen Shimakawa, *National Abjection: The Asian American Body Onstage* (Durham, NC: Duke University Press, 2002), 17.

14. Elena Tajima Creef, *Imaging Japanese America: The Visual Construction of Citizenship, Nation, and the Body* (New York: New York University Press, 2004), 46.

15. Sianne Ngai, *Ugly Feelings* (Cambridge, MA: Harvard University Press, 2005), 6.

16. Nyong'o, "Racial Kitsch and Black Performance," 380.

17. Elaine H. Kim, "Preface," in *Charlie Chan Is Dead 2: At Home in the World: An Anthology of Contemporary Asian American Fiction*, edited by Jessica Hagedorn (New York: Penguin, 2004), xix.

18. Sara Chin, "Red Wall," in *Charlie Chan Is Dead 2*, 74.

19. Tchen, "Who Is Roger Shimomura?" 8.

20. Clement Greenberg, "Avant Garde and Kitsch," *The Partisan Review* (1939): 34–49.

21. Josephine Lee, *The Japan of Pure Invention: Gilbert and Sullivan's* The Mikado (Minneapolis: University of Minnesota Press, 2010), 30–31.

22. Lee, *The Japan of Pure Invention*, 31.

23. Edward W. Said, *Orientalism* (New York: Vintage, 1978), 6; emphasis original.

24. For more on duplicity and inscrutability in Asian racialization, see Tina Chen, *Double Agency: Acts of Impersonation in Asian American Literature and Culture* (Stanford, CA: Stanford University Press, 2005); Sunny Xiang, *Tonal Intelligence: The Aesthetics of Asian Inscrutability during the Long Cold War* (New York: Columbia University Press, 2020).

25. Orientalist kitsch differs from Black kitsch in that it is not exclusively shaped by racist histories of minstrelsy but an earlier craze for Asian commodity items throughout the nineteenth century. Thus, American consumers have historically encountered the Orient through and as material objects, which became proxies for the cultures themselves. For an elaboration of how these consumerist patterns have transformed within the recent decades through the global popularity of cute, Asianized commodities, see Leslie Bow, "Racist Cute: Caricature, *Kawaii*-Style, and the Asian Thing," *American Quarterly* 71, no. 1 (2019): 29–58. See also Christopher Bush, "The Ethnicity of Things in America's Lacquered Age," *Representations* 99, no. 1 (2007): 74–98; Mari Yoshihara, *Embracing the East: White Women and American Orientalism* (New York: Oxford University Press, 2003).

26. Andrew Ross, "Uses of Camp," in *Camp: Queer Aesthetics and the Performing Subject: A Reader*, edited by Fabio Cleto (Ann Arbor: University of Michigan Press, 1999), 320.

27. For an astute analysis of popular culture as a central site for reproducing and contesting constructions of the Oriental, see Robert G. Lee, *Orientals: Asian Americans in Popular Culture* (Philadelphia: Temple University Press, 1999).

28. Ross, "Uses of Camp," 320.

29. Emily Roxworthy, *The Spectacle of Japanese American Trauma: Racial Performativity and World War II* (Honolulu: University of Hawai'i Press, 2008), 21; emphasis original.

30. Elizabeth Freeman, *Time Binds: Queer Temporalities, Queer Histories* (Durham, NC: Duke University Press, 2010), 62.

31. Ann Pellegrini, "After Sontag: Future Notes on Camp," in *A Companion to Lesbian, Gay, Bisexual, Transgender, and Queer Studies*, edited by George E. Haggerty and Molly McGarry (Malden, MA; Blackwell, 2007), 184.

Asian Men and the Construction of Racial Desire on Craigslist

C. WINTER HAN

Gay Racial Desire

In a 2010 magazine article titled "A state of Nanjing China," which appeared in *The Advocate*, the leading gay and lesbian publication in the country, author Michael Lowenthal chronicled his adventure "across 12 time zones to find a gay experience as foreign as the culinary delicacies his hosts won't stop serving." Filled with descriptions of dark alleys, strangely clad ambiguously gendered figures, and dimly lit rooms, Lowenthal describes his "foreign" adventure as one that culminated in a bathroom tryst with an Asian drag queen, whom the author goes to lengths to describe as someone with whom he would never have engaged in sexual activity with outside of his "foreign" adventure. In Lowenthal's narrative, sexual encounter with an Asian drag queen is enticing specifically because it is something that is "foreign" to him in every way. It is something for him to indulge in only when he is "twelve time zones away" rather than in his own backyard. There, in Nanjing, sex with an Asian drag queen becomes the ultimate act of engaging in sexual activity with the "other," an activity bell hooks reminds us is enticing specifically because it is seen as "a new delight, more intense, more satisfying than normal ways of doing and feeling."[1]

Here, in this faraway and foreign land, Lowenthal allows himself to engage in the "real fun" of "bringing to the surface all those 'nasty' unconscious fantasies and longings about contact with the other embedded in the secret (not so secret) deep structure of white supremacy." Only within the framework of a foreign adventure where one is expected to indulge in those delights that would normally be off-limits "back home," he is free to indulge in sex as he would indulge any other foreign delicacy. But as hooks also reminds us, the desire for the other isn't simply about desiring something different but is embedded in a larger process that helps to maintain the status quo of race. In this particular case, the "otherness" attributed to the gay Asian drag queen is simultaneously used to eroticize him while devaluing his worth compared to those Lowenthal might considered "normal." His sexual value to the author is only in relation to the other foreign delights indulged twelve time zones away. Rather than challenge existing racial hierarchies and boundaries, this episode of interracial desire is a deviation from the normal, and the abnormality of these desires is what needs to be explained or justified.[2]

This imagined foreignness of gay Asian men is not surprising given that gay Asian men and other gay men of color do not populate the everyday world of gay white men. Instead, they are cordoned off in those gay spaces specifically marked by race. Instead of racial diversity, "everyday" gay life is marked by an unrelenting onslaught of whiteness. As Allan Bérubé noted, various "whitening processes" creates a "gay community" made up of mostly male, and mostly white, upscale consumers with "mainstream, even traditional, values."[3] For example, gay bars, the epitome of gay spaces, are marked as racialized spaces, often with the specific goal of facilitating interracial sexual encounters outside of those gay spaces deemed "normal." Bars like the Blatino Brox Factory in New York and Red Dragon in Los Angeles mark their clientele as raced, whereas gay bars with largely white patrons are considered "mainstream." In fact, bars such as the Abbey in Los Angeles claim to be "for everyone," as owner David Cooley told the *LA Weekly*, despite numerous observations by men of color to the contrary.[4] Even when gay bars have a mixed race clientele, the bar itself is deeply segregated, with men of different races congregating at different sections of the bar.[5] Even when all the gay men are at the same place, they are not in the same space.

But why think about racialized desire at all? While desire for one race over another may be explained as personal preferences by those who hold them,[6] racialized desires are embedded with the larger narratives of race. What is considered desirable and beautiful is hardly a reflection of personal preferences but rather deeply embedded in a racialized system that assigns worth to some but not others.[7] More important, racialized desires help mark the boundaries of race by marking those partners who are normative and those who are to be engaged with only twelve time zones away. Thus, examining racialized desires offers us a glimpse into how race is constructed.

Orientalizing Gay Desires

In his analysis of gay porn featuring Asian men, Richard Fung noted that Asian men are uniformly depicted as submissive bottoms eager to please their white male partners.[8] Fung notes that whereas black men are hypersexualized, Asian men are "collectively seen as undersexed." But I want to extend this argument a bit further and note that Asian men are seen as undersexed only when it comes to being active sexual partners but are overtly sexual when eager to fulfil the sexual needs and desires of their white male partners. That is, within gay relationships, Asian men are expected to fulfil sexually submissive roles, and to do so eagerly.[9]

This isn't to imply that Asian men are uniformly portrayed as sexual bottoms in gay porn. In his analysis of porn star Brandon Lee, arguably the first Asian porn "star," Nguyen Tan Hoang points out that the performer is a sexual top.[10] Yet what makes Brandon Lee notable and worthy of academic inquiry as a performer is the very fact that he deviates from the norm. The attention he receives as an Asian "top" is due entirely to the peculiarity of an Asian top, thus reinforcing the Asian role as bottoms. His popularity comes not from the normalization of "masculine" Asian men in gay porn but his very peculiarity. In fact, he is the exception that proves the rule.

The gendered sexualization of gay Asian men and other men of color is hardly unique to the gay pornographic imagination. Rather, gendered tropes of sexuality are rampant. Not surprisingly, this gendered sexualization of Asian men has long historical roots deeply embedded in what it means to be an Asian or Asian American man. As Nayan Shah wrote:

> In the nineteenth and early twentieth centuries Chinese and Japanese American men and women were depicted as depraved, immoral, and racially inassimilable to US society. US immigration restrictions, labor migration, and recruitment patterns contributed to predominantly male Chinese, South Asian, and Filipino migration. This "bachelor society," with its lopsided gender ratios, has been cast as a tragedy of sexual and social alienation. Historians have critically interpreted the lurid and sensationalist imagery of Asian American bachelor vice to understand broader patterns of sexualized and gendered race-making that buttressed racial antipathy and segregation. The racial caricatures that circulate in the nineteenth and twentieth century media of effeminate men, treacherous women, and subservient women reinforced the perception of the "Oriental" race as gender atypical and sexually nonnormative, bereft of sexual agency.[11]

These historic stereotypes of Asian men served the purpose of positioning white sexuality as "normal." In fact, Wilson and his colleagues found that perceptions of gay white men lack the racialized gendered stereotypes associated with men of color, and both gay white men and gay men of color see those stereotypes by which gay men of color are measured as being normative.[12]

More important, the Orientalizing of gay desire not only marks who is desirable and who is not but also dictates expectations about how sexual interactions will occur.[13] In the first study to systematically examine the linkages between race and sexual roles, Lick and Johnson argued that "racial groups are imbued with gendered information, such that Asian men are perceived to be feminine."[14] If sexual performance is dictated by such sexual expectations, we need to examine the racialized and gendered implications that exist for the ways that such expectations are constructed, particularly given that sexual behaviors among gay men of color are sometimes dependent on the race of their sexual partners.[15]

Sexual Desires Online

Online personal ads often allow users to explicitly place and search for ads based on specific personal criteria such as age, race, sexual roles, and more, which that allow individuals to cater their ads to targeted readers. In fact, online spaces can be considered more authentic in terms of the articulation of sexual desires as they allow men to "engage more directly with their desires, develop and express their fantasies, and approach potential partners with these desires and fantasies in mind."[16] One does not become sexually excited by a potential sexual partner but becomes sexually aroused by an imagined other and goes online seeking someone to fulfil one's already existing desires. Because of this, examining personal ads allow us to explore the characteristics, both physical and behavioral, that users deem sexually desirable.[17]

Not only do these ads allow users to specifically target the demographic groups that they desire, but they also allow for users to market themselves by highlighting the traits that they believe will be desirable to others.[18] More important, personal ads can act as "a location of autobiography," where "advertisers [can] often construct their ideal selves in their personal narratives."[19] Because of this, advertisers not only construct an idealized sexual partner; they construct what they believe that sexual partner would want from them. As Neal Lester and Maureen Goggin note, personal ads allow for the "creation of a racially, gendered and sexualized self and others."[20] But more important, they become sites where negotiations of race and sexuality are publicly salient and "become public occasions for invoking and distributing a host of myths and fantasies about race and sex."[21]

The problem here is that stereotypes about sexual behaviors are always embedded with racial stereotypes, and vice versa. Within gay personal ads, these stereotypes get amplified rather than diluted. In fact, evidence suggests that these stereotypes are also widely shared among gay men of all races, and there is widespread agreement about the sexual proclivities of different men based on race.[22]

Studies of racial preferences in online personal ads are few, but Phua and Kaufman (2003) offer a glimpse into how race and sexuality might interact online.[23] After examining 2,400 online personal ads, the authors found that gay men were significantly more likely to explicitly state a racial preference for sexual partners than straight men. A later work by Lundquist and Lin (2015) found similar patterns among gay men.[24] In their study of the experiences of gay men of color who use online sex ads, Paul, Ayala, and Choi (2010) found that race was a was one of the primary criteria for online sexual partner selection, both to exclude potential sexual partners as well as to specifically facilitate interracial connections.[25] The authors also reported that gay men of color explicitly understood the racialized hierarchy of desire among gay men with white men at the top, followed by Latino men, with black and Asian men being viewed as less desirable. As can be expected, black and Asian men reported much higher levels of sexual rejection based on race than Latino men. These studies offer important insights, but they fail to capture the ways that racial preferences get articulated. This chapter addresses this gap in the literature by examining online personal ads placed by gay men to examine how racial desires are constructed through how men market themselves and how they virtually describe their preferred sexual partners. In doing so, it sheds light on the ways that "Asian-ness" comes to be perceived and marketed.

Racial Construction in Craigslist Ads

When examining ads placed by white men seeking Asian partners, a decidedly racial pattern can be observed. For example, one poster wrote:

> **Looking for asian son/daughter:** I'm a fatherly type white man who is attracted to nice, young (but legal) asian. Maybe you are a sweet asian boy who is curious about being with a guy, I'm basically straight but have an attraction to smooth and emo/fem asians. I can host at my home and we can enjoy some 420 and just relax together. I'm open to helping you explore your self identity, as well as any sexual fantasies that you many have. I'm very open minded—so feel free to be honest with me about what you need or want in terms of being with a dad type. If you have any interest in dressing, I have lots of things you could wear. My main objective is to meet a nice person and make you feel safe and comfortable. Please send a photo and I will return a photo of myself.

The above ad demonstrates a number of themes found among ads placed by white men seeking Asian partners. First, there is an expectation that the Asian partner would be more feminine than white men. In addition, the theme of Asian sexual inexperience was also prevalent in a number of ads.

The vast majority of ads placed by white men seeking an Asian sex partner are from self-described tops looking for bottoms. This isn't surprising given the long history of feminizing Asian men in contemporary American media, both gay and straight. Having roots in Western colonial domination of Asian countries, Asian men have long been stereotyped as being more feminine and more submissive than white men as part and parcel of colonial justification and Western homoerotic fantasies about the mysterious East.[26]

Not surprisingly, white men often sought Asian men with more "feminine" physical features. As one white poster wrote:

> **asian guys are hot:** I love the slim smooth asian guys I see at the gym and around town. they look great with their clothes on and even better with their clothes off. I'm a masculine bi white top 5'9" 170 uncut cock shaved crotch hiv-neg play safe looking for a sexy hiv-neg asian bottom (18–48) for daytime sex. host or travel. get back with pix and info. thx.

As the post demonstrates, desire for Asian men revolved around perceived conceptions of them being more feminine and sexually submissive than white men. In the way that black men fulfilled white sexual fantasies revolving around the need to be sexually dominated, Asian men were expected to fulfill white sexual fantasies of needing to dominate.

The perceived femininity of Asian male bodies is also reflected in the ways that white men talk about Asian penises. Very few ads from white men seeking Asian men specify penis size, but the majority of the ads placed by white men seeking Asian men that mention penis size specifically mention seeking men with smaller penises. For example, one poster wrote:

> **I love your small dick:** what's the big deal with big dicks? I like guys with small, boyish-looking dicks. I'm a masculine bi white top 5-9" 170 uncut hiv-neg play safe looking for a smooth small-hung hiv-neg white/asian/latino bottom (20–4) for daytime sex. host or travel. get back with pix and info.

While few of the ads placed by white men seeking Asian men specified that they were seeking sexual partners with a big penis, many of the white posters specified that they themselves possessed a big penis. For example, one white poster wrote:

> **Looking for young Twink that can host, Thick 7 inch's waiting:** Nice tall chill very clean thin strong white 38 155, 7" cut, thick 6.5 girth male hosting tonight for thin twink petite or tiny guys men

CD TS Asian ++++ Mostly top but verse here. Please be thin petite or small framed smaller the better younger the better 420 pnp

The ad demonstrates a number of themes found among ads placed by white men seeking Asian men. First, the Asian man is expected to be smaller, thinner, and younger than the white men. While the poster presents his "7" cut, thick 6.5 girth," the only physical demand he makes of his potential partner is a "thin petite or small frame."

The ads placed by Asian men indicate that many Asian men attempt to fit sexual stereotypes in order to attract white men. For example, one Asian poster wrote:

> **Come take my panties off daddy then fuck me:** I just got a new pair of panties and I would like to find an older married white or hairy top daddy to come pull them off as I suck your married cock then pull them off as I bend over so you can Fuck me like you do your wife. I live alone and discretion is a must. Your clear face pic and stats get mine. I am just a regular guy, not a cd or T girl. I am into kissing, sucking, massaging and if you like to rim a clean smooth tight asian asspussy ++.

The ad highlights the most common themes found among ads placed by Asian men seeking white men. First, white men are expected to be older and more masculine and to possess larger penises than Asian men. Second, white men must be willing to take charge of the sexual situation while the Asian man submits to him and provides him with sexual gratification. Within this fantasy, white men are always older and bigger and possess larger penises, and Asian men provide tight asses for them to use.

Discussion

In Craigslist ads, interracial sex is often presented as a "new delight," something that should be more intense and more satisfying, precisely because interracial sex is out of the ordinary. When men look for interracial sexual partners online, they are not looking for the "normal" ways of doing things but rather project their racialized sexual fantasies on potential sexual partners.

In writing their craigslist ads, white men seeking Asian men were likely to equate Asian sexuality with submission and innocence. In these ads, white men who sought Asian men specifically described seeking a more stereotypically feminine partner, whether it was for men who were physically smaller and smoother or who behaved in a more feminine manner. Asian men who specifically sought white sexual partners were also more likely to describe themselves as being more sexually submissive than their potential white partners. In describing their own bodies, Asian men often focused on their more "feminine" features and rarely discussed their penises, instead writing about their asses. Thus, it's clear that the characteristics attributed to Latino men had more to do with white sexual fantasies than actual realities.

The problem with racial objectification is that when taken to the extreme, people come to be seen purely in terms of stereotypical traits associated with the body.[27] It isn't simply that they come to be seen as objects for consumption; they are also seen as being a consumable good with predictable characteristics. This consideration is particularly important to consider now given the explosion of online ads for partner seeking among gay men. As more gay men utilize online resources to seek sexual partners, the ways that racialized desires get constructed in virtual spaces will become increasingly important in the ways that we come to perceive people of different races. Thus it becomes increasingly important that scholars attempt to understand the various ways that online spaces not only reflect racialized beliefs but also how they help to maintain and reinforce them.

While this article focused on men seeking inter-racial sexual partners, racial narratives rarely go unchallenged. That is, while dominant groups may create narratives of race about subaltern groups, members of subaltern groups do in fact challenge these dominant narratives.[28] Such counternarratives can be found in Craigslist ads posted by Asian men seeking other Asian men. While fewer in number, such ads challenge the dominant narratives of racialized sexual desires and norms. For example, one Asian man posted:

> **No Rice Queens:** VGL looking, in-shape Asian guy looking for other Asian guys for NSA sex. Mostly top but will bottom for the right guy.

Yet another posted:

> **Looking for regular fuck buddy:** Asian. 5'7". 145. 34. Always horny, looking for a regular buddy. Play safe only. Not into kink. Completely versatile here so you be the same. Not into older white dudes, so don't waste your time. Looking for a slim partner close to my age. Asian+.

Clearly, ads placed by Asian men seeking sex with other Asian men offer a stark counternarrative to the heavily racialized and gendered ads placed by those seeking sexual partners of another race, particularly ads placed by white men seeking an Asian partner. Not only are these ads devoid of racial stereotypes, but they also counter the larger narrative that white men are more desirable by specifically excluding white male partners and constructing white men as less desirable than Asian men. In doing so, they actively challenge the racialized hierarchy of desire that marks white men as having more worth than Asian men.

While not the focus of this article, ads placed by Asian men seeking other Asian men offer us a rich opportunity to examine the ways that larger narratives of race are actively confronted and challenged by members of subaltern groups. Members of subaltern groups rarely embrace dominant narratives without challenge. In both of these ads, what is notable is that they both challenge the taken-for-granted assumptions surrounding white and Asian sexual relationships, specifically that the normative interracial paring involves an older white man and a younger Asian man. In both these ads, the men specifically address this stereotype, rejecting them outright. In doing so, they construct a different sexual norm outside of the racialized framework.

NOTES

1. bell hooks, *Black Looks: Race and Representation* (Boston: South End, 1992), 21.

2. Neal A. Lester and Maureen Daly Goggin, "In Living Color: Politics of Desire in Heterosexual Interracial Black/White Personal Ads," *Communication and Critical/ Cultural Studies* 2, no. 2 (2015): 130–162.

3. Allan Bérubé, "How Gay Stays White and What Kind of White It Stays," in *The Making and Unmaking of Whiteness*, edited by B. B. Rasmussen, I. J. Nexica, E. Klinenberg, and M. Wray (Durham, NC: Duke University Press, 2001), 235.

4. Jonathan Tolliver, "Do We Need Black Gay Bars Anymore?" *LA Weekly*, June 12, 2015, http://www.laweekly.com/arts/do-we-need-black-gay-bars-anymore-5669980.

5. See Han, C. Winter, *Geisha of a Different Kind: Race and Sexuality in Gaysian America* (New York: New York University Press, 2015); Jason Orne, *Boystown* (Chicago: University of Chicago Press, 2017).

6. Brandon A. Robinson, "'Personal Preference' as the New Racism: Gay Desire and Racial Cleansing in Cyberspace," *Sociology of Race and Ethnicity* 1, no. 2 (2015): 317–330.

7. Dwight McBride, *Why I Hate Abercrombie & Fitch: Essays on Race and Sexuality* (New York: New York University Press, 2005).

8. Richard Fung, "Looking for My Penis: The Eroticized Asian in Gay Video Porn," in *Asian American Sexualities: Dimensions of the Gay and Lesbian Experience*, edited by Russell Leong (New York: Routledge, 1996), 181–198.

9. Chong-suk Han, "A Qualitative Exploration of the Relationship between Racism and Unsafe Sex among Asian Pacific Islander Gay Men," *Archives of Sexual Behavior* 37, no. 5 (2008): 827–837.

10. Tan Hoang Nguyen, *A View from the Bottom: Asian American Masculinity and Sexual Representation* (Durham, NC: Duke University Press, 2014).

11. Nayan Shah, "Race-ing Sex," *Frontiers* 35, no. 1 (2014): 27.

12. Patrick A. Wilson, Pamela Valera, Ana Ventuneac, Ivan Balan, Matt Rowe, and Alex Carballo-Dieguez, "Race-Based Sexual Stereotyping and Sexual Partnering among

Men Who Use the Internet to Identity Other Men for Bareback Sex," *Journal of Sex Research* 46, no. 5 (2009): 399–413.

13. Edward O. Laumann, Stephen Ellingson, Jenna Mahay, and Anthony Paik, eds., *The Sexual Organization of the City* (Chicago: University of Chicago Press, 2004).

14. David J. Lick and Kerri L. Johnson, "Intersecting Race and Gender Cues Are Associated with Perceptions of Gay Men's Preferred Sexual Roles," *Archives of Sexual Behavior* 44, no. 5 (2015): 1471.

15. See Han (2008) and Husbands et al. (2013).

16. Denton Callander, Martin Holt, and Christy E. Newman, "'Not Everyone's Gonna Like Me': Accounting for Race and Racism in Sex and Dating Web Services for Gay and Bisexual Men," *Ethnicities* 16, no. 1 (2016): 3.

17. Elizabeth M. Morgan, Tamara C. Richards, and Emily M. VanNess, "Comparing Narratives of Personal and Preferred Partner Characteristics in Online Dating Advertisements," *Computers in Human Behavior* 26 (2010): 883–888.

18. Elizabeth Jagger, "Is Thirty the New Sixty? Dating, Age and Gender in a Postmodern, Consumer Society," *Sociology* 39, no. 1 (2005): 89–106.

19. James D. Ross, "Personal Ads and the Intersection of Race and Same-Sex Male Attraction," in *Racialized Politics of Desire in Personal Ads*, edited by Neal A. Lester and Maureen Daly Goggin (Lanham, MD: Lexington, 2008), 97.

20. Lester and Goggin, "In Living Color," 131.

21. Ibid.

22. See Han (2008); Husbands et al. (2013). See also Patrick A. Wilson et al., "Race-Based Sexual Stereotyping and Sexual Partnering among Men Who Use the Internet to Identity Other Men for Bareback Sex," 399–413.

23. Voon Chin Phua and Gayle Kaufman, "The Crossroads of Race and Sexuality: Date Selection among Men in Internet 'Personal' Ads," *Journal of Family Issues* 24, no. 8 (2003): 981–994.

24. Jennifer H. Lundquist, and Ken-Hou Lin, "Is Love (Color) Blind? The Economy of Race Among Gay and Straight Daters," *Social Forces* 93, no. 4 (2015): 1423–1449.

25. Jay Paul, George Ayala, and Kyung-Hee Choi, "Internet Sex Ads for MSM and Partner Selection Criteria: The Potency of Race/Ethnicity Online," *Journal of Sex Research* 47, no. 6 (2010): 528–538.

26. Edward Said, *Orientalism* (New York: Pantheon, 1978).

27. Bartky, Sandra Lee. *Femininity and Domination: Studies in the Phenomenology of Oppression.* New York: Routledge, 1990.

28. Chong-suk Han, "Examining Identity Development among Gay Men of Color," *Sociology Compass* 11, no. 9 (2017): e12503.

"I Think I'll Be *More* Slutty"

*The Promise of Queer Pilipinx American Desire
on Mobile Digital Apps in Los Angeles and Manila*

Paul Michael Leonardo Atienza

took Victor to one of Silverlake's gay leather bars after we met for dinner at a Burmese restaurant.[1] I met Victor as an undergrad from my previous life as a college academic advisor and agreed to be part of my multisited ethnographic study focused on gay Filipinos and mobile digital media. He identifies as a second generation Pilipinx American gay cisgender man.[2] He moved to Los Angeles, California, soon after he graduated college and accepted a position with a nonprofit community service organization based in Koreatown. He is currently in an open relationship with his Asian American partner, Damon.[3] They met in college, and they have sustained their relationship even with an hour commute between the cities where they live. Victor and Damon negotiated their open relationship a few months after Victor's move to Los Angeles. Damon shuffles between his full-time job and responsibilities with his parents' business. Since Victor's move, they would spend weekends together. This arrangement allowed Victor to explore Los Angeles' app scene through Grindr and Jack'd.[4] "I only had sex with a handful of guys before I met Damon when I was nineteen. I couldn't imagine having sex with one person for the rest of my life. I wanted to experience more of what the world has to offer."

After ordering our drinks, Victor and I settled at the bar. We noticed two older Asian men across the room, perhaps in their late fifties or sixties, having an animated discussion. I leaned in to Victor and whispered, "Do you think we'd look like that when we get older?"

He said, "I think I'll be *more* slutty."

This essay follows the choices and experiences of Victor, a gay Pilipinx American, when finding sexual partners through geolocative dating apps. Even as virtual sites allow for more opportunities "to play [in the online] world" (Manalansan 2003), digital spaces are rife with the same offline social stigmas that (re)create hierarchies of difference. I ask how these hierarchies are experienced differently as people use the same platform in different places. I share some of Victor's online and offline stories in Los Angeles and Metro Manila, the National Capital Region of the Philippines, as he takes advantage of what I call the promise of intimacy—an investment in the idea that mobile digital media platforms will connect you to potential intimate partners quickly and with ease.

Victor's expectations of being "his best cis-gender queer self" did not provide a bounty of potential sex partners through the dating apps. Instead, he had to contend with complex social formations among the diverse group of app users. He also had to learn various app norms of communication. During his six months of active dating app use prior to our interview, Victor shared the criticisms and the affirmations he received based on his offline observations and online communication practices. But how do social discriminations work on mobile digital media for mobile queer Filipinx subjects? For Victor, particular sets of social and communicative norms in Los Angeles and Manila generated specific anxieties that inform the shifting meanings of desirability among gay men on these platforms.

I am interested in how gay Filipinos make sense of who they are through digital sites in the homeland and in the diaspora. Gay men learn how to be desirable subjects through a process of critique and evaluation based on feedback and conversations among others on digital platforms. They also reaffirm, solidify, and contest these qualities through offline discourse. I investigate how these digital translations of gay Filipinos affect the ways Victor understands themselves in and between city spaces and among digital media platforms, adding to rich scholarship that brings to life the messiness of the global gay figure (Benedicto 2014; Garcia 1996; Johnson 1997; Manalansan 2003). Through this brief analysis, my aim is to show how concepts of desirability shift as online and offline bodies move from place to place and also change through time. Thus, I invoke the charge to queer Asian studies in order to unmoor "queer studies" and "area studies" from their predictive sites and locations (Chiang and Wong 2017). I also extend a queer global Asias vantage invested in the pluralities of queerness and their unruly linkages around the world. Putting in conversation scholarship from Asian studies, Asian American studies, and queer of color critique strengthens the study of Asian cultures with a nuanced perspective on unequal power relations across multiple institutions and scales of time and space.

Ethnographic data for this essay was part of a combined fifteen-month field research in Metro Manila and Los Angeles mostly between January 2017 and January 2018. The study includes forty-three individuals with thirty-five based in the Philippines. Participants were recruited directly through one-on-one communication on several mobile dating app platforms in addition to snowball referrals from friends and colleagues. Platform switching practices were integral for my research participants, and therefore semistructured interviews were performed both in person and through several digital media applications. These include geolocative dating apps targeting gay and bisexual men (e.g., Grindr, Growler, Blued), social media (e.g., Facebook, Instagram), and messaging platforms (e.g., WeChat, Viber).

Mobile Filipina/o/x: Moving Bodies, Technological Expertise, and Digitized Race

As a highly mobile people with exceptional digital media skills, my transnational analysis provides insight into the "social traffic" of digital media use and its ties to social and material hierarchies in and between the homeland and diaspora. With more than 10 percent of its population dispersed in over two hundred countries as migrant laborers, Filipinos find ways to connect with each other as they move elsewhere (Madianou and Miller 2012). Material infrastructures such as telecommunication systems keep widely dispersed Filipinos in contact with their homeland (Cabañes and Uy-Tioco 2020; Francisco-Menchavez 2018; Ignacio 2005; Padios 2013). In 1995, the introduction of text messaging to the Philippines as a cheap alternative to telephone voice calls (Pertierra 2005), led to the proliferation of mobile phone use in the country, where it earned the title of texting capital of the world in the early 2000s (Ellwood-Clayton 2006). Despite having one of the slowest Internet speeds in Asia and one of the most expensive Internet services globally (Shahani 2015), many marketing studies designated the Philippines as the social media capital of the world (Revesencio 2015).

I situate Manila and Los Angeles as two important sites of diasporic connection for Filipinos. The cities are part of a transnational migration circuit supporting the movement of Filipinos around the world (Rodriguez 2010), but also as spaces where the exchange of ideas and beliefs about being Filipino are formed and questioned. I do not claim to provide a comparative study of Manila and Los Angeles, but I attempt to ethnographically trace associations with the disconnections and distinctions of social boundaries as gay Filipinos compose city life and their online selves in a seemingly hyperconnected world (Manalansan 2015).

I bring these formations in conversation with activist and scholar Daniel C. Tsang's (1994) assertion in *Notes on Queer 'N Asian Virtual Sex* that digital spaces are sites of reinvention for Asian American gay cisgender men. His qualitative analysis of online bulletin board systems demonstrated how virtual sites allowed people to take control of their sexual identities and forge new ways of understanding intimate relationships. But the acceleration and proliferation of new and different technologies since the mid-1990s have not changed the ways Asians and Asian Americans experience stereotypes and discriminatory practices, particularly while searching for intimate connections online.[5]

The works of Nguyen Tan Hoang (2014) and C. Winter Han (2015) highlight these experiences of sexual racism while providing alternate ways of thinking through the gendered, racialized, and a/sexualized stereotypes of gay Asian men in North American contexts.

Furthermore, I stress the importance of ethnographic studies about digital life and race in order to examine how cultural representations and subjectivities are recreated, shared, and contested online.[6] The work of media studies scholar Lisa Nakamura (2002, 2007) demonstrates that cyberspaces are not equally free and accessible to all. Nakamura argues that offline social differences such as race and gender are remapped and challenged online. Additionally, social differences such as race, class, and gender become quantified in simplistic statistical data (boyd and Crawford 2012). The digitization of race flattens out its complexities in order to make race easy to understand, store, move, and monetize in various forms online. Even as virtual sites allow for people to find others who share common interests and affiliations, they also recreate offline social hierarchies, stereotypes, and stigmas.[7]

"The Gays Be Judgy": Victor's App Experiences from LA to Manila and Back

When Victor started using Grindr and Jack'd soon after he and his partner agreed to open their relationship, he did not receive the responses he had expected. "The gays be judgy," he said. We laughed out loud together. His time on the apps made him feel empty. "I saw myself having the same scripted dialogues with every dude. Like 'Hey,' 'How are you,' 'You're cute,' or 'What are you into?'" Victor said these situations were more stressful than sexually liberating. He added, "I'm exposing myself to judgment and rejection, and being in LA I felt like everyone was a torso."

As cultural theorist Senthorun Raj (2011) explains about online social networking technologies, this digital space provides new forms of sociality and intimacy for gay men but warns of its disciplining structures in user digital formation and representation. Raj writes of Grindr, that it

> relies on normative categories of defining bodies (race, height, weight, age) in order to mediate sexual desire. Therefore, while new forms of social relations mediated by technology have the capacity to transform and (re)invent subjectivities, online social spaces such as Grindr recuperate sexual norms and aesthetical capital in the context of an online consumer space. (4)

He adds that investments in keeping up connections on these digital platforms require immense conversational and emotional labor. The generic statements and strict expectations of what type of bodies are found desirable affected Victor's initial beliefs and practices in Los Angeles. He developed feelings of emptiness and found interactions more stressful than fulfilling.

In the red-lit dark room of the bar, Victor also shared his stories from a trip to Manila earlier in the year. Before his visit, Victor contacted me for recommendations on places to go. He spent two weeks in the city. His experience on the apps and several of the gay bars in the Philippine capital reminded him of West Hollywood nights, he said, when most of the crowd were straight women and gay men performing the hardest version of masculine. "I guess I expected more attention from guys when I was in Manila," he said. "Do you follow the guys who write for *TEAM Magazine* on Instagram?[8] You can definitely see a big class difference on the apps versus what you see in real spaces of the city. It's like you have to be rich to be gay in Manila. Plus, everyone is so white. I thought that I would get more attention from guys."

I focused on Victor's comment about the whiteness of Manila's gay scene both online and offline. He was not talking about the large population of white foreigners and ex-pats; he was referring to attitudes and mannerisms of Filipinos that index qualities of whiteness.[9] Following how race and ethnicity become read through digital platforms challenges and upholds social discriminations. But ethnicities and colorisms also index values of desirability both when evaluating offline self-presentation and text and images on social app profiles (Rondilla and Spickard 2007). Victor experienced this when he first starting using the apps in Los Angeles. But there seemed to be an expectation from Victor that among a more homogenous group of men in the homeland, sexual racism and fetishistic expectations fall away.

In a comparative ethnic studies framework, Wendy Hui Kyong Chun (2009, 39) elaborates how race is itself a technology that works not only in purely biological or cultural logics but a mixture of "science, art, and culture." Race online is not just mere representation, discourse, or data. Technologies mediate ideologies and in turn uphold structures of social, political, and economic inequality. I hear this through Victor's story, where desirability among gay men in Manila constitutes gender norms of masculinity, an aspiration for a particular upper-class performance, and the preference for lighter skin tones. Victor experienced a new set of contextualized hierarchies familiar yet different from those he encountered in Los Angeles. The mention of *TEAM Magazine* and the social media platform Instagram confirmed the significance of these media in circulating contemporary gay Filipinx perspectives and images. In my own ethnographic observations the year before, these media generated content that introduced highly stylized depictions of youthful queer figures for consumption and reproduction in one of Manila's gay scenes.[10] Coming from the variety of ethnic differences in Los Angeles, Victor did not expect to encounter the diverse ways of being gay and Filipino in the Philippines.[11] Victor already experienced similar social dynamics in the United States. Filipinx America suspends its heterogeneity to forge seemingly unified affiliations with larger Asian American and people of color formations. Among gay communities in the United States, these racial groupings reshape themselves accordingly depending on social, economic, and political context. They also deploy their own sets of hierarchies with various systems of inclusion and exclusion.

Victor began eating healthier and started a regular gym regiment soon after he returned from Manila. The change in routine led to Victor losing thirty pounds. The change of Victor's offline body generated more attention from certain app users to his online profile. "Before I lost my weight, I would get messages from old white men. They were not what I was looking for. Or 'FOB'-by Asian guys."[12] Now he's receiving messages from muscular Asian guys and some younger white guys. "I guess when I lost my weight, my jawline became more prominent." I took note of how his app experiences changed alongside his new diet and exercise regime. Victor did not explicitly say that his experiences on the apps since the beginning of the year had influenced these recent life choices. He did note the stark difference in the frequency of response rates as well as the types of men that contacted him on digital media since his weight loss.

As we continued our conversation, Victor received a notification from Grindr. A handsome East Asian guy sent him a message. "Oh, my God. I've noticed this guy since I've moved in the neighborhood over a year ago. He never messaged me before." Proud of what had just happened, Victor shifted the conversation to share a recent sexual experience he had arranged through Jack'd. "This attractive older Asian man messaged me. He is like the vice president of marketing at a popular cosmetics chain. He lived all the way in Santa Monica [the west side of Los Angeles], so I had to arrange that on a Sunday to avoid the traffic. He was super nice and into me. He had a lot to say after sex too. We were cuddling, and all of the sudden he started asking me too many personal questions." Victor did not want to engage emotionally with the guys he met on the apps. "I just want a physical connection, you know?"

Modifications: Changes in Victor's App-Based Interactions

Victor's initial hope for a bounty of sexual encounters through digital app platforms are now starting to actualize with his new body. But the increase in attention Victor received brought out his own set of metrics in determining who is worth the consideration for a sexual encounter. Perhaps not intentionally recognizing his comment about "FOBby Asians" or his excitement for attention from handsome and rich East Asian men, Victor applied similar discriminations he encountered in Manila after he became more desirable among a wider variety of digital app users.[13]

The change in Victor's dating app experiences informed his modifications of both online expectations of communication and offline practices of self-improvement. He initially wanted to take advantage of the ability to pursue other men for sexual encounters, but the pressures to conform to different dating app norms in Los Angeles and Manila left Victor more frustrated than fulfilled. Whether or not these annoyances on mobile digital media influenced Victor's choices to eat healthier and exercise more consistently, months of immersing himself in regimes of app social norms coincided with changes in his physical appearance. These changes in Victor generated more attention from a larger pool and more diverse group of potential sexual partners. It also allowed Victor to articulate his own set of preferred characteristics that filtered digital app users as desirable or not.

Mobile digital media are becoming further embedded in everyday life and will require more studies that will unpack and articulate the different ways people, machines, and computational programs inform each other (Albury et al. 2017; Berry, Martin, and Yue 2003). Victor allows us to read the complex negotiations that inform metrics of desirability among a situated group of men on geolocative dating apps. What other forms of discipline may emerge in relation to the social traffic between places online and off? Victor's stories from his experiences on digital apps may be similar to many gay Filipinx American cisgender men, but I want to acknowledge how human social differences such as race, class, gender, ethnicity, ability, and more, further complicate interactions on these platforms. His assumptions about gay men in Los Angeles did not transfer to his experiences in Manila, yet there were shared forms of evaluation and criticism practiced among gay men both online and offline. These (dis)connections and (dis)locations are part of the method of queer Asia as critique. Studies of Asian cultures must attend to the plurality of possibilities within situated structures of inequality that loosely bind people, places, and institutions. Attending to the particularities and thick descriptions of the everyday is a possible intervention against the drive of digital infrastructures in flattening out the complexities of the human.

ACKNOWLEDGMENTS

Special thanks to Dr. Constancio Arnaldo, Dr. Douglas Ishii, Dr. Samantha Wettimuny, Khoi Nguyen, and Carleen Sacris for providing feedback in the expansion of this essay. My appreciation to Dr. Kale Fajardo for extending an invitation to submit work for this anthology. And, to Victor and Damon who agreed to share their process of queer companionship—an ongoing collaboration.

NOTES

1. "Victor" is a pseudonym I chose for the research participant with their consent and approval. They have read this piece and provided feedback on how I wrote about their story. Damon is also a pseudonym for the participant's partner. They also provided consent and approval.

2. I use "Filipino" when addressing the global Filipino diaspora, Filipinos in the Philippines, and referring to general studies about Filipino people. I also use "Filipinx" to acknowledge gender plurality when choosing how to identify the self. My study participants did not share the same categories and many shifted based on context and situation. I share the views of Professor Tuting Hernandez who beautifully writes about Filipinx in "Ekis: The Gigil Over Filipinx," September 10, 2020, *Subselfie.com*, https://subselfie.com/2020/09/10/ekis-the-gigil-over-filipinx/. I use "Pilipinx" when referring specifically to Victor since that is how he identifies. See Benjamin Pimentel, "Why Filipino Americans Say Pilipino Not Filipino," *Philippine Inquirer,* July 17, 2013, https://globalnation.inquirer.net/80871/why-filipino-americans-say-pilipino-not-filipino#ixzz5iuz1aagd. The use of Pilipinx instead of Pilipino or Filipino was Victor's choice. He combines the decolonial choice of "Pilipino" with the gender-neutral suffix "x." Debates whether or not to use "F" or "P" continue to animate decolonial movements in the United States. In the Philippines, "Pilipino" is used among the population. As comparative cultural studies scholar Theo Gonzalves explains, "When I started to learn about that larger frame of decolonization, I welcomed the switch from F to P, especially in writing. As for self-identification, I never made any hard rules. . . . I don't begrudge anyone the way they choose to identify themselves, whether Pinay, Pinoy, Pin@y, Pilipino America, Filipino/American, American Filipino. . . . In writing, I just prefer the rather generic and boring, 'Filipino American.'" in Benjamin Pimentel, "Why Filipino Americans Say Pilipino Not Filipino." Victor also purposefully chose to identify as cisgender to acknowledge his relation to his gender and how it raises awareness to a plurality of gender identities. According to the Oxford English Dictionary, cisgender is an adjective "designating a person whose sense of personal identity and gender corresponds to his or her sex at birth; of or relating to such persons. Contrasted with transgender." Read more about the term "cisgender" through Avery Dame, "Tracing Terminology: Researching Early Uses of 'Cisgender,'" *Perspectives on History,* May 22, 2017, https://www.historians.org/publications-and-directories/perspectives-on-history/may-2017/tracing-terminology-researching-early-uses-of-cisgender. Also see *Oxford Dictionaries*, "cisgender," accessed November 1, 2018, http://www.oed.com/view/Entry/35015487.

3. An open relationship is an arrangement of non-monogamy. There are varying forms based on agreements and negotiations among people involved. See David Blasband and Letitia Anne Peplau, "Sexual Exclusivity versus Openness in Gay Male Couples," *Archives of Sexual Behavior* 14, no. 5 (1985): 395–412. Also see Nena O'Neill and George O'Neill, *Open Marriage: A New Life Style for Couples* (New York: Rowman and Littlefield, 1984). For a discussion on managing homonormative perceptions on dating apps, see Jody Ahlm, "Respectable Promiscuity: Digital Cruising in an Era of Queer Liberalism," *Sexualities* 20, no. 3 (2017): 364–379.

4. Grindr and Jack'd are two types of geolocative dating apps designed for gay men. Grindr was conceptualized in the United States and became available for down-

load on mobile devices in 2009. In 2016, a 60 percent share of the company was purchased by Hong Kong–based tech firm Kunlun Group, which later purchased the remaining shares earlier this year. According to a market-based research group, in 2018, "Grindr reaches more than 196 countries and has more than 3 million daily active users. On average these users send 228 million messages and 20 million photos via the platform each day." See https://www.datingsitesreviews.com/staticpages/index.php?page=grindr-statistics-facts-history. Jack'd started in Cornell University in 2011. Its website boasts of 1.2 million users in 180 countries. Many queer people of color in the United States claim that Jack'd is less hostile to ethnic minorities and therefore a better platform to seek out potential partners. See Lisa Bonos, "What Is Jack'd? The Gay Dating App, Explained," *The Washington Post*, June 15, 2016, https://www.washingtonpost.com/news/soloish/wp/2016/06/15/what-is-jackd-the-gay-dating-app-explained/; Michael D. Bartone, "Jack'd, a Mobile Social Networking Application: A Site of Exclusion Within a Site of Inclusion," *Journal of Homosexuality* 65, no. 4 (2018): 501–523.

5. For a thorough overview on studies about gay digital life, see Andrew DJ Shield, *Immigrants on Grindr: Race, Sexuality and Belonging Online* (Cham, Switzerland: Palgrave Macmillan, 2019).

6. For an exceptional ethnographic study of the concept of mobility, everyday survival tactics, and gay Asian men, see Dai Kojima, "Migrant Intimacies: Mobilities-in-Difference and Basue Tactics in Queer Asian Diasporas," *Anthropologica* 56, no. 1 (2014): 33–44.

7. See also C. Winter Han, "They Don't Want to Cruise Your Type: Gay Men of Color and Racial Politics of Exclusion," *Social Identities* 13, no. 1 (2007): 51–67.

8. *TEAM Magazine* is a lifestyle gay publication founded in 2015. Its content addresses how gay Filipino men relate to social stereotypes in the country while providing an avenue for new perspectives and voices pertaining to gay rights. See also James McDonald, "Discover *TEAM*, the Philippines' New Gay Magazine," *Out.com*, October 9, 2015, https://www.out.com/interviews/2015/10/09/discover-philippines-first-gay-magazine-titled-team.

9. For a discussion of whiteness in the context among Asians, see Dredge Byung'chu Kang, "Eastern Orientations: Thai Middle-Class Gay Desire for 'White Asians,'" *Culture, Theory and Critique* 58, no. 2 (2017): 182–208.

10. For an analysis of dating app self-presentations in the Philippines, see Jonalou S. Labor, "Mobile Sexuality: Presentations of Young Filipinos in Dating Apps," *Plaridel* 17, no. 1 (2020): 261–292.

11. See also Lik Sam Chan, "How Sociocultural Context Matters in Self-Presentation: A Comparison of US and Chinese Profiles on Jack'd, A Mobile Dating App for Men Who Have Sex With Men," *International Journal of Communication* 10 (2016): 20.

12. FOB. refers to "fresh off the boat," a derogatory designation for recent immigrants (often from Asia) who have yet to assimilate to cultural norms of the new homeland. See Karen Pyke and Tran Dang, "'FOB' and 'Whitewashed': Identity and Internalized Racism among Second Generation Asian Americans," *Qualitative Sociology* 26, no. 2 (2003): 147–172.

13. See also Emerich Daroya, "Erotic Capital and the Psychic Life of Racism on Grindr," in *The Psychic Life of Racism in Gay Men's Communities*, ed. Damien W. Riggs (London: Lexington Books, 2018), 67–80, and C. Winter Han, "No Fats, Femmes, or Asians: The Utility of Critical Race Theory in Examining the Role of Gay Stock Stories in the Marginalization of Gay Asian Men," *Contemporary Justice Review* 11, no. 2 (2008): 11–22.

REFERENCES

Albury, Kath, Jean Burgess, Ben Light, Kane Race, and Rowan Wilken. 2017. "Data Cultures of Mobile Dating and Hook-Up Apps: Emerging Issues for Critical Social Science Research." *Big Data & Society* 4, no. 2: 1–11.

Benedicto, Bobby. 2014. *Under Bright Lights: Gay Manila and the Global Scene.* Minneapolis, MN: University of Minnesota Press.

Berry, Chris, Fran Martin, and Audrey Yue. 2003. *Mobile Cultures: New Media in Queer Asia.* Durham, NC: Duke University Press.

boyd, danah, and Kate Crawford. 2012. "Critical Questions for Big Data: Provocations for a Cultural, Technological, and Scholarly Phenomenon." *Information, Communication, & Society* 15, no 5: 662–679.

Cabañes, Jason Vincent A., and Cecilia S. Uy-Tioco. 2020. *Mobile Media and Social Intimacies in Asia: Reconfiguring Local Ties and Enacting Global Relationships.* Dordrecht, Netherlands: Springer.

Chiang, Howard, and Alvin Wong. 2017. "Asia Is Burning: Queer Asia as Critique." *Culture, Theory, and Critique* 58, no. 2: 121–126.

Chun, Wendy Hui Kyong. 2009. "Race and/as Technology; or, How to Do Things to Race." *Camera Obscura* 24, no. 1: 7–35.

Ellwood-Clayton, Bella. 2006. "All We Need Is Love—and a Mobile Phone: Texting in the Philippines." Paper presented at Cultural Space and Public Sphere in Asia, Seoul.

Francisco-Menchavez, Valerie. 2018. *The Labor of Care: Filipina Migrants and Transnational Families in the Digital Age.* Champaign, IL: University of Illinois Press.

Garcia, J. Neil C. 1996. *Philippine Gay Culture: Binabae to Bakla, Silahis to MSM.* Hong Kong University Press.

Han, C. Winter. 2015. *Geisha of a Different Kind: Race and Sexuality in Gaysian America.* New York: New York University Press.

Ignacio, Emily. 2005. *Building Diaspora: Filipino Cultural Community Formation on the Internet.* New Brunswick, NJ: Rutgers University Press.

Johnson, Mark. 1997. *Beauty and Power: Transgendering and Cultural Transformation in the Southern Philippines.* London: Berg.

Madianou, Mirca, and Daniel Miller. 2012. *Migration and New Media: Transnational Families and Polymedia.* London: Routledge.

Manalansan, IV., Martin F. 2003. *Global Divas: Filipino Gay Men in the Diaspora.* Durham, NC: Duke University Press.

———. 2015. "Queer Worldings: The Messy Art of Being Global in Manila and New York." *Antipode* 47, no. 3: 566–579.

Nakamura, Lisa. 2002. *Cybertypes: Race, Ethnicity and Identity on the Internet.* London: Routledge.

———. 2007. *Digitizing Race: Visual Cultures of the Internet.* Minneapolis: University of Minnesota Press.

Nguyen, Tan Hoang, 2014. *A View from the Bottom: Asian American Masculinity and Sexual Representation.* Durham, NC: Duke University Press.

Padios, Jan M. 2013. "Call Center Agent." In *Figures of Southeast Asian Modernity*, edited by Joshua Barker, Eric Harms, and Johan Lindquist, 38–40. Honolulu: University of Hawaii Press.

Pertierra, Raul. 2005. "Mobile Phones, Identity and Discursive Intimacy." *Human Technology: An Interdisciplinary Journal on Humans in ICT Environments* 1, no. 1: 23–44.

Raj, Senthorun. 2011. "Grindring Bodies: Racial and Affective Economies of Online Queer Desire." *Critical Race and Whiteness Studies. Special Issue: Future Stories/ Intimate Histories* 7, no. 2: 55–67.

Revesencio, Jonha. 2015. "Philippines: A Digital Lifestyle Capital in the Making?" *Huffington Post*, May 4. https://www.huffingtonpost.com/jonha-revesencio/philippines -a-digital-lif_1_b_7199924.html.

Rondilla, Joanne, and Paul Spickard. 2007. *Is Lighter Better? Skin-tone Discrimination among Asian Americans.* Plymouth: Rowman and Littlefield.

Shahani, Lila Ramos. 2015. "Why Is Our Internet so Slow?" *Philippine Star*, August 23. https://www.philstar.com/opinion/2015/08/23/1491398/why-our-internet-so-slow.

Tsang, Daniel C. 1994. "Notes on Queer 'N Asian Virtual Sex." *Amerasia Journal* 20, no. 1: 117–128.

(Re)Generations

A Queer Korean American Diasporic Response

ANTHONY YOOSHIN KIM AND MARGARET RHEE

> We cannot depend solely on histories to justify our existence. Queer
> and diasporic, wherever we are and whoever we fuck, the truth is that
> we always completely belong.
>
> —LEE, "Toward a Queer Korean American Diasporic History"

Over twenty years have passed since Jee Yeun Lee's evocative chapter "Toward a Queer Korean American Diasporic History" was published in the first groundbreaking volume *Q&A: Queer in Asian America* (1998), where she limns the historical and theoretical (im)possibilities of queer diaspora in order to reimagine the frameworks that underline the construction of Korean American history and belonging. As two interdisciplinary Korean American scholars and artists who are committed to Asian American studies and queer of color critique, we can recall the mixture of hunger and excitement we experienced in our initial reading early on in our intellectual trajectories, and even now we return to it in our thinking, writing, and teaching.

When we first embarked on our "maiden voyage" of this piece in July 2017, both of us were contingent faculty members in institutions located on opposite ends of the United States.[1] Yet that summer, we found ourselves back on the West Coast in the cities where we had spent the majority of our youths—Anthony in Oakland, and Margaret in Los Angeles—and in sites of our Korean immigrant parents' livelihoods. So many of the conversations that led to the ideas and arguments documented here transpired while we were behind the counter, at the register, and in between customers. These interactions—in the quotidian comingling of our intellectual, familial, and economic roles and responsibilities—revealed to us the "minor" contact zones of queer Korean American diasporic history taking shape through us.

We provide this brief glimpse into the material and physical conditions that led to the genesis of our work here without sentimentalism or solipsism; neither is it our intention to reinscribe the white liberal paternalism that undermines the way stories of immigrant lives and labors are told. We note the conditions simply because the controlling images for academia's production of scholarship conjures up a panoply of quiet libraries and offices and rooms with a lone figure (usually straight, white, cisgender, and male) who works away at a desk surrounded by crowds of papers and books. Academia's specifically bourgeois codes and conventions attain a presumed universality that disallows us to have a more capacious understanding of where queer diasporic theories and practices can emerge and who is conferred the license to theorize. To this end, Lee posits that the

> history of a queer and diasporic homeland is not about the Truth. It is about present-day investments and motivations. It is about present-day mediations, about the necessary interpretation and subsequent representation that go into producing a historical narrative.[2]

In this rendition, history is not an inert object or a mummified artifact whose narrative is foreclosed and cordoned off by the mandates of the imperial university, museum, and nation-state. History in its dominant register must always confront the collective histories that underwrite and contest its presumed singularity; it is a dialectical formation, a partial archive whose materials are always subject to re-collection and revision.

Although the political and cultural economies and reputations of South Korea and the United States have undergone dramatic shifts since 1998, Lee's conception of a queer Korean American diaspora as a critical terrain to interrogate and a contingent formation that (re)generates continues to give us—in the spirit of the late Korean American artist Theresa Hak Kyung Cha—a "motion of search" to propel our own scholarly and cultural productions.[3] Lee's use of the preposition "toward" to presage a conception of queer diaspora in her title also recalls the work of the late José Esteban Muñoz. In *Cruising Utopia: The Then and There of Queer Futurity* (2009),[4] Muñoz suggests that contrary to the opportune inclusion of LGBTQ differences into the preexisting social order, queerness is not a stable object of identification or inquiry. In his formulation, queerness is already here and not yet here at the same, a utopia. He also elaborates,

> Concrete utopias are relational to historically situated struggles, a collectivity that is actualized or potential. Concrete utopias can also be daydream-like, but they are the hopes of a collective, an emergent group, or even the solidarity oddball who is the one who dreams for many. . . . Hope along with its other, fear, are affective structures that can be described as anticipatory.[5]

While acknowledging that the world we live in is shaped by histories of often unimaginable loss, displacement, and violence, queerness is not just a negation but also contains the incantatory potential for people to forge new movements and visions—the "concrete utopias"—of that same world.

In this chapter for the second volume of *Q&A*, we take up Lee's anticipatory charge for "creative responses to these dilemmas and many queer Korean American diasporic histories to come" in conversation with Muñoz's queer horizons.[6] The geopolitical impasse of the Cold War and the arrested potentiality of national decolonization is one that extends beyond the territorial and symbolic borders of the Korean peninsula to those who inhabit the disparate geographies of the Korean diaspora. Therefore, we understand queer Korean American diaspora as situated by its intersectionality within multiple axes of power and difference while launching other forms and orientations of how to live, to labor, to invent, to be, and to be-in-relation to the world. We provide a survey of queerness in Korean American Studies and speculate on the recent developments of the Korean Wave in relation to the Korean Diaspora.

Queerness in Korean American Studies

Margaret's qualitative media and sociological analysis of Korean American LGBTQ issues has been prompted by questions of queer survival.[7] This research drew from *Q & A* and other formative texts in Queer Asian American Studies. As the late queer of color theorist José Esteban Muñoz writes,

> I always marvel at the ways in which nonwhite children survive a white supremacist culture that preys on them. I am equally in awe of the ways in which queer children navigate a homophobic public sphere that would rather they not exist. The survival of children who are both queerly and racially identified is nothing short of staggering.[8]

Muñoz's quote offers a depiction of how queer children of color and reflects the complicated ways queer Korean American youth negotiate homophobic and white supremacist spheres. In doing so, Muñoz frames how the survival of queer children of color is "staggering" and how their survival within a constraining and ill-fitting world is an astonishing feat. In his monograph, Muñoz argues for disidentification as a strategy for queers of color to negotiate majority culture by transforming mainstream works for their own transgressive cultural purposes. In this way, queer of color youth not only survive but also learn to disidentify and experience pleasure within these homophobic and racist spheres.

Survivance describes the ways queer of color youth and other marginalized subjects actively engage in practices of survival. The term survivance has been utilized prominently in Native American studies to refer to a space of survival where people actively struggle against historical absence and oblivion. The poetic writing of Diane Glancy on Gerald Vizor, who termed survivance, also reveals the power of the word through poetics: "Poetry is rebound. A turn of writing. (Sur) vivance: Sur-a urvival outside survival. Viviane-the vitality of it." Moreover, as Glancy writes, survivance is "formulating survival on one's own terms."[9] Along with Muñoz's compelling insights on queer of color children, the term "survivance" helps articulate the powerful ways queer of color youth navigate homophobic and racist mainstream worlds and ethnic communities.

Queerness provides locations and routes to practice survivance and refusals to normative mappings of the Korean American community. Within the diaspora, understanding Korean American immigration history helps us untangle the experiences of Korean American LGBTQ, and specifically how the Korean American community significantly values heterosexual endogamous marriage. While this kind of marriage has been seen as an adaptive mechanism for immigrants to the United States, the emphasis on heterosexual marriage and the structure of migration as a heterosexual process may marginalize LGBTQ identity and queerness within Korean America.[10]

Within this context, Jeong-Hyun An writes, "to most Koreans, being 'gay' and 'Korean' is an oxymoron, simply inconceivable."[11] Paralleling Asian American LGBTQ observations of their respective ethnic communities, communities of color may consider homosexuality a "white disease."[12] Same-sex sexuality conflicts with ideas of success and upward mobility in the Korean American community. Michael Kim argues that even if he attained the Korean American dream of Harvard but is gay, he ends up with a "big fat zero. He imagines a dialogue within the Korean community going something like, 'Well, my son didn't go to Harvard, but at least he's not gay.'"[13] The separation of ethnicity and homosexuality is further enforced by the notion that Koreanness and queerness are incompatible.[14] As scholar and activist Judy Han wrote in 2000:

> When I came out to my parents as a lesbian nearly ten years ago, they went through a lot of what other parents of lesbian, gay, bisexual, and transgender (LGBT) children experience: they blamed themselves, they blamed me, and they grieved the loss of the daughter they thought they had. And like other working-class immigrant parents whose sense of community relies heavily on family and church, my parents felt alone, and they found no resource available in Korean.[15]

Given the invisibility of LGBTQ people in Korean American communities and the lack of dialogue about queerness in Korean American communities, queer Korean Americans may appear "simply unconceivable."[16]

Whereas the gay community provides acceptance, queer Korean Americans are often hypervisible and marginalized within the queer community. Although same-sex sexuality is certainly not a Western white phenomenon, gay cultural identity privileges a homonormativity based on white middle-class gay consumers through signifiers such as gay pride parades, rainbow necklaces, and queer-specific media.[17] Notions of "coming out" and "same-sex marriage" are often framed within terms of individual liberties and rights, and in Asian American contexts, the valorization of discourses of individual rights over family harmony and community acceptance can fail to demonstrate the importance of family and community, especially in the context of racial discrimination and economic precarity.

The Horizon of Korean Waves and Diasporas

Anthony's research has focused on the Korean diaspora and its (dis)connection with South Korea's growing economic and cultural ascendancy. With the vastly globalized export and accumulation of commodities, popular culture, and tourism that constitute the Korean Wave (or *Hallyu*), the ties between South Korea, the United States, and the rest of the world seem closer than ever before. The Korean Wave (re)presents a South Korea that has, on the surface, miraculously recovered from the 1997 IMF Crisis that devastated its economy on the millennial cusp and rehabilitated its reputation as a powerful global brand name and partner. The "K" as a contemporaneous prefix to a litany of ever-expanding products (be it pop music, dramas, movies, barbeque, skincare, automobiles, and more) is one that confers an aura of high quality, upward mobility, and respectability to a global market of consumers. The "K" is thus a synecdoche for the commodity fetishization of Korean culture (and by extension South Korea), one that, within the logics of neoliberal capitalism, is captivatingly a priori and historyless (timeless).

What a critically queer diasporic framework can offer to the plasticized sheen and effortless (and endless) perfection of the Korean Wave's proffered neoliberal success story is perspective and context. Along with an examination of the capitalist vectors of state-sponsored creative industries and agents that make the momentum of the Korean Wave possible, we can also engage with the dissonant identities, interests, and values that are elided by and exceed state and market logics and are in difference to and from the hyperreal projection of Korea.

Urging caution, Lee necessarily observes that as Korean American diasporic subjects, we must name and confront our own "politics of position that recognizes embedment and complicity . . . in the structures and thought processes of the West" because "[there] is no pure space in which we stand outside of complicity."[18] These dominant representations, saturated as they are in the Orientalist masks of white supremacy, render opaque a turbulent and traumatic past, the "before" that both South Korean and American governments would rather forget, trivialize, or aggressively suppress in the volatile historical record of the Korean peninsula and its subsequently shadowed patterns and settlements of diaspora. Even without telling, the "before" refuses the terms and conditions of its postponement; its impacts continue to be felt within and across geographies and generations to this day.

Against a historical panorama of Japanese colonialism, national division, the Korean War, American imperialism, military dictatorships, violently suppressed people-powered movements and rebellions, and the shaky grounds of a just over three-decade-old modern democracy, the "before" that forms the dark underbelly of the Korean Wave is invisible in plain sight, obfuscating a throughline to a structurally altered "after" in this arbitrarily eternal present. A critically queer diasporic framework demands we turn toward these past histories and confront its lies and fallacies along with its submerged opportunities for justice and transformation. It also motivates us to turn toward the new histories yet to come, the ones we are envisioning and enacting everyday so that they may one day be our futures in the present.

We add to Lee's catalog of questions that serve as her conclusion about queerness in Korean American history to ponder the transnational dimensions of the present/future:

1. If "Korea/n" is a cultural, economic, and descriptive force, who or what does it or can it constitute?
2. Who or what has failed or been left behind?
3. What are the significant impacts of the "K" for those of us who reside in its diaspora in the United States—or KDiaspora?
4. Is the KDiaspora interpellated or eroded by the insertion of the "K"?
5. How does queerness put pressure on the "K" and imagine otherwise for what reunification projects can look like that exceed the logics of the heteronormative capitalist nation-state?

The End as Another Beginning

We return to the proud posture of Lee's final sentence, where her double adverb "always completely" is joined with belonging—regardless of "wherever we are and whoever we fuck," the multiple provocations of identity, location, and desire that might unsettle the accounts of civil society.[19] We also wonder about the nature and substance of what queer belonging entails—to whom, to what, and to what ends—as we simultaneously struggle to find and (de)construct such lucidity in a historical present that is marked by the destabilizing force of white supremacy, heteropatriarchy, neoliberal capitalism, working class sabotage, ecological disaster, pandemics, as well as differentiated vulnerabilities to harm. Can we find belonging when the world—quite literally—is on fire? Or put another way, we must, and we will find belonging—*because* the world is on fire.

ACKNOWLEDGMENTS

We would like to thank Paul Michael (Mike) Atienza for his compassion, good humor, and encouragement throughout the writing process.

NOTES

1. This is our nod to Dana Y. Takagi's seminal article, "Maiden Voyage: Excursion into Sexuality and Identity Politics," *Amerasia* 20, no. 1 (1994): 1–18.

2. Jee Yeun Lee, "Toward a Queer Diasporic Korean American History," in *Q & A: Queer in Asian America*, edited by David L. Eng and Alice Y. Hom (Philadelphia: Temple University Press, 1998), 199–200.

3. Theresa Hak Kyung Cha, *Dictee* (Berkeley: University of California Press, 2001), 81.

4. José Esteban Muñoz, *Cruising Utopia: The Then and There of Queer Futurity* (New York: New York University Press, 2009).

5. Ibid., 3.

6. Lee, "Toward a Queer Diasporic Korean American History," 204.

7. An earlier version of the argument in this section appears in Anthony Yooshin Kim and Margaret Rhee, "Toward Queer Korean American Horizons," in *A Companion to Korean American Studies*, edited by Rachael Miyung Joo and Shelley Sang-hee Lee (Leiden: Brill, 2018), 534–558.

8. José Esteban Muñoz, *Disidentifications: Queers of Color and the Politics of Performance* (Minneapolis: University of Minnesota Press, 1999).

9. Gerald Vizenor, *Survivance: Narratives of Native Presence* (Lincoln: University of Nebraska Press, 2008), 78.

10. Martin Manalansan critiques the tendency for scholars of international migration to assume heterosexual individuals who are part of a patriarchal family in depicting both the individuals who migrate and their conditions of migration. Martin Manalansan, "Queer Intersections: Sexuality and Gender in Migration Studies," *International Migration Review* 40, no. 1 (2006): 224–249.

11. Ibid.

12. Michael Kim, "Out and About: Coming of Age in a Straight White World," in *Asian American X,* edited by Arar Han and John Hsu (Ann Arbor, MI: University of Michigan, 2004), 146.

13. Ibid, 146.

14. Kim, "Out and About," 146; Lee, "Toward a Queer Diasporic Korean American History."

15. Judy Han, "Organizing Korean Americans Against Homophobia," *Sojourner* 25, no. 10 (2000): 4.

16. Larry Gross, *Up from Invisibility: Lesbians, Gay Men, and the Media in America* (New York: Columbia University Press, 2001), 13.

17. Joane Nagle, *Race, Ethnicity, and Sexuality* (New York: Oxford University Press, 2003), 48.

18. Lee, "Toward a Queer Diasporic Korean American History," 201.

19. Ibid., 204.

PART V

Burning Down the House—
Institutional Queerings

Model/Minority Veteran

*The Queer Asian American Challenge
to Post-9/11 U.S. Military Culture*

Long T. Bui

This chapter considers the way gay Asian American veterans challenged U.S. military policy and culture in the post-9/11 period, unearthing issues of discrimination within a state institution to which they committed their lives. Many scholars have written about the "War on Terror" as a pivotal experiential moment for South Asians and LGBTQ+ people, but less discussed is how they how queers of Asian descent were at the forefront of challenging the world's most powerful military force.[1] As individuals facing multiple forms of marginalization, there is a double bind faced by those seeking to serve their country while defending themselves against the oppressive conditions they meet in such capacity.

In her work on martial citizenship, Lucy Sayler argues for more work on Asian Americans in the armed forces as exemplars of "citizen soldiers," since military service offered one mechanism for Asians to naturalize and gain acceptance in a country that excluded them as sexual deviants and perverse subjects.[2] Simeon Man observes that during the Cold War, "bad" Asians were the targets of war, whereas the "good" ones were funneled into the military, but inclusion was partial.[3] Margot Canaday documents how gay men in particular were routed from military service due to their perception as potential communist agents and usurpers of the family and nation.[4] This kind of discrimination flies in the face of the U.S. military's credo that all soldiers are treated the same when they put on their uniforms. Whereas the dominant archetype of the good soldier has not traditionally included sexual minorities or people of color, the good minority, or "model minority," has been used to first construct Asian Americans and later gays and lesbians as passive beings who do not need to fight (or know how to).[5] Through a critical juxtaposition of the queer and Asian, I also scrutinize the figure of the model/minority veteran in order to expose ongoing political struggles related to those terms.[6] In doing so, I recognize the queer veteran of color as "a product of this contradiction between individual agency and collective racialization."[7]

In the following, I profile media cases that speak to the tense predicament of Asian gays as duty-bound model soldiers and obedient model minorities.[8]

The chosen examples involve controversies surrounding conscientious objection to preemptive war and gays serving in the military. My critical inquiries interrogate GIs' resistance to and complicity with state power, indexing their treatment as voluntary enlisted participants in an environment where difference is not always fully tolerated and where one must always obey the command of superiors.

Conscientious Dissenters and the Memory of Internment and Colonialism

The post-9/11 moment ushered in a new era of U.S. imperialism, pushing some military personnel to consider how the U.S. liberal affirmation of egalitarianism is "at once contradicted by the larger context in which that affirmation is advanced."[9] First Lieutenant Ehren K. Watada found instant notoriety when he became the first military officer in the country charged with "public dissent" since 1965. Watada refused his deployment to Iraq in June 2006 as part of Operation Iraqi Freedom. The Japanese Chinese American was the only commissioned officer at the time to relinquish his duties because he believed he had a personal duty to oppose an "immoral" war that would make him responsible for war crimes if he joined. Upon arrest, he said, "I think they will do their best to make an example of me."[10] Even though he did not think at first his was a case about race or racism, he found it curious the majority of soldiers who voiced their support for him have been nonwhites. In an interview, he says, "Whether they see me as giving a voice to minorities in the Army or simply fighting for minority rights I don't know."[11] Framing his protest as a form of service to country, Watada weighs in on his status as a model/minority soldier when he claims to follow the legacy of Nissei men who contributed to the U.S. war effort during World War II while their people were interned: "My decision brings honor to veteran JAs. Instead of perpetuating war crimes and a war of aggression, I am actively trying to put a stop to it. Instead of being the 'quiet, obedient Japanese,' I am fulfilling my oath to protect my soldiers and this country from our government."[12] As a former Eagle Scout and university graduate with a bachelor's degree in finance who needed no assistance from the army for his education, Watada presents a good Asian gone bad, but he is also trying to be the best soldier that he can be despite going rogue.

Watada's insurrection against hegemonic systems was preceded by another API veteran whose form of dissension could not be interpreted so nobly. Marine reservist Lance Corporal Stephen Eagle Funk was the first U.S. veteran of any rank to publicly object to the war. The noncommissioned officer made news appearing on television railing against the war, and pundits took note of his "strange" ethnic roots (Pilipino) and Funk's "second way out" of active-duty deployment after he admitted he was gay in violation of the military's standing "Don't Ask, Don't Tell" policy. Failing to report to duty, the reportedly "soft-spoken" man completed a half-year sentence in a military prison for desertion, punishment for the fact that he did not pursue the "smartest way" to get dissenter status, since one must show up to work first to claim it.[13] As a mixed race working-class queer, the Pinoy pacificist did not hold the same social status commonly associated with middle-class Japanese Americans like Watada, embodying instead a "bad" brown Asian of the Global South.[14] In his official public statement against the U.S. invading Iraq, Funk says this: "I could not remain silent. In my mind that would have been true cowardice, having a chance to do some good, but playing it safe instead . . . You don't have to be a cog in the machinery of war."[15]

Mainstream publications like *The Guardian* felt it necessary to mention that Funk had dropped out of classes at the University of Southern California, while working part-time in a pet shop.[16] The example of Funk sheds light on the plight of a "duped" derelict youth who joined the military for the wrong reasons and later admitted "there are so many more ways to get money for school."[17] As Robyn Rodriguez explains, Funk communicates the difficult experience of queers in not only the U.S. nation-state but in the Filipino diasporic nation, where heterosexual youth are venerated as the good example for poor immigrant communities aspiring toward model minority excellence.[18] In an interview for the leading gay magazine *Advocate*, Funk says his decision to become a conscientious objector was related to being a gay man in a military regime that is inherently immoral.[19] Meanwhile, ethnic media sources like *Filipinas* recognized Funk became politicized only after witnessing the people's power in ousting the Philippines' president Joseph Estrada, demonstrating how "Filipinos in all walks of war" can link the global "War of Terror" with domestic violence in the former colony of the United States.[20] Both Watada and Funk are gaysians who joined the military right after 9/11 only to reject warmongering, but Funk's case cannot be read as fully analogous to Watada since the two men inhabit different social strata and even ideological orientations. The latter's higher rank, ethnicity, and class privilege made him a cause célèbre of the antiwar left, whereas the former's "queerer than queer" image and decision to step back from the limelight—due to public pressures on his precarious personal life—demonstrate how the media "play an integral role in maintaining the norms of good from bad subjects, and [how] the subjects under its gaze not only consent to, but even participate actively in, the policing of this boundary line."[21]

These twenty-first-century examples of social containment dredge up the Cold War legacy of the model minority myth, which Robert Lee discusses as originally revolved around anxieties related to communism, race-mixing, and homosexuality. In such agonistic contexts, "accommodation would be rewarded," and "militancy would be contained or crushed."[22] In the delimitation of transgression, certain Asian groups like the Chinese and Japanese came to be seen as domesticated model minority types (though they resisted this label), while other groups like Southeast Asian refugees signified the unruly anti-model minorities that had to be corralled into the military due to their lower socioeconomic status and "violent nature." Here, we might ask how other "bad Asians" like gay Koreans upend the heteronormative racial order and "resist the status quo because they have already been excluded from it or oppressed, silence, or limited by it."[23] The next section turns to the issue of gays serving in the military to further explore this.

"Don't Ask, Don't Tell" and the Asian American Closet

One of the most divisive policies in the U.S. military is the longtime ban on gays and the policy of "Don't Ask, Don't Tell" (DADT), where one can be gay but is discouraged from publicizing it. LGBTQ+ activists have lambasted this policy for years and accused the military of enforcing a mandatory closet for all queer soldiers. DADT found its biggest public opponent in Lieutenant Dan Choi, a Korean American member of the National Guard who admitted, "I was afraid people would find out [I'm gay], and I thought the military would be a great way to hide."[24] Before Choi launched his invective against this military rule and outing himself in the process, another queer Asian received publicity for being terminated under DADT. Sandy Tsao, a Chinese American second lieutenant in the U.S. Army who is also a lesbian, sent a letter on the Chinese New Year to President Obama days after his inauguration. The letter was published in the *Windy City Times* as a cover story.[25] Tsao was discharge under the DADT implemented in 1993 under President Bill Clinton, which "tolerated" gays only if they do not tell or show anyone they are gay; any admission or revelation of a homosexual lifestyle provides grounds for immediate discharge. Coming on the heels of Tsao's announcement, Lt. Dan Choi became the poster child for the movement to end DADT (even though other veterans contributed) after publicly coming out on the popular TV news program *The Rachel Maddow Show*, and proclaiming that the law forced veterans to lie to their own officers, thus violating the military's own code against dishonesty. Choi was terminated right after appearing on the show. Like other gay servicemen found in specialty occupations, Choi was one of a few Arabic language experts. Despite their critical importance, fear of queer bodies and their potential disruption to the homosocial "unity" of combat units superseded the demand for talent and skills, which disrupts the American myth of meritocracy and education as the great leveler of social inequality.[26]

As an open test to the discriminatory policy, Dan Choi went to a recruiting station to rejoin the U.S. Army—a request that was rejected.[27] After his discharge, the lieutenant became the most visible campaigner against DADT, performing public stunts like taping his mouth or chaining himself to the front of the White House fence. As a main spokesperson for the Knights Out organization, Choi led marines, sailors, soldiers and those in the air force to demonstrate against the Democratic National Committee fundraiser. He began a hunger strike, declaring it would last until Obama repealed DADT and added a nondiscrimination policy to the military code. The strike ended in a week after a federal judge ordered the Department of Defense to stop enforcing the policy. Following its repeal by Congress, Choi was invited to President Obama's signing of the bill on December 22, 2010. It seemed gay equality had arrived, especially in the same period that saw same-sex marriage rights and more LGBTQ+ representation in popular culture. Leading gay magazine *Out* featured Dan Choi in their list of one hundred "People of the Year," placing him prominently on their 2012 cover of celebrities. As the only Asian face and only member of the armed forces within this Hollywood lineup, Choi epitomizes a minority (Asian) within a minority (gay) within another minority (vet). He queers the model minority sense of Asians as weak and invisible (pointing up their absence in white gay media), even if he might shore up what Jasbir Puar calls "homonationalism" and the production of gay patriots.[28]

Choi's battles with institutional homophobia appear unrelated to those of race, but these issues were not mutually exclusive. In an interview, the Korean American makes the following comments linking the gay closet with the "Asian American closet."[29] As he admits, "Being Asian American can be isolating at times . . . I experienced it at West Point and in the army; many times, I was the only 'openly Asian' member of my team. It is isolating and stressful. Racism hurts the entire team."[30] Choi's ardent fight for acceptance as an out gay member of the armed forces posits the dangers of being out as an Asian American. Choi's speech act stresses that racism and homophobia is harmful to teamwork. In this manner, Choi is hoping to reform or change the military, not entirely undermine it.

As the quagmire of Iraq and Afghanistan turned into the longest wars for the United States, the demand for higher recruitment numbers turned urgent. A push for diversity added to what Melani McAlister calls "multicultural militarism" and the need to conscript minorities to fight wars around the world.[31] Under the agenda of global counterterrorism, model/minority veterans like Choi provide a safeguard against the queer racialized foreign threat found everywhere.[32] The model/minority vet buoys the U.S.

empire as it seeks to expand external borders and reorganize its domestic order to reconfigure the insider-outsider dyad through "inclusive excellence." Recognizing Choi's complicity with power does not deny his bravery but instead forces recognition of the mainstreaming of identity politics vis-à-vis geopolitics. Though gay rights advocates made little mention of his Asian background, touting Choi as a new hero of the LGBTQ+ movement, the coastal guardsman often evoked the racial language of the model/minority vet as he stated in one API magazine interview: "When you are a stigmatized minority in the military, you put yourself in a mindset that says, 'I'm going to just show everybody that I'm the best at this.'"[33]

Before entering the spotlight as a model veteran gone bad, Choi was already ruled to be undisciplined, like when in 2005 he punched a platoon sergeant in the chest. His slowness in getting promotion respective to peers made him an anti-model minority, one unable to perform well under pressure or listen to orders. Amid railing against DADT, Lt. Dan Choi was admitted to the psychiatric ward due to mental breakdown and anxiety attacks.[34] Such events give the impression that Asian queers remain pathological, falling apart at any minute. Yet these personal "failures" are teachable moments to zoom into societal norms and expectations that never fully congeal within the individual.

Conclusion

The provocative opposition posed by gaysians against military dogma reposes the eternal question of who is a loyal citizen-subject and who is bad subject, something that has always haunted Asian Americans and queer people. While Choi's wish for a gay-friendlier military came true even as the battle for transgender rights heated up, his liberal stance still begs the question of how particular minoritarian subjects are subordinated to the larger system of power that unevenly interprets them as model/minority veterans. In the end, the ideological work of gay rights advocacy within the military must tackle the larger underpinnings of hypermilitarization that conscientious dissenters obviate.[35] Demands for minority civil rights and social justice coincide with the global call to arms within an expanding American war machine. This modern expansion of "freedom with violence," as Chandy Reddy calls it, urges attention to the intersectionality of race, ethnicity, sexuality, class, and even gender (e.g., cisgender gay men as political visible actors and activists compared to lesbians and others).

In telling a specific story about racial and sexual identity formation in the new millennium, my analysis complicates the model minority descriptor often attributed to gays and Asian Americans by examining it in conjunction with the trope of the good soldier.[36] At a time when increasing demand for equity, dignity, and personhood is matched by a disregard for the lives of so many communities of color, the queer Asian GI's complex rendering within policy and public discourse transacts a critical prism through which we can discombobulate matters of bigotry, democracy, empire, heroism, failure, and ethics. Insofar as the post-9/11 milieu intensified conversations about cultural belonging, the political work of gaysian veterans illustrates what it means to be inside and outside, and how perhaps to think beyond that duality.

NOTES

1. Jasbir Puar and Amit Rai, "The Remaking of a Model Minority: Perverse Projectiles under the Specter of (Counter) Terrorism," *Social Text* 22, no. 3 (2004): 75–104.

2. Lucy Salyer, "Baptism by Fire: Race, Military Service, and US Citizenship Policy, 1918–1935," *Journal of American History* 91, no. 3 (2004): 847–876. For general overview of the incorporation of Asian "aliens" in U.S. military, see Cara Wong and Grace Cho, "Jus Meritum: Citizenship for Service," in *Transforming Politics, Transforming America: The Political and Civic Incorporation of Immigrants in the United States*, edited by Taeku Lee, Karthick Ramakrishnan, and Ricardo Ramírez (Charlottesville: University of Virginia Press, 2010).

3. Simeon Man, *Soldiering through Empire: Race and the Making of the Decolonizing Pacific* (Berkeley: University of California Press, 2018).

4. Margot Canaday, *The Straight State: Sexuality and Citizenship in Twentieth-Century America* (Princeton, NJ: Princeton University Press, 2009).

5. Stewart Chang, "Is Gay the New Asian: Marriage Equality and the Dawn of a New Model Minority," *Asian American Law Journal* 23 (2016): 5–38.

6. Critical juxtaposition is a method of analysis from Yen Le Espiritu, *Body Counts: The Vietnam War and Militarized Refugees* (Berkeley: University of California Press, 2014).

7. Sylvia Shin Huey Chong, "'Look, an Asian!': The Politics of Racial Interpellation in the Wake of the Virginia Tech Shootings," *Journal of Asian American Studies* 11, no. 1 (2008): 45.

8. Melani McAlister, *Epic Encounters: Culture, Media, and US Interests in the Middle East since 1945* (Berkeley: University of California Press, 2005).

9. Chandan Reddy, *Freedom with Violence: Race, Sexuality, and the US State* (Durham, NC: Duke University Press, 2011), 245.

10. Hal Bernton, "Officer at Fort Lewis Calls Iraq War Illegal, Refuses Order to Go," *Seattle Times*, June 7, 2006, https://archive.seattletimes.com/archive/?date=20060607&slug=nogo7m.

11. Caroline Aoyai-Stom, "Exclusive: One on One With 1st Lt. Ehren Watada," *Pacific Citizen*, August 30, 2006, http://news.newamericamedia.org/news/view_article.html?article_id=0c13ccb6d447675317a9fb2094973a96.

12. Ibid.

13. Ji Hyun Lim, "APA Conscientious Objector Says He Couldn't Kill; Funk Warns Recruits about the Morality of Joining Military," *Asianweek* 24, no. 34 (2003): 7.

14. Eve Oishi, "Bad Asians: New Film and Video by Queer Asian American Artists," in *Countervisions: Asian American Film Criticism* 174 (2000): 221.

15. Stephen Funk, "Stephen Funk's Statement," in *Dissent: Voices of Conscience*, edited by Ann Wright and Susan Dixon (Kihei, HI: Koa Books, 2008), 152–153.

16. Duncan Campbell, "Marine Who Said No to Killing on His Conscience," *The Guardian*, April 1, 2003.

17. After he left the marines, Funk eventually enrolled in a city college before transferring to Stanford in 2005, working toward a degree in international relations. Funk used his position as the chapter president of the San Francisco Iraq Veterans Against the War organization to challenge educational barriers for many who may not know how to get into "elite" schools like Stanford University, where he eventually matriculated.

18. Robyn Rodriguez and Nerissa S. Balce, "American Insecurity and Radical Filipino Community Politics," *Peace Review* 16, no. 2 (2004): 131–140.

19. Ibid.

20. Vivian Araullo Zalvidea and Emmily Magtalas, "Filipinos from All Walks of War," *Filipinas* 12, no. 133 (2003): 28.

21. Sylvia Shin Huey Chong, "'Look, an Asian!'" 4.

22. Robert G. Lee, "The Cold War Construction of the Model Minority Myth," in *Contemporary Asian America: A Multidisciplinary Reader*, edited by Min Zhou and J. V. Gatewood (New York: New York University Press, 2007), 469–470.

23. Eve Oishi, "Bad Asians," 221.

24. "Lt. Dan Choi Talks Being Asian and Gay in the Military," *Nuasian*, January 20, 2012, http://nuasian.wordpress.com.

25. Tracy Baim, "Obama Responds to Lesbian Soldier's Letter," *Windy City Times*, May 6, 2009, www.windycitymediagroup.com.

26. He was also an active participant in international affairs like participating in a gay pride march in Moscow that turned violent in a country hostile to LGBT rights.

27. Jessica Green, "Gay Soldier Dan Choi Re-enlists in US Army," *Pink News*, October 20, 2010, www.pinknews.co.uk.

28. Jasbir K. Puar and Amit Rai, "Monster, Terrorist, Fag: The War on Terrorism and the Production of Docile Patriots," *Social Text* 20, no. 3 (2002): 117–148.

29. Jean Shin, Jean, "The Asian American Closet," *Asian Law Journal* 11 (2004): 1–21.

30. Mark Footer, "Dan Choi; The Gay-Rights Activist and Former US military Officer Tells Mark Footer about His Fight for the Right to Tell the Truth," *South China Morning Post*, January 8, 2012, 14.

31. Melani McAlister, *Epic Encounters: Culture, Media, and US Interests in the Middle East since 1945* (Berkeley: University of California Press, 2005).

32. Keith Aoki, "Foreign-ness and Asian American Identities: Yellowface, World War II Propaganda, and Bifurcated Racial Stereotypes," *UCLA Asian Pacific American Law Journal* 4 (1996): 1–61.

33. "Lt. Dan Choi Talks Being Asian and Gay in the Military."

34. Susan Donaldson James, "Gay Activist Dan Choi Hospitalized for Breakdown," *ABC News*, December 16, 2010, https://abcnews.go.com/Health/gay-activist-dan-choi-hospitalized-nervous-breakdown/story?id=12413069.

35. Choi's supported the whistleblower actions of transgender soldier Pvt. Chelsea Manning, who was arrested for leaking sensitive classified U.S. documents containing embarrassing revelations to the open online source WikiLeaks.

36. George H. Quester, "Demographic Trends and Military Recruitment: Surprising Possibilities," *Parameters* 35, no. 2 (2005): 27–40.

Disrupting Normative Choreographies

Queer Asian Canadian Interventions Making
a Mess with/in a "Too Asian" University

JOHN PAUL CATUNGAL

What Does It Mean to Be Here? Disrupting the University

At the University of British Columbia (UBC), where I work, the student body is majority Asian descent, a result in part of the demographics of UBC's locale and its aggressive efforts at targeted internationalization. Yet like in many other universities, there is a mismatch between the institution's demographic racial diversity and the whiteness of its leadership, curriculum, and institutional culture.[1] This renders scholars of color like me nonnormative subjects in white academic and educational spaces. We are queer, if we take queer to mean, capaciously, the failure to fit within normal arrangements.[2] In this chapter, I ask questions about racialized queerness at UBC and beyond. What does it mean to be Asian Canadian and Filipino Canadian at UBC and in the North American academy? How might we read for queerness in the ways that Asian Canadians and Filipino Canadians encounter institutional spaces of teaching and learning? What queer practices of critique, opposition, placemaking, and negotiation might Asian Canadians, including Filipino Canadians, engage in to navigate the academy? In this chapter, I call attention to the political possibilities offered by "disruptive choreography," those embodied practices of institutional intervention that Asian Canadians and Filipino Canadians engage in to articulate queer critiques of the normative arrangements of Canadian postsecondary educational spaces. Attention to "disruptive choreography" enables us to site and cite the fragile social construction of the academy and the need for its constant upkeep, as well as the politics of our place as (sometimes) provisional members in these institutions of higher learning. Considered thus, disruptive choreography is both analysis and vision: it attempts to make sense of socioeconomic, cultural, and political conditions of teaching and learning and prefigure different—more affirming, more just, more caring—ways of being in the university.

Despite the increasing enrolment of Asian scholars in the North American academic industrial complex, queerness remains apt as a descriptor for the provisional and conditional inclusion of Asian scholars within institutional settings that continue to emplace and enforce conditions of white, cishetero, and settler colonial normativity.[3] Yet Asian Canadian scholars, like other racialized scholars in white normative institutions, are agentive subjects who queer the university not only through our presence but also through the ways that we carve out space for our bodies, knowledges, and ways of being through conduct that attempts to chip away at normative institutional arrangements. At times, we imagine and enact alternative ways of relating with knowledge formations, with colleagues and students, and with institutionalized norms and practice that we have navigate. Following the conceptual and political spirit of José Esteban Muñoz's work, I argue that these "disruptive choreographies" are practices of queerness because they represent the indictment of an inadequate present and the possibility of another way forward.[4] They are also queer in Manalansan's sense of queerness as messiness—the refusal to clean ourselves up in alignment with normative institutional orders.[5]

In what follows, I locate my analysis within the institutional context of racial politics at UBC. I then discuss two autoethnographic vignettes featuring practices of disruptive choreography that I have participated in at UBC. I offer these vignettes both to reflect on the continuing queerness of Asian Canadianness and Filipino Canadianness within and beyond the university, and to recognize the potential power of the critiques that these practices represent. I end with reflections on the mess that disruptive choreographies make, which serve to highlight the limits of the university as we know it.

Location, Location, Location: UBC as Context

I write this reflection as a junior tenure-track faculty member at UBC. UBC is located on the traditional, ancestral, and unceded territories of the Musqueam peoples, for whom these lands have been sites of land-based and intergenerational teaching and learning since time immemorial.[6] Ongoing settler colonialism structures UBC's ongoing relationship to the Musqueam peoples. The university's name, reflective of the province on which it is located, clearly signals its colonial provenance. It was only relatively recently that the institution has begun reckoning with its complicity in the genocidal violence of settler colonialism, with UBC president Santa Ono issuing a formal apology in April 2018 for UBC's role in residential schooling, including training policymakers and bureaucrats who implemented this violent system of colonial education.[7] In addition, UBC has a checkered history of anti-Asian racism. The now infamous "Too Asian" Macleans article, published in 2010, serves as a vivid illustration of continuing anxieties over Asian descent members of the UBC community, who are said to be obsessed with academic success, overly traditional, joyless, and antisocial, and thus ruining university life for others.[8] During World War II, UBC also actively participated in the internment of Japanese Canadians, in part with the University's Canadian Officers Training Corps kicking out Japanese Canadian students even before internment became a formal national policy response.[9] In 2012, UBC formally recognized how its wartime anti-Japanese racism negatively shaped the lives of seventy-six Japanese Canadian students, who were unable to formally graduate or finish their degrees due to their eviction from the university and their internment. In response to the powerful activism of the community leader Mary Kitagawa on behalf of Japanese Canadian communities, UBC issued honorary degrees to these seventy-six students. It also launched the Asian Canadian and Asian Migration Studies (ACAM) program, of which I am an affiliated faculty member, as part of its response.

The previous examples, though not exhaustive, already clearly illustrate the racial politics of UBC as an institution, which inform my understanding of my place in this university and the analysis below. Following intersectional feminist and queer of color insights, I also want to reiterate that these racial politics are simultaneously gender and sexual politics. In recent work with Dai Kojima and Robert Diaz, I argue that Asian Canadian history is also queer history, in part because Asian communities were widely considered, in policy and public discourse, as threats to the reproductive heterofuturity of Canada as a white settler nation.[10] Considered within this broader context, UBC's participation in residential schools and in Japanese internment was arguably also evidence of the institution's complicity and indeed investment in national white reproductive heterofuturity. This is an ongoing process. While UBC has expressed contrition for these histories and in some ways have tried to make amends, it remains clear that the university as a space of teaching and learning continues to be shaped by within settler colonial, white supremacist, and cishetero normativities. Many things have changed, but many stay the same: the example of the 2010 Macleans article mentioned earlier exemplifies ongoing racism, as does the programming of anti-Indigenous and misogynistic chants within Commerce frosh orientation events at UBC in 2013.[11]

This is the ground on which I do my work, situated as it is at the nexus of critical race feminism, queer of color theorizing, urban geographies of social difference, Filipino Canadian studies, and migration and transnationalism studies. Doing this work in this institutional context requires facing up to the institution's historical legacies of, and continuing struggles against, white settler cisheteronormativity. These condition which bodies of knowledge, in the multiple senses of that phrase, can take place in this institution. I am aware, as a queer Filipino Canadian migrant settler who works at UBC in the areas that I do, that this context conditions how I understand myself vis-à-vis my institution. It also bears upon my capacity and motivation as an academic, particularly, as I note later, in terms of what and how I approach the task of teaching at UBC.

In this increasingly precarious academic job market, I should note that I have a lot of privilege in having a tenure-track appointment at the Institute for Gender, Race, Sexuality and Social Justice at UBC, in a faculty line specializing in critical race and ethnic studies. My institutional home base and the line of research that I was hired for give me wiggle room to launch the kinds of institutional critiques that I articulate in this chapter, as well as in my teaching and broader research. I do not take my position lightly. From the very beginning, even during my job interview, I recognized the gravity of my position. I recognized then, as I still do, that this position comes with tremendous responsibilities, particularly to queer students of color who do not always see themselves and their stories reflected in the bodies of knowledge—the professoriate and the curriculum—that they encounter in school. This sense of responsibility to other queer people of color is part of what fuels my practice as a teacher and scholar at UBC. It is part of what motivates the disruptive choreographies that I engage in as part of my job.

The presence of queer people of color on university campuses has the potential to disrupt the normative choreography—the way things are—of institutional spaces of teaching and learning. At times, we disrupt through our mere presence in these spaces, which transgresses the taken-for-granted normative arrangements of the university. More often than not, however, we do this through deliberate acts, including how we comport ourselves, what issues and ideas we foreground in our teaching, how we relate to our colleagues and students, and what ethical commitments we take on in our work. Our disruptive potential—and the racialized ways we are identified as disruptive killjoys—testify to the shakiness of the institution's normative construction.[12] Deliberately taking on the normative arrangements in these institutions thus constitutes a key form of intervention through which I and others attempt to remake the university and the constituent relations that comprise it. In other words, the possibility of reconfiguring the white settler cisheteronormativity that arranges UBC and other universities, and of dreaming up new ways that we can relate to, move with and act around each other: this is the disruptive choreography that I imagine as enacting in the now what might be possible at a larger scale in the future.

Disruptive Choreography at Work: Two Examples

In this section, I describe examples of disruption that I have been involved in at UBC. They move from the relatively mundane (clothing choices, speaking

Tagalog) to the highly institutional (course design and curriculum development). These examples signal the necessity of disruption in the multiple sites of the university. They also signal that disruption must be calibrated beyond the individual and placed at the level of the social and institutional. Just as the university's normative choreographies target collective ways of doing things, disruptive choreographies must also intervene at the level of the collective in order to articulate and enable the possibility of institutional shifts.

Vignette 1: Making Them Hear and See Us

I once attended a PhD examination at UBC dressed in a *barong tagalog* that I borrowed from a friend. The clothing choice was a statement, aesthetically and politically. Drawing on the familiarity of the *barong*, especially to other Filipinos, I wanted to center Filipino-ness in the event of a dissertation defense, and especially so since the work being examined was May Farrales's groundbreaking research on queering Filipinx geographies in settler colonial Canada. I wanted the *barong* to do two things: (1) communicate with May that she and I, as a fellow queer Filipinx subjects in the academy, share the space with each other and care deeply together about such highly personally significant work, and (2) signal to the audience that while there are not very many of us in these spaces, we are making our presence known.

The examination room was arranged such that the examining committee, of which I was a part, occupies the most space at the front. We were seated boardroom style, and the audience members were seated in rows of chairs set up against the back wall of the room, looking frontward to May and the committee. Given the work being examined, I knew that the audience was going to include members of the local Filipinx communities. With my body clothed in the way that it was, I wanted them to see that we, as Filipinxs, are active players in the production of knowledge about us. I knew that this has not always been the case. May Farrales's research was already a testament to work on the community and by the community, and it is one recent key work that advances queer Filipinx Canadian scholarship.[13] Beyond signaling affinity with Filipinxs in the room, I also wanted my fellow faculty members to take note of my positionality as a Filipinx Canadian academic in that space.

When it was my turn to ask my defense questions to May, I began by speaking in Tagalog. I know that none of my fellow faculty members would understand the language. I wanted to mark the possibility of an "insider" kind of conversation with May and Filipinxs in the audience even within the formal space of a dissertation defense. Though it is likely that Tagalog has been spoken in such a formal institutional event before, it is still a possibility that this is the first time that Tagalog has been spoken in a dissertation defense at UBC. Speaking in Tagalog worked against the institutional convention of English as academic lingua franca at UBC. It was my hope that beginning in Tagalog would enable even a momentary collectivity centered around a shared conversation among those of us in the room who knew Tagalog.

Because my eyes were trained on May—my comments were meant for her, after all—I did not see how the audience reacted to my speaking Tagalog. I saw May wipe a tear at some point, and it wasn't until later that I was told that this was partly because May's partner Leah also reacted emotionally to hearing Tagalog in this academic space. Attendees later told me that my speaking in Tagalog marked a memorable moment for them—of recognition, of representation, of community.

For a long time, Filipinx Canadians did not always see or hear ourselves in academic spaces. It was important for me to ensure, partly through clothing and language, that we do remain unseen or unheard.

Vignette 2: Queering Curriculum at UBC

I was first hired as a faculty member in the educational leadership tenure stream at UBC in January 2014. Teaching, curriculum development, and other tasks that contribute to the development of more effective education at UBC constituted my main responsibilities as part of this tenure stream. These tasks enabled me to approach practices and spaces of teaching and learning as important avenues for injecting queer of color and queer diaspora theorizing into undergraduate education at UBC.

As an affiliate faculty member in the Asian Canadian and Asian Migration Studies (ACAM) minor program at UBC, I contribute to the ACAM undergraduate program in several ways. Several of my upper-level courses in my home department (Gender, Race, Sexuality and Social Justice; GRSJ) count toward the fulfilment of the minor's course requirements because they feature significant ACAM related content. This past year, I also developed ACAM 250, a new second year course on Asian Canada and popular culture, which is envisioned as a lower level introduction to this scholarly field and as a recruitment course for students into the ACAM minor program. My first offering of ACAM 250 in Fall 2018 engaged works by LGBTQ Asian Canadians and cultural production on Asian Canadian sexualities, including films by Joella Cabalu, Richard Fung, Ali Kazimi, and Love Intersections, and music by Casey Mecija (of Ohbijou), Vivek Shraya and Kim Villagante, along with scholarly works on Asian Canadian gender and sexual politics.

In addition to my ACAM work, I have also been collaborating with GRSJ director Denise Ferreira da Silva to deepen offerings in the areas of critical racial and anticolonial studies (CRAS) within the GRSJ undergraduate program. One of my main interventions is ensuring the centrality of queer of color theorizing in the curriculum. I have designed and since offered GRSJ 316 (Queer and Trans of Colour Theorizing), which combined two upper level "special topics" courses that I taught previously. The course features significant content on queer Asian diaspora scholarship, including the works of Roland Sintos Coloma, Robert Diaz, David Eng, Richard Fung, Gayatri Gopinath, Yukiko Hanawa, Jin Haritaworn, Dai Kojima, Martin Manalansan, Nayan Shah, and Judy Tzu-Chun Wu. They will join the works of Gloria Anzaldúa, Cathy Cohen, the Combahee River Collective, Qwo-Li Driskill, Chris Finley, Audre Lorde, Donna Miranda, Cherrie Moraga, and Jose Esteban Muñoz to comprise the course curriculum.

Centering queer of color knowledge and cultural production, including works on and by queer Asians themselves, ensures that the critical race curriculum at UBC tarries with the intersectional politics that shape the nexus of race, gender and sexuality. It works to disrupt the sometimes unmarked settler whiteness of sexuality studies curricula and the cisheteronormativity of critical race studies.[14] Equally important, the centering of these thinkers and cultural producers disrupt the popular curriculum of Canadian exceptionalism, based as it is on triumphalist accounts of the nation-state's multiculturalism and LGBT friendliness.[15]

Toward a Different There and Then: Imagining and Enacting Alternatives in the "Too Asian" University

Over a decade ago, years before he became inaugural director of ACAM at UBC, Christopher Lee wrote of the urgent need for "coordinated institutional interventions . . . from Asian Canadian perspectives . . . in order to create spaces for alternative forms of knowledge and pedagogy in Canadian colleges and universities."[16] The "alternative forms of knowledge and pedagogy" that Lee envisioned then did not explicitly include queer Asian and queer of color theorizing, but they are nevertheless here, adding to the mess that Lee calls for. I participate in the making of these alternatives through the kinds of disruptions that I discuss above, but the work of messing with the normative order of things cannot be approached in individualistic ways. My examples signal that disruptive actions take place with broader social and institutional contexts, enacting different modes of community through the sharing sartorial and linguistic recognition or through the presenting of the queerness of Asian Canada in the curriculum. In other words, the messiness of these interventions are enabled by their very targeting of collectivities as key sites for imagining and enabling different institutional formations as well as shifted socialities and political arrangements. They thus tap into a broader ecology of interventions whose joint energies can challenge, in lockstep, the normative choreographies of institutional life. Indeed, the disruptive choreographies I describe above are part of and energized by the copresence of other ones that refuse to shore up the normative university. These include, for example, the work of colleagues in Critical Indigenous Studies at UBC, whose focus is on decolonizing and indigenizing the university and its relationship to Indigenous communities, including our Musqueam hosts, as well as that of many student organizations and activist groups who prefigure more just and more caring relations within the university.

Moreover, while the examples I have offered remain firmly ensconced within UBC, they are in fact plugged into queer Asian disruptions beyond this institution, not the least through tapping into the networked affective, political, and intellectual communities of scholars elsewhere. Indeed, disruptive choreography sometimes require crossing the bounds of institutions in order to enact collectivities whose fidelities are not bound, in neoliberal terms, to the local. For example, Banerjea et al. and Nagar et al. both illustrate the beauty of translocal and transnational friendships and the ways that they locate relational joy, support and collaboration in proximity and also beyond it, thus enacting a spatially capacious collective ways of being in the face of the neoliberal individualization of the academic subject.[17] In queer Asian Canadian studies, recent examples of scholarship in this collaborative vein, to which I have contributed and from which I have benefited, include a recent special focus section of the journal *TOPIA*, which I co-edited, on "Feeling Queer, Feeling Asian, Feeling Canadian," as well as the edited collection *Diasporic Intimacies: Queer Filipinos and Canadian Imaginaries*, which includes chapter contributors from across Canadian institutions and beyond (myself included).[18]

If the late José Esteban Muñoz is correct in defining queerness as the act of naming the inadequacy of the here and now and as the possibility of a different there and then, disruptive choreographies are queer both in their desire to mess up the university as we know it and in their "warm illumination of a horizon imbued with potentiality."[19] This is a horizon that imagines a university where queerness and Asianness are not framed as threatening forms of being but as productive for imagining a different university, both as an institution and as a space of being-in-difference.

NOTES

1. Annette Henry, "'We Especially Welcome Applications from Members of Visible Minority Groups': Reflections on Race, Gender and Life at Three University," *Race, Ethnicity and Education* 18, no. 5 (2015): 589–610.

2. Cathy Cohen, "Punks, Bulldaggers and Welfare Queens: The Radical Potential of Queer Politics?" *GLQ* 3 (1997): 437–465.

3. Long Bui, "A Better Life? Asian Americans and the Necropolitics of Higher Education." In *Critical Ethnic Studies: A Reader*, edited by the Critical Ethnic Studies Collective (Durham, NC: Duke University Press, 2016), 161–174.

4. Jose Esteban Muñoz, *Cruising Utopia: The Then and There of Queer Futurity* (New York: New York University Press).

5. Martin Manalansan, "The 'Stuff' of Archives: Mess, Migration, and Queer Lives," *Radical History Review* 120 (Fall 2014): 94–107.

6. "Musqueam and UBC—Aboriginal Portal," last accessed April 20, 2018, http://aboriginal.ubc.ca/community-youth/musqueam-and-ubc/.

7. "Statement of Apology," last accessed April 20, 2018, https://president.ubc.ca/speeches/statement-of-apology/.

8. Stephanie Finley and Nicholas Kohler, "Too Asian: Some Frosh Don't Want to Study at an Asian University" [Retitled to "The Enrollment Controversy"], *Macleans*, last accessed April 20, 2018, http://www.macleans.ca/education/uniandcollege/too-asian-2/; Dan Cui and Jennifer Kelly, "'Too Asian?', or the Invisible Citizen on the Other Side of the Nation?" *Journal of International Migration and Integration* 14, no. 1 (2013): 157–174; Roland Sintos Coloma, "'Too Asian?' On Racism, Paradox and Ethno-Nationalism," *Discourse: Studies in the Cultural Politics of Education* 34, no. 4 (2013): 579–598.

9. Heather Amos, "Righting a 70-Year Wrong," *Trek Magazine*, July–August 2012, https://trekmagazine.alumni.ubc.ca/2012/julyaugust-2012/features/righting-a-70-year-wrong/.

10. Dai Kojima, J. P. Catungal, and Robert Diaz, eds., "Focus Section: Feeling Queer, Feeling Asian, Feeling Canadian," *TOPIA* 38 (Fall 2017): 69–154.

11. Stephen Hui, "In Response to 'Pocahontas' Chant, UBC Plans to Tackle Students' Ignorance of Aboriginal Issues," *The Georgia Straight*, October 21, 2013, https://www.straight.com/news/513451/response-pocahontas-chant-ubc-plans-tackle-students-ignorance-aboriginal-issues; Yuliya Talmazan, "UBC's CUS Ends FROSH Orientation Event in Light of Rape Chant Controversy," *Global News*, September 11, 2013, https://globalnews.ca/news/834366/ubc-cancels-frosh-orientation-event-in-light-of-rape-chant-controversy/.

12. Sara Ahmed, *The Promise of Happiness* (Durham, NC: Duke University Press, 2010).

13. May Farrales, "Gendered Sexualities in Migration: Play, Pageantry and the Politics of Performing Filipino-ness in Settler Colonial Canada" (PhD diss., University of British Columbia, 2017).

14. Roderick Ferguson, *Aberrations in Black: Toward a Queer of Color Critique* (Minneapolis: University of Minnesota Press, 2004); Roderick Ferguson, *The Reorder of Things: The University and Its Pedagogies of Minority Difference* (Minneapolis: University of Minnesota Press, 2012).

15. Kojima, Catungal and Diaz, "Feeling Queer"; Robert Diaz, Marissa Largo, and Fritz Pino, eds., *Diasporic Intimacies: Queer Filipinos and Canadian Imaginaries* (Evanston, IL: Northwestern University Press, 2017).

16. Christopher Lee, "The Lateness of Asian Canadian Studies," *Amerasia* 33, no. 2 (2007): 1.

17. Niharika Banerjea, Debanuj DasGupta, Rohit K. Dasgupta, and Jaime M. Grant, eds., *Friendship as Social Justice Activism: Critical Solidarities in a Global Perspective* (Kolkata: Seagull, 2018); Richa Nagar, Özlem Aslan, Nadia Z. Hasan, Omme-Salma Rahemtullah, Nishant Upadhyay, and Begüm Uzun, "Feminisms, Collaborations, Friendships: A Conversation," *Feminist Studies* 42, no. 2 (2016): 502–519.

18. Kojima, Catungal and Diaz, "Feeling Queer"; Diaz, Largo, and Pino, *Diasporic Intimacies*.

19. Muñoz, *Cruising Utopia*, 1.

Open in Emergency

On Queer(ing) Asian American Mental Health

Mimi Khúc

I didn't know what wellness was until I became unwell. Then I learned that wellness is a Lie.[1]

Years later, queer and trans writer Kai Cheng Thom and queer writer and performance artist Johanna Hedva would teach me more about this Lie, this elaborate system that fails queer and trans folks, people of color, the most vulnerable, so spectacularly. Or more accurately, succeeds in differentially creating and participating in our vulnerabilities. Our unwellness.

———

For the last eight years, I've taught a university course on the experiences of second-generation Asian Americans, the children of immigrants and refugees. My story. The story of so many of my students. Our stories of life, and of death.

I start the class with two days on suicide.

Asian Americans have some of the highest rates of suicidal ideation, especially youth and young adults. Asian American women ages fifteen to twenty-four years have among the highest rates by age, race, and gender, and Asian American college students consider suicide more than any of their peers.[2] Add to this the gut-wrenching statistics about queer youth: that they seriously contemplate suicide at almost three times the rate of non-queer youth and are almost five times as likely to have attempted suicide.[3] Our stories are deeply structured by this unlivability, this horrifyingly close horizon of death.

A text that I teach across all my courses is Lisa Park's essay "A Letter to My Sister," a haunting, gut-wrenching indictment of processes of model minoritization in American society for their part in causing her sister's suicide. I often also teach an essay I wrote in response, describing my own experiences of surviving postpartum depression, contemplating suicide, and entering a new world structured by depression, exhaustion, dread—the intimate knowledge that there are structures and people on a mission to see me die.[4]

I'm not crazy. But sometimes it feels like I am. The illegibility of the violence striating my life is a chokehold. When no one around you sees or understands, when they all turn away from what is happening to you. When you are the only witness to your premature dying.

Lisa Park tells her sister she wasn't crazy. Not even for committing suicide. Park tells her sister that the madness that drove her to suicide is a madness born of violence, madness as a condition of life under siege as a second-generation Asian American woman, madness that is evidence not of her personal failure but the failure of the world around her. A world that shaped her immigrant parents into both "accomplices and victims," investing in the *civilizing terror* that is Americanization, model minoritization, driving themselves and their daughter(s) to shattering heartbreak. All in the name of the American Dream.[5]

Those of us living and dying under conditions of structural violence; those whose vulnerabilities are exploited to the point of *premature death*, as Ruth Wilson Gilmore defines racism; those who Lord(e) knows *were never meant to survive*—we know that we are trying to be sane in an insane world. We know that madness boils around us, seeping into our pores, our veins, the crevices of our minds; we are filled by it. By despair and rage and heartbreak and fear and loss and exhaustion and exhaustion and exhaustion. Madness is the psychic and affective life of living under siege.[6]

And so I started a project that we would end up calling *Open in Emergency*, a project on Asian American mental health that sees every day as an emergency, as a crisis of mental health, especially for communities under siege.[7]

Because what does mental health look like when we live within social structures that are trying to kill us?

Open in Emergency explores this question as an arts and humanities intervention that decolonizes mental health. It asks us to reconceive mental health in the context of historical and structural violence—and in the context of community meaning-making and practices of survival. It asks us to shift away from traditional models of wellness and unwellness that have historically been structured by and worked to bolster whiteness and white supremacy, capitalism, empire—and queer death. It asks us to look in different places, ask different questions, and make visible different things. It asks us to think and feel our way out of circuits that are killing us.

The World Health Organization defines mental health as "a state of well-being in which every individual realizes his or her own potential, can cope with the normal stresses of life, can work productively and fruitfully, and is able to make a contribution to her or his community."[8] In *Open in*

Emergency, several contributors directly engage this definition, pointing out its emphasis on work, its conflation of wellness with productivity. Is our health—and value—really determined by an ability to be productive? To participate in capitalism? Capitalism provides our frames for measuring our health; indeed, it frames precisely in ways that it can use, extract, exploit. Kill.

In her essay "The Myth of Mental Health," Kai Cheng Thom writes, "Mental health was invented to sell us something. . . . [It] is the language of power—the power to exist within, and sometimes define, the conventions of sanity, normalcy, the status quo, capitalism, white heteropatriarchy." Mental health as a normative construct—an ideal that defines for us how to be, what to become. In "Sick Woman Theory," Johanna Hedva shows us a dangerous consequence of this construction:

> What is so destructive about conceiving of wellness as the default, as the standard mode of existence, is that it *invents illness as temporary.* . . . Care, in this configuration, is only required sometimes. When sickness is temporary, care is not normal.

Neoliberal capitalism at its finest. Wellness as the normal state of being, illness—and only recognizable ones—as aberration, and thus care as aberration. Humanity requires nothing to sustain itself; humanity is owed nothing. We owe each other nothing. We owe ourselves nothing. Johanna Hedva asks us to do an exercise: "Go to the mirror, look yourself in the face, and say out loud: 'To take care of you is not normal. I can only do it temporarily.'" This seems a strange and awful thing to say to yourself—but it is what the world says to us every day.[9]

Mental health as "a state of well-being in which every individual . . . can cope with the normal stresses of life." What are normal stresses of life? For whom are they normal? Who gets to deem certain stresses as acceptable, and other kinds as too much, beyond some imagined threshold? Who gets to tell you what you should be asked to bear? And who gets to tell us how we must bear our burdens, what kinds of "coping" are healthy? Vulnerable communities have always been asked to bear too much. They have also always generated strategies of survival, both compromised and breathtaking. I started this project in order to take stock of what we've been asked to bear, what has been too much, what we have done and are doing in the face of too much. And I found that we need to look in many places, new places, different places to understand the scope and depth of the forces that structure Asian American life—and of the possibilities of agency, meaning, and care therein. "What hurts?" asks literary scholar erin Ninh.[10] I ask: How do we go on living while it hurts?

Perhaps to answer these questions, we look not in individual pathology or maladjustment but in the everyday burdens of structure, burdens best described in stories, in intimacies, in wounds, in crises of meaning. So we "hacked" the DSM. We asked, What would a Diagnostic and Statistical Manual of Mental Disorders look like if it was about Asian Americans, by Asian Americans, and from an arts and humanities approach? What kind of vocabulary could we develop for understanding wellness and unwellness in our communities if we took this untraveled route? So we made a mock DSM: Asian American Edition, framed as if we had taken an actual DSM for Asian Americans, torn out all the pages, and inserted new ones.

How does one "queer"—and "race"—the DSM? One way of answering this is to think back to the actual DSM: What in the actual DSM is queer? The DSM has a fraught history with queer life, with homosexuality listed as a mental disorder from the first edition in 1952 up until queer activists advocated for its removal in 1973 (with conditions related not entirely removed until 1987), and with trans identity taking many forms throughout editions of the DSM, including the most recent, the DSM-5 published in 2013.[11] So what does it look like to make an intervention crafted by queer folk that speaks to the needs of queer folk, to allow queer Asian Americans to diagnose their own lives—and to prescribe their own care practices?

Open in Emergency's DSM opens with an excerpt of "A Letter to My Sister" that situates Asian American life, and death, within racism and model minoritization. Kai Cheng Thom's essay is the DSM's first entry, asking us to question our most basic assumptions about mental health. What is it? Does it even exist? And she begins this questioning with the story of her first suicide attempt after coming out as trans to her family in high school.

> My parents drove me home from the hospital after my first suicide attempt on a Friday evening in spring. I remember because I was registered to take the SATs the following Saturday. My father, never an emotionally expressive man to begin with, drove in silence most of the way, clenching the wheel with white-knuckled hands. My mom was also silent, staring straight ahead through the windshield. I didn't have much to say either.

When her father does break the silence, he does so only to ask for more silence: *Please don't tell anyone about this.* And to insist that she must go on to take the SATs the next day, for their family's sake. Thom's response:

> Right there in car, as my father clenched the wheel like he wanted to kill it and my mother stared straight ahead, unblinking, I decided to be healthy, to get better, to be the kind of son my parents wanted. I was going to forget about all of this, about everything: heartbreak

and wanting to be a girl, feeling revolted by my own body, the nasty anonymous messages my classmates were sending me online, being sexually assaulted, not having any real friends.

I was going to be good. Sane. Normal. Better.

She was going to be good, sane, normal, better—as if all those are the same thing. Indeed, within circuits of love and guilt and pain in Asian immigrant families, within model minoritization and aspirational whiteness, within gender and sexual normativity—at the intersection of all these, "good," "sane," "normal," and "better" are easily conflated. The stakes are very high for a second-generation queer and trans Asian Canadian girl when success is defined through a kind of inclusion always out of reach, always strived for, and only precariously achieved, and when failure means a failure of personhood ("you are a failed person") and a failure of the deepest responsibility to the family to which you are indebted ("you have failed those you owe everything to"). In her book *Ingratitude*, erin Ninh traces the circuits of power and love within Asian immigrant families, the production of structures of feeling that create impossible burdens and cause incalculable pain for the children of Asian immigrants. How parental sacrifice turns into daughterly debt, the weaponization of parental suffering in order to extract "good" behavior and, ultimately, "good" personhood. Lives suffused with guilt and shame and worthlessness. All in the name of the American Dream. In Thom's opening story, she gives us a horrifying picture of what it is like to live in this system and then try to die and then try to live again through the abnegation of all her needs to the family's. "I was going to forget about all of this. . . . I was going to be good. Sane. Normal. Better."[12]

But this deep, urgent need to be "normal" isn't simply the work of heteropatriarchy or white supremacy or model minoritization or adaptive immigrant parenting tactics alone. Here, Thom gives us a new vector to consider: the imperative of wellness. Be normal, be well. Be productive. We define mental health through a neoliberal capitalist frame, defining health and "normalcy" through individual productivity, individual pathology and individual failure, individual effort to "achieve." Success through inclusion. You are healthy when you are normal, belong, can work.

Mental health as it is constructed by mainstream psychiatry, by capitalism and European colonization—that is to say, by dominant social forces—is, in the end about access to power, and to the status quo (normalcy).

That is to say, to be mentally healthy means to fit inside the confines of a job and heteronormative conceptions of sexuality/romance, to uphold social conventions of race and class and gender.

> Mental health is the language of power—the power to exist within, and sometimes define, the conventions of sanity, normalcy, the status quo, capitalism, white heteropatriarchy.[13]

We are told we must be well, and to be well looks like being "normal" as defined by dominant social structures and cultural narratives. And yet the majority of us cannot be "normal" and thus "well" in these ways. We cannot all be white, male, able-bodied, straight, cis, gender normative, middle-class, respectable. The world makes us sick and then tells us it is our fault.

> There is a reason why so many of us are anxious and depressed, traumatized and psychotic, self-loathing and suicidal—a reason greater than simple biological illness or personal failure.
>
> I would hazard to guess that the reason is colonization, capitalism, racial and gendered violence—the simple fact that the vast majority of people live oppressed (read: traumatic) lives, and are taught that we do not know it. It is, in a word, crazy-making.[14]

In centering her own suffering and the suffering of those around her and in contextualizing that suffering within structures of violence, Thom disrupts the imperative of wellness, queering mental health in ways that allow for vulnerable, exploited communities to claim pain and thus care. She asks, "What if, instead of clinging to the fantasy of mental health in order to deny our suffering, we asked our suffering what it is trying to say?"[15]

Part of what our suffering is telling us is that the world wants some of us, many of us, to die. So what is mental health, what is queer survival, in the face of this? Johanna Hedva's essay "Sick Woman Theory" also interrogates our assumptions about wellness, our frameworks' reliance upon normativity, capitalism, whiteness—we assume there is a normal to be achieved, and illness is deviance that can and should be corrected. And the normal is mapped onto certain bodies while others are rendered abnormal, pathological, in need of correction or eviction. And if wellness is normal, then it sustains itself; care is only corrective and is only necessary sometimes, when deviation occurs.

But what if we centered these sick bodies? What if to be ill is "normal"? Hedva centers the "Sick Woman"—the chronically ill, the disabled, the crazy, the weak, the marginalized, the exploited—and rethinks what care must look like in this context.

> The Sick Woman is an identity and body that can belong to anyone denied the privileged existence—or the cruelly optimistic *promise* of such an existence—of the white, straight, healthy, neurotypical,

upper and middle-class, cis- and able-bodied man who makes his home in a wealthy country, has never not had health insurance, and whose importance to society is everywhere recognized and made explicit by that society; whose importance and care *dominates* that society, at the expense of everyone else.

The Sick Woman is anyone who does not have this guarantee of care.

In centering the Sick Woman, Hedva opens up a new vision for care—what does it look like to guarantee care for her?

I used to think that the most anti-capitalist gestures left had to do with love, particularly love poetry: to write a love poem and give it to the one you desired seemed to me a radical resistance. But now I see I was wrong.

The most anti-capitalist protest is to care for another and to care for yourself. To take on the historically feminized and therefore invisible practice of nursing, nurturing, caring. To take seriously each other's vulnerability and fragility and precarity, and to support it, honor it, empower it. To protect each other, to enact and practice community. A radical kinship, an interdependent sociality, a politics of care.

This is the radical work to normalize and center suffering and therefore care, to ask for communal responsibility for each life. And ultimately, it is a rejection of the neoliberal capitalist notion of wellness that requires us to work, to be productive, in order to be worthy of life, of care. It is the radical reclaiming of the nonproductive body:

Because once we are all ill and confined to the bed, sharing our stories of therapies and comforts, forming support groups, bearing witness to each other's tales of trauma, prioritizing the care and love of our sick, pained, expensive, sensitive, fantastic bodies, and there is no one left to go to work, perhaps then, finally, capitalism will screech to its much-needed, long-overdue, and motherfucking glorious halt.[16]

So what are some ways we can take care of each other and ourselves? Queer performance artist and chef Genevieve Erin O'Brien gives us a set of queer Asian American self-care cards, meant to be cut out of the DSM and used as a wellness practice, that challenge mainstream ways of approaching self-care.[17] Let's step back for a moment to consider: What does it mean to include queer self-care cards in our DSM? To assert that the DSM should include methods of self-care is already a disruption in what we think a DSM is and what it should do; to assert that there is such thing as queer self-care, self-care designed by and for queer Asian Americans, asks us to think about care itself in new ways—who is allowed to diagnose pain, who is allowed to provide healing, who is allowed to receive care, and what care can and should look like for differential needs.

For example, one of the cards suggests that we "Fuck Shit Up." This is always my students' favorite. Why? Because it is a disruption of the normal, the rejection of the well-worn grooves of life they see in front of them, trajectories that they have inherited, that their families and larger communities push them into. This directly unsettles our reliance on the normal for defining mental health. There is no directive or even room for anyone to "fuck shit up" as part of the WHO definition of mental health. Indeed, this disruption of the normal opposes the WHO definition directly—and might even be seen by mental health authorities as signs of mental illness. Yet here, O'Brien is telling us that disruption is healthy, is needed, is curative. She invites us to disrupt the normal, to disrupt dominant structures and cultural narratives, because they can be what injures, what kills. Indeed, historically, they have formed the deathly conditions of queer life.

Another card suggests that we make a friendship bracelet and gift it to our "chosen family." "Chosen family" is a queer term to describe family that one chooses, especially in the face of families of origin that unchoose you, disown you. Disownment and disposability form stark horizons of queer family life, so this card suggests that in the face of that, we might rethink the concept of family: intimate relationships can be built and chosen with intentionality, and those kinds of relationships might be the sustenance that we need.

"Fuck Shit Up." Queer Asian American self-care cards by performance artist Genevieve Erin O'Brien. (From the author)

1) Make a friendship bracelet. 2) Gift your chosen family.

"Chosen Family." Queer Asian American self-care cards by performance artist Genevieve Erin O'Brien. (From the author)

Success comes in many forms.

"Success Comes in Many Forms." Queer Asian American self-care cards by performance artist Genevieve Erin O'Brien. (From the author)

The final example we'll examine is a meditation on the definition of success. "Success comes in many forms." The image here is curious, of a person mowing their lawn—not our usual idea of what success looks like. So what is success in this image? I know personally that the image is of one of O'Brien's closest friends. Is the success in the fact of her friend mowing their own lawn? That they are enjoying this work? That they feel competent? That the grass looks good? Is the success in their ability to simply be alive, doing an everyday, ordinary task? Or perhaps the success is in building community in the experience of being together while doing ordinary things like mowing the lawn? In framing mowing the lawn as a picture of success, O'Brien rejects neoliberal capitalist ideals of upward mobility and aspirations toward a white middle-class heteronormative life, as well as the model minority subject in the Asian American context. We see again an engagement with the American Dream, this time rejecting its horizons and reaching toward something else to define a life fulfilled.

To queer readers, these suggestions probably feel familiar, resonant perhaps with ways we are already enacting care in our lives but perhaps without that name. Here, O'Brien names these practices as self-care; together, these cards see the queer community as a source of knowledge for the forces that make life feel unlivable and as a resource for survival strategies. Queer life thus produces a kind of knowledge on what survival and wellness might look like outside of normative structures. We are forced out of "normal life," and so we build abnormal lives that can form roadmaps, blueprints, for fuller living for all. This is not to romanticize queer life, of course—queers are just as susceptible to normalization as others, leaning into privileges and access that leverage us some measure of inclusion and safety, especially if we are feeling too vulnerable along axes of gender and sexuality. But all of us engage the death machines that are capitalism and empire, and it is in finding ways to make life more livable that we open up possibilities. It is in the attempts, successful and failed, that queer flourishing lights the way.

Instead of starting with the traditional DSM and WHO's definition of mental health, O'Brien's cards, and the mock DSM more broadly, push us to see what is already happening as care and wellness practices in our communities, expanding what counts as care and making legible what psychology and psychiatry make illegible. Alongside Thom and Hedva's theoretical and personal offerings, O'Brien's whimsical and practical collection becomes part of a larger queer intervention in mental health, one that centers the pain of Asian American queer life, its horizons of illness and death, its spirit of survival, its explorations of healing, individually and as a community.

Open in Emergency's DSM: Asian American Edition includes many other queer contributions to queer the DSM and mental health more broadly: Mimi Thi Nguyen's Keanu Kares drawings bringing together pop culture, fandom, and Buddhism; Lydia X. Z. Brown on queer neurodivergence and its relationship to state structures of surveillance; Peggy Lee and Cynthia Wu on care work in the university; Jigna Desai on the body as a fraught site of wellness, illness, race, and agency; Shana Bulhan Haydock interrogating wellness and normality not just in dominant medicine but also in "alternative" or "holistic" wellness; Julie Thi Underhill's photography series documenting fears; and more. Other parts of *Open in Emergency* work to queer mental health in other ways: a redacted and annotated medical info pamphlet to correct and reframe how we understand postpartum depression and the literature we produce about it; handwritten family letters as both compromised testimony and agency; a tapestry of wounds, featuring voices from across the Asian American community, silent and not; and a deck of Asian American tarot cards renamed, refigured, and retheorized by and for Asian Americans, designed to reflect Asian American life and be a basis for wellness practices. As an arts and humanities project, *Open in Emergency* directly intervenes in normative psychological and psychiatric ideas about mental health—and places authority in other scholarly fields, in the hands of artists and writers, in the meaning-making strategies of communities. Together these art pieces, these scholarly interventions, these community creations are soulful offerings that we hope open up new pathways for thinking and feeling our way forward and outward, toward life fully felt, fully witnessed.

———

Queer Asian American survival has meant defining wellness and unwellness on our own terms, dissecting the institutional frameworks that have pathologized us and tried to norm us into wellness—and then disinvesting from these frameworks. To claim and build communities and structures of care. To build lives fully lived, fully felt.

May queer life—and death—continue to light the way.

———

What does mental health mean to you? To your communities? What kinds of vocabularies and lenses do you need to capture the depth and scope of your own suffering, of the suffering of those you love? What hurts? And how do we go on living while it hurts?

NOTES

1. Parts of this essay were previously published on the blog *Black Girl Dangerous*.

2. American Psychological Association, May 2012, http://www.apa.org/pi/oema/resources/ethnicity-health/asian-american/suicide-fact-sheet.pdf; Eliza Noh, "Asian American Women and Suicide: Problems of Responsibility and Healing," *Women and Therapy* 30, no. 3–4 (2007): 87–107.

3. "Sexual Identity, Sex of Sexual Contacts, and Health-Risk Behaviors among Students in Grades 9–12: Youth Risk Behavior Surveillance," CDC, U.S. Department of Health and Human Services, 2016.

4. Lisa Park, "A Letter to My Sister," in *Making More Waves: New Writing by Asian American Women*, edited by Elaine H. Kim, Lilia V. Villanueva, and Asian Women United of California (Boston: Beacon, 1997), 65–71.

5. Ibid., 65, 67, 69.

6. Ruth Wilson Gilmore, "Race and Globalization," in *Geographies of Global Change: Remapping the World*, 2nd ed., edited by R. J. Johnston, Peter J. Taylor, and Michael J. Watts, (Malden, MA: Blackwell, 2002), 261; Gilmore, *Golden Gulag: Prisons, Surplus, Crisis and Opposition in Globalizing California* (Berkeley, CA: University of California Press, 2007), 28; Audre Lorde, "A Litany for Survival," *The Black Unicorn: Poems* (New York: W. W. Norton, 1995).

7. Mimi Khúc, guest editor, "Open in Emergency: A Special Issue on Asian American Mental Health," *The Asian American Literary Review* 7, no. 2 (Fall–Winter 2016); "Open in Emergency, 2nd Edition," *The Asian American Literary Review* 10, no. 2 (Fall–Winter 2019).

8. World Health Organization. "Mental Health: A State of Well-Being," August 2014, accessed 20 May 2018, http://www.who.int/features/factfiles/mental_health/en/.

9. Kai Cheng Thom, "The Myth of Mental Health," in *Open in Emergency*, 9; Johanna Hedva, "Sick Woman Theory," in *Open in Emergency*, 150.

10. erin Khue Ninh, "Thesis," in *Open in Emergency*, 65.

11. "Diagnostic and Statistical Manual of Mental Disorders," https://en.wikipedia .org/wiki/Diagnostic_and_Statistical_Manual_of_Mental_Disorders.

12. erin K. Ninh, *Ingratitude: The Debt-Bound Daughter in Asian American Literature* (New York: New York University Press, 2011).

13. Thom, "The Myth of Mental Health," 9. Here, I'm reminded of my own father's regular pleading that I be "normal" all through my youth. How suffocating "normal" felt, how terrified my father was that I wasn't normal enough, how painful it was for me to knowingly cause him pain, how we had no way at all to talk about any of this.

14. Ibid., 11.

15. Ibid.

16. Johanna Hedva, "Sick Woman Theory," 149–150.

17. Genevieve Erin O'Brien, "#SELFCARE," in *Open in Emergency*, 127–136.

Religion and Ritual in the Lives of Queer Filipinx in Canada

MAY FARRALES

Since becoming one of Canada's top sources of immigrants, the Philippines has not only been credited for providing the country with a necessary labor force but is also being recognized for helping to reinvigorate its religious institutions. Asian migration in general has bolstered ailing religious institutions in the secularized landscapes of Canadian cities, Filipino/as in particular are touted for revitalizing Roman Catholic churches. Such a popular sentiment is echoed in a headline from one of Canada's national newspapers, "In a Time of Turmoil, Catholicism Is on the Rise in Vancouver."[1] The article goes on to describe how even as the Catholic Church has been wracked by scandal and beleaguered by dwindling numbers of parishioners over the past decade in Canadian cities, Catholic churches in Vancouver have experienced a revitalization. The archbishop interviewed in the article credits the surge in the number of parishioners to the arrival of recent immigrants from the Philippines. Adding to this assessment, the archbishop pontificates on the question of why the Church has had difficulty recruiting new parishioners, especially young Canadians: "How do you talk about God, in a world which seems in some ways, in particularly in the West, to be uninterested in that question. It's not that it [society] has articulated objections, it's just indifferent . . . The superficiality of modern life—that is the biggest enemy."

I am interested here in how the archbishop mobilizes the Filipino. In one breath, he credits Filipinos, who have recently migrated to the city, for regenerating the Church. In another cut, he muses that the West's ambivalence to "God" and questions of religion is inherently a condition of "modern life." When these two thoughts are brought together, the Filipino is cast as already and always outside the modern, a casting that pivots on the Filipino's natural devotedness to Catholicism.

In this essay, I explore this dominant configuration as religion intersects with questions of sexuality and race. I follow recent calls in Filipinx-Canadian scholarship urging that more serious attention be given to questions of religion,[2] and for further thought on how such questions relate to the formation of sexual, gendered and racial subjectivities.[3] To pay attention to the intersections of race, sexuality, gender, and religion, I play with the popular liberal Western and secular assumption that inherent in the devout Filipino are homophobic tendencies and repressed sexualities. I situate these assumptions in the context of the normative white heteropatriarchal settler colonial workings of Canada where liberal forms of secularism frame our experiences. I demonstrate how Filipino/as articulate our negotiations with religion and sexuality in relation to our experiences or knowledge of cultural norms in the Philippines and the liberal settler norms of Canada. I do so by working with interviews conducted with lesbian, gay, transgender, and queer Filipinxs on the unceded and traditional territories of the Musqueam, Squamish, and Tsleil-Waututh peoples (Greater Vancouver). In their interviews, I examine the moments and spaces where queer and Filipinx identifying subjects sometimes escape and push back on white liberal settler assumptions that presuppose Canada as secular and modern. I follow two particular narratives in the ways LGBTQ Filipinx in Vancouver articulate their relationship to religion. First, I explore how religion is articulated as way of marking our migration experiences from the Philippines to Canada in relation to sexuality and secularism. Second, I trace the role of religion and religious institutions in the lives of LGBTQ Filipinx in Vancouver that speak to a nuanced relationship between religion and sexuality that is not so easily legible by Canada's white liberal settler secular purview. Ultimately, I argue that while navigating dominant colonial logics from the Philippines and in Canada, their everyday negotiations with the Church, faith, and their families point to the limits of the dominant gender and sexual narratives associated with Filipinxs in Canada and the logic of liberal settler secularism itself.

"We Have More Reservations, Because We're Catholic": The Religious Markings of Filipinx Canadian Sexualities

Virgilio[4] tells me, "We have more reservations, because we're Catholic," when I asked him during our interview if he saw any differences being a Filipinx among his other Asian and white gay friends and acquaintances. He goes on to describe how he does not think white Canadians have to struggle with questions of religion and family, saying, "That doesn't mean that much to them." Based on his experience migrating to Canada as an adult and living as a gay male in Vancouver, he explains that the defining marker of being Filipinx and queer is "really just the religious background. That's main, that I think would be the main difference." Virgilio's truth that "it's really just the religious background," was common among those who participated in interviews.

Bernard, who migrated to Canada to join his mother in Vancouver in his late teenage years, shares a similar sentiment about how being religious distinguishes the Filipinx queer from other experiences. Bernard provides further insight into this marker of being gay and Filipinx, adding,

> So when I arrived in Canada, I kind of went to church with my mom for a good six months and I stopped because I was like well, if this is my identity and I'm gay, maybe I should kind of side with the gay people and not with the church.

With this statement, Bernard signals a tension that places devotion to religion as a condition of Filipinx queer subjectivities at odds with Canada where gay people and the Church do not mix. He shares further the impact this tension has had on his experience of being Filipinx and queer in Vancouver:

> Here, when I came to Canada, you know watching the news and everything, there's so many religions that they're just against all gay people. There's just so much hate for us. So that's really foreign to me.

Bernard's experience of shock and the foreignness of what he interprets as a hard and fast divide between queer sexualities and religion draws attention to the normative assumption that Canada, as modern and Western space, is inherently secular. For Filipinx like Bernard, where religion and nonnormative sexualities intersect, the presumed secular Canadian landscape conditions the ways in which Filipinx sexualities come to be. In such a normative secular space, the experience of religion is acutely experienced in Filipino immigrant families.

For example, Samonte shares of growing up with an appreciation for what makes their queer and transgender experience particular and different from the mainstream queer subject:

> For me, I knew that Catholicism was a huge deal in the Filipino community. So for me, I felt that automatically I was going to be rejected based on my sexuality from my home community because Catholicism is such a huge part of the culture. So speaking from my own experience, that's kind of where my fears were coming from around that. And just like, yah, just fears of being rejected.

Here, Samonte speaks to how, within the frames of their family and the Filipino community abroad, negotiations with sexuality and religion straddle two seemingly polar opposite worlds—one in which religious devotion delineates Filipino sexualities, and the other in which the liberal secularism holds such religious devotion with apprehension. I suggest that both these worlds condition the coming into being of Filipino sexualities in Canada.

In his ethnography of Filipino gay men in New York, Martin Manalansan outlines a similar set of negotiations wherein, as he puts it, "Religion, for many of my informants, stands in sharp opposition to secular America. For many of them, religious devotion is the mark of being Filipino."[5] Manalansan explains the various ways that Filipino gay men in America navigate this binary between religion and secularity by showing how in their everyday practices, the men make religion part of their lives through different practices and daily rituals. By doing so, the gay Filipino men push back against the assumption that America is a universally secular space as they carve out their lives and livelihoods in New York. I extend Manalansan's argument in two ways. First, in the section that follows, I trace the different means by which LGBTQ Filipinx in Vancouver productively navigate these two different yet overlapping worlds. Second, I want to suggest that the process of engaging with religion as a marker of being Filipinx is inherently racialized in the settler colonial context of Canada.

As Indigenous scholars have argued, religion, ideologies, and religious institutions are central in the colonial project in Turtle Island. Anishinaabe, Métis, and Norwegian scholar Melissa Nelson theorizes the ways in which Western religion, brought to bear by colonialism, systematically works to demonize Indigenous ways of relating to one another and other-than human beings.[6] She writes, "Tragically, these beautiful stories of embodied connection have been demonized and silenced by patriarchal, colonial, and Judeo-Christian ideologies."[7] Indigenous feminist, Two-Spirit, and queer scholars argue that these intimate, violent, and embodied forms of dispossession go hand in hand with the settler colonial drive to dispossess Indigenous peoples of their lands.[8] They point to specific instances when religion (i.e., Christianity and Catholicism) were used to justify and operationalize the violent removal of Indigenous women, Two-Spirit people, and communities from their bodies, ancestral lands, and relations. Cree scholar Alex Wilson, for example, writes of how gender and sexual disciplining in Indian Residential Schools (managed and operated by religious institutions) forced Indigenous children to conform to Western gender and sexual binaries.[9] Anishinaabe scholar Leanne Simpson theorizes a continuity in gender and sexual forms of violence of the past to the present:

> Two Spirit and queer [2SQ] people have always known from living as 2SQ in settler colonialism: 2SQ bodies and the knowledge and practices those bodies house as Indigenous political orders were seen as an extreme threat to settler society, sovereignty, dispossession, and the project of colonization, colonialism, and assimilation.[10]

As Simpson explains, even as Two-Spirit and queer Indigenous peoples pose an "extreme threat" to settler nations, their survival, resistance and the knowledge and relations they embody hold the possibility of wearing away at the settler colonial project.

I dwell on the interventions and knowledge of Indigenous scholars who insist on the persistence of settler colonial power relations and normative logics in present-day Canada as the settler colonial present is the setting and set of relations in which Filipinxs are negotiating sexuality, race, and religion. As I argue elsewhere, Filipinx subject and community formation is imbricated and implicated in contemporary settler colonial relations in Canada.[11] In the case of our negotiations at the intersections of religion and sexuality, the naturalization of Canada as a secular space can be seen as part of these processes and relations. More specifically, the presumption of Canada as wholly secular where the Filipinx's devotion to religion is cast as always and already outside the modern, and where religious ideologies and institutions form the basis for present day forms of colonialism can be brought into question.

These forms of questioning, though not directly articulated in the interviews shared in this essay, are nonetheless present among LGBTQ Filipinx in Vancouver. As I demonstrate in what follows, they are present in our everyday negotiations with religion and sexuality as Filipinx in Canada.

"Spiritual Shopping": Navigating Heteronormativity

In my interview with Telma, she describes what she calls "spiritual shopping," a process she embarked upon after leaving the Catholic Church and her husband. She shares that she left the Church and her husband over similar tensions embedded in the heteronormativity of both relationships. While "spiritual shopping," Telma went to different churches to "see what was different." She eventually ended her formal relationship with religious institutions while being groomed to become a leader in a Christian Filipino church because, as she puts it, "I was questioning whatever they were doing that's not congruent to the philosophy of what people believe in." In her search for congruency, Telma became active in a local LGBTQ group for Filipinx in Vancouver and continues to consider herself a spiritual person. She shares:

I'm okay with who I am now. I'm comfortable with my skin. I'm comfortable telling people. I really don't care anymore what people would think. I just know I have the right to be here just as you are. And the thing is, I don't have to be radical about it anymore, because I used to be radical about . . . you know . . . but now I'm just okay. I'm

just okay with it, it's not an issue, I don't even have to identify—
straight people don't have to identify themselves as straight.

I dwell on Telma's process of deciding to leave the heteronormative relations of her marriage and the Church, her "spiritual shopping," and her now
queer relationship with religion and spirituality as a means of appreciating
the complex and nuanced ways in which Filipinx negotiate religion and
sexuality while in Canada. Others I interviewed shared similar processes
of deciding to leave the Catholic Church for similar reasons, whereas some
find comfort and continuity through their involvement with the Church. For
example, Maritess explains:

> You know how Filipinos are—we are Catholic, we are a predomi-
> nantly Catholic . . . and I studied in a Catholic school so I'm still very
> religious. But at the same I'm a lesbian so I have to find a perfect mix.

Maritess believes she has found "that perfect mix" of being Filipina, Catholic,
and a lesbian, describing that she continues to attend mass, focusing on
spiritual lessons and the continuity of her relationship with her family that
she is able to draw from the Church. Telma and Maritess navigate the complicated terrain of sexuality, faith, religious institutions, family, and being
queer Filipinas in ways that overflow strict binaries between religion and
non-normative subjectivities. Their stories press upon framings that render
the Filipinx community in Canada as wholly repressed and homophobic by
presenting a more complicated picture of how they relate with other Filipinx
both despite and through religion. For Maritess, being religious, being
Filipina, and being a lesbian are not mutually exclusive. Instead, she insists
that all three experiences constitute and make possible her relationships with
her family and her connections with the broader Filipinx community. For
Telma, deciding to leave formal or institutionalized forms of religion while
remaining spiritual grows her relationships in the Filipinx community as
she continues to do work in the local LGBTQ organization. Although their
experiences with religion, sexuality, and being Filipina differ, both suggest
that there is a room to navigate and even push back on the heteronormativity
of the Filipino family and religion.

Conclusion

In his essay "Toward Queer(er) Futures: Proliferating the 'Sexual' in Filipinx
Canadian Sexuality Studies," John Paul Catungal urges those of us engaged
in knowledge production on, in, and about Filipino/as in Canada to "examine the intersections of religion and sexuality and their colonial genealogies

not only for LGBT Filipinx Canadian lives, but also, more capaciously, for the different configurations of intimacies and identifications that constitute and are constituted by Filipinx Canadian sexualities."[12] By highlighting the ways in which LGBTQ Filipinx in Vancouver negotiate religion as a marker of their Filipino-ness and sexuality as a means through which they negotiate religion, in this essay, I attempt to show how Filipina/o sexualities are constituted in these processes. I partially speak to the colonial bearings of these negotiations by attending to the ways that normative settler colonial relations and the presumed fixedness of Canada as a secular space relate to the ways in which we navigate the tensions between religion and sexuality. Overall, what I endeavour to do in this paper is underscore the ways in which the everyday engagements with questions of sexuality and religion trouble dominant framings of the devout Filipino and the secularity of Canada.

NOTES

1. Bitonti, Daniel Bitonti, "In a Time of Turmoil, Catholicism Is on the Rise in Vancouver," *Globe and Mail*, March 28, 2013, https://www.theglobeandmail.com/news/british-columbia/in-a-time-of-turmoil-catholicism-is-on-the-rise-in-vancouver/article10548277/.

2. Roland Sintos Coloma, Bonnie McElhinny, Ethel Tungohan, John Paul Catungal, and Lisa M. Davidson, eds., *Filipinos in Canada: Disturbing Invisibility* (Toronto: University of Toronto Press, 2012).

3. John Paul Catungal, "Toward Queer(Er) Futures: Proliferating the 'Sexual' in Filipinx Canadian Sexuality Studies," in *Diasporic Intimacies: Queer Filipinos and Canadian Imaginaries*, edited by Robert Diaz, Marissa Largo, and Fritz Pino (Evanston, IL: Northwestern University Press, 2018), 23–40.

4. Pseudonyms are used for interviewees who have chosen to remain anonymous.

5. Martin F. Manalansan IV, *Global Divas: Filipino Gay Men in the Diaspora* (Durham, NC: Duke University Press, 2003), 118.

6. Melissa K. Nelson, "Getting Dirty: The Eco-Eroticism of Women in Indigenous Oral Literatures," in *Critically Sovereign*, edited by Joanne Barker (Durham, NC: Duke University Press, 2017), 229–260, https://doi.org/10.1215/9780822373162-008.

7. Ibid., 232.

8. Leanne Betasamosake Simpson, *As We Have Always Done: Indigenous Freedom through Radical Resistance* (Minneapolis: University of Minnesota Press, 2017), https://muse.jhu.edu/book/55843; Sarah Hunt, "An Introduction to the Health of Two-Spirit People: Historical, Contemporary and Emergent Issues" (Prince George: National Collaborating Centre for Aboriginal Health, 2016), https://www-deslibris-ca.prxy.lib.unbc.ca/ID/10094398; Chris Finley, "Decolonizing the Queer Native Body (and Recovering the Native Bull-Dyke): Bringing 'Sexy' Back and out of Native Studies' Closet," in *Queer Indigenous Studies: Critical Interventions in Theory, Politics, and Literature* (Tucson: University of Arizona Press, 2011), 31–42.

9. Alex Wilson, "N'tacimowin Inna Nah': Our Coming in Stories," *Canadian Woman Studies* 26, no. 3–4 (Winter–Spring 2008): 193–199.

10. Simpson, *As We Have Always Done*, 126.

11. May Farrales, "Repurposing Beauty Pageants: The Colonial Geographies of Filipina Pageants in Canada," *Environment and Planning D: Society and Space*, October 10, 2018, https://doi.org/10.1177/0263775818796502; May Farrales, "Colonial, Settler Colonial Tactics, and Filipino-Canadian Heteronormativities At Play on the Basketball Court," in *Diasporic Intimacies, Queer Filipinos/as and Canadian*, edited by Robert Diaz, Marissa Largo, and Fritz Pino (Evanston, IL: Northwestern University Press, 2019), 183–189.

12. Catungal, *Toward Queer(Er) Futures*, 136.

Coming Back Around to a Place of Grace

A Personal Theological Reflection and Journey by a
1.5 Generation Korean American Transman

SUNG WON PARK

> Gather up
> In the arms of your love—
> Those who expect
> No love from above.
> —LANGSTON HUGHES, "Litany"

Clear as day, I can still remember the exact moment nearly thirteen years ago when an insurmountable wall was erected between my mother and me. We were at church at a revival[1] worship service with a renowned guest minister. As it is with most Korean American immigrant churches, revivals were big events, and the church was packed to capacity. I had attended the service because I was in a leadership role at the church and felt duty bound, and because I wanted to accompany my mom, with whom I shared a close relationship.

For some reason, this minister opened the revival with a sermon on the sins of transgender people. He started with sharing a story about a transgender woman who ultimately regretted transitioning and was seeking a way to transition back to being a male (the sex that was assigned at their birth). The case of this particular transgender woman made it clear to the minister that she had committed an atrocious sin. According to him, transgender people were defying the will of God by changing their gender assigned at birth—we were all specifically made to have the bodies God intended. He painted transgender people as confused and morally wayward people whose souls are doomed. To say I was shell-shocked would be an understatement. It was as if the air was sucked out of the room and the world around me was dissolving away.

While sitting there frozen, I felt as if the sermon was targeted specifically at me. Why? Why would the minister preach about this? Why was he doing this to me? To my knowledge, most people at the church our family belonged to did not even think about issues of transgender people, let alone hear an entire forty-five-minute sermon about it. Until that fateful evening, my mother was, in her own way, expressing her support around my queerness. She would randomly ask questions such as, "How would a person transition from being a female to male?" or, "Are there surgeries or procedures for people to change their physical attributes if they decide to change their gender?"

These were not isolated incidents; my mother had intermittently thrown similar questions at me since I was in my late teens. I had always known that it was her way of giving me an opening to come out to her without knowing exactly how to approach the subject. But I never took hold of that olive branch, usually with sterile responses—"There are hormones someone can take to assist them in transition if they wanted," and, "Yes there are surgical procedures for those who wish to make physical alterations." Although I knew that my mother was giving me an opening, I was too afraid of what her response would be once I told her the truth.

I grew up as a 1.5 generation Korean American[2] in a devout Christian family that has been active in the Korean American church since the day we immigrated to the United States in the mid-1980s. The churches our family belonged to ascribe to a fundamentalist doctrine, and I was taught that the Bible was inerrant and therefore held the ultimate authority in what the "truth" is. More often than not, sermons centered on living a life of piety lest you end up in the eternal fires of hell, and prayer meetings were driven by fervent wailings for forgiveness. In turn, I formed a deep sense of fear around God and sin.

Nevertheless, the Korean American church was a sanctuary for me, a place that echoed with the memory of my native home country—one that was preserved in my childhood as a place of happiness and joy. As with many Korean American immigrants, for me the church served as "the primary sources of comfort and compensation."[3] Within the walls of the church, I was able to be among those with whom I shared a kinship of home—I had finally found home in a new land. The Korean American church rooted me in the turbulence of settling into a life in America mired with isolation and hostility. It helped me hold on to my sense of self.

As I grew older, I knew my being queer and a transman did not align with the doctrines of the Korean American church, but I could not bring myself to sever ties with a place that gave me a sense of home and comfort. I continued to be actively involved in the church, taking on leadership roles and navigating sticky situations where questions of gender arose. By my midtwenties, I knew I was passing[4] as a male, although presenting my gender as male was not new to me (I had perceived myself as male since I was around four years old). I would get questions like, "I heard your mom has a daughter. Is she coming to church anytime soon?" Or, "I heard your brothers talking about their sister. How come I haven't seen her yet?" Or questions asked by a parishioner while I am helping my mom with something at church: "Oh! Is this your oldest son? The one you said you are so sad about because he doesn't go to church anymore?" And the best comment was, "This must be your son! How old is he? I have a niece who could use a nice young man like him."

After sitting through the transphobic sermon at the church revival service, I felt my time of reckoning was coming to a head. I decided to come out to the minister in charge of the young adult fellowship group I was a part of. That minister was a charismatic preacher who lived up to that word in every sense. Although his preaching and passion was a comforting familiarity, I was constantly living in fear that one day he would preach hell and brimstone against LGBTQ people. In a preemptive move, I decided to share with him about my gender identity even if I lacked the precise language to explain all the intricacies in Korean. I still remember my sweaty palms and my breath held in anticipation of his condemnation.

He listened very intently and asked me one question when I was done. "Do you love God? And do you know that God loves you? If you can say yes to both of those questions, nothing else matters." Needless to say, I was stunned into silence. I cannot adequately express the depth of relief and gratitude, mixed with a small dose of skepticism of course, that it could be okay. Then the minister received a calling to become a senior pastor of a church and took his leave.

The next minister was not so open and was aligned very much with the fundamental doctrines I was so familiar with. Emboldened by my meeting with the previous minister, I disclosed my gender identity with the new minister. The response I received was what I expected: that I should know what the Bible says, and that I should not live a life outside of it. He then promptly used the pulpit to preach one of the most homophobic sermons I have heard to date (though I am sure he would have made it transphobic if he knew how). My church home was no longer the place of refuge and comfort, and "when your own home has stirrings of 'unhomely' moments, to use Homi Bhabha's term, home can seem an unfamiliar and a strange place."[5]

Additionally, ever since that revival service, my mother ceased asking me questions about queerness and transitioning. It seemed the door she was cracking open had closed with that single sermon. For a time she was aloof, and I also kept my distance knowing what happened without needing to speak about it. I did not want to subject myself to the torments of condemnation, oppression, and inauthenticity any longer—both at the church and with my mother. I spoke to my mother about my being a transman, and although she had known all along, she was still shocked once the words were spoken and released. Her reaction was probably what I had feared: she did not want to accept the truth. How could I relegate my soul to eternal damnation? I knew there was nothing I could say to change her feelings. I left the church, and the close bond I shared with my mother became fraught with tension.

The next several years were harrowing, to say the least. During that time, inexplicably the call I felt to ministry in my youth returned in a louder and more persistent manner. I decided to pursue my faith deeper and more expansively, which led me to seminary. I was drawn to theology,[6] which spoke to the experiences of people in relation to God. Right before entering seminary, my interest in learning about Korean faith traditions, mainly indigenous shamanic practices, outside of Christianity was growing. Knowing that Koreans were introduced to Christianity by white Western missionaries, I became increasingly frustrated with the fundamentalist homophobic rhetoric from Korean American churches and their link to an oppressive colonialist history. Without gleaning a look into our past, I did not think it was possible to imagine a revisionist future that would embrace people like me. In other words, God needs to be righted in order for all those wounded by the church to be healed. After all, are we not all God's children?

I believe *Minjung* theology holds a way for us to be liberated from the chains of fundamentalist doctrine, and gain a distinct way of being for Korean Americans. *Minjung* theology (*minjung* is literally translated as suffering/oppressed people) was developed as a direct response to suffering of human lives (specifically in South Korea).[7] As with other theologies of liberation, *minjung* theology is contextual and holds the capacity to free us and can be adapted to the expanding lives of Korean Americans. Furthermore, it is a "revolution for social justice and revolution for individual spirituality."[8] Such an adaptation would help shed the Western cloak from the Korean American churches and reclaim what was lost as a result of Christian conversion.[9] Koreans are a stubborn and resilient people, and those seemingly lost shamanic roots still reside "deep in the Korean psyche."[10] The reclamation of our past and indigenous traditions can coexist with *minjung* theological practices—one that honors spirit.

I choose to believe that the church as an agent of harm has the potential to be transformed or reformed. *Minjung* theology is a testament that we as Korean Americans are a compassionate people who will stand in the face of injustice and cruelty. I am not ignorant of those voices that still seek to condemn people like me. But when I hear those voices now, I am reminded of what James Baldwin said: "People always seem to band together in accordance to a principle that has nothing to do with love, a principle that releases them from personal responsibility."[11] Those who spew messages of hate and condemnation are not doing it for God; it is a mask they hide behind to shirk their responsibility as Christians. "But now faith, hope, love, abide these three; but the greatest of these is love."[12]

The Baldwin quote also reminds me that most often, humans forget we possess a unique attribute: free will. And free will means we struggle and wrestle with what is right or wrong, to help or to harm, to love or to condemn. I believe I am a child of God, a child of spirits and ancestors, and I choose to love and live in grace with others, for the heart of faith beats with grace and love.

Afterword

There have been some changes in my spiritual development since I have written and submitted this essay. As of this moment, I have found a different path in pursuing traditional Korean shamanism as my spiritual practice and no longer identify as a Christian. I have long held a desire to find and study traditional Korean shamanism as a means to reconnect with ancestral practices, to heal the deep wounds of generational trauma. I am stretching my spiritual muscles to shed and unlearn those things imbedded by Western and Christian imperialism that have severed our ties to tradition and ancestors. Every person's spiritual journey is sacred, and I stand by what I have written in this piece: no religion or spiritual practice can condemn any soul. It has been an arduous passage at times, but I am finally making my way home.

NOTES

1. An early definition of Christian revival meeting is defined as "special religious services protracted for a term of days or weeks." Frank Grenville Beardsley, *A History of American Revivals*, 3rd ed. (New York: American Tract Society), 15.

2. The term "1.5 generation" Korean can be seen as "a concept that originated in the Korean community to describe immigrant children who are not quite first- or second-generation Korea." And, "Broadly, the term *Korean American 1.5 generation* has been used as an informal demographic marker to differentiate immigrant children from their parents (first generation) and from American-born (second generation) Koreans." Mary Yu Danico, *The 1.5 Generation: Becoming Korean American in Hawaii* (Honolulu: University of Hawai'i Press), 1–2.

3. Jonathan Y. Tan, *Introducing Asian American Theologies* (Maryknoll, NY: Orbis), 61.

4. There are countless ways the term "passing" can be defined. For the purpose of this paper, my usage of the term "passing" connotes being perceived in the gender I represent through my own gender presentation of a male.

5. Su Yon Pak, "Coming Home/Coming Out: Reflections of a Queer Family and the Challenge of Eldercare in the Korean Diaspora," *Theology and Sexuality* 17, no. 3 (2011): 340. The context of the quote is in having one's home disturbed by a change that seems outside of oneself. Pak's reference to the disturbance at home is having her elderly parents move in, due to her mother's illness, to the home she has built with her partner. The "strangeness" such a disturbance can create in one's home is a factor that is outside of that particular person whose home is being stirred. I felt it aptly describes the way my sense of the church as home was disturbed by homophobia.

6. In Merriam-Webster's Dictionary Online, the first definition of theology is "the study of religious faith, practice, and experience; *especially*: the study of God and of God's relation to the world." https://www.merriam-webster.com/dictionary/theology.

7. Andrew Sung Park, "Minjung Theology: A Korean Contextual Theology," *Pacific Theological Review* 18, San Francisco Theological Seminary, 1.

8. Ibid., 4.

9. The price of conversion to Christianity was paid when the Protestant missionaries "imposed Western Protestant Christian practices (particular way to worship, pray, and sing, for instance) over and against indigenous Korean practices." Su Yon Pak, Unzu Lee, Jung Ha Kim, and Myung Ji Cho, *Singing the Lord's Song in a New Land* (Louisville, KY: Westminster John Knox, 2005), 71.

10. Ibid., 71.

11. James Baldwin, "Down at the Cross," in *James Baldwin: Collected Essays* (New York: Library of America, 1998), 333.

12. 1 Corinthians 13:13, New American Standard Version.

BIBLIOGRAPHY

Baldwin, James. "Down at the Cross." *James Baldwin: Collected Essays.* New York: Library of America, 1998.

Beardsley, Frank Grenville. *A History of American Revivals*, 3rd ed. New York: American Tract Society, 1912.

Danico, Mary Yu. *The 1.5 Generation: Becoming Korean American in Hawaii.* Honolulu: University of Hawai'i Press, 2004.

Pak, Su Yon. "Coming Home/Coming Out: Reflections of a Queer Family and the Challenge of Eldercare in the Korean Diaspora." *Theology and Sexuality* 17, no. 3 (2011): 337–351.

Pak, Su Yon, Unzu Lee, Jung Ha Kim, and Myung Ji Cho. *Singing the Lord's Song in a New Land.* Louisville, KY: Westminster John Knox, 2005.

Park, Andrew Sung. "Minjung Theology: A Korean Contextual Theology." *Pacific Theological Review* 18. San Francisco Theological Seminary, 1985.

Tan, Jonathan Y. *Introducing Asian American Theologies.* Maryknoll, NY: Orbis, 2008.

"Save the Thai Temple"

Wat Mongkolratanaram, *Thai America, and the Heteronormative Logics of South Berkeley*

PAHOLE SOOKKASIKON

> We share the experience of using food to deal with migration and displacement; of going to extraordinary lengths for the right ingredients; of having little choice but to peddle our culture in restaurants; of toiling in kitchens without legal status; of being ridiculed for food; of being romanticized through it; of having it "columbused"; of living in a country that sees food service as our proper place in society; and of having America love our food but not our people.
>
> —MARK PADOONGPATT, *Flavors of Empire*

I am a part of a Thai American generation where *Wat Thai*(s), or Thai temples, have actualized themselves as ways to comprehend Thainess in the United States. For many of us, specifically the children of Thai immigrants, these religious strongholds represented our parents' survival, encouraging cultural maintenance, resilience, and defiance on foreign soil. Thai temples further became cultural bastions where Thai America, as a marginal sect of Asian America, could reimagine community and redetermine nonbelonging under the weight of larger groups. Elements of the Thai temple that helped nurture a sense of identity in the diaspora included studying and practicing Theravada Buddhism; learning or, in some cases relearning, how to speak, write, and read the Thai language; partaking in cultural immersion courses such as classical Thai dance, music, or martial arts; and, most popularly, celebrating identity through food festivals and the communal sharing of Thai fare. Thai Americanist Mark Padoongpatt claims that "thousands of Thais used *Wat Thai* as a transnational community space to maintain cultural practices, especially food festivals. *Wat Thai* food festivals brought Thai people together face-to-face to cultivate a Thai American suburban culture . . . foster[ing] the development of social capital, community, and a public sociability that crossed many boundaries: ethnicity, citizenship status, class, and religion."[1] In these ways, food is intrinsically linked to identity, budding as an "immigrant act."[2] In another way, diasporic fare, as Martin F. Manalansan IV contends, became an emotional and tangible bridge to maintain ethnic identity—triggering the homeland and past while making sense of one's present and future circumstances.[3]

As an extension of ethnicity, culture, and self, food is the most accessible and utilized route of return for Asian American immigrants netted in the diaspora.[4] However, as American history has painted, Asian fare has been a xenophobic medium measuring foreignness and difference, labeling who constitutes citizen or, as the case with many Asian Americans, the perpetual "other." Scholars insist that the trope of the Asian immigrant as unwashed, stinking, and unkempt parasitically latches itself onto ethnic foods in the United States, rehashing nativist rhetoric of immigrants unable to assimilate or fully access citizenship.[5]

In relation to the discriminations embalmed upon Asian American foods, this chapter examines a conflict in the late 2000s between *Wat Mongkolratanaram*, or the Berkeley Thai Temple—a Buddhist sanctuary around since the late 1970s, and neighbors on an adjacent road—the 1900 block of Oregon Street—who sought to regulate and censure the temple's rites and services that revolved around Thai food and Buddhist notions of merit making (or *tum boon*).[6] As a queer Thai American and one who helped organize for and rally around the *wat*, I contend that neighbors' arguments were predicated upon heteronormative and heterocentric logic, anchored within the domesticity of the South Berkeley neighborhood, that pervasively emphasized the temple as orientalist and queer. Neighbors' complaints drew upon popularized and nonnormative imagery casting the temple and its community through heteropatriarchal and imperial descriptors of race and foreignness, in addition to carnal and fleshly excess. Moreover, the complaints emphasized Thai America and *Wat Thai* as inherently queer, positioning them both as antithetical to the heteronormative domesticity of American neighborhoods and the suburban, nuclear family unit.

Focusing on this moment and the actions of my community, I contend that Thai America reoriented the neighborhood with a diasporic queerness, confronting the racial and sexual undercurrents that inform Berkeley's liberalism. I draw upon the symbolism weighted on this moment as ways to think of how compulsory heterosexuality marries racist notions of home, community, and family.

Theravada Buddhism: *Wat Mongkolratanaram* and *Tum Boon*

Attempting to fulfill the needs of a flourishing Thai and Southeast Asian American Buddhist population, a group of volunteers formed a small temple in 1978, inviting two monks from Thailand to spearhead that temple's materialization and offer spiritual guidance.[7] Three years later, the development resulted in *Wat Mongkolratanaram* and the establishment of a cultural center, which became recognized as a nonprofit by the State of California.[8] Since then, the Berkeley Thai Temple served as a cultural and religious pillar for the community, fulfilling religious needs as well as the preservation of Thai heritage, such as Thai dance, music, language and food.[9] The temple's uniqueness complimented the city's cultural vibrancy, so much so that it solidified what it meant to be Thai in the United States.[10] Lynda Tredway and Carrel Roumain, neighbors directly across from the temple, even boasted that *Wat Mongkolratanaram* is "a great asset to the life of the neighborhood . . . and are model neighbors."[11] It is surprising then that, even in all the years that the temple resided peacefully in the community, *Wat Thai* was met with xenophobia and aggression by neighbors who cited that temple was "overtly detrimental," "novel," "harm[ful]," and, as one neighbor flagrantly stated, a "'commercial enterprise' operating in a residential zone."[12] More egregiously, one complainant forcibly argued that "residents should not expect to be impacted by a weekly food service of any kind or culture."[13]

In August 2008, *Wat Mongkolratanaram* applied to Berkeley's Zoning Adjustments Board to construct an edifice to house sacred Buddhist statues, relics, and images. At the same time, Oregon Street residents banded together alleging that the Thai architecture would obstruct and diminish the "residential character" of the neighborhood, impacting "both the view and shade to immediately adjacent" inhabitants.[14] Accusers attested that, along with the proposed architecture, their major apprehension for the temple's "expansion" was its Sunday Food Offering which catered directly to Buddhist ideals of service and merit making, allowing practitioners to build upon goodwill and merit for their next lives, which are not defined monetarily.[15] These so-called neighbors cited that the Thai food and its preparation emitted "offensive odors" that nefariously affected South Berkeley.[16]

Tum Boon, which is practiced by approximately 90–95 percent of the Buddhist population in Thailand, involves giving back alms and contributions to the temple worshippers who attend.[17] In most cases, donations received by various *wats* cover miscellaneous expenses, determined by Western capitalism, which most Thai temples cannot fund directly—like custodial work, ground maintenance, utilities, mortgages, and living expenses for monks and laypeople. Jiemen Bao defines the action as "'giving gifts' to monks and the temple, and 'doing good things' throughout one's life . . . [to] positively influenc[e] a person's current and future lives."[18] Other scholars add that the rite is the primary means to which Thais accrue positive karma.[19] *Tum Boon* is therefore an amassment of merit that Buddhists sow while actively practicing their religious beliefs.

In these ways, merit making is a widespread religious phenomenon in Thailand, equating Buddhist acts to collective determinations of Thainess, civic engagement, and national pride. Penny Van Esterik even professes that "To be Thai is to be Buddhist" and that the religion "provides many Thai[s] with a way of viewing the world, a sense of reality, moral standards, and shared language and metaphors for analyzing their existing life situation."[20] Theravada Buddhism and its practices thus directly correlate with notions of Thainess and being. It is therefore not surprising that Buddhist practices, like *tum boon*, attached themselves to Thai immigrants and their quests to reimagine self and community overseas.

Suburbanization of Thai Food: Heteronormative Neighborhoods and Queer Foods

Thai food and Thainess have had a long history impacted by American heteronormativity and heteropatriarchal desires. For instance, Thailand has been contemporarily touted as "sexual Disneyland to the world," selling and serving "spectacle and fantasy" to an Americanized global imaginary.[21] Thais and the homeland are additionally rendered as docile and submissive—identities anchored in histories of militourism, branded as "genetically and culturally predisposed towards subordination and self-denial."[22] Much of these stereotypes emerged from the Cold War era, where Thailand was seen as a unique land of "stability," contending that among its Communist neighbors, the Thai nation-state could assume the submissive position of "eager student" in relation to the United States.[23]

Enthusiastic to also participate in U.S. global expansion, American housewives looked to the intimacies of food and home as to extend their gendered privilege and power over Thais. Mark Padoongpatt argues that American women engaged Thai food as an approach to U.S. global expansion, turning foodways, or "the production, representation, and consumption of food," into a site of gendered identity formation in addition to acts of participation in Cold War politics for the suburban housewife.[24] He contends, "White women who encountered food cultures of Asia and the Pacific attempted to replicate the enchantment [of being in and witnessing Asia] to fulfill their role as suburban housewives in the United States."[25] He further argues that white homemakers additionally used ethnic fare to "[play] dress up" for dinner parties, using food and the exotic to "elevate their *public* status in a private sphere."[26] Such whimsical uses of Thai food to reshape and empower white femininity indecorously tamed and domesticized Thainess through the kitchen. One could argue that white women tried to civilize Thais through their own acts of suburbanization, eerily mirroring the heteronormative practices found in Thai sex tourism. Western approaches to Thainess therefore made the foreign and exotic palatable for nuclear families, the white household, and white neighborhoods.

In the case of *Wat Mongkolratanaram*, Thai food and *tum boon*, as re-packaged by Thai America, pushed back against a heteronormative white-ness, its community, in addition to its perceptions of domesticity and neigh-borhood. Thai food and Buddhism espoused a queerness that, as Gayatri Gopinath argues, is resistant, "referenc[ing] an alternative hermeneutic" that "disturbs the space of the heteronormative home from within."[27] In another way, Berkeley Thai Temple's notions of merit making develops as queer diasporic cultural practices; it creates public cultural spaces that re-fashion dominant U.S. practices, notions of belonging within suburban spaces, and heteronationalist formations, like participation and citizen-ship.[28] Roderick Ferguson relatedly contends that "the concept of *home has been defined over and against people of color*, while also showing how het-erosexual households within racialized communities have been constituted at the expense of queer people of color."[29] Ferguson's statement accentuates how communities of color are rendered nonheteronormative and queer if they are unable to conform to heteronormative structures of community, neighborhood, and reproductive domesticity—suggesting that their inabil-ity to produce traditional forms of home, "proper heterosexual interaction," and belonging are due to a predisposed foreignness within the U.S. nation-state.[30] Whiteness and white heteronormative ideals emerge as baseline to how communities of color—like the immigrant figure—participate in the United States, illustrating how people of color are always marked as unable to transcend or assimilate into the normative structures of home and neigh-borhood.

Mongkolratanaram's apparently nonnormative and diasporic practices, though seen as a part of the community for decades, ultimately queered how residents on Oregon Street saw their small section of South Berkeley. Neigh-bors' actions asserted that Thai America was always foreign: a licentious and unmanageable identity, much in line with the Western sexualization of Thais and Thailand. In a letter to Greg Powell, senior planner for the City of Berkeley, Tom Rough violently states that

> The neighbors said the weekend cooking odors were overwhelming and unacceptable, and *the ingress of hundreds* each weekend over-whelmed their quiet streets and *their expected quiet lives*. They <u>insisted</u> *the feeding* be very sharply reduced in numbers and frequency, "or *find another place to do this feeding*."[31]

Rough's letter highlights the racist and beastly characterizations placed on Thai America, its revered temple, and its practices. His condescending lan-guage invokes depictions found in Western literature and media caricatur-izing Thais and their culture as subhuman and backward, or as Elizabeth Jennings, a complainant, claims, "distracting" irregularities.[32] Rough's use of "feeding" remarkably denotes savage and sexualized undertones, equating Thais and their religion as nothing more than animalistic and beneath American righteousness.

Beastly rhetoric is nothing new when defining or imagining Thainess and a Thai people. As an example, Victorian literature, like Margaret Landon's famed book *Anna and the King of Siam* (1944), based on the embellished adventures of Anna Leonowens, rendered Siamese as "human cattle," "poor reptiles on the floor," or "a bedlam of parrots."[33] The dehumanizing rhetoric used to describe the Siamese refers to Thais as nothing more than boorish, savage, and nonhuman. Such terminology, as used in Rough's argument, unsettles Thai America's legitimate claims to American citizenship and belonging—especially in the confines of South Berkeley. Such descriptors emphasize that Thai Americans, who they are, and their rights and rites are basically, as accuser Shari Ser maintains, "offensive and rude."[34]

Neighbors' arguments thus remark that Thai Americans are unassimilable to their perceived "sweet community dynamic" or "quality of life," declaring Thais' cultural practices as undesirable and uncontainable in the domesticated private sphere.[35] Sunday Food rites seemingly became too unruly for the Western and white home—developing as a radically queer site of identity, fundamentally disrupting the heteronormative logics and policed passivity of the City of Berkeley. Thainess, as it was historically disciplined by the West and the exotic curiosities of suburban housewives, now emanates as a queer counterpublic that dissembles the conservative logics of heteronormativity and the private sphere. *Wat Mongkolratanaram*, Thai America, and *tum boon* trouble and destabilize American labels of home and neighborhood, constituting a powerful challenge to domestic and nationalist ideologies.

Sunday Food Offerings and the Making of Thai America

Similar to *Wat Mongkolratanaram*, *Wat Thai* of Los Angeles was met with aggression and hostility as neighbors argued that the temple and its food festivals abused zoning laws, pushing against homeowners' utopic and muted visions of suburbia and home.[36] Nearby residents and zoning boards initially approved of *Wat Thai* because they thought that Thai Buddhism's stereotypically "contemplative, meditative nature" would not impact the expected and shallow tranquility of the community, assuming that Thainess was obscured and hidden.[37] In other words, Los Angelenos predetermined Thais to restrain their representation, performing manageable stereotypes that typecast the community as "Well-mannered," "graceful," and never ever "produc[ing] [disruptive] noise[s]."[38]

The Berkeley Thai Temple, like *Wat Thai* of Los Angeles, was confronted with the subsuming and heteropatriarchal expectations that drew Thais as nonconfrontational, even-keeled, and submissive—stereotypes that align themselves with imperial and Western histories of Thais and Thailand as malleable and ready to be civilized.[39] Yet migration and the diaspora changes communities—especially in regard to survival.

Mongkolratanaram evolved to survive as Theravada Buddhism and the Thai American community were marginalized in the United States. Transforming *tum boon* and how *Mongkolratanaram* and Thais operated in Berkeley were, in fact, diasporic acts of becoming, reiterating how an imperial and heteropatriarchal West—particularly the United States—manipulated and pervasively shaped Thainess and Thai being.[40] For the temple to endure and participate in American society, it needed the monetary donations accrued from Sunday services. In these ways, the Berkeley Thai Temple thus abided by America's rules, taking on the capitalist and heteronormative classifications of religion in the United States. Like the disidentificatory strategies of queerness, *Wat Thai* survived by working "within and outside the dominant public sphere" of Americanness, proving that it could adapt in a hostile environment.[41] However, it was Oregon Street complainants and their supporters who saw the temple and its services as an offensive perversion because they could not control us.

The fight for *Wat Mongkolratanaram* is a supremely significant moment for Thai America and its generations thereafter. Siwaraya Rochanahusdin, a Thai American and member of Save the Thai Temple, a grassroots campaign organized by diasporic Thai youth and members of *Mongkolratanaram*, argued that the temple and *tum boon* offer "an invaluable range of service[s] to an otherwise underserved population."[42] For many Thai Americans, especially diasporeans who express "homeland" through intersections of "religio-cultural and political activities," the temple and its queerness epitomize the difference between assimilating into what America expects Thais to be in contrast to what we, as Thai Americans, believe ourselves and our culture to entail.[43]

Grasping the significance of the Berkeley Thai Temple, the Berkeley City Council unanimously voted on September 22, 2009, with garnered support and pressure of many organizations in addition to the unfailing spirits of the Save the Thai Temple movement, in support of *Wat Mongkolratanaram*.

NOTES

This essay is an abbreviated and drastically altered version of a chapter from my master's thesis, "Fragrant Rice Queen: The Hungry Ghost of Anna Leonowens and Thai/America" (master's thesis, San Francisco State University, 2010). I am grateful for the advice and support of Mark Padoongpatt and Siwaraya Rochanahusdin, who listened to my thoughts and helped me craft this piece. Lastly, I write this chapter as a love ballad to my parents—Paitoon and Saisunee Sookkasikon—and my Save the Thai Temple family, in addition to the aunties, uncles, and monks of *Wat Mongkolratanaram*. This article is for you all.

1. Mark Padoongpatt, *Flavors of Empire: Food and the Making of Thai America* (Oakland: University of California Press, 2017), 118.

2. Lisa Lowe, *Immigrant Acts: On Asian American Cultural Politics* (Durham, NC: Duke University Press, 1996).

3. Martin F. Manalansan IV, "Beyond Authenticity: Rerouting the Filipino Culinary Diaspora," in *Eating Asian America: A Food Studies Reader*, edited by Robert Ji-Song Ku, Martin F. Manalansan IV, and Anita Mannur (New York: New York University Press, 2013), 292.

4. Ibid., 298.

5. Robert Ji-Song Ku, Martin F. Manalansan IV, and Anita Mannur, "An Alimentary Introduction," in *Eating Asian America: A Food Studies Reader*, edited by Robert Ji-Song Ku, Martin F. Manalansan IV, and Anita Mannur (New York: New York University Press, 2013), 3.

6. Yoram Shay to Greg Powell, letter, April 17, 2008.

7. Siwaraya Rochanahusdin and Christina Jirachachavalwong, "Application For A Broader Land Use Permit," (Prepared Report, Berkeley, CA, 2008), 1.

8. Ibid., 1.

9. Wat Mongkolratanaram, "Petition to Dismiss and Decist [*sic*] Zoning Board Actions to Curtail Berkeley Thai Temple's or 'Wat Mongkolratanaram's' Religious Activities on the Basis of U.S. Constitutional Right to Exercise Freedom of Religion," letter to Mayor Tom Bates and Calvin Fong, October 13, 2008.

10. Wat Mongkolratanaram, "Re: Application for a Broader Land Use Permit for the Continuance of Temple Activities," letter to Zoning Adjustment Board, January 26, 2009.

11. Lynda Tredway, "FW: Thai Temple," email to Steven D. Ross, September 12, 2008.

12. Oregon Street Neighbors, "Re: Appeal of Use permit #07-10000040/#08-70000019 and Request a Public Hearing before the City Council- 1911 Russell Street- Berkeley Thai Temple," letter to Mayor Tom Bates and Members of the City Council, April 5, 2009; Shari Ser, "Wat Mongkolratanaram—1911 Russell Street," email message to Steven D. Ross, August 27, 2008; Thomas Rough, "Hand out Distributed by the Thai Temple," email message to Greg Powell, September 8, 2008; Geoffrey A. Fowler, "Brunch as a Religious Experience Is Disturbing Berkeley's Karma," *The Wall Street Journal*, February 10, 2009, accessed July 31, 2018, https://www.wsj.com/articles/SB123422026431565295.

13. Oregon Street Neighbors, "Re: Appeal of Use permit #07-10000040/#08-70000019 and Request a Public Hearing before the City Council- 1911 Russell Street- Berkeley Thai Temple," letter to Mayor Tom Bates and Members of the City Council, April 5, 2009.

14. Carolyn Shoulders, "Thai Temple—Restaurant, Parking and Height Variance," email to Greg Powell and Steven D. Ross, September 11, 2008; and Residents of Oregon Street, "Appeal to Use Permit of the Berkeley Thai Temple," letter to Mayor Tom Bates and Members of the City Council, April 5, 2009.

15. Riya Bhattacharjee, "ZAB Allows Berkeley Thai Temple to Continue Sunday Brunch," *Berkeley Daily Planet*, February 13, 2009, accessed July 31, 2018, http://www.berkeleydailyplanet.com/issue/2009-02-12/article/32269; Wat Mongkolratanaram, "Wat Mongkolratanaram—Application for Broader Land Use Permit," 7.

16. Bhattacharjee, "ZAB Allows Berkeley Thai Temple to Continue Sunday Brunch"; and Wat Mongkolratanaram, "Wat Mongkolratanaram—Application for Broader Land Use Permit," 7.

17. Jiemen Bao, "Merit-Making Capitalism: Re-territorializing Thai Buddhism in Silicon Valley, California," *Journal of Asian American Studies* 8, no. 2 (2005): 120; Wat

Mongkolratanaram, "Re: Application for a Broader Land Use Permit for the Continuance of Temple Activities."

18. Bao, "Merit-Making Capitalism," 119.

19. Padoongpatt, *Flavors of Empire*, 123.

20. Penny Van Esterik, *Materializing Thailand* (Oxford: Berg, 2000), 65–66.

21. Ara Wilson, *The Intimate Economies of Bangkok: Tomboys, Tycoons, and Avon Ladies in the Global City* (Berkeley, CA: University of California Press, 2004), 78–79; Elizabeth Rho-Ng, "The Conscription of Asian Sex Slaves: Causes and Effects of U.S. Military Sex Colonialism in Thailand and the Call to Expand U.S. Asylum Law," *Asian Law Journal* 7 (2000): 103.

22. Krittinee Nuttavuthisit, "Branding Thailand: Correcting the Negative Image of Sex Tourism," *Place Branding and Public Diplomacy* 3, no. 1 (2007): 28.

23. Christina Klein, *Cold War Orientalism: Asia in the Middlebrow Imagination, 1945–1961* (Berkeley, CA: University of California Press, 2003), 197–198.

24. Mark Padoongpatt, "'Oriental Cookery': Devouring Asian and Pacific Cuisine during the Cold War," in *Eating Asian America: A Food Studies Reader*, edited by Robert Ji-Song Ku, Martin F. Manalansan IV, and Anita Mannur (New York: New York University Press, 2013), 187–188.

25. Ibid., 200.

26. Ibid., 201. Emphasis in original.

27. Gayatri Gopinath, *Impossible Desires: Queer Diasporas and South Asian Public Cultures* (Durham, NC: Duke University Press, 2005), 22, 84.

28. Ibid., 30.

29. Roderick Ferguson, "The Nightmares of the Heteronormative," *Journal for Cultural Research* 4, no. 4 (2009): 421. Emphasis mine.

30. Ibid., 420.

31. Thomas Rough to Greg Powell, August 26, 2008. Emphasis mine.

32. Elizabeth Jennings to Greg Powell, September 12, 2008.

33. Margaret Landon, *Anna and the King of Siam* (New York: John Day, 1944), 25, 54, and 33; Pahole Sookkasikon, "Fragrant Rice Queen: The Hungry Ghost of Anna Leonowens and Thai/America" (master's thesis, San Francisco State University, 2010).

34. Shari Ser to Steven D. Ross, August 27, 2008.

35. Carolyn Shoulders, "Thai Temple—Restaurant, Parking and Height Variance," email to Greg Powell and Steven D. Ross, September 11, 2008; Thomas Rough, "Hand out Distributed by the Thai Temple," email to Greg Powell, September 8, 2008.

36. Padoongpatt, *Flavors of Empire*, 119.

37. Robert Janovici, quoted in Padoongpatt, *Flavors of Empire*, 119.

38. Richard Basham, "Ethnicity and World View in Bangkok," in *Alternate Identities: The Chinese of Contemporary Thailand*, edited by Chee Kiong Tong and Kwok B. Chan (Singapore: Times Academic, 2001), 132.

39. Klein, *Cold War Orientalism*, 198–199.

40. Stuart Hall, "Cultural Identity and Diaspora," in *Identity: Community, Culture and Difference*, edited by Jonathan Rutherford (London: Lawrence and Wishart, 1990).

41. José Esteban Muñoz, *Disidentifications: Queers of Color and the Performance of Politics* (Minneapolis: University of Minnesota Press, 1999), 5.

42. Save the Thai Temple, "Press Release," May 14, 2009.

43. Jonathan H. X. Lee and Mark S. Leo, "Performing Thai and Indigenous Igorot American Folklore and Identities: Ethnic and Cultural Politics Revealed," *Journal of Southeast Asian Studies* 18 (2013): 190.

PART VI

Mediating Queer

KAY ULANDAY BARRETT

In Which I Watch YouTube to Watch Fan Video Edits of You: For Nico Minoru on Marvel's Runaways

1.
There was a time which I made us all up, you see. Which is what you do when you are the only one in an all white school. Picture an Asian queer with lopsided hair trimmed short, which is only acceptable for aunties over forty-five, of course. Ripped jeans, kissing white girls during spin the bottle. Because this is considered accomplishment in college. The American dream, if you will. At that time, there is not one face like mine in books. But there you were in comics, smirking subtext like *maybe maybeeeee she's bisexual?* and that was just enough to be satiated, right? To think, parts of me reflected. Somewhere.

2.
Sure, we had Jubilee, spritely genderqueer, if we squinted, but she followed around everyone but her own self. Certainly Psylocke, though Filipina, was a white villain shape shifted into a yellow or brown woman's body, armed with her skin, something to put on, something made of evil plot twists, secondhand Asian. White people like Asian women, because they think they can put them on, like an article of clothing, absorb our lives and skills that come with, call it appreciation, when in fact it a succubus story. I know they think dragon or demure whenever we might sigh away.

3.
Okay, fast-forward: about your face, it is on screen now. A friend and I watch you gloating, *She totally has Gay Face*, which is wishing you into existence. Lush lips in black lipstick and nail polish, wiccan witch, tears over a bonfire, boss of complications. You chart merciless combat this version, you are no theory, and kiss sparkly white girl in slow tempo,

kiss her again as music swells, kiss in camera view. The white girl's smirk is the last focused shot. Your possible gay bi teen—rainbow shiny and skinny pale LA archtype, who feels more sure of herself each time you glance at her.

4.
This is how Asian women are, in service, making things clearer for everybody else. When you kissed the white girl back, it was like a bird of prey. You were pulled apart and splayed everywhere. I could google your name, and hundreds of videos of teenagers, Asian and Brown, yelped *OHMYGOD OHMYGOD IT'S HAPPENING, YesYesYes, or OH My GAY heart!* Each in reaction, rocking back and forth, palms on their cheeks, mouth agape—How is it a miracle to witness people like us possibly loved?

5.
And I won't lie, I was one of them, Tisha in Ohio, Sam in NYC, Vera in San Diego, Me in Jersey City, leaned in close, near tears, edited brief 10, 15, 30 second videos of footage of you hopelessly falling for another woman. I wonder, if we could all sing a hymn, cast a spell, consider the love rising up in us, consider it without whiteness, quiet the still air, and not question what it would be like to feel the spit of our own? Assimilation will not protect you, but I think just kill you, slowly. A wound may still be a wound without the blood.

6.
Tell me, do you wonder what it would be like to not have to explain your culture or your family's migration to the person you love? Why can't you be a superhero with your own people? A theory: I bet there's someone who can hold your howl. Even if no wand or sparks are left for the upcoming battle, somewhere someone is ready to kiss the forehead of a person, and what's better than incantation, than somebody who doesn't mispronounce your last name?

Anomaly: a poem sponsored by TSA

On the 5th city, but really, every city, TSA dumps out
all your belongings. Your journal tumbles to the floor,
all your poetry coats the tile. All your hard work.
An agent screams loudly, *Anomaly!! We've found an ANOMOLY.*
Do you want a Female or Male agent to search you?
Female or Male, I said!!!
Her tenor spills you over much like your stuff. What
once was organized and beautiful, is now a ransacked mess.
You've become what cis white middle america fears
something truly Other, unidentifiable, the breath between
the boxes, beyond. *Female or Male* she demands again.
She explains where her hands will go, if I have pain on my
body. I say solemnly, look her in the eye,
Pain is everywhere. It hurts everywhere.
Of course, in standard procedure, presumably cis
white men in suits zoom passed. Do I want to be
searched in plain sight or enclosed room? Plain sight
I mumble. I lock eyes with a brown Sikh man who's
also being searched. Our faces focused, we raise arms
up in unison like two birds frozen, smirk an out of
place slant as white strangers' hands touch corners
and sacred under some guise of freedom.
But what actually, they mean is police.
After we each almost miss our boarding time, we are
cleared. I ask him if he's okay and he shakes his head no,
You? I look down like maybe I've got answers, but
nothing comes. We both apologize to one another for this
system that needs to scan our bodies until we're checked
out of our skin. We don't say exactly that, but it's what
we mean. We agree, we never get used to this. There's nothing
to get used to. There's just ache where you're reminded
who you are equals threat– not person, not real, not worthy.
Over our heads, we hear news announcements
of Trump's inauguration splayed with orchestral music.
Horns sound loudly. Before we go rush to our respective
gates, we lock eyes again on the tv monitor as the bombast
of the music persists. Both of us with our faces fallen as
we keep watch, hold our breath, without a word,
together   in tears

You Are SO Brave: A Found Poem

& those scars i had hidden wit smiles
& good fuckin
lay open
& i dont know i dont know any more tricks
i am really colored & really sad sometimes & you hurt me
—NTOZAKE SHANGE

W hat happened? Aw, sweetie, let me get that for you. What do you mean "no thank you," you don't want my help? Some people are ungrateful, I was helping YOU. You are SO brave! *Please step on the scale. Please step on the scale. Please step off the scale.* You are SO brave! I've never seen someone one on a dancefloor/protest move like that! What a pimp! Can I touch your cane? *Does it hurt?* **"People with disabilities are often seen as 'flawed' beings whose hope of normalcy rests in becoming more like non-disabled people or by becoming 'cured.'"—Sins Invalid.** (When will you get better?) Don't worry everything will be normal soon. If you just try hard enough you will heal. If you just pray hard enough you will heal. (Have you tried acupuncture, water therapy, meditation?) If you take these herbs enough you can be like you were, better, normal. Why are you walking so slow? This is the city of the hustle, son. buck up. **Dear _____, I understand that you have accessibility needs, and we as a queer progressive organization <u>love</u> your work but we unfortunately, we find your requests to be unrealistic. We understand that you are a queer and transgender person of color with limited income but we cannot fund you at this time.** *Please do send us samples of your work so that we may distribute them to our participants for free! <u>Dear—insert assigned at birth name you no longer identify with—</u>it has come to our attention that you are 100 percent disabled. you cannot work at all.* Does it hurt still? *Classification: No prolonged standing, walking, steel pin impacted osteoctomy aiken mcbride. Constant deviance in the foot based on affected use. Constant deviance. Constant deviance. Cane usage to support impediment and prolonged limp.* Oh, my! Look at that hair! Don't you have a boyfriend to come to physical therapy with you? **"Seen as 'flawed' beings whose hope of normalcy rests in becoming more like non-disabled people or by becoming 'cured.'"** *For the report, we're going to need to see some ID. That cannot possibly be you, you were attractive. What happened? Please step on the scale.* So, you were attacked? What did you do to motivate the attack? What does LGBTQ mean? *Well, ma'am, we have to use the biological sex it says on paperwork.* It'd be nice if you wore some lipstick, maybe some makeup? It might make this whole process easier. *Does it hurt still? Hasn't it been years now? Why aren't you better?* Based on your old life, Don't you want to be more like me? Do you have a fundraiser**? I don't know any disabled people personally,** but we can raise funds to help you, because we think you deserve it. This is the city of the hustle, son, buck up. YOU DON'T KNOW WHAT YOU ARE DOING! Give me that; you don't know how to take care of yourself! Ugh, you are so slow. **It's hard to imagine you could do anything yourself at all, so pathetic!** Does it hurt? Still? Yo, _____, we're all going to the club! Should be some cuties there. Oh, yeah, sorry, dude, I forgot. The march is 2.5 miles long; maybe you can meet us at the rally? Aw, look at that little boy with the cane. Why do I have to get up? **You want my seat, faggot?** So, you were attacked? Why do I have to get up, chink? **He doesn't even look disabled.** If you have any concerns around safety at this event/conference/protest, you should really bring up these concerns this cisgender rad, skinny, able-bodied person who confuses wellness work for "everybody gets better work"! Wait (laughs) is that a girl? Aw, you look so cute when you dance! Let me take a picture of you holding your back, *show the cane! Show the cane!* What did you do for someone to attack you? We'll help you because we think you deserve it, <u>not like some people with disabilities</u>, the ones who drool and make a fuss. You'll be normal soon, won't you? It's not far, just a few blocks? Aw, I know you're in pain, but you can make it, dude. What do you mean "No, thank you," you don't want my help? *Please step on the scale. Please step on the scale. Please step off the scale.*

PhilippinExcess

Cunanan, Criss, Queerness, Multiraciality, Midwesternness, and the Cultural Politics of Legibility

THOMAS XAVIER SARMIENTO

> Chicago and Minneapolis were among his [Andrew Cunanan's] favorite U.S. cities.
>
> —MAUREEN ORTH, *Vulgar Favors: The Assassination of Gianni Versace*

On April 27, 1997, Jeffrey Trail was bludgeoned to death with a hammer twenty-seven times in a Minneapolis loft.[1] A few days later, David Madson was fatally shot once in the back and twice in the face in Chisago, Minnesota.[2] While local police in Minneapolis had suspected Andrew Cunanan was involved in these murders, the discovery of Lee Miglin's gruesomely stabbed body and almost severed head in his Chicago garage on May 4, 1997, catapulted Cunanan to the national stage.[3] And although Cunanan shot bystander William Reese in the back of the head on May 9, 1997, in Pennsville, New Jersey, to escape law enforcement,[4] he likely targeted Gianni Versace, fatally shooting Versace twice in the face on July 15, 1997, in Miami Beach and rising to the world's attention.[5] When Cunanan shot himself eight days later, "the largest failed manhunt in U.S. history" came to an end.[6] But the drive to make meaning of his actions had only just begun, and people continue to ponder what drove a multiracial Filipino American gay man to murder.

Scholars have written about the sexual, racial, and gendered dimensions of Cunanan's spree killing. For example, Allan Isaac muses on Cunanan's "enigmatic unrecognizability," which for him stems from Cunanan's multiraciality and dominant U.S. culture's reluctance to avow its imperial past and neocolonial present with the Philippines.[7] Less attention however has been devoted to Cunanan's geographic ties. But as this chapter's epigraph suggests, the place of the Midwest is central to Cunanan's story. His mother, MaryAnn Schillaci Cunanan, was born and raised in Ohio; her parents had settled there from Sicily.[8] The lead investigator for the national manhunt, Kevin Rickett, was an FBI agent in charge of the Minnesota Fugitive Task Force for the bureau.[9] Cunanan's first and second victims lived in Minneapolis, and his third victim lived in Chicago. Moreover, according to Darryl Cooper, former chairman of Gay Men and Lesbians Opposing Violence,

"Cunanan didn't come to the nation's attention until Chicago."[10] These Midwestern threads are essential to understanding Cunanan's notoriety and "enigmatic unrecognizability."

Considering his spree killing started in Minneapolis and traversed the Eastern Seaboard, this chapter uses Cunanan's presence "east of California" as a prism to reframe Filipinx illegibility in dominant U.S. culture as spatial-racial-sexual excess.[11] By revisiting Cunanan some twenty years later via multiracial Filipino actor Darren Criss's portrayal on FX's *The Assassination of Gianni Versace: American Crime Story* (2018), I explore how the intersection of queerness, multiraciality, and Midwesternness engenders Filipinx subjects who exceed racial, sexual, geographic, imperial, national, and diasporic formations. As a play on "Filipinxs," my chapter title, "PhilippinExcess," highlights the limits of heteronormative Filipina/o formations and the impulse to position the Philippines as the automatic origin of U.S. diasporic Filipinxs. Criss as Cunanan reveals how diasporic queer Filipinxs who occupy the Midwest exceed (1) the affective pull of the Philippines as homeland, (2) the compulsory heterosexuality of ethnoracial nationalisms, (3) the homonormativity of white gay male culture, and (4) the oceanic coastal geographies of queer and Asian America. By reorienting toward diasporic Filipinxs who are excessive in their sexual-racial-geographic embodiments, my inward turn to the heartland of U.S. empire aims to reimagine the politics of racial-sexual recognition.

Queer Filipinx American Crime Story

FX premiered *The Assassination of Gianni Versace*, its second television installment of *American Crime Story*, on January 17, 2018. The nine-episode program is based on *Vanity Fair* special correspondent Maureen Orth's book *Vulgar Favors: Andrew Cunanan, Gianni Versace, and the Largest Failed Manhunt in U.S. History*, published in 1999 and reprinted with the subtitle *The Assassination of Gianni Versace* in 2017 as a tie-in to FX's then forthcoming series. Versace might be perceived as the show's focus based on its title, but Cunanan is truly its star.[12] Whereas Orth's book clearly centers on Cunanan—composing a profile of the infamous Filipino Italian American spree killer that takes readers on a journey from his childhood in San Diego, California, to his suicide in Miami Beach, Florida—the series attempts to balance its coverage of Cunanan and Versace, drawing viewers into the opulent world of the Versaces (siblings Gianni and Donatella) while also establishing a refracted parallel between murderer and victim. *Versace* follows up on the success of *The People v. O. J. Simpson* (2016) and invites viewers to explore once again how individual crimes are symptomatic of national strife; in its use of the adjective "American" in its subtitle, it interpellates such criminal acts as belonging to the nation's story about itself, albeit often dis-avowed. And with Filipinx America's ambivalent claims on Cunanan as one of our own, reading the FX series as a story about America provides another entry point to destabilize national and diasporic scripts and to redraw the boundaries of racial-sexual belonging.

Ryan Murphy is an executive producer for *American Crime Story*, so it is not surprising Criss was cast to play Cunanan given his breakout success on *Glee* (2009–2015), another Murphy production. What might be surprising is the casting of an actor of Filipinx descent, mirroring the person's ethnic identity he portrays, in an industry that often whitewashes race. On *Glee*, Criss's character's ethnoracial identity is never resolved: Blaine Anderson is the openly gay teenage dream who is "vaguely Eurasian."[13] However, Cunanan's own racial ambiguity was at the center of "the largest failed man-hunt in U.S. history," and thus casting a multiracial Filipino actor is apro-pos. This is not to say the series prominently features Criss's/Cunanan's Filipinxness; rather, like Orth's book, it is not disavowed but functions as a subcutaneous presence.[14]

Not until episode seven ("Ascent") does Andrew's Filipino raciality come to the fore.[15] In both the series and its book source, his Filipino identity is never hidden, but neither is it a focal point. Instead, his sexuality—in par-ticular his homosexuality and his alleged penchant for BDSM—figures as the mark of his identity. In an essay on Criss's portrayal of Blaine on *Glee*, I argued that show foreclosed intersectional subjectivity by marking Blaine's homosexuality and unmarking his potential Filipino identity, which resem-bles Criss's portrayal of Cunanan on *Versace*, even as the latter avows the character's ties to the Philippines.[16] I argue this is symptomatic of queer mul-tiracial visual cultural representations. As LeiLani Nishime provocatively illumines, "the very perception of sexuality as 'nonracial' makes it an ideal location for public expressions of racial anxieties in a post-racial era." More-over, "In the popular imagination, queer culture is predominantly *white* queer culture."[17] Rather than conceptualize queerness and multiraciality as simply analogous, however, Nishime calls for an intersectional analysis that frames both vectors of identity as mutually constitutive. Reading Criss as Cunanan holds in tension actors' and characters' embodied raciality and sexuality and suggests that even when one vector of identity is being ex-plored, other vectors of identity are always there; it is our job as viewers and critics to entertain the plausibility of what has not necessarily been rejected.

Exceeding Nation and Homeland: A Case for the "X"

This chapter uses the case of Cunanan as a prism to conceptualize racial-sexual-geographic excess not only in diaspora but also in the imagined homeland. Accordingly, "PhilippinExcess" operates as a referent for both Filipinx excess, regardless of geographic location, and diasporic Filipinxs who exceed the geographic boundaries of the Philippine archipelago. This is not a call to separate Philippine Filipinxs and diasporic Filipinxs per se, but a recognition that home for diasporic Filipinxs is not always the Philippines; such a conceptualization aligns with queer diasporic scholars like Jigna Desai, David Eng, and Gayatri Gopinath, who have problematized the nation as homeland, and thus origin, and diaspora as always an extension of the nation, and thus epiphenomenal of an abstracted homeland.[18]

"PhilippinExcess" also is related to its homonym "Filipinxs." Here, I am making a case for the "x" when generally describing people of Philippine descent. Whereas "Filipino" is legible as an ethnoracial marker, it can be construed as masculinist, as Filipinx feminists/peminists have articulated.[19] And while the alternative "Filipino/a" or "Filipina/o" draws attention to the gendered dimensions of ethnoraciality, it nevertheless presupposes a binary view of gender. "X," on the other hand, is amorphous, much like queerness, and it leaves open yet simultaneously refuses gender interpellation. Often representative of the unknown algebraic variable, "x" similarly functions as an indeterminate gender marker for people ethnoracially tied to the Philippines. However, unlike algebra, the "x" in "Filipinx" is not meant to be solved. Rather, it is a deliberate signification of unknowability that at once is hyperaware of gender even as it works to undo it. In the context of this chapter, conceptualizing Cunanan as Filipinx is not so much to interpellate him as not cisgender (given trans* and nonbinary people's early adoption of "Filipinx"); instead, it calls attention to how he falls short and exceeds normative notions of masculinity, which imbricates with his diasporic subjectivity.[20] Cunanan's identity is very much about gender and sexuality as it is about race and place.

My use of "Filipinx" draws on Latinx activists and scholars who seek to create a more expansive vision of Latinidad and gestures toward relational experiences with Spanish colonialization. In their introduction to *Las Américas Quarterly*, a special issue of *American Quarterly*, Macarena Gómez-Barris and Licia Fiol-Matta employ "Latinx" to "signal a route out of gender binaries and normativities we can no longer rehearse. From the South and in the borderlands, the 'x' turns away from the dichotomous, toward a void, an unknown, a wrestling with plurality, vectors of multi-intentionality, and the transitional meanings of what has yet to be seen."[21] They go on to explain that the "x" marks queer potentiality, a capacious future yet to materialize but ephemerally glimpsed in our present, as the late José Esteban Muñoz so beautifully put it.[22] The special issue reworks the idea of America by reconsidering its geotemporal boundaries, shifting away from an exclusive focus on the United States and toward a transnational, transhemispheric orientation that encompasses Latin America, the Caribbean, and Latinidad. Similarly, my chapter reworks the geographic boundaries of the U.S. imperial-nation-state and Filipinx America by reorienting inward, toward ostensibly the nation's heartland and the diaspora's hinterland. Moreover, using the "x" in "Filipinx" as both a mark of excess and unknown potentiality works to reimagine the geographic and symbolic place of people of Philippine descent in the heartland of the metropole.[23]

In "Creator/Destroyer" (episode eight), Andrew's father, Modesto "Pete" Cunanan (played by Jon Jon Briones), flees the United States, seeking refuge in the country of his birth, the Philippines, to avoid indictment for embezzling from his stock clients. Teenage Andrew travels to Baliuag to find out whether his father has stashed away the money for the family, only to discover Pete has abandoned them to preserve himself, leaving them bankrupt. After spending only one night in the tropics, Andrew realizes the Philippines is not his home. Upon arrival in Manila, the camera shows a sweat-drenched Andrew. When the taxi drops him off, he meets his *tito* (uncle) who does not speak much English. Tito asks, "Do you speak Tagalog?" to which Andrew replies, "No. No, I'm sorry." Tito follows up, "Ah. Is this your, uh, first time home?" This time, Andrew does not respond, instead remaining silent and scanning Tito and the front porch for a moment before changing the subject and inquiring, "Is my father here?" In this brief exchange, the narrative subtly hints at Andrew's disorientation in the homeland of his father. That he neither confirms nor denies the Philippines as home suggests his ambivalence as a diasporic, U.S.-born Filipino.

In the middle of the night, Andrew walks over to his father's netted hammock, turns on the light, and silently stands over him. Startled but immediately recognizing it is only his son, Modesto rhetorically asks, "Can't sleep?" The camera cuts to a medium-low angle of Andrew, who silently remains standing behind the netting and looks down at Modesto. Modesto continues, "I'm not surprised. It's the heat," to which Andrew subtly nods. Modesto proceeds, "Me, I'm used to it. Grew up in it. Played in it. Worked in it. It's been a while since I've been back, but . . . the body remembers. You can pretend you belong somewhere else, but the body knows." As he utters these words, the camera remains focused on a close-up of his face that gradually zooms in ever so slightly as he remains lying down on his hammock and looks up at Andrew. Modesto's second-person address is a reference to his immigrant experience in the United States, but it also operates as an indirect address to his son, whose body signals (through sweating and an inability to sleep) that the Philippines is not where he belongs. And yet Andrew neither belongs completely in the United States, as evidenced by his calculated efforts to assimilate into high society, though certainly influenced by his Filipino father. Thus, the Philippines is part of Andrew but not of him.

Whereas the series embellishes Andrew's transoceanic trip to his patri-lineal homeland, its source material (Orth's book) devotes only three short paragraphs to it and ends with a quote from one of his Bishop's School (a prestigious private school in La Jolla) teachers: "When Andrew saw the crude poverty in which his father was living . . . a thriving madness took over his mind."[24] Again, not to disavow diasporic Filipinxs' ties to the Phil-ippines, Cunanan's estrangement from the archipelago demands a rethink-ing of diasporic connections to home as always beyond the host country. If diaspora is about homelessness, then diasporic subjects like Andrew belong neither here (the United States) nor there (the Philippines). Accordingly, Cunanan's struggles could be interpreted as queer diasporic nonbelonging in both the social and geographic senses.

Diasporic Queer Multiracial Filipinx Excesses

On the television screen, Andrew hears the sound of his father's voice declaring, "My son is not, and has never been, a homosexual" (episode nine, "Alone").[25] Viewers might interpret these words as proof of immigrant homophobia, and while part of my argument highlights dominant Filipinxness's exclusion of homosexuality, I do not want to suggest Filipinxs are any more homopho-bic than other ethnoracial groups, including white people. Rather, Modesto's words underscore gay identity and embodiment as being excessive to racial-ethnic-national-cultural identity and the politics of racialized respectabil-ity engendered by white supremacy. And while Cunanan's family may have been oblivious to or in denial of his sexuality, some of his former Bishop's classmates' recollections of Andrew quoted by Orth further illustrate how Cunanan is emblematic of PhilippinExcess.

One classmate remarks, "Whatever he [Andrew] was looking for, he was getting it, and he just got progressively worse—louder and more exagger-ated."[26] Another recounts, "He wanted to experience the arts, culture, im-portant people. But his longing bypassed intelligence, insight, and judgment to become histrionic: Look at me, I'm flamboyant, I'm entertaining to be around—take me out to dinner."[27] To be sure, his penchant for histrionics and gay flamboyance coupled with his desire for high culture and wealth signifies his excessive persona. However, the particularity of his postcolo-nial diasporic subjectivity provides a necessary context for understanding his performative excess. As Homi Bhabha illumines, mimicry is constitutive of colonial intimacies with the colonized Other that simultaneously main-tains and threatens to undo the colonial project of subjugation. The latter actually describes the menace of mimicry: "a difference that is almost total but not quite."[28] Cunanan's determination to fashion himself in the image of affluent European immigrants (e.g., Miglin, Versace) and to fulfill and even exceed the American dream under his Filipino immigrant father's tutelage illustrates the danger—the menace—of enticing racial-colonial Others to desire the colonial world that they will never truly be a part of to maintain the relations of power between colonizer and colonized.

In her analysis of the decolonial aesthetics of contemporary Filipinx American art and performance, Sarita See argues, "The Filipino American cultural moment is marked by excessive embodiment, which constitutes an aesthetic response to the relegation of Filipino America to invisibility and absence in an imperial culture of forgetting."[29] Here, See positions the Filipinx subject as excessive in both their ability to obfuscate Asian American raciality vis-à-vis postcoloniality and their impulse to overdramatize the legacy of multiple colonial violences. That is, Filipinx ontology is a performative archive of disidentification with the U.S. imperial-racial system.

Likewise, Lucy Burns forwards puro arte "as an episteme, as a way of approaching the Filipino/a performing body at key moments in U.S.-Philippine imperial relations." Puro arte's literal translation from Spanish and Filipino/Tagalog to English is "pure art," but its connotative meaning aligns more with irony. It "gestur[es] . . . to the labor of overacting, histrionics, playfulness, and purely over-the-top dramatics." As an admonishment, it basically casts doubt on "one's veracity and authenticity." However, despite its engendering of discipline and derision, it also evokes admiration in its "attention-seeking," "performative extravagance."[30] As such, puro arte names a mode of being that plays with normative performative scripts and can be interpreted as a Filipinized version of Muñoz's theory of disidentification.[31]

Burns's theory of puro arte is instructive for making sense of Cunanan's hedonistic persona as well as Criss's performance of him on Versace. As an interpretive frame, puro arte refuses the essentialist constraints of racialization based on phenotype and allows for Filipinx ways of knowing that enable Filipinxs to recognize one another through bodily gesture. As a component of mise-en-scène, figure behavior encodes meaning. Although Criss's performance as Cunanan may not be viewed as a racial performance, race nevertheless appears as a televisual excess akin to cinematic excess. Brett Farmer defines cinematic excess as "the proposition that the film-text is the site of a complex semiotic heterogeneity that can never be totally reduced or exhausted by a film's dominant narrative structures. . . . Moments of excess appear as deviations from or a going beyond the motivations of dominant narrative demands either at the level of narrative content . . . or at the level of textual form."[32] So while Criss may come across performing as more of a sociopath than a racial minority, attending to the series's moments of televisual excess reveals the narrative's racial unconscious.

In "Ascent" (episode seven), Andrew applies to be a gay escort with an agency but appears to exceed the expectations of race and sexuality. When the manager (played by Molly Price) opens the door of the office, she looks him up and down and reluctantly lets him in. After taking a Polaroid of him, she asks, "Age?" to which he replies, "Twenty-three." Then she asks, "What are you?" Andrew is slightly taken aback, asking, "Um, what am I?" Initially the manager guesses he is Latino, but after he explains his mother is Italian American and his father is from the Philippines and declares, "I'm Asian American," she no longer sees him as possibly Latino but as Asian, which is seen as a liability since "gay clients don't ask for Asian men." Despite Andrew's refusal to be pinned down as Asian, suggesting he could assume a Latino racial identity, the manager consistently returns to his Asianness. She concludes, "I can't sell a clever Filipino. Even one with a big dick."

Although Andrew is undesirable in the gay escort world because he figures as a sassy gaysian, his well-endowment, implied by the manager's gaze since the camera never pans down as he unzips his pants, intrigues the manager and invites viewers to rethink the stereotype of the Asian bottom.[33] While Criss's speech act betrays his ambiguous raciality, the scene's televisual excesses materialized through his arguably puro arte style of subtle head tilts and eye rolls that complement such phrases as "I *am* the dinner table conversation" should be read not only as queer confidence but also Filipinx pride.[34]

Midwesternizing Cunanan's Excess

Central to my polysemous conceptualization of Cunanan's racial-sexual excess is the role of geography in discursively shaping his illegibility in mainstream U.S. public culture. Mapping Cunanan in the middle of the country necessarily revises how we ought to think of his "enigmatic unrecognizability." As the introduction to the *GLQ* special issue *Queering the Middle* indicates, "The middle creates less a magisterial panoramic perspective than a queer vantage—a troubled, unstable perch buttressed by the dominance of the coasts and the 'South.'"[35] Geographically and symbolically the middle of the United States, the Midwest functions as both a physical location in which to interrogate racial-sexual subjectivity and, more important, as an epistemic standpoint from which to unsettle normative notions of identity and belonging. Kale Fajardo's contribution to the special issue specifically addresses the case of diasporic Filipinxs in the United States and Canada, inviting readers to rethink transnational connections not through land but through water, namely the Great Lakes.[36] In queering and transing lacustrine contact zones, Fajardo situates the regional Midwest as a translocal nodal point where racial-gender-sexual nonconformity can inhabit.[37]

Interpreting Cunanan's confounding elusiveness from a Midwestern standpoint reveals how space and place influence social perception. For instance, Sergeant Bob Tichich of the Minneapolis police force, who was at the scene of Trail's murder, had originally filed charges against Madson for Trail's death. Orth obtained the file a year later and noted "it contained some sloppy errors. 'Cunanan' was spelled incorrectly throughout the document."[38] This is not surprising given that a friend of Madson had described Andrew as "a dark-haired former lover of David's from California who might be into something 'shady'"[39] and whose last name was "definitely Kunanen or Cunanen."[40] Accordingly, Tichich's file would have multiple spellings of Andrew's surname. However, Orth notes "Cunanan" is "a not uncommon Filipino name in California."[41] Here, race and region become vectors for imagining Cunanan. Cunanan's multiracial Filipino heritage seems illegible in the Midwest—at least from the perspective of non-Filipinx Midwesterners—whereas his multiraciality does not eclipse his Filipinxness along the West Coast, the capital of Filipinx America.

For Christine Balance, Cunanan is a universal emblem of Filipinx America: "We Filipinos always knew that Andrew Cunanan—with his telltale last name—was one of us. . . . We could relate to . . . his experience of being outside a group yet wanting to belong. . . . His violent actions were excessive forms of the intricate and improvised steps we who are outside the norm perform daily in this cultural cha-cha with America."[42] Balance's reflections on Filipinx Americans' ambivalent, affective ties to Cunanan position him at an extreme end of a continuum defined by postcolonial mimicry that enjoins Filipinx Americans to aspire to a hegemonic national culture that petitions their submission but denies them belonging. For her, Cunanan is a synecdoche of diasporic Filipinxs' structural queerness in the postcolonial U.S. metropole. While her intersectional reading of Cunanan posits race as a grossly overlooked factor in dominant narratives of the infamous spree killer, which often focus on his deviant sexuality, Balance's reading overlooks the geographic dimensions of his illegibility. Not unlike most Filipinx American studies scholarship, Filipinx America often is conceptualized as an amorphous universal abstractly tied to the territorial United States. Surely, Cunanan's exclusion from normative U.S. society resonates with Filipinxs across the U.S. nation. However, not considering how Cunanan's particular presence in different parts of the country not readily imagined to be a node of Filipinx America takes for granted how geography transforms sociality.

Conversely, rethinking the place of Cunanan also works to unsettle Middle America's shock that such violence could happen (t)here. As Edward Ingebretsen argues, "The crisis triggered by the serial killer . . . can be seen as less about killing than about the perceived disarray of cultural intimacies themselves," and in Cunanan's case, "the overheated paranoia . . . originates not in the streets of San Diego, but in the homes of middle America, which admits itself to be as much threatened by the fragmentation of gender codes as by killers."[43] Ingebretsen's analysis of the unsavory media coverage of Cunanan rests on the prurient nature of Cunanan's extravagant lifestyle, which transgressed normative standards of gender performance and sexual identity for men and thus trespassed upon national fictions for appropriate social citizenship.[44] Unfortunately, his reading ignores that Cunanan's gender and sexual transgressions may in fact be racialized and colonial in form.[45] That is, Ingebretsen's domestic frame to interpret Cunanan's violation of the decidedly white social contract overlooks how Asian bodies historically have been casts as an invading Yellow Peril and how Filipino men in particular have been viewed as hypersexual deviants.[46] Suturing Balance and Ingebretsen's conceptual gaps, I forward intersectional, relational readings of Cunanan's curious figuration in public culture must consider space and place as pivots on which social identities are made and remade.

Conclusion: Facing the Middle; Toward a Cultural Politics of Illegibility

What are the epistemic and ontological possibilities of Cunanan's "enigmatic unrecognizability" that refer not only to his multiracial heritage but also to his geographic traversal of the heartland of U.S. empire? While his ambiguous raciality and ability to perform multiple personas may have foreclosed the opportunity for mainstream U.S. culture to recognize him as "one of us," such an illegible subject position can figure as a productive fissure to minoritarian calls for visibility. That is, figures like Cunanan and Criss who elude interpellation offer alternative ways to conceptualize the project of Filipinx critique.

Regarding (il)legibility, Gómez-Barris and Fiol-Matta note, "Recognition . . . has historically functioned as an important category of coloniality in the Americas. It has also been, in reverse, a place of social activation, where subaltern groups petition the state as a way to access resources and normalization."[47] They acknowledge both the possibilities and limits of legibility. While coloniality in the Americas has violently produced illegible subjects, dehumanizing them beyond recognition, the decolonial move to humanize and make legible minoritarian being can unwittingly reinscribe coloniality's power to name subjects. Thus, Cunanan's illegibility, his unrecognizability, reveals a moment of rupture, an unconscious refusal to be subjected to U.S. racial-colonial regimes. Fittingly, Muñoz posits queerness as one form of interpellative refusal: "Queers are people who have failed to turn around to the 'Hey, you there!' interpellating call of heteronormativity."[48] And for me, heteronormativity is not simply constituted by race and sexuality but necessarily by geography.

Throughout this chapter, I have argued queerness is spatial and place-based just as much as it is sexual, gendered, racial, and classed. Andrew Cunanan's geographic mobility across the United States—as being "everywhere and nowhere," or more aptly everywhere in nowhere—speaks to his diasporic queering of space and place.[49] He was able to penetrate the upper echelons of urban gay white male society while also whisking in and out of America's heartland, a place imagined to be so far removed from the saturated multiculturalism of California. Revisiting the case of Cunanan enjoins us to rethink the parameters of queerness and to realize its geographic specificities, the latter of which contributes to the negation of queerness as ahistorical and universally coherent. Instead of seeing excess as too much, we might recognize those who are excess remind us that our current frameworks are not enough.

NOTES

1. Maureen Orth, *Vulgar Favors: The Assassination of Gianni Versace* (New York: Bantam, 2017), 223.

2. Ibid., 251.

3. Ibid., 275.

4. Ibid., 324.

5. Ibid., 412–413.

6. Ibid., 11.

7. Allan Punzalan Isaac, *American Tropics: Articulating Filipino America* (Minneapolis: University of Minnesota Press, 2006), xxiii.

8. Orth, *Vulgar Favors*, 16.

9. Ibid., 5.

10. Ibid., 386.

11. Stephen H. Sumida, "East of California: Points of Origin in Asian American Studies," *Journal of Asian American Studies* 1, no. 1 (1998): 83–100.

12. Criss won the Emmy for Outstanding Lead Actor in a Limited Series or Movie in 2018 and the Golden Globe for Best Performance by an Actor in a Limited Series or a Motion Picture Made for Television in 2019 for his performance in *Versace*, becoming the first Filipinx American to earn each accolade.

13. See Thomas Xavier Sarmiento, "The Empire Sings Back: *Glee*'s Queer Materialization of Filipina/o America," *MELUS: Multi-Ethnic Literature of the United States* 39, no. 2 (2010): 211–234.

14. In a promotional interview for *Versace*, Criss proudly claims his Filipino heritage, which he has consistently done over the years, while not identifying as Asian American because of his phenotypic whiteness (from his perspective); the latter statement has not been met without controversy, prompting Criss to clarify in a tweet that "1 of my favorite things about myself is that I'm half Filipino. PERIOD. I happen to not look like it, but THAT fact is not what I like." E. Alex Jung, "Darren Criss on Playing Serial Killer Andrew Cunanan in *ACS: Versace* and Passing as White," *Vulture*, March 14, 2018, https://www.vulture.com/2018/03/darren-criss-american-crime-story-versace-and-race.html?utm_campaign=vulture&utm_source=tw&utm_medium=sl; Darren Criss (@DarrenCriss), Twitter, March 14, 2018, 10:50 p.m., https://twitter.com/DarrenCriss/status/974161008553013250.

15. I refer to Cunanan by his first name when discussing depictions of him in Orth's book and in the FX program.

16. Sarmiento, "The Empire Sings Back."

17. LeiLani Nishime, *Undercover Asian: Multiracial Asian Americans in Visual Culture* (Urbana: University of Illinois Press, 2014), chapter 2.

18. Jigna Desai, *Beyond Bollywood: The Cultural Politics of South Asian Diasporic Film* (New York: Routledge, 2004); David L. Eng, *The Feeling of Kinship: Queer Liberalism and the Racialization of Intimacy* (Durham, NC: Duke University Press, 2010); Gayatri Gopinath, *Impossible Desires: Queer Diasporas and South Asian Public Cultures* (Durham, NC: Duke University Press, 2005); Gayatri Gopinath, *Unruly Visions: The Aesthetic Practices of Queer Diaspora* (Durham, NC: Duke University Press, 2018).

19. For more on peminism, see Melinda L. de Jesús, ed., *Pinay Power: Peminist Critical Theory; Theorizing the Filipina/American Experience* (New York: Routledge, 2005).

20. Another way to frame Cunanan's masculinity would be to think of it as proximate. See Isaac, *American Tropics*, chapter 5.

21. Macarena Gómez-Barris and Licia Fiol-Matta, introduction to *Las Américas Quarterly*, *American Quarterly* 66, no. 3 (2014): 504n1.

22. Gómez-Barris and Fiol-Matta, introduction to *Las Américas Quarterly*, 504; José Esteban Muñoz, *Cruising Utopia: The Then and There of Queer Futurity* (New York: New York University Press, 2009).

23. The "x" among people of Philippine descent (as with people of Latin American descent) remains contested. MT Vallarta's work on queer Filipinx poetics, which conceptualizes "Filipinx" as method, and Sony Coráñez Bolton's work on queerness, disability, and Filipinx indigeneity during the late Spanish period of the Philippines resonate with my usage. MT Vallarta, "Brown Shout Outs: Trans and Non-binary Filipinx American Poetry," University of Victoria Transgender Archives, posted November 27, 2019, YouTube video, https://www.youtube.com/watch?v=SSGafrmkuZo; Sony Coráñez Bolton, "Dos X: Filipinx and Latinx Queer Temporalities" (paper presentation, American Studies Association, Atlanta, GA, November 10, 2018).

24. Orth, *Vulgar Favors*, 59.

25. In Orth's book, an excerpt from Modesto's film pitch includes, "I had never known my son, Andrew, to be a homosexual" (35).

26. Orth, 47.

27. Ibid., 49.

28. Homi Bhabha, "Of Mimicry and Man: The Ambivalence of Colonial Discourse," *October* 28 (Spring 1984): 132.

29. Sarita Echavez See, *The Decolonized Eye: Filipino American Art and Performance* (Minneapolis: University of Minnesota Press, 2009), 34.

30. Lucy Mae San Pablo Burns, *Puro Arte: Filipinos on the Stages of Empire* (New York: New York University Press, 2013), introduction.

31. José Esteban Muñoz, *Disidentifications: Queers of Color and the Performance of Politics* (Minneapolis: University of Minnesota Press, 1999).

32. Brett Farmer, "Queer Negotiations of the Hollywood Musical," in *Queer Cinema: The Film Reader*, ed. Harry Benshoff and Sean Griffin (New York: Routledge, 2004), 79.

33. Orth actually mentions Cunanan preferred to top while engaging in sex with men (168, 172, 187). See Nguyen Tan Hoang, *A View from the Bottom: Asian American Masculinity and Sexual Representation* (Durham, NC: Duke University Press, 2014), for a critical reimagining of Asian bottomhood.

34. In episode two ("Manhunt"), another moment of televisual excess materializes when viewers see Gianni Versace (played by Édgar Ramírez) and his longtime partner Antonio D'Amico (played by Ricky Martin) strut through the dance floor of the Miami gay nightclub Twist to Filipina American singer Jocelyn Enriquez's 1997 dance hit single "A Little Bit of Ecstasy." This subtle nod to Filipinx American culture is fitting given Enriquez's own racial misrecognition; see Elizabeth H. Pisares, "Do You Mis(recognize) Me: Filipina Americans in Popular Music and the Problem of Invisibility," in *Positively No Filipinos Allowed: Building Communities and Discourse*, ed. Antonio T. Tiongson Jr., Edgardo V. Gutierrez, and Ricardo V. Gutierrez (Philadelphia: Temple University Press, 2006), 172–198.

35. Martin F. Manalansan IV, Chantal Nadeau, Richard T. Rodríguez, and Siobhan B. Somerville, introduction to *Queering the Middle: Race, Region, and a Queer Midwest*, *GLQ: A Journal of Lesbian and Gay Studies* 20, no. 1–2 (2014): 1.

36. Kale Bantigue Fajardo, "Queering and Transing the Great Lakes: Filipino/a Tomboy Masculinities and Manhoods across Waters," *GLQ: A Journal of Lesbian and Gay Studies* 20, no. 1–2 (2014): 115–140.

37. For more on contact zones, see Mary Louise Pratt, *Imperial Eyes: Travel Writing and Transculturation* (New York, Routledge, 1992).

38. Orth, *Vulgar Favors*, 515.

39. Ibid., 232.

40. Ibid., 233.

41. Ibid., 62.

42. Christine Bacareza Balance, "Notorious Kin: Filipino America Re-imagines Andrew Cunanan," *Journal of Asian American Studies* 11, no. 1 (2008): 87–88.

43. Edward J. Ingebretsen, *At Stake: Monsters and the Rhetoric of Fear in Public Culture* (Chicago: University of Chicago Press, 2001), 72.

44. See also Ingebretsen's "Gender-Deviancy and Crime: An American Fantasy," *International Journal of Sexuality and Gender Studies* 5, no. 3 (2000): 255–277.

45. Ingebretsen, toward the end of his chapter, does mention Cunanan as being "ambiguously racialized" and how "the moralized deviancy of Andrew Cunanan was used to clarify . . . jealousies over race, class privilege, access to sex, finances and drugs as well" (*At Stake*, 85).

46. See Linda España-Maram, *Creating Masculinity in Los Angeles's Little Manila: Working-Class Filipinos and Popular Culture, 1920s–1950s* (New York: Columbia, 2006); Mae M. Ngai, *Impossible Subjects: Illegal Aliens and the Making of Modern America* (Princeton, NJ: Princeton University Press, 2004); Rhacel Parreñas, "'White Trash' Meets the 'Little Brown Monkey': The Taxi Dance Hall as a Site of Interracial and Gender Alliances between White Working Class Women and Filipino Immigrant Men in the 1920s and 30s," *Amerasia Journal* 24, no. 2 (1998): 115–134.

47. Gómez-Barris and Fiol-Matta, introduction to *Las Américas Quarterly*, 497.

48. Muñoz, *Disidentifications*, 33.

49. Quoted in Isaac, *American Tropics*, xxiii.

Balang's Dance

Puro Arte as Queer Affect

CASEY MECIJA

Balang, a ten-year-old from Cavite, a small province located on the southern shores of the Philippines, has garnered worldwide attention for his dancing. Balang is a talented dancer who is best known for his performances of elaborate dance routines to American pop hits. His You-Tube videos have amassed millions of viewers, and he is a frequent guest on the TV talk show *Ellen*. On Balang's debut performance on *Ellen*, his arms flail, his hips gyrate, and he flutters his eye lashes while he lip-syncs to "Bang Bang," a pop song performed by Jessie J, Ariana Grande, and Nicki Minaj.[1] Outfitted in a golf shirt that hugs his round body, his wrists flick from side to side while his face bursts with exaggerated expressions. In a fedora and dark rimmed glasses, he aims to impress on his first visit to the United States. His choreography and lip-syncing awkwardly drifts off time while the audience laughs and cheers at his efforts to entertain them. He ends his performance with the splits, causing the crowd to erupt with applause. Balang, whose full name is John Phillip Bughaw, is adored for the expressive and arguably queer passion with which he performs. Through the expression of queer affects, Balang's performance possesses reparative potential. In this article, I argue that Balang absorbs that which has aimed to assimilate his difference and uses it to feed his desire for pleasure. In Balang's performance, we are witness to a reinterpretation of American culture that is motivated by the need to express the affective residues of imperialism. He excavates the vexed site of American popular culture, which has historically had a colonizing hold on Filipinx culture, for energy and sustenance.[2]

On *Ellen*, Balang's facial expressions are overpronounced, and he lip-syncs to a pop song in English, a language he does not know how to speak (he uses a translator for an interview with the show's host). He stands on a little stage opposite to an audience that expects to be entertained, and they are, laughing at his femininity and fatness. There's no way to predict what Balang's gendered embodiment will mean to him, however the online responses to his performances that have identified him as gay, queer, and bakla raise questions about how queer discourse is written upon this Filipinx

332 / Casey Mecija

child.[3] After the performance, Ellen comments, "That was so entertaining, I could watch that for another hour."[4] Although his appearance on American television is a moment of entertainment, there is more to consider in relation to postcolonial framings of masculinity in Balang's performance. Each of Balang's movements playfully tests representations of Filipinx acceptability and belonging; perhaps unknowingly, the child's performance sits within a long history of Filipinx bodies read by Americans as entertaining, excessive, and, even when embraced as exceptional, running the risk of being perceived as a "cheap trick or mindless aping" of American greatness.[5] Following the example of other Filipinx YouTube stars like Jake Zyrus, Balang admits he's learned to dance through copying performances he has watched on American television.[6] Along with his capacity to entertain Ellen's studio audience, his videos have amassed over twelve million views on YouTube, evidence that he is undoubtedly successful at attracting worldwide attention. Watching Balang's performance on *Ellen* is at once pleasurable and uncomfortable. I can imagine my Filipinx family enjoying his performance but also calling the child "puro arte" in an effort to distance themselves from his queer excess. In Tagalog, one might say that Balang is puro arte, or overacting. A person is referred to as puro arte if they are deemed dramatic, flamboyant, or excessive.

In this article, I theorize the affective excess of Balang's performance and argue that it elucidates intimacies between empire, performance, race, and gender. I read Balang's dancing through the work of Lucy Mae San Pablo Burns, who uses "puro arte" as a conceptual framework to describe the performing Filipinx body on a global stage.[7] Building on Burns's work, I argue that puro arte, as affective terrain, accounts for the unassimilated residues of difficult experience that circulate around Balang's performance.[8] Burns's theory of puro arte helps to describe the affective engagements that audiences have with Balang as reliant on a history of colonial encounters between the Philippines and the United States. I suggest that the affective excesses of Balang's performance enable an alliance with queerness not as an embodied certitude but as a method that creates new iterations of gendered and racial difference. A critical reading of the child's dance and its reception also offers commentary on how queerness emerges as both recognizable and politically contested in the Philippines and in the diaspora. Second, by drawing our attention to the history of Filipino taxi dance hall dancers in the United States, I argue that we can grasp at how colonial histories of race and bio-power, masculinity and sexuality, have a genealogy that predates Balang's performance. Here, I consider what Balang's dancing does to affirm, rupture, or adjust expectations of the Filipinx body on stage. What political meanings can be found in the ways this child moves and holds the gaze of the camera? How might Balang's performance animate affective traces that interrupt a fraught history of globalization and American and Philippine relations? How does Balang's performance illuminate the "asymmetries of innocence" assigned to children from the global south?[9] Why is his body read as gay by those who watch his videos, and what meaning can we glean from this queer association?

In addition to theorizing puro arte as affective excess, underscoring my ideas in this article is the work of Dina Georgis, who insists that queer affect accounts for the "abject perversions of difference, not easily nameable."[10] Queer affects are emotions that are attached to unconscious knowledge. They are sensations that undo us and that exceed the confines of identity. As a phrase that registers the circulation and expression of queer affect, puro arte helps me to describe the historical racialization of the Filipinx performer while excavating the enigmatic agency that is in excess of Balang's cultural subjectivity. Queerness is used here as a methodology that challenges hegemonic understandings of identity formation to make space for the creative ways Balang contests and reimagines his racialized subjectivity. By examining the affective excesses of Balang's performance, we can begin to examine how Filipinx diasporic experiences are complexly enunciated in pursuit of building a creative relation to difficult affects created by histories of homophobia, colonialism and imperialism. Performance offers a surrendering to the unknowable affects inspired by movement and sound. Despite the structure of choreography and the predetermined length and lyrics of American pop songs, Balang's relation to his performance is full of queer affect. He is unpredictably impacted by the music he performs to and how he is received by his audience. Performance provides room to encounter the unexpected and each one of Balang's performances possesses the possibility of difference, something Eve Sedgwick might call "queer possibility."[11] Through dancing, Balang symbolizes both conscious and unconscious phantasies and anxieties. Dancing is a site where affects are represented and elide the demands of language. His performance is a site of play where the unconscious and difficult histories of race, gender, and nation-state manifest and are reworked.

Puro Arte and the Child Who Acts Out

Translated from Spanish to English, "puro arte" means "pure art," however in the Philippines it "performs a much more ironic function."[12] For Filipinos, puro arte embodies a more playful meaning, gesturing at that which is deemed over the top or overdramatic behaviour. In *Puro Arte: Filipinos on the Stages of Empire*, Burns contends that to be puro arte is to resist knowable expressions and that in the invocation of the phrase there is a recognition of the creativity and theatrics required to "put on a show."[13] Overacting is aligned with creativity, aesthetics, and artful expression; the term attempts to capture the potentiality of Filipino corporeality as it is acted out on stage. In this way, dancing, like Balang's, is an aesthetic intervention that expresses puro arte as a means to insist on the agency of the racialized performer despite a history of colonial subjugation. Balang's dramatic charisma is in defiance of the history that has tried to erase him. Burns suggests that calling someone puro arte is an attempt to discipline an unruly body or emotional response, an attempt to point out "the body's performative extravagance, a spectacle making that must be disciplined [and] reined in."[14] Differently, psychoanalytic theories of child development suggest that healthy development involves some "acting out."[15] I suggest that Balang's dancing is a form of acting out unconsciously at a history of Filipinx performers being read through discursive constructions of race and racism.

Balang's status as an Internet sensation earned him recognition in the United States, where representations of the Filipinx performing body have been largely determined through the lens of sensationalism. Because of the colonial histories between the Philippines and the United States, Allan Punzalan Isaac proposes that there is often a psychic desire for Filipinx people to belong to the U.S. nation as a "sensation."[16] However, we might also be interested in sensation as an index of how the performing body feels and how the performing body is perceived by audiences. The sensations cathected onto Balang and his simultaneous creative reworking of them are a possible disruption of colonial intelligibility. Katherine Sugg describes how a "distinct economy of sensation" possesses the potential to push somatic expression into "unfamiliar territory."[17] In the context of dealing with the psychic repercussions of colonialism, Sugg suggests that an excess of sensation "signals a rebellion against the codes of recovery" and proper "affective relations."[18] Balang acts out against assumptions of a docile and submissive Asian body, falling in line with a history of Filipino dancers who are called "sensational" for their kinesthetic performances. Balang's "distinct economy of sensation" possesses the potential to undermine pathologies of race and gender.[19]

A reading of Balang through the lens of puro arte opens up a discussion of queer childhood. Receiving a variety of responses from online audiences, Balang's acting out is most commonly read as "gay," "homosexual," "bakla," or "queer," an association with sexuality and gender that I want to unsettle. In *The Queer Child, Or Growing Sideways in the 20th Century,* Kathryn Bond Stockton suggests that the child that doesn't seamlessly grow in line with heterosexual demands instead grows sideways.[20] This sideways growth relies on adult theories of childhood development that determine what conditions are appropriate for a child to advance to adulthood. Stockton contests normative teleologies of childhood development by pointing out the queerness of childhood. Stockton's queer theory of childhood, in which some subjects aren't deemed worthy of complete development, is useful for thinking about Filipinx subjectivity as it relates to the American nation-state. Referred to as the "little brown brother" by Americans during the period of U.S. colonial rule, the Philippines is the country that isn't allowed to grow up. The infantalization of the Philippines by the United States has determined Filipinx people as always already "queer." The reception of Balang as gay should be read as an inheritance of this history. However, I don't employ this term to suggest I know how Balang will identify his sexual orientation in the future. As Hannah Dyer has written, "queer" can potentially describe a child's sexuality or identity, but it can also provide language with which to describe the child's creative resistances against normalcy.[21] In her work, queerness offers a critical framework that accounts for the creative ways children interrupt the social contract that underwrites their relation to the future. Balang may be considered a queer child who pushes against ideas of acceptable gender, race, and sexuality. If queerness is loosened out of the holds of identity, it offers a mode with which to address feelings, objects and relations that contest normativity.

I do not want to sentimentalize Balang's performance or reify racialized stereotypes of Filipinx people as overly dramatic copycats. Instead, I want to highlight how Balang's dancing creates conditions for repair of a difficult past and uncertain future. Melanie Klein suggests that reparation involves the infant creatively integrating what it wants to nurture and destroy in order to sustain its world.[22] For her, reparation is motivated by the depressive position, whereby the ego communes the good and bad aspects of an object. In Balang's performance, we witness a child seeking pleasure, and for Klein, this would be motivated by the desire to repair. A reparative reading of Balang's performance on *Ellen* could argue that Balang reworks American culture in an effort to more seamlessly belong despite a history of subjection. He works through the tight hold American culture has on the Philippines by through dance. Despite the Philippines being called the "little brother" of the United States, Balang interrupts this history and affective hierarchy by remaining ambivalent to the demands of his colonial ruler. Instead of wanting to straightforwardly spoil or destroy American culture, Balang reinterprets American pop hits; he takes the original song and performance and makes it his own.

In Balang's performance, we are witness to a child interacting with the world in ways that are both cognitive and unconscious. Klein describes reparation as a process where the ego undoes harm done in phantasy. It is a psychic process whereby the infant seeks to make amends for injuries caused by both its real and phantasmatic attempts to experience pleasure of its mother's breast. Balang's performance is impulsively reparative.[23] His dancing is a site of play where the unconscious manifests, whereby new articulations of diasporic experience are generated. Through the repetition of these performances, Balang reexperiences his emotions and phantasies in relation to his Filipinx subjectivity. These encounters stage an opportunity to revise his relations to difficult encounters caused by racism, homophobia, and histories of colonization and thus begin to tolerate any anxieties. In Balang's performance, we are witness to a reinterpretation of American Filipino history that is motivated by repair and a recentering of Filipinx desire and pleasure.

Balang's "Splendid" Dancing

In *Puro Arte: Filipinos on the Stages of Empire*, Burns provides an account of the history of Filipino taxi dance hall dancers in 1920s and early 1930s United States, reading this historical moment as one which archives how Filipinos have been deemed exceptional performers by Americans.[24] In this section, I point out similarities between Balang and these dancers, and I more broadly read the Filipino dancing body as queer within a context of American imperialism. I suggest that we can read Balang's dancing as an attempt to shake the hold of empire, still energetically present in the Philippines. His body is always already enmeshed in the legacies of American imperialism in the Philippines, yet he fervently moves to disentangle the mess of his own subjectivity as constituted through a history of empire.

In the 1920s and early 1930s, in large American cities such as Detroit, Chicago, and Los Angeles, Filipino men made up "at least a fifth of the total patronage."[25] A taxi dance hall was a nightclub, where working class white women were paid by men, most of whom were migrant workers, to dance with them. Like taxi rides, the female dancers expected some form of tip for their services. Taxi dance halls functioned as an important hub for socializing between immigrants during a tense political moment of heightened racial segregation and anti-miscegenation sentiment in the United States.[26] In these spaces, Filipino men came into close proximity with white women taxi dancers. Burns explains that "for many Filipino patrons going to taxi dance halls was often referred to as 'going to class.'"[27] The taxi dance hall was a social institution where the Filipino man could access "whiteness" and become acquainted with the social practices required to perform and mimic American practices. Through them, Filipino men gained tenuous access to American life and sociality by purchasing dances with white women. The Filipino taxi dance hall dancer is "an archival embodiment" of the palimpsestic relations between "immigration, foreign policy, social institutions and Filipino corporeal colonization."[28]

In the taxi dance hall, Filipino dancers were observed as arguably the most talented dancers. Often referenced to as "splendid," "spectacular," and "fancy," the Filipino male was suggested to exhibit unparalleled kinesthetic abilities and moved in ways that demanded attention.[29] The Filipino's knowledge of American dance steps was regarded as exemplary, and his quick learning of "American ways" was made sense of alongside discourses of racial exceptionality. In this summation of his skill, the trope of exceptionalism works to simultaneously veil and reveal the history of American imperial rule over Filipinos in the United States. The Filipino performing body was deemed "gifted" and "exceptional" through his perfection of American dance steps. And yet, as Burns explains, "these markers of recognition highlight the Filipino performing body as 'excess.' That is, the very markers that make Filipinos visible are also the very signs that make impossible their acceptability in and belonging to American political, social, and cultural fabric."[30] Deemed "hypersexual," Filipino men in taxi dance halls were often understood as the cause of a "miscegenation and contagion" between Filipinos and white women.[31] Burns argues that the Filipino body deemed splendid or exceptional "sediments and extends U.S. Colonial modes of commodification and racism."[32] However, the taxi dance hall was not simply a site where Filipino men were subjugated or disciplined. The "splendid dancing" was as much about a structural and reciprocal exchange as it was about pleasure. And yet the Filipino body, despite its freedom on the dance floor, was never wholly apart of the nation outside the dance hall.

Balang's performance is an ontological offspring of the history of the Filipino taxi dance hall dancer. Within the framework of puro arte, Balang's consumption can be understood as complexly gendered and racialized in exceptional ways. He performs on a stage where the history of American occupation in the Philippines is attempted to be erased. But if we read Balang's performance beside a history of the "splendid" Filipino taxi dance hall dancers, we can grasp at a historical present in which this child comes to be recognized as exceptional for his ability to entertain. Burns uses the term "corporeal colonization" to register the ways in which the Filipino body comes into contact with "the uneven successes and limits of U.S. empire."[33] In Balang's case, the Filipino body has been disciplined by the residues of U.S. empire even before his arrival in the United States. He is celebrated for his dancing but only in relation to "material rule" of the Filipino body. The Filipino body remains a "complex mobility" in which she must traverse a web of U.S.-Philippine relations that surface in a multitude of emotional and historical entanglements.[34]

For Rhacel Parreñas, Filipino taxi hall dancers contested subjection "through the maximization of their bodies as machines."[35] Dancing is an assertion of presence that allows one to imagine a new embodied strength. Perhaps Balang dances despite the psychic impossibility of ever breaking free from the hold of a history of empire into which he was born—and also the stigma that comes from homophobia. For Filipino taxi dance hall dancers, the mastering of American dance steps or the exceptional performance of these moves never securely guaranteed access to national belonging and citizenship. Balang's waving arms and his whirling waist create an aesthetic space that is in excess of markers of acceptability and belonging, and thus in his performance, one catches a glimpse of what Jose Muñoz might deem queer futurity.[36]

Balang extends his limbs to test his relations to the social world. His movements are rehearsed, but despite the discipline of choreography, his expressions of those calculated steps are full of unpredictable affect. Balang symbolizes his world through dance, both pleasing his audience but also pleasing himself. In *History of Sexuality: An Introduction, Volume 1*, Michel Foucault reminds us that pleasure has unruly manifestations that are not always legible in ways we might expect, and that escape our capacity to theorize.[37] Foucault suggests that the ways our bodies materialize pleasure are perhaps incalculable, and the more we attempt to assign meaning or casualty, the more we detract from the pleasure itself. There is no way to surmise the pleasure Balang might feel from the movement of his body that may be in excess of his choreography. However, within the discipline of lip-synced words and timed-out steps, there is an aesthetic space for Balang to express an unknowable agency that is outside the hold of empire and is solely his.

Conclusion

Balang creatively symbolizes his desire and subjectivity through dance. His act of puro arte wrestles with the affective residues of imperialism. His queer presence on stage in California raises important questions about how and why a Filipinx child both inherits and resists a legacy of aesthetic expression within the context of American imperialism. As I have described, there is important scholarship written on the traditions of Filipino performance as being deeply rooted in mimicry and imitation of American culture.[38] I do not intend to elide the complicated colonial dynamics that play out in the necessary act of imitating American ways in order to more smoothly gain access to notions of acceptability and belonging. Rather, I mean to argue that Balang's dance sits within a history of hegemonic standards of masculinity and thus can be read as a queer act of remaking gendered futures for children. The reappropriation of American culture by postcolonial subjects like this child's interpretation of American song and dance offers us something new and not yet imagined.

In his interview with Ellen, Balang is asked what he wants to be when he grows up. His translator says, "He wants to be a Zumba instructor for us to be healthy."[39] Against fat-shaming, I read this comment for Balang's desire to help an audience be psychically healthy, which involves "acting out." How might Balang's dancing create an aesthetic intervention that interrupts a fraught history of American and Philippine relations? Balang comments that "when he watches TV [presumably American TV] and when he hears a song, he can easily jive with it."[40] Perhaps we can learn from Balang how creativity gives expression to that which is difficult to know and understand. Balang's level of awareness of the political and social dynamics that create the conditions of his subjectivity do not undermine how his dancing contributes to a new understanding of the world around him. Burns's theory of puro arte opens up an aesthetic space with which to theorize the psychic liminalities and contradictions of Filipino subjectivity through performance. I have reflected on the genealogy of Filipino taxi dance hall dancers in order to contextualize the ongoing negotiation of Filipino belonging within the hold of American empire. I have argued that Balang's dancing and performance shares a palimpsestic kinship to that of the Filipino taxi dance hall dancer, both of which could be described as "queer" and as "acting out" in order to make sense of and be made sense of in the world.

NOTES

1. "Balang's US Debut," YouTube, accessed February 14, 2020, https://www.youtube.com/watch?v=m0taQOtvxfU.

2. Recently, "Filipinx" has emerged as a popular term for describing people and experiences related to the Philippines. Without a gendered imperative for either male or female (i.e., "Filipino" or "Filipina"), I employ this term in my own writing. However, since much of the literature that I have read and will discuss does not, at times I use "Filipino" and/or "Filipina."

3. Robert Diaz (2015) explains that *Bakla* is a Filipinx sexual/gender term that "denotes gay male identity, male-to-female transgender identity, effeminized or hyperbolic gay identity, and gay identity that belongs to the lower class. The term is thus conditional and contextual, and its deployment often points to the geographic, temporal, and material constraints of its usage" (721). Diaz recommends Martin Manalansan's book *Global Divas* (2003) for a more comprehensive examination of the term and its social implications.

4. "Balang's US Debut."

5. Lucy Mae San Pablo Burns, *Puro Arte: Filipinos on the Stages of Empire*, Postmillennial Pop (New York: New York University Press, 2013), 12.

6. See Christine Balance's work for an in-depth analysis on Asian American YouTube performance. In *Tropical Renditions: Making Musical Scenes in Filipino America (2016)*, Balance explores the impacts of going viral on Filipinx performer Jake Zyrus.

7. Burns, *Puro Arte*.

8. Dina Georgis, "Discarded Histories and Queer Affects in Anne Carson's Autobiography of Red," *Studies in Gender and Sexuality* 15, no. 2 (2014): 154–166, https://doi.org/10.1080/15240657.2014.911054.

9. Hannah Dyer, *The Queer Aesthetics of Childhood: Asymmetries of Innocence and the Cultural Politics of Child Development* (Rutgers University Press, 2020), https://doi.org/10.2307/j.ctvscxrd5.

10. Georgis, "Discarded Histories and Queer Affects in Anne Carson's Autobiography of Red," 154.

11. Eve Kosofsky Sedgwick and Adam Frank, *Touching Feeling: Affect, Pedagogy, Performativity*, Series Q (Durham, NC: Duke University Press, 2003).

12. Burns, *Puro Arte*, 2.

13. Ibid., 1.

14. Ibid., 1.

15. Dyer, *The Queer Aesthetics of Childhood*; Jen Gilbert, "Risking a Relation: Sex Education and Adolescent Development," *Sex Education* 7, no. 1 (2007): 47–61, https://doi.org/10.1080/14681810601134736; D. W. Winnicott, *Playing and Reality* (New York: Basic Books, 1971).

16. Allan Punzalan Isaac, *American Tropics: Articulating Filipino America*, Critical American Studies Series (Minneapolis: University of Minnesota Press, 2006).

17. Katherine Sugg, *Gender and Allegory in Transamerican Fiction and Performance*, 1st ed. (New York: Palgrave Macmillan, 2008), 144.

18. Ibid., 144.

19. Ibid., 144.

20. Kathryn Bond Stockton, *The Queer Child, or Growing Sideways in the Twentieth Century*, Series Q (Durham, NC: Duke University Press, 2009).

21. Dyer, *The Queer Aesthetics of Childhood*.

22. Melanie Klein, *Love, Guilt, and Reparation, and Other Works, 1921–1945* (London: Hogarth, 1975).

23. Melanie Klein, "The Psychoanalytic Play Technique*," *American Journal of Orthopsychiatry* 25, no. 2 (1955): 223–237, https://doi.org/10.1111/j.1939-0025.1955.tb00131.x.

24. Burns, *Puro Arte*.

25. Paul Goalby Cressey, *The Taxi-Dance Hall: A Sociological Study in Commercialized Recreation and City Life*, University of Chicago Sociological Series (Chicago: University of Chicago Press, 1932), 45.

26. Rhacel Salazar Parreñas, "'White Trash' Meets the 'Little Brown Monkeys': The Taxi Dance Hall as a Site of Interracial and Gender Alliances between White Working Class Women and Filipino Immigrant Men in the 1920s and 30s," *Amerasia Journal* 24, no. 2 (January 1, 1998): 115–134, https://doi.org/10.17953/amer.24.2.760h5w08630ql643.

27. Burns, *Puro Arte*, 49.

28. Ibid., 56.

29. Ibid., 51.

30. Ibid., 65.

31. Ibid., 65.

32. Ibid., 52.

33. Ibid., 63.

34. Ibid., 73.

35. Parreñas, "'White Trash' Meets the 'Little Brown Monkeys,'" 119.

36. José Esteban Muñoz, *Cruising Utopia: The Then and There of Queer Futurity*, Sexual Cultures (New York: New York University Press, 2009).

37. Michel Foucault et al., *The History of Sexuality*, 1st American ed., Social Theory, 2nd ed. (New York: Pantheon, 1978).

38. Burns, *Puro Arte*; Hsuan L. Hsu, "Mimicry, Spatial Captation, and Feng Shui in Han Ong's Fixer Chao," *Modern Fiction Studies* 52, no. 3 (October 4, 2006): 675–704, https://doi.org/10.1353/mfs.2006.0065; J. Lorenzo Perillo, "'If I Was Not in Prison, I Would Not Be Famous': Discipline, Choreography, and Mimicry in the Philippines," *Theatre Journal* 63, no. 4 (2011): 607–621.

39. "Balang's US Debut."

40. "Balang's US Debut."

BIBLIOGRAPHY

Balance, Christine Bacareza. "How It Feels to Be Viral Me: Affective Labor and Asian American YouTube Performance." *WSQ: Women's Studies Quarterly* 40, no. 1–2 (2012): 138–152. https://doi.org/10.1353/wsq.2012.0016.

———. *Tropical Renditions: Making Musical Scenes in Filipino America*. Refiguring American Music. Durham, NC: Duke University Press, 2016.

"Balang's US Debut." YouTube. Accessed February 14, 2020. https://www.youtube.com/watch?v=m0taQOtvxfU.

Burns, Lucy Mae San Pablo. *Puro Arte: Filipinos on the Stages of Empire*. Postmillennial Pop. New York: New York University Press, 2013.

Cressey, Paul Goalby. *The Taxi-Dance Hall: A Sociological Study in Commercialized Recreation and City Life*. University of Chicago Sociological Series. Chicago: University of Chicago Press, 1932.

Dyer, Hannah. *The Queer Aesthetics of Childhood: Asymmetries of Innocence and the Cultural Politics of Child Development*. New Brunswick, NJ: Rutgers University Press, 2020. https://doi.org/10.2307/j.ctvscxrd5.

———. "Reparation for a Violent Boyhood: Pedagogies of Mourning in Shane Meadow's This Is England." *Pedagogy, Culture and Society* 25, no. 3 (2017): 315–325. https://doi.org/10.1080/14681366.2016.1255244.

Foucault, Michel, et al. *The History of Sexuality*, 1st American ed. Social Theory, 2nd ed. New York: Pantheon, 1978.

Georgis, Dina. "The Aesthetic Archive and Lamia Joreige's Objects of War." *Canadian Network for Psychoanalysis & Culture: The Freudian Legacy Today* (2015): 46–61. https://cnpcrcpc.com/cnpc-1-the-freudian-legacy-today-2015/.

———. *The Better Story: Queer Affects from the Middle East*. Albany: State University of New York Press, 2013.

———. "Discarded Histories and Queer Affects in Anne Carson's Autobiography of Red." *Studies in Gender and Sexuality* 15, no. 2 (2014): 154–166. https://doi.org/10.1080/15240657.2014.911054.

———. "What Does the Tree Remember? The Politics of Telling Stories." *Topia*, no. 25 (Spring 2011): 222.

Gilbert, Jen. "Risking a Relation: Sex Education and Adolescent Development." *Sex Education* 7, no. 1 (2007): 47–61. https://doi.org/10.1080/14681810601134736.

Hsu, Hsuan L. "Mimicry, Spatial Captation, and Feng Shui in Han Ong's Fixer Chao." *Modern Fiction Studies* 52, no. 3 (October 4, 2006): 675–704. https://doi.org/10.1353/mfs.2006.0065.

Isaac, Allan Punzalan. *American Tropics: Articulating Filipino America*. Critical American Studies Series. Minneapolis: University of Minnesota Press, 2006.

Klein, Melanie. *Love, Guilt, and Reparation, and Other Works, 1921–1945*. London: Hogarth, 1975.

———. "The Psychoanalytic Play Technique*." *American Journal of Orthopsychiatry* 25, no. 2 (1955): 223–237. https://doi.org/10.1111/j.1939-0025.1955.tb00131.x.

Muñoz, José Esteban. *Cruising Utopia: The Then and There of Queer Futurity*. Sexual Cultures. New York: New York University Press, 2009.

Parreñas, Rhacel Salazar. "'White Trash' Meets the 'Little Brown Monkeys': The Taxi Dance Hall as a Site of Interracial and Gender Alliances between White Working Class Women and Filipino Immigrant Men in the 1920s and 30s." *Amerasia Journal* 24, no. 2 (January 1, 1998): 115–134. https://doi.org/10.17953/amer.24.2.760h5w08 630ql643.

Perillo, J. Lorenzo. "'If I Was Not in Prison, I Would Not Be Famous': Discipline, Choreography, and Mimicry in the Philippines." *Theatre Journal* 63, no. 4 (2011): 607–621.

Stockton, Kathryn Bond. *The Queer Child, or Growing Sideways in the Twentieth Century*. Series Q. Durham, NC: Duke University Press, 2009.

Sugg, Katherine. *Gender and Allegory in Transamerican Fiction and Performance*, 1st ed. New York: Palgrave Macmillan, 2008.

Winnicott, D. W. *Playing and Reality*. New York: Basic, 1971.

"I Will Always Love You"

Queer Filipino Performances of Blackness,
Death, and Return

THEA QUIRAY TAGLE

ike Barthes's punctum, these queer performances haunt me, taunt me,
ask me to write them into posterity, like angry ghosts calling beyond the
grave. No wonder, as their contents are haunting. Between 2007 and 2012,
a rash of viral videos on YouTube emerged from the Philippines: all featured
amateur queer, *bakla,* or trans performers lip-synching and dancing to hits by
Michael Jackson, Whitney Houston, and other American pop singers—with
a twist. Diverging from the music video or live concert choreography of the
originals, the Filipino performers in these videos spectacularly transform over
the course of the song, from flashy divas into the walking undead. Stranger
still, these goth covers from the Philippines predate the deaths of Houston and
Jackson by two years or more, portending these legends' tragic ends. Haunted
by these apparitions years after their first appearance, I ask: Why meld
Blackness with monstrosity in these queer Filipino performance scenes? What
connections remain between ways of living and dying in the Philippines
and United States? Finally, what modes of survival amid and among the
dead do these seemingly throw-away entertainments help us imagine?

The so-called *Filipino aswang lip-sync* is the most unusual of these videos,
though it begins innocently enough: a young person (perhaps a drag queen or
bakla performer) dressed like Wednesday Addams from *The Addams Family*
is lip-syncing to Whitney Houston's hit song "I Will Always Love You."[1] According to the YouTube's caption, this performance occurred in May 2010 in
Malabon City, a municipality of Metro Manila, for the annual Fiesta Sulucan
Gaya-Gaya Puto Maya competition.[2] "Gaya-gaya puto maya" is a colloquial
Tagalog phrase for "copycat," a fitting phrase for this lip-sync and cover song
competition, yet for the "aswang lip-sync," it was the performer's failure to be
loyal to the original—or to Whitney Houston's cover of Dolly Parton's original,
to be more exact—that was its precondition for success. As the chorus crescen-
dos, the goth-styled girl begins to transform into a monstrous being: as the
sound glitches abruptly, the audience hears a high-pitched scream and batlike
noises as she begins to flap her arms like wings. Breaking momentarily from
singing to screech, wail, and writhe on the stage, the girl transitions into a

manananggal, one of a class of folkloric monsters in the Philippines known as *aswang* that "incorporate aspects of five creatures: witch, self-segmenting viscera sucker, were-beast, bloodsucker, and corpse eater."[3] The manananggal menaces the audience and sends children screaming in terror, before the performance climaxes with the figure transforming once again, to birth from the seeming void of its black dress two "children." Two mechanized white dolls crawl onstage and emit a cry of "Mama!," a sound culled from *The Poltergeist* (1982) intercut over the song's final notes. Since its YouTube debut in 2010, this absurd performance's power to turn an already cinematic song into an even more excessive spectacle has led to its virality and its being celebrated as a truly Filipino cultural production, or "Filipino *talaga.*"

As the live audience in Malabon City responded that night, so too do we—globally gazing, far-removed online voyeurs—continue to experience pleasure, discomfort, and shock at this scene, not for its verisimilitude to Houston's performance of "I Will Always Love You" in *The Bodyguard* (1992) but for its cultural uncanniness. Yet this is not the first such instance of the Filipino uncanny. Across times and spaces, through their perfected American accents and gestures, Filipino performers embody the hierarchies between the Philippine urban and the rural, and between the United States and the Philippines—even as their performances contain within them destabilizing possibilities. Like other appearance of the Filipino uncanny, I contend that the Filipino aswang lip-sync is a gestural and sonic act of witness to the palimpsestic violences informing the contemporary conditions of life and death in the Philippines: from U.S. military and political intervention to the labor exportation of Filipina women across the globe, to the Philippine president's ongoing War on Drugs. Reading queerly, I attend to the appropriated Filipino myth and the stolen Black woman's voice deployed in this viral performance of "I Will Always Love You," and the possibilities contained therein. Ultimately, I am interested in the ways that the monstrous drag of the aswang lip-sync is productive of what scholar, activist, and filmmaker Che Gossett and artist Juliana Huxtable call "temporary fabulous zones."[4] Through a process of "underworlding," this monstrous performance is one that creates, momentarily or ephemerally, "parallel spaces and sustaining underworlds beneath the world of the status quo" that allow Filipino peoples to resurrect themselves and others after materialized (and not simply metaphorized) violence and death.[5]

The Failed Mimicry and Temporal Drag of the Manananggal

That this performance was staged in the Philippines nearly renders banal the performer's choice of an American pop single since, in the global imaginary, the Filipino entertainer is notable only for being an exemplary mimic of American musical cultures: Journey's replacement lead singer Arnel Pineda, Bruno Mars, and *Glee*'s Jake Zyrus and Darren Criss are only several high-profile examples from the 2010s. Cultural studies scholars Christine Balance and Karen Tongson have historicized this phenomenon, writing of the exceptional status of Filipino karaoke and cover band singers, both before and after the official American colonization of the Philippines. Tongson uses her family's history as touring musicians as evidence for the ways that Filipino cover bands in Tokyo and Hong Kong soothed white European and American homesickness with a serving of colonial nostalgia in their renditions of American jazz and pop standards.[6] Within the Philippine archipelago, the feminized singer's affective labor also serves to comfort, whether she is performing American torch ballads or the Philippines' homegrown *kundimans*. Balance argues that Imelda Marcos's rendition of "Dahil Sa Iyo," sung to President Lyndon B. Johnson, functioned as a "romanticized musical urtext that performed the Philippines's dependence on the United States" during the Cold War, to reaffirm the policies of benevolent assimilation through song.[7]

Yet the form and content of the aswang lip-sync troubles this genealogy of the Filipino performing body as mimic par excellence, even as it initially appears to be more of the same. If the Filipino singer is exceptional because of her nuanced practice of *palabas*, a performative process and artistic practice based on "concealing the device of drama," the aswang lip-sync instead presents us a drag performance that has intentionally failed to pass.[8] As is common to the genre of drag, the performer relies on a strategy of denaturalization rather than verisimilitude: refusing to merge seamlessly into another identity and maintain it for the duration, they continually and repeatedly transgress boundaries of race, gender, sexuality, nationality, and humanity itself over the course of the performance. Significantly, however, this performer uses a Black woman's voice to animate their monstrous transformation, letting Houston's song become the soundtrack for acts both destructive and reproductive of new life.

By calling the aswang lip-sync a drag or a queer performance, I am less interested in what makes it "drag" or "queer" from a U.S.-centric lens; while the performer's real or perceived bakla subjectivity matters, analyzing this performance through the frame of gender play is less productive an entry point. Instead, drawing from Elizabeth Freeman, I argue that this performance is one of "temporal drag," where the transformation of young girl into a manananggal enacts a "counter-genealogical practice of archiving culture's throwaway objects, including the outmoded masculinities and femininities from which usable pasts may be extracted."[9] The uncanny appearance of the manananggal "drags" not only because the monster is out of place (it is on stage instead of in the shadows; it appears in the city rather than in the countryside) but also because it is out of time: that is to say, its apparition calls forth palimpsestic histories of Indigenous and Black genocide occurring on both sides of the Pacific Ocean that most would prefer buried or forgotten. This performance arrests because, with the sight and sound of the manananggal before us, viewers are confronted with the racialized and gendered surplus of modernity. It is the excess that survives despite all attempts to extinguish it, to extinguish *her.*

As Freeman reminds us, "some bodies register on their very surfaces the co-presence of several historically-specific events, movements, and collective pleasures."[10] The transformation of this surface—from that of a beautiful woman into a fearsome manananggal—taps into the live audience's indigenous knowledge of the creature, passed down through oral tradition and gossip, or apprehended in regional news or popular Philippine horror films. This indigenous knowledge is sexualized as well as gendered: of all the aswang, the manananggal is unique for its presentation as "an attractive woman by day, buxom, long haired, and light-complexioned" and its nocturnal ability to "discard its lower body from the waist down [to fly] in search of human prey."[11] Its prey is also feminized—manananggal hunt pregnant women, by piercing women's bellies with their long, threadlike tongues to suck out the fetus.[12] Stories of the manananggal in the Philippines were first documented in sixteenth-century colonial missionaries' accounts to discredit *babaylans*, or the Indigenous women who served as healers, midwives, and respected elders in their local communities.[13] In order to turn natives away from their "backwards" spiritual and medicinal practices and toward the guidance of the Catholic Church, Spanish missionaries sowed fear of the babaylan by casting her as a sexualized threat to others' husbands and children, and ultimately as a menace to the entire social order. The babaylans' destruction at the hands of colonial emissaries was not only discursive but was part of a three hundred-years-long campaign of sexual violence, mass genocide, and land expropriation that did not cease but merely changed hands with the Philippine archipelago's conquest by the United States.

As Bliss Cua Lim argues, contemporary manananggal sightings are attempts to work through forms of economic and bodily violence being experienced by the nation in its present state; manananggal apparitions are symptomatic of patriarchal anxieties over female labor migration and rural-to-urban labor flows brought about by the global demand for flexible, exploitable workers from Third World nations like the Philippines.[14] As Philippine citizens have migrated internationally to work as nannies, nurses, and other exploited laborers, so too has the manananggal gone global; sighting the manananggal across the Pacific is thus to bear witness to the exploitation and devaluation of feminized Filipino affective, reproductive, and productive labor across geographic spaces and scales. With help from its viral dissemination in this YouTube video, the manananggal queerly resurfaces subaltern narratives of life and death under regimes of terror no longer containable to the Philippine state.

For the local crowd at the *barrio fiesta*'s annual lip-sync contest, the monster's appearance might register quite differently than it does for global audiences encountering the spectacle online. The monster's ghostly white face, wild hair, and its evil undead babies have been (mis)read by foreign viewers as other Asian horror figures, such as the Japanese vengeance spirit *Onryō* or the Malaysian spirit *kuntilanak,* a vampiric spirit of a pregnant woman. This failure of sight as a productive one, however, as substituting another Asian demon's unholy attendance at a local barrio fiesta is to be reminded of the fate of Filipina women preyed upon by and in other Asian nations—of the disappearance of Filipina "comfort women" trafficked during Japan's occupation of the islands during World War II, or the death sentence cast upon "unruly" domestic worker Flor Contemplacion by the Singaporean government in 1995.[15] Reading across generic borders of Asian horror figures bridges the sociospatial distance between the Philippines and other Asian nations, revealing how the Philippine state works as co-conspirator to the vampiric drainage of Filipina lives and labor. In mistaking the manananggal for another Asian monster, one uncovers the sites throughout Asia where Filipina women go to live and, sometimes, to horrifically die.

Sounds of Black Mo'nin': Whitney Houston's Voice as Punctum

While the aswang lip-sync works partially because of its visual recall of the manananggal, its most powerful form of temporal drag registers through the grain of the singer's voice: Whitney Houston's 1992 rendition of Dolly Parton's 1974 track "I Will Always Love You." When it first premiered, Houston's cover was praised for "transforming a plaintive country ballad into a towering pop-gospel assertion of lasting devotion to a departing lover," by appropriating a tune from a lily-white genre and modifying it with vocal stylings drawn from Black Southern gospel music. The song accompanied Houston's starring role in *The Bodyguard*, where it served as anthem for Houston's character, a Black femme pop singer being stalked by an unhinged fan and who ultimately falls in love with the white bodyguard (Kevin Costner) assigned to protect her. At the film's climax, the bodyguard nearly loses his life protecting Houston, and viewers are conditioned to understand his actions as driven by selfless love despite the wage economics underwriting this exchange—Costner is Houston's employee, after all. For the romance to ring true, viewers must forget that the bodyguard's "love" is paid for and ends with his contract's expiration; the repeated refrain of "I Will Always Love You," recurrent at key moments in the film, performs this ideological work of forgetting by rerouting Houston's debt of life to Costner as eternal love.

Even as the film and its musical soundtrack labor so that we forget, outside the cinematic frame we must remember the woman behind the character, the person behind the voice. As we know in hindsight, the physical and metaphorical shield of whiteness that was supposed to protect Whitney Houston in the real world failed her; watching the singer who loves in perpetuity stings in the wake of Houston's tragic death in 2012, two years after the aswang lip-sync first appeared online. Houston's death from drug overdose, from domestic violence, and from a parasitic media industrial complex that profited from her televised downfall is exceptional but also endemic within a capitalist economy that preys on Black life and profits from Black death. The white savior narrative of a "bodyguard" who will look after you if you acquiesce and submit to his benevolent guidance has been repeatedly revealed as a farce, with those who proclaim their "love" for the state discarded once they are no longer of value. To hear Houston's voice from beyond the grave in the aswang lip-sync is to hear what Fred Moten calls "black mo'nin'," an utterance that breaks through the spectacle and that gestures elsewhere and otherwise to a place more proximate to the Real.[16] Houston's voice breaks through the fourth wall, or all walls, allowing us to hear the sounds of endurance and of despair within global regimes of racialized, gendered, and classed violence that seek to end the lives of Black women, Indigenous women, bakla, queer, and trans folk in the United States, in the Philippines, and around the world.

Even before the goth girl transforms into the manananggal, I am stirred by the sound of Whitney's voice pouring forth from this body. I know that I am not the only one so moved, as the sonic presence of Houston's "I Will Always Love You" undeniably animates this overwrought drag scene into something extraordinary. Being "Filipino talaga," this performance appears uncanny, but perhaps it is more than a replay of the same old love song—in its promise to "always love you," the manananggal of the aswang lip-sync directs its love elsewhere than to a white bodyguard, and in doing so generates a different vision of the world.

The ending of the aswang lip-sync, you'll recall, is of her improbably birthing two children, in an inversion of the manananggal myth that constructs it as a fetus-eater. This monstrous birth, if it remained true to the source storyline of The Bodyguard, would serve as a cautionary tale for those who confuse debt for true love: as Houston perpetually sings to a man who has already left her, so too must the babies born from this manananggal's dead-end love be nothing but "future dead persons," the damaged products of never-ending cycles of violence.[17] This cynical reading would be a realist one, as poor, queered, and feminized Filipinos who continue to profess their loyalty and love for the Philippine state are consistently met with death: by 2018, Philippine president Rodrigo Duterte's War on Drugs had claimed over twenty thousand lives, and as of 2020, the discarding of wasted populations by extrajudicial militias continues unabated, despite Pulitzer Prize–winning photojournalistic coverage and widespread international exposure.[18] The Philippine president justifies these killings under the cover of national security and the protection of innocent youth; his discourse mirrors the vampiric and genocidal logics of the United States' twinned War on Drugs and War on Terror. It is routine to look away from the plight of these "future dead persons" with no hope within or outside the Philippines, to fail to witness or to simply see.

To imagine otherwise, however—to imagine that the manananggal directs her affection not to an abandoning lover but to her children instead—proposes we radically rethink the terms of life and death. What if the manananggal serenades her (un)dead children with Houston's song? Singing in the keys of "black mo'nin'," this voice uncovers not only "the hidden transcript of repressed knowledge of alienation" but also contains "the reservoir of a certain knowledge of freedom, a counter-inscription anticipatory of the power/discipline that it overwrites and the life-situation against which it prescribes."[19] As the affective power of Houston's voice will always exceed the limitations placed upon it by scriptwriters and media moguls keen to exploit, so too does this manananggal cast off the colonial discourses marking her as "savage" and "non-reproductive" and performs otherwise, creating alternative forms of life in the process. I believe that this act of queer (re)generation and redirection offers inspiration for all of us brown and queer folks to transform our collective monstrosity, to live and love in otherworlds and underworlds, in order to survive among and beyond death.

NOTES

1. Following queer of color theorists such as Roderick Ferguson and Filipino American studies scholars including Martin Manalansan on the problematics of claiming and naming subjects' genders and sexualities, I want to be clear that I do not presume that the performer of the aswang lip-sync self-identifies as *bakla*; rather, I understand that mainstream Filipino audiences in the late twentieth and early twenty-first centuries would apprehend this performer's gender and sexual identity as *bakla* for their participation in such a *barrio fiesta* drag contest.

2. Alphabeta2, "Creepy Lip Sync Contestant Totally WTF! (Philippines)," YouTube video, May 10, 2010, https://youtu.be/ri5-uR8-3AE.

3. Bliss Cu Lim, *Translating Time: Cinema, the Fantastic, and Temporal Critique* (Durham, NC: Duke University Press, 2009), 97.

4. Che Gossett and Juliana Hutaxtable, "Existing in the World: Blackness at the Edge of Trans Visibility," in *Trap Door: Trans Cultural Politics and the Politics of Visibility*,

edited by Reina Gossett, Eric A. Stanley, and Johanna Burton (Cambridge, MA: MIT Press, 2017), 52.

5. Ibid.

6. Karen Tongson, *Why Karen Carpenter Matters* (Austin, TX: University of Texas Press, 2019), 2–3.

7. Christine Bacareza Balance, "*Dahil Sa Iyo*: The Performative Power of Imelda's Song," *Women and Performance: A Journal of Feminist Theory* 20, no. 2 (2010): 130–131.

8. Ibid., 125.

9. Elizabeth Freeman, *Time Binds: Queer Temporalities, Queer Histories* (Durham, NC: Duke University Press, 2010), xxiii.

10. Elizabeth Freeman, "Packing History, Count(er)ing Generations," *New Literary History* 31, no. 4 (Autumn 2000): 720.

11. Lim, *Translating Time*, 99.

12. Ibid., 97.

13. Katrin De Guia, *Kapwa: The Self in the Other* (Pasig City: Anvil, 2005), 46.

14. Lim, *Translating Time*, 129.

15. Robyn M. Rodriguez, "Migrant Heroes: Nationalism, Citizenship, and the Politics of Filipino Migrant Labor," *Citizenship Studies* 6, no. 3 (2002): 341–356.

16. Fred Moten, *In the Break: The Aesthetics of the Black Radical Tradition* (Minnesota: University of Minneapolis Press, 2003), 210.

17. Carla Freccero, quoted in Carolyn Dinshaw et al., "Theorizing Queer Temporalities: A Roundtable Discussion," *GLQ: A Journal of Gay and Lesbian Studies* 13, no. 2–3 (2007): 184.

18. Antony Lowenstein, "Only the Law Can Stop Duterte's Murderous War on Drugs," *Foreign Policy*, February 26, 2018, http://foreignpolicy.com/2018/02/26/only-the-law-can-stop-dutertes-murderous-war-on-drugs/.

19. Moten, *In the Break*, 227.

BIBLIOGRAPHY

Alphabeta2. "Creepy Lip Sync Contestant Totally WTF! (Philippines)." YouTube Video, May 10, 2010. https://youtu.be/ri5-uR8-3AE.

Balance, Christine Bacareza. "*Dahil Sa Iyo*: The Performative Power of Imelda's Song." *Women and Performance: A Journal of Feminist Theory* 20, no. 2 (2010): 119–140.

De Guia, Katrin. *Kapwa: The Self in the Other*. Pasig City: Anvil, 2005.

Dinshaw, Carolyn, et al. "Theorizing Queer Temporalities: A Roundtable Discussion." *GLQ: A Journal of Gay and Lesbian Studies* 13, no. 2–3 (2007): 177–195.

Freeman, Elizabeth. "Packing History, Count(er)ing Generations." *New Literary History* 31, no. 4 (Autumn 2000): 727–744.

———. *Time Binds: Queer Temporalities, Queer Histories*. Durham, NC: Duke University Press, 2010.

Gossett, Che, and Juliana Hutaxtable. "Existing in the World: Blackness at the Edge of Trans Visibility." In *Trap Door: Trans Cultural Politics and the Politics of Visibility*, edited by Reina Gossett, Eric A. Stanley, and Johanna Burton, 39–55. Cambridge, MA: MIT Press, 2017.

Lim, Bliss Cua. *Translating Time: Cinema, the Fantastic, and Temporal Critique*. Durham, NC: Duke University Press, 2009.

Lowenstein, Antony. "Only the Law Can Stop Duterte's Murderous War on Drugs." *Foreign Policy,* February 26, 2018. http://foreignpolicy.com/2018/02/26/only-the-law-can-stop-dutertes-murderous-war-on-drugs/.

Moten, Fred. *In the Break: The Aesthetics of the Black Radical Tradition.* Minnesota: University of Minneapolis Press, 2003.

Rodriguez, Robyn M. "Migrant Heroes: Nationalism, Citizenship, and the Politics of Filipino Migrant Labor." *Citizenship Studies* 6, no. 3 (2002): 341–356.

Tongson, Karen. *Why Karen Carpenter Matters.* Austin: University of Texas Press, 2019.

The Opposite of Performance

M. Butterfly *in 2017*

I n the 2017 revival version of *M. Butterfly,* Rene Gallimard, the hapless French diplomat, visits the opera singer Song Liling's apartment under slight duress. Having initially thought Song to be a woman, he realizes, upon seeing Song perform in a Chinese opera in a local theatre, that he "made a mistake," and rather than being about to "plow an exotic Chinese babe," he has merely "made a friend" of "Monsieur Song."[1] He arrives at the apartment planning to give Song "a final word. A cursory farewell." Yet when Song appears in her apartment, she is dressed not in the "androgynous Mao suit" he last saw her in, but instead in a "prerevolutionary qipao," standing "like Anna May Wong" in the doorway.

> Gallimard: Is this some sort of performance?
> Song: Quite the opposite.
> Gallimard: But—
> Song: Most of my life is a performance. Except onstage, and here. Within the walls of my flat. Alone. Most of the time. And now, with you.
> Gallimard: I'm afraid I don't understand.
> Song: But you do. All along, you have known. From the first time you called me "mademoiselle."[2]

Song proceeds to reveal to him that his initial, seeming misrecognition of her as a woman was in fact correct; her parents, she confesses, in need of a legal heir and having only had daughters, decided upon Song's birth to pretend she was a boy. Gallimard remains confused: "So you're telling me that you are . . . ?" She finishes the sentence: "A woman. What you see onstage is who I really am."[3]

If Asian American studies can be said to have a canon, *M. Butterfly* is on it. Debuting to wide acclaim on Broadway in 1988, the play remains the only one written by an Asian American to win a Tony for Best Play; B. D. Wong, who originated the role of Song Liling, remains the only Asian

American actor to win a Tony for Best Actor. Throughout its long career as an object of study, *M. Butterfly* has primarily been read through, and for, its deconstructing, alienating tendencies. David Henry Hwang's insistence that the play is "not a docudrama," combined with the play's use of irony and alienation, have led critics to take Hwang at his word and read the play for the way that it unsettles the audience's understanding of reality as shaped by nationalist, gendered, and raced discourses. In other words, Asian American critics have consistently read *M. Butterfly* for the ways in which it disturbs audience's notions of essential racial and gender identities, arguing that in doing so, *M. Butterfly* forces audiences to reconsider their own investments in whiteness and heterosexuality as codependent structures.[4]

The 2017 revival, however, is interested not so much in performance but in its opposite, coded throughout the play as truth, authenticity, and love. Where the original shadowed Gallimard and Song's relationship in ambiguity, the revival, in its promotional materials and in the rewritten script itself, invests heavily in biographical and biological truths—information taken from the "real" subjects of the play, Bernard Boursicot and his lover Shi Pei Pu—as a scaffold to restructure the play as a cathartic romance rather than an alienating and highly symbolic drama. In particular, both Julie Taymor, the revival's director, and Hwang himself discursively code this return to the bio—graphical and logical—as part of a broader social trend toward knowledge and acceptance of gender fluidity, articulated alongside a renewed investment in truth and authenticity in the stead of relativism and irony. These investments are embodied on the one hand in the play's shift from regarding Song as queer to discursively treating Song as trans*, and on the other in a recasting of whiteness as an abject particularity that has been heretofore ignored and now can (and must) return to the center of American national culture and sentiment.

The shifts in focus from Gallimard the pathetic to Gallimard the lovable, and from Song Liling, queer Oriental spectacle, to Song Liling, nonbinary or gender fluid individual, reveal both continuities and disjunctures between the two cultural eras in which the plays debuted: liberal multiculturalism, reaching its height in the late 1980s as *M. Butterfly* first came onto the scene, and what I call post-multiculturalism, which cohered most insistently in the aftermath of Donald Trump's election in 2016. The revival's stark distinctions from the original have the effect of revealing the crude workings of multiculturalism in the original: despite its declared commitments to alienation, which uses performance to interrupt and trouble consumption, the original *M. Butterfly* is revealed to be heavily invested in the spectacle of multicultural ethics, in which bad whiteness and Orientalism (acting as metonyms for racism) are vanquished and good, multicultural subjects, both Asian American and white, emerge triumphant. With respect to the way the play has been read within Asian American studies, the re-vival version lays bare the operations of the multicultural Asian American in the original, who functions to anxiously channel and ritually alleviate the white multicultural audience's racial guilt. And just as the Asian American body cohered both multicultural anxieties and ethical imperatives in the late 1980s, the trans* or gender nonbinary body similarly coheres a different set of both anxieties and imperatives in the post-multiculturalist moment, with both serving as stages upon which the normative can be stabilized.

M. Butterfly debuted in 1988, a year after the publication of Allan Bloom's notorious *The Closing of the American Mind,* and ran through 1990, with a film version premiering in 1993. Its popularity was entirely circum-scribed by the raging of the canon wars in American universities, in which, according to Jodi Melamed, neoconservatives and liberal multiculturalists alike consumed literature and culture as mediums for fulfilling normative political horizons.[5] Critics' reviews of *M. Butterfly*'s Broadway run revealed the ways in which the play was being contextualized within the imperative for minority culture to fulfill the dreams of multiculturalism for its audi-ence, in which "the author's racialized identity was of utmost importance because information retrieval for liberal multiculturalism was tied to ide-ologemes of representativeness, authenticity, and 'gaining voice.'"[6]

Whether or not the play was considered successful, critics framed this success in terms of the play's potential for advancing the audience's "under-standing" and empathy about issues that apparently preoccupied Hwang as a racially marked playwright. The *Christian Science Monitor* deemed *M. Butterfly* "the latest satire on East-West relations by the Chinese-American author of such plays as 'F.O.B.'"[7] The *U.S. News and World Report* identified Hwang as "one of a number of Asian American artists who . . . examine the psychological underpinnings of discrimination and wrestle with the tension between assimilation into mainstream America and the preservation of Old World traditions."[8] While these reviewers saw Hwang's play as successful, John Simon let forth a somewhat infamous invective against Hwang's eth-nicized failure in *New York Magazine,* arguing that Hwang was "obsessed" with personal resentments: "The son of affluent Chinese Americans, he has scores to settle with both America and the new China, the former for mak-ing him embarrassed about his ethnicity, the latter for repudiating his bour-geois status and Armani suits." "Unfortunately," Simon concluded, "pot-shots, sarcasms, double entendres . . . are no substitutes for making us care and leave with more understanding than we came with."[9]

These reviews mark the critics' endeavors to treat the play, despite its stated intentions, as a source of information retrieval and truth about Asian American experience—a somewhat strained reading given that although the play insistently collapses "Western" and "Eastern" identities, there are no actual Asian American characters in the actual play. The play's putative success or failure, as Simon's review reveals, hinged for these critics on its ability to make the audience "care" and "understand"—that is, on its ability as an artifact of minority culture to instruct white audiences on the importance of minority experience.

The lexicon with which critics introduce this reading is itself instructive. The use of the terms "Asian American" and "Chinese American" to delineate Hwang's ethnicity reveal the long reach of multiculturalism's ethical imperatives. "Asian American" is a term that began to be used in the late 1960s and 1970s by activists and scholars who sought to name a panethnic collectivity that could serve as the basis for organization. Here, however, the usage of "Asian American" connotes multicultural savvy while establishing the reviewer's ethical relationship to the play's themes. Hwang himself delineates this ethical usage in the afterword to the original *M. Butterfly*: "In general, by the way, we prefer the term 'Asian' to 'Oriental,' in the same way 'Black' is superior to 'Negro.' I use the term 'Oriental' specifically to denote an exotic or imperialistic view of the East."[10] By recognizing the play's "true" meaning as a reflection of Asian American experience, and by utilizing multicultural terms like "Asian American" and "Chinese American," reviewers signaled their distance from the Orientalism on display in the play itself and their capacity to be folded in to a knowing multicultural audience, whose empathy for Hwang's experiences marked them as ethical consumers of minority culture.

Given this context, it is possible to return to moments in the text that have served as key for Asian American readings' emphasis on deconstruction and performativity and read them anew for their capacity to be consumed as the fulfillment of a normative multicultural politics, rather than their capacity to unsettle such political horizons. David Eng reads Gallimard's application of white paint to his face before his on-stage suicide as a "hyperbolic illustration" of whiteness and heterosexuality as anxious performances that are always threatening to be undone.[11] Yet when considering a white audience primed by the invectives of multiculturalism to reject racism and embrace liberal pluralism, it is possible to read Gallimard's suicide in white face as, indeed, revealing the nonuniversality of whiteness, demarcating its particularities so that *bad* and nonethical whiteness can be ritually sacrificed and good whiteness can be assumed by the consuming audience. Gallimard's painting of his face might not serve to highlight to the audience the way all whiteness is performed and regulated; rather, his assumption of white face productively severs him from the white audience, as he definitively takes on the burden of racist whiteness and becomes the bad object that must be sacrificed in the name of multicultural modernity. Rather than alienating the audience, Gallimard's suicide can then function as a "ritual of identification and absolution," as Patricia Stuelke describes in a different multicultural context, one that "purges" the white audience of their racial complicity and creates a "space of innocence" from which they can perform their multicultural citizenship.[12]

For Karen Shimakawa, the apex of *M. Butterfly*'s deconstructive capacity is during the break between acts two and three, when Song, who has broken out of Gallimard's imaginative constraints to take over the narrative, changes costumes on stage from her Butterfly costume to his Armani suit, despite Gallimard's pleas to stop.[13] This moment is Song's ultimate moment of insubordination, as her on-stage transformation exceeds the audience's ability to fix her race and gender, revealing the unstable and contingent boundary between abject Oriental feminine object and agential white/ Western masculine subject. The extent to which Song's transformation registers as excessive and insubordinate, however, depends on the audience's investment in Song's abject figuration of the Butterfly in the first place. An audience that came to *M. Butterfly* hoping for Orientalist spectacle—for the *Madame Butterfly* of it all—might indeed be unsettled and alienated by the ease in which the abject object can transform into subject before their very eyes. Yet for a multicultural audience, this transformation does not exceed normative horizons but fulfills them: it is this very transformation of abject, historical minority object to multicultural modern subject that a multicultural audience came to see. Extratextually, this scene extends into "reality" through the Tony awards and the scenes of David Henry Hwang and B. D. Wong accepting their awards in front of adoring and applauding audiences; "Song," the Oriental, not only gets to shed his imprisoning Butterfly outfit in this transformation and put on the garb of the modern multicultural Asian American, but also gets to receive his just reward for his tribulations and triumphs. Thus, the original version's proclaimed commitment to deconstruction, alienation, and irony did not interrupt, and even functioned to disguise, the workings of what Roderick Ferguson calls "archontic power," which "worked through the 'recognition' of minoritized histories, cultures, and experiences and . . . used that 'recognition' to resecure its status."[14]

The 1988 version of *M. Butterfly* ends with an ambiguous tableau. Gallimard, having just painted his face white and committed suicide, lies dead, wearing the Butterfly costume. Song, in his Armani suit, stands over him, smoking. Two words, the stage directions tell us, leave his lips: "Butterfly? Butterfly?"[15] The play ends with these directions: "Smoke rises as the lights fade to black." In the 2017 version, however, Song's reaction—and the play's direction—is anything but ambiguous. Upon entering the stage to find Gallimard on the floor, Song runs to him, calling out, "Butterfly? Butterfly?" He collapses on top of Gallimard's body. A projected image of two butterflies, paths intertwining, "flutter[s] upwards from their bodies."[16] This projection also occurred earlier in the play, as Song performed the Chinese opera, "The Butterfly Lovers," for Gallimard in act 1; after describing the plot, in which a girl disguises herself as a boy but falls in love with a male classmate and embarks on a doomed romance with him, she asks, "Isn't that more beautiful than your Cio-Cio-San? [. . .] In mine, the girl and boy love as equals."[17] If, in the original, Gallimard's suicide enabled multicultural audiences to purge themselves of racist whiteness and assume a position of white innocence, Gallimard's revised suicide does different work for the post-multicultural audience of 2017. In moving affective registers from pity and disgust to empathy and grief, Gallimard's death now raises the post-multicultural possibility that, after humiliation, whiteness can again be a loved object.

In using the term "post-multicultural," I intend to delineate this racial structure of feeling from both the liberal multiculturalism and neoliberal multiculturalism that Jodi Melamed outlines, yet also to gesture toward the ways in which a "post-" structure does not mean a definitive end to what came before, but rather moves uneasily alongside, within, and in reaction to its precedents.[18] As the term implies, the post-multicultural is not merely an outright rejection of the lexicons of the multicultural but also a complex adaptation of them. Thus Donald Trump's rise to prominence in the presidential race and eventual election was cast, by him and his followers, in the terms of a return to a national citizenship that is always collapsed with whiteness. Yet rather than figure whiteness as an unspoken and unmarked universal, aggrieved white citizens emerged in the particular. In books like *Hillbilly Elegy* and *White Rage,* the rural white male subject cohered as both aggrieved and ungrieved: left out of multiculturalism's modernity, unprotected by the state, and yet forced to endlessly apologize for past racisms that had clearly been resolved, whiteness staked out its particularity as that which had been punished enough, and now, abject, asked only to be loved again, and to take its place among the other particularities as a rightful participant in the nation.[19]

Enter Clive Owen's Gallimard. The revival Gallimard is a different beast than the original: he is younger (aged down ten years, to a fairly unbelievable twenty-seven, according to the script, although Owen himself was fifty-three at the time of the premiere); he is never referred to as ugly or bad-looking, as his predecessor was constantly; and he drags with him all the cultural cache that Owen's longstanding reputation as "the thinking man's hunk" has accrued.[20] He is, in short, attractive, in a manner that neither John Lithgow nor Jeremy Irons embodied, and that the script bends over backward to assist. Rendering Gallimard lovable rather than pitiable effects the revision's transformation from alienating drama to cathartic romance. Butterfly and Gallimard's final embrace, as butterflies rise from their bodies, suggest that only in death, and only in Butterfly drag, can Song and

Gallimard love as equals. This final tableau displaces Song's transformation in the original. Rather than transform himself into degraded Asian feminine object in response to Song's metamorphosis into ascendant, masculine subject, this version of Gallimard relinquishes the position of subject to join Song as degraded fantasy object. That is, Gallimard's revised suicide is still a purging of bad, racist whiteness—this time not just for the audience but also for Gallimard himself. It also literalizes the expected results of such purging—whiteness's just rewards, that is, for reckoning with its own flaws. Where the multicultural Gallimard had to commit suicide in order for the audience to purge their own sins, the post-multicultural Gallimard has earned his happy ending and can return to us as both lovable and beloved.

If Gallimard comes to us as a loved and lovable object in 2017, what becomes of Song, his lover, and the multicultural Asian American subject I suggest subtends her performance? Like Gallimard, Song is transformed in the revival version of the play, although her revision is coded as a return: in rewriting the script, both Hwang and Taymor say, they returned to the biographical and archival material about Shi Pei Pu, Song's real life counterpart, to uncover a version of Song that was simultaneously more "contemporary," "nuanced," and "true"—and, importantly, "less gender-binary."[21] The result is the double, then triple, then quadruple take on Song's gender as the play unfolds: rather than focusing on one profound misrecognition, the play traffics in multiple (mis)recognitions, performances that are also the opposite of performance.

Given these multiplied early revelations about Song, her transformative intermission, discussed earlier, has been excised entirely from the revival version. Yet where the revival refuses the spectacularity of Song's transformation, it gives granular detail about her bodily transformation, and how she transformed her body during sex with Gallimard to disguise "its truth." In the original, Song is asked multiple times about how she and Gallimard had sex without Gallimard noticing the "little flap of flesh" that would reveal her deception.[22] Both times, under the pressure of interrogation, Song implies or says outright that she and Gallimard had anal sex. The answer isn't fully satisfactory, of course, as it elides the question at the heart of the specifics of Song and Gallimard's sex; as the Judge repeatedly asks, "Did Monsieur Gallimard know you were a man?" In response to clear requests for anatomical details that would clarify Gallimard's knowledge about Song's "true" sex—and thus, Gallimard's sexuality—Song emphasizes that such details are unimportant. As Song puts it in arguably the play's most famous line, the truth is that it didn't matter whether Gallimard encountered Song's penis: "I am an Oriental," he concludes, "and being an Oriental, I could never completely be a man."[23]

In the revival, however, Song gives a very different answer when pressed for details by the Judge. Initially, Song demurs, much like the original courtroom scene, but then under pressure confesses.

Judge: Did Monsieur Gallimard ever touch your genitals?

Song: You really want me to—?

Judge: Did the two of you have anal intercourse? Or what?

Song: No, he didn't put it up my ass!

Judge: Ugh, disgusting business. But at least we're finally getting somewhere.

Song: When we fucked, I pushed my balls up into a cavity between my legs, which left my scrotal sack dangling, like the lips of a vulva. I tucked my cock between my balls, held my legs together, and used cooking oil for lubrication. Apparently, when I put all that together, it must have felt like a very shallow pussy. Which is probably what he imagined of a delicate Chinese girl. Anyway, I never got any complaints. And every month, the butcher down the road supplied me with bloody rags, which I left in my trash for him to discover. Is that graphic enough for you?

Judge: I still don't . . . completely understand.

Song: I can't account for your lack of vision.[24]

This account is taken straight from reality, as it were; Shi Pei Pu was indeed forced to demonstrate his "unusual ability" to retract his testicles into his body as part of his and Bernard Boursicot's espionage trials.[25] Here, the revision effects multiple substitutions: spectacular performance for granular biology and biography, anal for a "shallow pussy" created by the manipulation of the scrotal sack, and multicultural Asian American for an individualized trans/nonbinary body.

These substitutions reveal how post-multiculturalism formulates itself as a response to and corrective for multiculturalism. Alana Lentin and Gavin Tilley, writing about the figure of multiculturalism in the rise of proto-fascist movements in Europe, observe that anti-multicultural narratives consolidate around calls for a return to certainties and values that multiculturalism weakened or relativized.[26] Thus is a return to biological certainty held up in response to multiculturalism's cultural relativism, which overemphasized performative identifications and deconstruction to the point where nothing was certain and no facts or moral hierarchies could be established. In the contemporary moment, Taylor and Hwang suggest, audiences are fatigued with narratives of performance and demand something more, or indeed, the opposite.

Song Liling's graphic description—and its attendant denial of anal sex—lacks the ideological richness of meaning attached to white-Asian anal sex.[27] It turns us firmly away from a contemplation of the racial and gendered scripts that inform, and often control, sexuality and sexual experience, toward a scrutiny of Song's individual body, and even more specifically toward

Shi Pei Pu's seemingly unusual anatomy and possibly nonbinary or trans*
status. By replacing one with the other, the revision figures both the problem
of race as a structure of desire and the problem of sexuality as a vector of
social alienation as structurally resolved and without potency. Having understood the structural, this substitution suggests, we can now turn to the
individual and attend to specificities, a move both more "real" and more
"nuanced" than the ideological critique staged by multiculturalism. Just as
whiteness, having reckoned with its particularity, can move into the next
stage of being "just" a mode of difference in a sea of differences, post-multiculturalism here figures the return to individualism as a triumph of progress
and a sign that the intellectual work has been done, and now the audience
can enjoy its just rewards.[28]

The narrative framework of post-multiculturalism, through which
Hwang and Taymor articulate their revisions of *M. Butterfly,* thus holds up
truth and authenticity as a break with and response to multiculturalism. Yet
as discussed earlier, multiculturalism, as a structure of consumption, was
itself never not engaged with ideologemes of authenticity. Even when minority texts themselves disavowed authenticity or realism as a formal structure,
they were nevertheless enmeshed in a market structure that consumed them
for their ability to both transmit information about minority subjects and
convey cultural capital onto their audience. In this way, we can see that the
move from spectacular performance to granular biography is actually a continuity, not a rupture. If Song's performative transformation functioned, as
I argued, to allow the audience to ritualize their knowingness as multicultural subjects who always knew the Butterfly story was pitiful, her biographical recitation of the "truth" of her sex with Gallimard similarly deploys a
trans* individual as a figure through which post-multicultural audiences
can ritualize and enunciate their progressive political affect—that is, their
"devastation" with the state of national politics today.[29]

Lentin and Titley point out that multiculturalism was not a true institutional regime but emerged only in unsettled fragments that never quite cohered into a hegemonic ethics. In the same way, the post-multiculturalism
sketched out in *M. Butterfly*'s revival is but one of many competing structures of racial and gendered feeling in the contemporary moment. The fact
that the revival was not a commercial success—the play closed almost two
months early, after a mere sixty-one regular performances, a stark contrast
to the original's two-year, 777-performance, Tony Award–winning run—
might imply that this version of post-multiculturalism is not compelling. Or
it might simply reveal that post-multiculturalism's cultural center of gravity
is distinct from multiculturalism's, which was still invested in elite institutions of cultural production. As the mainstream success of the 1988 *M. Butterfly* reveals, multiculturalism's central technology is the absorption of even

the most stringent of critiques, and even the most excessive of performances, for the purposes of generating literal and social capital for those who consume it. Multiculturalism feeds on the elaboration of cultural critique in order to channel the progressive and ethical impulses of consumers towards more consumption. The 2017 *M. Butterfly* reminds us that, whether it transforms on stage or in the wings, multiculturalism's next phase is something to keep our eye on.

NOTES

1. Hwang, *M. Butterfly* (2017), 24.
2. Ibid., 31.
3. Ibid., 31.
4. See Kondo, "M. Butterfly"; Eng, *Racial Castration*; Shimakawa, *National Abjection*.
5. Melamed, *Represent and Destroy*, 112.
6. Ibid., 114.
7. Quoted in Pao, "The Critic and the Butterfly," 6.
8. Ibid., 7.
9. Ibid., 10.
10. Hwang, *M. Butterfly* (1993), 94.
11. Eng, *Racial Castration*, 143, 165.
12. Stuelke, "The Reparative Politics of Central America Solidarity Movement Culture," 777.
13. Shimakawa, *National Abjection*, 123–28.
14. Ferguson, *The Reorder of Things*, 13.
15. Hwang, *M. Butterfly* (1993), 93.
16. Hwang, *M. Butterfly* (2017), 105.
17. Ibid., 22.
18. To use Raymond Williams' terms, the post-multicultural was emergent within cultural structure of feelings long before it became dominant. We see the post-multicultural emerge, for instance, within the backlash to multiculturalism in both the U.S. and Europe that followed September 11, 2001, wherein Muslims became the figure of "multiculturalism's pathology" and Islamophobia was coded, not as a rejection of culturalism as a principle, but rather a resistance to the specific excesses of Muslim populations, who took their cultural license "too far." The post-multicultural similarly comes into focus at the time of Barack Obama's election and throughout his tenure as President, as the insurgent Tea Party swept into office under the auspices of an aggrieved white polity that had been left out of Obama's multicultural visions. Most recently, and pressingly, the post-multicultural in the U.S. consolidated in 2016 with the election of Donald Trump. Williams, *Marxism and Literature*.
19. Anderson, *White Rage*; Vance, *Hillbilly Elegy*.
20. Owen's brand of brooding sex appeal is not a neat fit for Gallimard's character—as one review put it bluntly, "Hwang wrote Gallimard as a repressed and dweebish colonial [...] Owen does not evoke that quality." Even reviews that seemed impressed with his performance noted that it ran against type and counter to expectations: the *New York Times* exclaimed that Owen is "surprisingly convincing as someone who could never get a date in high school," while *The Guardian* noted that it was "tough to believe" that Owen, "a long-limbed pleasure," was ever unpopular. Brantley, "Review"; Soloski, "M. Butterfly Review."

21. Hwang, *M. Butterfly* (2017), vi; Fierberg, "Substance and Spectacle."
22. Hwang, *M. Butterfly* (1993), 55.
23. Ibid., 83.
24. Hwang, *M. Butterfly* (2017), 95.
25. Wadler, "The True Story of M. Butterfly; The Spy Who Fell in Love with a Shadow."
26. Lentin and Titley, *The Crises of Multiculturalism*.
27. See Eng, *Racial Castration*; Fung, "Looking for My Penis"; Nguyen, *A View from the Bottom*; Lim, *Brown Boys and Rice Queens*.
28. Think of a common reaction to 2017's surprise film hit *Call Me by Your Name*: a general sigh of relief that queer romance can be enjoyed as just romance, without forcing the audience to engage with a narrative of structural violence.
29. I want to clarify here that the post-multicultural figuration of trans* is not the only, nor even the hegemonic, invocation of trans* in the contemporary moment. There are, as Treva Ellison, Kai M. Green, Matt Richardson, and C. Riley Snorton lay out succinctly, any number of critical figurations of trans* that do not articulate alongside notions of biological truth, elaborate toward regimes of authenticity and individuality, or deploy the resolution of race and sexuality as their own grounds for emergence. For a longer account of how trans* came to be a preoccupying figure in post-multiculturalism, see Halberstam, *Trans**; Ellison et al., "We Got Issues: Toward a Black Trans*/Studies."

BIBLIOGRAPHY

Anderson, Carol. *White Rage: The Unspoken Truth of Our Racial Divide*. Reprint ed. New York: Bloomsbury USA, 2017.
Brantley, Ben. "Review: 'M. Butterfly' Returns to Broadway on Heavier Wings." *The New York Times*, October 26, 2017. https://www.nytimes.com/2017/10/26/theater/review-m-butterfly-david-henry-hwang-julie-taymor-broadway.html.
Ellison, Treva, Kai M. Green, Matt Richardson, and C. Riley Snorton. "We Got Issues: Toward a Black Trans*/Studies." *TSQ: Transgender Studies Quarterly* 4, no. 2 (May 1, 2017): 162–169.
Eng, David L. *Racial Castration: Managing Masculinity in Asian America*. Durham, NC: Duke University Press, 2001.
Ferguson, Roderick A. *The Reorder of Things: The University and Its Pedagogies of Minority Difference*. Minneapolis: University of Minnesota Press, 2012.
Fierberg, Ruthie. "Substance and Spectacle: How Julie Taymor Is Transforming M. Butterfly for Its First Broadway Revival." *Playbill*, October 2017.
Fung, Richard. "Looking for My Penis: The Eroticized Asian in Gay Video Porn." In *A Companion to Asian American Studies*, 235–253. New York: Wiley-Blackwell, 2004. https://onlinelibrary.wiley.com/doi/10.1002/9780470996928.ch15.
Halberstam, Jack. *Trans**: A Quick and Quirky Account of Gender Variability*. Oakland: University of California Press, 2018.
Hwang, David Henry. *M. Butterfly: Broadway Revival Edition*. New York: Plume. Accessed March 26, 2018. https://www.amazon.com/M-Butterfly-David-Henry-Hwang-ebook/dp/B071R1H2Y6/ref=tmm_kin_swatch_0?_encoding=UTF8&qid=1522093630&sr=8-3.
———. *M. Butterfly: With an Afterword by the Playwright*. New York: Plume, 1993.
Kondo, Dorinne K. "'M. Butterfly': Orientalism, Gender, and a Critique of Essentialist Identity." *Cultural Critique*, no. 16 (1990): 5–29. https://doi.org/10.2307/1354343.

Lentin, Alana, and Gavan Titley. *The Crises of Multiculturalism: Racism in a Neoliberal Age*. New York: Zed, 2011.

Lim, Eng-Beng. *Brown Boys and Rice Queens: Spellbinding Performance in the Asias*. New York: New York University Press, 2013.

Melamed, Jodi. *Represent and Destroy: Rationalizing Violence in the New Racial Capitalism*. Minneapolis: University of Minnesota Press, 2011.

Nguyen, Hoang Tan. *A View from the Bottom: Asian American Masculinity and Sexual Representation*. Durham, NC: Duke University Press Books, 2014.

Pao, Angela. "The Critic and the Butterfly: Sociocultural Contexts and the Reception of David Henry Hwang's M. Butterfly." *Amerasia Journal* 18, no. 3 (January 1, 1992): 1–16. https://doi.org/10.17953/amer.18.3.w380674743173pll.

Shimakawa, Karen. *National Abjection: The Asian American Body Onstage*. Durham, NC: Duke University Press, 2002.

Soloski, Alexis. "M. Butterfly Review—Clive Owen Impresses in Julie Taymor's Revision | Stage." *The Guardian*, October 26, 2017. https://www.theguardian.com/stage/2017/oct/26/m-butterfly-clive-owen-review.

Stuelke, Patricia. "The Reparative Politics of Central America Solidarity Movement Culture." *American Quarterly* 66, no. 3 (September 8, 2014): 767–790. https://doi.org/10.1353/aq.2014.0058.

Vance, J. D. *Hillbilly Elegy: A Memoir of a Family and Culture in Crisis*. New York: Harper, 2016.

Wadler, Joyce. "The True Story of M. Butterfly; The Spy Who Fell in Love with a Shadow." *New York Times Magazine*, August 15, 1993. https://www.nytimes.com/1993/08/15/magazine/the-true-story-of-m-butterfly-the-spy-who-fell-in-love-with-a-shadow.html.

Williams, Raymond. *Marxism and Literature*. Oxford: Oxford Paperbacks, 1978.

The Craft

QTBIPOC Tarot in Mariko Tamaki and Jillian Tamaki's Skim

XINE YAO

The Major Arcana represents life's universal archetypes: twenty-two cards numbered from The Fool (0) to The World (XXI). The Minor Arcana speaks to everyday life: fifty-six cards grouped into four suits—Wands, Cups, Pentacles, Swords—from ace to ten followed by the court cards Page, Knight, Queen, King. These seventy-eight cards constitute the Rider-Waite Tarot, the most popular deck in the Western occult tradition. Tarot as an object is in tension with tarot as practice: the deck's white heteronormative hierarchies contrast with tarot readings as a creative hermeneutics of self-knowledge. This generative dynamic between overdetermination and self-determination speaks to the prominence of tarot in the assemblage of occult practices reclaimed by contemporary queer feminist culture: practising tarot divination reflects critical agency while acknowledging the situatedness of subjecthood emergent through interlocking structures.[1] Queering the tarot, however, has meant not only queering the practice but the cards themselves. In 2008 the Portland-based Collective Tarot signaled a political shift challenging the traditions represented by the Rider-Waite: the cult status deck radically reimagined the cards' visuals and meanings to be inclusive of all peoples of color, genders, bodies, and abilities.[2] Currently out of print after three runs, this activist tarot opened the way for decks for and by queer and trans Black, Indigenous, and other peoples of color—popularly referred to as QTBIPOC tarot decks—that attend to their spiritual, affective, and communal needs.[3]

"Interests: Wicca, tarot cards, astrology (me = Aquarius = very unpredictable), philosophy," writes Kimberly Keiko "Skim" Cameron in her diary.[4] Mariko Tamaki and Jillian Tamaki's acclaimed graphic novel *Skim* explores the ways in which the occult occupies a vital role in queer subculture, particularly the disidentificatory tactics that anticipate the development of QTBIPOC tarot decks. Armored with her Goth identity, this queer mixed Japanese Canadian teen's jaded depression is a symptom of her disaffection from her parents' acrimonious divorce and her predominantly white all-girls Catholic high school in Toronto. Set in 1993, the narrative begins with Skim and fellow Goth Lisa as distanced spectators of a popular girl's breakup, which turns to tragedy with that unseen ex-boyfriend's suicide over his unrequited love for another boy. The school's performance of public mourning is unsettled by whispers about his queerness: presuming Skim would be affected by a stranger's death, adults and peers pathologize her Goth disaffection under the aegis of care, oblivious to Skim's own burgeoning queerness exploited by her teacher Ms. Archer. Skim's occult practices index her eventual heartbreak and fraying friendship with these two white women, Ms. Archer and Lisa, but also catalyze an unexpected connection with Katie, the once popular girl likewise pathologized by her ex's death.

Critics have commented on the Tamakis' nuanced representations of race and sexuality, reflecting what Hillary Chute has identified as a feminist tradition of destabilizing memory and identity in graphic narratives: as Monica Chiu phrases it, race and sexuality are "imagistically present but absent in prose," thus requiring a mode of reading attentive to silence and suggestion.[5] Unaddressed is how race and sexuality are not merely hidden but occulted—I suggest this figuration as a playful take on Roderick Ferguson's definition of queer of color critique as "an epistemological intervention" attentive to how the "transparency" of liberal ideology "*occludes* the intersecting saliency of race, gender, sexuality, and class in forming social practices" (emphasis added).[6] Like readers deciphering comics panels, Skim reads the panel-like cards of the classic Rider-Waite as her primary technology of self-making and self-care. Tarot mobilizes her affects, desires, and relations so she can process her psychic life, mediating her attachments and eventual detachments to Ms. Archer and Lisa. I argue Skim crafts a queer of color sensibility to and through the Western occult's traditions, with tarot key to her disaffection and eventual disidentification. Finally, I speculate about the ways in which the Asian American Tarot, conceived in 2016 by the Asian American Literary Review, might be read by someone like Skim.

The Sacred Is Not a Luxury

Despite the disenchantments of Western secularism, the Sacred endures.[7] In defiance of the colonial norms of modernity, M. Jacqui Alexander calls for transnational feminisms to acknowledge the importance of the Sacred: these cosmologies allow people to make their lived experiences intelligible to themselves through the tangibility of everyday praxis, affirming the link between embodiment and knowledge in ways irreducible to materiality. Taking these metaphysical systems seriously respects how Sacred practices engage personal and collective matrixes of history and embodiment toward healing, meaning-making, interdependence. Focusing her discussion on the Black diaspora, Alexander's theory in the flesh arises from her practice of

Vodou and Santería. She references Indigenous and Asian spiritual systems alongside African-based cosmologies: access to the Sacred emerge from the confluences of the aesthetic, secular, and everyday. Belief does not exclude criticality, nor does critique invalidate faith: "the spiritual is lived in the same locale in which hierarchies are socially invented and maintained," she states, elaborating how feminists and queers of color negotiate their spiritual lives with imaginative devotion attentive to apparatuses of power.[8] This relationship with the Sacred challenges the modern virtue of demystification, recalling disidentification, those subversive transformations of culture articulated by José Esteban Muñoz that are foundational to queer of color critique.

Tarot offers access to a symbolic grammar of universal human experience and self-knowledge. The cards were first designed for gambling in fifteenth-century Italy. In eighteenth-century Paris, tarot was reconceived as a medium for divination and became established in the Western occult by the nineteenth century. Its origins were deliberately obscured: practitioners fabricated traditions, falsified ascriptions, and invented lineages, understanding the codependence between mystery and hermeneutics. Occultists produced different tarot decks that generally retained the structure of the Major and Minor Arcana and relied upon a faux-medieval European aesthetic with Orientalist influences derived from Jewish mysticism and ancient Egypt. In 1909 the occultist Arthur Edward Waite collaborated with artist Pamela Colman Smith to design a fully illustrated tarot deck. Their deck, published by the Rider Company, was the first commercially available tarot pack in England, thereby standardizing the cards' imagery. U.S. Games Systems Inc. bought the publication rights in 1970 and continues to keep the deck on the market. In their history of tarot, Ronald Decker and Michael Dummett lament the lack of a "internally coherent and historically plausible" system that can explain tarot's chosen subjects, symbolism, and ordering.[9] From a disenchanted perspective, tarot's uneven strata of obfuscation and fraud invalidates a Sacred praxis for queers of color.

Tarot's appeal to queer of color spiritual practices comes from viewing its dubious history and false universality as potential for reappropriation rather than grounds for dismissal. From this angle, tarot is a dynamic cultural site for ways of reading and storytelling that inspires queers of color to remake that Western occult tradition in their own image. Describing her creation of Dust II Onyx, a "Melanated Tarot" designed to reflect the Black diaspora's complexity, Courtney Alexander writes of her choice to use tarot as a medium: "I felt conflicted about jumping into other African spiritual traditions within the diaspora to find myself. I didn't want to be appropriative."[10] These QTBIPOC decks are conceived as decolonial disidentificatory projects that revise the Rider-Waite archetypes for marginalized cosmologies. The Asian

American Tarot, for instance, acts as "an anti-racist hack" by offering a re-imagined Major Arcana meant to be incorporated into a traditional deck.[11] Adapting the logic of occult hermeneutics, the project's Kickstarter proclaims that this redesigned tarot works "to reveal the hidden contours of our Asian American emotional, psychic, and spiritual lives, as well as the systems of violence that bear down upon them."[12] Suppressed identities and histories can be reimagined as occulted: specialized knowledges as well as esoteric histories a practitioner can access through the therapeutic pleasures of the Sacred practice of reading for one's self and others.

Drawing Cards: Desire and Detachment in *Skim*

"Maybe she thought that's how people left parties in Canada. Asians first," recounts Skim about when she and a Vietnamese adoptee classmate were bullied by the white popular girls.[13] Eventually she tires of waiting for acceptance: "I decided I'd rather be alone in the dark."[14] In this moment featuring the narrative's only textual acknowledgment of race, Skim reappropriates her childhood association with darkness from when she was cast as the "Night Sky" in a production of *Our Town*, marking her as an outcast since there were no actual roles available.[15] As a teen in Catholic school, Skim has become an occult-practising Goth, expressing her antisocial embrace of this alienation. Although for queers of color the Goth subculture presents a model for disrupting norms of gender and sexuality, the aesthetic fascination with pallor reflects the subculture's whiteness—a racial dimension both epidermal and structural that is easier for East Asian Goths to navigate than Black or brown Goths.[16] Goth subculture's fixation with darkness allows for her ambivalent, negative feelings as affective coping and resistance against the performances of positivity imposed by those who marginalize her.[17] Disaffection, according to Martin F. Manalansan IV, operates as an affective and political composure in the face of gendered, racialized demands for emotional labor, "a form of strategic emotional flow combined with self possession that is part of quotidian survival and an economy of affect."[18] As a closeted, fat, mixed race Asian teen, Skim is justifiably jaded—a defensive mode of adolescent disaffection. For Skim, however, being Goth is not only about jadedness as dissent; her Sacred praxis of the occult centered upon her therapeutic use of the Rider-Waite Tarot.

The graphic novel tracks Skim's struggle to understand her affects and desires through spiritual practice. Lisa and Ms. Archer are introduced in relation to the occult. Lisa signs her cast with a pentacle.[19] Meanwhile, Ms. Archer's declaration that Skim has "the eyes of a fortune teller" galvanizes the teen's infatuation—a recognition of Skim's occult practices.[20] The graphic novel segues to the occult still-life of her altar that dominates the page:

her Rider-Waite deck is centered, with a Major Arcana card, The Sun, face up. Next to it is her note: "(Must be GIVEN to you or they don't work)."[21] Skim understands tarot's powers as facilitated by personal attachments; we are invited to read The Sun as signifying her deck, associated with the promise of joyful flourishing in contrast to her general feelings of estrangement from school and family.

Her tarot reading acts as a technology of self-knowledge, allowing her to interpret her relationships with both Ms. Archer and Lisa; on another level, her reading of cards draws attention to reading comics panels.[22] Overcome with anxiety about her illicit romance with Ms. Archer, she continually re-reads her fortune, during which Skim draws The Lovers as her "'self' card" five times, once reversed.[23] The Lovers is presented twice in the middle of the page, first upright and then reversed: the Rider-Waite depicts the heteronormative dyad of a white Adam and Eve with an angel overhead. The cards float in this blank space: their shape recalls the standard comics panel, while the tarot spread echoes the layout of panels. Skim's exegesis of tarot grammar is reminiscent of guides to understanding comics by theorists like Scott Mc-Cloud: the card itself symbolizes "love and relationships, new beginnings, new connections" while analyzing the visuals, "The Angel on the card = FATE."[24] The spatial position of the card is significant: "if you get this card reversed = upside down . . . it means a bad decision, an untrustworthy person, a state of imbalance."[25] Although ostensibly concerned about her crush, she speculates, "I have an untrustworthy person in my life (?Lisa?)."[26] This scene demonstrates her management of her complicated feelings about both white women through tarot's mutable meanings, reminding the reader of the careful attention needed to divine meaning. While for McCloud the gutter, the space between the panels, is "the magic and mystery" of comics, for Skim both the cards and the embodied process of reading are magic itself, every drawing of a card presenting new interpretive possibilities.[27] She resignifies the Rider-Waite's white heteronormative pairing to read the contours of her own life.

The ambiguity of The Lovers card upright and reversed speaks to the changes in her desire for Ms. Archer and her identification with Lisa. The obvious correlate of The Lovers is Ms. Archer, who embodies Skim's desire for the occult's queer potentiality; however, she acts as The Lovers reversed, willing to exploit her student's feelings. For Halloween, Ms. Archer dresses up as a fortune teller, masquerading as the practitioner Skim hopes to become. Skim obscures the details of their affair, ending that diary entry, "Technically nothing has happened."[28] In the following entry, Skim occults her emotions by quoting from her new Wiccan book: "It is that moment in our lives when we feel the Magic of the Universe coursing through us for the very first time, and we know beyond all real and imagined shadows that this calling to the mysteries is indeed there."[29] On the next page, like flipping a card, we are shown a wordless two-page spread of Skim and Ms. Archer kissing, a lesbian iteration of The Lovers. Skim associates her deck with Ms. Archer, the object of her lovesick divinations: her teacher's house has a sun-shaped mailbox akin to The Sun card into which Skim feeds her artwork as gifts.[30] Later, frustrated, she leaves her deck in the house and walks out. This act of distancing surrenders her technology of self-care, which she soon regrets after an unsettling dream: "I wish I had my tarot cards so I knew what it meant."[31] After departing from a terrible heterosexual double date, Skim decides to reclaim her Sacred practices and dissociate her queerness from Ms. Archer by leaving a note in the sun mailbox: "I want my TAROT CARDS back.—Skim."[32] As Ferguson remarks of Muñoz's concept, "to disidentify in no way means to discard."[33] With their return, Skim regains a measure of control over her heart rather than languishing after Ms. Archer, who has left the school.

The Lovers reversed marks Skim's souring friendship with Lisa. A questionable best friend who often belittles Skim, Lisa is a fellow jaded Goth; through her evolving occult practices, Skim articulates her detachment from Lisa, whose cynicism manifests as heteronormative cruelty. Crushing hard, Skim lists what she withholds from her friend, namely her queer feelings and her independence as an occult practitioner: "I feel like I am definitely a witch."[34] After Lisa's callous comment about suicide and Wicca, Skim confronts her friend, to which Lisa responds, "Fuck you. So now you're this all-powerful witch or something, and you know everything about Wicca?"[35] Undeterred, Skim pursues her own practice, tarot finally enabling her to recognize her ambivalence about their friendship. The Rider-Waite Lovers represent Lisa's toxic heteronormativity, reinforcing their Catholic school's repressiveness. Lisa slut-shames other girls, and when news emerges that the deceased John was gay, she delves into homophobia. For Lisa, queerness is pathological: laughing at John's ex-girlfriend Katie, assumed to have failed at her own suicide attempt, Lisa sneers, "[S]he will still be the girl whose boyfriend committed suicide because he was a fag."[36] While Skim silently nurses her broken heart, Lisa pressures her to join her on a double date with unremarkable white boys. Eventually, Lisa is preoccupied with an unseen boyfriend, living her own version of The Lovers.

The new beginnings and connections signified by The Lovers gesture to an unforeseen third possibility for cathexis as Skim detaches herself from her unhealthy relationships. Following Katie's accident, Goth outsider and popular girl are paired by teachers based on their broken arms; the girls end up supporting each other in the healing of their broken hearts. "So is it true you're a witch?" Katie asks, admiring Lisa's pentacle on Skim's cast.[37] After getting back her tarot, Skim critiques an overemphasis on the Death card as signifying change: "But almost all the cards = change," she muses as she bleaches her hair, unexpectedly resulting in shades of brown and red, not white.[38] "It's nice. It's like, kind of sunny," compliments Katie, an allusion linking Skim back to The Sun's salutary promise.[39] Skim helps Katie confront her hypocritical friends: together, they leave the school dance and walk into the night, their friendship symbolically confirmed when Katie asks Skim to sign her cast, which she does with a pentacle.[40] The enigmatic final pages suggest ambiguity about this new relationship: with two panels portraying Skim walking away from school and Lisa, the full page depicts overgrown plants with a head barely visible, adorned with a beret.[41] An attentive reader might recognize Katie's hat and the location as Skim's former meeting place with Ms. Archer seen from a new angle, Skim's perspective. We are invited to wonder at the queer potential of this visual symbolism, to divine the possibility of an aleatory configuration of The Lovers. The last page is blank save for an abandoned origami fortune teller, the future indeterminate.

QTBIPOC Tarot Divinations

The reimagined Major Arcana of the Asian American Tarot reflects the dimensions of the Asian diaspora: twenty-two cards running from Death (I) to The Devil (XXII), haunted by the addition of an unnumbered card, The Ghost. This QTBIPOC tarot project led by Mimi Khúc seeks to address the Asian American mental health crisis, the decks meant to be a resource at QTBIPOC and multicultural centers. Drawing upon her experiences with postpartum depression, Khúc articulates what Skim understands intuitively: tarot acts as "a resource for and a means to build new practices for reading the forces shaping our lives."[42]

We can try to divine the therapeutic possibilities if Skim had this disidentificatory intervention incorporated into her Sacred practice of tarot. Simi Kang's artwork for The Ghost mirrors the worlds of the living and the dead: the card invokes John as the specter of queerness that brings Skim and Katie together, a felt but absent presence. But perhaps most importantly for Skim, this iteration of The Lovers depicts two figures of ambiguous race and gender in an embrace framed by stars and flowers, holding a cloth below them with no angel overhead. According to Wo Chan's accompanying text, this represents "their shared traumas" and the processes of healing toward "a practice of love with no impulse to possess."[43] QTBIPOC tarot gives us the reassurance that neither readings nor events are ever fixed—and even the cards we are dealt can be transformed.

NOTES

1. For instance, *Autostraddle*, a website for queer women, femmes, and nonbinary people, features occult lifestyle columns, and the feminist website *Little Red Tarot* supports the series "Queering Tarot."

2. "The Collective Tarot: Round III," Kickstarter, May 8, 2012. https://www.kick starter.com/projects/1249459446/the-collective-tarot-round-iii.

3. Asali, "Tarot of the QTPOC: Deck Listing," Asali Earthwork, June 27, 2015.

4. Mariko Tamaki and Jillian Tamaki, *Skim* (Toronto: Groundwood, 2008), 7.

5. Hillary L. Chute, *Graphic Women : Life Narrative and Contemporary Comics* (New York: Columbia University Press, 2010); Monica Chiu, "A Moment Outside of Time: The Visual Life of Homosexuality and Race in Tamaki and Tamaki's Skim," in *Drawing New Color Lines: Transnational Asian American Graphic Narratives*, edited by Monica Chiu (Hong Kong: Hong Kong University Press, 2014), 29.

6. Roderick A. Ferguson, *Aberrations in Black: Toward a Queer of Color Critique*, Critical American Studies Series (Minnesota: University of Minnesota Press, 2004), 3, 4.

7. Jane Bennett, *The Enchantment of Modern Life* (Princeton, NJ: Princeton University Press, 2001).

8. M. Jacqui Alexander, *Pedagogies of Crossing: Meditations on Feminism, Sexual Politics, Memory, and the Sacred* (Durham, NC: Duke University Press, 2005), 310.

9. Ronald Decker and Michael Dummett, *A History of the Occult Tarot* (London: Duckworth Overlook, 2002), 315.

10. Courtney Alexander, "Statement," n.d.

11. "Asian American Tarot: A Mental Health Project," Kickstarter, July 19, 2016.

12. Ibid.

13. Tamaki and Tamaki, *Skim*, 86.

14. Ibid., 87.

15. Ibid., 48.

16. Lauren M. E. Goodlad and Michael Bibby, "Introduction," in *Goth: Undead Subculture*, edited by Lauren M. E. Goodlad and Michael Bibby (Durham, NC: Duke University Press, 2007), 25–26.

17. Michelle Miller, "'I Hate You Everything': Reading Adolescent Bad Feelings in Tamaki's Skim," *English Studies in Canada* 43, no. 1 (2017): 83–102.

18. Martin F. Manalansan IV, "Servicing the World: Flexible Filipinos and the Unsecured Life," in *Political Emotions*, edited by Janet Staiger, Ann Cvetkovich, and Ann Morris Reynolds (New York: Routledge, 2010), 217.

19. Tamaki and Tamaki, *Skim*, 9.

20. Ibid., 13.

21. Ibid., 14.

22. See Rita Felski, *Uses of Literature* (Malden: Blackwell, 2008) on reading and enchantment.

23. Tamaki and Tamaki, *Skim*, 59.

24. Ibid.

25. Ibid.

26. Ibid.

27. Scott McCloud, *Understanding Comics: The Invisible Art* (New York: Harper Perennial, 1994), 66.

28. Tamaki and Tamaki, *Skim*, 38.

29. Ibid., 39.

30. Ibid., 51.

31. Ibid., 79.

32. Ibid., 122.

33. Ferguson, *Aberrations in Black*, 5.

34. Tamaki and Tamaki, *Skim*, 28.

35. Ibid., 33.

36. Ibid., 97.

37. Ibid., 109.

38. Ibid., 126.

39. Ibid., 136.

40. Ibid.

41. Ibid., 142.

42. Mimi Khúc, "Decolonizing Mental Health with the Asian American Tarot," *Masq*, January 30, 2017. http://www.masqmag.com/blog/asian-american-tarot.

43. *Asian American Literary Review*, "Asian American Tarot: The Lovers card," 2017.

PART VII

Finding One's Way

Routes of Lives and Bodies

Loving Our Children, Finding Our Way

MARSHA AIZUMI

She was my daughter who liked girls, and so she came out as a lesbian at the age of fifteen. I was ashamed that I wasn't a better mother and was afraid for my child, but I accepted her sexual orientation, slowly realizing from an early age she had been telling me in subtle ways who she was. Flash-forward five years, and she hesitantly comes out to me a second time. She discovered the idea of gender identity and understood that she was assigned the wrong gender at birth. Despite what others thought, in her mind and in her heart, she was a boy. And so my husband and I took the next year to align Aiden to be the boy that he has always been.

Initially, Tad and I grieved for the loss of our daughter of twenty years and were even more fearful of her future. But our child was depressed, withdrawn, and suicidal. Instinctively, we felt if we didn't get this right, we would lose this child, and that prospect was not an option for us. Therefore, we stood by Aiden as he transitioned to be our son . . . most of the time listening to our hearts, but often just praying we weren't making a mistake.

Once Aiden was living as his true self, he blossomed. We knew that he was moving in the right direction and breathed a sigh of relief. Listening to our hearts and supporting our son brought hope and joy back into his life and ours. By no longer having to hide who he was, he could use that energy for something more meaningful. He volunteered in various places: The Trevor Project, his PFLAG chapter, and any opportunity that seemed to call to him.

Now feeling so much gratitude, I wanted to learn everything I could about being transgender. I signed up for lesbian, gay, bisexual, transgender, and queer (LGBTQ) events, conferences, and workshops. I researched on the Internet and bought books. When people asked me to share our story, I gradually began to do so. Then one morning I woke up and thought, *If this world is going to be safe for my son, then I have to find a way to be part of this change.* Not knowing what being "part of this change" meant, I began to find ways to show up and get involved. At a meeting one afternoon, someone introduced me as an activist. I turned to him and said, "Oh, no, I am not an activist, just a mother who loves her son." He didn't argue with me but smiled back knowingly. He saw my path before I saw it myself.

With every opportunity to learn more about this community that my son was a part of, I found myself drawn to vulnerably speaking about our journey. I also felt compelled to write a book about how we transitioned our family along with Aiden's transition. After consulting with Aiden and the family, I decided to risk sharing our story to others in print. We realized that once our book was published, there was no going back into the closet. *Two Spirits, One Heart* ended up being a bonding and healing experience for all of us. And our wish to help both our transgender community and our Asian Pacific Islander (API) community has been part of this experience as well. The 2nd edition of our book was released at the end of 2020.

As I went around the country and talked about our book, I met many wonderful people. I was asked to join the PFLAG National Board of Directors in 2011 and am still serving on this board nine years later. PFLAG is a national organization that supports, educates, and advocates for families, friends, and allies of LGBTQ individuals, as well as LGBTQ individuals themselves. PFLAG is one of the reasons our family has been able to navigate our journey to grow in love and acceptance. Another organization that has supported us is the National Queer Asian Pacific Islander Alliance (NQAPIA), which focuses on the Asian, Southeast Asian, South Asian, and Pacific Islander LGBTQ communities. I am so grateful for both of these organizations and their work.

When President Joe Biden created the Biden Foundation with one of their pillars being LGBTQ Equality. I am so honored to have served on their LGBTQ Advisory Council while it was active. I hope that I brought greater visibility and family acceptance for the API LGBTQ community through my voice.

When Aiden first came out, I felt so all alone. At the first PFLAG meetings I attended, I never saw a parent who looked like me and understood the cultural uniqueness of our API families. People weren't aware of how much shame, saving face, and honor played into our culture. Whereas Caucasian families value being an individual, Asian families value taking care of family, honoring family, and respecting our elders over individual achievements. There is also a language barrier for many API families, so how could they get support and resources when so much was in English? And a misconception that being LGBTQ was an American disease was often reinforced because wherever API families turned, they saw only faces that were non-Asian.

Three things seemed to converge to point me in a direction to all I am doing today. First, I met Harold and Ellen Kameya, parents of a gay daughter, who had been doing this work for twenty-five years. I talked to them about forming a PFLAG chapter focused on the API LGBTQ community. They supported me 100 percent. Next, because of the publication of *Two Spirits, One Heart*, I began touring the country to talk about our book. I met parents who yearned for a space and connection to other API parents who loved their queer and transgender children. And finally, I connected with the leaders of NQAPIA, who had a vision that API parents around the country could unite in support of their queer and transgender children.

With the help of the Kameyas and a few others, we formed a PFLAG satellite with the support of PFLAG Pasadena, the chapter I first attended. Our satellite program was located in the San Gabriel Valley, which is in Southern California and is heavily populated with API families. As a satellite program, we were able to build our leadership. One year later, we became the first PFLAG chapter focused on the API community through the efforts of Carol Mannion, our first chapter president. In May 2021, we celebrate nine years of providing a safe space for API LGBTQ families and eight years as a chapter. We are also so proud of bringing other forms of support like afternoon teas and family circles to families that need a more private way to get support or want to talk in a language other than English.

Traveling around the country gave me a chance meet more and more parents. At one of my events, I met Aya Yabe, who expressed these feelings: "Until I met several young Asian queer individuals at Marsha's book reading, I was the happy mother of a gay daughter, not realizing there were many families unable to accept their children's queerness. I want to change the perception of the public on LGBTQ individuals that makes them marginalized. My child and other LGBTQ individuals deserve to feel safe, respected, and loved for all of who they are." Today, Aya is leading our family acceptance work with Japan and supporting Japanese-speaking parents in the United States.

Through NQAPIA, we had our first API parent convening in 2012. Clara Lee, founder of the API Rainbow Parents (a program that is a part of the PFLAG New York City chapter) and one of the parents who participated in our first convening, shared with me recently, "To accept and love my transgender, bisexual son, unconditionally, I had to re-examine my own prejudice and value system. It was liberating to feel I could break out of my traditional Korean immigrant upbringing to see my son as a precious gift and source of courage to live my life bravely." Clara has also created a Korean American Rainbow Parents group, which has meet-ups in New York City; Washington, DC; and Los Angeles.

Our movement has grown thanks to the parents I have mentioned above and more parents who are bringing their passion for change and love of their children to this work. We have worked with NQAPIA to produce a one-sheet informational leaflet that has been translated into over twenty API languages. We have trained parents around the country to speak as part of NQAPIA's Family Acceptance Campaign. One of the parents we have trained to speak is Glenn Murakami, the father of two gay sons. Glenn says, "My journey started out with many questions and misconceptions. I was especially fearful knowing how hurtful religious institutions have been towards LGBTQ individuals. But the countless personal stories shared by brave parents, young people, and clergy have helped to open my heart, educate my mind, and manage my fear. I want to give back by sharing my journey of unconditionally loving both of my sons as I processed through my feelings, my faith and most of all my hope for their future."

Our Family Acceptance Campaign has taken us around the country. We have traveled the West Coast, the East Coast, and cities in between like New Orleans, Chicago, Houston, and Denver. We have taken our stories across the ocean to Korea, China, and Japan. We brought greater awareness, more resources, but most of all a sense that there are parents around the globe who love their queer and transgender children and are courageously willing to stand up for them.

Through NQAPIA and my work with Okaeri: A Nikkei LGBTQ Community, we have started to expand our work in the faith community, because we know that this work is so needed. In 2019, we worked with churches, temples, and organizations around the country to share our stories about the importance of inclusion and love in the faith community. One of the individuals who is helping us with this work is a Filipino father and ordained Southern Baptist minister. Pastor Danny Cortez has been speaking about his evolution of previously recommending LGBTQ individuals go through conversion therapy to now being a visible and loving advocate for the LGBTQ community, no longer advocating for conversion therapy. When his son Drew came out and told his family, "If there was a pill that could make me straight, I would take it," Danny replied, "If there was a pill that could make you straight, I would not want you to take it. You were made this way by God, and you are loved by him just as you are." Today, Drew is an out and proud gay man and was a leader at his college for LGBTQ rights. Pastor Danny has now started Estuary Space, a nonprofit to help churches who want to be more welcoming and LGBTQ individuals who struggle with reconciling their sexual orientation and/or gender identity with their faith.

One of the most powerful things I have seen is Pastor Danny standing up in front of an audience of hundreds and apologizing for his and the Church's judgment of LGBTQ individuals. Aiden was asked to leave the Church until he could come back not being LGBTQ, so every time I hear Pastor Danny's apology, I feel my heart healing just a little bit more from the painful rejection our family faced.

As parents continue to find ways to show up, connect, and march with pride for their children, we want our API LGBTQ community to know that we are standing here with you. You are not alone. Your parents are not alone. And regardless of where your parents are on this journey of love and acceptance, we can be your chosen family while your own family is finding their way.

I began this journey because I loved my son, but this love for Aiden has become a passion and commitment to the queer and transgender API community. I see that passion and commitment in the eyes of so many parents who are doing this work. This journey has shown us how much more strength, courage, and love we have, and what a gift our children have given us.

When I talk with parents around the country, I hear the same messages. Don't judge our children by who they love or how they identify. Look at the kind of person they have become. Parents dream that their children are given the same opportunities as others, to make a positive contribution to the world because they are seen and valued for all the gifts they bring. This is my vision for the world, my dream for the API LGBTQ community, and my hope for Aiden.

Needles and Cushions

A Reflection on Memory

Syd Yang

"This land is my land, this land is your land," the voices of my grade school classmates lifted up, our right hands over our hearts as we walked into our homeroom each day. I could feel a visceral longing pushing up against the palm of my hand each time we sang that song, the beat of a heart begging to be heard, desperate to understand where "my land," my home, was.

How critical it is for us, as human beings, to remember who we are, even in an ever-present void of disruption, disconnection, and erasure. For so many of us in Asian America, the threads that tie us to our lineage(s), our heritage(s) have been severed—over and over and over again—by the sharp blades of colonialism, Christian missions, genocide, forced and chosen migration, assimilation, foreign greed, tourism, and capitalism.

As queer, trans, and nonbinary beings, we have the privilege of wandering the spaces in between, of hearing the words left unspoken, and of being adept in the shadows. These are some of the gifts that tug at many of us who have been called back into the healing arts, of reclaiming and reimagining the medicines of our ancestors in modern times.

For me, it was in the searching for ways to regulate a body torn down by depression and eating disorders and to calm a mind devastated by ancestral and emotional trauma that thrust me on the path of remembering, of reclaiming a right to healing and medicine, which I would later learn already resided within me.

I remember.

My eyes scattered across the rows and rows of bulk herbs along the far wall, my fingers itching to know which ones to grab, which ones held the secrets my body longed to hear. My gaze focused on the swift hands opening and closing the worn, wooden drawers taking a pinch of this herb, a handful of another and piling them gently onto a small square of white paper on the counter. How did the herbalist know exactly what I needed?

I had recently begun work with an acupuncturist to help my body resolve a life-threatening relationship to food. At the time, I struggled fiercely with bulimia, depression, and anxiety, along with a myriad of digestive challenges that made being far from a toilet deeply unbearable.

I had spent many years—decades, even—navigating Western psychiatry, pharmaceuticals, and humbling visits with gastroenterologists before making that first appointment with the acupuncturist. None of the previous interventions seemed to help (and at times seemed to make things worse), but I was still hesitant to turn to Chinese medicine. It felt too tied to the shame I experienced as a child, being told that I was "too Chinese" or "too exotic," that my dad was "too weird," and that my house smelled gross— especially on the days my father brewed his herbal decoctions. My resistance held strong, until accessing help literally had me wedged between possible death (a side effect of an experimental drug the most recent Western medical doctor wanted to prescribe) and facing my shame. In that moment, shame felt like the easier path.

While lying down on the treatment table on my first acupuncture visit, needles forming spikes around my navel and resting in a crown at the top of my head, I could hear my breath singing out beyond the confines of my rib cage, remembering a tale my young body had once been told:

"Long before you were born. Long before your birth was even an idea in the consciousness of your own people, the earth loved you. She birthed you. She called out your name and invited you into the cycles of life and death and rebirth, guiding your feet gracefully across the lush landscape of her belly. She whispered your name into the ears of your ancestor's ancestors, filling their hearts with a promise of who you were to become, how your name would be the sweet leaves that, when picked, would gather up all the dreams—both realized and misspent—into a single cup of tea. In that time, those dreams would be brought home, across oceans, across mountains, and across the deep fissures in the sea—so that even though scattered, our people could once again be made whole."

It was a story I was afraid to believe, yet was so hungry for it to be true. What would I need to release in order to remember my name, to remember who I was?

Buddhist meditation and Chinese medicine became my companions as I wandered deeper into my recovery from an eating disorder and into a journey toward a more sustainable mental health. These weren't the paths I actively sought out. In fact, one might say they remembered me.

When I first began working with my acupuncturist, pretty much the only food I could reliably eat without digestive offense was rice. Plain white rice. Luckily, I love rice, but I was confused. Why only rice? My acupuncturist explained that in many ways, our bodies remember that which sustained our ancestors, the foods that kept them alive. Rice became a guiding metaphor for body wisdom as I healed—letting me know that even at the cellular level, my body was remembering where it came from, the lands and plants it was connected to and its relationship to the Earth. What else was I remembering? What else would rise up from within me if I could get quiet enough inside?

With each step I took in recovery, I began to remember a little bit more.

"Yang Mei-Yi. That is the name your Ah-Gong has given you," my father announced to me on my third birthday, his eyes betraying a sweet pride as he stared into my face. The deep lacquer brown of my pupils eagerly drank up his joy. "This is who you are," he continued. "Remember this. Your name means born in America, but your heart is in Taiwan."

While growing up in Southern California, in the years that followed, I got so caught in trying to fit in that I soon forgot the spell cast within that name.

Many, many years later, seated in stillness on my meditation cushion, my body would find rest in this name—a name that had been whispered across the generations of ancestors until it would be spoken aloud through my grandfather, through my father, and then into me. Remembering who I am is the unending, ever-unexpected healing path journey to walk myself home . . . and home, for me, is a plural word.

In my remembering what was, I began to reimagine, to remember forward into what could be.

During my eating disorder recovery, I learned how to sit every day, contemplating silence as an urban monk in training, a dragon watching, waiting, always ready to fly. My breath is the rope that keeps me tethered to the here and now.

————

One evening, after a challenging session with one of my healers, I dropped my hips onto my meditation cushion and lowered my gaze to the floor. Three deep exhales later, I realized that I was no longer in my bedroom. I was seated before my ancestors and guides in a realm and in a time far, far away.

My knees greeted the floor as I bowed before my council, the Goddess Quan Yin before me, one of the ancients beside her, his long white beard hanging down, grazing the arc of a silk dragon at his waist. They were waiting for me to speak, pearls of expectation blinking back at me.

"Rise," the elder commanded with his breath, but my knees refused to release the floor's embrace. The stillness of the marble columns beside me reminded me of the twists and turns of the Taroko Gorge in Taiwan, a place my Ah-Gong would take me as a child, and I gave in to a comfort of what finally felt like home.

"Why am I here?" I tentatively expressed.

"You have called us here today. What is it that you seek?" the Silk Dragon spoke.

"Answers. I need answers," I responded, my voice exhausted from so many years wandering a lonely road.

My breath caught on my next inhale, and suddenly they all were gone. I was back in my bedroom, and the final edges of a sunset I didn't get to see crept through the windows behind me. I had never felt so lonely in my life, in this room, in this practice, my body seated on a cushion for the third time today. I took yet another deep breath in as a sharp pain shot down from behind my ear and into my left shoulder blade, lodged into the space where my kidneys greeted my lower back—a body fighting to stay alive. My breath faltered one more time on my next exhale, a staccato of hope connecting me to the earth.

"Keep breathing," I told myself. "Bodily pain is temporary. Right now you just need to breathe."

My eyes closed this time, and in a few moments I was back again in the golden temple with my council before me. My breath continued, in and out, expanding more and more light into the spaces that surrounded me.

"Dear one," the elder began again, "whom are you fighting?"

My knees were weary of the hard floor beneath them, and my body greeted an awareness of pain in every one of its cells. I breathed into the filaments of this pain that wove through the doorways and passageways of my body, depositing grief and sorrow, trauma and loss at each turn. I was battle worn, exhausted, from the inside out.

"I promised myself that I would find a way to survive, but I am dying, and I don't know how to make it stop," I responded, my words mingling with the salty tears of surrender.

"My dear, yes, but whom are you fighting?" the elder asked again.

"Her! I am always fighting her," I cried out. "Always her!" The words unfurled with anger as they were released. "I am fighting her. A white mother who never saw me, who refused to see past her own sorrow and her own grief. I am fighting the unending deluge of her tears that she never explained but always blamed me for. Her! A mother who tried to make me atone for her sins by being the perfect daughter, and despite it all, I never was. I was never good enough."

"Ah. But whom are you fighting?" he gently prodded me again.

"I just told you," I snapped back, wanting him to take away the pain so I could breathe easy again.

"No," he continued, "you are making up stories. That is all. Whom are you really fighting?"

"Then it is the patriarchy," I cried out, exasperated with this line of inquiry. "That is what holds me down! It is the patriarchy. It is racism! It is the blood-stained fangs of capitalism! It is the tight-waisted puritanical sexuality of my ancestors! It is Christianity! It is white supremacy! Is that what you want to hear?"

His body remained perfectly still as my words stirred up the dust and cobwebs from underneath his feet, and my list continued.

"It is elitism! It is the stench of colonialism! It is the sting of a diaspora that stole my ancestor's languages from my tongue. And yes, I am fighting against a world that every day tells me that I am wrong, that I am too much and not enough in the same breath! I am fighting against that world, whose hands have shackled me up against a decaying wall and leaves me there to rot with everything else—because who I am is not supposed to exist. I am not white enough, not Asian enough, not straight enough, not queer enough, not feminine enough, not radical enough, not mainstream enough, not quiet enough, not loud enough to warrant space."

I looked up at the elder as I paused to take a breath, my lungs spewing fire. He nodded slowly, holding my gaze.

"That is whom I am fighting," I closed.

"Again, you are telling stories. You are not fighting that world."

"What do you mean?" I responded, my eyes expanding into large pools of disbelief. I threw my hands up in the air.

"To see whom you are fighting, my dear one, you must look deeper inside yourself." He posed the question once again. "Whom are you really fighting?"

Exasperated, I sat back on my hips and exhaled my breath into the spaces between his words, and we sat together in silence for a painfully long time.

"I don't know," my heart eventually emptied out, despair coating each word.

My ears perked up just then as a pair of brocade-covered feet shuffled toward me, twin yellow canaries embroidered onto them, two sets of eyes pulling me into their tarry depths.

"Look up!" one of the canaries commanded, and I lifted my face to greet the person standing before me, a young girl no older than eight, a spark of recognition passing from her face to mine as she handed me an unadorned porcelain bowl that felt as light as feathers in my hands.

Looking down, I noticed that the bowl was half filled with clear water whose gentle ripples had settled into a stillness on its surface as it rested in my embrace. Unsure of what to do next, I watched the canaries shuffle back into the shadows to my left. I turned my attention to the council before me.

"Am I supposed to drink this?" I asked, and the room came alive with the laughter of a thousand ancients.

"This is whom you are fighting," one of them shared as he bowed his head down to greet mine.

"I'm fighting a bowl?" I responded, incredulous and exasperated all over again.

"Look inside," he replied.

As I lowered my gaze to the water, I saw myself, my face, my body reflected back, and with a gust of errant wind, it hit me. *I have always and only been fighting myself.* The muscles in my arms gave out, the delicate bowl tumbling roughly onto the ground. I watched as it shattered into three distinct pieces, small waves of water spilling out across the gold tiled floor.

All this time, it was me.

All this time, I was only ever fighting myself.

A warm cadence to my breath returned, my inhale catching my exhale in a lover's embrace, and my spine found her throne again. "I am the answer," I responded to the elders. "All this time, the answer has always been within me. I am remembering! I am the one I have been looking for. I am the one I have been waiting for."

Each word ushered a new sobriety into my body that interlaced the sacred and the profane. The stillness in the temple reached out to capture each one, the claws of the silk dragon pulling them into his heart. Quan Yin and the ancients moved closer to me, encircling me as I sat on the floor, my cushion holding my body as the gale of breaths between us became one.

"Your body is not the enemy anymore," Quan Yin declared. "Now is the time to let her remember, to set her free."

My forehead lowered to the ground in response, kissing the smooth lacquer of the temple floor. I felt the wind that spoke before me: "Rise, our beloved. It is time."

In the background, the sound of a small metal bowl chimed out of the timer on my phone, and my body was called back to waking life. I sensed my spine rise up out of hips seated in another room, finding balance on a cushion waiting patiently in another dimension. Breathing in, I called myself back through the billowing fabric of time, back into a set of lungs whose hands then released me back into the present moment, back into the here and now. Breathing out, I promised my body that it would finally be free.[1]

In my queerness, I have been asked, invited perhaps, to weave new possibilities with my body, with my desire, with my breath—with the mere fact that I exist.

"You are an edge walker," my therapist declared, in a moment when my resolve to ever know myself would falter. "You walk purposefully at the boundaries, because you belong in many worlds. You navigate at the thresholds—the edges—as you hold the keys to each one."

"Then there's no place I really belong?" I inquired slowly, my heart prepping itself to sink deeper into despair depending on how she might respond.

"You belong to the Earth," she replied. "It is not so simple for you, given your history and lineage, to say that you belong in just one place. This is also something our ancestors knew, but we have forgotten. They knew that they belonged to the Earth. That was their first allegiance. Reweave your relationship to her and then see how you feel."

As a mixed race, queer, nonbinary/genderqueer being, I have never quite felt at home in any one space. I need multiple landing strips, multiple places and spaces to call home.

A woman I briefly dated once declared to me that being mixed race must one of the most confusing and painful identities ever.

I disagreed.

To be mixed is to call on a myriad of lineages that feed me. To be mixed is to root into the wisdom and healing of the earth at multiple locations. It is to be connected and rooted into my first Mother (the Earth) anywhere and everywhere I go.

I remember.

"*Nimen shi zhong wen ma*?" the waiter asked, his gleeful smile spreading all the way to the tips of his fingers as they rapped gently at the edge of the table we were seated at.

I tried to stifle a small laugh in my side belly at the assumption that I might be Chinese, from China, as opposed to being so blatantly Chinese American. My partner at the time, whom I was traveling with, simply nodded and explained that we lived in LA.

"Oh! You are overseas Chinese!" he proclaimed, his eyes sparking with recognition. "I knew it!" "Hao, hao." He bowed respectfully as another server placed a hotpot of young cauliflower, chives, and pork belly in the space between us. As we lifted our chopsticks in our right hands and our rice bowls in our left and began to eat, I could feel the muscles in my body remembering, affirming that it was true. This land once was home; the body never forgets.

We were in Shanghai for the first time, my partner and I, celebrating our marriage a few months earlier. It felt appropriate to travel to a land where so many of both of our ancestors had come from, even if no one in either of our families had any known living connections there. My Chinese ancestors had migrated to Taiwan centuries ago, mingling their blood with the aboriginal peoples there. That is the blood memory I carry. For my partner, they were born in Vietnam, their parents and grandparents all raised in Southeast Asia (Vietnam and Cambodia). Our histories are different, and yet ethnically we both are Chinese, living in America, speaking English, navigating queerness through both a Western and Eastern lens.

We have been overseas Chinese for generations, holding the lonely threads of a forgotten lineage that the hungry belly of diaspora had severed long before we were born. It can be said that diaspora breeds a powerful loneliness, one whose fingers wrap around the throat and constricts the breath. There is an ancient grief in that hold, inspiring tears to fall that do not know from whence they came, wails rising deep within the chest for a loss that has no name. This is the body in diaspora, groping for remnants of stories, shards of broken ceremonies, whispers in the shadows of who we might be.

Amid that pain, I remember forward.

There is healing in a forgotten body too. As we individually and collectively remember—as many of us are individually and collectively called back to the healing and resilience practices of our ancestors—we are being invited back into a dance with our own becoming. Our present-day realities are reweaving and resewing the threads that were once so brutally severed. In doing so, we are perhaps becoming more capable of walking each other home.

NOTE

1. This is an excerpt from Stephanie Syd Yang, *Release: A Bulimia Story* (Los Angeles: Blue Jaguar Healing Arts, 2018).

Queercore Prepped Me for Cancer

LESLIE MAH

Despite my pleading, my girlfriend at the time preferred drinking and fighting to coming out, claiming the Colorado punk scene was no place to be gay. Which was true, but I wanted to fuck with that. We were harassed all the time anyway, called diesel dykes, which is preferable to standard sexual harassment. When Doods shouted, "Faggots!" out the window as they drove by, I would correct them by yelling, "No, we're dykes!" You can bet after our breakup, I fled Colorado for the rainbow shores of the San Francisco. It wasn't long before Act Up presented a backdoor rage portal, perfect for punk rock.

"Do it yourself," claims the very foundation of punk. As a triple-threat minority, this proved to be a time-saving, lifesaving trajectory for me. My band would network in real life with a few other scruffy queirdos, erecting Queercore on the shoulders of feminist punk, homocore, and Queer Nation. I still can access sublime moments of transcendence when I felt surrounded by the most incredible people; it felt like we could truly transform the world.

My punk rock nineties were spent in the shelf (sleeping loft), in a van, on the road, putting in miles and kilometers throughout what is described as the Western world. The first world underground punk world, our youthful idealism fortifying a brave new world. We gleefully included safe sex and self-defense demos at our events.

The whole band would be exhausted, passing viral then bacterial infections in the van, emotional puddles of protoplasm held together with the promise that we were doing something important. Everything would suck, but then when we took to the stage, each of us conjured the magic. I would act as if the revolution had already happened and we were simply here to commemorate the brave queers and girl warriors.

Careening through seasonal touring that became annual road warrior campaigns, the band developed highly tuned bodily function management skills. Public restrooms at gas stations, at dive bars, at squats, and often on the side of the road became the site of lost privacy and an unintentional gain of political activism. Despite being the lone femme gendered band member, we traveled as a nebulous entity of intimately connected parts. Scouting the safety of a bathroom site was often my duty. Truth was I don't have an exclusive feminine presence, but I chose to embody the most femme part of myself 'cause I felt it was my most revolutionary route to confronting sexism. I loved the bewildered reaction to the spectacle of physically aggressive, head-banging, guitar-shredding femme performance.

This coincided with the trans community's increasing visibility, which became an incredible opportunity for growth for me. I got to learn and unlearn things about gender that my original coming out paradigm adhered to.

Today, I'm navigating a whole different world but am often amused when my old queercore skills come into play. Even with good insurance, a do-it-yourself approach is vital when you're lost in the freefall that is an advanced cancer diagnosis.

For a few years, I sensed something was different, and not in a good way. My concerns were dismissed, reasons received for not performing a pap smear: perimenopause, too many false positives, scanning and screening for something else instead, performing an unwanted transvaginal ultrasound (twice) instead. I was denied a pap three times in the year leading up to the first diagnosis. Now I know, via women of Black Twitter, that if your healthcare provider dismisses your requested test, you can ask to have their refusal noted in your file, and often they will take your concerns more seriously and perform the task.

I have been opening the gifts from all the generous queers who have lit my ass on fire, challenging me over the decades. When I began training for the AIDS Lifecycle, a 545-mile route to raise funds for HIV and AIDS research and support for folks living with the disease, I learned that those same patients were riding with us. Proudly flagging their bikes with neon banners, they challenged stigma just by living their lives. Less than two months after completing my third San Francisco to Los Angeles Lifecycle ride, I received my first diagnosis and gathered my people, sharing my life-altering news. Outing myself as a cancer patient, delivering realness throughout the whole process. Honoring the spirit of those with AIDS who refused to be burdened with the shame of sickness.

The second diagnosis was horrible. Six months after my initial chemo, external beam radiation, and internal surgical radiation, my oncologist detected cancer again. I was offered only two shitty options, one being to do nothing and die; the other gave me only a 25 percent chance of a cure, a major radical surgery to remove all of my pelvic organs. This included uterus, ovaries, fallopian tubes, bladder, rectum, and vagina. The surgery would be two parts: removing everything, and then reconstructing the vagina, then pouches fashioned from intestines to collect waste. The only question

I could think of was whether I would still be able to ride a bike. My surgeon said yes, so I agreed to the procedure. Then I was informed that about half the patients who receive a pelvic exenteration die from the surgery, and only half of those remaining are cured of cancer, and everybody has complications. I inquired about the vaginal reconstruction, and it required taking a muscle out of my leg, or my stomach, to fold over, creating a tube. This would take six to seven hours, making the surgery twice as long. Increasing risk. So, I asked, why is it necessary? Blank stares. Could I just not do that part? Perplexing both surgeons, I didn't understand why this was normal procedure in a high morbidity surgery. The doctors agreed it wasn't necessary. I asked if it would increase my chances of surviving the surgery if I didn't get a fake vagina. The answer was: absolutely. Daymn, why is fake vagina standard?

"There are lots of women who don't have vaginas," I stated. A coupla beats passed, and then my nurse practitioner validated me by repeating my statement. Lots of women don't have vaginas. I'm so grateful I live in a world where biology is not destiny, and destiny is not defined by anatomy. Thankful for all the transfolks' labor for this surprise gift. My surgery went well, taking seven hours instead of thirteen.

Side note: If you see a woman in a restroom standing to pee (firstly, why the fuck are you creeping her?), you don't know shit. Literally. Add to the reasons why minding your own business while handling your business, there is the chance she's a cancer patient hoping to enjoy a few more good times on our gorgeous planet. She who bestowed the altar of life with sacrificial vital organs may also be experiencing medical menopause, and you really do not want to fuck with her.

The final pathology dealt the most devastating blow. The disease had already spread. Recurrent metastatic cervical cancer is not curable. The only option at that point was maintenance chemo, which slows disease growth. My triple chemo cocktail usually gets a patient just a few extra months. After living in this medical grey area for three years and thirty-one chemo infusions, I have massively outlived my life expectancy. The clinical trial saved nearly 7 percent of us with a poor prognosis. I'm in remission. My oncologist has never had someone with my diagnosis survive. He called me a miracle.

I am not religious, but I view art and music as evidence of something spiritual, connecting us all to the mysteries of which we emerge and will return. But I am not going anywhere anytime soon. I am in remission. I am living as if the revolution has already happened. And I am still here to honor you brave queers and warrior women.

From *We Are All the Descendants of Survivors*. Charcoal and chalk on hand toned roma paper of live models. (From the artist's collection)

WIP the O's. Charcoal and chalk on hand toned roma paper of live models. (From the artist's collection)

From *We Are All the Descendants of Survivors*. Charcoal and chalk on hand toned roma paper of live models. (From the artist's collection)

This One Body

An Excerpt from a Multimedia Poetry Performance in Progress

Maiana Minahal

Blood (haynaku series)

Bleeding's
daily terror:
toilet roses bloom.

Scarlet,
garnet, crimson,
cherry, black, vermilion.

Flooding
soaks ruby
pad after pad.

Gurgle
ghost children
down the drain.

Poems,
flushed, trickle,
pink, forfeit, anemic.

Can
clenching muscles
stop hemorrhage gush?

Will this bleeding
ever never
end?

Instructions

Don't sneeze, cough, pass gas, defecate, urinate, or laugh. You'll bleed even more.
Don't stand up, don't stretch, don't exercise.
And definitely no sex.

Sleep on your side, wear three overnight pads, two pairs of tight-fitting underwear.
Always wear dark pants, very dark, solid black is best, always bring extra.
Sit on a towel, sleep on two. Don't ruin the furniture.

Don't turn around in class, don't stand near students, don't let them smell blood.
Change pads during breaks, don't bleed onto your clothes, don't let them see blood.

Stay on schedule, answer emails, attend committees, grade homework.
Don't cancel class, don't have cramps while lecturing.

Don't pass out from walking up the stairs between classes.
Don't dwell on the size of the clots dropping from your cervix.

Jello

Curled up on the library floor,
pressed against the sweaty smell
and assorted detritus
of the well-worn carpet,
you can only pray for time to skip forward
and to end class, to send students away,
because your insides feel like a meat grinder
                                    is slicing through each layer
                    of your uterus
                        with mind-shattering
            slowness, meticulously
                                                carving
                    the perimetrium,
                            myometrium,
                                    endometrium—
            the cells of your cervix leisurely
                                        pierced
                        by lava
            that razors down
                                    the vaginal canal
                    to deposit
                        onto your pad,
finally,
                this animal
                        memento, this wobbly
                jewel, this
        sticky
        dark Jell-O
of coagulated blood.

MRI

A magnetic resonance imaging (MRI) scan is a medical test that uses power-ful magnets, radio waves, and a computer to create images of the inside of the body.

The hospital machine hum is a cocoon
in the narrow light blue tunnel
that the hard platform you've been strapped to
slowly slides into.
Contrast dye IV menthols your left arm
and coats your tongue with tin.

Through the plugs in your ears, mechanical sounds pop,
ping bang whirr ping whoosh,
kicked cans and metallic cracks
like echoes in a dark and empty cave:
Who's there? there? there?
and only faint sea whispers in response.

With all of your cells' water molecules aligned,
the machine moves down your abdomen
to tap its dolphin song of your uterus
and image black and white pixels of tissue
that ob-gyn #3 will later report: adenomyosis.

Mamang, or *Death in Vegas*

Karen Tongson

Linda Oñas Katindig remarked throughout her lifetime that she had "many suitors." I knew this to be true. When I was about three years old, Mamang—the honorific I bestowed upon her for "grandmother" instead of the more traditional "lola"—would occasionally bring me along for her various rendezvous around Manila with men who were more than friends. She would often, for the sake of efficiency, refer to these admirers by their profession (e.g., "Attorney"), or as "Tito Something-or-Other." As she liked to brag about Attorney, he had to enter the priesthood after they broke up because "he could never love so powerfully again." The titos usually stuck around a little longer.

She was my favorite family member, our matriarch in the truest sense of that word. And though Mamang was once married to my grandfather, the popular and charming yet wildly untrustworthy jazz pianist Romeo Katindig, for an indeterminate period of time starting in their early twenties, she spent much of her life as a fiercely independent woman. She molded, nurtured, and disciplined all of us in her family—in her many families by blood and by choice—with a certain jovial tenacity.

Developmental logics are likely to arrive at the overdetermined conclusion that I was so attached to Mamang because she raised me as an infant and a toddler in Manila. She did this so that my own very young mother, Elizabeth "Maria" Katindig, could continue her burgeoning singing career. The mythos I ascribe to my and Mamang's relationship—something I've referenced in the acknowledgments to every book I've written thus far—is that she was the first person who taught me that writing was a beautiful thing. As soon as I achieved sentience and mobility, I would crawl onto our round dining table, where she would write and translate radio soaps into Visayan. I'd plop myself onto the center of the lazy Susan, and twirl myself round and round while I festooned her with toilet paper and decreed that she was "the queen." I believed it then, and still believe it now.

In 2014, I planned a big party for Mamang's eightieth birthday at the Max's of Manila in Las Vegas. She retired to Vegas to live with my youngest aunt, Abby, after two decades of living in Riverside, California, first with my mom, dad, and me and then on her own—or rather, with one of her ex lovers turned roommates, Tito Ernie. She rushed to us in California after my mom was diagnosed with type 2 diabetes at the end of the 1980s. In retrospect, it seems like an extreme measure to have sold everything and uprooted one's entire life back home to move all the way across the Pacific for a manageable diabetes diagnosis. But this all transpired in the era of *Steel Magnolias*, and I can't help but think Mamang's fears were fueled by Sally Field's fierce maternal monologue after her daughter Shelby (played by Julia Roberts) dies of diabetes-related causes.

Mamang's eightieth was to be grand yet also functional and familiar, hence the decision to book a place all the Pinoys would already have a feel for, like Max's. Relatives and friends scattered throughout the states in Pennsylvania, Missouri, Texas, California, and Nevada would all converge in Sin City to sup on endless platters of sisig, lechon kawali, pancit palabok, and that signature Max's chicken rumored to be fried in pork fat.

Mamang was always a party girl at heart and hosted huge, nightly, multitable mahjong games for what felt like all of Antonio Village at our home in Manila, with ample *ihaw-ihaw* and a bottomless supply of San Mig. It was at these epic mahjong gatherings that queer and trans people, who comprised a substantial demo in Mamang's *barkada*, nurtured my budding queerness. One of her best friends, and my aunt Abby's godmother, was Lisa Amor, who boasted that she was the first transwoman in the Philippines to have all of her surgeries done in Amsterdam. Lisa also claimed—and I haven't been able verify whether or not this is true—that she was the first postoperative Filipina transsexual *ever*.

Mamang was incredibly proud of the fact that, in her words, she was "always very popular among the gays." In fact, I always appreciated her willingness to call me "pogi" in person and on social media, even though some folks wouldn't find that normal. Linda Katindig was many things, but she was definitely not normal.

Her landmark eightieth birthday—momentous, because Mamang's older sister, Mellie, had been the only one in our family, at least thus far, to achieve octogenarian status—would be a prime occasion to honor her festive energies. We would recapture the mood of all those Manila nights in the 1970s and early 1980s, with everyone together instead of scattered into our atomized, nuclear units leading much lonelier existences. Plus, it was Vegas, baby: the city that she loved, and that captured her spiritual scale of bigness and largesse, even if she was no longer much of a gambler.

But beyond its glitz and tawdry glamor, Las Vegas is also a veritable Filipino town, and that's what inevitably enticed my grandmother to retire there and live with Tita Abby. Las Vegas nurtures the lives and careers of the

Linda Katindig in front of the Roman Catholic Shrine of the Most Holy Redeemer, Las Vegas, NV, July 31, 2013, on her seventy-ninth birthday. (From the author)

Philippines' diasporic empires of care and domestic labor, as well as entertainment. According to data compiled in the 2010 census, Filipinos are the largest growing minority population in the state of Nevada. More than half of all the Asians in the state of Nevada are Filipino.

Most of my family and our extended circle of friends either lived or spent significant time in Las Vegas as entertainers, primarily as musicians, working in places like the Trop and the Bellagio. Even my grandfather and his brothers performed in Vegas in the late 1960s at the Sands. Those among us who weren't in the entertainment industry worked in the health-care profession as nurses, nurse practitioners, or physicians' assistants. Amid the outsized flashing lights, yardstick margaritas, nightly Celine Dion spectacles, and opulent king crab buffets were everyday Filipino lives unfolding in environs not too dissimilar from the ones back home, like Max's, Nanay

Glorias, or Seafood City. Mamang relished being recognized as the Katindig matriarch whenever she moved through these spaces, and like a true Leo, she would make sure to casually drop the information that she was indeed from *those* Katindigs, the ones who pioneered Latin jazz and ruled the smooth jazz charts back home.

A day before her eightieth birthday, and several days before our decadent fête, Mamang didn't feel well. She was digestively blocked and hadn't been able to go the bathroom or pass gas for at least forty-eight hours after feasting and cavorting with some of the guests who arrived early, like her former sis-ter-in-law Tita Letty, who came in from Poplar Bluff, Missouri. Mamang took herself to the ER, and they admitted her for observation. With any luck, things would move while she was there, and we'd all be on track for the big celebration. My wife, Sarah, and I arrived directly from Germany, where I had a visiting gig at Bielefeld University that summer. I'd been bragging to the Germans about flying directly from Deutschland to Las Vegas to celebrate my grandmother's eightieth. They all thought it was incredibly exotic, and I felt almost as glamorous—if a little *mayabang*—as I'm sure Mamang did when people would recognize her (or at least her name) at the local turo-turo joint.

Our primary concern when we all converged in Vegas was what to do about the party, because all the guests had already touched down. Surely this wasn't anything a little psyllium husk or some hospital grade laxatives couldn't solve. The plan, largely spearheaded by Mamang, was to press on. Even from her hospital bed, Mamang remained sanguine. "There's still a few days yet with everyone in town. We'll continue the party at home if I can't make it to Max's," she reasoned.

She didn't make it to Max's. Her condition didn't improve.

Though we hadn't received a diagnosis or any grave warnings from the physicians attending to her, I still cried when I gave the toast at the eightieth birthday party she couldn't come to, surrounded by all the food she wasn't allowed to eat unless something shifted. Everyone from out of town visited her in the hospital, and she remained in good spirits, already planning ahead for a taste of leftovers, as well as future celebrations—maybe in Ore-gon where her cousin, Tito Roger, lived. The doctors couldn't figure out what was happening, so an exploratory surgery was scheduled for two days later, after I'd already be back in Los Angeles.

My mother called me from Vegas with the postsurgery update after I got back home: "The doctors say Mamang has only one week to live. There's cancer everywhere, and they can't do anything. She can't eat. She can only have fluids. Pedialyte and water. We're bringing her back to her house later today for hospice care."

Our matriarch, my queen, had been given a death sentence within days of achieving her milestone eightieth. Turning eighty was supposed to be

Mamang's big "Fuck you!" to anyone and everyone who zealously cautioned her that her immodest, indulgent lifestyle would be curtailed as punishment from the Lord. She got to eighty with such panache, despite dodging Japanese bullets in Visayan rice fields during World War II and enduring the abusive machismo of her philandering husband in midcentury Manila. Eighty seemed like another beginning. But as the Lord giveth, he just as swiftly and cruelly taketh away.

I immediately drove back to Las Vegas, mourning clothes hastily packed, sobbing the entire length of the four-hour drive from Los Angeles, pausing only to stuff an In-N-Out burger into my face during a pit stop in Barstow. I was eating my grief and feeling selfish for doing so, because I knew my grandmother wouldn't be able to eat anything again for the rest of the little time she had left. Mamang and I had stopped at this same In-N-Out back in 2005, when she still lived in California and we were driving back from a visit to my aunt's. That time it was Mamang who cried over her double-double with grilled onions, because my mom had just been diagnosed with cancer and was undergoing a brutal six months of chemo. My mom thankfully survived her intensive treatment before going into remission. "I just don't want to lose my daughter," Mamang said as we held each other tight, briny tears and American cheese smeared across our mouths.

Mamang's stubbornness triumphed over the doctors' most dire predictions. She stretched out the week she was given into two complete months. She refused to have her bed—her deathbed—set up in her bedroom. Instead, she insisted on being at the center of the house, smack in the middle of the open-plan living room where she had a full view of the big screen playing TFC all day. She also wanted to make sure that all of us could see and be with her at all times, that guests could flow in and through the house, and that those coming to pay their respects or to pray with her from near and far couldn't avoid her, even if they lost their nerve and tried. She was ever the pragmatic hostess.

She could no longer eat—she could only taste, chew, and spit things out—but she nevertheless demanded to monitor the kitchen and dining area adjacent to her setup, where she had her last rites conferred not once but twice. Mamang corrected recipes, obsessively posted pictures of Filipino food on Facebook, and insisted she be photographed with everything we prepared in her kitchen. She sucked on popsicles, Pedialyte, fruit, and morphine while the rest of us gorged on afritada, adobo, paksiw, and all of her other favorite foods that she insisted we prepare for her to experience indirectly through scent and vision, despite the circumstances. She even snuck small sips of halaan, tinola, and nilaga broth whenever she could, all of us praying that it wouldn't trigger any additional pain or distress. By the time Mamang was nearing the end, this woman with a palate for complex flavors in life as in food said the only thing she wanted was a cup of coffee and a warm piece of bread smothered with butter.

During the first week of our vigil, I didn't quite know when or where to express my fear, anger, and grief, so I booked a room at the M Resort, which was near Mamang and Abby's house. I never spent the night at the hotel, but I'd occasionally sneak away for an hour or two to scream, sob openly, drink heavily, work out, or swim. It felt at once like a relief and a special species of Vegas torture to be poolside at the M, which offered such an incongruous scene of people partying like there was no tomorrow. Meanwhile, a couple of miles down the road, my family was lying in anxious wait, terrified at the inevitable end of all tomorrows. My parents and other family members would also use that room at the M in shifts for their own ministrations of grief, rage, and despair. I often wonder how they felt about having their tragedy, our tragedy, scored to the incessant ringing of slots machines.

Nearly every weekend, I'd come back to Las Vegas after a week of teaching, usually by car. On November 1, 2014—*dia de los muertos*—something told me I needed to fly back right away. I had just FaceTimed with Mamang the night before, and she was having a red-letter day because my family was celebrating Abby's birthday. We talked about the feast she wanted us to make at Christmas, and she cracked a silly joke that the only thing she'd be bringing would be ice cream from Thrifty's.

There is nothing more antipodal to grief than a Southwest Airlines flight direct from Burbank to Las Vegas on Halloween weekend. Flight attendants hammily sling jokes about hangovers and bachelorettes, and roving packs of budget party seekers push their way past you on board so they can get to the business of downing bloody marys and shots of Cuervo at 7:00 a.m.

I landed in Vegas at in the morning and rushed to Mamang's, just in time for her to register my presence and utter a few words before she couldn't speak anymore. "My eyes hurt," she whispered to me. I told her she could close them. I brushed her hair, lay next to her, held her, and sobbed openly, no longer compelled to sequester my fear and grief in the borrowed privacy of a casino hotel room. I put on a playlist of her favorite music, and she smiled when I joked (as Julie Andrews sang "Getting to Know You" from *The King and I*) that Mamang always liked it when people said she looked like a Filipina Julie Andrews. Her fingers waved weakly in the air, and a smile wavered across her face as she listened to the music, eventually fading along with it.

To Fukaya Michiyo

TRACI KATO-KIRIYAMA

> *We are daughters*
> *Of the sea, moon and sun.*
> —MICHIYO FUKAYA

A dream
shook me awake too soon.

We sat in a circle of fire
formed by your fingernails
to surround us in the Meiji era of
womxn, shouting:
Kusunose Kita
wielding tongue of suffrage, of
anarchist, iconoclast:
Kanno Sugako, Kaneko Fumiko
weaving through the flames with us, they
urging us toward revolution, faced you
coaxing them from the men who drove them away, me
collecting my desire in the path of your ashes.

i woke to your words at my bedside:

> *There is no way out*
> *Except madness or death*

and
see the cracked mirror reflections
of our mothers
in the pinch of yesterday's light.

We share:
the
same
    wrong dirty name,

an ease with
confrontation,

hunger for the
luscious food.

I have searched
endlessly, dire histories of
our ancestors to
find what earns your spirit.

i suspend myself
in your life's tether, cut
from the same cloth, your
sanity's nomenclature,
loving and cursing
the verses that link
us.

> *We search all our lives*
> *For beauty*   there,

           is your ember.

My mere pledge:

> Take every chance to burn old
> self,
> Ignite every fire
> inside,
> Evoke you, the inferno
>
> *Who will always be with me.*

About the Contributors

Marsha Aizumi is the proud mother of a transgender son. She has shared her story of moving from shame, sadness, and fear to unconditional love and acceptance to over two hundred schools, corporations, and organizations in the United States and Asia. Marsha is the cofounder of the PFLAG San Gabriel Valley Asian Pacific Islander (SGV API) chapter, the first API focused chapter in PFLAG's history, and also serves on the PFLAG National Board of Directors. She is founder of Okaeri: A Nikkei LGBTQ Community, which is a biennial conference and various community events drawing people from all over the United States, Canada, and Asia since 2014. Her book, *Two Spirits, One Heart*, written with Aiden, is a heartfelt love story about a mother and son finding their way back to each other and then using their visibility and voices to bring greater awareness, support, and hope to the LGBTQ community and their families.

Kimberly Alidio is the author of three books of poetry: *why letter ellipses* (selva oscura press, 2020), *: once teeth bones coral :* (Belladonna*, 2020), and *After projects the resound* (Black Radish Books, 2016). Her most recent poetry chapbook is *a cell of falls* (Portable Press at Yo-Yo Labs, 2019). Her work has been supported by the Jack Kerouac School of Disembodied Poetics, the Center for Art and Thought, and Kundiman. She holds a Ph.D. in history from the University of Michigan and an MFA candidacy in poetry from the University of Arizona.

Paul Michael (Mike) Leonardo Atienza (@pmlatienza) is a doctoral candidate of anthropology with a graduate minor in gender and women's studies at the University of Illinois, Urbana-Champaign. He is also a research affiliate with the Seeing Systems INTERSECT group, an interdisciplinary collaboration among Urbana-Champaign scholars interested in the role of vision in technological systems. He is one of the first to receive a master of arts degree in Southeast Asian studies at the University of California, Riverside's SEATRiP program. A classically trained tenor, Mike is one of the original vocalists for the California-based keroncong group, Orkes Pantai Barat. He is also a performance collaborator with drag artist Ma. Arte Susya Purisima Tolentino (@dragmaarte).

Long T. Bui is associate professor in the Department of Global and International Studies at the University of California, Irvine. He is the author of *Returns of War: South Vietnam and the Price of Refugee Memory* (New York University Press, 2018).

John Paul (JP) Catungal (he/him/his) is an assistant professor in the Institute for Gender, Race, Sexuality and Social Justice, University of British Columbia. Born in Manila to Pangasinense parents, JP is a queer first generation Filipino Canadian migrant settler currently living in unceded Musqueam, Squamish, and Tsleil-Waututh territories in so-called Vancouver. JP's research concerns queer, immigrant, and racialized community organizing as a set of knowledge production practices illuminating lived materialities of ongoing systemic violence as well as a prefiguration of more socially just futures. JP has too many guilty pleasures, among them gummy worms, dried mangoes, and bad TV shows.

Ching-In Chen is author of *The Heart's Traffic* (Arktoi/Red Hen, 2009) and *recombinant* (Kelsey Street Press, 2017; winner of the 2018 Lambda Literary Award for Transgender Poetry), as well as the chapbooks *how to make black paper sing* (speCt!, 2019) and *Kundiman for Kin :: Information Retrieval for Monsters* (Portable Press at Yo-Yo Labs, 2020; finalist for the Leslie Scalapino Award). Chen is also the coeditor of *The Revolution Starts at Home: Confronting Intimate Violence Within Activist Communities* (South End Press, 2011; AK Press, 2016) and *Here Is a Pen: an Anthology of West Coast Kundiman Poets* (Achiote, 2009). They have received fellowships from Kundiman, Lambda, Watering Hole, Can Serrat, and Imagining America and are a part of Macondo and Voices of Our Nations Arts Foundation writing communities. As a community organizer, they have worked in Asian American communities in San Francisco, Oakland, Riverside, Boston, Milwaukee, and Houston.

Jih-Fei Cheng has worked in HIV and AIDS social services, managed a university cultural center, been involved in media production and curation, and participated in queer and trans of color grassroots and nonprofit organizations in Los Angeles and New York City. He is coeditor, with Nishant Shahani and Alexandra Juhasz, of *AIDS and the Distribution of Crises* (Duke University Press, 2020). His first monograph, tentatively titled *Queer Code: HIV/AIDS and the History of Virology*, examines the science, activism, and media of HIV/AIDS in relation to the colonial history of virology and the historical transformations of global capitalism. A second research project addresses the role of genetics and virology in the development of the People's Republic of China, commencing with an investigation of the HIV epidemic among blood donors in his paternal grandfather's province of Henan.

Kim Compoc teaches U.S. history at University of Hawai'i–West O'ahu. Her research focuses on U.S. empire in the Philippines and Hawai'i; Asian/American studies; as well as diasporic Filipinx Studies with an emphasis on Indigenous, Feminist, and Queer critique. In both her activism and scholarship, she is interested in how the story of empire becomes more evident through continued engagement with each other's stories of resistance. The title of her manuscript-in-progress is *Outsmarting Empire: Filipinx in Hawai'i and Contemporary Visions of Decolonization.*

Sony Coráñez Bolton is an assistant professor of Latinx and Latin American studies in the Department of Spanish at Amherst College. He enjoys queering the Spanish language as an unexpected and deviant speaker and teacher. He is working on his first book on histories of mestizaje and disability in the colonial Philippines.

D'Lo is a queer/transgender Tamil Sri Lankan American actor, writer, and comic. His solo shows have toured the college circuit, theaters, and festivals internationally. His work has been published in various anthologies and academic journals, including *Desi Rap: Hip Hop and South Asia America and Experiments in a Jazz Aesthetic* (coedited by Sharon Bridgforth) and *Troubling the Line: Trans and Genderqueer Poetry and Poetics*, with features in the *Guardian*, NBC, and the *Advocate*. He created the "Coming Out, Coming Home" writing workshop series with South Asian and immigrant LGBTQ organizations nationally.

Patti Duncan is an associate professor of women, gender, and sexuality studies at Oregon State University, where she specializes in women of color feminisms, transnational feminisms, queer studies, and motherhood studies. Duncan is the editor of the scholarly journal *Feminist Formations*, the author of *Tell This Silence: Asian American Women Writers and the Politics of Speech* (University of Iowa Press, 2004), the coeditor of *Mothering in East Asian Communities: Politics and Practices* (Demeter, 2014), and the coeditor of *Women's Lives Around the World: A Global Encyclopedia* (ABC-CLIO, 2018). Her work has been published in *Women's Studies Quarterly*, *Frontiers: A Journal of Women's Studies*, *The Journal of the Motherhood Initiative for Research and Community Involvement (JMI)*, and *Atlantis: Critical Studies in Gender, Culture, and Social Justice*, as well as many anthologies, including the original *Q&A: Queer in Asia America*, edited by David Eng and Alice Y. Hom. Her current research focuses on narratives of rescue, migration, and motherhood in the global South.

Chris A. Eng is an assistant professor of English at Washington University in St. Louis. The thinking in this chapter draws from his book project, *Extravagant Provisions: Constraint and Queer Conviviality in Asian America*. His writings have also appeared in *American Quarterly*, *GLQ*, *Journal of Asian American Studies*, *Lateral*, *MELUS*, and *Theatre Journal*. He received a 2020 Career Enhancement Fellowship from the Institute for Citizens & Scholars (formerly the Woodrow Wilson Foundation).

Kale Bantigue Fajardo is an interdisciplinary anthropologist, writer, and photographer and is an associate professor of Asian American studies at the University of Minnesota, Twin Cities. Born in Malolos, Bulacan, Philippines, and raised in Portland and Gladstone, Oregon, he is the author of *Filipino Crosscurrents: Oceanographies of Seafaring, Masculinities and Globalization* (University of Minnesota Press, 2011; reprinted by the University of the Philippines Press, 2013). Kale has other publications in the journal *GLQ*, *The Transgender Studies Reader*, and *Filipino Studies: Palimpsests of Nation and Diaspora*, among others. He is currently writing his second and third books, respectively titled *Another Archipelago: Filipinx Diasporic Migrants, Immigrants, and Photography in the 20th Century* and *Fish Stories: Photos/Essays from the Mississippi River to Manila Bay*. Kale dedicates his work on this anthology to his mother, Concepcion (Baby/Connie) Bantigue Fajardo (1939–2013), and his daughter, Baía/Nia Amihan Tinsley Fajardo.

May Farrales, Ph.D., is a Filipinx interdisciplinary scholar whose research centers on the embodied and lived experiences of people of colour in settler colonial urban geographies. She is an Assistant Professor in Urban Social Change in Geography, cross appointed with the Department of Gender Sexuality and Women's Studies at Simon Fraser University located on the unceded territories of the Squamish (Sḵwx̱wú7mesh Úxwumixw), Tsleil-Waututh (səlilw̓ətaʔɬ), Kwikwetlem (kwikwəƛ̓əm), and Musqueam (xwməθkwəy̓əm) Nations. Before joining SFU, she completed a postdoctoral fellowship as a Michael Smith Foundation for Health Research Trainee at the University of Northern British Columbia. She holds a Ph.D. (2017) in Geography from the University of British Columbia.

Joyce Gabiola MSLIS is the head archivist for Lambda Archives of San Diego. They are a coeditor for @uprootknowledge, the We Here publication that centers work by Black, Indigenous, and people of color in and about archives, libraries, education, and other information environments. As a charter class member of alpha Kappa Delta Phi at the University of Houston, they penned the organization's history and they have a complicated relationship with Texas but call it home.

C. Winter Han is an associate professor of sociology at Middlebury College. Prior to becoming an academic, he was an award-winning journalist and served as the editor in chief of the *International Examiner*, the oldest continuously publishing pan-Asian Pacific American newspaper in the United States.

Alice Y. Hom is a community builder invested in bridging diverse and overlapping communities for social change. She is the director of equity and social justice at Northern California Grantmakers. Alice serves on the board of Borealis Philanthropy and on the advisory council for the Conscious Style Guide. She is a cofounder of Beyond Two Cents, a LGBTQ AAPI giving circle, and is the host of *Historically Queer*, a podcast of historical and contemporary stories of activism by LGBTQ people of color. Alice coedited the anthology *Q & A: Queer in Asian America* and has published articles in various journals and anthologies.

Douglas S. Ishii is an assistant professor of Asian American Literature and Culture in the Department of English at the University of Washington. He is currently completing his first book project, *Something Real: Asian American Arts Activism and the Racialization of Sophistication*, and working on his second, tentatively titled *Lateral Diasporas: The Queer Language of Generation in Asian Settlement*. His writing has appeared in *Camera Obscura: Feminism, Culture, and Media Studies*, *American Quarterly*, and *The Account: A Journal of Poetry, Prose, and Thought*, as well as the edited collections *Techno-Orientalism: Imagining Asia in Speculative Fiction, History, and Media*; *Global Asian American Popular Cultures*; and *The Oxford Encyclopedia of Asian American Literature and Culture*.

traci kato-kiriyama (she/they) is an award-winning artist, community organizer, and cultural producer; performer and principal writer of PULLproject Ensemble; director and cofounder of Tuesday Night Project (presenter of Tuesday Night Cafe, which is in its twenty-third year—the longest-running Asian American–produced public arts series in the country). traci has been presented in hundreds of venues throughout the country as an author, actor, storyteller, theatre deviser and performer, artist organizer, educator, and arts and culture consultant. traci's writing, commentary, and work have been presented by media (including NPR, PBS, C-SPAN, Elle.com, and the *Hollywood Reporter*) and publishers including Regent Press, Heyday Books, Bamboo Ridge Press, Chaparral Canyon Press, Tia Chucha Press, and Entropy. traci's forthcoming book is being published in 2021 by The Accomplices/Writ Large Press.

Jennifer Lynn Kelly is an assistant professor of feminist studies and critical race and Ethnic Studies at University of California, Santa Cruz. She received her Ph.D. in American studies with a portfolio in women's and gender studies from University of Texas at Austin, her master's degree in interdisciplinary humanities from New York University, and her bachelor's degree in feminist studies and literature from University of California, Santa Cruz. Her research broadly engages questions of settler colonialism, U.S. empire, and the fraught politics of both tourism and solidarity. She is currently completing the manuscript for her first book, a multisited ethnographic study of solidarity tourism in Palestine.

Mimi Khúc is a writer, scholar, and teacher of things unwell and Scholar/Artist/Activist in Residence in Disability Studies at Georgetown University. She is the managing editor of *The Asian American Literary Review* and guest editor of *Open in Emergency: A Special Issue on Asian American Mental Health*. She oversees the Open in Emergency Initiative, a multiyear national project developing mental health arts programming with universities and community spaces. She is very slowly working on several book projects, including a manifesto on contingency in Asian American studies and essays on mental health, the arts, and the university. But mostly she spends her time baking, as access and care for herself and loved ones.

Anthony Yooshin Kim, Ph.D., is a writer, scholar, and artist originally from the San Francisco Bay Area. He is currently working on a collection of essays titled *Motions of Search: A Personal Film History*, which brings together film criticism, personal memoir, and Korean diasporic history and culture. He has been visiting faculty in Asian American studies at Hunter College and Williams College. His future is as yet an improvisation.

Việt Lê is an artist, writer, and curator. Lê is an associate professor in visual studies at California College of the Arts. Recent exhibitions include *The Foot Beneath the Flower: Camp, Kitsch, Art, Southeast Asia* (ADM, Nanyang Technological University, Singapore, 2020), *lovebang!* (Kellogg University Art Gallery, LA, 2016), *vestige* (H Gallery Bangkok, 2015), and *tan nÁRT côi lòng | heARTbreak!* (Nhà Sàn Collective, Hà Nội, 2015). *White Gaze* is an art book (poetry, images, performance) in collaboration with Latipa (née Michelle Dizon) and Faith Wilding (Sming Sming Books and Objects | Candor Arts). Lê cocurated *humor us* (with Leta Ming and Yong Soon Min; Los Angeles Municipal Art Gallery, LA, 2008), *transPOP: Korea Việt Nam Remix* (with Yong Soon Min; Seoul, Sài Gòn, Irvine, San Francisco, 2008–2009), the 2012 Taipei Kuandu Biennale, and *Love in the Time of War* (UC Santa Barbara and SF Camerawork). Lê is the author of *Return Engagements: The Traumas of Modernity and History in Phnom Penh and Sài Gòn* (Duke University Press, 2021) and has coedited special issues of *Asian American Literary Review* ("[Re]Collecting Vietnam," 2015), *BOL Journal* ("Việt Nam and Us," 2008) and *Reflections: A Journal of Writing, Service Learning, and Community Literacy* (Syracuse University Press, 2008). He has coedited with Professor Lan Duong a special issue of *Visual Anthropology* (Routledge, Winter 2018). Visit his website, vietle.net.

Danni Lin (b. 1992) was raised in LA, was schooled at SFAI, and works in NY. Lin is a multimedia artist with an emphasis in oil painting and experiential installations. They have exhibited across the United States, including shows at the Diego Rivera Gallery in San Francisco, Art Share in Los Angeles, and Local Projects Art Space in Queens. Lin's most recent project is producing a traveling art history podcast, *Art Sistory*.

Glenn D. Magpantay is a longtime LGBTQ rights activist, civil rights attorney, and professor of Asian American studies. He is the former executive director of the National Queer Asian Pacific Islander Alliance (NQAPIA). He inspires future advocates by teaching at Brooklyn Law School and Hunter College/CUNY. Glenn attended the State University of New York (SUNY) at Stony Brook and, as a beneficiary of affirmative action, graduated *cum laude* from the New England School of Law, in Boston.

Leslie Mah. Music: guitar, bass, vocals. For Anti Scrunti Faction, Tribe 8, Slow Club, Dragon Ladies, Comrade Lover—a social justice loving Lion Slam Dance troupe, and a multitude of side projects. Select films: *Estrofemme* (director), *Shut Up White Boy* (director: Vu T. Thu Ha'), *Rise Above: The Tribe 8 Documentary* (director: Tracy Flannigan). Professional tattoo artist since 1996. Fine artist since 2015. Lives in Oakland, California.

Martin F. Manalansan IV is an associate professor of American studies at the University of Minnesota, Twin Cities. He has taught at the University of Illinois, Urbana-Champaign; University of the Philippines; New York University; New School University; and City University of New York. He is presently chair of the Minority Scholars Committee of the American Studies Association. He is the author of *Global Divas: Filipino Gay Men in the Diaspora* (Duke University Press, 2003; Ateneo de Manila University Press, 2006). He is editor or coeditor of four anthologies, *Filipino Studies: Palimpsests of Nation and Diaspora* (New York University Press, 2016), *Eating Asian America: A Food Studies Reader* (New York University Press, 2013), *Cultural Compass: Ethnographic Explorations of Asian America* (Temple University Press, 2000), and *Queer Globalizations: Citizenship and the Afterlife of Colonialism* (New York University Press, 2002). He has published in numerous journals, including *GLQ, Antipode, Cultural Anthropology, positions: east asian cultural critique*, and *Radical History*, among others. Among his many awards are the Ruth Benedict Prize from the American Anthropological Association in 2003, the Excellence in Mentorship Award in 2013 from the Association of Asian American Studies, the Richard Yarborough Mentoring Prize in 2016 from the American Studies Association, and the Crompton-Noll Award for the best LGBTQ essay in 2016 from the Modern Language Association. Before going back to academia, he worked for ten years in AIDS and HIV research, program evaluation, and prevention education at the Gay Men's Health Crisis and the Asian Pacific Islander Coalition on HIV/AIDS, both in New York City.

Casey Mecija is an assistant professor in the Department of Communication Studies at York University and holds a Ph.D. from the University of Toronto. Her current research examines sound as a mode of affective, psychic, and social representation, specifically in relation to diasporic experience. Her work communicates across the fields of queer theory, Filipinx studies, psychoanalysis, and cultural studies. She is also a filmmaker and musician.

Maiana Minahal is a queer femme, interdisciplinary artist, writer, and social justice educator. An immigrant born in the Philippines and raised in California, she currently lives and works in Honolulu as an assistant professor of English at Kapi'olani Community College. Maiana formerly directed the Poetry for the People program at UC Berkeley, authored the poetry collection *Legend Sondayo*, and cofounded the Bay Area Filipinx artist group Kreatibo. She is an old soul with a young heart, leveraging queer femme superpowers to instigate good things in community.

Sung Won Park is a 1.5 generation Korean American immigrant who grew up in Brooklyn, New York, and continues to hold it down in spite of a massive and invasive gentrification wave. A church dropout with a master's degree in divinity, Sung has found a deep passion for all things urban farming, slow cooking, making and fermenting sauces, throwing pottery, and most of all studying traditional Korean shamanism. Sung dreams of days when all these elements will come together seamlessly.

Thea Quiray Tagle is a curator, art writer, and assistant professor of gender and sexuality studies and critical ethnic studies at the University of Massachusetts, Boston. Her transdisciplinary research investigates socially engaged art and site-specific performance, visual cultures of violence, and modes of survival amid waste in the expanded Pacific Rim. Thea holds a Ph.D. in ethnic studies from the University of California, San Diego, and her writing has been published in popular and academic venues including *American Quarterly*, *ACME: An International Journal for Critical Geographies*, *Asian Diasporic Visual Cultures and the Americas*, *ASAP/J*, *Journal of Critical Ethnic Studies*, and *Hyperallergic*. She has curated exhibitions, written exhibition and catalog texts, and produced public programs for and with queer Asian diasporic artists alejandro t. acierto, Eliza O. Barrios, Zulfikar Ali Bhutto, Romson Regarde Bustillo, Leeroy New, Jovencio de la Paz, Azin Seraj, and Super Futures Haunt Qollective.

Emily Raymundo is a presidential fellow in American studies at the University of Manchester (UK). She earned her doctorate in American studies and ethnicity at the University of Southern California, and she was a dean's fellow in Asian American studies at Dartmouth College from 2017 to 2019. She is currently working on her first monograph, *Asian America at the End of Multiculturalism*, and her work has been published in *Journal of Asian American Studies*, *Women and Performance*, and *Theatre Journal*, as well as in the anthology *Fashion and Beauty in the Time of Asia* (New York University Press, 2019).

Vanita Reddy is a feminist scholar and cultural theorist whose research focuses on the intersections of race, sexuality, and gender in global contexts. She is an associate professor of English at Texas A&M University with a faculty affiliation in women's and gender studies. Dr. Reddy's research examines practices of cultural identity, belonging, and political community within the South Asian American and the global South Asian diaspora. It seeks to make visible subjects and populations who have occupied a historically marginal place within studies of diaspora and globalization, such as women, girls, service sector workers, undocumented migrants, and sexual minorities. She has published widely on beauty and fashion cultures in diasporic communities, and is the author of *Fashioning Diaspora: Beauty, Femininity, and South Asian American Culture* (Temple University Press, 2016). She is also the coeditor of a special issue of the journal *The Feminist and Scholar Online*, "Queer and Feminist Afro-Asian Formations" (2018), and she is currently writing a book about comparative South Asian diasporas from a feminist and queer perspective, tentatively titled *Global Intimacies*.

Eric Estuar Reyes currently teaches as an associate professor of Asian American studies at California State University at Fullerton. Besides teaching, he enjoys creating ceramic artwork and traveling abroad.

Margaret Rhee is a poet, scholar, and new media artist. She is the author of the poetry collection *Love, Robot*, named a 2017 Best Book of Poetry by *Entropy Magazine* and awarded a 2018 Elgin Award by the Science Fiction Poetry Association and the 2019 Best Book Award in Poetry by the Asian American Studies Association. Currently, she is completing her monograph *How We Became Human: Race, Robots, and the Asian American Body* and a Queer Film Classics title on *The Watermelon Woman*. She was a college fellow in digital practice in the English Department at Harvard University and a member of MetaLab at Harvard. She received her Ph.D. from UC Berkeley in ethnic studies with a designated emphasis in new media studies. She is an assistant professor in the Department of Media Study at SUNY Buffalo.

Thomas Xavier Sarmiento, Ph.D., is assistant professor of English at Kansas State University. He specializes in diasporic Filipinx American literature and culture, cultural representations of the Midwest, and queer theory. His research appears in the journals *Amerasia Journal, MELUS: Multi-Ethnic Literature of the United States*, and *Women, Gender, and Families of Color* and in the edited collections *Asian American Feminisms and Women of Color Politics* (University of Washington Press, 2018), *Curricular Innovations: LGBTQ Literatures and the New English Studies* (Peter Lang, 2019), and *The Oxford Encyclopedia of Asian American Literature and Culture* (Oxford University Press, 2020).

Pahole Sookkasikon, Ph.D., received his doctorate in American studies at the University of Hawai'i at Mānoa. His doctoral work and dissertation intervene in the burgeoning field of Thai American studies, theorizing gender and sexuality as they operate through performance and cultural productions of Thai American (non)belonging and becoming. He has written a handful of articles published by different presses such as Routledge, ABC-CLIO/Greenwood, Anglistica AION, Duke University Press, and a forthcoming piece with University of Wales Press. Beyond the academe, Pahole is highly active in the community and was crowned Mr. Hyphen 2009—a faux pageant created to showcase more nuanced images of Asian American men—by *Hyphen Magazine*, where he supported the Thai American Scholarship Fund as well as the Asian American Donor Program (AADP) by way of Helping Janet and Project Michelle.

Amy Sueyoshi is the dean of the College of Ethnic Studies at San Francisco State University. They are a historian by training with an undergraduate degree from Barnard College and a Ph.D. from University of California at Los Angeles. Amy has authored two books, *Queer Compulsions: Race, Nation, and Sexuality in the Affairs of Yone Noguchi* and *Discriminating Sex: White Leisure and the Making of the American "Oriental."* Additionally, they served as a founding cocurator of the GLBT History Museum, seeded the intergenerational Dragon Fruit Oral History project at API Equality Northern California, and cochaired the inaugural Queer History Conference 2019 hosted by the Committee on LGBT History. Amy is the recipient of numerous awards, including the Clio Award for her contribution to queer history and the Phoenix Award for her service to the Asian and Pacific Islander queer women and transgender community.

Karen Tongson is the author of *Why Karen Carpenter Matters* (University of Texas Press, 2019) and *Relocations: Queer Suburban Imaginaries* (NYU Press, 2011). In 2019, she received the Lambda Literary Jeanne Córdova Award for Lesbian/Queer Nonfiction. She is chair of gender and sexuality studies, and professor of English, gender and sexuality studies, and American studies and ethnicity at USC, as well as coeditor (with Henry Jenkins) of the award-winning book series *Postmillennial Pop* at NYU Press. She also cohosts the podcast *Waiting to X-hale* with Wynter Mitchell-Rohrbaugh. For more information, visit www.karentongson.org, as well as her socials on Twitter (@inlandemperor) and Instagram (@tongsonator).

Kim Tran is a facilitator, writer, and organizer whose work centers on a simple concept: "Be the person you needed when you were younger." As a queer woman of color, the projects and initiatives she builds center on her communities and their intersectional needs. In 2008, Kim was one of a handful of people who established the LGBTQ Youth Space, a therapeutic safe space for queer youth in the South Bay Area. In 2013, she became an executive publisher for Third Woman Press, a Queer and Feminist of Color Publisher. In 2017, Kim was a core planner for Hai Bà Trưng Organizing School for Organizing, a social justice incubator run by VietUnity. In her consulting practice, she approaches organizational change from a practical, liberatory perspective. Kim holds a Ph.D. in ethnic studies from UC Berkeley. Her writing has been featured in *Vice*, *Teen Vogue*, and *Bitch Media*. She is currently writing a book manuscript titled *The End of Allyship: A New Era of Solidarity*.

Kay Ulanday Barrett, aka @Brownroundboi, is a poet, performer, and cultural strategist. Named one of "9 Transgender and Gender Nonconforming Writers You Should Know" by *Vogue*, K. has been featured at the Lincoln Center, the United Nations, Symphony Space, Princeton University, Tucson Poetry Festival, NY Poetry Festival, the Dodge Poetry Foundation, the Hemispheric Institute, and Brooklyn Museum. Their contributions are found in *Academy of American Poets*, the *New York Times*, *Buzzfeed*, *Asian American Literary Review*, *PBS News Hour*, *Race Forward*, *NYLON*, the *Huffington Post*, *Bitch Magazine*, and more. *More Than Organs* (Sibling Rivalry Press, 2020) is their second collection. Currently, Kay lives outside of the NYC area with his jowly dog and remixes his mama's recipes whenever possible. Visit his website, www.kaybarrett.net.

Reid Uratani is a doctoral candidate in the Department of American Studies at the University of Minnesota, Twin Cities. His dissertation articulates the logics by which U.S. imperialism and neoliberal capital selectively incorporate and enfranchise minorities as new markets. In conversation with critical tourism studies, it elaborates the processes by which queer subjectivities, refracted through colonial fantasies of indigeneity and race, are regulated in post-statehood Hawai'i. Specifically, it examines tourism's role in the ambivalent labor of representing Hawai'i's unique confluence of racial difference, indigeneity, militarism, and globalization.

Eric C. Wat is a storyteller. Sometimes he makes up his own stories, like his novel *SWIM* (The Permanent Press, 2019). Other times, he weaves together stories from amazing and inspirational people, as he did in *The Making of a Gay Asian Community: An Oral History of Pre-AIDS Los Angeles* (Rowman and Littlefield, 2002). His next book, *Love Your Asian Body: AIDS Activism in Los Angeles*, will be published by the University of Washington Press in fall 2021. He was a LGBTQ research fellow at the ONE Archives Foundation in 2018.

Sasha Wijeyeratne is the former organizing director at the National Queer Asian Pacific Islander Alliance (NQAPIA), working to build the power of LGBTQ API communities toward a world where all queer and trans people of color can thrive. Sasha is currently the executive director of CAAAV: Organizing Asian Communities, organizing working-class Chinese, Bangladeshi, and Korean immigrants in Chinatown and Queens in New York City. Sasha has been part of a number of grassroots and national organizing campaigns and deeply believes in the power of organizing to win impossible battles. They are confident that we have what we need to transform ourselves and our world and that working-class immigrant and people of color organizing will get us free. Sasha has also been part of a variety of organizing and political education, projects including South Asian Youth Movement, No Dane County Jail Coalition, VigilantLove, Asians for Black Lives, DC Desi Summer, hotpot!, and Queer South Asian National Network.

Syd Yang (they/them) is a mixed race Taiwanese queer, non-binary writer and personal essayist who also weaves together magic, prayer, and intention as an energy healer in the world through their practice, Blue Jaguar Healing Arts. Their work locates its resonance at the intersections of memory, body, sexuality, and mental health, finding spaciousness in a nonlinear breath. Learn more at bluejaguarhealingarts.com.

Xine Yao, Ph.D., is a lecturer in American literature to 1900 at University College London. Her book *Disaffected: The Cultural Politics of Unfeeling in Nineteenth-Century America* is forthcoming with Duke University Press in 2021. Her work has appeared in *J19*, *Occasion*, and *American Quarterly*. Xine is the cohost of *PhDivas*, a podcast about academia, culture, and social justice across the STEM and humanities divide. She shares certain convergences with Skim of the eponymous graphic novel, among them attending Catholic school in 1990s Toronto as a disaffected youth inclined toward the occult and excessive amounts of black clothing.

Index

1.5 generation Korean Americans, 296, 299n2

9/11, xii, 184, 195, 198, 257–259, 361n18; Israel and, 128, 134n11

ability, 183, 243, 277. *See also* disability

abnormality, 228, 280, 284. *See also* normativity

Abu El-Hajj, Nadia, 51

Abu-Lughod, Lila, 126

academia, 17–21, 23–24; and archives, 209; and Israel, 125, 137n38; and Korean American diasporas, 248–249; and queer API activism, 152; queer Asian Canadian interventions in, 265, 267–270, 272

activism, 1, 3–4, 9–10, 12, 17–19; and Asian American term, 355; and cultural production, 5; and Filipinx term, 321; and Korean American diaspora, 251; Marsha Aizumi as, 375–376; and media representation, 73; and mental health, 278; and Palestine, 126, 129; QTBIPOC tarot as, 364; and queer APA history, 171–177; queer API, 151, 153–159, 162–166, 167–168n22, 193–197, 199; queercore and, 389; South African, 113, 115; and U.S. military, 260, 262; and Viet Unity, 187

acupuncture, 316, 380–381

Adams, Ansel, 218

administrative aloha, 8, 139, 142–145

advertising, 73, 99, 124, 138, 156. *See also* personal ads

advocacy, 18; API LGBTQ, 10, 195–196, 201, 376; environmental, 131; and faith communities, 378; HIV, 152, 155, 157; gay rights in military, 262; transgender, 163–164, 173, 175, 376

aesthetics, 8; and Balang, 334, 338–339; and comparative racialization, 112; and Filipinx American art, 324; and popular media, 74; and Roger Shimomura, 217–220, 223–224

affect: and administrative aloha, 138, 141; and Black and Asian diasporas, 112; and comedy, 74; and Filipinx representation, 319, 326, 345–346, 349; and puro arte, 331–333, 335, 338; and QTBIPOC tarot, 365, 367; and Roger Shimomura, 217–219; and Viet Unity, 188–191

Afghanistan, 174, 261

Africa: African cosmologies, 366; and racialization, 42, 50, 121n23; South Africa, 8, 113–118, 121n23

African American communities: and activism, 152; Afro-Asian intimacies, 112, 115, 120; criminalization of, 171;

African American communities *(continued)* and HIV/AIDS, 23. *See also* Black communities

age, 23, 152, 164, 234, 275, 375; coming-of-age narratives, 72–77, 103

agriculture, 41–42, 47–48, 141, 188

Aguhar, Mark, 38–39

Aguilar-San Juan, Karin, 151, 173

AIDS, xii, 1, 22, 50; and activism, 23, 151–158, 162–165, 174–176; AIDS Coalition to Unleash Power (ACT-UP), 152, 388; AIDS Lifecycle, 389; Asian AIDS Project (AAP), 174–175; Asian AIDS Taskforce (AAT), 174; Asian American Recovery Services (AARS), 174; Asian Pacific AIDS Intervention Team (APAIT), 152–158, 162

Aizumi, Marsha, 13, 163–164

Alexander, Courtney, 366

Alexander, M. Jacqui, 95, 99–101, 134n4, 365

Alidio, Kimberley, 7

alienation, 75, 154, 229, 349, 353, 355–357

allyship, 160–161, 164–165, 168n22, 184, 199, 376

Aloha, 8, 138–145; administrative, 8, 139, 142–145

American dream, 279, 284, 313, 324; Korean American dream, 251

American Son (novel), 8, 103–104, 106, 108

Americanness, 104, 220, 307

Amor, Lisa, 397

Amsterdam, Netherlands, 89, 397

An, Jeong-Hyun, 251

Andrews, Julie, 401

anthropology, 21, 46, 48–49, 100

antiracism, 101, 115, 175, 223, 367

Anzaldúa, Gloria, 107–108, 110, 271

apartheid, South African, 8–9, 113–120; post-apartheid, 113, 114, 120

API Equality: Los Angeles (APIELA), 153, 159, 177; Northern California, 177, 196

API Rainbow Parents, 377

apps, dating, 10, 124, 238–243

archives, 10–11, 45; archival studies, 207; and Filipino dancing, 336; institutional, 209, 212; LGBTQ+, xiii, 206–210, 212; and Sinitic Jews, 45–47

area studies, xiii, 3, 23, 238

art, 5, 7–8, 89, 212, 390–391; and Asian Pacific American activism, 177; D'Lo and, 57, 60; Filipinx, 324, 333, 344–345; and Korean American diaspora,

248–249; and *Open in Emergency*, 275, 281–283, 285; and QTBIPOC tarot, 366; and Roger Shimomura, 217–222

Ascalon Roley, Brian, 105

Asian AIDS Project (AAP), 174–175

Asian AIDS Taskforce (AAT), 174

Asian American communities: Asian American closet, 260–261; Asian American Legal Defense and Education Fund (AALDEF), 200; Asian American Movement, 72, 172–173; Asian American Tarot, 285, 365, 370; Asian Lesbians of the East Coast (ALOEC), 174–176, 193; Asian Pride Project (APP), 200. *See also* Asian American studies

Asian American Recovery Services (AARS), 174

Asian American studies, xi, 3, 8–9, 18–19, 23, 216; and comparative colonial studies, 123, 133n1, 137n8; and *M. Butterfly*, 352, 354; queer, 3, 20, 22, 108, 238, 248

Asian American Tarot, 285, 365, 370

Asian Australian identity, 73

Asian Canadian communities, 3, 265–272, 279; Asian Canadian and Asian Migration Studies (ACAM), 267, 270–271

Asian Lesbians of the East Coast (ALOEC), 174–176, 193, 197

Asian Pacific AIDS Intervention Team (APAIT), 152–158, 162

Asian Pacific American (APA) communities, 67, 170–177; Asian Pacific AIDS Intervention Team (APAIT), 152–158, 162; Asian Pacific Lesbian Bisexual Transgender Network (APLBTN), 193, 197, 201n3; Asian/Pacific Lesbians and Gays (A/PLG), 155, 166n3, 166n5, 174

Asian Pacific Islander (API) communities, 18, 23; and antiracist activism, 181; API Equality, 153, 159, 177, 196; API Rainbow Parents, 377; and archives, 207–208, 213, 214n12; Asian Pacific AIDS Intervention Team (APAIT), 152–158, 162; Asian Pacific Lesbian Bisexual Transgender Network (APLBTN), 193, 197, 201n3; Asian/Pacific Lesbians and Gays (A/PLG), 155, 166n3, 166n5, 174; National Queer Asian Pacific Islander Alliance (NQAPIA), 181–185, 194, 197–201, 376–378; queer API activism, 9–10, 151–166,

163, 210, 212, 353; genderqueer, 210, 313, 386; inclusivity, 109, 152, 162, 199, 364; nonbinary, 51, 153, 210, 321, 354, 358–360, 380, 386; nonconforming, 7, 22, 60, 181–182, 198, 325; norms, 114–115, 120, 229, 241, 279–280, 288, 304, 327; and performance, 230, 241, 327, 331, 358, 389. *See also* transgender; men; women
generations, xii, 10, 23, 253, 266, 275; 1.5 generation Korean Americans, 296, 299n2; and Chinese American communities, 382, 386; in Hawai'i, 141, 145; and lateral diasporas, 120; and LGBTQ+ API activism, 153, 157, 163–165, 176; and Thai American, 301, 307
genetics, 41–52
genocide, 43, 52, 79, 346, 380
gentrification, 22, 184, 191n4
geographies, 2–3, 22, 75, 99; Filipinx, 267, 269, 319–322, 325–328; and Korean American diasporas, 250, 253; and Sinitic Jews, 41, 43
geolocative dating apps, 237–238, 243, 244n4
geopolitics, 40–42, 44, 52, 65, 139, 250
Georgis, Dina, 333
Ghetto Bill, South African, 114–115, 121n11
Gidlow, Elsa, 171
Gilmore, Ruth Wilson, 188–189, 276
Glancy, Diane, 251
Glazer, Diane, 40
Glazer, Guilford, 40
Glee (TV show), 320, 345
global contexts, xii, 2, 144; and Asian American studies, 4, 22; and China, 40–42, 45, 52; and economies of desire, 8; and Filipinx communities, 238–239, 244n2, 332–333, 346–348; Global North, xii; Global South, xii, 2, 259; globalization, 21, 99–100, 333; and Korean American diasporas, 252; and lateral diasporas, 73–74, 77, 79; neoliberal, xii; and racial capitalism, 105, 108; and U.S. expansion, 258, 261–262, 304
Goggin, Maureen, 230
Goishi, Dean, 153, 155, 157
Gómez-Barris, Macarena, 321, 327
Gopinath, Gayatri, 73–74, 109, 271, 305, 321
Gossett, Che, 344
goths, 343, 348, 364–365, 367, 369
Gramsci, Antonio, 41

Grant, Oscar, 187
Greenberg, Clement, 219
greenwashing, 131
grief, 7, 38, 88, 383, 387, 400–401
Grindr, 10, 237, 239–240, 242, 244n4
Guam, 175
Gyeltsen, Geshela, 91

Hai Bà Trưng School for Organizing (HBT), 187
Hak Kyung Cha, Theresa, 64, 70n1, 249
Halkin, Hillel, 42–43, 51
Hall, Katherine, 174
Han, C. Winter, 10, 240
Han, Judy, 251
Han people, 44–46, 52
Hanawa, Yukiko, 271
happiness, 188, 190, 296
harassment, 160, 173, 182–183, 197, 388
Haritaworn, Jin, 271
Hawai'i, 8, 95, 131, 138–145, 170
Hayashi, Kris, 170
Haydock, Shana Bulhan, 285
health, 13; and access, xii, 389; and Balang, 339; cancer, 389–390, 399–400; and Chinese medicine, 381; and genetics, 51; healing arts, 380; and HIV/AIDS, 23, 153–156, 174–175; and illness, 13, 23, 277, 280, 282, 284; mental health, 11, 181, 276–282, 284–285, 370; public, 48, 174
heartland, United States, 319, 322, 327–328
Hedva, 275, 277–278, 281, 284
Hernández, Robb, 46–47
heteronormativity: and Afro-South Asian intimacies, 114–115, 120; and API LGBTQ+ activism, 171, 211, 213; and Asian American histories, 10; and Asian American mental health, 277, 279–280, 283; compulsory heterosexuality, 46, 73, 302, 319; and Filipinx communities, 100, 259, 266–268, 271, 288, 291–292; heterofuturity, 267; heteromasculinity, 114; heteronationality, 109, 305; heteropatriarchy, 42, 44, 51–52, 206, 280, 288, 304, 306–307, 319, 327; and Korean American diasporas, 251, 253, 260; and *M. Butterfly*, 353, 355; and QTBIPOC tarot, 364, 368–369; and Roger Shimomura, 217, 223; and Thai American communities, 12, 302, 304–307

Hinaleimoana, Kumu, 177
hip-hop, 7, 61
history, xi–xiii, 2–3, 7–11, 170–173, 177, 229,
    267; and API LGBTQ+ activism, 155,
    157, 162, 193–194, 196–197; and archives,
    206–207, 209–210, 212–213; and Black
    and South Asian diasporas, 112, 114,
    120; and Chinese Jews, 41–52; Filipinx,
    98, 108–110, 318–320, 331–339, 346; in
    Hawaiʻi, 139–142; and Israel, 127–129;
    and Korean American diasporas, 64–66,
    68, 248–253; and mental health, 276,
    278, 281; in Oakland, 189, 191; and
    Orientalism, 216, 218, 220–221, 224–225;
    and tarot, 366–367; and Thai American
    communities, 302, 304, 306–307
HIV/AIDS, xii, 1, 22, 50; and activism,
    23, 151–158, 162–165, 174–176; AIDS
    Coalition to Unleash Power (ACT-UP),
    152, 388; AIDS Lifecycle, 389; Asian
    AIDS Project (AAP), 174–175; Asian
    AIDS Taskforce (AAT), 174; Asian
    American Recovery Services (AARS),
    174; Asian Pacific AIDS Intervention
    Team (APAIT), 152–158, 162
Hom, Alice Y., xi, 1, 20
home, 67, 101, 304–306, 332–333, 380–383,
    386; homelessness, 144, 323; Israeli
    representations of, 127; and LGBTQ+
    API activism, 151, 166, 181, 183; and
    religion, 296–297
homonationalism, xiii, 133–134n2, 261
homonormativity, xiii, 144, 252, 261, 319
homophobia, 1; and *American Son*, 106;
    and *Brokeback Mountain*, 95; and
    Filipinx communities, 292, 323, 333,
    338; and Israel, 124–126, 128, 134n4;
    and Korean American diasporas,
    250–251; LGBTQ+ API organizing, 154,
    157–159, 165, 194, 196–197; and religious
    communities, 297, 299n5; television
    representations of, 73, 76–78; and the
    U.S. military, 261; in *The World Unseen*,
    113–114
homosexuality: and Andrew Cunanan, 320,
    323; and Balang, 334; and friendship,
    190–192; and Israel, 131; and LGBTQ+
    API activism, 195, 198, 200, 251; and
    mental health, 278; and religion, 160; and
    U.S. military, 260
Honda, Mike, 164

Honda-Phillips, Michelle, 164
Hong, Grace K., 112, 120
Hong Kingston, Maxine, 218
hooks, bell, 227
housenboys, 8, 104, 106, 108
Houston, Whitney, 343–349
Huang, Eddie, 72
Huang, Hsinya, 45
Hughes, Langston, 78
human rights, xiii, 123, 131, 153, 158, 195
human trafficking, 197, 347
humanities, 276, 278, 285
Hutchins, Loraine, 176
Huxtable, Juliana, 344
Hwang, David Henry, 208, 353–356,
    358–360
hybridity, 47, 49–50

I Can't Think Straight (film), 113
"I Will Always Love You" (song), 344, 348
identities, 2, 9; Filipina/o/x, 96–97, 103, 289,
    297, 320–321, 325, 335, 339; gender, xii,
    152, 166, 297, 353, 375; in Hawaiʻi, 141,
    145; identity politics, 9, 262; and Korean
    American diasporas, 251–253, 297;
    and LGBTQ+ API activism, 152–153,
    156–157, 164; mixed-race, 66, 69, 118;
    national, xiii, 41–42, 45; sexual, 103, 239,
    262, 327, 349; and Sinitic Jews, 43, 45–46,
    52; in South Africa, 113–114, 116, 118,
    120; and Thai communities, 301–302,
    304–305; trans, 164, 278
Ige, David, 143–144
illegibility, 115, 276, 284, 319, 325–327
illness, 13, 23, 277, 280, 282, 284
immigrant communities, 68; and activism,
    152–153, 162, 181, 188, 193, 197–201, 377;
    and families, 62, 64, 67, 245, 275–276;
    Filipinx, 287, 289, 322–324, 336; and
    Hawaiʻi, 140; immigration histories, 3,
    44, 47–49, 171; and Korean American
    diasporas, 245, 248, 251, 295–296; and
    mental health, 275–276, 279; Thai,
    301–302, 304–306; TV representations of,
    73–75, 77–78, 322–324; undocumented,
    193, 198–199; and visas, 198–199
imperialism, 3–4, 109, 170, 253; and China,
    42, 48; Christian, 299; and Filipinx
    communities, 101, 318–319, 322, 324, 331,
    336–338; and Hawaiʻi, 138, 140; in *M.
    Butterfly*, 355; and Thai communities,

302, 307; and tourism, 73, 100–101; and
U.S. military, 258
incarceration, 2, 13, 52, 188; prisons, xii,
113, 129, 289; Japanese American, 216–
218, 220–223; military, 259
Indian communities, 61–62; and activism,
174, 195; and indenture, 114; in South
Africa, 113–120, 121n11
Indigenous communities: Anishinaabe,
290; in Canada, 267, 272, 290–291;
Cree, 290; Hawaiian, 138–141, 173;
indigeneity, 24, 39, 46, 51, 139, 177, 329;
Indigenous studies, 42, 272; Kanaka
Maoli, 138, 140–141, 143, 145, 146n17;
Métis, 290; Musqueam, 266, 272, 288;
Native American studies, 250; "native"
representations, 74, 76, 95, 100, 346;
Paiwan, 45; in the Philippines, 346, 348;
and race, 50–52; and religion, 298; and
residential schooling, 266–267, 290;
Sinitic, 45–46; and sovereignty, 73; and
tarot, 364, 366; Two Spirit and queer
(2SQ), 290–291
industrialization, 42, 48, 219
inequalities, 1, 11, 96, 100, 115, 128, 261
Ing-Wen, Tsai, 45
Ingebretsen, Edward, 326–327
Inouye, Daniel, 131
Instagram, 127, 239, 241
Institute for Gender, Race, Sexuality and
Social Justice (GRSJ), 268, 270–271
institutions, 11–12, 15, 23–24, 238, 336;
and API LGBTQ+ activism, 153, 157–
159, 162, 175; and archives, 206–207,
209, 212; in Hawai'i, 141, 146n17;
institutionalization of disciplines, xiii,
1, 4, 40; Israeli academic, 125, 137n38;
multiculturalism as, 360; religious,
287–288, 290–292, 378; University of
British Columbia as, 265–272; U.S.
military as, 257, 261
interdisciplinary fields, xi, 23, 41, 212,
248
Interfaith Council of Vietnamese
Americans, 160–161
intergenerational trauma, 64, 163
internment, Japanese American, 52, 141,
258, 267
interracial intimacies, 10; Afro-South
Asian, 113, 115, 120; and Craigslist ads,
228, 231, 233, 235

intersectionality, 11, 18, 123, 250, 271, 365;
and activist movements, 165, 197, 199,
209; and Andrew Cunanan, 320, 327–
327; Mexican American and Filipino,
103, 108, 110; and religion and sexuality,
291–291
intersex people, 51, 212
intimacies, 13, 293, 304, 332; Asian-
Asian, 156; Black and Asian diasporic,
112–113, 115, 117–118; cross-racial, 113,
115, 120; and dating apps, 238–240;
heteronormative, 223; Latinx and
Filipinx, 109; and the *mulato* figure,
46–47, 51–52
Iraq, U.S. invasion of, 258–259, 261, 264n17
Isaac, Allan Punzalan, 318, 334
Ishii, Douglas S., 7
Islam: Islamophobia, xii, 52, 77, 183,
361n18; Muslims in China, 48, 52;
Muslims in Malaysia, 77–78; Muslim
queers, 182–184
Israel, 4, 8; birthright trips to, 123, 126–127,
135n19; Brand Israel, 128, 133n2; and
checkpoints, 129–132; and construction
of safety, 123–126; Hebron, 130;
Israel Defense Forces (IDF), 123–132;
and Jerusalem, 127–130, 135n22;
pinkwashing, xiii, 99, 123–124, 131–132;
and Sinitic Jews, 40–43, 45, 52; and state
violence, 123–132; Taglit-Birthright
Israel trips, 126–127, 135n19; Tel Aviv in,
124–130

Jack'd, 240, 242, 244, 245–245n4
Jackson, Michael, 343
Jacobs, Joseph, 49
Jang, Crystal, 172
Japanese communities: and activism,
153, 170, 173–175, 212, 377–378;
Ainu, 212; anti-Japanese racism, 223,
267; and archives, 208; "enemy Jap"
representations, 218–221; in Hawai'i,
131, 138–141, 144; Japanese American
internment, 10, 52, 14, 216–218, 220–223,
258, 267; Japanese Canadians, 13, 267,
364; Japanese colonialism, 98, 253, 347;
Nikkei, 154, 163, 165, 378; Nissei, 141,
258; and Roger Shimomura, 217–224;
U.S. discrimination of, 48, 170–171; and
U.S. military, 258–260
jazz, 345, 396, 399

Lee, Jee Yeun, 10
Lee, Joon Oluchi, 104
Lee, Josephine, 219
Lee, Peggy, 284
Lee, Robert, 259
leftist politics, 45, 101, 176, 259, 281
Lei (magazine), 138–139, 143
Lentin, Alana, 359–360
Leonowens, Anna, 306
lesbian communities, 68; and activism, 152–156, 158, 166n3, 171–176, 193–194, 197, 375; Asian Lesbians of the East Coast (ALOEC), 174–176, 193; Filipinx, 292; and Korean American diasporas, 251; lesbians of color, 17; March on Washington for Lesbian and Gay Rights, 145; South Asian lesbian desire, 112–115, 120; and the U.S. military, 260
lesbian, gay, bisexual, transgender, and queer (LGBTQ+) communities, xii–xiii, 1–3, 9–10, 316; and APA/API activism, 152–164, 171–177, 193–201, 375–379; and the archives, 206–211, 213; in Canada, 270–271, 288, 290–293; and Hawai'i, 138, 142, 144, 145n3; and Israel, 123–124, 126–127, 131–132; and Korean American diasporas, 250–251; LGBT Center, 158; National Gay and Lesbian Task Force, 194, 197; and nationalism, 101; and religion, 297; in South Africa, 113; and the U.S. military, 257, 260–262
Lester, Neal, 230
Lew, Steve, 174–175
liberalism, 74–77, 112, 248, 288–289, 355, 365; and capitalism, xi; liberal multiculturalism, 131, 353–354, 357; and militarism, 258, 262; queer, xiii. *See also* neoliberalism
Lick, David J., 230
Lim, Bliss Cua, 346
Lim-Hing, Sharon, 176
Lin, Danni, 7
Lin, Jeremy, 78
Lin, Ken-Hou, 231
Lingle, Linda, 143
Link, Matthew, 142–143
lip-syncing, 331, 338, 343–345, 347–348, 349n1
literature, xii, 13–14, 109, 170–171, 354, 365; and Sinitic Jews, 40, 42, 50; and Thai representations, 305–306

Little Saigon, 152, 161, 168
local, the, 8–9; and API LGBTQ+ activism, 153, 160–162, 164–165, 193–194, 199, 291–292; and Hawai'i, 139–143; translocal, 272, 325; TV representations, 73; and queer Asian disruptions, 272; and U.S. militarism, 67
Lorde, Audre, 271, 276
Los Angeles, California, 8; and borderlands, 103, 107–108; and Craigslist ads, 228; dating apps in, 237–243; Jewish communities in, 40; LGBTQ+ API activism in, 153, 156–159, 163, 171, 189, 195–196; Los Angeles Asian Pacific Islander Sisters, 156, 166n5, 167n9; riots in, 8, 103, 107, 189; Thai temples in, 12, 306; University of California, Los Angeles (UCLA), 59, 142, 152, 156, 193, 198
Lougani, Greg, 176
love, 64, 83, 314; and activism, 183, 200, 376–379; in *The Bodyguard*, 347–349; and Chinese medicine, 381; family, 63, 396–397; in *M. Butterfly*, 353, 357–358; and mental health, 279, 281; and religion, 298–299; and tarot, 368–370
Lowe, Lisa, 46–47, 74
Lowenthal, Michael, 227
Lunar New Year, 20, 75, 159, 195
Lundquist, Jennifer H., 231
Lyon, Phyllis, 171

M. Butterfly, 12, 208, 352–361
Mackintosh, Cameron, 176
Madson, David, 318, 326
Magpantay, Glenn D., 9–10
Mah, Leslie, 13
Mahmood, Saba, 126
Mahu, 152
Malaysia, 77–78, 347
Mamang, Karen Tongson's, 13, 396–401
Man, Simeon, 257
Manalansan, Martin F., IV, 73, 109, 266, 271, 290, 301, 349n1
manananggal, the, 344–349
Mangaoang, Gil, 172–173
Manila, Philippines, 96–100, 238–243, 332, 343, 396–397
Mannion, Carol, 377
Marcos, Ferdinand, 96
Marcos, Imelda, 345

396–397; martial law in, 96, 100, 141; PhilippinExcess, 318–319, 321; queer performances in, 343–349; Tagalog language, 96–97, 172, 269–270, 322, 324, 332, 343; taxi dance hall in, 332, 336–339; and U.S. military, 259; U.S.-Philippine relations, 324, 337; War on Drugs in, 344, 349. *See also* Filipina/o/x communities

photography, 87, 89, 94, 207–208, 213, 218, 234

Phua, Voon Chin, 230

Pilipinx communities, 237, 244n2, 259

Pinay/Pinoy identities, 7, 39, 244n2, 259, 397

Pineda, Arnel, 345

pinkwashing, xiii, 99, 123–124, 131–132

pleasure, 9–10, 174, 219, 346, 367; and Balang, 331, 335–338

police: activism against, 173, 177, 182, 187, 189; border, 101; Israel and, 125, 129–130; of Muslims, 183; in South Africa, 116–117; and TSA, 183, 315

political organizing, xii; API LGBTQ, 9–10, 18, 151–165, 181–185, 187, 193–201, 376; labor, 140; in Palestine, 129, 131–132; and queer APA history, 170–177; and Thai activism, 302, 307

politics, xii, 2–3; and APA LGBTQ+ history, 171; and Balang, 332, 336–337, 339; class, 8, 101; and disruptive choreographies, 265–266, 272; and Filipinx and Latinx diasporas, 104, 106, 108–110; global, 41; in Hawai'i, 139–140, 142, 144; of Japanese American incarceration, 216, 218–219, 223; and liberal modernity, 112; multicultural, 355, 360; political power, 182–185; queer, 13, 113; racial, 267, 271; respectability, 163. *See also* political organizing; progressive politics

Ponce, Joseph Martin, 109

pop art, 217, 220–222

popular culture, 2, 7, 13, 217–218, 220, 223–223, 320; and Balang, 331, 333, 335; Canadian, 270–271; and Dan Choi, 261; and *Fresh Off the Boat*, 78; and LGBTQ+ API activism, 157; and *Open in Emergency*, 284; pop art, 217, 220–222; popular knowledges, 41; and queer Filipinx performance, 343–345, 347; and South Korea, 252

postcoloniality, 12, 99, 109, 112, 324, 326, 332, 338

postpartum depression, 58, 275, 284, 370

potlucks, 173, 182–183, 185

poverty, xii, 2, 67, 97, 259, 323, 349

Powell, Greg, 305

pride events, 8, 252; and APA history, 173; and API activism, 157, 163, 195, 200; in Israel, 123–124, 127; in San Francisco, 20

prisons, xii, 113, 129, 289; incarceration, 2, 13, 52, 188; Japanese American internment, 216–218, 220–223; military, 259

privilege, 9, 66, 252, 280, 284, 304; and Filipinx communities, 96–97, 100; and LGBTQ+ API activism, 163, 181, 183, 185

progressive politics, 2, 172, 187, 316; Israel as progressive, 125–126, 128, 132; and LGBTQ+ API activism, 154, 156, 193; and multiculturalism, 360–361

Proposition 8, California, 159, 167n14, 196

Proposition 22, California, 153, 158, 167n14

protests, 168n22, 281; Black Lives Matter, 125, 187–188, 190–191; LGBTQ+ API, 152, 154, 159, 161, 175–176, 185, 195; and Palestinians, 125, 135n15; protest songs, 188; in South Africa, 114, 116; and U.S. military, 258; and Vietnamese Unity (VU), 187–188, 190–191

psychiatry, 262, 279, 284–285, 381

Puar, Jasbir, 101, 131, 261

public health, 48, 156, 174

puro arte, 324–325, 332–334, 337–339

Qing Dynasty, 42, 44

Quan Yin, 382, 385

queer communities; and API activism, 152, 154–155, 159, 162–164, 176; queer Asian American communities, 17, 20, 22, 170, 181, 281–283, 285; queer Asian American studies, 3, 108; queer of color critique, xi–xii, 11, 112, 238, 248, 250–251, 270–271, 365–366; queer comparative framework, 114–115; queer diasporic framework, 72, 109, 114, 188, 248–249, 252–253, 305, 321, 323; queer feminism, 112, 364; queer methodology, 190; Queer Nation, 152, 176; queer people of color, 20, 105, 109, 113, 172, 248, 257, 268, 305; queer possibility, 333; queer studies, xiii, 2–3, 22–26, 42, 123, 133, 238; queer

Filipinx communities, 98, 344, 346–348; Jewish, 49–50; in *M. Butterfly*, 352; and Orientalism, 223, 229; in South Africa, 113, 115, 117–120; and queer APA history, 171–173, 175–176; trans women, 162, 164, 175, 295, 390, 397; white, 223, 304, 336; women of color feminisms, xii, 4, 112. *See also* lesbian communities
Wong, Ali, 78
Wong, Alvin K., 4
Wong, B. D., 352, 356
Wong, Connie, 156
Wong, Marshall, 159
Wong-Kalu, Kumu Hinaleimoana, 177
workers, 11; agricultural, 47; domestic, 104; Filipinx, 99, 128, 336, 346–347; in Hawai'i, 140–141; immigrant, 198–199, 335; and racism, 48, 113, 116; sex, 171, 173
working-class communities, 24, 251, 253, 336; and API organizing, 182, 185; Filipinx, 100, 259
World Journal, 75, 195
World Unseen, The, 8, 113–115

World War II, 44, 52, 140–141, 188, 217, 223, 267, 347, 400
Wu, Cynthia, 284
Wu, Judy Tzu-Chun, 271

xenophobia, 1, 48, 52, 76, 302–303

Yabe, Aya, 377
Yang, Syd, 13
Yao, Xine, 12
yellowwashing, 131
Yin, Quan, 382, 385
Yoshikawa, Yoko, 176
youth: diasporic Thai, 307; and LGBTQ+ API activism, 153, 158, 187; queer, 126–128, 250–251, 275; and the U.S. military, 259
YouTube stars, Filipinx, 332, 343–344, 347
Yu, Timothy, 72–73

Zamora, Linmark, R., 8, 96
Zia, Helen, 172
zoning politics, 12, 303, 306
Zyrus, Jake, 332, 345

Also in the series *Asian American History and Culture*

Vanita Reddy, *Fashioning Diaspora: Beauty, Femininity, and South Asian American Culture*

Audrey Wu Clark, *The Asian American Avant-Garde: Universalist Aspirations in Modernist Literature and Art*

Eric Tang, *Unsettled: Cambodian Refugees in the New York City Hyperghetto*

Jeffrey Santa Ana, *Racial Feelings: Asian America in a Capitalist Culture of Emotion*

Jiemin Bao, *Creating a Buddhist Community: A Thai Temple in Silicon Valley*

Elda E. Tsou, *Unquiet Tropes: Form, Race, and Asian American Literature*

Tarry Hum, *Making a Global Immigrant Neighborhood: Brooklyn's Sunset Park*

Ruth Mayer, *Serial Fu Manchu: The Chinese Supervillain and the Spread of Yellow Peril Ideology*

Karen Kuo, *East Is West and West Is East: Gender, Culture, and Interwar Encounters between Asia and America*

Kieu-Linh Caroline Valverde, *Transnationalizing Viet Nam: Community, Culture, and Politics in the Diaspora*

Lan P. Duong, *Treacherous Subjects: Gender, Culture, and Trans-Vietnamese Feminism*

Kristi Brian, *Reframing Transracial Adoption: Adopted Koreans, White Parents, and the Politics of Kinship*

Belinda Kong, *Tiananmen Fictions outside the Square: The Chinese Literary Diaspora and the Politics of Global Culture*

Bindi V. Shah, *Laotian Daughters: Working toward Community, Belonging, and Environmental Justice*

Cherstin M. Lyon, *Prisons and Patriots: Japanese American Wartime Citizenship, Civil Disobedience, and Historical Memory*

Shelley Sang-Hee Lee, *Claiming the Oriental Gateway: Prewar Seattle and Japanese America*

Isabelle Thuy Pelaud, *This Is All I Choose to Tell: History and Hybridity in Vietnamese American Literature*

Christian Collet and Pei-te Lien, eds., *The Transnational Politics of Asian Americans*

Min Zhou, *Contemporary Chinese America: Immigration, Ethnicity, and Community Transformation*

Kathleen S. Yep, *Outside the Paint: When Basketball Ruled at the Chinese Playground*

Benito M. Vergara Jr., *Pinoy Capital: The Filipino Nation in Daly City*

Jonathan Y. Okamura, *Ethnicity and Inequality in Hawai'i*

Sucheng Chan and Madeline Y. Hsu, eds., *Chinese Americans and the Politics of Race and Culture*

K. Scott Wong and Sucheng Chan, eds., *Claiming America: Constructing Chinese American Identities during the Exclusion Era*

Lavina Dhiṅgra Shankar and Rajini Srikanth, eds., *A Part, Yet Apart: South Asians in Asian America*

Jere Takahashi, *Nisei/Sansei: Shifting Japanese American Identities and Politics*

Velina Hasu Houston, ed., *But Still, Like Air, I'll Rise: New Asian American Plays*

Josephine Lee, *Performing Asian America: Race and Ethnicity on the Contemporary Stage*

Deepika Bahri and Mary Vasudeva, eds., *Between the Lines: South Asians and Postcoloniality*

E. San Juan Jr., *The Philippine Temptation: Dialectics of Philippines–U.S. Literary Relations*

Carlos Bulosan and E. San Juan Jr., eds., *The Cry and the Dedication*

Carlos Bulosan and E. San Juan Jr., eds., *On Becoming Filipino: Selected Writings of Carlos Bulosan*

Vicente L. Rafael, ed., *Discrepant Histories: Translocal Essays on Filipino Cultures*

Yen Le Espiritu, *Filipino American Lives*

Paul Ong, Edna Bonacich, and Lucie Cheng, eds., *The New Asian Immigration in Los Angeles and Global Restructuring*

Chris Friday, *Organizing Asian American Labor: The Pacific Coast Canned-Salmon Industry, 1870–1942*

Sucheng Chan, ed., *Hmong Means Free: Life in Laos and America*

Timothy P. Fong, *The First Suburban Chinatown: The Remaking of Monterey Park, California*

William Wei, *The Asian American Movement*

Yen Le Espiritu, *Asian American Panethnicity*

Velina Hasu Houston, ed., *The Politics of Life*

Renqiu Yu, *To Save China, To Save Ourselves: The Chinese Hand Laundry Alliance of New York*

Shirley Geok-lin Lim and Amy Ling, eds., *Reading the Literatures of Asian America*

Karen Isaksen Leonard, *Making Ethnic Choices: California's Punjabi Mexican Americans*

Gary Y. Okihiro, *Cane Fires: The Anti-Japanese Movement in Hawaii, 1865–1945*

Sucheng Chan, *Entry Denied: Exclusion and the Chinese Community in America, 1882–1943*